D0003861

NETWORKING COMPLETE
THIRD EDITION

SYBEX®

SAN FRANCISCO ▸ LONDON

Associate Publisher: Neil Edde

Acquisitions and Developmental Editor: Elizabeth Hurley

Compilation Editor: Brad Price

Production Editor: Erica Yee

Technical Editor: John Price

Book Designer: Maureen Forys, Happenstance Type-o-Rama

Electronic Publishing Specialist: Interactive Composition Corporation

Proofreaders: Nelson Kim, Dave Nash, Denise van den Berg, Yariv Rabinovitch, Nancy Riddiough

Indexer: Lynnzee Elze

Cover Designer: Design Site

Library of Congress Card Number: 2002108071

ISBN: 0-7821-4143-9

Manufactured in the United States of America

10 9 8 7 6 5 4 3 2 1

CONTENTS AT A GLANCE

CONTENTS

Part II ▶ Network Hardware and Software 143

Appendices

INTRODUCTION

*N*etworking Complete, Third Edition, is a one-of-a-kind computer book—valuable both for the breadth of its content and for its low price. This nearly thousand-page compilation of information from many Sybex books provides comprehensive coverage of networking topics. This book, unique in the computer book world, was created with several goals in mind:

- ▶ To offer a thorough guide covering all the important elements of networking at an affordable price.

- ▶ To help you become familiar with the essential networking topics so you can design, maintain, install, and administer networks with confidence.

- ▶ To acquaint you with some of our best authors—their writing styles and teaching skills, and the level of expertise they bring to their books—so you can easily find a match for your interests as you delve deeper into networking and the opportunities it opens up to you.

Networking Complete, Third Edition, is designed to provide all the essential information you'll need to get the most from networking your home or business computers, while at the same time inviting you to explore the even greater depths and wider coverage of material in the original books.

If you've read other computer "how-to" books, you've seen that there are many possible approaches to the task of showing how to use software and hardware effectively. The books from which *Networking Complete,* Third Edition was compiled to represent a range of the approaches to teaching that Sybex and its authors have developed—home and small business networkers, students, technicians, and network and system administrators should all be able to learn from this format. The source books range from our *Mastering* series books, which are designed to bring beginner and intermediate level readers to a more advanced understanding, to many of our *Study Guides*, which are intended for readers who are looking to boost their IT careers to the next level. As you read through various chapters of *Networking Complete,* Third Edition you'll see which type of material is most useful for you. You'll also see what these books have in common: a commitment to clarity, accuracy, and practicality.

You'll find in these pages ample evidence of the high quality of Sybex authors. Unlike publishers who produce "books by committee,"

Sybex authors are encouraged to write in individual voices that reflect their own experience with the software at hand and with the evolution of today's personal computers.

Nearly every book represented here is the work of a single writer or a pair of close collaborators. Chapters were edited only to minimize duplication, omit coverage of non-related topics, and update or add cross-references so that you can easily follow a topic across chapters.

Who Can Benefit from This Book?

Networking Complete, Third Edition is designed to meet the needs of a wide range of people—from those who are thinking about implementing networks to those that have already implemented them. Networking is an extraordinarily complex topic, with some information that everyone needs, as well as details that may be essential to some users but of no interest to others. Therefore, while you could read this book from beginning to end—from networking fundamentals through network security—you may not need to read every chapter. The table of contents and the index will guide you to the subjects you're looking for.

Home and Small Business Networkers Even if you have only a little familiarity with networks and the basic terminology associated with them, this book will start you working with the concepts of networking. You'll find descriptions of different kinds of networks and how they are suited for certain functions, as well as introductions to related networking material; each topic is covered with clear explanations of essential concepts. You may want to start with chapters from the Networking Fundamentals and Networking Hardware and Software sections. As you plan and set up your home and small-office networks, you also find the information on network design, troubleshooting, disaster recovery, and security very useful. This information will better equip you to handle any network-related problems you may encounter.

Students and Technicians Chances are, you already know how to do routine networking tasks and are familiar with much of the material discussed in the fundamentals section. You know your way around a network and at least one network operating system, but you also know that there is always more to learn about working more effectively. As you prepare for networking certifications, many sections in the early part of the book with provide the foundational knowledge you will need. The latter part of *Networking Complete*, Third Edition, will bring you up to speed on more advanced topics, and give you opportunities to augment your knowledge base. You'll also find the glossary of networking terms to be a valuable daily reference and the information on certification may help you decide how best to prepare for the next step in your career. You'll find that throughout this book nearly every chapter has nuggets of knowledge from which you can benefit.

Network and System Administrators   As a network administrator, you are probably well versed on many of the topics presented in this book, but here you will also find information on network operating systems other than the ones you use every day. This book will also provide you with a chance to review topics you are less comfortable with, as well as provide ideas for ways that you can expand and enhance your own network. There's plenty for you here, too. In particular, you might find the sections on real-world troubleshooting, remote access, thin client networking, and security to be the most useful.

This book is for anyone who uses or manages a network. Regardless of whether you are designing and implementing your first network or your hundredth, you'll find useful information in this comprehensive compendium. With topics ranging from networking essentials and media to administering extranets and network security, there truly is something to please everyone. Whether you are pursuing one of the many networking certifications, or just learning about the myriad facets of networking, *Networking Complete*, Third Edition, will provide a quick and inexpensive way for you to access a wide range of information.

How This Book Is Organized

Networking Complete, Third Edition has five parts, consisting of twenty-four chapters and six appendices.

Part I: Networking Fundamentals

This first part, as the name suggests, is dedicated to networking fundamentals. Chapter 1, "An Introduction to Networks," introduces the reader to networks and why they are so important. Chapter 2, "Networks in the Workplace," deals with how networks are used in the workplace and what their powers and limits are in this capacity. Chapter 3, "Network Topologies and Types," describes the type of networks in detail and how these networks are connected. Chapter 4, "The OSI Model," explains the Open Systems Interconnect reference model, which is the basis for most networks and is an essential ingredient to attaining a deep understanding of networking. Chapter 5, "Major Protocol Suites," provides a detailed discussion of TCP/IP, NetWare IPX/SPX, and AppleTalk, the most important protocol suites.

Part II: Network Hardware and Software

Part II discusses the various components of a network. Chapter 6, "Installing Cards and Cables," discusses installing network cards and cables to build networks to connect your computers. Chapter 7, "Network Connectivity Devices," covers the hardware that makes it possible to connect numerous small networks to make a larger one. Chapter 8, "Network Operating Systems," explains how different network operating systems provide functionality, supply protocol support, deal with file and print sharing, and other activities. Chapter 9, "Configuring Network Hardware," discusses the basic concepts needed to configure network hardware for your client operating system. Chapter 10, "Network Applications," discusses the useful features of applications that have developed because of networks and comparisons that should be made when deciding between various products. Chapter 11, "Thin Client Networking," describes common thin client networking solutions and how to implement them in a server-based network. Finally this section will close with Chapter 12, "Extending Terminal Services."

Part III: Network Design, Maintenance, and Troubleshooting

Part III covers different types of network designs, how to maintain your network, and how to troubleshoot problems that come up. Chapter 13, "The Principles of Network Design" covers the details of networking an enterprise. Chapter 14, "Home Networking Technologies," describes how each type of home network works. Chapter 15, "Network Troubleshooting," provides tips on how to ascertain the cause of many network problems you experience. Chapter 16, "Diagnosing Real-World Problems," discusses some common problems that networks experience. Chapter 17, "Disaster Recovery," discusses how to avoid potential problems and how to rebuild your system after a major crash.

Part IV: Intranets and Interconnecting Networks

Part IV discusses various types of networks: intranets and interconnected networks. Chapter 18, "Managing Network Connections," discusses network protocols. Chapter 19, "Intranet, Extranet, and Internet Services," introduces various WAN topologies build on WWW technologies. Chapter 20, "Web Site Content and Design," looks at techniques used to create and design an effective Web site for your intranet or the Internet.

Part V: Network Security

Chapter 21, "Security with Certificates," covers the use of x.509 certificates to control Web site and LAN/WAN security including PKI services. Chapter 22, "Firewalls and your Network," explores the basics of security and some approaches to be used to secure your system; company policies, and NOS security features. Chapter 23, "Securing Your NetWare 6 Network," discusses areas of security concern in a NetWare 5 environment. Chapter 24, "Unix Security," gives a little Unix history and then explains how to keep a Unix system secure. Chapter 24, "Remote Connectivity," explains what remote access and Virtual Private Networks are, how to set them up, and how to keep them secure.

Appendixes

Appendix A, "Beyond Network Administration," is a sneak peek of a day in the life of an IT administrator turned consultant. Appendix B, "Glossary of Networking Terms," provides definitions of common networking terms. Appendix C, "Internet Resources," and Appendix D, "Certification Resources," offer useful URLs to networking resources and certification programs. Appendix E, "ASCII Charts," and Appendix F, "EBCDIC Charts" are additional reference charts.

A Few Typographical Conventions

When a networking operation requires a series of choices from menus or dialog boxes, the ➢ symbol is used to guide you through the instructions, like this: "Select Programs ➢ Accessories ➢ System Tools ➢ System Information." The items the ➢ symbol separates may be menu names, toolbar icons, check boxes, or other elements of the operating system interface—anyplace you can make a selection.

This typeface is used to identify Internet URLs and HTML code, and lines of programming. **Boldface** type is used whenever you need to type something into a text box.

You'll find these types of special notes throughout the book:

TIP

Denotes quicker and smarter ways to accomplish a task, as well as any helpful tidbits you should know.

NOTE

You'll see these Notes, too. They usually offer some additional information that needs to be highlighted.

WARNING

In some places, you'll see a Warning like this one. Because networks can be very complex—and you *really* don't want your network to crash—these appear when there is a possibility of goofing something up. If you see one, read it carefully to make sure you don't get into trouble.

YOU'LL ALSO SEE SIDEBAR BOXES LIKE THIS

These boxed sections provide added explanations of special topics, examples of how certain people or companies might handle a situation in a real life scenario, or ways to perform a specific networking function. Each sidebar has a heading that announces the topic so you can quickly decide whether it's something you need to know about.

For More Information...

See the Sybex Web site, www.sybex.com, to learn more about all the books that went into *Networking Complete*, Third Edition. On the site's Catalog page, you'll find links to any book you're interested in.

We hope you enjoy this book and find it useful. Happy networking!

Part I
NETWORKING FUNDAMENTALS

Chapter 1

AN INTRODUCTION TO NETWORKS

Imagine 20 years ago working in an office with little or no computer equipment. It's hard to imagine now, isn't it? One could say that we take for granted a lot of what we have gained in technology the past few decades. Now, imagine having to send a memo to everyone in the company. Back then we used interoffice mail; today we use e-mail. This is one form of communication that only became available due to the introduction and growth of networks.

This chapter focuses on the basic concepts surrounding how a network works, including the way it sends information and what it uses to send information. This information is covered only to a minor degree by the A+ certification exam. However, if you have interest in becoming a service technician, this information will prove to be very useful, as you will in all likelihood find

Adapted from *A+ Complete Study Guide, Deluxe Edition* by David Groth and Dan Newland

ISBN 0-7821-4052-1   976 pages $59.99

yourself asked to troubleshoot both hardware and software problems on existing networks. Included in this chapter is information on:

- ▶ What is a network?
- ▶ Network types
- ▶ Media types
- ▶ Connectivity devices

NOTE

If you find that the material in this chapter interests you, you might consider studying for, and eventually taking, CompTIA's Network+ exam. It is a generic networking certification (similar to A+, only it is for network-related topics). You can study for it using Sybex's Network+ Study Guide materials available at www.sybex.com.

WHAT IS A NETWORK?

Stand-alone personal computers, first introduced in the late 1970s, gave users the ability to create documents, spreadsheets, and other types of data and save them for future use. For the small business user or home computer enthusiast, this was great. For larger companies, however, it was not enough. The larger the company, the greater the need to share information between offices, and sometimes over great distances. The stand-alone computer was not enough for the following reasons:

- ▶ Their small hard drive capacities were inefficient.

- ▶ To print, each computer required a printer attached locally.

- ▶ Sharing documents was cumbersome. People grew tired of having to save to a diskette, then taking that diskette to the recipient. (This procedure was called "sneakernet.")

- ▶ There was no e-mail. Instead, there was interoffice mail, which was not reliable and frequently was not delivered in a timely manner.

To address these problems, *networks* were born. A network links two or more computers together to communicate and share resources. Their success was a revelation to the computer industry as well as businesses.

Now, departments could be linked internally to offer better performance and increase efficiency.

You have heard the term "networking" in the business context, where people come together to exchange names for future contact and to gain access to more resources. The same is true with a computer network. A computer network allows computers to link to each other's resources. For example, in a network every computer does not need a printer connected locally to print. Instead, one computer has a printer connected to it and allows the other computers to access this resource. Because they allow users to share resources, networks offer an increase in performance as well as a decrease in the outlay for new hardware and software.

LANs vs. WANs

Local area networks (LANs) were introduced to connect computers in a single office. *Wide area networks (WANs)* came to expand the LANs to include networks outside of the local environment and also to distribute resources across distances. Today, LANs can be seen in many businesses, from small to large. WANs are becoming more widely accepted as businesses are becoming more mobile and as more of them are spanning greater and greater distances. It is important to have an understanding of LANs and WANs as a service professional, because when you're repairing computers, you are likely to come in contact with problems that are associated with the computer being connected to a network.

Local Area Networks (LANs)

The 1970s brought us the minicomputer, which was a smaller version of the mainframe. Whereas the mainframe used *centralized processing* (all programs ran on the same computer), the minicomputer used *distributed processing* to access programs across other computers. As depicted in Figure 1.1, distributed processing allows a user at one computer to use a program on another computer as a "back end" to process and store the information. The user's computer is the "front end," performing the data entry. These allowed programs to be distributed across computers rather than centralized. This was also the first time computers used cable to connect rather than phone lines.

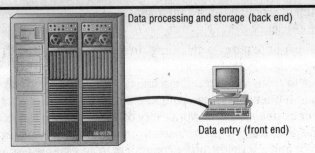

Data processing and storage (back end)

Data entry (front end)

FIGURE 1.1:   Distributed processing

By the 1980s, offices were beginning to buy PCs in large numbers. Also, portables were introduced, allowing computing to become mobile. Neither PCs nor portables, however, were efficient in sharing information. As timeliness and security became more important, diskettes were just not cutting it. Offices needed to find a way to implement a better means to share and access resources. This led to the introduction of the first type of PC LAN: ShareNet by Novell. LANs are simply the linking of computers to share resources within a closed environment. The first simple LANs were constructed a lot like Figure 1.2.

FIGURE 1.2:   A simple LAN

After the introduction of ShareNet, more LANs sprouted. The earliest LANs could not cover a great distance. Most of them could only stretch across a single floor of the office and could support no more than 30 users. Further, they were still simple, and only a few software programs supported them. The first software programs that ran on a LAN were not capable of permitting more than one user at a time to use a program (this constraint was known as *file locking*). Nowadays, we can see multiple users accessing a program at one time, limited only by restrictions at the record level.

Wide Area Networks (WANs)

By the late 1980s, networks were expanding to cover ranges considered geographical in size and were supporting thousands of users. Wide area networks, first implemented with mainframes at massive government expense, started attracting PC users as networks went to this whole new level. Businesses with offices across the country communicated as if they were only desks apart. Soon the whole world would see a change in its way of doing business, across not only a few miles but across countries. Whereas LANs are limited to single buildings, WANs are able to span buildings, states, countries, and even continental boundaries. Figure 1.3 gives an example of a simple WAN.

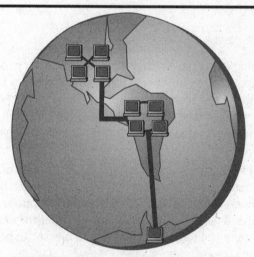

FIGURE 1.3: A simple WAN

Networks of today and tomorrow are not limited anymore by the inability of LANs to cover distance and handle mobility. WANs play an important role in the future development of corporate networks world-wide. Although the primary focus of this chapter is LANs, we will feature a section on WAN connectivity. This section will briefly explain the current technologies and what you should expect to see in the future. If you are interested in more information on LANs or WANs, or if you plan on becoming a networking technician, check your local library resources or the Internet.

Primary Network Components

Putting together a network is not as simple as it was with the first PC network. You can no longer consider two computers cabled together a fully functional network. Today, networks consist of three primary components:

▶ Servers

▶ Clients or workstations

▶ Resources

No network would be complete without these three components working together.

Servers

Servers come in many shapes and sizes. They are a core component of the network, providing a link to the resources necessary to perform any task. The link it provides could be to a resource existing on the server itself or a resource on a client computer. The server is the "leader of the pack," offering directions to the client computers regarding where to go to get what they need.

Servers offer networks the capability of centralizing the control of resources and can thus reduce administrative difficulties. They can be used to distribute processes for balancing the load on the computers and can thus increase speed and performance. They can also offer the departmentalizing of files for improved reliability. That way, if one server goes down, then not all of the files are lost.

Servers perform several tasks. For example, servers that provide files to the users on the network are called file servers. Likewise, servers that host printing services for users are called print servers. (There are other tasks as well, such as remote access services, administration, mail, etc.) Servers can be *multi-purpose* or *single-purpose*. If they are multi-purpose, they can be, for example, both a file server and a print server at the same time. If the server is a single-purpose server, it is a file server only or print server only.

Another distinction we use in categorizing servers is whether they are dedicated or nondedicated:

Dedicated Servers   These are assigned to provide specific applications or services for the network, and nothing else.

Because a *dedicated server* is specializing in only a few tasks, it requires fewer resources from the computer that is hosting it than a nondedicated server might require. This savings in over-head may translate to a certain efficiency and can thus be considered as having a beneficial impact on network performance.

Nondedicated Servers These are assigned to provide one or more network services and local access. A *nondedicated server* is expected to be slightly more flexible in its day-to-day use than a dedicated server. Nondedicated servers can be used not only to direct network traffic and perform administrative actions, but often to serve as a front end for the administrator to work with other applications or services. The nondedicated server is not really what some would consider a true server, because it can act as a workstation as well as a server.

Many networks use both dedicated and nondedicated servers in order to incorporate the best of both worlds, offering improved network performance with the dedicated servers and flexibility with the nondedicated servers.

Workstations or Client Computers

Workstations are the computers that the users on a network do their work on, performing activities such as word processing, database design, graphic design, e-mail, and other office or personal tasks. Workstations are basically nothing more than an everyday computer, except for the fact that they are connected to a network that offers additional resources. Workstations can range from a diskless computer system to a desktop system. In network terms, workstations are also known as *client computers*. As clients, they are allowed to communicate with the servers in the network in order to use the network's resources.

It takes several items to make a workstation into a client. You must install a *network interface card (NIC)*, a special expansion card that allows the PC to talk on a network. You must connect it to a cabling system that connects to another computer (or several other computers). And you must install some special software, called *client software*, which allows the computer to talk to the servers. Once all this has been accomplished, the computer will be "on the network."

To the client, the server may be nothing more than just another drive letter. However, because it is in a network environment, the client is able to use the server as a doorway to more storage or more applications, or through which it may communicate with other computers or other networks. To a user, being on a network changes a few things:

- They can store more information, because they can now store data on other computers on the network.

- They can now share and receive information from other users, perhaps even collaborating on the same document.

- They can use programs that would be too large for their computer to use by itself.

Network Resources

We now have the server to share the resources and the workstation to use them, but what about the resources themselves? A *resource* (as far as the network is concerned) is any item that can be used on a network. Resources can include a broad range of items, but the most important ones include:

- Printers and other peripherals

- Files

- Applications

- Disk storage

When an office can purchase paper, ribbons, toner, or other consumables for only one, two, or maybe three printers for the entire office, the costs are dramatically lower than the costs for supplying printers at every workstation. Networks also give more storage space to files. Client computers are not always able to handle the overhead involved in storing large files (for example, database files) because they are already heavily involved in the day-to-day work activities of the users. Because servers in a network can be dedicated to only certain functions, a server can be allocated to store all the larger files that are worked with every day, freeing up disk space on client computers. Similarly, applications (programs) no longer need to be on every computer in the office. If the server is capable of handling the overhead an application requires, the application can reside on the server and be used by workstations through a network connection.

NOTE

The sharing of applications over a network requires a special arrangement with the application vendor, who may wish to set the price of the application according to the number of users who will be using it. The arrangement allowing multiple users to use a single installation of an application is called a *site license*.

BEING ON A NETWORK BRINGS RESPONSIBILITIES

You are part of a community when you are on a network, which means that you need to take responsibility for your actions. First of all, a network is only as secure as the users who use it. You cannot just randomly delete files or move documents from server to server. You do not own your e-mail, so anyone in your company's management can choose to read it. Additionally, printing does not mean that if you send something to print now it will print immediately— yours may not be the first in line to be printed at the shared printer. Plus, if your workstation has also been set up to be a nondedicated server, you cannot turn it off.

Network Operating Systems (NOSs)

PCs use a disk operating system that controls the file system and how the applications communicate with the hard disk. Networks use a network operating system (NOS) to control the communication with resources and the flow of data across the network. The NOS runs on the server. Many companies offer software to start a network. Some of the more popular network operating systems at this time include Unix, Novell's NetWare, and Microsoft's Windows NT Server (or Windows 2000). Although several other NOSs exist, these three are the most popular.

Back in the early days of mainframes, it took a full staff of people working around the clock to keep the machines going. With today's NOSs, servers are able to monitor memory, CPU time, disk space, and peripherals, without a baby-sitter. Each of these operating systems allows processes to respond in a certain way with the processor.

With the new functionality of LANs and WANs, you can be sitting in your office in Milwaukee and carry on a real-time electronic "chat" with a coworker in France, or maybe print an invoice at the home office in

California, or manage someone else's computer from your own while they are on vacation. Gone are the days of disk-passing, phone messages left but not received, or having to wait a month to receive a letter from someone in Hong Kong. NOSs provide this functionality on a network.

Network Resource Access

Now that we have discussed the makeup of a typical network, let's discuss the way resources are accessed on a network. There are generally two resource access models: peer-to-peer and server-based. It is important to choose the appropriate model. How do you decide what type of resource model is needed? You must first think about the following questions:

- ▶ What is the size of the organization?
- ▶ How much security does the company require?
- ▶ What software or hardware does the resource require?
- ▶ How much administration does it need?
- ▶ How much will it cost?
- ▶ Will this resource meet the needs of the organization today and in the future?
- ▶ Will additional training be needed?

Networks today cannot just be put together at the drop of a hat. A lot of planning is required before implementation of a network to ensure that whatever design is chosen will be effective and efficient, and not just for today but for the future as well. It is the forethought of the designer that will create the best network with the least amount of administrative overhead. In each network, it is important that a plan be developed to answer the previous questions. The answers will help decide the type of resource model to be used.

Peer-to-Peer Networks

A peer-to-peer network is a network where the computers act as both workstations and servers. An example of a peer-to-peer resource model is shown in Figure 1.4.

Peer-to-peer networks are great for small, simple, and inexpensive networks. In fact, this model can be set up almost immediately, with little extra hardware required. Windows 3.11, Windows 95, and Windows NT are popular operating system environments that support a peer-to-peer resource model.

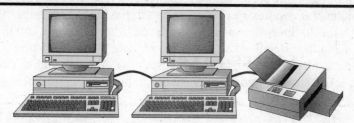

FIGURE 1.4: The peer-to-peer resource model

There is no centralized administration or control in the peer-to-peer resource model. However, this very lack of centralized control can make it difficult to "administer" the network; for the same reason, it's not very secure. Moreover, because each computer is acting as both a workstation and server, it may not be easy to locate the resources. The person who is in charge of the file may have moved it without anyone's knowledge. Also, the users who work under this arrangement need more training, because they are not only users but also administrators.

Will this type of network meet the needs of the organization today and in the future? Peer-to-peer resource models are generally considered the right choice for companies where there is no expected future growth. For example, the business might be small, possibly an independent subsidiary of a specialty company, and has no plans on increasing its market size or number of employees. Companies that are expecting growth, on the other hand, should not choose this type of model. Although it could very well meet the needs of the company today, the growth of the company will necessitate making major changes over time. If a company chooses to set up a peer-to-peer resource model simply because it is cheap and easy to install, it could be making a costly mistake. The company's management may find that it will cost them more in the long run than if they had chosen a server-based resource model.

Server-Based Resource Model

The server-based model is better than the peer-to-peer model for large networks (say 25 users or more) that need a more secure environment and centralized control. Server-based networks use a dedicated, centralized server. All administrative functions and resource sharing are performed from this point. This makes it easier to share resources, perform backups, and support an almost unlimited number of users. It also offers better security. However, it does need more hardware than that used by the typical workstation/server computer in a peer-to-peer resource model. Additionally, it requires specialized software (the NOS) to manage the server's role in the environment. With the addition of a server and the NOS, server-based networks can easily cost more than peer-to-peer resource models. However, for large networks, it's the only choice. An example of a server-based resource model is shown in Figure 1.5.

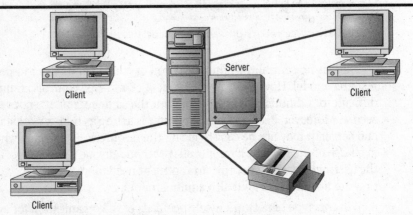

FIGURE 1.5:   The server-based resource model

Will this type of network meet the needs of the organization today and in the future? Server-based resource models are the desired models for companies that are continually growing or that need to initially support a large environment. Server-based networks offer the flexibility to add more resources and clients almost indefinitely into the future. Hardware costs may be more, but, with the centralized administration, managing resources becomes less time-consuming. Also, only a few administrators need to be trained, and users are only responsible for their own work environment.

TIP

If you are looking for an inexpensive, simple network with very little setup required, and there is really no need for the company to grow in the future, then the peer-to-peer network is the way to go. If you are looking for a network to support many users (more than 25), strong security, and centralized administration, consider the server-based network your only choice.

Whatever you decide, be sure to take the time to plan. A network is not something you can just "throw together." You don't want to find out a few months down the road that the type of network you chose does not meet the needs of the company. This could be a timely and costly mistake.

Network Topologies

A *topology* is a way of "laying out" the network. Topologies can be either physical or logical. *Physical topologies* describe how the cables are run. *Logical topologies* describe how the network messages travel. Deciding which type of topology to use is the next step when designing your network.

You must choose the appropriate topology in which to arrange your network. Each type differs by its cost, ease of installation, fault tolerance (how the topology handles problems like cable breaks), and ease of reconfiguration (like adding a new workstation to the existing network).

There are five primary topologies (some of which can be both logical and physical topologies):

- ▸ Bus (can be both logical and physical)
- ▸ Star (physical only)
- ▸ Ring (can be both logical and physical)
- ▸ Mesh (can be both logical and physical)
- ▸ Hybrid (usually physical)

Each topology has its advantages and disadvantages. Chapter 3, "Network Topologies and Types," covers each of these topologies and compares and contrasts each one.

Network Communications

You have chosen the type of network and arrangement (topology). Now the computers need to understand how to communicate. Network communications use protocols. A *protocol* is a set of rules that govern communications. Protocols detail what "language" the computers are speaking when they talk over a network. If two computers are going to communicate, they both must be using the same protocol.

There are different methods used to describe the different protocols. We will discuss two of the most common types in Chapter 3, "Network Topologies and Types," and Chapter 4, "The OSI Model."

Network Architectures

Network architectures define the structure of the network, including hardware, software, and layout. We differentiate each architecture by the hardware and software required to maintain optimum performance levels. The major architectures in use today are Ethernet, Token Ring, ARCNet, and AppleTalk. Chapter 3, "Network Topologies and Types," covers this information in greater detail.

NETWORK MEDIA

We have taken a look at the types of networks, network architectures, and the way a network communicates. To bring networks together, we use several types of media. A medium is the material on which data is transferred from one point to another. There are two parts to the medium, the network interface card and the cabling. The type of network card you use depends on the type of cable you are using, so let's discuss cabling first.

Cabling

When the data is passed from one computer to another, it must find its way onto the medium that is used to physically transfer data from computer to computer. This medium is cable. It is the network interface card's role to prepare the data for transmission, but it is the cable's role to properly move the data to its intended destination. It is not as simple as just plugging it into the computer. The cabling you choose must support both the network architecture and topology. There are four main types of cabling methods: twisted-pair cable, coaxial cable, fiber-optic cable, and wireless. We'll summarize all four cabling methods following the brief descriptions below.

The Network Interface Card (NIC)

The network interface card (NIC) provides the physical interface between computer and cabling. It prepares data, sends data, and controls the flow of data. It can also receive and translate data into bytes for the CPU to understand. It communicates at the Physical layer of the OSI model and comes in many shapes and sizes.

Different NICs are distinguished by the PC bus type and the network for which they are used. This section describes the role of the NIC and how to choose the appropriate one. The following factors should be taken into consideration when choosing a NIC:

- ► Preparing data
- ► Sending and controlling data
- ► Configuration
- ► Drivers
- ► Compatibility
- ► Performance

Preparing Data

In the computer, data moves along buses in parallel, as on a four-lane interstate highway. But on a network cable, data travels in a single stream, as on a one-lane highway. This difference can cause problems transmitting and receiving data, because the paths traveled are not the same. It is the NIC's job to translate the data from the computer into signals that can flow easily along the cable. It does this by translating digital signals into electrical signals (and in the case of fiber-optic NICs, to optical signals).

Sending and Controlling Data

For two computers to send and receive data, the cards must agree on several things. These include the following:

- ► The maximum size of the data frames
- ► The amount of data sent before giving confirmation
- ► The time needed between transmissions
- ► The amount of time needed to wait before sending confirmation
- ► The amount of data a card can hold
- ► The speed at which data transmits

If the cards can agree, then the sending of the data is successful. If the cards cannot agree, then the sending of data does not occur.

In order to successfully send data on the network, you need to make sure the network cards are of the same type (i.e., all Ethernet, all Token Ring, all ARCNet, etc.) and they are connected to the same piece of cable. If you use cards of different types (for example, one Ethernet and one Token Ring), neither of them will be able to communicate with the other (unless you use some kind of gateway device, such as a router).

Additionally, network cards can send data in either full-duplex or half-duplex modes. *Half-duplex communication* means that between the sender and receiver, only one of them can transmit at any one time. In *full-duplex communication*, a computer can send and receive data simultaneously. The main advantage to full-duplex over half-duplex communication is performance. Network cards (specifically Fast Ethernet network cards) can operate twice as fast (200Mbps) in full-duplex mode than they do normally in half-duplex mode (100Mbps).

Configuration

The NIC's configuration includes things like a manufacturer's hardware address, IRQ address, base I/O port address, and base memory address. Some may also use DMA channels to offer better performance.

Each card must have a unique hardware address. If two cards have the same hardware addresses, neither one of them will be able to communicate. For this reason, the IEEE committee has established a standard for hardware addresses and assigns blocks of these addresses to NIC manufacturers, who then hard-wire the addresses into the cards.

Configuring a NIC is similar to configuring any other type of expansion card. The NIC usually needs a unique IRQ channel and I/O address, and possibly a DMA channel. Token Ring cards often have two memory addresses that must be excluded in reserved memory to work properly.

Drivers

For the computer to use the network interface card, it is very important to install the proper device drivers. These drivers communicate directly with the network redirector and adapter. They operate in the Media Access Control sublayer of the Data Link layer of the OSI model.

PC Bus Type

When choosing a NIC, use one that fits the bus type of your PC. If you have more than one type of bus in your PC (for example, a combination ISA/PCI), use a NIC that fits into the fastest type (the PCI, in this case).

This is especially important in servers, as the NIC can very quickly become a bottleneck if this guideline isn't followed.

Performance

The most important goal of the network adapter card is to optimize network performance and minimize the amount of time needed to transfer data packets across the network. There are several ways of doing this, including assigning a DMA channel, using a shared memory adapter, and deciding to allow bus mastering.

If the network card can use DMA channels, then data can move directly from the card's buffer to the computer's memory, bypassing the CPU. A shared memory adapter is a NIC that has its own RAM. This feature allows transfers to and from the computer to happen much more quickly, increasing the performance of the NIC. Shared system memory allows the NIC to use a section of the computer's RAM to process data. Bus mastering lets the card take temporary control of the computer's bus to bypass the CPU and move directly to RAM. This is more expensive, but can improve performance by 20 to 70 percent. However, EISA and MCA cards are the only ones that support bus mastering.

Each of these features can enhance the performance of a network interface card. Most cards today have at least one, if not several, of these features.

Media Access Methods

You have put the network together in a topology. You have told the network how to communicate and send the data, and you have told it how to send the data to another computer. You also have the communications medium in place. The next problem you need to solve is how do you put the data on the cable? What you need now are the *cable access methods*, which define a set of rules for how computers put data on and retrieve it from a network cable. The four methods of data access are:

- ▶ Carrier Sense Multiple Access with Collision Detection (CSMA/CD)
- ▶ Carrier Sense Multiple Access with Collision Avoidance (CSMA/CA)
- ▶ Token Passing
- ▶ Polling

For more information on these methods, see Chapter 3, "Network Topologies and Types."

CONNECTIVITY DEVICES

It's the cabling that links computer to computer. Most cabling allows networks to be hundreds of feet long. But what if your network needs to be bigger than that? What if you need to connect your LANs to other LANs to make a WAN? What if the architecture you've picked for your network is limiting the growth of your network along with the growth of your company? The answer to these questions is found in a special class of networking devices known as *connectivity devices*. These devices allow communications to break the boundaries of local networks and let your computers talk to other computers in the next building, the next city, or the next country.

There are several categories of connectivity devices, but we are going to discuss the six most important and frequently used. They are:

- Repeaters
- Hubs
- Bridges
- Routers
- Brouters
- Gateways

These connectivity devices have made it possible to lengthen the distance of the network to almost unlimited distances. For a complete discussion of these devices, check out Chapter 7, "Network Connectivity Devices."

WHAT'S NEXT

In the next chapter, you'll be introduced to computer networks and how they evolved. You'll learn how to decide whether setting up a network will work for your company, and, if you decide that it will work, this chapter will help you determine the qualities to look for when hiring staff to maintain your network.

Chapter 2

NETWORKS IN THE WORKPLACE

Networking has been with us since man first decided to become a communal animal. We have relied on communication to manage the growth of the human race. From simple communication methods such as the telegraph system and the postal service, networks have become more sophisticated as we advance technologically.

Computer networks have existed for many years, far longer than personal computers. Mainframe systems consisted of a central unit with terminals networked throughout an enterprise that allowed users to process requests and view reports. Although this was a great concept, many users found that trying to get information from the system was not as easy as it seemed. For the most part, any data that users needed had to be requested from the Data Processing department, which in turn had to program the system to retrieve the correct information. This could take several days, weeks, or even months to develop, depending on the complexity of the data.

Written Expressly for *Networking Complete*
by Brad Price

In the early 1980s, personal computers became prevalent within corporate environments; however, they were mainly used to process individual requests. Most Data Processing departments did not recognize the benefit of the personal computer. They resisted change and wanted to keep the data "where it belonged," on the safe, secure mainframe. Other departments took advantage of personal computers and started using canned software to input data into rudimentary databases and spreadsheets so that they could manipulate it, often far faster than the mainframe programmers could program a new report.

As data was modified and manipulated, it could be transferred to other systems. Transferring data from computer to computer via floppy diskettes soon became known as *sneakernet*, because users had to run around from computer to computer to deliver all of the data.

THE FIRST NETWORKS

Sneakernet contained some serious limitations. Foremost, whenever someone needed access to the data, they had to copy it to their computer. Many copies of the same information could be kept on multiple systems at once, and all of them could conceivably contain different information. If someone changed the data contained on their system, they would have to copy it to a floppy diskette and walk it to every other computer that needed the data. Time consuming and not very efficient, safe, or reliable!

As Data Processing departments started to realize the benefit of personal computers, they realized that the independent processing power of the PC had some distinct advantages. These advantages did not come without some serious limitations. After a report was printed out from the mainframe, the data had to be reentered on the PC. Eventually someone figured out a way to get the data from the mainframe onto media that could be read from a PC, but most companies chose to reenter the data.

Eventually, software and hardware became available for personal computers to "talk" to one another. Although originally slow and sometimes unreliable, the ability to transfer information from one computer to another and to share peripherals was invaluable. Most companies took advantage of printer sharing, but they soon evolved into sharing resources on their computers, such as files and applications. As software became more complex, and networks more sophisticated, PCs were networked with mainframes to allow the PCs to offload the mainframe data to its own applications.

COMING FULL CIRCLE

The early Data Processing departments were responsible for making sure that the company's information was safe, secure, and accessible to users. Although "accessible" at the time meant that users requested data reports, they could at least receive those reports on a daily or weekly basis so they could make decisions for the company.

As personal computers proliferated and networks became prominent, the processing of information moved from a centralized model (mainframe-held data) to a decentralized model (personal computers holding and processing information). This did not sit well with many administrators. They wanted to control the data that was available, and for good reason. If the data were to be distributed to personal computers, and the data was replicated to many systems, which one would hold the definitive copy?

Slowly Data Processing departments started taking control of the data again, as well as control of the personal computers within the organization. Most departments took on a new moniker: Information Systems (IS) or Information Technology (IT). Instead of individual departments purchasing and "owning" their PCs, the IS department started controlling what types of PCs would be allowed in the organization. This standardization allowed the IS department to better control the assets it managed. As networks grew, specialized PCs were added that became dedicated computers for tasks such as database, file, and printer sharing. These high-end, powerful "servers" were under the control of the IS department, which managed the same type of control over these resources as they did the mainframes. Centralized management was again obtained.

Users did not relinquish their ability to manipulate the data. Their desktop PCs were able to access the data stored on the servers. Decentralized processing with centralized data control. The best of both worlds? Almost. Although IS departments were not inundated with requests to format new reports based on the data held in the mainframe, controlling the applications and "putting out the fires" caused by novice, or sometimes overtly curious, users proved to be a little costly as far as man hours were concerned.

Many companies are now moving to what is known as the *client-server model*. In this model, users have bare-bones computer systems on their desktops devoid of the luxuries of fast processors, extensive memory, and large hard drives. These systems are merely responsible for displaying information. The server is then responsible for processing all of the information that users request. Also called *server-based computing*, all of the resources are controlled by the IS department, which has control of every application that is used within the organization. If one of the users' computers happens to fail, another unit can replace it very quickly because the applications do not have to be reloaded onto the new unit.

So we have come full circle to a completely centralized model where users have access to terminals, and the IS department controls the information. The PC platform allows users to manipulate data and use applications that are more user-friendly than the mainframe model.

ENTER THE INTERNET

Certain technologies impact the way everyone sees the world. The Internet is one of those life-altering technologies. Although it has been around in one form or another since the early 1970s, it was not until the 1990s that the Internet started to infiltrate our everyday lives. Now, everyone who accesses the Internet, even just to look at a web page or to read their e-mail, is on a network.

As the Internet has grown and matured, the technologies that make it easy for everyone to communicate have become part of nearly every other network. Software that companies use in their day-to-day business is being reworked so that these technologies are available. Companies such as Microsoft, Citrix, Oracle, Novell, and many others understand the benefit of making software user-friendly, and since people are growing more accustomed to the Internet, the applications are taking on the same feel.

Many applications now utilize a web browser as the interface for users to access data. Although this may not be the most efficient method of accessing data as far as the operating system and network are concerned, it is a huge benefit to the organization as a whole. How many people do you know who do not understand how to click on a hyperlink within a web page? The web-based interface is almost second nature because we have been using it so much over the past 10 years. Using software that takes advantage of the web-based feel reduces the total training required by the user. The more familiar the feel of the application, the more readily users will adopt the application.

HOW DO YOU KNOW IF YOU NEED A NETWORK?

Unless you run such a small business that you only have one computer and printer, you probably need some type of network. You can ask yourself several questions to determine if you need to network your computers. Of course, the first question is probably the most obvious:

Are you currently using sneakernet? If you are transferring files from one computer to another, via floppy diskette, CD-ROM, or some other type of media, chances are that you need to look into putting a network in place. Having multiple copies of the same information residing on more than one computer is an accident just waiting to happen. Imagine putting together information based on data that someone else has updated on their machine but neglected to tell you. Both of you go to your boss and present your findings, but your data doesn't match. Not good.

Are you currently supporting multiple versions of the same hardware for several users? Buying printers for every user in the organization is very wasteful, especially if they only use the printer once or twice during the day. Sharing resources amongst many users is not only efficient, but you can make a case for implementing a network by proving the cost savings from sharing resources.

Do you want to centralize administrative capabilities? As mentioned earlier, moving to a networked environment allows administrators to manage and control resources from a central location. Depending on the extent to which you want to take it, you can control access to files and printers, manage e-mail and databases, and control software deployment and access.

WHO MAKES UP THE NETWORK TEAM?

Going with the standard consultant's response: it depends. Smaller organizations may have one administrator who becomes the jack-of-all-trades. Larger organizations will have many administrators who are specialized in specific functions of the network. Part of the planning stage should include identifying your strengths and weaknesses. Know when to admit that your expertise does not match the skills needed to operate an efficient network. You can bring other administrators on board, or you can hire consultants to fill in the gaps. There are numerous options for organizations of every size.

The responsibilities will usually be split among the individual specialties. In smaller organizations, you may find yourself wearing many of these hats, while in larger organizations you may be more specialized.

Infrastructure   The infrastructure specialists program and design the underlying technologies that make up the network. From routers, switches, and hubs to the wires and the wiring closets to the network addressing, they control and manage all aspects of the network communication.

Server administrators   Servers can take on many different faces. Databases, web servers, e-mail servers, and file and print servers are the most common server types. Again, in a small- to mid-sized organization, these roles are often combined, but larger organizations have individuals who specialize in one server type.

Technicians/help desk   Just as users have questions and applications, and computers have a tendency to fail when we most need them, networks can have their own fair share of problems. The technical support group and help desk team should be well versed in the typical problems that may arise and have the expertise to troubleshoot those problems that don't fit the "norm."

Choosing a Network Administrator

Far too often, management decides to invest in a network, and they look around the company to see who is most proficient with computers. This may not be the best choice for the company. Knowing how to work with Windows 98 and knowing how to use Microsoft Office efficiently is not the same as implementing and supporting a network. You should find someone who is proficient with the technologies you are planning on implementing. Neglecting this fact could end up costing you more than hiring someone to perform the duties.

When hiring or promoting someone for the position, you *must* choose someone you can trust. Putting all your eggs into one basket requires that you find someone you can trust to not make an omelet. Remember that the network administrator(s) will have access to all of the data within the organization. No matter how much security is applied to the network and the systems included within it, someone must have enough privileges to access all the files. Trust can be a hard thing to come by, but your administrator will need your trust so they can perform their roles efficiently and successfully.

A network is only as good as the administrator running it. There is a difference between good administrators and great administrators. Good administrators have learned how to use the tools given to them by the designers of the software. They can configure operating systems and the network and make it work. A great administrator, on the other hand, not only knows how to utilize the tools, but also understands the underlying technology and what happens when those tools are used. A good interviewing process will help you determine which candidates are good and which are great administrators.

Finally, you need to have someone who is not resistant to change. Computer systems and networks are in a constant state of flux. Administrators need to constantly stay on top of technology and have the desire to learn. Training is available in several formats: books, computer-based tutorials, and instructor-led classes. Your budget will prove to be the best guideline to which of these you can use, but historically, instructor-led training has been the most effective because it is usually coupled with hands-on labs and immediate feedback.

What's Next

In the next chapter, we'll discuss network topologies and types in detail. We'll cover the distinction between clients, servers, and peers; the many different types of servers; and the software and hardware resources they require. We'll introduce the ways in which computers and other media get linked together to form a network. Finally, we'll outline different types of protocols (the language computers speak).

Chapter 3

NETWORK TOPOLOGIES AND TYPES

In this chapter, you will learn about different types of networks and how they may be connected using different topologies. If you are responsible for a network, you will need to understand these concepts. Although networks are very sophisticated, if you learn the material presented in this chapter, as well as in the other chapters in this book, you will be able to make such a system work effectively for your purposes.

Adapted from *MCSE: Networking Essentials Study Guide*, Third Edition by James Chellis, Charles Perkins, and Matthew Strebe

ISBN 0-7821-2695-2   720 pages $49.99

CLIENTS, SERVERS, AND PEERS

There are three roles for computers in a local area network:

- ▶ Clients, which use but do not provide network resources
- ▶ Peers, which both use and provide network resources
- ▶ Servers, which provide network resources

The type of operating system a computer uses determines each of these computer roles. Servers run network operating systems such as Windows 2000 Server or Novell NetWare. Clients run client operating systems, such as Windows 95/98/Me, Windows 2000 Professional, or Windows XP. Peers run peer network operating systems, such as Windows 95/98/Me or the Macintosh operating system. Each of these operating systems is optimized to provide service for the role it plays.

Many times the role of a computer is also determined simply by use. For instance, a computer running Windows 95 is not a peer unless it is actually sharing network resources. This means that it may be in use only as a client or that it may not be on a network at all. It is also possible to run Windows 2000 Server simply as a client operating system, although it does not make much sense to use a powerful operating system in that role.

Based on the roles of the computers attached to them, networks are divided into three types:

Server-based (also called client-server) Contains clients and the servers that support them.

Peer (also called-peer-to-peer) Has no servers and uses the network to share resources among independent peers.

Hybrid network Is a client-server network that also has peers sharing resources. Most networks are actually hybrid networks.

Server-Based Networks

Server-based networks are defined by the presence of dedicated servers on a network that provide security and resources to the network. Servers have many roles, as discussed later in this chapter.

Server-based (or client-server) networks divide processing tasks between clients and servers. Clients (often called the "front end") request services, such as file storage and printing, and servers (often called the "back end") deliver them. Server computers typically are more powerful than client computers, or they are optimized to function as servers.

In Windows 2000, server-based networks are organized into what are called *active directory domains*. Domains are collections of networks and clients that share security information. Special servers called domain controllers control domain security and logon permission. Computer users cannot access the resources of servers in a domain until a domain controller has authenticated them. In a Novell NetWare network, all users are organized into an NDS tree. All NetWare servers know about the tree, so if one server goes down, another server simply provides resources to the user. Like Windows 2000, user information is stored centrally so users only need to log on once.

Advantages of Server-Based Networks

Server-based networks have a great many advantages, including:

- ▶ Strong central security

- ▶ Central file storage, which allows all users to work from the same set of data and provides easy backup of critical data

- ▶ Ability of servers to pool available hardware and software, lowering overall costs

- ▶ Ability to share expensive equipment, such as laser printers and mass storage

- ▶ Optimized dedicated servers, which are faster than peers at sharing network resources

- ▶ Less intrusive security, since a single password allows access to all shared resources on the network

- ▶ Freeing of users from the task of managing the sharing of resources

- ▶ Easy manageability of a large number of users

- ▶ Central organization, which keeps data from getting lost among computers

Disadvantages of Server-Based Networks

Server-based networks do have some disadvantages, although they are mostly related to the cost of server equipment, including:

- ▶ Expensive dedicated hardware
- ▶ Expensive network operating system software and client licenses
- ▶ A dedicated network administrator (usually required)

Peer Networks

Peer networks are defined by a lack of central control over the network. There are no servers in peer networks; users simply share disk space and resources, such as printers and faxes, as they see fit.

Peer networks are organized into workgroups. Workgroups have very little security control. There is no central login process. If you have logged in to one peer on the network, you will be able to use any resources on the network that are not controlled by a specific password.

Access to individual resources can be controlled if the user who shared the resource requires a password to access it. Because there is no central security, you will have to know the individual password for each secured shared resource you wish to access. This can be quite inconvenient.

Peers are also not optimized to share resources. Generally, when a number of users are accessing resources on a peer, the user of that peer will notice significantly degraded performance. Peers also generally have licensing limitations that prevent more than a small number of users from simultaneously accessing resources.

Advantages of Peer Networks

Peer computers have many advantages, especially for small businesses that cannot afford to invest in expensive server hardware and software:

- ▶ No extra investment in server hardware or software required
- ▶ Easy setup
- ▶ Little network administration required
- ▶ Ability of users to control resource sharing
- ▶ No reliance on other computers for their operation
- ▶ Lower cost for small networks

Disadvantages of Peer Networks

Peer networks, too, have their disadvantages, including:

- ▶ Additional load on computers because of resource sharing
- ▶ Inability of peers to handle as many network connections as servers
- ▶ Lack of central organization, which can make data hard to find
- ▶ No central point of storage for file archiving
- ▶ Requirement that users administer their own computers
- ▶ Weak and intrusive security
- ▶ Lack of central management, which makes large peer networks difficult to work with (10 or fewer computers recommended)

Hybrid Networks

Hybrid networks have all three types of computers operating on them and generally have active directory domains and workgroups. This means that while most shared resources are located on servers, network users still have access to any resources being shared by peers in your workgroup. It also means network users do not have to log on to the domain controller to access workgroup resources being shared by peers.

Advantages of Hybrid Computing

Hybrid computing provides these advantages:

- ▶ The advantages of server-based networking
- ▶ Many of the advantages of peer-based networking
- ▶ Ability of users and network administrators to control security based on the importance of the shared resource

Disadvantages of Hybrid Computing

Hybrid computing shares the disadvantages of server-based networking.

Peer Security vs. Server Security

One large difference in the way peer-to-peer and server-based networks operate is in how they implement security. Peer-to-peer networks are usually less secure than are server-based networks, because peer-to-peer networks commonly use share-level security, while server-based networks commonly use file-level or access permission security.

In Windows 95, for example, the computer user can allow any other computer on the network to access a shared directory or device. The user can assign a password to the shared resource if some degree of security is required. However, the user cannot specify which users on the network can access the resource—any user on the network that knows the password can access the resource.

Another limitation of peer-to-peer shares implemented in this manner is that each shared resource that you wish to control access to must have its own password. The number of passwords to resources that you must remember can quickly grow unwieldy in a large network.

Most server-based networks implement security differently. Instead of requiring a password for every shared resource you wish to access, the server-based network requires only one password for you to access all resources on the network that you have permission to use.

The security advantage of peer-to-peer networking is that each user controls access to their own resources. The security disadvantage of peer-to-peer networks is that you cannot differentiate among network users when you allow access to a resource. The security advantage of server-based networking is that each user is allowed access to only those resources that the user has the privilege to access. A disadvantage is that someone must centrally administer the security on your network.

Selecting the Right Network Type

When deciding which type of network to use, your primary consideration will be whether you can afford a network file server, network operating system software, and the cost of an administrator. If you can, you should consider using a hybrid networking environment to get the advantages of both types of networking. If you cannot, you should use a peer-based network.

It is possible to organize a peer-based network in a fashion similar to a server-based network by using a single powerful peer computer to store network files and share such resources as printers. Then you will be able to administer shared resources centrally and back up your network in one location. This computer will be loaded down, though, so it should be reserved for light computer use only. Peers used this way are called *nondedicated servers*.

REAL-WORLD PROBLEMS

Here are some possible real-world problems; you will find several such sidebars in this chapter. Use the material covered so far to determine the best way to answer the questions posed at the end of each scenario.

You are installing a small network for a collections agency. There will be only five stations on the network. Cost is an issue, and the company would prefer not to dedicate an individual's time to maintaining a network. However, the agency is also concerned about keeping its data safe, and the users are not sophisticated computer users.

▶ In what ways is a peer-to-peer network appropriate for this company? In what ways is it inappropriate?

▶ In what ways is a server-based network appropriate for this company? In what ways is it inappropriate?

You are replacing the minicomputer and terminals in a travel agency with a network of 35 personal computers. The computers will be installed with Windows Me, which includes built-in peer-to-peer networking. You must justify the additional cost of a server and server software.

▶ Why is it a good idea to make this a server-based network instead of or in addition to a peer-to-peer network?

Server Types

Not all servers are alike in a server-based network. A server in a network is dedicated to performing specific tasks in support of other computers on the network. One server may perform all these tasks, or a separate server may be dedicated to each task. A file server, for instance, is dedicated to the task of serving files. A print server provides print services to client computers on the network.

Common server types include these:

▶ File servers

▶ Print servers

▶ Application servers

▶ Message servers

▶ Database servers

Server operating systems support all of these capabilities. In fact, one server can, by itself, serve in all of these capacities simultaneously on a small network. On larger networks, however, you need to spread these roles among multiple servers. Let's take a look at what services each of these server types provides.

File Servers

File servers offer services that allow network users to share files. File services are the network applications that store, retrieve, and move data. This type of service is probably the most important reason companies invest in a network. With network file services, users can exchange, read, write, and manage shared files and the data contained in them. File servers are designed specifically to support the file services for a network. There are several popular types of file servers, such as Windows NT, NetWare, and AppleShare.

The following sections consider these types of file services:

▶ File transfer

▶ File storage and data migration

▶ File update synchronization

▶ File archiving

File Transfer   Before networking computers became a popular way of sharing files, sneaker net was the dominant method. To transfer a file from one computer to another, you would save the file to a floppy disk, put on your sneakers, and walk it over to the other computer. Even in a small office this was an inconvenience, especially when files were too large for a single floppy. For longer distances, it was impossible. The most sophisticated option was to dial the other computer and transfer your files with a modem or across a direct serial connection. But this, too, is an impractical method of sharing files regularly. Fortunately, networks became more sophisticated and began to offer file transfer services. Users can now typically transfer files between clients and servers and between multiple servers.

With all this file transferring taking place, the need for file security arises. Every network operating system has its own level of file security. Higher levels use passwords to control system access, file attributes to limit file usage, and encryption schemes to prevent data from being obtained by unauthorized individuals.

File Storage and Data Migration   One by-product of the era of the "information explosion" is a huge amount of data that must be stored somewhere. Nowhere is this more evident than on the networks of the world.

Twenty years ago, the idea of gigabytes of data would have made your average computer enthusiast's eyes roll. Now, there exist teenage Internet surfers whose 20-gigabyte hard drives are completely full. On networks, terabyte storage systems may become fairly common before too long. As a network administrator, you must find the most affordable and efficient means of storing all this data.

NOTE

A megabyte equals 1,048,576 bytes. A gigabyte equals 1,073,741,824 bytes. A terabyte equals 1,099,511,627,776 bytes!

Not long ago, most storage took place on hard drives. Hard drives can be accessed quickly, but, despite the fact that you can practically set your watch by the falling cost of gigabytes on hard drives, there are still more affordable network storage devices.

Three main categories of file storage are these:

▶ Online storage

▶ Offline storage

▶ Near-line storage

Online storage consists, most notably, of hard drive storage. Information stored on a hard drive can be called up very quickly. For this reason, hard drives are used to store files that are accessed regularly. However, hard drive space is, as mentioned earlier, relatively expensive. There is also another limitation specific to internal hard drives (but not external hard drives): because they are a fairly permanent part of a computer, they cannot be conveniently removed, placed in storage, and replaced when needed.

Much of the heavy load of data most file servers take on is not urgent data. For example, financial records from previous years may be stored on a company's network, waiting only for the day when an audit is necessary. This type of data can be stored just as well on less accessible, less expensive devices.

Offline storage devices include media such as data tapes and removable optical disks. This type of storage offers a high-capacity, low-price alternative to online storage. One disadvantage of this type of storage, however, is that it requires a person to retrieve the disk or tape and mount it on the server. In this age of convenience, that is enough to make a network administrator want to cry. This type of storage is best for data that is rarely used and for data backup.

Fortunately, there is a happy medium. Near-line storage devices offer fairly low costs and high storage capacities, without requiring the network administrator to wake up, go to the archive shelf, and mount the tape or disk on the server. Instead, a machine, such as a tape carousel or jukebox, automatically retrieves and mounts the tape or disk. These systems tend to offer faster, more efficient data access than offline systems, but they are still only fast enough for infrequently used data and applications.

The process by which data is moved from online to offline or near-line storage is called data migration. Network operating systems usually have some type of facility available as an option, possibly from a third party that automatically migrates files from hard drives to near-line or offline storage. Files are selected for migration based on factors such as the last time the file was accessed, the file owner, or the file size.

File Update Synchronization   File update synchronization has the lofty goal of ensuring that each user of a file has the latest version. By using time and date stamping and user tracking, file synchronization works to ensure that changes made to a file are organized in the chronological order in which they actually took place and that files are properly updated.

Imagine that you download some files from a network server onto a laptop. You then take the laptop on a trip to Africa. Meanwhile, back on the network, people are changing those same files left and right. You also make some changes to your copies of the files. When you log in to the network and begin to copy those files back to the network, all the changes will need to be synchronized in some way to make sure the server keeps them in order and your files are updated with the latest changes. Both your files and the server files need updates to put everything in order. This is where file update synchronization comes into play.

File synchronization is usually a third-party option or an upgrade package for most network operating systems. Also, a network operating system cannot synchronize data within files if it is not aware of the file format. For this reason, many database and other information management programs include their own data-synchronization mechanisms.

NOTE

Ideally, update utilities would be able to solve any conflicts. However, at present, there are many cases in which update utilities cannot resolve problems. These utilities merely alert you by flagging files when there are conflicting updates.

File Archiving   File archiving is the process of backing up files on offline storage devices, such as tapes or optical disks.

Because you can back up all the servers on a network onto a single backup storage, archiving files is really not very difficult. Some backup systems even allow central backup for client workstations. In other words, you can back up files that reside on multiple client workstations without leaving your chair. This way, you may be able to store every file on a network on a single central storage device.

TIP

It's best not to procrastinate when it comes to file archiving. Do it now, or you'll later wish you had.

Print Servers

Another important factor in the genesis of computer networking was the demand for the ability to share printers. Before networks made this possible, there were few alternatives. You could employ sneaker net. You could use a manual switching device that hooked up a few computers to a single printer. Or you could keep your printer on a cart and wheel it from computer to computer.

The advent of networking represented a whole new level of computer printing, because a network can

▶ Allow users to share printers

- ▶ Allow you to place printers where convenient, not just near individual computers
- ▶ Achieve better workstation performance by using high-speed network data transfer, print queues, and spooling
- ▶ Allow users to share network fax services

Print services manage and control printing on a network, allowing multiple and simultaneous access to printing facilities. The network operating system achieves this by using print queues, which are special storage areas where print jobs are stored and then sent to the printer in an organized fashion. When a computer prints to a queue, it actually functions as though it were printing to the printer. The print job is simply stored in the queue and then forwarded to the printer when the printer has finished the jobs scheduled ahead of it.

Jobs in print queues may be forwarded in the order received, or they may be prioritized in accordance with other criteria (such as by the size of the egos of the users whose jobs are in the queue).

TIP

To keep everyone happy, you might consider setting up a separate printer for "important" users. Then other users won't need to wait for their lower-priority print jobs.

You can place printers anywhere on a network, and anyone on the network can use any one of those printers. For example, if you want to print on a special 11- by 17-inch network printer that resides five miles away, you can do that.

Printing on a network with queues can be a more efficient way for users to work. The print data is transferred to the queue at network speed. The user can then continue working in an application while the network takes care of the printing.

Network printing also cuts costs by allowing shared access to printing devices. This is especially important when it comes to the more expensive varieties of printers. High-quality color printers, high-speed printers, and large-format printers and plotters tend to cost a lot. It is seldom feasible for an organization to purchase one of these for every individual computer that should have access to one.

Another print service is fax services. Fax machines are now a fundamental communication device around the world. With network print services, you can fax straight from your workstation to a receiving fax machine. This way, you can eliminate the step of printing a hard copy and scanning it into a fax machine. From an application, you can send a document to a fax queue, which then takes care of the faxing. Furthermore, with a fax server, you can receive faxes directly on your workstation. Optical character recognition (OCR) software can even convert these faxes into editable text, thereby saving a lot of time and effort.

Application Servers

Application services allow client PCs to access and use extra computing power and expensive software applications that reside on a shared computer. You can add specialized servers to provide specific applications on a network. For example, if your organization needs a powerful database, you can add a server to provide this application.

NOTE

Application servers are used when efficiency or security requires a program to stay close to the data, and the data stays in one place—for example, to handle large databases or transaction processing.

Application servers can be dedicated computers set up specifically for the purpose of providing application services, or they can serve multiple functions. A single server, for example, can provide file, print, communication, and database services.

TIP

An application server dedicated solely to the task of providing application services can be useful. An organization with such a server can accommodate growth simply by upgrading that server. Windows NT 4 Server and Windows 2000 Server make excellent application servers.

Although in the earlier days of networking, application services were not often found on networks, they have recently become more popular. In terms of network models, they reflect more directly the centralized processing model of the mainframe world. When they do appear on a network, application servers are usually dedicated machines, minimizing the drain on file servers' resources. For example, an accounting department of a large corporation might have an IBM AS400 machine running OS 400 to handle its accounting database software.

Message Servers

Message servers provide message services in a wide variety of communication methods that go far beyond simple file services. With file services, data can pass between users only in file form. With message services, data can take the form of graphics, digitized video, or audio, as well as text and binary data. As hypertext links (electronic connections with other text, images, sounds, and so on) become more common in messages, message services are becoming an extremely flexible and popular means of transmitting data across a network.

Message services must coordinate the complex interactions between users, documents, and applications. For example, with message services, you can send an electronic note, attached to a voice-mail message, to a fellow user on a network.

Four main types of message services are

▶ Electronic mail

▶ Workgroup applications

▶ Object-oriented applications

▶ Directory services

Electronic Mail   Electronic mail, or e-mail, is an increasingly popular reason for installing a network. With e-mail you can easily send a message to another user on the network or on other networks, including the Internet (once your network is connected to other networks, of course).

Originally, e-mail was text-based—it contained only text characters. Now e-mail systems can transfer video, audio, and graphics, as well. With e-mail, sending this data halfway around the world is usually much easier than by any other method. E-mail is much faster than traditional "snail mail" (regular postal mail delivery), much cheaper than courier services, and much simpler than dialing the recipient's computer and transferring the files to it.

E-mail systems are quickly becoming more complex. Integrated voice mail is one of the most popular of the recent developments, rapidly fusing computers and telephones into a single communication system.

Part I

> **NOTE**
>
> Users can now call into the network from a distant telephone and, using a text-to-speech program, have their computer convert their e-mail messages to a synthesized voice that will deliver those messages. In the not-too-distant future, speech-to-text systems that allow you to talk to your computer and convert your speech to an e-mail message may be perfected.

Workgroup Applications   Workgroup applications produce more efficient processing of tasks among multiple users on a network. The two main workgroup applications are

- ▶ Workflow management applications
- ▶ Linked-object documents

Workflow management applications route documents, forms, and notices among network clients. Tasks that require the input of multiple network users are often much easier using this type of application. Scheduling programs are one application of this sort. More complex applications can take care of otherwise difficult paperwork processes. For example, for a supply clerk to complete a requisition at a military base, approval from several higher-ups may be needed. This process could be automated so that each person whose approval is routinely needed would receive the requisition form on the network. The application would send the form around from one person to the next, in the correct order, until all approvals had been granted (or refused).

Linked-object documents are documents containing multiple data objects. A variety of types of data objects can be linked to construct a document. For example, a single linked-object document could contain voice, video, text, and graphics linked together. A network message service can then act as an agent for each of these objects, passing messages between the object and its originating application or file.

Object-Oriented Applications   Object-oriented applications are programs that can accomplish complex tasks by combining smaller applications, called objects. By using a combination of objects, object-oriented applications gain the ability to handle large tasks.

Message services facilitate communication between these objects by acting as a go-between. This way, objects do not need to communicate with other objects on the network. Instead, an object can simply pass data to the agent, which then passes the data to the destination object.

Directory Services   Directory services servers help users locate, store, and secure information on the network. Both Active Directory and Novell Directory Services store information about users and computers. For example, a user can request the postal address of another user from one of these services.

NOTE
You can configure a single server computer to perform any one or all of the preceding directory services functions in a server-based network.

Database Servers   Database services can provide a network with powerful database capabilities that are available for use on relatively weak PCs. Most database systems are client-server based. This means that the database applications run on two separate components:

- ► The client-end portion of the application runs on the client, providing an interface and handling less intensive functions, such as data requests.

- ► The server-end portion of the application handles the intensive performance of database operations. It runs on the database server, managing the database, processing queries, and replying to clients.

For example, imagine a network with a 100-gigabyte database. This database could be managed by a centralized database application based on the client-server model. Clients could request information from the server, which would then perform a query and report the results to the client. The client could then access the data, process it on the client end, and return it to the server.

Database servers are becoming increasingly powerful, providing complex services including security, database optimization, and data distribution. Distributed databases, utilizing database management systems, are becoming increasingly popular.

Distributed databases maximize network efficiency by storing data near where it is needed. From the user end, the database appears as a single entity, even though the data might be stored across the network, close to the users who need those parts. This can boost performance by helping to ensure that users are using local resources to access data, rather than, for example, using WAN lines to access it.

REAL-WORLD PROBLEMS

You have a 40-node network with a single server. You run a Microsoft Exchange Server on your server computer to route e-mail to and from the Internet and your corporate headquarters, and you run Oracle on it to keep track of organizational data. All three of your printers are attached to the server, and all organizational files are stored to the server's hard disk.

▶ What can you do to improve the performance of your network?

Your network installation company uses Microsoft Access to keep track of customers, potential customers, and the various aspects of running a network installation job. The database has grown rather large, and as your company expands and more people access the database, the response time lags.

▶ How can you improve the performance of the database system?

It is essential that your organization not lose data.

▶ What aspects of a dedicated file server will help keep your data safe?

Server Software

Network servers are computers, just like the personal computers used for more mundane tasks, such as word processing and spreadsheet calculations. It is the server operating system software that makes the server computer unique. A server operating system must meet a different and more stringent set of requirements than a network client operating system, such as Microsoft Windows 95/98/Me or the Macintosh operating system.

For example, several characteristics of server operating systems set them apart from most client systems, as described in Table 3.1.

TABLE 3.1: Characteristics of the Server Operating System

Category	Description
Symmetric multiprocessing (SMP)	SMP allows the work of a server to be spread evenly over more than one processor in a single computer.
Multiple-platform support	Computer chip makers constantly produce faster and better chips, and they are not necessarily all compatible with each other. A server operating system should be able to adapt to the fastest chip available.
Log-based file system	A log-based file system is not corrupted by the failure of a disk operation to complete. This keeps data much safer in the face of hardware and software failures.
Filename/directory length	255 characters.
File size	16EB (exabytes).
Partition size	16EB (exabytes).

NOTE

An exabyte is slightly larger than one billion gigabytes. This should be plenty for a while.

Server Hardware

Although the server computer is much like a personal computer, it is often considerably more powerful. With many clients requiring its services, the network server needs a more powerful processor, more memory, a larger hard drive, and more powerful network adapter cards to keep the information flowing. A typical server computer has at least a Pentium III Xenon processor and 512MB or more of RAM.

TIP

As computers get faster and network demands grow, you may find yourself replacing your server computer with a more powerful one. Often, you can recycle your old server as an excellent client computer.

Client Hardware

With the shared services concentrated in network servers, client computers do not need the extra RAM or hard drive storage that would be required if they were to serve the information themselves. A typical client computer now has at least a Pentium III processor and 64 to 128MB of RAM.

NETWORK TOPOLOGY

In the preceding section, you learned how computers are organized into networks to share information and hardware resources. In this section, you will see the ways in which the wires (or other media) can be run to link those computers together.

The way in which the connections are made is called the *topology* of the network. Network topology specifically refers to the physical layout of the network, especially the locations of the computers and how the cable is run between them. It is important to select the right topology for how the network will be used. Each topology has its own strengths and weaknesses.

PHYSICAL TOPOLOGIES

The physical topology you choose for your network influences and is influenced by several factors:

- ▶ Office layout
- ▶ Troubleshooting techniques
- ▶ Cost of installation
- ▶ Type of cable used

First, there's the simple matter of looking at how your office is arranged. Those people setting up only a few computers in a single room will have more options than those with many computers distributed throughout several floors of a building.

Second, troubleshooting techniques and requirements are determined to some degree by the physical topology you use. For example, some topologies have built-in physical redundancy to prevent breaks in the cable from interrupting communications. Other topologies isolate each cable in the network so that a single break won't bring everything down.

Third, not all physical topologies are equal in terms of cost. Some of this cost is going to depend on your office layout, to be sure; it's more work to wire a network that extends over a larger area, and cost will reflect that extra effort. However, some of the cost will be affected by the complexity of the topology you choose and more important, how hard it is to make the topology fit into your space. The bus topology, for example, is simple when done in a small area but could be a major headache to cable if you attempted to run it through a multi-floor network.

Finally, to a significant degree, the physical topology you choose for your network determines what kind of cable you'll get for it and vice versa. UTP uses RJ-45 connectors to connect each computer on the network to a central hub. This particular configuration is called the *star topology* because it looks like rays radiating from a central point. You can't use coaxial cable in the star physical topology because the cables simply don't fit together that way.

That said, let's take a look at the most common physical topologies you're likely to encounter.

The Bus Physical Topology

For simple networks in a small area, the bus physical topology (known in the Mac world as *daisy-chaining*) may be the best solution. In the bus topology, the cable runs from computer to computer, making each computer a link of a chain. All computers on the network share a single cable and this cable is typically coaxial cable.

NOTE
A network using twisted pair cable could use the bus physical topology if you connected the individual PCs with patch cables, but this really isn't practical for connecting more than a couple of computers.

You can connect a bus topology in two different ways, depending on the type of cable you're using. If your network is using the Thicknet coaxial cable, then the bus network will have a central backbone cable that's the thick coaxial cable. Smaller, thinner (and more flexible) cables called *taps* or *drops* will run from the backbone to each PC in the network. A small device called a *transceiver* actually connects the thinner cable to the Thicknet backbone. You can see an example of this topology in Figure 3.1.

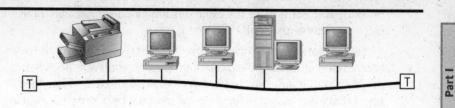

T = terminator

FIGURE 3.1:   The bus physical topology using Thicknet coaxial cable.

The thick Ethernet configuration is normally used in mainframe and minicomputer networks in a setup like the one illustrated in Figure 3.1, but its popularity is diminishing as PCs get smarter and mainframe-based networks become less common. For new networks using the bus physical topology, you're much more likely to use thin coaxial cable.

As opposed to thick Ethernet, *Thinnet* eschews the backbone idea and connects all network devices directly. Rather than using thick cable, Thinnet uses the more flexible coaxial cable shown in Figure 3.2. This is a more popular version of the bus physical topology today than the thick counterpart that uses taps and transceivers. It's mostly a matter of simplicity; the thick cable that thick Ethernet uses is a pain to work with—it's very stiff and clumsy.

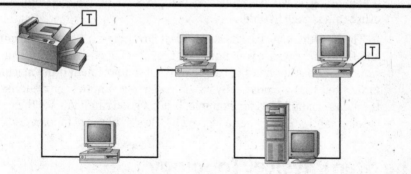

T = terminator

FIGURE 3.2:   In the bus physical topology, PCs can also connect directly to the backbone.

The biggest potential problem with a bus network is that if it's not terminated correctly, then your network can't transmit properly. If you are using the bus physical topology, you must do what you can to prevent breaks in continuity along the cable. Malfunctioning nodes and cable breaks can cause problems for all computers.

The network won't transmit correctly if even one node on the network is malfunctioning because the system depends on every node being in proper working order so that it can pass along the data. This doesn't mean that every machine on the network must be powered up and logged on to the network for the network to work. There is an important distinction between malfunctioning (the cable connection being not quite snapped together, for example) and the node being off. If the node is turned off, then data will pass through the T-connector plugged into the network interface card (NIC) to the next active node. In this case, the network is unaware that an inactive node is present. However, if the node is active and malfunctioning, then problems will occur. The active node will still attempt to process packets but will do it inaccurately, thus slowing down the whole network or bringing it to a screeching halt.

Cable breaks will also cause problems for the bus topology because proper functioning of the network is dependent on the cable running unbroken between its terminated ends. If the cable is damaged at some point along the way, the network won't work, and it can be time consuming trying to figure out just where that break took place so you can replace the broken segment of cable. You might need to inspect every node to make sure that the cables are securely fastened, that no one tried to reboot or log off when a signal was being passed, or that any number of other things were in order.

The bus topology does have one great advantage: it's cable-efficient and therefore can save you money on the most expensive part of your network. On the other hand, it can be difficult to implement if the machines in your network are not neatly lined up in a row. A network extending throughout a building, for example, is not a good candidate for the bus topology and would be better served by the star physical topology.

The Star Physical Topology

In the *star topology*, each server and workstation plugs into a central hub that provides connections to all other devices connected to the hub. If seen from above, a network using the star topology would look something like the schematic shown in Figure 3.3.

The first data communications networks used a star topology to connect dumb terminals to the mainframes. Why is this topology still around? Mostly because it's really easy to work with. Each workstation and server on the network has its own connection to the central switching point. This means that each connection is independent of all other connections; a break in workstation A's cable won't affect workstation B's connection. It also means that the network is relatively easy to cable because you don't have to worry as much about where the computers on the network are in relation to each other. So long as each workstation and server is no more than the maximum cable length from the hub, then that's all you need to worry about.

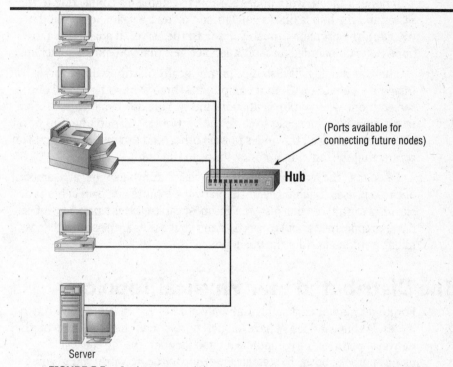

(Ports available for connecting future nodes)

Hub

Server

FIGURE 3.3: In the star topology, all resources connect to a central device.

The centerpiece of the star topology is a hub. Hubs come in several different flavors, but the basic design is simple: they're devices that provide a central junction point for all network cables, providing a connection between each port to permit the computers plugged into it to talk to each other. Another big advantage to the star topology is that it's easy to troubleshoot. As described earlier in the section "The Bus Physical Topology," if your bus network fails, it can be very difficult to pinpoint exactly where the problem lies without a node-to-node search. On a star network, it's very easy to find the source of a problem. If one node doesn't work, the problem probably lies somewhere between the port on the hub and the node that it is physically attached to. You should check to see if the problem lies with one of the following:

▶ The terminal itself

▶ The cable between the hub and the terminal

▶ The port on the hub that services the troubled terminal

If none of the network nodes are able to establish a connection to the server and the hub is fine (a good reason to keep a spare hub around if you can), the problem probably lies with the server. If so, it's time to hope that you planned for fault tolerance and that you did your backups.

The star topology is also nice for physically distributed networks. Imagine a network with four computers—three workstations and one server. If one workstation is upstairs and two are downstairs but in separate rooms, it's a lot easier to cable the network if you don't have to worry about connecting all the nodes to each other, and can just concentrate on connecting the individual workstations to the hub.

Of course, the star topology has one major drawback: the large amount of cable it uses. Each piece of the network requires its own cable run. Having a centralized hub just isn't the most cable-efficient arrangement, so if you're concerned about cable costs and your nodes are close together, you might want to consider the bus topology.

The Distributed Star Physical Topology

For larger networks, a single hub may not be able to support all the nodes. Perhaps it doesn't have enough ports for all the computers on the network; perhaps the computers are too far apart for the cable you're using—perhaps both. To connect everyone to the network, you're going to need more than one hub, but the idea of having three or four separate networks in the same building isn't very appealing. How do you get around this problem?

That's where a variation on the star physical topology comes in. This variation, called the *connected star* or *distributed star*, daisy-chains together the hubs on your network so that all the hubs can communicate (see Figure 3.4). This configuration does have some of the drawbacks of the bus network in that a break in the cable connecting two hubs will isolate the part of the network beyond the break. However, this drawback is compensated for by the fact that without the bus the hubs would be isolated anyway.

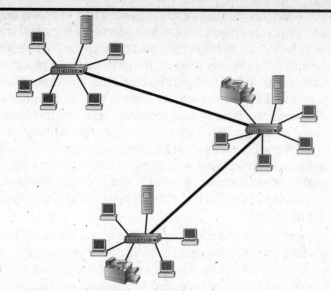

FIGURE 3.4:   Use a distributed star topology to connect multiple star networks.

The Ring Physical Topology

Finally, there's a physical topology that you're not likely to encounter but is worth mentioning. The *ring* physical topology (see Figure 3.5) connects all PCs on the network in a loop, running double cables between each node in order to maintain network integrity. It could work, but it's a real pain in the neck to cable and puts your costs through the roof because of the double cabling costs.

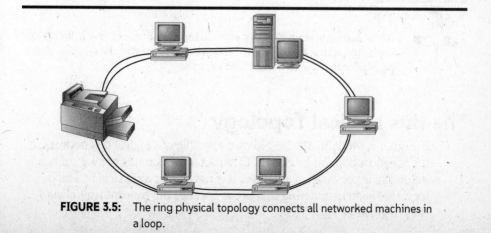

FIGURE 3.5:   The ring physical topology connects all networked machines in a loop.

The ring physical topology has its applications. Fiber wide area networks sometimes use this physical topology because it's not a bad way to give a number of sites in a metropolitan area access to the fiber network. However, the only LAN I've ever seen use the physical ring topology was an old IBM office automation system called the 8100. You're not likely to come across one of these and even less likely to want to cable one if you're building a network from scratch, so you can note that this topology exists and then forget about it. An exception to this rule is fiber channel technology (see "Speed Demons—Fast Ethernet and Gigabit Ethernet" later in this chapter), which may use a physical ring to create a high-speed physical layer path between network nodes and other hardware. Due to the high cost of fiber channel, this isn't one you're likely to see either, but it does exist.

Maybe some of you are scratching your heads at this, saying, "I know of someone who's got a ring network!" You're probably thinking of a Token Ring network. Token Ring is an IBM wiring system that uses the ring *logical* topology of token passing, and we'll learn about that in just a minute.

LOGICAL TOPOLOGIES

Logical, or *electrical,* topologies describe the way in which a network transmits information from one node to the next node, not the way the network looks. It's not all theory, however, because the way you want your network to transmit information can directly affect your options when it comes to purchasing cable and network interface cards.

TIP

It is important to remember that physical topology does not have a direct bearing on the logical topology. You can have a physical star and a logical ring, a physical star and a logical bus, and so forth.

The Bus Logical Topology

Ethernet is probably the best-known example of a logical bus network; it's the most popular LAN type. Ethernet is an example of a *logical* bus topology; as you'll see in a minute, it is not always a *physical* bus topology. (We keep hammering that home because the concept isn't always easy to grasp.)

How does the logical bus topology work? Simply put, each time a node on the network has data for another node, the sending node broadcasts the data to the entire network. The various nodes hear it and look to see if the data is for them. If so, they keep the data. If not, they ignore the data. Every Ethernet card has a 48-bit address peculiar to itself, and each piece of data that travels the network is directed to the address of the card in the node that should receive the data.

NOTE

What if a packet is intended for more than one workstation? Network software can set an Ethernet card to listen for specific multicast addresses. If a packet is intended for the entire network, then the destination address will be entirely 1s, thus signifying that every card should collect that packet.

Whatever anyone on the bus says, everyone hears. It's something like the old telephone party lines, where a number of neighbors would share a telephone number. Each person sharing the telephone was assigned a distinctive ring to determine who was receiving a call. If your code was, say, three quick rings, and you heard the telephone ring three quick rings, you could pick it up and know it was for you. On the other hand, if you heard two long and one short, you'd know that the call was for your neighbor Burt and you'd ignore it. In all cases, everyone heard the rings, but only one person responded—the person who was supposed to receive the call. The bus topology works in a similar fashion, although the bus networks work better than the old party lines in that your neighbor's machine won't gossip with the other PCs on the network about data not sent to it.

If that's how data finds its destination on the network, how do networked computers send it in the first place? On a bus network, every workstation can send out information in a package called a *packet*. Data transmitted on a network of *any* type must conform to the strict format, called the *Data Link Layer Frame* format, which that network type uses for arranging data.

NOTE

Ethernet packets can be of varying lengths, but each packet can be no longer than 1518 bytes, just to make sure that one workstation doesn't hog the network for too long.

Before a workstation broadcasts to the network, it listens to see if anyone else is using the network. If the coast is clear, then the workstation broadcasts.

What if the coast isn't clear? The biggest problem with the broadcast method of network transmittal is distance. If the distance between two computers on the same network (let's call them Node A and Node B) is too great, they may not hear each other on the line. If they can't "hear" each other, then Node A can't tell whether Node B is transmitting or not. Thinking that all is quiet, Node A may therefore begin its transmittal when Node B is already transmitting data. If this happens, and two nodes transmit at the same time, an event called a packet collision occurs, causing a frequency "ripple" on the cable. The first node to detect this increased frequency ripple will send out a high-frequency signal that will cancel out all other signals. This signal tells all nodes that a collision has occurred and that all nodes on the network should stop sending packets. At this point, each node waits a random amount of time, and then tries broadcasting again. They will do this up to 16 times before giving up. Take a look at the sidebar "How Nodes Recover from Collisions" for more details on how this works. Figure 3.6 illustrates this process for Ethernet networks.

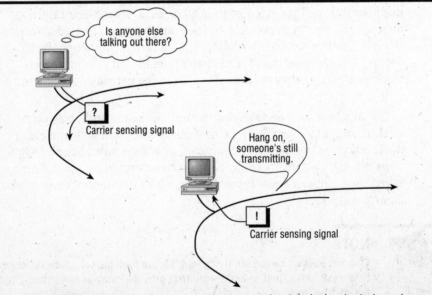

FIGURE 3.6:   How packets are sent on a network using the bus logical topology.

HOW NODES RECOVER FROM COLLISIONS

The system that nodes use to decide when to resend their data is known by the unfortunate name *truncated binary exponential back-off*. (No, unlike almost everything else in the LAN world, it doesn't have a convenient and commonly used acronym or abbreviation.) In plain language, this means that after two nodes collide, each node on the network randomly generates a whole number between one and two, multiplies that number by one half, and then waits that number of milliseconds before retransmitting. Of course, the first time out the chances are 50/50 that A and B will pick the same number, so they might have to retry again. The next time, A and B will each randomly pick a number between one and four and do the same thing. If they pick the same number again, they'll each pick a number between one and eight. This goes on, doubling each time, either until A and B choose different numbers and send their information, or the 16 attempts are up and they stop trying. The chances are pretty good that both A and B will get to send their data, but by the time they get to the sixteenth try, this could be up to half a second delay. Realize that for a network transmitting data at 100 million bits per second, half a second is an eternity. It's very rare for a bus network to need that many retries.

How likely are collisions? Having cable no longer than it's supposed to be decreases your chance of a collision because the nodes can hear other nodes broadcasting. (For example, on Ethernet networks that means a cable can be no longer than 185 meters before the signal must be boosted.) In fact, the way the bus logical topology works *increases* the likelihood of packet collisions. If a node can't broadcast until the network is clear and more than one node has information to send, what's going to happen as soon as the line's free? Both nodes will leap to get their information out first, and the result is a collision.

Keep in mind that all of this processing takes place at the Ethernet NIC. Therefore, if you are going to use the Ethernet topology, all of your nodes must have Ethernet cards. Ethernet can run on top of a physical bus, physical star, or physical ring.

NOTE

Ethernet isn't the only example of a bus logical topology, but it is the most common one. Other networks using the bus logical topology include ArtiSoft's LANtastic and the LocalTalk/AppleTalk network built into Macintosh computers. LocalTalk only transmits at one quarter of a million bits per second, but employs many of the basic design principles of Ethernet.

The Ring Logical Topology

The bus logical topology is a broadcast system—what one station says, all stations hear—but the ring topology doesn't work that way. In the ring topology, used by Token Ring and Fiber Distributed Data Interface (FDDI) networks, every station must repeat what it hears from the previous station, making a kind of "bucket brigade" of data. When a piece of data gets back to the originator, it stops. An entire file can't be transmitted in one packet, so its pieces will be transmitted in succession as illustrated in Figure 3.7.

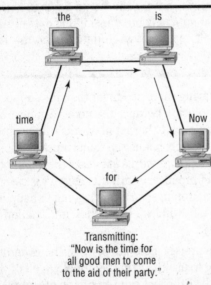

Transmitting:
"Now is the time for
all good men to come
to the aid of their party."

FIGURE 3.7: Sending data with the ring logical topology.

The heart of the ring logical topology is the *token packet*. To avoid packet collisions, the ring topologies ensure that only one workstation can send information across the network at any given time. Only the node that has control of the token packet can send information across the network.

How does the token packet move around the network? When a workstation is done with the token packet, it releases it to whatever station is next in line. If nobody grabs it, the workstation releases it a second time. If nobody responds to the token packet for a second time, then the workstation sends out a general query, known as a *solicit successor frame*. This frame goes out over the network, asking, "Who's supposed to get the token next?" If a workstation responds, the sending workstation addresses the token to that workstation and passes the token. Because no single node can transmit for longer than it takes for a piece of data to make a complete circuit of the network, no PC ever waits more than one circuit's worth of information before getting a chance to transmit.

In the ring logical topology, data is not broadcast on the network but passed from node to node. Thus, timing is important to make sure that frames passed on the network are received properly, and the token is responsible for maintaining this timing. Given the token's importance in keeping order on a network using the ring logical topology, one computer is dedicated to token management. This computer, called the *token master* or *active monitor*, detects lost tokens, monitors frame transmissions, and creates a new token when necessary. The active monitor also maintains a regular clock tick on the network that keeps all other nodes synchronized.

IEEE STANDARDS

The Institute of Electrical and Electronics Engineers (IEEE) has standardized some network types. They're defined at the physical and data link layers of the Open Systems Interconnect (OSI) model. These layers overlap, as the standards describe both physical media and methods of packet transmittal. In other words, you can know how a network that conforms to one of these standards will behave and how that network is designed to work. In this section, we'll review some of the IEEE standards for which you're likely to see references when dealing with networking.

NOTE
All of these standards begin with "802" because the 802 committee of IEEE is in charge of LAN standards.

The 802.2 Standard

The 802.2 standard defines the rules for data link communications for networking topologies 802.3–802.5. Working for both Token Ring and Ethernet, it provides the interface between networking protocols such as TCP/IP and the network types. The 802.2 standard can function either in connectionless mode (for protocols that don't require an explicit connection to be established before they start transmitting data) or in connection-oriented mode for protocols that do require such an explicit connection to be made.

The IEEE divides the data link layer into two sections: the *logical link connection* (LLC, or *data link connection*; both terms are used) and *media access control* (MAC). The LLC handles the interface between all networking topologies and their network-layer communication protocols. To do this, the LLC relies on the MAC layer to provide it with certain addressing information. The method of addressing information it uses defines the network type.

The Ethernet (802.3x) Standard

Ethernet was originally designed in the 1970s by Dr. Robert Metcalfe as part of an "office of the future" project. At that point, it was a 3Mbps network. In 1980, Ethernet was standardized as a 10Mbps network by the DEC-Intel-Xerox (DIX) consortium, and then in 1985 standardized by the 802 committee of IEEE. Since then, new Ethernet technologies have followed the basic pattern of that original Ethernet design, which called for a logical bus topology and a method of error detection and recovery called carrier sense multiple access with collision detection (CSMA/CD, described in a moment). The various forms of Ethernet use different physical topologies (bus and star, for example) and cabling types (such as UTP, coax, and fiber).

NOTE

All Ethernet-type networks—10Base2, 10Base5, 10BaseT, or 10BaseF—use variations of the 802.3x or "Ethernet" standard.

Ethernet Basics

Information travels an Ethernet network in packets consisting of six parts:

Preamble   Consists of eight bytes of information used to coordinate the rest of the information in the packet.

Destination address   Consists of the hardware address (burned into the Ethernet card) of the workstation or workstations that are to receive this information.

Source's address   Allows the receiving workstation or workstations to recognize the workstation that sent the information.

Type   Designates the type of information that is held within the data part of this packet, whether it is graphic information, ASCII text information, or whatever.

Actual data   Can be anywhere from 46 to 1500 bytes long.

Frame checked sequence   Resembles a packing slip; it's used to verify that the rest of the packet reached its destination intact.

You can see the parts of an 802.3 Ethernet frame in Figure 3.8.

Preamble 7 bytes	Start delimiter 1 byte	Destination address 2-6 bytes	Source address 2-6 bytes	Length 2 bytes	Data 46-1500 bytes	Frame check sequence 4 bytes

FIGURE 3.8:   The structure of an 802.3 Ethernet RAW frame.

There are several different kinds of Ethernet, each with its own number and its own name by which it's more commonly known. These types are described in Table 3.2.

INTERPRETING ETHERNET NAMES

The various Ethernet types have common names by which they're more often known than by their IEEE committee numbers. These names take the form of numbers and letters and may not appear much more descriptive than the IEEE numbers. They're not perfectly descriptive, but the basic idea is that the first number represents the top speed of the network in megabits per second. The word "base" means that the transmission is *baseband*, or transmitted serially, as opposed to broadband networks such as those sometimes used for WAN connections, in which data may be transmitted along a parallel path. Finally, the last letter indicates something about how long (in meters) a segment of the network may be.

This final part isn't really very helpful as it's not always accurate. For example, 10Base2 networks have an actual run length of 185 meters. Also, it isn't always a number but instead refers to cable type, as in 100BaseT (twisted pair) or 100BaseF (fiber) networks. However, if you've ever wondered why a 10Base2 network was called that, this is why.

TABLE 3.2: Some Ethernet Types and Descriptions

IEEE NUMBER	COMMON NAME	PHYSICAL TOPOLOGY AND MEDIA	BANDWIDTH
802.3	10Base2	Thin coaxial cable in a bus topology	10Mbps
802.3	10Base5	Thick coaxial cable for the backbone; taps to the backbone from each PC	10Mbps
802.3u	100BaseT or Fast Ethernet	Unshielded twisted pair in a star topology	100Mbps (10Mbps version is 802.3)
802.3z	Gigabit	Ethernet fiber-optic for the backbone, coaxial cable for the taps to the hub, all in the star topology	1000Mbps

NOTE

No matter what the physical topology of the network, an Ethernet network always uses the bus logical topology, which means that all cables in the LAN are part of the same path and are available to all networked PCs.

Whichever type of network it's running on, the 802.3n standard's most salient feature is the *carrier sense multiple access with collision detection* (CSMA/CD) designation. Carrier sense multiple access with collision detection; quite a mouthful, eh? It gets to the heart of the basic Ethernet problem discussed before: how can you send vast amounts of information simultaneously across the network without causing collisions?

The short answer is that you can't. However, that's not bad news; Ethernet is *supposed* to experience collisions from time to time. To understand CSMA/CD, let's break it apart. "Carrier sense" means that all nodes on the network listen to the network to see whether it's clear before attempting to transmit. "Multiple access" means that all nodes on the network have access to the same cable—that signals are broadcast across the entire LAN. "Collision detection" means that each node can tell if another node starts transmitting data at the same time the first node is already sending data. In short, CSMA/CD provides a means for reducing packet collision by having each PC broadcast a signal known as the *carrier-sensing signal* before transmitting in order to see if any other workstations are broadcasting. If not, the signal gives the workstation the "all-clear," and the workstation transmits its packet. However, if the carrier-sensing signal detects another workstation's transmittal, the workstation waits before broadcasting.

Part I

This process avoids collisions so long as network traffic isn't heavy and the LAN's cables aren't any longer than their rating. If either of those conditions exist, then collisions are likely to happen regardless of CSMA/CD. CSMA/CD isn't in charge of making sure that only one workstation transmits at a time, it's in charge of making sure all workstations are quiet before one transmits. If two workstations happen to begin transmitting at the same time, there's nothing that CSMA/CD can do to avoid the collision.

If two packets collide, CSMA/CD tries to avoid a repeat collision. As I discussed earlier in this chapter, the first time a collision happens, each workstation chooses a random number between one and two before transmitting again. If the workstations choose the same number, causing another collision by beginning their broadcasts at the same time, they each choose a number between one and four and try again. This process goes on until either the workstations have both successfully completed their transmissions or they've tried 16 times without success. If they flunk out by the sixteenth try, both workstations have to pause and give the other workstations a chance to transmit.

TIP

If 16 tries doesn't produce a successful transmittal, then something is wrong. Check for broken cables or a heavily overloaded network.

The list below shows the range of numbers possible at each repeated attempt to transmit:

Retry Number	Range of Numbers
1	1–2
2	1–4
3	1–8
4	1–16
5	1–32
6	1–64
7	1–128
8	1–256
9	1–512
10–16	1–1024

In short, CSMA/CD isn't designed to prevent every collision, but it tries to minimize the time that collisions tie up the network. You can see the entire process in Figure 3.9.

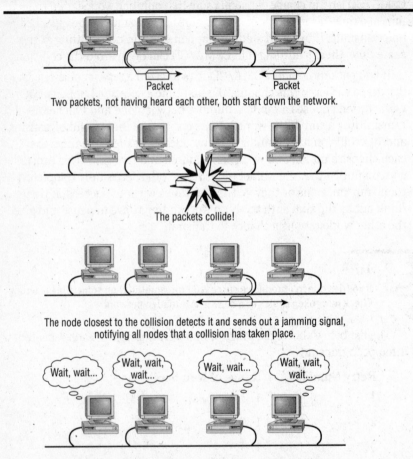

Two packets, not having heard each other, both start down the network.

The packets collide!

The node closest to the collision detects it and sends out a jamming signal, notifying all nodes that a collision has taken place.

Wait, wait...

Wait, wait, wait...

Wait, wait...

Wait, wait, wait...

Each node on the network waits a random number of milliseconds before transmitting, in hopes that they won't coincidentally wait the same amount of time and send the packets at the same time again.

FIGURE 3.9:   How CSMA/CD recovers from collisions.

Speed Demons—Fast Ethernet and Gigabit Ethernet

As noted, Ethernet originally ran at 3Mbps and was upgraded to 10Mbps. This 10Mbps speed lasted for quite a while until Fast Ethernet, running at 100Mbps over Category 5 UTP, was released as an official standard in 1995. This trend has been continued with the development of Gigabit

Ethernet, a backbone technology designed to allow Ethernet networks to operate at line speed over fiber-optic cable and has been proven to work using all four of the pairs of twisted-pair wiring. As its name implies, Gigabit Ethernet runs at 1000Mbps, or 1Gbps.

Generally speaking, the main differences between the various types of Ethernet lie in the physical media used and the speeds derived from using the faster media. All types of Ethernet use CSMA/CD, and all use the same frame type illustrated in Figure 3.8. The greater transmittal speeds of Fast Ethernet and Gigabit Ethernet come about largely because of the media used, not from significant changes to the framing standards or transmission methods. This means that Ethernet networks of varying speeds can be connected without requiring changes to the packet structure. In fact, it's fairly common for an Ethernet network to combine a couple of different speeds, perhaps supporting both 10Mbps and 100Mbps connections, or supporting 100Mbps to the desktop with a 1Gbps backbone. That's why you can have one network card that supports both 10Mbps Ethernet and Fast Ethernet with a single connection. Each type of Ethernet works a little differently on the physical layer, but all use the same data link layer standards, so they can interoperate.

Gigabit Ethernet supports half-duplex transmission for shared areas of the network (those on which nodes are contending for bandwidth) and full duplex for unshared switch-to-switch areas. The shared areas, which use CSMA/CD to manage packet collisions, operate slightly differently than shared areas under slower types of Ethernet. The problem is the high line speeds. As the network speeds are so fast, the timing had to change; otherwise, nodes wouldn't be able to "hear" each other before their transmission was over. Thus, in Gigabit Ethernet, for devices operating in half-duplex mode (network nodes), the minimum time slot available for each packet has been increased from 64 bytes to 512 bytes—that is, each node will be given windows sufficient to transmit 512 bytes instead of 64 bytes. Packets smaller than 512 bytes will be padded to accommodate this increased time slot. As this larger time slot slows down packet transmission by reducing the "clock tick," Gigabit Ethernet supports packet bursts so that groups of smaller packets can be sent during a single time slot. However, this change to timing doesn't affect interoperability with slower types of Ethernet, particularly because the full-duplex areas of the Gigabit Ethernet network use the same 64-byte time slots as slower versions of the 802.3n standard.

This change in network timing led to another innovation especially for Gigabit Ethernet networks to be used on the backbones—a device called a *buffered distributor*. The buffered distributor is a hub-like device connecting two or more Gigabit Ethernet segments, like a repeater. The main difference between a buffered distributor and a repeater is that a repeater forwards packets to the outgoing segments as it gets them, while the buffered distributor can buffer frames to get better use out of existing bandwidth.

USING FIBER FOR HIGH-SPEED NETWORKS

Gigabit Ethernet wasn't created in a vacuum. Its methods of getting line-speed network transmission out of a channel are related to those originally developed for fiber channel networks.

Fiber channel was originally conceived as a method of blurring the distinction between network hardware and the network, but not in the way that this kind of blurring is usually done. Rather than logically making all parts of the network accessible from a single location (as networking attempts to do), fiber channel physically makes all parts of the network a single unit by replacing network cables and high-speed data channels, such as SCSI connectors with high-speed fiber channels that run at gigabit speeds. Thus, a server can be connected to a hard disk across the room from it, but still treat that hard disk as though it were a locally attached piece of hardware.

Fiber channel conceives of connections as possibly being one of three types. First, a connection can be point-to-point, connecting two devices. Second, it can be arranged in a physical ring, with all devices looped together. Third, it can be arranged in what's called a *fabric*, in which devices are part of a physical and logical mesh.

As fiber channel is a high-end and high-cost technology, it's not one you're likely to encounter often. However, it's worth noting now both as a contributor to Gigabit Ethernet and as a rival to SCSI because it allows all parts of the network to be physically distributed in the manner most convenient to the people using it, not by the limitations of the data channels.

You're not likely to see Gigabit Ethernet to the desktop any time soon; it's too expensive. You will find this technology deployed as a means of creating a high-speed connection between routers or switches and servers on an Ethernet network. Deployment to the desktop will come when prices fall, as they did with Fast Ethernet.

The Token Bus (802.4) Standard

In an effort to design a standard less prone to collisions than the 802.3, the IEEE 802.4 subcommittee designed a combination bus/ring topology that transmitted information via a token but would use the bus physical topology. The 802.4 standard is designed around the observation that computers are prone to the same fallibility as humans: give 'em half a chance, and they'll talk right on top of each other. To get around this problem, the 802.4 committee described a token packet that the network could use to decide which machine got to "talk." So it is with the 802.4 standard.

Only the workstation that has the token can send information, and once that workstation has received acknowledgment of the receipt of that information, it must then pass the token to the next workstation in line. How does the network determine who's next in line? In the 802.4 standard, the network keeps track of who gets the token next. Just as the business manager could get the talking stick more often than the person in charge of office decorations, it's possible for some workstations to have higher priority to get the token than others.

The method of controlling collisions isn't the only way in which the 802.4 standard differs from the 802.3 standard. First, the medium is different to some degree; a Token Bus network runs on either 70-ohm coaxial cable (unlike the 50-ohm used by 10Base2) or fiber. Second, as you can see in Figure 3.10, an 802.4 Ethernet frame looks different than an 802.3 frame in that it contains the following: a preamble, a start frame delimiter, a frame control, a destination address, a source address, information, a frame check sequence, and a frame delimiter.

Preamble	Start frame delimiter	Frame control	Destination address	Source address	Information	Frame check sequence	Frame delimiter

FIGURE 3.10:   An 802.4 Ethernet frame.

Although the token/bus combination avoids collisions, the 802.4 standard still has some disadvantages that have kept it from common usage. Most shortfalls of the token/bus format come from malfunctioning hardware, which can result in the token being lost, or shadowed tokens that make it look as though there are multiple tokens on the network. Imagine a board meeting with more than one talking stick!

The Token Ring (802.5) Standard

The IEEE 802.5 committee developed the 802.5 standard in conjunction with IBM. This standard is specifically designed for Token Ring networks that use the token specification to pass information from one workstation to another.

As in the 802.4 standard, the workstations on a Token Ring network use a token to determine which workstation gets to transmit data at any given time. If a workstation doesn't need to transmit anything, it passes the free token to the next workstation and so on until it gets to a workstation that needs to transmit something.

Data travels from the originating workstation to every node on the network in succession. Each workstation examines the address on the data packet. If the data is for that station, it keeps a copy of the data and sends the original on. If the data isn't for that station, it merely sends it to the next workstation on the network. When the sending workstation gets back the copy of its first data packet, it knows that it is time to stop transmitting and passes the free token to the next workstation. This process is illustrated in Figures 3.11, 3.12, and 3.13.

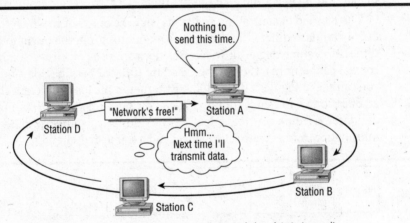

A free token is passed from node to node until one node has data to transmit.

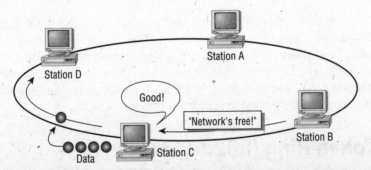

Station C has data to transmit to station B. Upon receiving the free token, station C begins to transmit data instead of passing the free token to the next station.

FIGURE 3.11:   How token passing works (stage 1).

The 802.5 standard has some qualities to recommend it. With a smart hub, the Token Ring standard can help the network recover from problems due to malfunctioning hardware—a nice feature that the Token Bus standard doesn't have. If a workstation malfunctions, either not releasing the token when its turn is up or jabbering over the network, the smart hub can tell that there's trouble and cut that workstation from the LAN, allowing the rest of the network to function normally. An 802.5 network can also extend for longer distances than either the 802.3 or the 802.4 because the packet travels from one workstation to another, retransmitted at every step, and so it never has very far to go before being retransmitted.

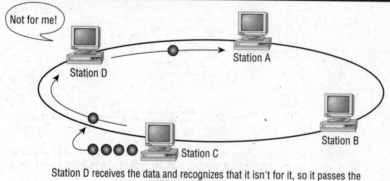

Station D receives the data and recognizes that it isn't for it, so it passes the data along and forgets about it.

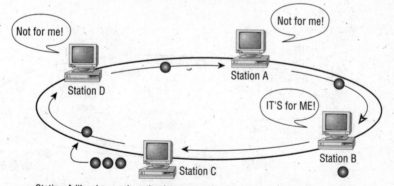

Station A likewise receives the data, notes that it isn't for it either, and passes it along. Station B, however, recognizes that it is the destination address and makes a copy of the data for itself. Then, instead of halting the transmission, it continues to send the data around the ring.

FIGURE 3.12: How token passing works (stage 2).

A Token Ring board attaches to the multistation access unit (MAU) with a D-shell type connector on one side and an odd-looking IBM connector on the other. The Token Ring connector just pops into the MAU.

Eight PCs can attach to one MAU; from there, those MAUs attach to other MAUs. There are no terminators on Token Ring networks; one end of the cable plugs into the board, the other plugs into the MAU.

As with the hubs for 10BaseT, you can most easily arrange your Token Ring network so that cables extend from a central wiring closet on each floor to workstations on that floor and put the MAUs in the wiring closet. The cables between the MAU and the network device can be up to 45 meters long, providing enough space for most floor plans to be cabled with a wiring closet.

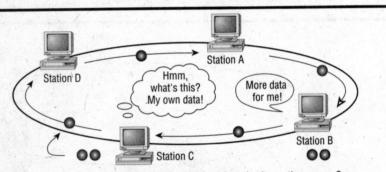

Station C sees the incoming frame of data and recognizes that it was the source. Once it notices its own data, it quits sending data (regardless of whether it's finished) and releases a free token instead.

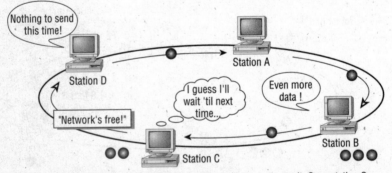

The free token gives someone else on the ring a chance to transmit. Once station C receives the free token ring, it can finish sending its data to station B.

FIGURE 3.13: How token passing works (stage 3).

Although the Token Ring network has a ring logical topology, it uses a star physical topology. Instead of hubs, Token Ring uses either concentrators or, more commonly, MAUs. Don't confuse this MAU with the media attachment unit, which is a transceiver connecting to the AUI port on an Ethernet adapter.

NETWORK MEDIA

In the preceding section, you were introduced to several ways of physically linking computers. In this section, we will briefly discuss what their connection media are made of and how that affects computer networking.

What Are Media?

Media are what the message is transmitted over. Different media have different properties and are most effectively used in different environments for different purposes. For example, television is a good medium for quick coverage and dramatic presentation of news events, whereas newspapers are better suited for a more in-depth presentation of issues. A scholarly journal or technical report might marshal facts more convincingly than television or newspapers. Figure 3.14 illustrates the concept of media.

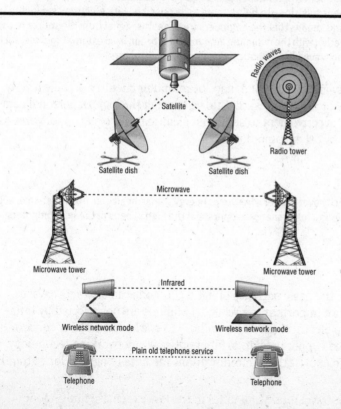

FIGURE 3.14: Media can be anything that carries a message.

In computer networking, the medium affects nearly every aspect of communication. Most important, it determines how quickly and to whom a computer can talk and how expensive the process is.

Copper

The most common network medium is copper. This metal has served our communications needs for over a century and will most likely be widely used for another century. Engineers have become very good at sending electrical signals over copper wires and detecting them with a great deal of fidelity at the other end.

NOTE
Fidelity is how precisely the signal that is received corresponds to the signal that was sent. High-fidelity audio equipment attempts to give the listener an experience as close to being there as is possible with electronics. Fidelity in networks means that the engineers try to get the signal from the source to the destination with the minimum amount of distortion from external sources, such as radio waves or magnetic fields from electric motors.

Electricity is the native language of computer circuitry. It is electricity, not photons or radio waves, that flows through the logic of personal computers, so it is convenient to send that electricity out over copper wires to be detected by other computers.

NOTE
Electricity over copper wires loses energy the farther it gets from its source, and it requires a lot of energy to operate at the high speeds of today's computers.

Glass

Photons are the basic particles of light. (Photons can also act as waves, but that is not important to this text.) Photons are not affected by interference from electrical devices or radio waves, which is a major concern in high-speed copper networks. Fiber optics is a networking technology developed to exploit the communications medium of light in long strands of glass.

Light can travel for several miles in the less expensive multi-mode fiber-optic cable without signal loss. The more expensive single-mode fiber-optic cable long-distance telephone companies use can carry a light signal for several hundred miles without signal degradation.

> **NOTE**
>
> A single strand of fiber-optic cable can transmit data at over 2 gigabits per second. Two thousand novels of average length could be transmitted over fiber-optic cable in one second.

Unfortunately, properly installing fiber optics requires more skill than installing copper wire, and an adapter card for a computer to send data at several gigabits is very expensive. Fiber optics is used mainly in environments where copper will not work and where the faster speed is really needed—for instance, a machinery shop where interference would disturb signals on copper wire or an animation studio where the large animation files would take a long time to exchange over copper wire.

Air

Both fiber optics and copper cabling have the drawback that you need a cable to connect the computers. Infrared technology can send the data right through the air—no cabling required! Infrared provides an effective solution for temporary or hard-to-cable environments, or where computers (such as laptops) are moved around a lot. For example, a worker equipped with a laptop or other mobile computer can connect to a network or print to a printer by lining up the computer's infrared port with an infrared port attached to the network or printer.

Infrared is a line-of-sight technology. The photons will not go through walls, which limits the usefulness of infrared in office environments. Figure 3.15 illustrates an infrared network in an office environment.

Infrared is not a very high-speed network when compared to copper and fiber-optic networks. Most local area networks today operate at a speed of 10Mbps, and networks that operate at 100Mbps are becoming affordable. Infrared adapters operate at speeds ranging from .3Mbps (adapters designed for serial printing) to 4Mbps (the new IRDA standard for infrared communication). Some infrared equipment, such as infrared laser bridges, operate at data rates of 100Mbps and beyond, but the cost and complexity of such specialized hardware make it impractical to use them in local area networks. The limited amount of infrared equipment produced for local area networks keeps costs high, but as infrared technology improves and gains wider acceptance, the prices will drop.

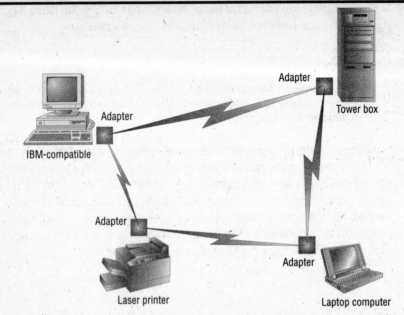

FIGURE 3.15:   Infrared network interface adapters connect computers without wires.

Radio

Another through-the-air method is via radio. Engineers have been sending information over electromagnetic waves for almost as long as they have over copper wires.

Radio waves will go through walls. Radio waves will also reach places it is difficult to get a network cable to. There is a very dynamic industry providing radio links to connect networks together.

Radio links can connect computers without regard to walls or line of sight. Radio is also immune to rain and snow, unlike external infrared installations.

WARNING

Radio is a carefully regulated technology. Some radio communications equipment can be operated without a license, but your organization may need to have a license or permit to operate the higher-power or more sophisticated systems.

One problem with radio is that there is only so much electromagnetic spectrum to go around. Much of it is already occupied by television, radio, and important government and military communications systems, so there is little left for networking computers. This situation is changing, though, and as more sections of the spectrum become available and engineers learn to better exploit the areas left over, more and more exciting networking solutions will be in radio.

REAL-WORLD PROBLEMS

You are designing a network for an office complex. Several buildings must be linked together with high-performance long-distance links, and servers within the buildings must be linked together with a high-speed backbone. Hundreds of client computers in each building must be linked together inexpensively.

▶ Which media types will you use in this network, and where will you use them?

You are considering an infrared laser link between two buildings on your company's campus in Aspen, Colorado.

▶ What are the drawbacks of using a laser wireless link in this instance?

You need to link the computers on your marine research ship with the LAN on your shore facility. The research ship stays within line-of-sight of the shore facility (about 15 miles), exploring local ocean conditions.

▶ How will you link the ship to the shore?

NETWORK PROTOCOLS

The preceding section covered what computers talk over (the medium), and the section before that described how the computers are linked together (the topology). Now we'll look at the languages or protocols computers speak.

What Are Protocols?

Protocols are the agreed-upon ways that computers exchange information. Networks are full of protocols. A computer needs to know exactly how messages will arrive from the network so it can make sure the message gets to the right place. It needs to know how the network expects the message to be formatted (for instance, which part of the message is the data and which part of the message identifies the recipient) so the network can convey the data to its destination. As a comparison, consider the road-traffic protocols employed at an intersection to allow cars to cross safely (see Figure 3.16).

Green – Go
Yellow – Slow Down
Red – Stop

It is green, I can go.

Green – Go
Yellow – Slow Down
Red – Stop

It is red, I must stop.

FIGURE 3.16:   The protocol at an intersection allows cars to safely cross.

There are many levels of protocols in a network. Protocols can be broadly divided into hardware and software categories.

Hardware Protocols

Hardware protocols define how hardware devices operate and work together. The 10BaseT Ethernet protocol is a hardware protocol specifying exactly how two 10BaseT Ethernet devices will exchange information and what they will do if it is improperly transmitted or interrupted. It determines such things as voltage levels and which pairs of wires will be used for transmission and reception. There is no program involved; it is all done with circuitry.

The Hardware-Software Interface

Whenever a program in a computer needs to access hardware, such as when a message has arrived from the network and is now waiting in the adapter card's memory, ready to be received, the computer program uses a predefined hardware-software protocol. This basically means that the computer program can expect the data to always be in the same place; that certain registers on the card will indicate what is to be done with it; and that when other registers are accessed in the proper order, the card will do something logical, such as receive another message or send a message out.

Software Protocols

Programs communicate with each other via software protocols. Network client computers and network servers both have protocol packages that must be loaded to allow them to talk to other computers. These packages contain the protocols the computer needs to access a certain network device or service.

There are different protocol packages for different networks and even for different kinds of servers on the same network. Microsoft Windows 2000 Server and Novell NetWare come with a large number of network protocols so you can make the best use of your network.

TIP

All the computers on your network must have at least one set of protocols in common in order to communicate. To communicate with the Internet, your computers must have the TCP/IP set of protocols.

WHAT'S NEXT

In Chapter 4, we'll discuss the makeup of network models—more specifically, that of the OSI Reference Model. We'll divide the model into three layers—top, middle, and bottom—and explore the composition, function, and duty of each layer as a part of the entire system.

Chapter 4
THE OSI MODEL

You can't open a book on networking technologies without reading about the Open Systems Interconnect (OSI) model. This book is no exception, and for good reason. The OSI model helps us understand the fundamentals of network data transmission by offering a guideline to sending data from one computer to another. In this chapter, we will discuss the makeup of the various network models and, specifically, the most commonly discussed network model, the OSI model.

Adapted from the *Network+ Study Guide*, Third Edition by David Groth

ISBN 0-7821-4014-9   624 pages $49.99

INTRODUCING THE OSI MODEL

The OSI model was designed to promote interoperability by creating a guideline for network data transmission between computers that have different hardware vendors, software, operating systems, and protocols. For example, look at the simple process of transferring a file. From a user's perspective, a single operation has been performed to transfer the file. In reality, however, many different procedures had to take place behind the scenes to accomplish this seemingly simple task. Network data transmission (like the file transfer) is performed through the use of a protocol suite, also known as a protocol stack.

A *protocol suite* is most easily defined as a set of rules used to determine how computers communicate with each other. It is similar to language. If I speak English and you speak English, then we can communicate. But if I speak only Spanish and you speak only English, we won't be able to communicate.

The OSI model is used to describe what tasks a protocol suite performs as you explore how data moves across a network. Keep in mind that not all protocols map directly to the guideline provided for us through the OSI model, but there are enough similarities so that you can use the OSI model to examine how these protocols function. There are a myriad of protocol suites in use today, including IPX/SPX, NetBIOS, and TCP/IP. Each performs a specific function. Many of these functions that are provided through the use of a protocol stack and its components are standard functions performed by other components in other protocol stacks.

The most commonly referenced protocol model, the OSI model, was developed in 1977 by the International Organization for Standardization (ISO) to provide "common ground" when describing any network protocol (see Figure 4.1).

NOTE

ISO is really not an abbreviation for the International Organization for Standardization but is instead derived from the Greek word isos, which means "equal," and was adopted by the organization. For more information, go to www.iso.ch.

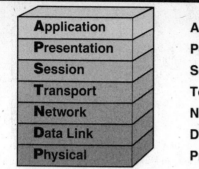

Application	All
Presentation	People
Session	Seem
Transport	To
Network	Need
Data Link	Data
Physical	Processing

FIGURE 4.1:   The Open Systems Interconnect (OSI) model

TIP

You can use mnemonic devices to help you remember the order of the OSI model layers: APSTNDP (from top to bottom). The most popular mnemonic for this arrangement is All People Seem To Need Data Processing. A reverse mnemonic (from Physical to Application, bottom to top) is Please Do Not Throw Sausage Pizza Away. (Good advice, don't you think?)

As you can see in Figure 4.1, the OSI model consists of seven layers. Each layer performs a specific function and then passes on the result to another layer. When a sending station has data to send, it formats a network request and then passes that request to the network protocol at the top layer, the Application layer. The protocol that runs at the Application layer performs an operation on the request and then passes it to the next, lower layer. Each protocol at each layer below the Application layer performs its own calculations and appends its own information to the data sent from the layer above it. At the receiving station, the process happens in reverse. Figure 4.2 illustrates this basic process.

The OSI model is only a model; it is not a protocol. Nobody is running the "OSI protocol" (at least no one has developed one at the time of this writing). Let's take a brief look at the layers of the OSI model and the basic protocol functions they describe. We'll start at the top with the Application layer and work our way down to the Physical layer.

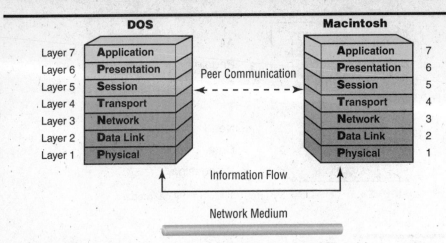

FIGURE 4.2:   How data travels through the layers of the OSI model

The Application Layer

The Application layer, the top layer of the OSI model, does not refer to applications such as word processors, but rather refers to a set of tools that an application can use to accomplish a task, such as a word processor application requesting a file transfer. This layer is responsible for defining how interactions occur between network services (applications) and the network. Services that function at the Application layer include, but are not limited to, file, print, and messaging services. The Application layer may also support error recovery.

The Presentation Layer

The Presentation layer is responsible for formatting data exchange. In this layer, character sets are converted, and data is encrypted. Data may also be compressed in this layer, and this layer usually handles the redirection of data streams.

The Session Layer

The Session layer defines how two computers establish, synchronize, maintain, and end a session. Practical functions, such as security authentication, connection ID establishment, data transfer, acknowledgments, and connection release, take place here. This list is not all-inclusive. Any communications that require milestones—or, put another way, require an answer to "Have you got that data I sent?"—are performed here. Typically these milestones are called *checkpoints*. Once a checkpoint has been crossed, any data not received needs retransmission only from the last good checkpoint. Adjusting checkpoints to account for very reliable or unreliable connections can greatly improve the actual throughput of data transmission.

The Transport Layer

The Transport layer is responsible for checking that the data was delivered error-free. It is also used to divide a message that is too long into smaller segments and, in the reverse, take a series of short messages and combine them into one longer segment. These smaller or combined segments must later be correctly reassembled. This is accomplished through segment sequencing (usually by appending a number to each of the segments).

This layer also handles logical address/name resolution. Additionally, this layer can send an acknowledgment that it got the data packet. Frequently you will see this referred to as an ACK, which is short for acknowledgment. This layer is responsible for the majority of error and flow control in network communications.

The Network Layer

The Network layer is responsible for logical addressing and translating logical names into physical addresses. A little-known function of the Network layer is prioritizing data. Not all data is of equal importance. Nobody is hurt if an e-mail message is delayed a fraction of a second. Delaying audio or video data a fraction of a second could be disastrous to the message. This prioritization is known as *Quality of Service (QoS)*.

In addition, the Network layer controls congestion, routes data from source to destination, and builds and tears down packets. Most routing protocols function at this layer.

The Data Link Layer

The Data Link layer takes raw data from the Physical layer and gives it a logical structure. This logic includes information about where the data is meant to go, which computer sent the data, and the overall validity of the bytes sent. In most situations, after a data frame is sent, the Data Link layer then waits for a positive ACK. If one is not received or if the frame is damaged, another frame is sent.

The Data Link layer also controls functions of logical network topologies and physical addressing as well as data transmission synchronization and connection.

The Physical Layer

The Physical layer is responsible for controlling the functional interface, such as transmission technique, pin layout, and connector type.

THE OSI MODEL'S LOWER LAYERS

Now that you have a broad overview of the OSI model and its seven layers, you will now learn about the functions of each layer in a little more detail, starting with the lower layers. In addition to the concepts, you'll read about some of the devices that operate at those layers and some of their installation concepts.

The Physical Layer

The easiest way to think about the Physical layer is that it deals with measurable, physical entities. Any protocol or device that operates at the Physical layer deals with the physical concepts of a network.

Physical Layer Concepts

Generally speaking, Physical layer concepts deal with a network component that is tangible or measurable. For example, when a protocol at the Physical layer receives information from the upper layers, it translates all the data into signals that can be transmitted on a transmission medium. This process is known as *signal encoding* (or *encoding*, for short). With cable media (also called *bounded media*), the protocols that operate at the Physical layer translate the ones and zeros of the data into electrical ons and offs.

Additionally, the Physical layer specifies how much of the media will be used (in other words, its *signaling method*) during data transmission. If a network signal uses all available signal frequencies (or, to put it differently, the entire bandwidth), the technology is said to use *baseband* signaling. Most LAN technologies, such as Ethernet, use baseband signaling. On the other hand, if a signal uses only one frequency (or only part of the bandwidth), the technology is said to use *broadband* signaling. This means multiple signals can be transmitted on the media simultaneously. Television signals use broadband signaling.

Finally, the Physical layer specifies the layout of the transmission media (its topology, in other words). A physical topology describes the way the cabling is physically laid out (as opposed to a logical topology, discussed later in the section titled "The Data Link Layer"). The physical topologies include the following:

▶ Bus

▶ Star

▶ Ring

▶ Mesh

The Bus Topology   In a physical bus topology, every computer is directly connected to a common medium. A physical bus network uses one network cable that runs from one end of the network to the other. Workstations connect at various points along this cable. The main advantage to this topology is simplicity: only one cable is used, and a physical bus topology typically requires less cable than other physical topologies. However, a cable fault can bring down the entire network, thus making a physical bus topology the least fault tolerant of all the physical topologies. Figure 4.3 shows a sample physical bus network.

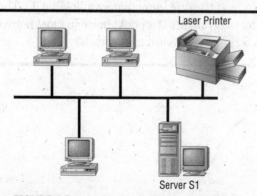

FIGURE 4.3:   A sample physical bus topology

The Star Topology   In a physical star topology, a cable runs from each network entity to a central device. This central device (called a *hub*) allows all devices to communicate as if they were all directly connected. The main advantage to a physical star topology is its fault tolerance. If one node or cable malfunctions, the rest of the network is not affected. The hub simply won't be able to communicate with the station attached to that port. An Ethernet 10BaseT network is one example of a network type that requires a physical star topology. Figure 4.4 shows a sample network that uses a physical star topology.

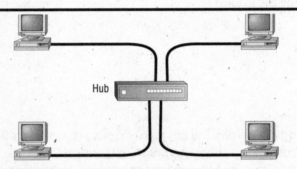

FIGURE 4.4:   A physical star topology

The Ring Topology   A physical ring topology isn't seen much in the computer-networking world. If you do see it, it's usually in a wide area network (WAN) environment. In a physical ring topology, every network entity connects directly to only two other network entities (the one immediately preceding it and the one immediately following it). The complexity of the ring topology makes it a poor choice in most network environments. Figure 4.5 shows a physical ring network.

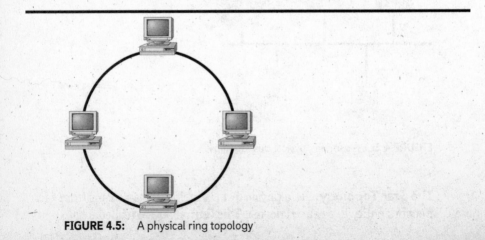

FIGURE 4.5:   A physical ring topology

The Mesh Topology   A physical mesh topology is another physical topology that isn't widely used in computer networks (except in special WAN cases). In a physical mesh topology, every computer is directly connected to every other computer in the network. The more computers that are on a mesh network, the more cables that make up the network. If a mesh network has n computers, there will be $n(n-1)/2$ cables. With 10 computers, there would be $10(10-1)/2$, or 45 cables. As you can see, this topology quickly becomes unmanageable with only a few computers. Figure 4.6 shows a sample mesh network.

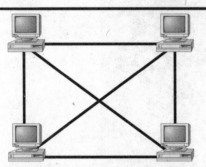

FIGURE 4.6:   A physical mesh topology

Physical Layer Devices

Several devices operate primarily at the Physical layer of the OSI model. These devices manipulate mainly the physical aspects of a network data stream (such as the voltages, signal direction, and signal strength). Let's take a quick look at some of the most popular:

- ▶ NIC
- ▶ Transceivers
- ▶ Repeaters
- ▶ Hubs
- ▶ MAUs

The Network Interface Card (NIC)   Probably the most common component on any network is the network interface card (NIC). A NIC is the component that provides the connection between a computer's internal bus and the network media. NICs come in many shapes and sizes. They vary by the type of bus connection they employ and their network media connection ports. Figure 4.7 shows an example of a network interface card.

FIGURE 4.7: A sample network interface card

The Transceiver   In the strictest definition, a *transceiver* is the part of any network interface that transmits and receives network signals (transmitter/receiver). Every network interface has a transceiver. The appearance and function of the transceiver vary with the type of network cable and topology in use.

NOTE

Some network interface cards have an Attachment Unit Interface (AUI) port (typically a 15-pin DIN connector) that allows a different, external transceiver type to be used, thus changing the media types to which the NIC can connect. For example, if you are using an Ethernet 10Base2 network interface card with an AUI port, you can connect to an Ethernet 10BaseT network by using an external transceiver attached to the AUI port. A DIN connector meets the specification of the German national standards body, Deutsche Industrie Norm, or DIN.

The Repeater   The simplest of all the Physical layer devices is the repeater, which simply amplifies the signals it receives on one port and resends (or "repeats") them on another. Repeaters are used to extend the maximum length of a network segment. They are often used if a few network stations are located far from the rest of the network. Figure 4.8 shows a network that uses a repeater.

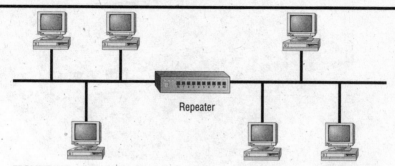

FIGURE 4.8:   A repeater installed on a network

The main downfall of a repeater is that it repeats everything it receives on one port, including noise, to its other ports. This has the ultimate effect of limiting the number of repeaters that can practically be used on a network. The 5-4-3 Rule dictates how many repeaters can be used on a network and where they can be placed. According to this rule, a single network can have five network segments connected by four repeaters, with three of the segments populated. If this rule is violated, one station may not be able to see the rest of the network. Figure 4.9 illustrates the 5-4-3 Rule.

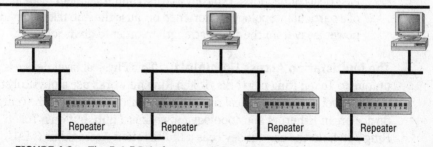

FIGURE 4.9:   The 5-4-3 Rule for network repeaters

The Hub   After the NIC, a hub is probably the most common Physical layer device found on networks today. A hub (also called a *concentrator*) serves as a central connection point for several network devices. At its basic level, a hub is nothing more than a multiport repeater. A hub repeats what it receives on one port to all other ports. It is, therefore, also subject to the 5-4-3 Rule. Figure 4.10 shows an example of a hub.

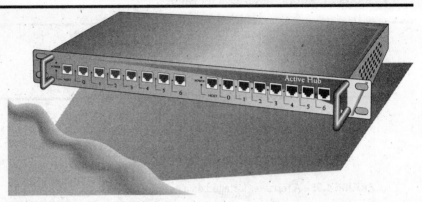

FIGURE 4.10:   A standard hub

There are many classifications of hubs, but two of the most important are active and passive:

▶ An *active* hub is usually powered, and it actually amplifies and cleans up the signal it receives, thus doubling the effective segment distance limitation for the specific topology (for example, extending an Ethernet segment another 100 meters).

▶ A *passive* hub is typically unpowered and makes only physical, electrical connections. Typically, the maximum segment distance of a particular topology is shortened because the hub takes some power away from the signal strength in order to do its job.

The Multistation Access Unit (MAU)   This Physical layer device is unique to Token Ring networks. Token Ring networks use a physical star topology, yet they use a logical ring topology (discussed later). The central device on an Ethernet star topology network is a hub, but on a Token Ring network, the central device is a Multistation Access Unit (MAU, sometimes called MSAU). The functionality of the MAU is similar to that of a hub, but the MAU provides the data path that creates the logical "ring" in a Token Ring network. The data can travel in an endless loop between stations. MAUs are chained together by connecting the Ring Out port of one MAU to the Ring In port of another and connecting the last Ring Out port to the Ring In of the first MAU in the chain, thus forming a complete loop. In a Token Ring network, you can have up to 33 MAUs chained together. MAUs are shown in Figure 4.11.

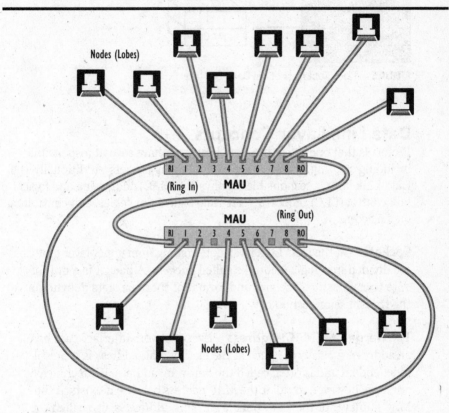

FIGURE 4.11:   MAUs in a Token Ring network

The Data Link Layer

The Data Link layer is actually made up of two sublayers:

▶ The Media Access Control (MAC) sublayer

▶ The Logical Link Control (LLC) sublayer

Figure 4.12 illustrates this arrangement.

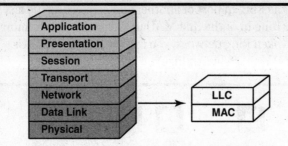

FIGURE 4.12: Sublayers of the Data Link layer

Data Link Layer Concepts

Protocols that operate at the Data Link layer have several responsibilities, including creating, transmitting, and receiving packets. Additionally, the Data Link layer is responsible for physical (MAC) addressing and logical link control (LLC) processing, creating logical topologies, and controlling media access.

Packets   At the Data Link layer, data coming from upper-layer protocols are divided into logical chunks called *packets*. A packet is a unit of data transmission. The size and format of these packets depend on the transmission technology.

The Hardware (MAC) Address   Every network interface card has an address, typically assigned at the factory. This address is protocol-independent and is often called the hardware address. It's technically accurate, however, to call it the *MAC address* because it exists at the MAC sublayer of the Data Link layer. This address is also called the *Ethernet address* or the *physical address*.

The MAC address itself is a 12-digit hexadecimal number. A hexadecimal number uses all digits from 0 through 9 and A through F. Each two-digit set is separated by colons, like so:

07:57:AC:1F:B2:76

Normally, the MAC address of a network interface card is set at the factory and cannot be changed. For this purpose, all NIC manufacturers keep track of the MAC addresses they use so they don't duplicate addresses between vendors. As of late, however, some manufacturers have started reusing their blocks of MAC addresses. This makes it necessary for administrators to be able to change the MAC addresses of the cards they receive (using a factory-supplied program), so if they discover a duplicated MAC address, they can resolve the conflict.

Logical Topology   In addition to these responsibilities, the Data Link layer can also dictate the logical topology of a network, or the way the packets move through a network. A logical topology differs from a physical topology in that the physical topology dictates the way the cables are laid out; the logical topology dictates the way the information flows. The types of logical topologies are the same as the physical topologies, except that the information flow specifies the type of topology to use.

Finally, the Data Link layer can describe the method of media access. The three main methods of media access are as follows:

▶ Contention, in which every station "competes" with other stations for the opportunity to transmit, and each has an equal chance at transmitting. If two stations transmit at the same time, an error, referred to as a *collision*, occurs, and the stations try again.

▶ Polling, in which a central device, called a *controller*, polls each device, in turn, and asks if it has data to transmit. This type of media access virtually eliminates collisions.

▶ Token passing, which uses a special data packet called a *token*. When a station has the token, it can transmit. If it doesn't have the token, it can't transmit. This media access technology also eliminates collision problems.

Media Access   With many stations on the same piece of network media, there has to be a way of vying for time on the cable. This process is called media access, and there are three main methods: CSMA/CD, token passing, and CSMA/CA.

Carrier Sense/Multiple Access with Collision Detection (CSMA/CD)

This media access technology with the extremely long acronym is probably the most common. When a protocol that uses CSMA/CD has data to transmit, it first senses if a signal is already on the wire (a *carrier*), indicating that someone is transmitting currently. That's the "Carrier Sense" part. If no one else is transmitting, it attempts a transmission and then listens to hear if someone else tried to transmit at the same time. If someone else transmits at the exact same time, a collision occurs. Both senders "back off" and don't transmit until some random period of time has passed. Then they both retry. That's the "Collision Detection" part. The final part ("Multiple Access") just means that more than one station can be on the network at the same time. CSMA/CD is the access method used in Ethernet and wireless Ethernet networks.

Token Passing

This media access method uses a special packet called a token. The first computer that is turned on creates the token. It then passes on the token to the next computer. The token passes around the network until a computer that has data to send takes the token off the network, modifies it, and puts it back on the network along with the data it has to send. Each station between the sender and the receiver along the network reads the destination address in the token. If the destination address doesn't match its own, the station simply sends the package on its way. When the destination station recognizes its address in the destination address of the token, the NIC copies the data into the station's memory and modifies the token, indicating it has received the data. The token continues around the network until the original sender receives the token again. If the original sender has more data to send, the process repeats itself. If not, the sender modifies the token to indicate that the token is "free" for anyone else to use. With this method, there are no collisions (as in CSMA/CD networks) because everyone has to have "permission" to transmit (via the token).

Carrier Sense/Multiple Access with Collision Avoidance (CSMA/CA)

This technology works almost identically to CSMA/CD, but instead of sending the whole data chunk and then listening to hear if it was transmitted, the sender transmits a request to send (RTS) packet and waits for a clear to send (CTS) before sending. When it receives the CTS, the sender sends the chunk. AppleTalk networks use this method of media access. The difference between CSMA/CD and CSMA/CA has been described like this: Say you want to cross a busy street and you want to use one of these protocols to cross it. If you are using CSMA/CD, you just cross the street. If you get hit, you go back to the curb and try again. If you're using CSMA/CA, you send your little brother across. If he makes it, it's probably OK for you to go.

Project 802

One of the major components of the Data Link layer is the result of the Institute of Electrical and Electronics Engineers' (IEEE) 802 subcommittees and their work on standards for local area and metropolitan area networks (LANs/MANs). The committee met in February 1980, so they used the "80" from 1980 and the "2" from the second month to create the name Project 802. The designation for an 802 standard always includes a dot (.) followed by either a single or a double digit. These numeric digits specify particular categories within the 802 standard. Currently, there are 12 standards. These standards, shown in Figure 4.13, are listed in Table 4.1 and described in more detail in the following sections.

NOTE

Some standards have a letter to further distinguish the standard (for example, 802.11b). The letters usually refer to different versions or interpretations of the standard.

TABLE 4.1: IEEE 802 Networking Standards

Standard	Topic
802.1	LAN/MAN Management (and Media Access Control Bridges)
802.2	Logical Link Control
802.3	CSMA/CD
802.4	Token Bus
802.5	Token Ring
802.6	Distributed Queue Dual Bus (DQDB) Metropolitan Area Network (MAN)
802.7	Broadband Local Area Networks
802.8	Fiber-Optic LANs and MANs
802.9	Integrated Services (IS) LAN Interface
802.10	LAN/MAN Security
802.11b	Wireless LAN
802.12	Demand Priority Access Method

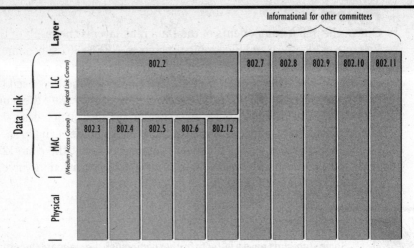

FIGURE 4.13:   The IEEE standards' relationship to the OSI model

The 802.1 LAN/MAN Management (and Media Access Control Bridges)   IEEE 802.1 discusses standards for LAN and MAN management, as well as for MAC bridges. One of the derivatives of 802.1 is the spanning tree algorithm for network bridges (bridges are discussed later in this chapter). The spanning tree algorithm helps to prevent bridge loops in a multibridge network.

The 802.2 Logical Link Control   This standard specifies the operation of the Logical Link Control (LLC) sublayer of the Data Link layer of the OSI model. The LLC sublayer provides an interface between the MAC sublayer and the Network layer. The 802.2 standard is used by the IEEE 802.3 Ethernet specification (discussed next), but not by the earlier Ethernet 2 specifications (used in early implementations of Ethernet).

The 802.3 CSMA/CD   This standard specifies a network that uses a bus topology, baseband signaling, and a CSMA/CD network access method. This standard was developed to match the Digital, Intel, and Xerox (DIX) Ethernet networking technology. So many people implemented the 802.3 standard, which resembles the DIX Ethernet, that people just started calling it Ethernet. It is the most widely implemented of all the 802 standards because of its simplicity and low cost.

Recently the 802.3u working group updated 802.3 to include Ethernet 100BaseT implementations.

The 802.4 Token Bus   This standard specifies a physical and a logical bus topology that uses coaxial or fiber-optic cable and a token-passing media access method. It is used mainly for factory automation and is seldom used in computer networking. It most closely resembles the Manufacturing Automation Protocol (MAP), developed by General Motors and used by many manufacturing companies. Some people think that the IEEE 802.4 standard is for a technology known as the Attached Resource Computer Network (ARCnet). That is an incorrect assumption. Although the technologies are similar, the IEEE 802.4 standard more closely resembles MAP, not ARCnet.

The 802.5 Token Ring   This standard is one example of a commonly used product becoming a documented standard. Typically, a standard is developed and then products are written to conform to the standard. Token Ring was developed by IBM in 1984, and the 802.5 standard soon followed. The 802.5 standard and Token Ring are almost identical.

Like Ethernet, Token Ring can use several cable types. Most often, it is installed using *twisted-pair* cabling, which can be either *shielded* or *unshielded*. Shielding adds to the cable investment but offers the advantage of resistance to unwanted electrical signals that could impair the network signal.

Possible transmission rates for Token Ring have increased with time; after 4Mbps Token Ring came 16Mbps Token Ring. Token Ring uses a physical star, logical ring topology with token-passing media access. If you install 4Mbps NICs on a network that otherwise uses 16Mbps NICs, your entire ring speed is reduced to 4Mbps. Unlike Ethernet, a computer cannot talk unless it has a token. This can cause some grief if a token gets "stuck."

Unlike ARCnet, Token Ring is still used in a number of locations for two reasons:

▸ IBM made sure that Token Ring did a fine job of talking to IBM mainframes, which are still commonly used.

▸ Token Ring network performance "degrades with grace."

The latter means that as network traffic increases, the network slowly gets slower, because the single token, which can travel in only one direction, gets busy carrying all that traffic. Ethernet, on the other hand, can become so flooded as network traffic increases that the entire network fails. Now, suppose you were wiring a computerized fire alarm system for a large building. Which would you rather use: Ethernet or Token Ring? To increase performance, some Token Ring technologies implement early token release, whereby the sending station doesn't hog the token. It simply grabs the token, sends its data, and frees the token.

In Token Ring, just as in all ARCnet and most Ethernet schemes, there is a central device to which stations connect. It isn't, however, called a hub. IBM calls it a MAU. IBM often has a different name for things. Even their name for Token Ring cabling is different. In telephone and computer networks, twisted cable is rated by *categories*. IBM rates Token Ring cable by *type*.

One final difference between Token Ring and the others is the *regeneration process*. Data signals are read, amplified, and repeated by every device on the network, to reduce degradation. This includes MAUs and NICs and is one reason that Token Ring is fairly expensive. An average Token Ring NIC is upward of $200, whereas a similar Ethernet card can be less than $20.

The 802.6 Distributed Queue Dual Bus (DQDB) Metropolitan Area Network   In some ways, asking what defines a metropolitan area network (MAN) is like asking how long a rope is. We can safely say that a MAN reaches beyond the area of a LAN. The interesting question is, "When does a MAN become a WAN?" Sorry to say, there is no easy answer. Like a WAN, a MAN can support many computers. How many miles a MAN can cover has more to do with regulations than with geography. For example, from a geographical standpoint, Portland, Oregon, and Vancouver, Washington, are separated by nothing more than several hundred feet of water. From a political standpoint, they are in different states, and, therefore, different telecommunication regulations apply to each city. This could mean that no MANs can connect Portland and Vancouver. For our purposes, we need to know only that a MAN generally encompasses a city-sized area and can support many-to-many connections. Transmission speeds vary with the size of an enterprise's bank account. The standard recommends the use of Distributed Queue Dual Bus (DQDB) technologies for MANs.

The 802.7 Broadband Local Area Networks   Don't let the fancy phrasing fool you. You have already used broadband if you have seen cable TV. When one cable carries multiple signals, that is broadband. The most common method for separating signals is to have them on different frequencies, which is called *Frequency Division Multiplexing (FDM)*. For example, each channel on a TV uses a different frequency. It is as simple as that. Maybe you can win a beer from some friends by seeing if they can explain Frequency Division Multiplexing. If they can't, collect your reward and tell them that is how all those TV channels get into their TV from one cable. The alternative to sending a set of signals this way is to use the entire cable for one signal. This is known as baseband and is used by standards such as Ethernet.

The 802.8 Fiber-Optic LANs and MANs   As the name implies, this working group handed down guidelines for fiber-optic usage on networks defined by 802.3 through 802.6, which includes *Fiber Distributed Data Interface (FDDI)* as well as *10BaseFL*. 10BaseFL defines Ethernet over fiber-optic cable. As you can see, some of the 802 definitions have more to do with your day-to-day work than others do.

The 802.9 Integrated Services (IS) LAN Interface   For a while, it seemed that this definition would have a profound effect on daily networking, because it laid out how *Integrated Services Digital Network (ISDN)* behaves. Late in 1998, however, many industry watchers began to call for the slow death of ISDN, because both cable modems and *asymmetrical digital subscriber line (ADSL)* had overtaken ISDN with less-complicated setup, higher performance, and lower cost.

The 802.10 LAN/MAN Security   This standard provides a secure pathway for data across a shared path. An implementation of this standard is using the public Internet as a backbone for a private interconnection between locations. The term for this form of connecting is known as *virtual private networking (VPN)*. Because VPN costs less than direct private connections, VPN is likely to become popular in the near future.

The 802.11 Wireless LAN   Wireless networking usually requires a higher up-front investment than cable-based networking. Still, the cost can be justified if an office is rearranged with any regularity or must be moved from location to location to satisfy business requirements. A famous example of this is the Red Cross. This agency would not be effective if it had to wire computers together before assisting at each disaster area.

Recently, 802.11 was updated to include the 802.11b standard, which specifies higher wireless speeds (11Mbps instead of 1Mbps for the original 802.11 standard). This demonstrates that the 802 standards have not been static for 20 years; instead, they've been a dynamic set of rules that continue to be updated as technology moves forward.

The 802.12 Demand Priority Access Method   First developed by Hewlett-Packard, this standard combines the concepts of Ethernet and ATM. The communication scheme used is called Demand Priority (thus, the name of the standard). It uses "intelligent" hubs that allocate more bandwidth to frames that have been assigned a higher priority by the sending computer. The hub scans its ports and then allocates bandwidth according to each frame's priority. This is extremely valuable for real-time audio and video transmissions.

The 802.12 standard is also known as *100VG (Voice Grade)*, *100VG AnyLAN*, *100BaseVG*, and *AnyLAN*. The 100 is short for 100Mbps, or 10 times faster than the original Ethernet speeds. Other manufacturers didn't buy into the ideas of 100VG, perhaps in part because of the higher overhead of demand priority due to port scanning. Instead, they updated the original Ethernet to *Fast Ethernet*, which also supports 100Mbps while maintaining the 802.3 standards.

Table 4.2 summarizes the main features—including speed, access method, topology, and media—of various network technologies, such as 802 standards and FDDI.

TABLE 4.2:   Main Features of Various Network Technologies

Technology	Speed (s)	Access Method	Topologies	Media
IEEE 802.3	10, 100, or 1000Mbps	CSMA/CD	Logical bus	Coax or UTP
IEEE 802.5	4 or 16Mbps	Token passing	Physical star, Logical ring	STP
IEEE 802.11b	1 or 11Mbps	CSMA/CA	Cellular	None (Wireless)
FDDI	200Mbps	Token passing	Physical star, Logical ring	Fiber-optic (UTP implemented as CDDI)

Data Link Layer Devices

Three main devices manipulate data at the Data Link layer:

- Bridges
- Switches
- NIC

They are more complex than their Physical layer counterparts and thus are more expensive and more difficult to implement. But they each bring unique advantages to the network.

The Bridge   A bridge is a network device, operating at the Data Link layer, that logically separates a single network into two segments, but it lets the two segments appear to be one network to higher layer protocols. The primary use for a bridge is to keep traffic meant for stations on one side of the bridge and not let it pass to the other side. For example, if you have a group of workstations that constantly exchange data on the same network segment as a group of workstations that don't use the network much at all, the busy group will slow down the performance of the network for the other users. If you put in a bridge to separate the two groups, however, only traffic destined for a workstation on the other side of the bridge will pass to the other side. All other traffic stays local. Figure 4.14 shows a network before and after bridging.

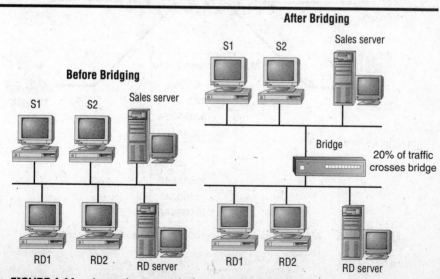

FIGURE 4.14:   A sample network before and after bridging

TIP

Bridges can connect dissimilar network types (for example, Token Ring and Ethernet) as long as the bridge operates at the LLC sublayer of the Data Link layer. If the bridge operates only at the lower sublayer (the MAC sublayer), the bridge can connect only similar network types (Token Ring to Token Ring and Ethernet to Ethernet).

The Switching Hub   In the past few years, the switching hub has received a lot of attention as a replacement for the standard hub. The switching hub is more intelligent than a standard hub in that it can actually understand some of the traffic that passes through it. A switching hub (or switch for short) operates at the Data Link layer and is also known as a Layer 2 Switch. Layer 2 switches build a table of the MAC addresses of all the connected stations (see Figure 4.15).

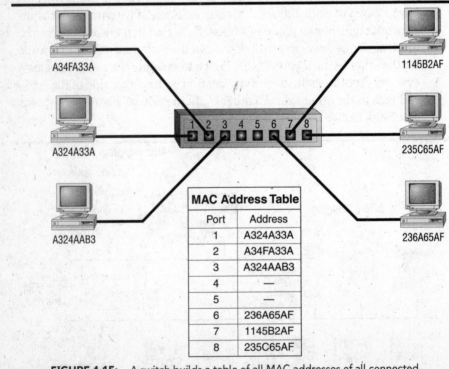

FIGURE 4.15:   A switch builds a table of all MAC addresses of all connected stations

When two stations attached to the switch want to communicate, the sending station sends its data to the switch. This part of the process is similar to the way a standard hub functions. However, when the switch receives the data, rather than broadcasting it over all its other ports as a hub would, the switch examines the Data Link header for the MAC address of the receiving station and forwards it to the correct port. This opens a virtual pipe between ports that can use the full bandwidth of the topology.

Switches have received a lot of attention because of this ability. If a server and several workstations were connected to the same 100Mbps Ethernet switch, each workstation would need a dedicated 100Mbps channel to the server, and there would never be any collisions.

THE OSI MODEL'S MIDDLE LAYERS

As you move up the OSI model, the protocols at each successive layer get more complex and have more responsibilities. At the middle are the Network and Transport layers, which perform the bulk of the work for a protocol stack. You'll see why in the sections to follow.

The Network Layer

The Network layer of the OSI model defines protocols that ensure that the data arrive at the correct destination. This is probably the most commonly discussed layer of the OSI model.

Network Layer Concepts

The most important Network layer concepts are these:

- ► Logical network addressing
- ► Routing

Logical Network Addressing In the last section, you learned that every network device has an address (the MAC address) assigned at the factory and that this address is protocol-independent. But, as you know, most networks communicate using protocols that must have their own addressing scheme. If the MAC address is the Data Link layer physical address, the protocol-addressing scheme at the Network layer defines the logical address.

NOTE

If IP addresses are duplicated on Windows 9*x*/Me/NT/2000/XP workstations, the first station that is assigned an address gets to use it. Any other station that has that address receives error messages about duplicated IP addresses. The address is then unassigned. The first station receives error messages as well, but it can continue to function.

Each logical network address is protocol-dependent. For example, a TCP/IP address is not the same as an IPX address. Additionally, the two protocols can coexist on the same computer without conflict. However, two different stations using the same protocol cannot have the same logical network address on the same network. If that happens, neither station can be seen on the network (see Figure 4.16).

Address: 204.153.163.2

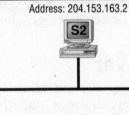

Since S2 and S3 have conflicting network addresses, neither station can be "seen" on the network.

Address: 204.153.163.4

Address: 204.153.163.2

FIGURE 4.16:   Address conflicts on a network

NOTE

Address conflicts can be common with TCP/IP because an administrator often needs to assign IP addresses. IPX addresses don't suffer from conflict nearly as often, because they use the MAC address as part of the IPX address. The MAC address is unique and can't be changed.

USING NETWORK ADDRESS FORMATS

Whenever you have to set up a network or add a station, it is important to have an understanding of how network addresses work. Every network address in either TCP/IP or IPX has both a network portion and a node portion. The network portion is the number that is assigned to the network segment to which the station is connected. The node portion is the unique number that identifies that station on the segment. Together, the network portion and the node portion of an address ensure that a network address will be unique across the entire network.

IPX addresses use an eight-digit hexadecimal number for the network portion. This number, called the IPX network address, can be assigned randomly by the installation program or manually by the network administrator. The node portion is the 12-digit hexadecimal MAC address assigned by the manufacturer. A colon separates the two portions. Here is a sample IPX address:

```
Network Address    Node Address
       |                |
|00004567:006A7C11FB56|
```

TCP/IP addresses, on the other hand, use a dotted decimal notation in the format xxx.xxx.xxx.xxx as shown in the following:

199.217.67.34   IP Address

255.255.255.0   Subnet Mask

The address consists of four collections of eight-digit binary numbers (or up to three decimal digits) called octets, separated by periods. Each decimal number in an IP address is typically a number in the range of 1 through 254. Which portion is the network and which portion is the node depends on the class of the address and the subnet mask assigned with the address. A subnet mask is also a dotted decimal number with numbers in the range of 0 through 255. If a subnet mask contains 255 in any position (corresponding to a binary number of all ones), the corresponding part of the IP address is the network address. For example, if you have the mask 255.255.255.0, the first three octets are the network portion, and the last portion is the node.

Routing   *Routing* is the process of moving data throughout a network, passing through several network segments using devices called routers, which select the path the data takes. Placing routers on a network to connect several smaller routers turns a network into an entity known as an *internetwork*. Routers get information about which paths to take from files on the routers called routing tables. These tables contain information about which router network interface (or port) to place information on in order to send it to a particular network segment. Routers will not pass unknown or broadcast packets. A router will route a packet only if it has a specific destination. Figure 4.17 illustrates these components and their participation in the routing process.

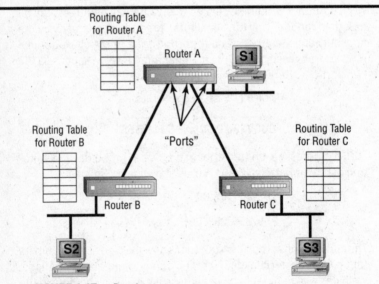

FIGURE 4.17:   Routing components

Information gets into routing tables in two ways:

▶ Through static routing

▶ Through dynamic routing

In *static routing*, the network administrator manually updates the router's routing table. The administrator enters every network into the routing table and selects the port on which the router should place data when the router intercepts data destined for that network. Unfortunately, on networks with more than a few segments, manually updating routing tables is time-intensive and prohibitive.

NOTE

When using a Windows NT server as a router, use the ROUTE command to add, change, or remove static routes.

Dynamic routing, on the other hand, uses route discovery protocols (or routing protocols for short) to talk to other routers and find out which networks they are attached to. Routers that use dynamic routing send out special packets to request updates of the other routers on the network as well as to send their own updates. Dynamic routing is the most popular routing technology.

With dynamic routing, the two categories of route discovery protocols are distance vector and link state. Older route discovery protocols, such as Routing Information Protocol (RIP) for TCP/IP and RIP for IPX, use the distance vector method. In distance vector routing, a router sends out its routing table when the router is brought online and the contents of its routing tables every 30 seconds thereafter. When another router receives the contents of the other router's table, it adds 1 to the hop count of each route in the list of routes and then rebroadcasts the list. A *hop* is one pass through a router. This process typically takes place every 30 seconds.

The main downside to distance vector route discovery is the overhead required in broadcasting the entire routing table every 30 seconds. Link state route discovery is more efficient. Routers using link state route discovery routers send out their routing table via a multicast, not a broadcast packet, every five minutes or so. If there is an update, only the update is sent. NetWare Link Services Protocol (NLSP) for IPX and Open Shortest Path First (OSPF) for TCP/IP are two link state route discovery protocols.

Several protocols can be routed, but a few protocols can't be routed. It is important to know which protocols are routable and which aren't so that you can choose the appropriate protocol when it comes time to design an internetwork. Table 4.3 shows a few of the most common routable and nonroutable protocols and the routing protocols they use, if any.

TABLE 4.3:   Routable and Nonroutable Protocols

Protocol	Route Discovery Protocol	Routable?
IPX	RIP	Yes
IPX	NLSP	Yes
NetBEUI	None	No
TCP/IP	RIP	Yes
TCP/IP	OSPF	Yes
XNS	RIP	Yes

NOTE

When setting up routing on your network, you may have to configure a default gateway. A *default gateway*, when configured on a workstation, is the router that all packets are sent to when the workstation doesn't know where the station is or can't find it on the local segment. TCP/IP networks sometimes have multiple routers as well and must use this parameter to specify which router is the default. Other protocols don't have very good routing functions at the workstation, so they must use this feature to "find" the router.

Network Layer Devices

Three devices operate at the Network layer:

▶ Routers

▶ Brouters

▶ Layer 3 Switches

The Router   The router is the device that connects multiple networks or segments to form a larger internetwork. It is also the device that facilitates communication within this internetwork. It makes the choices about how best to send packets within the network so that they arrive at their destination.

Several companies manufacture routers, but probably the two biggest names in the business are Bay Networks and Cisco. Bay Networks is a conglomeration of smaller networking companies bought out by networking giant Synoptics. Cisco has always been a built-from-the-ground-up router company. Both companies make other products, to be sure, but their bread and butter is routing technologies.

Routers have many functions other than simply routing packets. Routers can connect many small segments into a network, as well as connect networks to a much larger network, such as a corporate WAN or the Internet. Routers can also connect dissimilar lower-layer topologies. For example, you can connect an Ethernet and a Token Ring network using a router. Additionally, with added software, routers can perform firewall functions and packet filtering.

Routers are probably the most complex devices on a network today. Consequently, they are likely to be the most expensive. But simple low-end routers have been introduced by Bay Networks, Cisco, and other companies in the sub-$1,000 range that make Internet connectivity more affordable. Hub vendors have begun to introduce basic intranetwork routing functionality into their products as well.

The Brouter   The *brouter* is a unique device that combines the functionality of a bridge and a router. It routes most packets, but if it can't route a particular packet, it will try and bridge it. Unfortunately, if you try to use a brouter as either a bridge or a router, it will fall short in the functionality of either.

The brouter was mainly used to connect different network topologies and to bridge them, but it is not used much anymore.

Layer 3 Switches   A fairly new Network layer device that has received much media attention of late is the Layer 3 Switch. The Layer 3 part of the name corresponds to the Network layer of the OSI model. It performs the multiport, virtual LAN, data-pipelining functions of a standard Layer 2 Switch, but it can also perform basic routing functions between virtual LANs. In some workgroups, a Layer 3 Switch can replace a workgroup router.

The Transport Layer

The Transport layer defines the protocols for structuring messages and checks the validity of transmissions.

Transport Layer Concepts

The Transport layer reminds me of what my old Net Tech instructors used to pound into my head: "Reliable end-to-end error and flow control."

(Thanks, Doug and Al!) The Transport layer does other things as well, but the protocols that operate at the Transport layer mainly ensure reliable communications between upper peer layers.

The Connection Type   To provide error and flow control services, protocols at the Transport layer use connection services. The two types of connection services are these:

- ▶ Connection-oriented
- ▶ Connectionless

Connection-oriented connection services use acknowledgments and responses to establish a virtual connection between sending and receiving stations. The acknowledgments are also used to ensure that the connection is maintained.

Connection-oriented connections are similar to phone calls. You dial the intended recipient, and the recipient picks up and says hello. You then identify yourself and say that you'd like to talk about something, and the conversation begins. If you hear silence for a while, you might ask, "Are you still there?" to make sure the recipient is still on the line. When finished, you both agree to end the connection by hanging up. Connection-oriented services work in the same way, except that instead of mouths, phones, and words, they use computers, NICs, and special packets. Figure 4.18 shows an example of the beginning of communications between two computers using connection-oriented services.

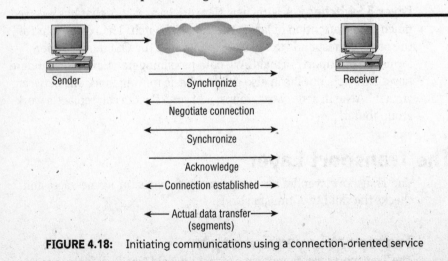

FIGURE 4.18:   Initiating communications using a connection-oriented service

Connectionless services, on the other hand, don't have error and flow control. They do have one simple advantage: speed. Because connectionless services don't have the overhead of maintaining the connection, the sacrifice in error control is more than made up for in speed. To make another analogy, connectionless services are similar to a postcard. Each message is considered singular and not related to any other. So, if one part of the message is lost, it can simply be resent.

Name Resolution   The Transport layer also handles logical address–to–logical name resolution. In some protocols, a node address, such as 185.45.2.23, isn't the best way to reference a host. Some protocol stacks (TCP/IP and IPX/SPX, for example) can use Transport layer logical names for hosts in addition to their Network layer logical addresses. These logical names make it easier for you to find hosts on the network.

At the Transport layer, various protocol stacks implement a protocol to translate Network layer addresses into Transport layer logical names.

Transport Layer Implementations

Before we discuss the other layers of the OSI model, let's take a look at the IPX/SPX, TCP/IP, and NetBEUI implementations of the Transport layer.

The IPX/SPX Protocol   As far as the connection services of IPX/SPX are concerned, there are two transport protocols: IPX and SPX. IPX is connectionless and thus enjoys the benefits of connectionless transports, including increased speed. SPX, on the other hand, uses connection-oriented services.

IPX/SPX has no name resolution system by default. That functionality is employed when a NetWare server is running Novell Directory Services (NDS) and the NDS directory requester (which runs at the Session, Presentation, and Application layers) can make requests of an NDS database.

The TCP/IP Protocol   Like the IPX/SPX protocol stack, the TCP/IP protocol stack has two transport protocols:

▶ Transmission Control Protocol (TCP)

▶ User Datagram Protocol (UDP)

TCP is connection-oriented, and UDP is connectionless. Some upper-layer protocols, such as FTP and HTTP, require reliable connection-oriented service and, therefore, use TCP. Other upper-layer protocols, such as

Trivial File Transfer Protocol (TFTP) and Network File System (NFS), require increased speed and will trade reliability for that speed. They, therefore, use UDP.

NOTE

For network address–to–name resolution, TCP/IP uses Domain Name Services (DNS). It is my belief that the name resolution of the OSI model's Transport layer was designed for DNS. Many operating systems use DNS for name resolution, but Unix (whose networking is based on TCP/IP) uses DNS almost exclusively. DNS is probably the most cross-platform name resolution method available.

The NetBEUI Implementation   Because it is based on the NetBIOS protocol, NetBEUI (NetBIOS Enhanced User Interface) has datagram support and, thus, has support for connectionless transmission. It doesn't, however, have support for connection-oriented services. NetBIOS does allow hosts to have logical names (using WINS), but the naming service, as with NDS, functions at the upper layers of the OSI model.

THE OSI MODEL'S UPPER LAYERS

The upper layers of the OSI model deal with less esoteric concepts. Even though we're still discussing computer networking, the top three layers (Session, Presentation, and Application) seem easier to understand. Because the Network+ exam doesn't cover the upper layers (and many times these top three layers are grouped together), the following sections will give only a brief overview.

The Session Layer

Protocols that operate at the Session layer of the OSI model are responsible for establishing, maintaining, and breaking sessions, or *dialogs*. This is different from the connection services provided at the Transport layer, because the Session layer operates at a higher level and looks at the bigger picture—the entire conversation, not just one sentence. Many gateways operate at the Session layer.

The Presentation Layer

The Presentation layer does what you might think it does: it changes the look, or *presentation*, of the data from the lower layers into a format that the upper-layer processes can work with. Among other services, the Presentation layer deals with encryption, data compression, and network redirectors.

In addition, the Presentation layer deals with character-set translation. Not all computer systems use the same table to convert binary numbers into text. Most standard computer systems use the American Standard Code for Information Interchange (ASCII). Mainframe computers (and some IBM networking systems) use the Extended Binary Coded Decimal Interchange Code (EBCDIC). The two are totally different. Protocols at the Presentation layer can translate between the two.

The Application Layer

Now I know what you might be thinking: "This layer is for my programs, right?" Wrong. The Application layer defines several standard network services that fall into categories such as file transfer, print access, and e-mail relay. The applications that access these network services are located above the Application layer (although some people say that applications are an extension of the Application layer).

Upper-Layer Devices

There are only a few upper-layer devices, none of which operate at any specific layer. Because they perform a range of functions for the network, they fall into the class of devices known as gateways. A *gateway* translates one type of network data into another. Gateways can be either hardware or software, but the most popular way to run a gateway is as a software program on a dedicated computer.

There are many, many types of gateways, but the one most people think of is an e-mail gateway. E-mail gateways translate e-mail messages from one type of e-mail system so that they can be transmitted on another (for example, from GroupWise e-mail to SMTP mail for the Internet).

WHAT'S NEXT

In Chapter 5 we will discuss the major protocol suites. NetWare IPX/SPX, TCP/IP, and AppleTalk are considered the most important of these suites, and we will explore these three in great detail. We will also highlight some other protocols and protocol standards.

Chapter 5
MAJOR PROTOCOL SUITES

This chapter provides a detailed discussion of the most important of these suites and takes a look at some other protocols and protocol standards. Although your Networking Essentials exam will not require that you have mastered much of this material, a further understanding of protocol suites broadens your knowledge base as a network administrator.

These are the protocol suites examined in this chapter:

▶ NetWare IPX/SPX, Novell NetWare's proprietary protocol suite

▶ TCP/IP, the nonproprietary protocols that make up the Internet

▶ AppleTalk, Apple Computer's proprietary protocols, which began with the Macintosh

• •

Adapted from *MCSE: Networking Essentials Study Guide*, Third Edition by James Chellis, Charles Perkins, and Matthew Strebe

ISBN 0-7821-2695-2   720 pages $49.99

Review of Protocols, Models, and Implementations

A *protocol* is a set of rules for communication. A simple example of a protocol from the realm of human communications is the different ways of greeting people: should you bow, shake hands, or kiss both cheeks of the person you're greeting? It depends on where you are and whom you are greeting. If you make a mistake, you could be misunderstood.

Although in the data communications world protocols are more complex and precise, the same idea holds true. For example, a protocol may define the shape of a packet that will be transmitted across the network, as well as all the fields within the packet and how they should be interpreted. Obviously, both the sender and receiver must agree on the exact way the packet should be formatted in order for communication to occur.

NOTE

Any protocol product available on the market will necessarily be a protocol implementation, which means any one company's interpretation of the protocol definition or standard. Therefore, one company may interpret a standard in a different way than another, which can cause incompatibility.

A *protocol suite* is a group of protocols that evolved together, whether created by the same company, as in the case of IBM's SNA, or used in the same environment, such as the Internet protocol suite. Protocol suites have definitions for the interface between protocols that occur at adjacent layers of the Open Systems Interconnect (OSI) model, such as IPX and SPX in the NetWare suite.

NetWare IPX/SPX Protocols

The NetWare protocol suite takes its name from the two main protocols at the network and transport layers of the OSI model: IPX and SPX.

NOTE

NetWare was first developed by Novell, Inc., in the early 1980s. Its design was based on a network developed by Xerox at its Palo Alto Research Center (PARC) called Xerox Network System (XNS).

The NetWare IPX/SPX protocol suite provides file, print, message, and application services. This architecture is server-centric because workstations make requests for file services or other services from the server. To the user at a workstation, all resources appear local to that workstation. For example, saving a file to a file server on the network is simply a matter of saving it to drive F (or another mapped drive) in the same way it would be saved to the user's C hard drive.

The NetWare protocols are modular; you can use them with many different hardware configurations. You can also use other protocols, such as TCP/IP and AppleTalk, with NetWare, making it very flexible. NetWare, therefore, is not limited to its proprietary protocols, IPX and SPX. Allowing additional protocols provides more interoperability with other computer systems.

The NetWare protocol suite can be mapped to the OSI model as shown in Figure 5.1. The following sections discuss the NetWare protocols, organized by their function with respect to the OSI model.

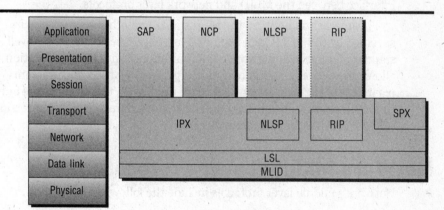

FIGURE 5.1:   The NetWare protocol suite mapped to the OSI model

NetWare Lower-Layer Protocols

NetWare normally runs over standard lower-layer protocols, such as Ethernet (IEEE 802.3) and Token Ring (IEEE 802.5). The lower-layer protocol discussed here, MLID, is a proprietary standard for network interface card drivers.

MLID (Multiple Link Interface Driver)

The MLID protocol operates at the MAC sublayer of the OSI model's data link layer. It is concerned with medium access and uses these methods:

- Contention
- Token passing
- Polling

The MLID is a standard for network drivers. Each type of network board has a unique MLID driver. The MLID is implemented in software. A common example is the DOS file called NE2000.COM, written for the Novell/Eagle NE2000 network card.

The MLID is also called the network driver or LAN driver. Its job is to communicate directly with the hardware network card. The MLID is independent of upper-layer protocols because of the LSL (link support layer) module at the LLC sublayer of the data link layer, which acts as an interface between the MLID and network layer protocols.

The interaction between the MLID, LSL, and other components is specified by the ODI (Open Data-link Interface) specification, a Novell standard for modular network communications. The ODI specification allows you to easily configure client software using the same programs, regardless of the type of network board used. With this architecture only the MLID changes; before ODI, you needed to create a customized version of the IPX driver for each network card.

NetWare Middle-Layer Protocols

NetWare's middle-layer protocols include the following:

- **IPX:** Used for transporting packets
- **RIP and NLSP:** Routing protocols
- **SPX:** Runs at the transport layer and adds connection-oriented service when added reliability is required

IPX (Internetwork Packet Exchange)

Novell's main network layer protocol is IPX. It deals with addressing (the logical network and service addresses), route selection, and connection services. IPX provides connectionless datagram service, which means that data is sent over the whole network segment rather than across a direct connection. IPX is based on the IDP (Internetwork Datagram Protocol) of XNS (Xerox Network System).

Because of its connectionless nature, IPX is not suitable for some types of network communications. Most of the communication on a network, including workstation connections and printing, uses the SPX protocol, described later in this chapter. Simple IPX is used for broadcast messages, such as error notifications and time synchronization.

IPX performs dynamic route selections based on RIP tables, which contain a list of identified and reachable networks. In NetWare 4.1, IPX is usually implemented by the IPXODI.COM program, which follows the ODI specification. Earlier NetWare versions used a program called IPX.COM. As discussed in the section "MLID (Multiple Link Interface Driver)" earlier in this chapter, before ODI, a custom version of IPX was required for each type of network card and settings.

RIP (Routing Information Protocol)

RIP is the default protocol NetWare uses for routing. RIP uses the distance-vector route discovery method to determine hop counts. The hop count is the number of intermediate routers a packet must cross to reach a particular device.

RIP functions at the network layer of the OSI model, although it has a service address assigned to it. Because it is a distance-vector routing protocol, RIP periodically broadcasts routing table information across the internetwork. This can create a bottleneck when the information must be transmitted over wide area links. For WANs, you should use a link-state routing protocol instead, such as NLSP.

NLSP (Network Link Services Protocol)

NLSP is another routing protocol that functions at the network layer. NLSP uses the link-state route discovery method to build routing tables. It is based on an OSI routing protocol called IS-IS (Intermediate System-to-Intermediate System).

Link-state routing protocols do not broadcast routing tables periodically, as distance-vector routing protocols do. Instead, they broadcast only when a change occurs in the state of the network, such as when a link goes down or an additional router is installed. NLSP can support mesh and hybrid mesh networks for increased fault tolerance.

SPX (Sequenced Packet Exchange)

SPX is a transport layer protocol that adds reliability to IPX. This protocol is concerned with addressing, segment development (division and combination), and connection services (segment sequencing, error control, and end-to-end flow control).

SPX provides connection-oriented packet delivery and is used when IPX datagram packet delivery is not reliable enough, such as for a print server. It provides reliability through virtual circuits that are identified as connection IDs. Packets that arrive at their destination correctly are acknowledged. If the receiving system does not acknowledge the packet, that packet must be retransmitted. IPX is less reliable because it does not send acknowledgments.

NOTE

A Xerox protocol called Sequenced Packet Protocol was the basis for SPX.

NetWare Upper-Layer Protocols

Novell's two upper-layer protocols, NCP and SAP, both cover multiple layers of the OSI model. NCP functions at the transport, session, presentation, and application layers. SAP functions at the session and application layers.

NCP (NetWare Core Protocols)

NCP functions at four layers of the OSI model:

- ▶ At the transport layer, it provides connection services, with segment sequencing, error control, and end-to-end flow control.

- ▶ At the session layer, NCP handles session administration for data transfer.

- ▶ At the presentation layer, NCP is responsible for translation (character code and file syntax).

- ▶ At the application layer at the top, this protocol deals with service use, providing an operating system (OS) redirector.

NCP provides a group of function calls that define the interchange between client and server. For example, a client might call on a server to open a file or write to a file. Other NCP functions support printing, name

Part I

management, file services, synchronization, and file locking and unlocking. Because NCP functions at the transport layer (in addition to its functionality at the higher layers), it provides reliable, connection-oriented packet delivery and therefore makes SPX unnecessary in many cases.

SAP (Service Advertising Protocol)

At the session layer, SAP is concerned with session administration for file transfer. At the application layer, SAP provides active service advertisement.

Service providers, such as file servers and print servers, use SAP to advertise their services to the network. Each service provider broadcasts a SAP packet every 60 seconds. This packet lets clients know that the server is available and what its address is. Clients can also request service information, such as the location of the nearest file server, on the internetwork by transmitting a Service Query Packet.

WARNING

On WANs, SAP can become a problem because of the quantity of broadcasts from multiple servers over sometimes slow links. In that case, network administrators can turn SAP off for particular servers.

INTERNET PROTOCOLS

The Internet protocol suite was developed along with its namesake, the Internet. The Internet began as a project funded by the United States Department of Defense in the 1970s to interconnect educational institutions and government installations. At that time it was called ARPAnet (Advanced Research Projects Agency Network). Over time it has evolved into the huge, worldwide network known as the Internet. The protocols that make up the Internet protocol suite, the best known being TCP (Transmission Control Protocol) and IP (Internet Protocol), have become de facto standards because of the success of the Internet. The entire protocol suite is sometimes referred to as TCP/IP.

The Internet protocol suite is unique in that it is made up of nonproprietary protocols. This means that they do not belong to any one company and that the technology is available to anyone who wishes to use it. As a result, the Internet protocol suite is supported by the widest variety of vendors.

The Internet suite was developed about 10 years before the OSI model was defined and can therefore be only roughly mapped to it. The Internet protocol suite was defined according to its own model, known as the Internet or Department of Defense (DOD) model. Figure 5.2 illustrates the relationship between the Internet protocol suite and the OSI reference model.

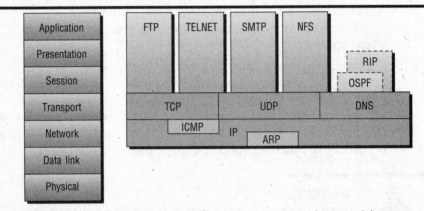

FIGURE 5.2:   The relationship between the Internet protocol suite and the OSI model

The four DOD model layers (shown in Figure 5.3) and the OSI model layers to which they correspond are as follows:

▶ The network access layer corresponds to the physical and data link layers of the OSI model.

▶ The Internet layer corresponds to the OSI network layer. Protocols at this layer are concerned with transporting packets through the internetwork. The main Internet layer protocol is IP.

▶ The host-to-host layer corresponds roughly to the OSI transport layer. Protocols at this layer communicate with peer processes in other hosts or networked devices. An example of a host-to-host protocol is TCP.

▶ The process/application layer corresponds to the OSI session, presentation, and application layers. Protocols at this layer provide application services on the network. Examples of protocols at this layer are Telnet (a terminal emulator) and FTP (File Transfer Protocol).

Figure 5.3 shows the Internet (DOD) model mapped to the OSI model.

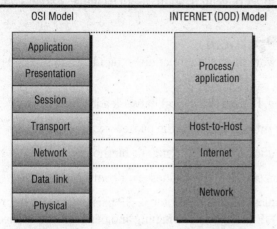

FIGURE 5.3: The Internet (DOD) model mapped to the OSI model

The Internet protocols do not cover the lower two layers of the OSI model. This is because the designers of TCP/IP used existing physical and data link standards, such as Ethernet and Token Ring, to make TCP/IP hardware independent. As a result, the protocols of the Internet suite are widely used to connect heterogeneous systems.

Since the Internet protocol suite does not include lower-layer protocols, we will begin our discussion of the individual protocols at the middle layers.

Internet Middle-Layer Protocols

As you have learned, the protocols at the OSI model's network and transport layers are concerned with transporting packets across the internetwork. TCP/IP and other Internet protocols use three types of addresses for network addressing:

▶ The data link and physical layers use hardware or physical addresses. Physical addresses are usually hard-coded into the network cards at each device.

▶ IP addresses provide logical node IDs. IP addresses are unique addresses assigned by an administrator according to certain guidelines. They are expressed in four-part, dotted-decimal notation—for example, 123.144.131.12.

▶ Logical node names, which an administrator can also assign, are easier to remember than an IP address—for example, Barney.com.

IP (Internet Protocol)

IP works at the network layer. The functions it handles and methods it uses are as follows:

▶ For addressing, IP uses the logical network address.

▶ For switching purposes, it uses the packet-switching method.

▶ For route selection, it uses the dynamic method.

▶ For connection services, IP provides error control.

IP is a connectionless, datagram protocol. (IP packets are also referred to as IP datagrams.) IP uses packet switching and performs route selection by using dynamic routing tables that are referenced at each hop. The packets making up a message could be routed differently through the internetwork depending on the state of the network at each hop. For example, if a link were to go down or become congested, packets could take a different route.

Appended to each packet is an IP header, which includes source and destination information. IP uses sequence numbering if it is necessary to fragment a packet into smaller parts and reassemble it at its destination or at an intermediate point. IP performs error checking on the header information by way of a checksum.

NOTE

A *checksum* is an error-checking method in which the data is submitted to an algorithm and the result is appended to the packet. When the packet arrives at its destination, the same calculation is performed on the data to see whether it matches the checksum value.

IP addresses are unique, four-byte addresses that must be assigned to every addressable device or node on the internetwork. Depending on the class of IP address, a certain number of bytes specifies the network portion and a certain number of bytes specifies the host or node portion. If a connection to the Internet is desired, a unique IP network address must be requested from a governing body called the SRI Network Information Center. This ensures that the new network will have an address different from any other on the Internet. IP addresses are assigned according to three classes of networks:

▶ **Class A addresses:** Used for systems with a small number of networks and a large number of hosts. These addresses use the first byte to specify the network and the last three bytes to specify the host. The first byte of a Class A address can be in the range from 0 to 127—for example, 80.23.102.3. The available IP addresses for this class have already been assigned.

▶ **Class B addresses:** Provide for an equal number of networks and hosts by assigning the first two bytes to the network and the last two bytes to the host. The range of values for the first byte of a Class B address is 128 to 191—for example, 132.45.67.28. This class is most often assigned to universities and commercial organizations.

▶ **Class C addresses:** Use the first three bytes of the address to specify the network and the last byte to specify the host. Because there is only one byte available for host addresses, a Class C network will only support a small number of hosts (or nodes). The range of values for the first byte of a Class C address is 192 to 223— for example, 194.123.45.7.

ARP (Address Resolution Protocol)

ARP is a network layer protocol concerned with mapping node names to IP addresses. It equates logical and physical device addresses. ARP maintains tables of name-to-address mappings and can send out discovery packets if a desired name or address is not currently in its table. The discovery packet requests that the entity corresponding to the known name or address respond with the needed information.

A related protocol, RARP (Reverse Address Resolution Protocol) performs the same function in reverse; that is, given an IP address, it determines the corresponding node name.

ICMP (Internet Control Message Protocol)

ICMP is a protocol used with IP to augment error handling and control procedures. It works at the network layer and is concerned with connection services. ICMP provides error control and network layer flow control.

ICMP detects error conditions such as internetwork congestion and downed links and notifies IP and upper-layer protocols so packets can be routed around problem areas.

RIP (Routing Information Protocol)

RIP is a network layer protocol. It is a distance-vector routing protocol, which means it periodically broadcasts routing tables across the internetwork. Similar to NetWare RIP, Internet RIP causes bottlenecks in WANs and is therefore being replaced by OSPF.

OSPF (Open Shortest Path First)

OSPF is another network layer protocol that addresses route discovery. It is a link-state routing protocol similar to NetWare's NLSP, described earlier in this chapter. It was developed to be more efficient and to create less overhead than RIP. It provides load balancing and routing based on class of service.

TCP (Transmission Control Protocol)

TCP is the Internet protocol suite's main transport layer protocol. It also provides addressing (with service addresses) services at the network layer.

TCP provides reliable, full-duplex, connection-oriented transport service to upper-layer protocols. TCP works in conjunction with IP to move packets through the internetwork. TCP assigns a connection ID (port) to each virtual circuit. It also provides message fragmentation and reassembly using sequence numbering. Error checking is enhanced through the use of TCP acknowledgments.

UDP (User Datagram Protocol)

UDP is a connectionless protocol that works at the transport layer. UDP transports datagrams but does not acknowledge their receipt. UDP also uses a port address to achieve datagram delivery, but this port address is simply a pointer to a process, not a connection identifier, as it is with TCP. The lack of overhead makes UDP more efficient than TCP.

DNS (Domain Name System)

DNS is a distributed database system that works at the transport layer to provide name-to-address mapping for client applications. DNS servers maintain databases that consist of hierarchical name structures of the various domains in order to use logical names for device identification. This type of address/name resolution is called service-provider initiated. The largest use of DNS is in the Internet. Name servers (DNS servers) are used to translate site names, such as Sybex.com, to actual network addresses.

Internet Upper-Layer Protocols

The upper-layer Internet protocols generally provide applications or services for use on the Internet, such as file transfer and electronic mail.

FTP (File Transfer Protocol)

As its name implies, FTP is used for file transfer between internetwork nodes. In addition, it allows users to initiate processes on the remote host. FTP enables users to log in to remote hosts. It functions at the top three layers of the OSI model, as follows:

- At the session layer, FTP provides session administration, handling connection establishment, file transfer, and connection release.

- At the presentation layer, FTP is concerned with translation, using a machine-independent file syntax.

- At the application layer, this protocol supplies network services, namely file services and collaborative service use.

FTP is a peer-to-peer protocol. FTP supports the ability to transfer files between dissimilar hosts because it uses a generic file structure that is operating-system independent.

Telnet

Telnet is used for remote terminal emulation. It enables users to access host-based applications by emulating one of the host's terminals. Telnet provides connectivity between dissimilar operating systems.

Telnet functions at the top three layers of the OSI model, as follows:

- At the session layer, it provides dialog control, using the half-duplex method. It also provides session administration, handling connection establishment, file transfer, and connection release.

- At the presentation layer, Telnet is concerned with translation, using the byte order and character codes.

- At the application layer, this protocol supplies the service use functions for remote operation.

SMTP (Simple Mail Transfer Protocol)

SMTP is a protocol for routing e-mail messages. It works at the application layer to provide message service.

SMTP does not provide a user interface for sending and receiving messages, but many Internet e-mail applications interface with it. SMTP uses TCP and IP to route the mail messages across the internetwork.

NFS (Network File System)

NFS is an application layer protocol that provides file services and remote operation service use. A major advantage of NFS is its transparency; it allows remote file systems to appear as though they were part of the local machine's file system.

NOTE

NFS is a family of protocols developed by Sun Microsystems and is considered part of the Internet protocol suite. This group of protocols comprises Sun's ONC (Open Network Computing) platform. NFS is also the name of one of the protocols in Sun's family of protocols.

XDR (External Data Representation)

XDR is a presentation layer protocol that handles translation. It uses the methods of byte order, character codes, and file syntax.

XDR is used for the representation of data in a machine-independent format. It allows data descriptions and encoding through the use of a library of C routines that allow a programmer to create arbitrary data structures that can be ported between different machine environments.

RPC (Remote Procedure Call)

RPC is a session layer protocol concerned with session administration (connection establishment, file transfer, and connection release). With this protocol a software redirector determines whether a request can be satisfied locally or whether it requires network access. The redirector handles the packaging of the network request, and the interchange is transparent to the user.

RPC servers are usually specialized for the purpose of handling RPC requests. They tend to have large amounts of file storage and the ability to handle many procedure calls. The server executes the request and generates a reply packet to the originating host.

APPLETALK PROTOCOLS

AppleTalk is the name given to the protocol suite designed for the Apple Macintosh. Apple Computer began the development of AppleTalk in 1983. Phase 1 of AppleTalk was limited in scope. It did not provide support for internetworks because the addressing scheme did not include a network address. In 1989, Apple Computer expanded the capabilities of AppleTalk with the release of AppleTalk Phase 2. Phase 2 allows for internetworking by supporting network addresses. It allows multiple protocols to coexist with AppleTalk on large, complex networks.

Table 5.1 summarizes the differences between AppleTalk Phase 1 and Phase 2.

TABLE 5.1: Differences between AppleTalk Phases 1 and 2

CHARACTERISTIC	PHASE 1	PHASE 2
Maximum zones on a network segment	1	255
Maximum nodes per network	254	About 16 million
Dynamic addressing based on	Node ID	Network + Node ID
Link-access protocols supported	LocalTalk EtherTalk	LocalTalk IEEE 802.3 IEEE 802.5
Split-horizon routing	No	Yes

The protocols that make up AppleTalk can be mapped to the OSI model, as illustrated in Figure 5.4.

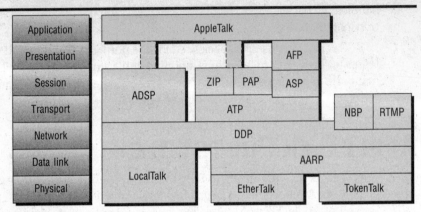

FIGURE 5.4:   AppleTalk and the OSI model

AppleTalk Lower-Layer Protocols

The lower-layer protocols of AppleTalk include Apple's original LocalTalk, as well as versions of Ethernet and Token Ring. Another protocol included here is the AppleTalk Address Resolution Protocol (AARP), which functions at the OSI model's data link and network layers.

LocalTalk (LLAP)

The LocalTalk Link Access Protocol, or LocalTalk, is Apple's original data link and physical layer protocol.

At the physical layer, LocalTalk handles the following:

Connection types:	Multipoint
Physical topology:	Bus
Digital signaling:	State-transition
Bit synchronization:	Synchronous
Bandwidth use:	Baseband

At the MAC sublayer of the data link layer, this protocol is concerned with the following:

Logical topology:	Bus
Media access:	Contention
Addressing:	Physical device

Finally, LocalTalk has these functions at the LLC sublayer of the data link layer:

Transmission synchronization:	Synchronous
Connection services:	LLC flow control and error control

LocalTalk was developed for small workgroups. It is slow—at 230.4Kbps—and is limited to 32 devices and 300-meter segment lengths. It is still useful for small offices, however. LocalTalk uses a dynamic addressing scheme, which allows each workstation to negotiate a unique node address with the other workstations at startup.

EtherTalk (ELAP)

EtherTalk (the EtherTalk Link Access Protocol) is an implementation of AppleTalk that uses the Ethernet protocol (contention access, collision detection, and star/bus topology). Like Ethernet, EtherTalk corresponds to the data link and physical layers of the OSI model.

TokenTalk (TLAP)

TokenTalk (the TokenTalk Link Access Protocol) is an adaptation of AppleTalk at the physical and data link layers. It uses the Token Ring protocol (token-passing access and star/ring topology).

AARP (AppleTalk Address Resolution Protocol)

AARP maps AppleTalk addresses to Ethernet and Token Ring physical addresses. AARP allows upper-layer protocols to use data link layer protocols other than LocalTalk.

AppleTalk Middle-Layer Protocols

The AppleTalk protocols that run at the OSI middle layers include the following:

- ▶ **DDP:** For datagram packet delivery
- ▶ **RTMP:** A distance-vector routing protocol
- ▶ **NBP:** To map logical names to addresses
- ▶ **ATP:** A transport layer protocol that uses acknowledgments to keep track of transactions

Datagram Delivery Protocol (DDP)

DDP is the workhorse of AppleTalk's network layer protocols. It provides connectionless or datagram service.

Using the concept of sockets or service addresses, DDP specifies the source and destination upper-layer protocol. DDP uses the complete address to route packets through the internetwork. The complete address consists of a logical network address, a node address, and a socket number. An address such as logical network 1002, node 1, socket 3, refers to an exact connection.

DDP works with the RTMP, NBP, and ZIP protocols to provide datagram packet delivery. It uses dynamic route selection and supports interoperability by providing network layer translation.

Routing Table Maintenance Protocol (RTMP)

RTMP is a distance-vector routing protocol, similar to RIP, which functions at the network layer. This protocol creates and maintains routing tables that DDP uses to make dynamic route selections.

Name Binding Protocol (NBP)

AppleTalk uses NBP at the transport layer to match a logical device name with its associated address. Because AppleTalk allows dynamic node addressing, NBP must obtain the current address for a given node name. This address resolution method is service-requester-initiated.

AppleTalk Transaction Protocol (ATP)

ATP is an acknowledged connectionless protocol that functions at the transport layer. It is based on transactions instead of connections. A transaction consists of a request followed by a response and is identified by a transaction ID. ATP acknowledges packet delivery and initiates retransmission if a packet remains unacknowledged for too long.

AppleTalk Upper-Layer Protocols

These AppleTalk protocols work at the upper layers of the OSI model:

- ▶ **ADSP:** Actually runs at both the transport and session layers
- ▶ **ASP:** Manages dialogs
- ▶ **PAP:** Mainly used for printing

- ▶ **ZIP:** For managing logical groups called zones
- ▶ **AFP:** For file sharing
- ▶ **AppleShare:** For application layer services

AppleTalk Data Stream Protocol (ADSP)

ADSP is categorized as a session layer protocol even though it also performs transport layer functions. The session layer functions it performs are establishing and releasing connections. The transport layer functions are segment sequencing and flow control. ADSP is an alternative to ATP as a transport protocol. ADSP does not keep track of transactions; it uses connection identifiers instead and transmits data in byte streams.

AppleTalk Session Protocol (ASP)

ASP provides session layer services by establishing, maintaining, and releasing connections. It works in conjunction with ATP to provide reliable packet delivery. ASP allows multiple sessions to be established with the same service provider, as long as requests are made individually by service requesters.

Printer Access Protocol (PAP)

You can use PAP for more than just printing, in spite of its name. It is a session layer protocol that permits sessions to be initiated by both service requesters and service providers. PAP allows connections between file servers and workstations, as well as between workstations and print servers.

Zone Information Protocol (ZIP)

ZIP allows devices to be organized into logical groups called zones. A zone can reduce the apparent complexity of an internetwork by limiting the number of service providers viewed to the subset the user needs to see. Routers and other network nodes use ZIP to map between zone and network names. The ZIP protocol falls in the OSI network layer.

AppleTalk Filing Protocol (AFP)

AFP was developed to facilitate file sharing. It works at the session and presentation layers to translate local file system commands into a format that can be used for network file service. AFP provides file-syntax translation for other applications as well. It enhances security by verifying login names and passwords at connection establishment and by encrypting login information before sending it across the network.

AppleShare

AppleShare is a suite of three protocols or applications that provide Apple-Talk's application layer services. The following protocols make up AppleShare:

▶ **AppleShare File Server:** The Macintosh's network operating system. It uses AFP to provide access to remote files. AppleShare File Server registers users and allows those users to log in and access resources.

▶ **AppleShare Print Server:** Uses lower-layer protocols (such as NBP and PAP) to provide printer sharing on the network. Similar to NetWare, AppleShare Print Server stores print jobs in a queue before sending them to the selected printer. AppleShare Print Server's utilization of NBP allows users to refer to a printer using a name of their choice; NBP maps that name to the printer's address.

▶ **AppleShare PC:** Allows DOS workstations to access AppleShare file services. An MS-DOS user running an AppleShare PC can read or write files to an AppleShare File Server and print to an AppleTalk printer.

AppleShare provides active service advertisement and collaborative service use.

MISCELLANEOUS PROTOCOLS AND STANDARDS

The rest of this chapter covers some miscellaneous protocols and standards. Some are LAN protocols; others, including those used for public data networks, primarily make up WANs.

Serial Line Internet Protocol (SLIP)

The SLIP and PPP protocols (discussed in the next section) are used with dial-up connections to the Internet. If you connect to the Internet from your home computer, chances are you're using one or the other of these protocols. SLIP was the first of the two to be developed, and it is the simplest. It functions at the physical layer only and does not provide error control or security. Despite these drawbacks, SLIP is a popular protocol for Internet access. Most users don't need a secure connection, and most high-speed modems provide their own error control.

NOTE
Although SLIP functions at the physical layer of the OSI model, it is frequently referred to as a data link communications protocol.

Point-to-Point Protocol (PPP)

PPP was developed as an improvement to SLIP, and the functions it provides encompass both the physical and data link layers. PPP's additional functions include error control, security, dynamic IP addressing, and support for multiple protocols. Both SLIP and PPP are point-to-point protocols. PPP provides physical device addressing at the MAC sublayer and LLC-level error control.

Figure 5.5 shows SLIP and PPP mapped to the OSI model.

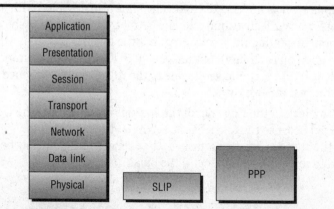

FIGURE 5.5: SLIP and PPP mapped to the OSI model

Fiber Distributed Data Interface (FDDI)

FDDI is a LAN and MAN standard based on the use of fiber-optic cable wired in a physical ring or star. Because the use of fiber-optic cable allows a network to span greater distances than the typical LAN, it is commonly used for campus-wide and even larger networks. FDDI uses a token-passing media access method, similar to IEEE 802.5 Token Ring. Like IEEE 802.5, the FDDI standard covers the physical and MAC sublayers of the OSI model and uses the LLC defined by IEEE 802.2. Figure 5.6 shows FDDI mapped to the OSI model.

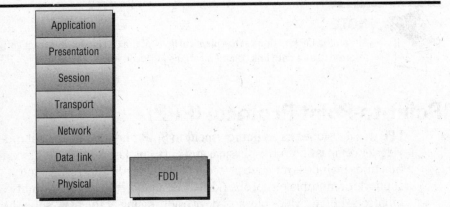

FIGURE 5.6:   FDDI mapped to the OSI model

FDDI has a very high bandwidth at 100Mbps, which makes it suitable for applications such as multimedia and video. It is also designed with the potential for very effective fault tolerance. An FDDI ring can be cabled with dual counter-rotating rings (meaning that the token is passed in the opposite direction on each ring). Stations on an FDDI ring can be either single-attached stations, connected to one of the rings, or dual-attached stations, connected to both rings.

If there is a break in the ring and all the stations are single attached, the ring will fail because the token cannot arrive at the next station. However, if the stations are dual attached, the ring will automatically be reconfigured to route the token around the break.

X.25

The international standards organization CCITT (International Tele-graph and Telephone Consultative Committee), since renamed to the

International Telecommunications Union (ITU), developed X.25 in 1974 as a WAN standard using packet switching.

As you can see in Figure 5.7, X.25 functions at the network layer. It normally interfaces with a protocol called LAPB (Link Access Procedures–Balanced) at the data link layer, which in turn runs over X.21, or another physical layer CCITT protocol, such as X.21bis or V.32.

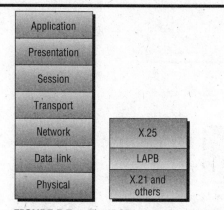

FIGURE 5.7: The X.25 protocol mapped to the OSI model

X.25 provides permanent or switched virtual circuits, which imply reliable service and end-to-end flow control. However, line speeds used with X.25 are too slow to provide LAN application services on a WAN.

At the physical layer, X.21 allows for a hybrid mesh topology and a point-to-point connection type.

LAPB is a data link layer protocol based on SDLC that provides LLC-level flow control and error control.

At the network layer, X.25 uses a type of addressing called channel addressing, which is similar to logical network addressing except that the address is maintained for each connection.

Frame Relay

Frame relay is a newer packet-switching technology, similar to X.25, that uses virtual circuits. Like X.25, frame relay is used in WANs. Frame relay assumes that certain error-checking and monitoring tasks will be performed by higher-level protocols, and this allows it to be faster than X.25. Frame relay functions at the physical and data link layers of the OSI model, as illustrated in Figure 5.8. Frame relay is defined by CCITT recommendations I.451/Q.931 and Q.922.

At the physical layer, frame relay handles point-to-point connections in mesh (hybrid) physical topologies. At the LLC sublayer of the data link layer, frame relay provides error detection but not error recovery.

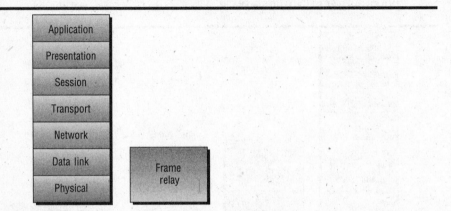

FIGURE 5.8:   Frame relay mapped to the OSI model

NOTE

Frame relay services generally allow customers to specify committed information rates according to their bandwidth requirements.

Integrated Services Digital Network (ISDN) and Broadband ISDN (B-ISDN)

ISDN is a set of standards designed to provide voice, video, and data transmission over a digital telephone network. B-ISDN provides greater bandwidth, which can be used for applications such as video, imaging, and multimedia. B-ISDN can be used with SONET and ATM, which are described in the next two sections.

At the physical layer, ISDN provides time-division multiplexing (TDM). At the network layer, the ISDN standard is defined by CCITT recommendations I.450/Q.930 and I.451/Q.931. Figure 5.9 shows ISDN mapped to the OSI model.

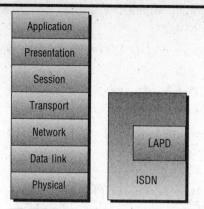

FIGURE 5.9: ISDN mapped to the OSI model

ISDN functions as a transmission media service only. The ISDN specification uses the LAPD (Link Access Procedure, D Channel) protocol at the data link layer to provide acknowledged, connectionless, full-duplex service. At the MAC sublayer, LAPD provides physical device addressing. At the LLC sublayer, it handles flow control and frame sequencing.

The ISDN standard for integrating analog and digital transmissions using digital telecommunications networks allows for circuit-switched or packet-switched connections. These connections are provided by means of digital communication channels, or bit pipes. Using the ISDN bit pipes, several standard rate multiplexed channels are available. These channels are classified as follows:

- **Channel A:** 4KHz analog channel
- **Channel B:** 64Kbps digital channel
- **Channel C:** 8 or 16Kbps digital channel (used for out-of-band signaling)
- **Channel D:** 16 or 64Kbps digital channel (used for out-of-band signaling). Includes three subchannels: *s* for signaling, *t* for telemetry, and *p* for low bandwidth packet data
- **Channel E:** 64Kbps digital channel (for internal ISDN signaling)
- **Channel H:** 384, 1536, or 1920Kbps digital channel

LAPD operates on the D channel.

The following three channel combinations have been standardized by CCITT as international service offerings:

- **Basic rate:** Includes two B channels (at 64Kbps) and one D channel (at 16Kbps)

- **Primary rate:** Includes one D channel (at 64Kbps), 23 B channels in the U.S. and Japan, or 30 B channels in Europe and Australia

- **Hybrid:** Includes one A channel (4KHz analog) and one C channel (8 or 16Kbps digital)

Synchronous Optical Network (SONET) and Synchronous Digital Hierarchy (SDH)

Bell Communications Research developed SONET. It is a physical layer protocol standardized by ANSI and generally used for WANs. ITU (formerly CCITT) created a similar standard called SDH. Regional variations, developed because of local differences in telecommunications, are SDH-Europe, SDH-SONET (North America), and SDH-Japan. Figure 5.10 shows SONET and SDH mapped to the OSI model. SONET and SDH provide point-to-point connections, work with mesh or ring physical topologies, and use the TDM multiplexing method.

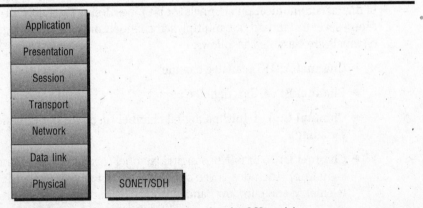

FIGURE 5.10:   SONET and SDH mapped to the OSI model

Asynchronous Transfer Mode (ATM)

ATM is a standard developed by the ITU Telecommunications Standards Sector and the ATM Forum. It is most frequently considered for WANs, but it can be used for LANs and MANs as well. This protocol covers the OSI model's data link and network layer functionality and can operate over physical layer protocols such as FDDI and SONET/SDH. Figure 5.11 maps ATM to the OSI model.

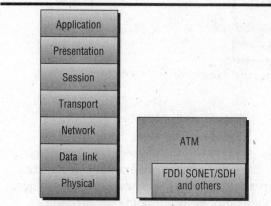

FIGURE 5.11: ATM mapped to the OSI model

A distinguishing feature of ATM is that it uses cell switching. A cell is a 53-byte packet that follows a virtual circuit. Its other network layer function is static route selection.

At the LLC sublayer of the data link layer, ATM provides isochronous transmission synchronization and error control.

Switched Megabit Data Service (SMDS)

SMDS is a cell-switching technology developed by Bell Communications Research. Like ATM, it uses small packets, called cells. It can be mapped to the data link and network layers of the OSI model, and it is normally used with physical layer protocols such as the DQDB standard for MANs (IEEE 802.6) and SONET/SDH. At the LLC sublayer of the data link layer, SMDS provides isochronous transmission synchronization. Figure 5.12 shows SMDS mapped to the OSI model.

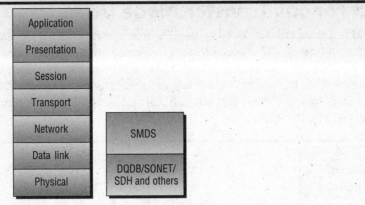

FIGURE 5.12:   SMDS mapped to the OSI model

WHAT'S NEXT

In the next chapter, we'll move on to basic card and cable installation. This chapter will focus on what you need to know about your physical installation before the cabling process begins and then take you through installation procedures so that you can build your own networks and connect your PCs.

Part II
NETWORK HARDWARE AND SOFTWARE

Chapter 6

Installing Cards and Cables

I n this chapter, we will cover installing cards and cables to build networks that will connect your PCs.

Adapted from *Mastering Local Area Networks*
by Christa Anderson with Mark Minasi
ISBN 0-7821-2258-2   784 pages $39.99

CABLE INSTALLATION CONSIDERATIONS

Most of what this section covers concerns how to prepare for a contractor's help and what you need to know about your physical installation before the cabling process begins. This is not a complete tutorial in cable installation. First, there's not enough room. Second, it's difficult to tailor such instructions when you can't see the environment in which the cable will be installed. Third, complex cabling is often a specialist's job. Therefore, we'll cover the basics, so far as you need to know them for simple cabling jobs or for overseeing someone else doing a more complex one. After reading this, you'll be better prepared to instruct the cable installer in what you need done. Outsourcing this kind of work isn't cheap, and the meter's always ticking, so it's best to be prepared.

Plan Ahead

This is one of those really obvious but easily overlooked hints: don't just think about what your needs are now, think about what they'll be five or 10 years down the line. Cabling a building is not so much fun that you're going to want to do it twice, so plan ahead.

First, know your situation. Get the blueprints for the building you're in and study them. Where is the ductwork? Where's the electrical wiring and how is it shielded? Are there any surprises waiting to happen? What are the fire codes for your area? What do they say about where you can use polyvinylchloride (PVC) coated cable and where you must use plenum?

Get the fastest cable you can afford. Even if you don't need it now, the chances are excellent that sooner or later you'll use it, when your company starts implementing databases, or video to the desktop, or some such thing. Buy that 100Mbps Cat 5 now, or even fiber if you can justify it, and you'll save yourself money later in not having to pay for two cabling installations.

Give Yourself Some Slack

Don't plan out your cabling needs to the last foot, but anticipate quite a bit of extra cable. First, you'll need this because you can't just plug PCs into the network on top of each other; if you're using the bus physical topology, you'll need about 10 feet between taps or connections to the

PC. The extra room will give you flexibility. If you have just enough cable for your needs, then sooner or later Joe User is going to want to move his PC 5 feet to the left and that's going to completely throw off your entire network if your plan has no flexibility built into it. When running the cable along the ceiling or floor, leave a few loops (6 to 8 feet for backbone cable) at each corner, or each doorway, or anywhere that's a permanent physical feature in the building so you can find it again. Secure the loops with electrical tape to keep them neat and out of the way. When you need a little more length in your cable, you'll have it. Otherwise, you'll have two options: splicing the cable yourself, or paying someone else to do it. Contractors typically charge not only for the length of the cable they run but also for the number of terminations they must do. Splicing the cable means paying for two useless terminations that don't do anything but give you more length that you could have had from the beginning with a little planning. Similarly, when running taps from a backbone or hub, give yourself a spare 10 to 15 feet so that you can move the PC at a later time if you need to do so.

WARNING

If you haven't planned for flexibility and need to extend your cable, splice it rather than attempting to stretch it. Stretching can damage cable—especially stranded cable—and damaged cable is far more prone to interference.

Giving yourself elbow room applies to conduit, too. In big installations with high security needs, you'll often have a central backbone run in a large duct, with smaller conduits branching off from it. This is an expensive configuration, and larger conduits will make it more expensive yet. Regardless, you should seriously consider getting conduit a little larger than you need now. For example, if the 1/2-inch variety will let you run two taps from the backbone, get the 3/4-inch variety so that you can run three or four taps if you need to do so. Once again, even if it's more expensive up front, giving yourself room to grow will save you money down the road when you don't have to buy new conduit, pay to have it installed, and scrap the stuff you already paid for.

Neatness Counts

Keep in mind that you're going to have to deal with this cable at some point after it's installed, so make it as easy as possible to access. When it comes to ceiling installations, you may be tempted to just throw the cables across the "floor" of the ceiling because it's less work. It's true, this is less work initially, but when you have to work up in that ceiling later, you're not going to like it if you have to trip over cable snaking across the floor. To avoid this, secure the cables to something such as the supports of the drop ceiling; clamps are made for the purpose, or you can use plastic snap ties. You may also want to consider attaching the cables to air conditioning or heating ductwork.

As a last resort, leave all the cables on the floor of the ceiling, but bundle and tie them so that they're out of the way. That way, if you have to move them, you only have to move one lump, not six individual cables all tangled up together.

NOTE
Not all drop ceilings can support cable, so you may have to secure the cables to the supports or ductwork to make this work at all.

Running cables under the floor requires similar planning. Again, lay the cables neatly so they're easy to get to. If you've got the money, consider getting ductwork or conduit to run the cables in so they stay in one place. Also, put the cables somewhere you can get to them *after* the furniture has been put into the room. It might look neater to have the cables running along the wall, but the chances are excellent that cubicles or a table will be along the wall. The middle of the room, where there's less likely to be furniture, is a better bet.

If you're running cable *on* the floor, then the rules are a little different. In that case, you'll do well to keep the cables against the wall and out of harm's way. That way, people will be less likely to trip over them (injuring themselves and/or the network in the process). Also, janitorial staff are less likely to damage them with enthusiastic cleaning. Tape down cables as best you can to avoid the chances of them being tripped on or wandering away.

Finally, label *everything*. At troubleshooting time, you're going to want to know which cables go where without doing this routine: "Okay, Karen, when I say 'Go,' shake the cable so I can tell which one it is." That exchange is normally followed by this routine: "Okay, it wasn't that cable. When I say so, shake the one next to it."

To avoid this scenario, use different colors of electrical tape wrapped around the ends of the cables, or little adhesive numbers, or (if you've got deep pockets) color-coded cables themselves. These make it easier to tell which cable you've got at the end and also make it possible to tell which cable you're holding when you're crouched in the ceiling. I don't recommend hand-printed labels, as they can be hard to read. Unless you've got a really complicated cabling system that requires extensive description, symbols are probably the way to go. You can identify them at a glance and don't have to decipher someone else's handwriting or turn the cable over to read the whole thing. Keep a legend of cable codes around so people can tell what they're looking at even if you're out of the office.

TIP

A little more than 10 percent of the male population can't tell red from green, so consider using symbols or avoiding green and red cables.

Play Well with Others

Think about what's going to be running in the same place as your network cable. Got lots of interference-producing devices around? Consider cable with extra shielding, such as coaxial or STP, or, better yet, RFI-immune fiber.

TIP

Fluorescent lights emit a lot of electromagnetic interference, or EMI, so don't run cables over the top of them.

Are electrical cables already in place? Don't run your network cables parallel to them, particularly if you're looking at big bundles, such as those leading up to a fuse box. If new electrical cables are going in after the network has been installed, avoid introducing new interference problems by asking for armored cable (run in a metal sheath) rather than the ones enclosed in the plastic sheath. Once again, it will cost more up front, but these extra precautions may save you money later.

Things to Know Ahead of Time

We've looked at some of the specifics you need to be aware of before the cabling process begins. Here are some questions for your contractor. Figuring out these details early in the process can save you time, money, and lots of headaches.

Part II

Do you have wiring conduits?   Many buildings provide you with built-in places in the walls and ceilings where you can run your cable. Often, these wiring conduits are themselves plenum-rated. This means that you *may* be able to use a cheaper PVC cable.

How are you testing your cables?   You will want to know the precise method that is being used to test the cables after they are installed. Common sense reigns supreme on this issue. (Keep in mind that common sense really isn't that common.) Make sure that you get a written description of the testing method and follow the testing logic from start to finish to ensure that it makes sense for installation.

How are you documenting your cables?   Make sure that the cables are being documented and labeled according to your company's set standard. If your company has not set one, then it should do so. You want to be sure that the labeling system makes sense to you, so I recommend that your company set the labeling standard, not the contractor.

What is the repair policy for the cable installation?   You will want at least a 24-hour on-site response from your contractor. Many contractors say they have a 24-hour response to cable problems, when what they mean is, "We will call you back within 24 hours, and it may take us up to a week to actually get there." You don't want that; you want the contractor at your site in 24 hours or less. Cable problems are mission-critical problems.

Can you get at least three local references from the contractor? You will want three local references from your contractor so you can personally see the quality of his or her work and documentation of it. Most companies will not mind taking you on a tour of their cable systems if they are happy with the work the contractor has done. Don't forget to reciprocate when prospective clients call you to come see your expertly designed and installed cable system.

Are you following building and fire code requirements?   To ensure the safety of all your employees, follow all local building and fire codes. You want to select a contractor who can demonstrate by experience and references that she or he is well versed in the local regulations. When in doubt, call the city or county offices yourself and ask questions.

Do you need to notify anyone else in your building or locale of your plans?   You may need to check with other tenants in your building to make sure that the cable installation will not conflict with their workflow. This is usually more of a courtesy than a requirement. Often, if you notify building management, they will notify all the other tenants in your building.

How long is the guarantee on the cable installation valid? Verify the length of time the contractor will guarantee his or her labor and the cables themselves. A service contract at least one year long is advisable. Reasonable costs for an annual service contract should not exceed 12 percent of the overall cable installation cost.

Wireless Networking

Preparing for a wireless network—or, more likely, a wireless portion of a wired network—isn't significantly different from preparing for a wired one. You still have to think about environmental factors and how the data is going to get from point A to point B.

Two kinds of wireless networking are used in LANs. Most commonly used are the radio-frequency (RF) wireless networks, which can be used to connect PCs and servers over a fairly wide area, but have low transmission speeds (around 1Mbps). More specialized applications, such as wireless printers and keyboards, use infrared (IR) technology to create a high- speed, short-range link.

Interference is the biggest problem you're likely to encounter with wireless networks. Infrared communications have an extremely high frequency, so in order to use them, the sender and receiver must be close and in the line of sight. If you can't stretch a piece of string between the sending device and the receiving one, they can't communicate. Therefore, if you've got an IR printer, it's a good idea to place it somewhere that IR notebook users can access it without people walking between the two devices.

NOTE

Frequency determines the amount of data that can be sent during a specified interval. Because of this, high-frequency communications are more easily interfered with than low-frequency ones.

Part II

RF devices are less prone to interference because their lower frequencies mean that the signal can more or less go around obstacles instead of being blocked by them. For this reason, although IR devices are confined to the room in which they operate, RF wireless devices can roam up to about 300 to 500 feet away from their source if indoors, or 800 to 1000 feet away if outdoors. Thick walls or metal barriers will interfere with the signal, but otherwise RF signals are pretty flexible.

INSTALLING AND CONFIGURING NETWORK CARDS

The cables are in. Now you're ready to attach them to something. If you're not familiar with card installation and configuration, read on. You'll learn how to get the card in the box in the first place and how to make it work with the other cards in the box once it's in there.

Installing Network Cards

If you have any experience at all in installing cards in a PC, the mechanics of installing a network card are pretty straightforward. Power down the PC, don your antistatic strap, open the computer case, and find a slot in the PC that's free and fits the kind of card you have.

TIP

If you can, choose a slot that's not next to another card in order to keep the air-flow inside the PC's box as open as possible.

If you're removing another card to insert the new one, follow these steps:

1. Make sure that the card is disconnected from any outside cables.

2. Unscrew the small screws attaching the card to the PC case and lay them aside.

TIP

Keep an egg carton around to hold screws. They're perfect for the task—they are cheap and accessible, they have lots of little slots where you can put the different kinds of screws, and you can close the tops to keep screws from flying everywhere if you knock the carton off the table. The only risk lies with well-meaning people who don't understand why you have egg cartons lying around and throw them out.

3. Pull gently on the card, using both hands to wiggle it back and forth slightly to disengage it from the connectors. This may take a little tugging, but if the card doesn't come fairly easily, stop and make sure that the card is indeed fully disconnected from the PC.

4. When you've got the card out, set it aside. If you plan to use the card again, wrap it back up in its original sheath. Don't touch the gold connectors on the card: the oils in your skin can corrode the gold and thus reduce the card's connectivity.

Installing a card is much the same process, in reverse:

1. Unwrap the card, being careful not to touch the gold connectors, and set it aside.

2. Power down the PC and open it up.

3. Find an open slot on the motherboard that matches the bus required by the card. An ISA card needs an ISA slot; a PCI card needs a PCI slot.

NOTE

ISA and PCI are the two card types you're most likely to be dealing with. MCA and EISA cards are very rare, and I'd be surprised if you found a network card that required you to use either bus type. It's possible to find EISA network cards, but they're fairly uncommon.

4. Unscrew the plate that covered the open slot's opening to the rear of the computer and set the plate and screws aside. You may need the plate later, and you'll need the screws in just a minute.

Part II

5. Align the network card with the slot in the PC, and push gently but firmly to seat the card in its slot. You may need to push fairly hard for this to work, which can be somewhat intimidating if you're not used to inserting cards. If you've got the right slot and push straight in, then the card should snap into place.

6. Using those screws that you set aside in step 4, screw the card into the little holes in the case to hold it in place. If the card is in all the way, this extra step won't affect the card's positioning all that much, but will keep it from sagging or working loose.

7. Replace the case and, if the cables are already in place, connect them to the card.

Installing Network Card Drivers

The process for installing the drivers for the card depends on your operating system. Like other add-in cards, network cards come with a disk containing drivers. To install these drivers, follow the instructions that come with the network card.

TIP

The operating system may include drivers for the card, but if the operating system is more than a year old, the drivers that come with the card itself are likely to be newer.

More recent versions of operating systems may include drivers for the cards that you can load using an interface within the operating system. For example, Windows 95/98/Me includes the Add New Hardware Wizard, which you can use to detect the card and automatically load the required driver. That said, you may end up using the disk anyway, as the drivers on the floppy disk may be more recent, or may be better optimized for the card than are the drivers included with the operating system. Consider the 3Com EtherLink III NIC (see Figure 6.1). When installing the card for use with Windows 2000, you can use the drivers that come with the operating system, or you can manually select the card to be installed and install the drivers from the disk. Not sure what you should do? Read the documentation for the card included in the package or on the manufacturer's website.

Add/Remove Hardware Wizard

Select Network Adapter
Which network adapter do you want to install?

Click the Network Adapter that matches your hardware, then click OK. If you have an installation disk for this component, click Have Disk.

Manufacturers:

| 3Com |
| Accton |
| Acer |
| Addtron |
| Advanced Micro Devices (AMD |
| Aironet |

Network Adapter:

| 3Com 10/100 Mini PCI Ethernet Adapter Version: 1.10.16.0 |
| 3Com EtherLink III Bus-Master EISA Ethernet Adapter |
| 3Com EtherLink III EISA (3C579) |
| 3Com EtherLink III EISA (3C579-TP) |
| 3Com EtherLink III ISA (3C509/3C509b) in Legacy mode |
| 3Com EtherLink III ISA (3C509b) in EISA mode |

Have Disk...

< Back   Next >   Cancel

Part II

FIGURE 6.1:   Installing network cards from a floppy disk by using the Have Disk button in the Windows 2000 Add/Remove Hardware Wizard.

Speaking of websites, if you've got Internet access, you may not want to use the drivers provided on the disk *or* in the operating system because they're both extremely likely to be outdated. Instead, turn to the website for the network card's manufacturer and find the section for software downloads. Select the type and model of card you're using. There will often be a page like the one shown in Figure 6.2 from which you can download drivers for that particular model of card.

When you compare drivers from the Web with the drivers on the disk that were saved in 1993, you can see the advantage of checking out websites and FTP sites for the most recent versions of card drivers.

TIP

This tip about downloading drivers from the Internet applies not only to network cards but also to any device you're installing. Not all device drivers are frequently updated, but it's always worth looking.

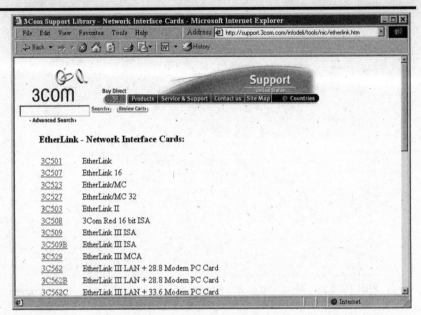

Configuring Card Resources

In a lot of ways, physically installing the card is the easy part: you plug it
in and you're ready to go. Configuring it is another matter entirely. Cards
use logical addresses and they must be unique on the network, but that's
not the hard part. The hard part lies in making sure that the network card
has access to the CPU and a place to store its data while it's waiting for
the CPU to process that data. In other words, it needs its own interrupt,
I/O address space, and (rarely) DMA channels.

If you're familiar with all these terms, you can skip the next few pages
that contain a review of what these configuration settings are and why
you'll need them.

TIP

On modern cards, interrupts, I/O buffers, and DMA settings are software configured, either with a SETUP program or by automatic detection in the operating system. On older cards, some of these settings may be set with hardware jumpers or switches on the card itself. So, before installing a card in the machine, note whether the card is software configurable or hardware configurable.

TIP

If you're using only PCI cards and have installed an operating system that supports Plug and Play, you don't have to worry about any of the configuration issues mentioned in the remainder of this chapter. PCI cards support Plug and Play, in which the cards are self-configuring. The cards still use the same resources described here—you just don't have to manually configure them.

Getting the CPU's Attention—Interrupt Requests

The network card is in charge of sending and receiving information across the network. However, it can't *do* anything with that information. All number crunching, moving to main memory, or data manipulation must be handled by the CPU.

This is fine, but every other device in the PC or attached to it—the keyboard, hard disk, video card, sound card, and what have you—is also contending for access to the CPU. Those peripheral devices could get access in one of two ways. First, every few milliseconds (thousandths of a second), the CPU could periodically go over to the NIC and ask, "Excuse me, NIC, but have you any information that needs to be processed?" This method of "nagging" the cards in your system periodically is known as *polling*, and you can see how it would work in Figure 6.3.

This works, and some older network cards really do require the CPU to poll them to find out their status. The trouble is, this process is terribly inefficient. If the CPU were to do this, it would constantly have to stop doing what it loves to do best (processing), just to nag the NIC for information that may or may not be there. That's a whole lot of wasted CPU time, especially as there are many other devices in the PC that would also be polled. In a polling-only computer, the CPU could conceivably spend all of its time virtually rushing from device to device, asking, "Have you got anything for me?" This doesn't leave a lot of time for number crunching, which is what the CPU is best at and designed for.

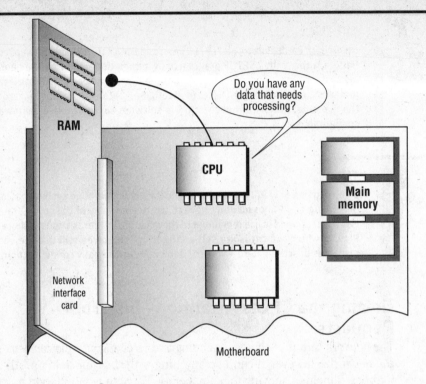

Polling: The CPU periodically asks the networking card
if it has any information to transfer.

FIGURE 6.3:   The CPU polling the NIC for data.

The alternative is the method preferred in modern systems: interrupts. When the network card has packets waiting to be processed, as shown in Figure 6.4, they're stored in the NIC's memory. When a packet arrives in the "waiting room" or memory on the NIC, the NIC goes over to the CPU, taps it on the shoulder, and says, "Excuse me, CPU, but there is some information sitting in the memory of the NIC. When you get a chance, will you please interrupt what you are doing and process this information or move it over to main memory?" When the NIC does this, it is making an *interrupt request*.

Once the CPU receives this request, it goes ahead and continues working. However, when it gets a free moment, the CPU will then go over to the NIC and start processing the information or move the information from the NIC to main memory.

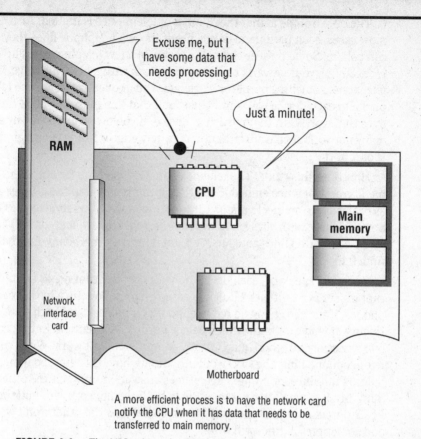

A more efficient process is to have the network card
notify the CPU when it has data that needs to be
transferred to main memory.

FIGURE 6.4:   The NIC asking the CPU to move data.

Having trouble imagining this? Think of the CPU as the CEO of your
PC, and each peripheral device as a department head. The CPU keeps its
door locked, but has an array of telephones on its desk, each a different
color so it can tell them apart. Each telephone is a hotline from one
department or another. So, if the pink telephone rings, it's the hard disk
requesting that data be pulled from cluster 492 into main memory. If the
green telephone rings, it's the keyboard insisting that the keystrokes in
its buffer be registered before they're lost. If it's the black telephone...
well, you get the idea. Each device gets its own hotline to the CPU so that
it can ask the CPU to do something for it. When a particular telephone
rings, then the CPU can immediately identify who needs help, and if it's
already dealing with someone else's request, the CPU can prioritize based
on the urgency of requests associated with that particular telephone.

Part II

The only trouble is that the number of telephones is limited. Also, in most cases, each peripheral device needs its own telephone line—they can't share. Some devices can only use one of a few telephones at all; for example, your network card may only work with a blue or orange telephone, not with a purple or black one. Thus, you must assign one telephone to each device you want to use, and that line must be one of the ones that work with that particular device. If you ever wondered why so many network people are either prematurely gray or losing their hair, this is part of the reason.

How does this work? The telephone analogy isn't too far off. There are metal traces or wires embedded in the motherboard, and those wires act as pathways to connect various cards sitting in their bus slots to the CPU. Some of these pathways are known as *interrupt request lines,* or *IRQ lines.* There are 16 IRQ lines going to each slot on the motherboard, numbered from 0 to 15.

Generally speaking, each device on your network that needs an interrupt must have a different IRQ line assigned to it. To return to the telephones, if the CPU had two red telephones on its desk and both were ringing, it wouldn't know which device needed its attention. In that case, one device or the other—maybe both—simply wouldn't work. When the red telephone rang, the CPU wouldn't know who was calling, so it might ignore both lines, or it might sometimes answer one and not the other. Similarly, if you assign the same IRQ to both the network card and the LPT2 port, sometimes one won't work, sometimes the other won't work, and sometimes neither will work.

How do you find out which interrupts your network card can use and which of those are free? The first question can be answered by reading your network card's documentation. Somewhere, it should list supported interrupts. Most network cards support two or three interrupts, one of which is likely to be IRQ 5.

TIP

If no supported interrupts are available for your network card but some interrupts are available, look to see whether a device in your system could switch to the one that's free. For example, suppose that your network card supports only IRQs 5 and 10, but IRQ 7 is the only one available. If your sound card is using 5 but will support 7, switch the sound card's interrupt to 7.

You can answer the second question in a couple of different ways. One method is to meticulously document each interrupt, I/O buffer area, and used DMA channel and write them down on a sheet of paper that's kept in an envelope taped to the computer case. There are a couple of advantages to this method. First, you can always get a good idea of your system's configuration, even when the computer is turned off. Second, it's easy to see the configuration at a glance—something not always true when dealing with software diagnostics. The only catch to this method is that you *must* keep it updated, or you're lost.

Well, not entirely lost. Although software diagnostics have historically not been all that great at correctly identifying which devices were using which resources (including IRQs), with Windows 95 the situation got a lot better. The Device Manager tab in the System applet available in the Windows 95/98/Me Control Panel can tell you what resources some devices are using. As shown in Figure 6.5, select the device for which you want information, then click the Properties button. You'll move to the Properties sheet for the device. Turn to the Resources tab, as shown in Figure 6.6, and you'll be able to see the system resources that a particular network card is using.

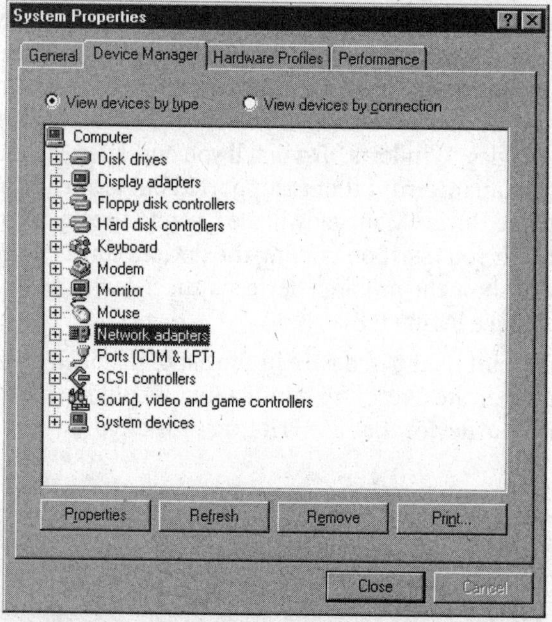

FIGURE 6.5:   The Windows 95 Device Manager.

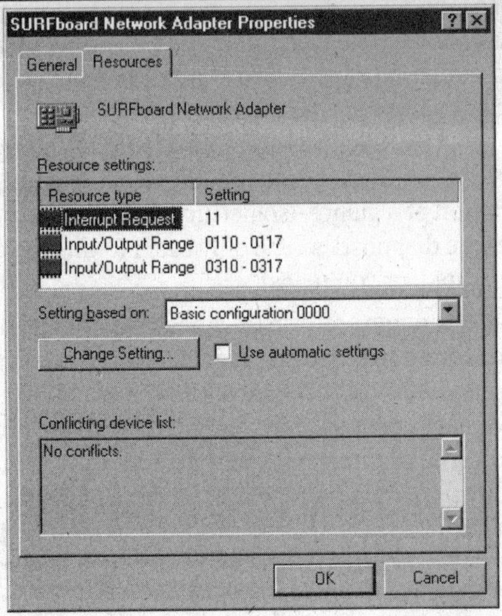

FIGURE 6.6: The properties of a network card.

You can use the Device Manager not only to determine current system configuration but also to change it. To change the interrupt a device is using, click the Change Setting button on the Resources tab and enter a new IRQ number in the space provided. If you choose an interrupt not supported by that device, Windows 95 will tell you and offer you another option. If you choose an interrupt that *is* supported but is already in use by another device, the Device Manager will alert you to the problem, as shown in Figure 6.7. If you insist on making the devices conflict, the Device Manager will show the problem device in the list with an exclamation point next to it (see Figure 6.8).

An exclamation point next to a device in the list of installed devices doesn't necessarily indicate a resource conflict, but it could herald some other problem with the device that keeps it from working.

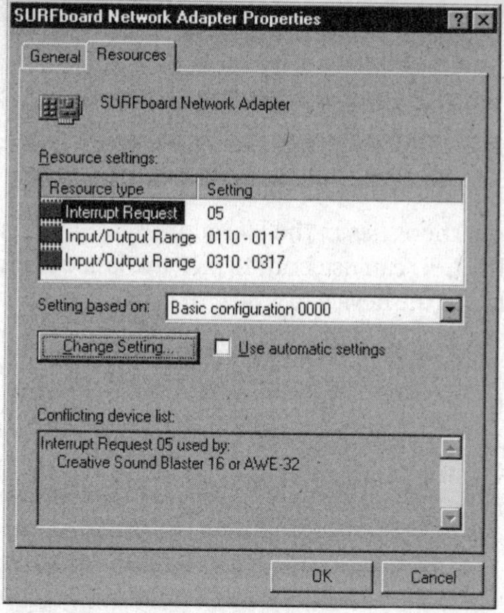

FIGURE 6.7:   The Device Manager will warn you if you assign an interrupt already in use by another device.

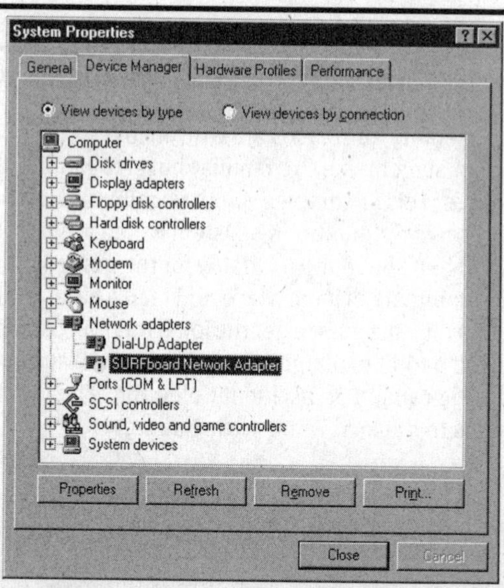

FIGURE 6.8:   Devices currently not working will have an exclamation point next to their entries in the list of installed devices.

Where Does This Data Go? Choosing a Base I/O Address

Now you know how the network card gets the CPU's attention when it has information to pass along. Where is this information stored? For that matter, when the CPU passes instructions to the peripheral device, where are those instructions stored?

The answer to both questions lies in the I/O addresses. Essentially, they're a mailbox that the CPU can use both to pick up data waiting for it and drop off instructions for the device to which that I/O area belongs. Each device must have its own I/O area so that the CPU will drop off the appropriate instructions to each device; it's going to cause no end of confusion if the CPU asks the network card to play a sound. Therefore, you'll either need to tell the device which I/O addresses to use or let the system configure itself to avoid conflicts. The *base* I/O address is the one defining the bottom of the range.

NOTE

Normally, you'll configure the base I/O address and the rest is taken care of for you. However, some cards will require you to define a range, letting you pick from one of the ranges supported by that card.

WHY DO MEMORY ADDRESSES HAVE LETTERS IN THEM?

I/O addresses and memory addresses are written in hexadecimal, a base-16 numbering system like the familiar base-10 numbering system. The reason for this is complex, but basically it's because computers think in a base-2 numbering system called *binary*, and binary numbers tend to be long and unwieldy for the human brain. If you're like an old roommate of mine who could read a binary number on a license plate and at a glance get the joke, then you can feel superior to me. If she hadn't explained after she started laughing, I probably would have caused an accident doing the "Okay, carry the one" conversions to decimal while driving along.

In an effort to make these numbers easier to absorb, programmers began using first a base-8 system and now hexadecimal, so as to express the numbers in a more efficient form. Why not use decimals? Mostly because of bytes, which are eight bits. The 10-based decimal system didn't accommodate the 8-based bytes all that well; a system more easily divisible by four made the conversions easier.

CONTINUED ➡

As the base-10 numbering system we're used to doesn't have 16 distinct characters used to express numbers, the hexadecimal system must be supplemented with letters in the alphabet. A–F make up the missing six digits. Therefore, up to the number 9, hex and decimal numbers look just alike. At 10, things start looking a bit off. In hexadecimal, 10 is A, 11 is B, 12 is C, and so forth until we get up to 16 and run out of letters. The decimal 16 is 10 hexadecimal, 17 is 11 hexadecimal, and so on. Hexadecimal numbers are often written with a lowercase "h" at the end so that you can tell that the number is written in hex, not decimal, like so: 330h. The "h" is not part of the number

You can do conversions if you want to, but for most of us, the simplest way to convert hexadecimal to decimal is to break out the Windows calculator and run it in Scientific mode. Make sure that the calculator is set to display in the number system you're starting out in (say, hexadecimal), type in the number, and then change the display to the numbering system to which you're converting. This doesn't impress people the same way that converting in your head does, but you don't have to *tell* anyone you used the Windows calculator.

Getting Information to the CPU—Direct Memory Access

We have already learned about getting the CPU's attention to let it know that there is a packet of information sitting on the NIC. However, once the CPU is aware of this, how does the information actually get from the NIC to main memory?

On the first PCs in the early 1980s, the CPU was in charge of moving data from the NIC to main memory, and the CPU was not happy about this. More to the point, the users were not happy about this. Why? Because when information was moved from a card in your computer to main memory, it had to go through the CPU one bit at a time (see Figure 6.9). This method of transferring information is referred to as *Programmable Input/Output (PIO)*. PIO is very processor-intensive, which means that your processor has less time to get any real work done.

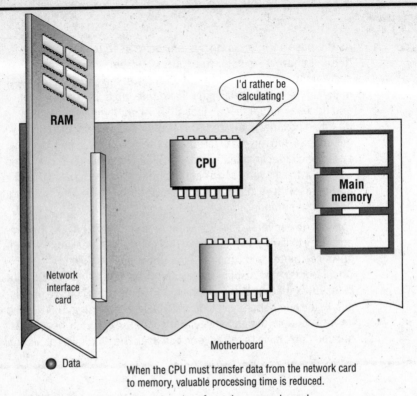

When the CPU must transfer data from the network card
to memory, valuable processing time is reduced.

FIGURE 6.9:   The CPU moving data from the network card.

In the mid 1980s, a new chip known as a *direct memory access* (DMA) chip was developed, delivering a whole new way to move data around in your computer. We already know that when a packet arrives at your workstation, it goes to the memory of the network card. At that point, the network card issues an interrupt to the CPU to ask it to do something with this data that it's just received. With the advent of DMA chips on the motherboard, the CPU no longer had to stop what it was doing and move the data itself. Instead, it could pause for a moment in its calculating of that really engrossing spreadsheet and tell the DMA chips on the motherboard, "Please move this information for me and let me know when you're finished." The real power of direct memory access is that the DMA chips now can move information back and forth while the CPU is still calculating.

When the DMA chip is finished moving the information, it lets the CPU know that it is done. With DMA chips on board, we can now process and move information faster and more efficiently on each computer system, as demonstrated in Figure 6.10.

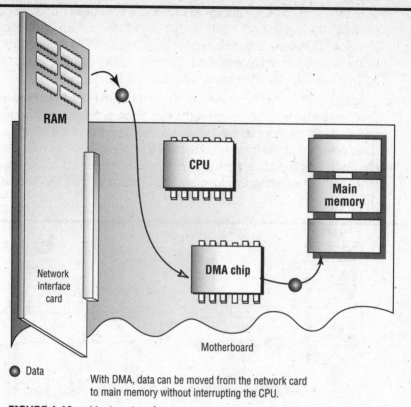

Part II

○ Data

With DMA, data can be moved from the network card to main memory without interrupting the CPU.

FIGURE 6.10: Moving data from memory using a DMA chip.

On modern motherboards, there are two DMA chips. Each DMA chip supports four *DMA channels* (dedicated pathways across which information is moved), so there is a total of eight DMA channels on the motherboard, numbered 0 through 7.

As with IRQ lines, every device on your network that needs to use DMA must use a unique DMA channel to avoid traffic jams and system crashes. There are really no software utilities that document this information well. The best way to keep track of your DMA channels is to document the settings of your cards as you install them. As most cards—especially newer ones—don't use DMA channels, this isn't too hard to do.

DMA isn't just for motherboards. A special type of network card known as a *bus-mastered network interface* card (actually, this could be any kind of card) has a DMA chip on the card itself. Why do they call it bus-mastered? The slots where you place your video card, sound card,

SCSI card, and so on are known as expansion slots or *bus* slots. The card sitting in the bus slot will control—that is, *master*—its own DMA transfer, hence the title, bus-mastered. As soon as you put a DMA chip on any card, you now have a bus-mastered card. Today you can purchase bus-mastered NICs, hard disk controller cards, and SCSI cards.

In 1989, IBM introduced some of the first bus-mastered cards, asserting that by putting the DMA chip on the card itself, the card could process and do direct memory access transfers faster than the two DMA chips on the motherboard. As it turned out, they were right. With its own DMA chip, a bus-mastered network card can communicate with main system RAM without additional processing intervention by the CPU. You can see this in Figure 6.11.

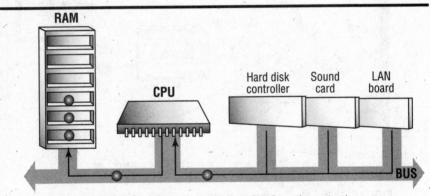

Without bus mastering, all data transfers from the system's interface cards to memory must be processed through the CPU.

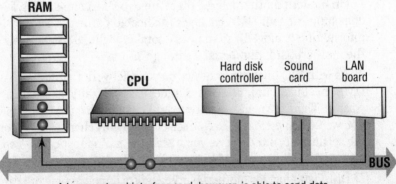

A bus-mastered interface card, however, is able to send data directly to memory, avoiding any bottlenecks at the system CPU.

FIGURE 6.11: Bus-mastered network cards can transfer information without the help of the CPU.

SUMMARY

The previous pages covered the basics of installing your cabling system and network cards. Neither are difficult tasks, but both are made much harder if you don't prepare ahead of time.

When installing cables, the most important thing to keep in mind is planning ahead. Know what you're dealing with before you start. Build flexibility into your design. If need be, spend a little more money on cables or wider conduit now so that you can expand later. The most expensive part of your network is not going to be the machines that are part of it, but the cable. It's hard to install and harder to upgrade; plan ahead so that you only have to do the installation once. Finally, document everything so that when troubleshooting time comes around, you're prepared and can tell which cable is the problem child.

Network cards are like any other add-in card for your computer. When installing them, you must configure them to have their own interrupts, I/O buffers, and perhaps DMA channels for quick transfer of data between network card and motherboard. Once again, proper documentation—whether by hand or with the help of diagnostic programs—is key to trouble-free card installation.

WHAT'S NEXT

The next chapter will cover networking hardware used to interconnect multiple smaller networks to form larger ones. This is an essential skill when building medium-sized and larger LANs and WANs. The content will range from repeaters and hubs to learning how to split your network into two or more segments, allowing traffic on each portion to flow faster and more efficiently.

Part II

Chapter 7
NETWORK CONNECTIVITY DEVICES

Thus far, we've talked about many of the common network architectures that you may encounter and some points you may need to know relating to providing a cabling infrastructure to support them. We've looked at the products you can use to bring your communication endpoints to a central location. But is there any communication taking place over your infrastructure? What you need now is a way to tie everything together.

This chapter focuses on the rest of the pieces you need to establish seamless communication across your internetwork.

Adapted from *Cabling: The Complete Guide to Network Wiring,* Second Edition by David Groth, Jim McBee, and David Barnett

ISBN 0-7821-2958-7   816 pages $49.99

REPEATERS

Nowadays, the terms *repeater* and *hub* are used synonymously, but they are actually not the same. Prior to the days of twisted-pair networking, network backbones carried data across coaxial cable, similar to what is used for cable television.

Computers would connect into these either by BNC connectors, in the case of thinnet, or by vampire taps, in the case of thicknet. Everyone would be connected to the same coaxial backbone. Unfortunately, when it comes to electrical current flowing through a solid medium, you have to contend with the laws of physics. A finite distance exists in which electrical signals can travel across a wire before they become too distorted. Repeaters were used with coaxial cable to overcome this challenge.

Repeaters work at the physical layer of the OSI reference model. Their job is to simply boost an electrical signal's strength so that it can travel farther across a wire. Figure 7.1 illustrates a repeater in action.

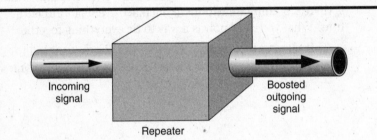

Incoming signal

Boosted outgoing signal

Repeater

FIGURE 7.1:   Repeaters are used to boost signal strength

Being passive in nature, repeaters do not look at or alter the contents of the packets flowing across the wire.

Theoretically, repeaters could be used to extend cables infinitely, but due to the underlying limitations of communication architectures like Ethernet's collision domains, repeaters were used to tie together a maximum of five coaxial-cable segments.

HUBS

Because repetition of signals is a function of repeating hubs, *hub* and *repeater* are used interchangeably when referring to twisted-pair networking. The semantic distinction between the two terms is that a repeater joins two backbone coaxial cables, whereas a hub joins two or more twisted-pair cables.

In twisted-pair networking, each network device is connected to an individual network cable. In coaxial networking, all network devices are connected to the same coaxial backbone. A hub eliminates the need for BNC connectors and vampire taps. Figure 7.2 illustrates how network devices connect to a hub versus to coaxial backbones.

FIGURE 7.2:   Twisted-pair networking vs. coaxial networking

Hubs work the same way as repeaters in that incoming signals are amplified before they are retransmitted across its ports. Like repeaters, hubs operate at the OSI physical layer, which means they do not alter or look at the contents of a packet traveling across the wire. When a hub receives an incoming signal, it amplifies it and sends it out over all its ports. Figure 7.3 shows a hub at work.

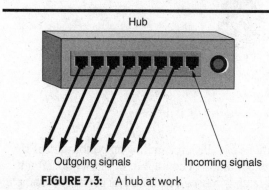

FIGURE 7.3:   A hub at work

Hubs typically provide from 8 to 24 twisted-pair connections, depending on the manufacturer and model of the hub (although some hubs support several dozen ports). Hubs can also be connected to each other (cascaded)

by means of BNC, AUI ports, or crossover cables to provide flexibility as networks grow. The cost of this flexibility is paid for in performance.

As a media-access architecture, Ethernet is built on carrier-sensing and collision-detection mechanisms (CSMA/CD). Prior to transmitting a signal, an Ethernet host listens to the wire to determine if any other hosts are transmitting. If the wire is clear, the host transmits. On occasion, two or more hosts will sense that the wire is free and try to transmit simultaneously or nearly simultaneously. Only one signal is free to fly across the wire at a time, and when multiple signals meet on the wire, they become corrupted by the collision. When a collision is detected, the transmitting hosts wait a random amount of time before retransmitting, in the hopes of avoiding another data collision. Figure 7.4 shows a situation where a data collision is produced, and Figure 7.5 shows how Ethernet handles these situations.

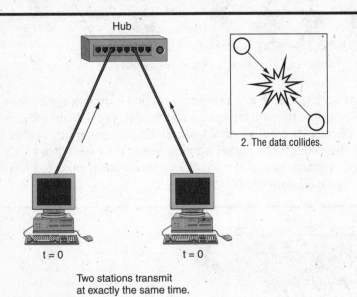

Hub

2. The data collides.

t = 0   t = 0

Two stations transmit
at exactly the same time.

FIGURE 7.4:   An Ethernet data collision

So what are the implications of collision handling on performance? If you recall from our earlier explanation of how a hub works, a hub, after it receives an incoming signal, simply passes it across all its ports. For example, with an eight-port hub, if a host attached to port 1 transmits, the hosts connected to ports 2 through 8 will all receive the signal. Consider the following: if a host attached to port 8 wants to communicate with a host attached to port 7, the hosts attached to ports 1 through 6 will be barred from transmitting when they will sense signals traveling across the wire.

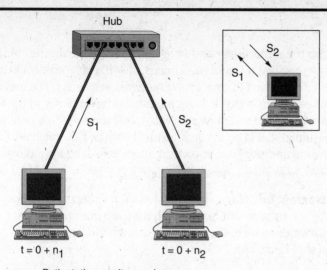

Hub

S_2

S_1

S_1

S_2

$t = 0 + n_1$

$t = 0 + n_2$

Both stations wait a random
amount of time and retransmit.

FIGURE 7.5: How Ethernet responds to data collisions

NOTE

Hubs pass incoming signals across all their ports, preventing two hosts from transmitting simultaneously. All the hosts connected to a hub are therefore said to share the same amount of bandwidth.

On a small scale, such as our eight-port example, the shared-bandwidth performance implications may not be that significant. However, consider the cascading of four 24-port hubs, where 96 hosts share the same bandwidth. When one host transmits, 95 others cannot. The bandwidth that the network provides is finite (limited by the cable plant and network devices). Therefore, in shared-bandwidth configurations, the amount of bandwidth available to a connected host is inversely proportional to the number of hosts sharing that bandwidth. For example, if 96 hosts are connected to the same set of Fast Ethernet (100Mbps) hubs, they have only 1.042Mbps available each. For Ethernet (10Mbps), the situation is even worse, with only 0.104Mbps available each. All hope is not lost, however. We'll look at ways of overcoming these performance barriers through the use of switches and routers.

As a selling point, hubs are relatively inexpensive to implement.

BRIDGES

When we use the terms *bridge* and *bridging*, we are generally describing functionality provided by modern switches. Just like a repeater, a bridge is a network device used to connect two network segments. The main difference between them is that bridges operate at the link layer of the OSI reference model and can therefore provide translation services required to connect dissimilar media access architectures such as Ethernet and Token Ring. Therefore, bridging is an important internetworking technology.

In general, there are four types of bridging:

Transparent bridging   Typically found in Ethernet environments, the transparent bridge analyzes the incoming frames and forwards them to the appropriate segments one hop at a time (see Figure 7.6).

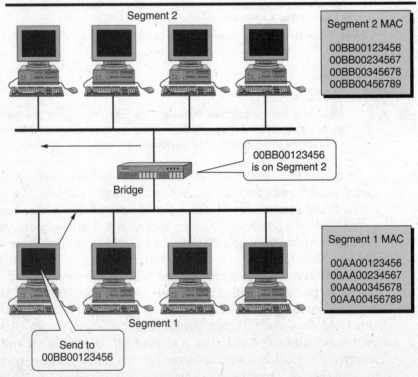

FIGURE 7.6:   Transparent bridging

Source-route bridging Typically found in Token Ring environments, source-route bridging provides an alternative to transparent bridging for NetBIOS and SNA protocols. In source-route bridging, each ring is assigned a unique number on the source-route bridge port. Token Ring frames contain address information, including a ring number, which the bridge analyzes to forward the frame to the appropriate ring (see Figure 7.7).

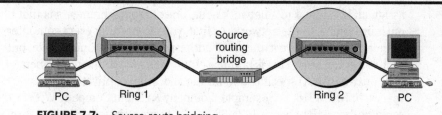

FIGURE 7.7: Source-route bridging

Source-route transparent bridging Source-route transparent bridging is an extension of source-route bridging whereby non-routable protocols such as NetBIOS and SNA receive the routing benefits of source-route bridging and a performance increase associated with transparent bridging.

Translation bridging Translation bridging is used to connect network segments with different underlying media-access technologies such as Ethernet to Token Ring or Ethernet to FDDI, etc. (see Figure 7.8).

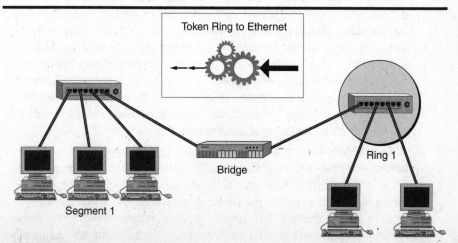

FIGURE 7.8: Translation bridging

Compared to modern routers, bridges are not complicated devices; they consist of network interface cards and the software required to forward packets from one interface to another. As previously mentioned, bridges operate at the link layers of the OSI reference model, so to understand how bridges work, a brief discussion of link-layer communication is in order.

How are network nodes uniquely identified? In general, OSI network-layer protocols, such as the Internet Protocol (IP), are assumed. When you assign an IP address to a network node, one of the requirements is that it must be unique on the network. At first, you might think every computer in the world must have a unique IP address in order to communicate, but such is not the case. This is because of the Internet Assigned Numbers Authority's (IANA) specification for the allocation of private address spaces, in RFC 1918. For example, Company XYZ and Company WXY could both use IP network 192.168.0.0/24 to identify network devices on their private networks. However, networks that use a private IP address specified in RFC 1918 cannot communicate over the Internet without network-address translation or proxy-server software and hardware.

IP as a protocol merely provides for the logical grouping of computers as networks. Because IP addresses are logical representations of groups of computers, how does communication between two endpoints occur? IP as a protocol provides the rules governing addressing and routing. IP communication occurs at the link layers of the OSI reference model.

Every network-interface card has a unique 48-bit address, known as its *MAC address*, assigned to the adapter. For two nodes to converse, one computer must first resolve the MAC address of its destination. In IP, this is handled by a protocol known as the *Address Resolution Protocol* (ARP). Once a MAC address is resolved, the frame gets built and is transmitted on the wire as a unicast frame. (Both a source and a destination MAC address exist.) Each network adapter on that segment hears the frame and examines the destination MAC address to determine if the frame is destined for them. If the frame's destination MAC address matches the receiving system's MAC address, the frame gets passed up to the network layer; otherwise, the frame is simply discarded.

So how does the communication relate to bridging, you may ask? In transparent bridging, the bridge passively listens to all traffic coming across the wire and analyzes the source MAC addresses to build tables that associate a MAC address with a particular network segment. When a bridge receives a frame destined for a remote segment, it then forwards that frame to the appropriate segment so that the clients can communicate seamlessly.

Bridging is one technique that can solve the shared-bandwidth problem that exists with hubs. In the hub example where we cascaded four 24-port hubs through the use of bridges, we can physically isolate each segment so that only 24 hosts compete for bandwidth; throughput is therefore increased. Similarly, with the implementation of bridges, you can also increase the number of nodes that can transmit simultaneously from one (in the case of cascading hubs) to four. Another benefit is that collision domains can be extended; that is, the physical distance between two nodes can exceed the physical limits imposed if the two nodes exist on the same segment. Logically, all of these nodes will appear to be on the same network segment.

Bridging does much for meeting the challenges of internetworking, but its implementation is limited. For instance, bridges will accommodate a maximum of seven physical segments. And although you will have made more efficient use of available bandwidth through segmentation, you can still do better with switching technologies.

SWITCHES

A *switch* is the next rung up the evolutionary ladder from bridges. In modern star-topology networking, when you need bridging functionality you often buy a switch. But bridging is not the only benefit of switch implementation. Switches also provide the benefit of micro-LAN segmentation, which means that every node connected to a switched port receives its own dedicated bandwidth. And with Layer 3 switching, you can further segment the network into virtual LANs.

Like bridges, switches also operate at the link layers of the OSI reference model and, in the case of Layer 3 switches, sometimes extend into the network layer. The same mechanisms are used to build dynamic tables that associate MAC addresses with switched ports. However, whereas bridges implement store-and-forward bridging via software, switches implement either store-and-forward or cut-through switching via hardware, with a marked improvement of speed.

Micro-LAN segmentation is the key benefit of switches, and most organizations have either completely phased out hubs or are in the process of doing so to accommodate the throughput requirements for multimedia applications. Although switches are becoming more affordable, ranging in price from $10 to slightly over $20 per port, their price may still prevent organizations from migrating to completely switched infrastructures. At a minimum, however, servers and workgroups should be linked through switched ports.

Part II

ROUTERS

Routers are packet-forwarding devices just like switches and bridges; however, routers allow transmission of data between network segments. Unlike switches, which forward packets based on physical node addresses, routers operate at the network layer of the OSI reference model, forwarding packets based on a network ID.

If you recall from our communication digression in the discussion on bridging, we defined a network as a logical grouping of computers and network devices. A collection of interconnected networks is referred to as an *internetwork*. Routers provide the connectivity within an internetwork.

So how do routers work? In the case of the IP protocol, an IP address is 32 bits long. Those 32 bits contain both the network ID and the host ID of a network device. IP distinguishes between network and host bits by using a subnet mask. The *subnet mask* is a set of contiguous bits with values of one from left to right, which IP considers to be the address of a network. Bits used to describe a host are masked out by a value of 0, through a binary calculation process called *ANDing*. Figure 7.9 shows two examples of network IDs calculated from an ANDing process.

192.168.145.27 / 24

Address:
11000000 10101000 10010001 00011011

Mask:
11111111 11111111 11111111 00000000

Network ID:
11000000 10101000 10010001 00000000

192.168.145.0

192.168.136.147 / 29

Address:
11000000 10101000 10001000 10010011

Mask:
11111111 11111111 11111111 11111000

Network ID:
11000000 10101000 10001000 10010000

192.168.136.144

FIGURE 7.9:   Calculation of IP network IDs

NOTE

We use IP as the basis of our examples because it is the industry standard for enterprise networking; however, TCP/IP is not the only routable protocol suite. Novell's IPX/SPX and Apple Computer's AppleTalk protocols are also routable.

Routers are simply specialized computers concerned with getting packets from point A to point B. When a router receives a packet destined for its network interface, it examines the destination address to determine the best way to get it there. It makes the decision based on information contained within its own routing tables. Routing tables are associations of network IDs and interfaces that know how to get to that network. If a router can resolve a means to get the packet from point A to point B, it forwards it to either the intended recipient or to the next router in the chain. Otherwise, the router informs the sender that it doesn't know how to reach the destination network. Figure 7.10 illustrates communication between two hosts on different networks.

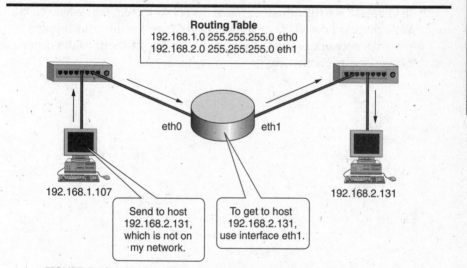

FIGURE 7.10:   Host communication between internetworked segments

Routers enabled with the TCP/IP protocol and all networking devices configured to use TCP/IP make some sort of routing decision. All decisions occur within the IP-protocol framework. IP has other responsibilities that are beyond the scope of this book, but ultimately IP is responsible for forwarding or delivering packets. Once a destination IP address has been resolved, IP will perform an AND calculation on the IP address and subnet mask, as well as on the destination IP address to the subnet mask. IP then compares the results. If they are the same, then both devices exist on the same network segment, and no routing has to take place. If the results are different, then IP checks the devices routing table for explicit instructions on how to get to the destination network and forwards the frame to that address or sends the packet along to a default gateway (router).

A detailed discussion on the inner workings of routers is well beyond the scope of this book. Internetworking product vendors such as Cisco Systems offer certifications in the configuration and deployment of their products. If you are interested in becoming certified in Cisco products, Sybex also publishes excellent study guides for the CCNA and CCNP certification exams. For a more intimate look at the inner workings of the TCP/IP protocol suite, check *TCP/IP: 24seven* by Gary Govanus (Sybex 1999).

WHAT'S NEXT

In Chapter 8, we will introduce you to the network operating system (NOS). We'll discuss how NOSs provide network functionality and supply you with network protocol support, file and print sharing, and other network-centric activities.

Chapter 8

NETWORK OPERATING SYSTEMS

Picking an operating system can be a daunting task. By understanding what each brand of operating system brings to the table—and by comparing those features with the needs of your organization—choosing the best fit is simply a matter of making a list.

As computer networks have progressed over the years, so have the operating systems that make them function. This chapter will evaluate the latest network operating systems (NOSs) powering computing today, as well as examine the strengths and weaknesses of each system.

Written Expressly for *Networking Complete*
by Mark Lierley

COMMON FEATURES OF DIFFERENT OPERATING SYSTEMS

Although network operating systems have distinct differences, network operating systems also have many features in common. Before we analyze the various NOSs, let's look at some common features. Each operating system can be broken down into one of five general categories:

- ▶ Type
- ▶ Processing
- ▶ Memory
- ▶ Storage
- ▶ Additional features

Using these categories as measuring sticks, you can make a fair comparison of the various operating systems.

Type

Operating systems are generally one of three types: client, server, or hybrid. Depending on the size of your network, any combination of these operating systems may be appropriate.

Client Operating Systems

A *client* operating system (OS) uses resources such as printers or files. These operating systems have network capability but generally don't provide a service to the network. There are no true client operating systems on the market today except for set-top Web interface boxes, such as WebTV.

NOTE

Client-only operating systems have lost favor in the market due to their limited functionality. Even the less expensive set-top or Web-interface-only devices are a poor choice compared with the low cost of PCs today. Many industry insiders believe, however, that as the Web continues to expand in size and increase in speed, a slim but feature-rich embedded (built into hardware) OS may someday be as common as a telephone or cable box.

Server Operating Systems

Unlike a client operating system, the *server* operating system functions to provide resources instead of use them. Most server NOSs have a limited interface and work only to provide information to a client. Thus the server OS is generally very lean and efficient. Novell NetWare is an example of this type of NOS.

NOTE

The true server OS has many advantages. By stripping the server of a complex interface, the code becomes much leaner and less prone to bugs. In addition, because the server bears no resemblance to the client OS, users are less likely to bother it. In environments that use this structure, administration can be accomplished from any client computer with the necessary security or through a Web interface.

Hybrid Operating Systems

A *hybrid* OS server is both a client and a server in a network environment. The portion of the operating system acting as a server can share resources. The portion running as a client can access resources from other servers.

The Windows 95/98/Me and 2000/XP series of operating systems fit best in this category. For example, Windows 95 and 98 are most often used as a client to a Windows 2000 server, but they can still act as servers in their own right. For example, many confidential company data files can be stored on the secured and protected server, while less critical data can be created and shared from the user's computer.

A *peer-to-peer* server refers to multiple hybrid NOSs communicating with one another without the need for a central server. This type of system is less expensive, but it becomes difficult to manage with more than 10 computers.

The Windows NT and Windows 2000 Server operating systems are specifically tuned to perform the tasks necessary to make them efficient server platforms. These are ideal choices for companies that grow beyond the needs of a peer-to-peer system.

Processing

Regardless of the type of OS you choose, all NOSs will need to process data. Processing is accomplished by the *central processing unit* (*CPU*) inside the computer. As the complexities of networks and the number of users accessing the server increase, so do the demands placed on the CPU. And with these demands comes the need for increased processing power.

The processing power of the computer can be increased with the following techniques:

- ▸ Symmetric multiprocessing

- ▸ Multithreading

We will look at both techniques in the next sections.

Symmetric Multiprocessing and Multiple CPUs

In the early days of personal computer networking, having a single CPU was sufficient. In fact, the processing power was far beyond what many thought would ever be needed. As software has become more complex, however, the demand for processing power has also increased. In response to this demand, the major PC chip vendors have increased the speed at which processors crunch data, as well as the amount of data that is processed in each cycle. However, having only one high-speed processor is a limitation. Multiprocessor systems are nothing new; in fact, they have been around since the very early days of computing.

The advantage of a multiprocessor system is that you can use two or more lower-speed processors to accomplish more work than a single, high-speed processor. The downside is that a NOS must manage the work sent to each processor and schedule time efficiently enough to make that work flow quickly through the computer. This scheduling involves some overhead and, as you might expect, results in a less than 100 percent speed increase with a second processor.

The most common implementation of multiple processors is *symmetric multiprocessing (SMP)*. SMP views all processors as equal, thus symmetric, and allows any processor that is free to do the work.

When you consider using SMP operating systems, you should evaluate the specific need. For example, file and print sharing are basic activities that require minimal processing power on the server. A database server, however, may need many CPUs to complete complicated searches and analysis.

Don't be fooled by all this talk of multiple processors. While your computer hardware may allow you to add an additional processor, the operating system you are running may not take full advantage of it. Windows 95/98/Me doesn't support a second processor. Novell NetWare and the Windows NT/2000/XP series support a number of processors, but even then, this can be deceptive. While Novell can support as many as 32 CPUs in NetWare 5.*x*, not all of the services you may run on the server will take advantage of these processors. The Microsoft family of server OSs experiences the same limitations. In the next few years, NOSs will use multiple CPUs much more efficiently.

When you compare operating systems, examine the application running on the OS; it will dictate the demand for multiple CPUs.

Multithreading

In the early days of personal computers, only one application ran at once on only one CPU. As operating systems have become more complex, so have the ways in which applications and the OSs have been written.

Multithreading is the process of taking the applications—or operating systems—that run on your computer and dividing them up into much smaller pieces, or threads. By making each piece of the processing job its own thread, multiple threads can be run simultaneously through the CPU or CPUs. Multithreading makes it possible for you to run Solitaire and Microsoft Word at the same time on your computer, or for a server to perform multiple tasks at once.

All of the operating systems on the market today take advantage of multithreading. However, the rules that govern each thread vary between OSs. For example, Windows NT/2000/XP imposes much stricter control over threads as they run in the CPU. Windows 95/98/Me, however, tries to remain backward compatible with Windows 3.1, and therefore is much looser, resulting in Windows 9.*x* being less stable but more compatible. As newer software has been developed, this issue has become less critical. Many business users opt for the Windows NT technologies for the increased stability.

Memory

Along with the processor, memory is one of the major components of any computer system. A NOS is generally responsible for using *random access memory*, or RAM, for both application code and user data. Let's evaluate the different ways the many NOSs use memory.

RAM Usage

The primary job of an operating system is to control computer hardware and resources. As PC operating systems evolve, the amount of RAM they can address, or use, steadily grows. For instance, the original MS-DOS operating system could only use 640KB of memory. Today some operating systems can address 64GB of RAM.

Protecting the information stored in RAM by various applications is another important role of the operating system. In the early days of computing, when two programs ran on the same computer, they had the potential of modifying each other's data. This situation caused problems if one of the programs incorrectly stored information that wasn't expected. This caused programs, or the OS, to crash or ABEND (abnormal end). Other problems also resulted; for example, if a program required a chunk of memory to operate, the OS would allocate that amount. However, some programs would terminate incorrectly, not returning as much memory as they took. This memory fragmentation is referred to as a *memory leak*: as programs continue to run, the system progressively has less and less memory until it simply doesn't have enough to operate.

To address these issues, modern operating systems use a *memory manager*, which is responsible for all requests of memory to the operating system. Programs are never allowed to directly modify each other's data but must instead contact the memory manager. This solution allows programs to run much more reliably and the OS to manage memory much more efficiently.

MEMORY PROTECTION

Memory protection can make or break an operating system. If the system uses memory inefficiently, it will eventually run out and crash. This is an area where Novell NetWare excels. Ask a NetWare administrator how long their server has been running. Many will tell you 60, 90, or even 300 days. NetWare is very good about reclaiming memory and managing memory efficiently.

Windows 9x has a terrible time managing memory. To illustrate, try leaving your Windows 95 computer on for three days straight and see how well it functions. You will probably notice that performance will be very sluggish and eventually will become unstable. Windows NT is better but still may require a reboot to clean everything out. Windows 2000 and Windows XP seem to be the best Microsoft systems so far. Many users are reporting that they can run reliably for long periods of time without needing a reboot.

Virtual Memory

As we have learned, modern applications are becoming more complex. As complexity increases, so do memory requirements. While operating systems can use ever-increasing amounts of RAM, the physical resources are still costly. One of the ways to strike a balance between hardware cost and the need for additional RAM is the use of virtual memory.

The memory manager component makes use of not only the physical RAM in the computer but also a special storage area on the hard drive called a *swap file*. As programs request memory from the memory manager, the system evaluates its physical resources against the request. If there is not enough physical RAM, the memory manager will take data in RAM that is not currently active and move it to the disk swap file. When that information is called later, other data will move to the swap file and the needed data moves back into free RAM. This swapping process is generally done with small areas of memory called *pages*. Each page of memory is generally between 4 and 64Kb, depending on the operating system.

Virtual memory increases RAM utilization, but it also has a drawback. Suppose that your computer doesn't have enough physical RAM to run all the programs you require. Virtual memory will use the larger capacity hard disk to swap information, but if the physical RAM is simply not big enough, the system can spend all its time swapping data, a process called *disk thrashing*. With disk thrashing, the system performance slows to a crawl as the hard disk tries to keep up with the constant swapping of the memory manager.

Caching

We have now learned that a NOS will use a great deal of physical memory and that the virtual memory manager will make up for memory inadequacies. But how do we improve performance? RAM is one of the fastest components of a computer, as it is not a mechanical resource. Many server NOSs exploit this fact by storing frequently used information in RAM rather than looking for it on the local, and slower, disk storage. This process is known as *caching*. Cache memory is RAM set aside for frequently used data from both users and the operating system. For example, if a server often receives a request for a large file, the NOS will copy the file to RAM and thus send it to the client directly from memory rather than going to the hard disk each time.

Caching occurs at many levels in your computer. The processor caches its information both internally and externally. Hard disks have local caches for information before it is sent to the computer. And of course the OS can cache user data and settings. Caching is so efficient that it can result in a 10- to 300-percent performance gain. For a NOS to most efficiently use a cache, it must have extra physical RAM to work with. Therefore, it is generally best to install as much physical RAM in a server as possible. After the needs of the OS and programs are met, the system will use the remainder of RAM to increase caching.

When selecting an operating system for file and print sharing, caching can make a tremendous difference in speed. Novell NetWare is very efficient at caching data from the disk and providing information to clients straight from RAM. For instance, if all users run the same application from the server, NetWare will cache the files in RAM after the first user accesses them. All subsequent users will pull the file out of RAM, thus reducing the access time and increasing the access speed.

All Microsoft operating systems will cache data, as well. Windows 2000 is much more efficient than Windows NT at file caching; however, Novell NetWare has them both beat, hands down.

Storage

So you have a server. It has several fast processors and plenty of RAM. But without storage, it is useless. After all, the purpose of a server is to store and provide resources.

Each server OS stores the data in a proprietary format on its local disk, but it is accessible to network clients, as they would expect. This proprietary file system helps to enforce the security and special features that the server OS may support.

File storage can occur with many types of media, from slow tape backup to very high-speed disk arrays. No matter what type of storage media you use, all of them share some common characteristics.

Hard Disks

In the early days of computing, information was stored on large reels of tape, much like an audiotape. While this method worked well—and is still in use today—it has a major drawback. If you want to access information at random, you have to go back and forth through a lot of tape to find the information. The solution is the modern hard disk. Using the same technology as tape, hard disks store information magnetically on spinning disks. This allows users to find information very quickly anywhere on the disk.

Hard disks have significantly progressed over the years in three ways:

Size They are much smaller. The difference in size contributes to the second big change, speed.

Speed They are faster. The smaller the disk, the less time it takes to search for information.

Capacity Although hard disks have gotten smaller, their storage capacity has steadily increased. Of course, like all computer equipment, the capacity has increased as the relative cost has decreased. For example, in 1994 a 170MB hard disk cost approximately $250. Today you can purchase a 60GB hard disk for $125, and prices continue to drop.

There are many other types of storage media in use today: CD-RW, DVD, DLT, and various other backup tapes. But the venerable hard disk still provides the fastest access to information at a relatively low cost.

Fault Tolerance

If you've ever heard the phrase, "Don't put all your eggs in one basket," you know why putting all your data in one location can be a bad thing. Wisdom teaches us that by spreading the information in multiple places, we have a much-reduced chance of loss. This process can be accomplished through several different means. The first is backup. Backing up information to CD or tape is a very reliable way to keep a record of information. Even better is storing your backup media away from the server that has been backed up. This prevents loss due to fire or natural disaster.

While a backup is always necessary, an operating system that can both accept and recover from system failure is preferable. This feature is called *fault tolerance*. Fault tolerance comes in several forms, including on-the-fly software recovery as well as hardware fault tolerance. The most common implementation of hardware fault tolerance is a system known as Redundant Array of Inexpensive Disks, or RAID. RAID comes in many different varieties, each having strengths and weaknesses. However, the most common implementation of RAID is RAID level 5, disk striping with parity. With RAID level 5, the system stores all saved data across all physical disks with an additional piece of information called *parity*. Parity is like a math problem. Let's say you have the equation $3 + x = 5$. What is

Part II

x? It is 2, of course. Now let's suppose you have $3 + 2 = x$. Again, you can determine what is missing. In RAID 5, a single hard disk can fail, but as long as all the other disks are still working, the system doesn't lose any data. The administrator has the opportunity to install a new, good hard disk, and the system re-creates the data.

Another RAID technology called RAID level 1, or disk mirroring, works a different way. In RAID level 1, two hard disks keep exactly the same information. All data stored on disk 1 is also stored on disk 2. This works well, as there are always two copies of the data. RAID level 1 has one major disadvantage over RAID level 5. With RAID level 1, you have to buy twice the storage space for your data; with RAID level 5, you can have only slightly more storage than you really need, as parity info is not a complete copy of the data.

WHICH OS OFFERS THE GREATEST FAULT TOLERANCE?

Windows NT/2000 supports the two levels of RAID discussed here. Novell NetWare provides disk-mirroring support with software. While many operating systems can provide some or all of these features, it is generally best to buy hardware that provides this service.

Due to many factors, some operating systems are inherently more fault tolerant than others. For example, Windows NT is more fault tolerant than Windows 95. With each generation of OSs, the products become more stable and more reliable. Windows 2000 is a huge step in the right direction for Microsoft in this area. While NT is a good OS, 2000 has support for many different types of system recovery. Novell NetWare has long enjoyed a reputation for being a "bullet proof" and very reliable OS.

When choosing the perfect OS for your needs, evaluate what fault tolerance needs your network has, along with the hardware you will be purchasing. For example, NetWare has less built-in RAID support but works with all major hardware vendors' offerings.

File System

With the physical disk in place, the next consideration you need to take into account when deciding which operating system to use is which file system you prefer. Some operating systems give you many choices; others allow only one. A *file system* is the way in which the OS organizes information on the physical disk. The differences in file systems generally relate to file size, file and folder naming, and security features.

The initial file system used by PCs was known as FAT or FAT16. FAT stands for *file allocation table*, and it describes the way in which the file system keeps track of the files stored on the disk. FAT16 has several limitations, the major one being a 2GB limit in the maximum size of a volume. The Windows 95 Operating System Release 2 (OSR2) introduced FAT32, which removed many of the restrictions imposed on the original FAT16. The major drawback was that earlier versions of Windows, including Windows NT, could not read this new file system. Windows NT introduced a new file system called NTFS (New Technology File System). This system significantly increases the volume size as well as the size of a single file. As hard disks increase in size, this has become a major issue. The NetWare OS also has its own file system called NWFS, or NetWare File System. Both NWFS and NTFS include many security features and additional enhancements that make them a better choice on the server's storage media.

It is worth mentioning that with Windows 2000, NTFS added some new features, including disk quotas and file encryption. Novell, not to be outdone, also released a new file system called NSS, or Novell Storage Services. NSS uses a network-like approach to storing files that allows collections of free space to be pulled from various locations and logically grouped together as one.

In addition to the file system, the server OSs provide additional file system features. For example, NetWare has a feature called *block sub allocation*. With sub allocation, the system assigns each file a large (64KB) block on the hard disk. If the actual data were only 1KB, then 63KB would be wasted. However, in NetWare the 1KB files are then moved into a sub allocation unit inside of the wasted space in an existing file. This feature can reclaim gigabytes of wasted space on a large server.

Windows 2000/XP has a feature called *file level encryption*. With this feature, even if the physical hard disk is compromised, the data on the disk is encrypted and, thus, inaccessible.

TIP

When selecting a NOS, determine what your security and storage needs are, and then look for the OS that will address the majority of those needs.

Part II

Regardless of the file system, if computers have taught us anything, it is that what we think will suffice today will most likely not meet the needs of the future.

Additional Features

As you can see, many network operating systems perform the same basic tasks. So what separates the different vendor offerings? Probably the easiest answer is the additional features that each OS provides. For example, Novell includes *Novell directory services*, or NDS. With NDS, an administrator can manage any resource on the network from any location within the network through a common interface. On the other hand, Microsoft Windows products provide a common user interface and have excelled at providing a foundation for network applications.

While there are many differences between the various offerings, it is generally best to evaluate a NOS on three key points:

- Open standards compatibility

- Application availability

- Specific organizational needs

Open Standards Compatibility

Open standards compatibility has become a common buzzword in computer networking. Open standards systems can work well with others by using industry-accepted protocols and standards to exchange and process data. The reason behind this push is the idea that being locked into a single hardware or software vendor limits a company's choice for the best technology. With open standards, an organization can choose the best product for a given job. In the late '80s, IBM learned the value of open standards the hard way. IBM had developed a new interface standard for internal devices call Micro Channel. The design was really quite ahead of its time. But because IBM developed the technology, many hardware vendors chose not to implement it, instead using the jointly developed EISA standard. In the end, only IBM and a few other vendors ever took advantage of the superior system.

Application Availability

In the past, each company that purchased a computer system would spend time and money to custom-write software to fulfill their needs. As the pace of computing and business has increased, many companies have neither the time nor the funds to spend on custom software development. Choosing a NOS that has the applications you need already written can save a considerable amount of money. If an application isn't available that meets your needs, choosing a NOS that has the necessary tools to build one quickly may be the second best thing.

Organizational Needs

The third—and probably the most critical—factor is to determine what your needs are and to choose a NOS that meets those requirements. For example, Organization X may need to have a platform that is consistent from client to server. In this case, Microsoft may be a very good solution. Organization Y may need a system that is very scalable and has shown a proven growth curve in very large organizations. In this case, Novell NetWare may be the best choice. Again, evaluate what will work best in your situation.

COMPARING POPULAR NETWORK OPERATING SYSTEMS

Now that we have a common foundation for understanding some of the core features of various NOSs, let's take a detailed look at some of the more popular operating systems on the market today.

Client Operating Systems

We'll start with a comparison of the various client operating systems on the market today.

Apple MacOS

If cats have nine lives, then Apple must be a cat. The Macintosh has been a dead product more times than anyone can remember. But with the introduction of a super-fast CPU, a new operating system, and the iMac, Macintosh looks to be around for some time to come. Apple has never been a major market share leader when compared to Windows, nor has it been considered a serious business contender. However, the MacOS may be one to watch in the future as Apple reinvents itself and its still-revolutionary products.

So why choose a Mac? Apple has long enjoyed the reputation for being the best OS for graphics, video, and desktop publishing. While these applications have moved to the Microsoft platform, many designers still prefer Macintosh. Apple is also heavily instilled in schools and universities; thus, there is a great deal of educational software. Many people still believe the Mac to be one of the easiest computers to use.

Microsoft Windows 95, 98, and Me

The Microsoft Windows 9x and Me (Millennium) family of operating systems was originally released in late 1995. At the time, Windows 95 was one of the most progressive operating systems on the market. It provided multitasking, multithreading, a graphic user interface (or GUI), and many high-end features. To Microsoft's credit, it also provided an easy-to-use interface to connect to the Internet, thus spurring on the Internet revolution.

The Windows 9x/Me platform is a good workstation solution for most businesses. The interface is clean and easy to use, there are many helpful features, and with built-in networking, many companies find it a perfect fit. Microsoft has tried to move the 9x platform to the home market, to speed the sale of its more powerful NOSs to corporations, but business has been slow to begin using the platform, probably due to the cost of an upgrade to 2000 or XP. Choose Windows 98 or Me when cost, ease of use, and application support is necessary.

Microsoft Windows NT Workstation, Windows 2000 Professional, and Windows XP Professional

Windows NT Workstation 4, Windows 2000 Professional, and Windows XP Professional are among the most robust NOSs ever. The NT and 2000/XP Pro lines add high-end features such as SMP support and a much more stable OS. They also have a great deal of built-in security and are more efficient on lesser hardware. With these features, NT and 2000/XP Pro are superb choices in corporate LAN environments.

Windows NT and 2000/XP Pro are the best choices for business and workplace needs. These OSs provide most of the features of the Windows 9x series but add greater system stability and support for much larger hardware. Windows 2000 and Windows XP are fast becoming the client solution in many companies due to their significant array of remote management and security features.

Table 8.1 compares the various client operating systems we have just explored.

TABLE 8.1: Comparison of Client Operation Systems

	APPLE MAC OS	WINDOWS 95, 98, AND ME	WINDOWS NT AND 2000/XP PROFESSIONAL
Offers a large number of applications		X	X
Is easy to use with full GUI	X	X	X
Runs on standard PC hardware		X	X
Supports multiple processors			X
Is multithreaded	X	X	X
Provides full network support	X	X	X
Manages RAM efficiently	X		X
Provides a low-cost solution	X	X	

Server Operating Systems

Now let's look at those operating systems most often found on back-room servers. Table 8.2 shows the minimum requirements of the server operating systems we will be examining in this section.

TABLE 8.2: Server Operating System Minimum Requirements

	CPU	MEMORY	STORAGE	OTHER
Novell NetWare 5.1	1 CPU Pentium II or higher	128MB	1.3GB	VGA video card, CD-ROM drive, network card, PS/2 mouse
Windows 2000 Server	133MHz Pentium or higher	128MB minimum, 256MB recommended	1GB minimum, 2GB recommended	VGA video card, CD-ROM drive, network card, PS/2 mouse

Part II

TABLE 8.2 continued: Server Operating System Minimum Requirements

	CPU	MEMORY	STORAGE	OTHER
Windows 2000 Advanced Server	133MHz Pentium or higher	128MB minimum, 256MB recommended	1GB minimum, 2GB recommended	VGA video card, CD-ROM drive, network card, PS/2 mouse
Windows 2000 Data Center Server	1 CPU Pentium III Xenon or higher	256MB minimum	1GB minimum, 2GB recommended	VGA video card, CD-ROM drive, network card, PS/2 mouse
Red Hat Linux	1 CPU Pentium or higher	32MB minimum, 64MB recommended	500MB minimum, 600MB recommended	VGA video card, CD-ROM drive, network card, PS/2 mouse

Linux

Linux is a fairly recent phenomenon with an old history. Linux, named after its author Linus Torvalds, is a collection of code that has been collaboratively developed by a host of various software writers. It uses what is called an *open source model*, meaning that the technology of the operating system is available to anyone to read and change. The only requirement is that changes made to the system also be made available to the public.

Because no one company or individual owns Linux, it has been free to grow and develop at an astounding pace. While you probably won't see Linux on your co-worker's desktop any time soon, it is making great inroads as a server operating system, especially with Internet-related companies.

Linux is most popular for special-purpose applications such as Web servers or firewalls. While many administrators are not proficient with Linux, they are investigating its features. The fact that the OS itself is free makes it an active solution for many organizations. At the time of this writing, Internet Service Providers most commonly use Linux.

Microsoft Windows NT Server and Windows 2000 Server Family

In addition to all of the features of the NT and 2000 Pro client operating systems, Microsoft has released server versions, as well. The NT Server family and the 2000 Server family build on the same easy-to-use GUI, as well as a solid foundation for application services. Many back-end network applications have been developed on the Windows platform, probably because of its tight client and server integration.

Windows 2000 took the success of the NT system and added some much-needed and anticipated enhancements, including Active Directory. Active Directory is a central database of settings and user and other configuration information that can be accessed by and from any computer for management and configuration. In addition, Windows 2000 increases the performance, capacity, and reliability of the Windows 2000 product line. Although Microsoft hoped its customer base would move to Windows 2000, the adoption has been slow due to the much higher system requirements and the necessity of planning for an upgrade.

Windows 2000 Server comes in three flavors: 2000 Server, 2000 Advanced Server, and 2000 Data Center Server. Each product varies in its processor and memory capacity, as well as the services they support, but all are built on the same core OS.

Windows NT is the best choice for small-to-medium networks. With an easy-to-use setup and interface, and broad application support, NT is a good choice for the novice administrator. As NT has gained popularity, however, the lack of a true directory service has become a cumbersome limitation. With the introduction of Windows 2000, Microsoft is capturing large enterprise networks. Still, many companies like what they see in 2000, but have been holding off, believing it to be an as yet unproven new technology for Microsoft.

One of the other major advantages for using NT or 2000 is the cradle-to-grave solution. Microsoft supports open standards but would rather you use its products throughout your organization (for example, Windows 2000/XP Pro on the desktop running Office 2000/XP, and Windows 2000 Server for the back-end server applications). Many companies like this type of tight integration; however, Microsoft may not have the best solution at every level.

Novell NetWare 5.x

Novell has been in the PC networking business for quite some time. Its original product, NetWare, was one of the first to allow various and separate PCs to share information. Novell has taken that product over the years and built one of the most reliable and popular server OSs ever.

NetWare is different from other server NOSs in that it is only run on the server, or, in other words, it is a true server OS. The NetWare server has a minimal user interface and is basically a box that sits in a server room. The administration is achieved remotely from any client workstation.

Novell's flagship product is actually a service of NetWare called NDS, a central database of information on all resources on the network. NDS can store any type of information and can retrieve it very quickly. NDS was introduced in NetWare 4 around 1993 and, therefore, is a mature and scalable product. In the last year, Novell has been able to demonstrate an NDS database with over one billion user objects. In addition, the speed of access is roughly equivalent to a much smaller system. NDS has one other major advantage over the competition, that being its cross-platform compatibility. NDS can be run on Linux, NetWare, Windows NT, and other high-end operating systems.

Despite what you may read in some magazines, NetWare is one of the most popular and installed OSs in corporations today. NetWare's robust directory service and tremendous reputation for reliability and stability make it the best choice for large enterprise environments. Most Novell products and services can be run on multiple OSs, allowing companies to pick the best pieces for their network.

Table 8.3 compares the various client operating systems we have just discussed.

TABLE 8.3: Server Operating System Comparisons

	NETWARE 5.x	WINDOWS SERVER	WINDOWS NT SERVER	LINUX
Multitasking and multithreading	X	X	X	X
Virtual memory	X	X	X	X
Memory management	X	X	X	X
X.500 directory service	X	X		

TABLE 8.3 continued: Server Operating System Comparisons

	NETWARE 5.x	WINDOWS SERVER	WINDOWS NT SERVER	LINUX
File system security features	X	X	X	X
Many applications available	X	X	X	
Enterprise-level management tools	X	X		
Internet/open standards support	X	X		X
Bundled Web and FTP servers	X	X	X	X
Bundled media and news servers	X	X		X
Included Web-based administrator	X	X—Limited		
Central network administrator	X	X		

SUMMARY

As you can see, there are many factors when considering the best operating system for your needs. In the end, evaluate what you need the system to do and what types of services you need, and then pick the OS that includes the best set of those features.

WHAT'S NEXT

We have looked at the various operating system choices available. In the next chapter, we will discuss the setup of some of the networking hardware you will use to build your network.

Chapter 9

CONFIGURING NETWORK HARDWARE

In Chapter 8, we looked at the various network operating systems used on both servers and clients. In this chapter, we will further expand on the necessary hardware components that allow the network to communicate.

This chapter will use Windows 95 as a model, but the concepts are similar for any network operating system, even if the method varies.

Adapted from *MCSE: Networking Essentials Study Guide*, Third Edition by James Chellis, Charles Perkins, and Matthew Strebe

ISBN 0-7821-2695-2   720 pages $49.99

NETWORK INTERFACE CARDS

In order for a network operating system (NOS) to communicate on the network, it must have a network interface card, or NIC. In this section, you will learn how to install a network card in a client computer and configure a client operating system (Windows 95) to use that card to talk to the network.

Card Installation

The first step in putting a client computer on the network is to put the network interface card in the computer. This usually involves opening the computer and inserting the card in an empty expansion slot on the computer's motherboard (see Figure 9.1).

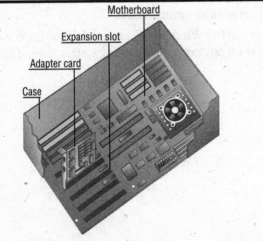

Motherboard

Expansion slot

Adapter card

Case

FIGURE 9.1:   Network interface cards are placed in expansion slots on the personal computer's motherboard.

WARNING

Computer circuitry is sensitive, and electricity can be deadly, so use caution. Turn off the power and remove the power source (unplug the computer) before opening the case. You should also use a ground strap to prevent your body's electrostatic charge from damaging the components in the computer. You can find this strap at most electronics stores.

Some network interface cards use jumpers or switches on the card to configure such settings as the IRQ and DMA. Figure 9.2 shows an adapter card with jumpers and DIP switches. You need to know the settings for the card when you put it in the computer so you can tell the client operating system how to talk to the card. Some cards use software to configure their settings, so you may have to run a DOS configuration program to configure the card before you configure the client operating system to talk to the card.

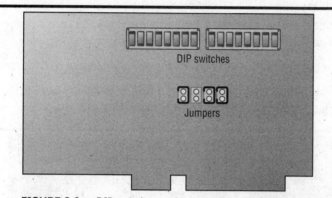

FIGURE 9.2: DIP switches and jumpers can configure card settings.

In Windows 95, you have the option of using device drivers from DOS or Windows 95 device drivers. One common type of network driver for DOS and earlier versions of Windows is ODI, an interface for device drivers. Novell introduced ODI drivers for use when connecting to Novell NetWare. ODI makes device drivers interchangeable—one device driver for one card that implements the ODI interface can be exchanged for another device driver and card. ODI also allows several network protocols to all talk to the same card.

Included with Windows 95 is another type of interface for device drivers, called NDIS. NDIS performs the same function as ODI, but NDIS is written for Windows 95 and is integrated into the operating system.

You should use ODI device drivers if you are using software that requires the ODI interface to function or if no NDIS driver is available; otherwise, choose NDIS device drivers for use with Windows 95.

OS Configuration

Once you have installed the network adapter card, you need to configure the client operating system to recognize the card. Windows 95 provides you with several ways of doing this:

- The Add New Hardware Wizard attempts to find new hardware you have installed and then guides you through the process of configuring the hardware.

- The Windows 95 Plug and Play software may autodetect and autoconfigure the operating system to match your card if you have a Plug and Play motherboard and a Plug and Play network interface card.

- You can install the network card driver and set the card's parameters in the Network Control Panel yourself.

To add network adapter software to Windows 95, follow these steps:

1. Double-click the Network icon in the Control Panel (see Figure 9.3). The Configure Network dialog box appears.

FIGURE 9.3: Select the Network icon in the Control Panel to add a network adapter to Windows 95.

2. Select the Add button to add a networking component.

3. Select Adapter to add an adapter.

4. Find the network interface card installed in the computer (see Figure 9.4). If your adapter is not included in the list,

select Have Disk and select the adapter from the floppy disk provided by the manufacturer.

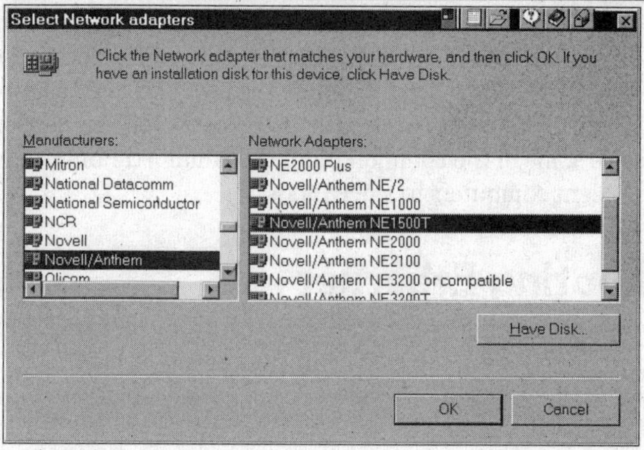

FIGURE 9.4: Windows 95 comes with drivers for many network adapters. You can select Have Disk if your adapter is not included with Windows 95.

5. Back at the Configure Network dialog box, double-click the adapter card that is now listed in the window.

6. Set the software to match the settings (DMA, IRQ, Base Address, and so on) you used when you installed the card. Figure 9.5 shows the Configure Network Card Control Panel.

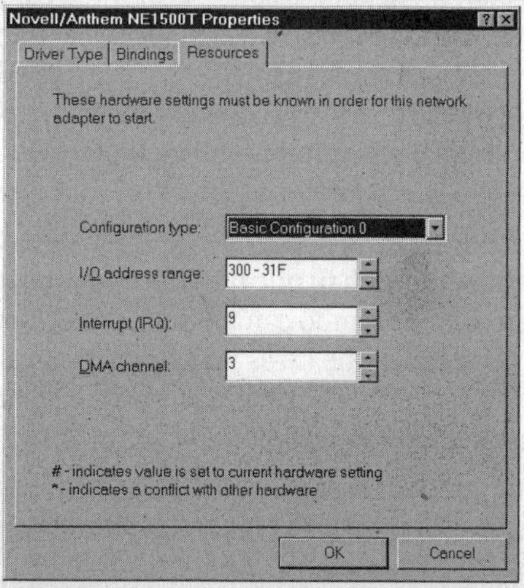

FIGURE 9.5: You can configure the network adapter card from the Configure Network Control Panel.

TROUBLESHOOTING CLIENT CONNECTIONS

Once you have installed the network adapter in the client computer and configured the operating system to talk to the card and to the network, you still may have problems connecting to the network. This section will help you solve some of the common problems administrators face when connecting client computers to a network.

Troubleshooting Ethernet

Ethernet troubleshooting involves checking cards (including IRQ and port settings) and cables (10Base2 being the cable type most likely to require troubleshooting).

Ethernet Card Problems

Each Ethernet adapter on a network must have a unique MAC address. This is normally not a problem because Ethernet adapters are made with unique addresses burned in at the factory. Unfortunately, an Ethernet adapter manufacturer once shipped a batch of Ethernet cards with duplicate MAC addresses by mistake, which caused address conflicts on a few networks.

To prevent this problem from occurring again, some Ethernet adapters allow you to override the default MAC address burned into the card at the factory with your own setting. This ability is provided for the extremely rare possibility that you have two network adapters with the same MAC address setting. You should not use this feature unless you know for certain that you have a MAC address duplication problem. If you are having MAC address problems, reset all the Ethernet adapters on your network to the default factory MAC addresses.

Some Ethernet adapters have more than one transceiver on board. These cards are usually referred to as combo cards because they have a combination of transceivers available. The cards may have any combination of twisted-pair, AUI, BNC, and optical-fiber transceivers. Generally they have two, but in rare cases they have three.

These cards either have a jumper setting or a software-configurable setting to select which transceiver is in use. You must select the transceiver for the type of cable you are using in your network. If you have the wrong transceiver selected, the card will not work.

Some cards have an "autosense" feature that allows the adapter to select the transceiver to use if one of the ports has electrical current or light present. This feature does not always work properly on every card in every situation, so if you have a combo network adapter set to autosense that appears to be malfunctioning, try setting the port you are actually using.

When a workstation's NIC goes out and begins to talk continuously and incoherently on the network, it will create packets that are larger than 1518 bytes and have CRC errors. This type of packet is called a *jabber packet*. To find the faulty card, disconnect workstations or hubs one at a time until you pinpoint the rogue card.

In some cases, resource conflicts can cause network communications problems. You may need to take all the boards out of your system except the network adapter. Once you have it working, add one board at a time until you find the board that has the conflicts. Reconfigure and continue adding cards until the system is up and running.

Remember that COM1 uses IRQ 4 and COM2 uses IRQ 3. Try to avoid these when configuring IRQs, because they are commonly used by a serial mouse and modem. Sometimes just the presence of the serial port will interfere with these IRQs.

Check for the frequent error of not having common frame types bound to the workstation and the file server. If they are not bound, your workstation will respond with the message "File server not found."

Be sure to use the diagnostics program that ships with the LAN card. You will be able to test and configure the card in the machine rather than having to remove it. If you use a card that has two or more ports, be sure you have set the jumpers or configuration to use the correct port on the card.

Some network adapter cards do not make a very good connection in the card socket. Cleaning the card connector and resetting the card can usually solve this problem.

TIP

To clean any component, first unplug the power and make sure you have a ground strap. On circuit connectors, the best method is a lint-free cloth dampened with a little rubbing alcohol. Be very careful to clean only the flat edge of the card, not the socket it goes into.

Don't be tempted to use an eraser to clean the connector—it will leave grit on the card. If you have checked the settings and cleaned the card and it still doesn't work, replace it with a spare that you know is functional.

10Base2 Problems

If your 10Base2 network goes down, it is likely that the bus continuity has been damaged or disconnected. (Perhaps someone moved a PC.) Check terminators at both ends of the cable with a volt-ohm meter to be sure they still read 50 ohms resistance. Check the resistance of the entire segment of cable by using the center conductor of a T and the T's outside shield. It should measure 25 ohms or slightly above. If it measures close to 50 ohms, you may have a faulty terminator, a missing terminator, a break in the wire, or a missing T-connector. Also, check that one end of the cable is still grounded.

If you are working with 10Base2, make sure the cable has not grown too long as a result of the consistent addition of users without consideration of wiring lengths. This is a very common problem with bus topology networks.

Because some people see no difference between RG-59, RG-58A/C, and RG-62, make sure someone did not just add a black piece of coax to extend or repair the cable. Also check for the wrong connector types on your cable.

TIP

If only one workstation is having a problem on a 10Base2 or 10Base5 network, you can be sure it is not the cabling but rather the LAN card, the transceiver, or the AUI cable. You will probably need to swap out the card to nail this one down, so make sure you have a spare. Remember to configure the card before you attempt this solution.

Ethernet, IPX, and Frame Types

One frequently encountered problem with the IPX protocol stack is frame type incompatibility. IPX comes with four frame types:

- Ethernet_802.2
- Ethernet_802.3
- Ethernet_SNAP
- Ethernet_II

The differences between these frame types are minor, involving such issues as checksum and addressing. They are incompatible with each other, however. For any two computers to communicate on your network, they must both support the same frame type.

The simplest way to deal with this problem is to set each device in your network to the same single frame type. Microsoft and Novell both recommend using Ethernet_802.2. This is, unfortunately, difficult for some users because many early Ethernet adapters support only one frame type, usually Ethernet_802.3. To avoid this problem, your server should be configured to support all necessary frame types. Doing so may cause a slight performance penalty, but it will allow all computers on the network to communicate with the server.

> **NOTE**
> This problem with frame type incompatibility is also common in NWLink.

Note that although many operating systems support frame type autodetection, some Ethernet cards do not. For this reason, you should set the frame type manually if you know what it should be.

If you have a computer using IPX that does not appear to be communicating on the network, set the IPX frame type to the frame type supported on the network file server.

Cable Problems and Cable-Testing Tools

Check to make sure the cabling does not run near high-voltage cables or is wrapped in cable trays. Fluorescent lights can also cause electromagnetic interference. Check that the wires are not run against or across these lights. Electrical motors also cause EMI if wires are run across them.

Network cable-testing equipment can locate wiring faults quickly. If you suspect you will be troubleshooting on a regular basis, a network cable tester is a good investment.

A time-domain reflectometer is a cable-testing device that can tell you whether the cable is shorted, broken, or crimped, and how far down the cable the problem resides. The device sends a signal down the wire and measures the characteristics of the reflected signal. From the reflection, it can determine the type of problem with the cable. (This is like throwing a rock down a well and determining how long it takes before you hear it hit the bottom, as well as sensing whether it hit water, dirt, or other rocks.)

Troubleshooting Token Ring

Most Token Ring problems come from obvious mistakes. You can begin troubleshooting by asking questions such as these:

- Are the patch cables and adapter cables to the workstations of the correct specifications?

- Are the correct types of cables in the right places?

- Are the connectors tight and properly secured?

Token Ring Card Problems

Start your troubleshooting of card problems by confirming that there are no resource conflicts with the Token Ring NIC and other devices installed in the workstation. This is especially important if you are adding a card or have recently added other devices to the workstation.

Check the Token Ring card's custom statistics to see whether any internal errors are listed. Internal errors are usually a sign that the card has malfunctioned and should be replaced.

Token Ring card addresses are hard-coded into the ROMs, but some cards allow you to override these addresses with custom addresses. Make sure you do not have two cards with exactly the same node address. This has been known to happen with Ethernet, Token Ring, and ARCnet networks.

Be sure all Token Ring cards are configured for the same speed. In other words, if a network is set for 16Mbps, make sure the card you are troubleshooting is configured for 16Mbps as well. If the system is an IBM/PS2 and the user used the IBM reference disk to set up a new or existing piece of hardware in the machine, the Token Ring card is automatically reset to the 4Mbps speed. If you do happen to place a card in the network that is configured with an inappropriate Token Ring speed, it will cause network traffic to halt temporarily while the ring reconfigures.

You can specify three settings for a Token Ring card merely by using the device drivers supplied with the card:

- The adapter address, which you can change to override the internal address built in by the manufacturer

- Shared RAM locations the card uses

- Activation of the early token release feature (but only with 16Mbps Token Ring cards set to 16Mbps)

Cabling and MSAU Problems

Be sure your network cabling and associated hardware are well documented. This will help you quickly identify the cable and MSAU of a malfunctioning station. This type of information is critical when isolating a hardware-related problem.

WARNING

Do not mix MSAUs from different vendors. Internal electrical characteristics, such as impedance, can cause problems with Token Ring networks.

If your network does not have bridges or routers, you can try a troubleshooting fix that is often used to reset the Token Ring network:

1. Disconnect all of the patch cables from the MSAUs.

2. Use the Setup tool to reset each port.

3. Reconnect each port one at a time with the patch cables.

It's also a good idea to have on hand special cable testers and equipment that are built specifically for troubleshooting Token Ring.

Troubleshooting Multiple Adapters

When you have multiple adapters in your server, you are introducing the possibility of conflict and the necessity of routing data between the cards. These problems, which can prevent client connections, appear to originate on the client side—some clients will work and other clients will not.

Each adapter in a server must have its own unique IRQ and port setting and may require its own upper memory address space. If two cards try to occupy the same hardware resource, neither will work reliably.

You must make sure each adapter is bound to a transport protocol and has a unique network number (IPX) or IP number (TCP/IP). Adapters with conflicting network or IP numbers will not operate correctly. Conflicting network or IP numbers may allow some clients to attach and others to be denied service.

You will need to enable routing between multiple adapters unless your server is the only destination for traffic on your network. Peer computers attached to networks on different adapters in the server will not be able to see one another unless the server is routing traffic between the network adapters. In Windows NT, routing is enabled between all transport

Part II

protocols and adapters by default. In most other network operating systems, you must specifically enable routing between network adapter cards.

Troubleshooting FDDI

The common problems that occur on FDDI networks involve connectors, cabling, and communication delays.

Connector Problems

Dirty connectors can cause problems in FDDI networks. To allow clear communication, the connector must be free of dirt and dust. Remember that the signals are being transmitted using light. If the connectors are dirty, you can clear them using a lint-free cloth and alcohol. (You should use only alcohol as a solvent to clean connectors.)

Another problem may be a bad connector or an open segment of cable. Faulty connectors, bad connections, or open segments (segments that are incorrectly terminated) may be responsible.

Cable Problems

If you use the wrong type of cable between nodes, you will experience problems. Multi-mode fiber is good for distances up to 2 kilometers (1.2 miles). Use single-mode fiber for longer distances.

The type of fiber-optic cable you use can affect network speed. You should probably replace any plastic fiber-optic cable if you want throughput of more than 10Mbps. Glass fiber-optic cable is the best alternative. Plastic should not be used on runs longer than 50 meters (165 feet).

There are several ways to find cable problems. If a complete break occurs in a cable segment, you can find the break using a flashlight by searching for light escaping from the cable. For small breaks, you can use an optical power meter and a source of light energy to test the cable. You can also use an optical time-domain reflectometer (OTDR), although this is the most expensive option.

SUMMARY

The client operating system must be given the same settings the network adapter card was configured with to allow the operating system to recognize the card.

To troubleshoot Ethernet networks, check for faulty NICs and be sure NICs are connected properly. To look for cable problems, use cable-testing tools, such as a time-domain reflectometer. Check for incorrect cable types. Also check for the wrong connector types on your cable.

When troubleshooting a Token Ring system, start by confirming that there are no resource conflicts with the Token Ring NIC and other devices installed in the workstation. Then check the Token Ring card (such as its custom statistics for internal errors, which indicate a faulty NIC, and for duplicate node addresses) and your network cabling. Be sure all Token Ring cards are configured for the same speed (4 or 16Mbps).

Some common problems in an FDDI network are dirty connectors, bad connectors, open segments of cable, inappropriate cable usage, and breaks in the cable.

WHAT'S NEXT

With the cables in place and the hubs powered up, you're ready to start moving data. The next chapter discusses some of the applications that can use the power of a network to increase your productivity.

Part II

Chapter 10

CONTROLLING NETWORK APPLICATIONS

Part II

From an end user's viewpoint, it's very easy to take software for granted. For example, many of us have come to expect our computers to run messaging applications and productivity applications. However, from the view of systems administrators and help desk staff, deploying and maintaining software can be a troublesome and time-consuming job. Regardless of how much time is spent installing, updating, reinstalling, and removing applications based on users' needs, there seems to be no end to the process!

Fortunately, Windows 2000 and Active Directory provide many improvements to the process of deploying and managing software. Through the use of Group Policy objects and Microsoft Installer (MSI), it's easy to configure software deployment options. The applications themselves can be made available to any users who are part of the Active Directory environment. Furthermore, systems administrators can automatically assign

Adapted from *MCSA/MCSE: Windows 2000 Network Management Study Guide* by Michael Chacon, James Chellis, Anil Desai, and Matthew Sheltz

ISBN 0-7821-4105-6   832 pages $49.99

applications to users and computers and allow programs to be installed automatically when they are needed.

In this chapter, we'll look at how to use Windows 2000 and Active Directory to deploy and manage software throughout the network.

OVERVIEW OF SOFTWARE DEPLOYMENT

One of the key design goals for Active Directory was to reduce some of the headaches involved in managing software and configurations in a networked environment. To that end, Windows 2000 offers several features that can make the task of deploying software easier and less prone to errors. Before we dive into the technical details, though, let's examine the issues related to software deployment.

The Software Management Life Cycle

Although it may seem that the use of a new application requires only the installation of the necessary software, the overall process of managing applications involves many more steps. When managing software applications, there are three main phases to the life cycle of applications:

Deploying Software   The first step in using applications is to install them on the appropriate client computers. Generally, some applications are deployed during the initial configuration of a PC, and others are deployed when they are requested. In the latter case, this often used to mean that systems administrators and help desk staff would have to visit client computers and manually walk through the installation process.

TIP

It is very important to understand that the ability to easily deploy software does not necessarily mean that you have the right to do so! Before you install software on client computers, you must make sure that you have the appropriate licenses for the software. Furthermore, it's very important to take the time to track application installations. As many systems administrators have discovered, it's much more difficult to inventory software installations after they've been performed.

.**Maintaining Software**   Once an application is installed and in use on client computers, there's a need to ensure that the software is maintained. Changes due to bug fixes, enhancements, and other types of updates must be applied in order to ensure that programs are kept up-to-date. As with the initial software deployment, software maintenance can be a tedious process. Some programs require that older versions be uninstalled before updates are added. Others allow for automatically upgrading over existing installations. Managing and deploying software updates can consume a significant amount of time for the IT staff.

Removing Software   At the end of the life cycle for many software products is the actual removal of unused programs. Removing software is necessary when applications become outdated or when users no longer require their functionality. One of the traditional problems with uninstalling applications is that many of the installed files may not be removed. Furthermore, the removal of shared components can sometimes cause other programs to stop functioning properly. Also, users often forget to uninstall applications that are no longer needed, and these programs continue to occupy disk space and consume valuable system resources.

Each of these three phases of the software maintenance life cycle is managed by the Microsoft Installer application. Now that we have an overview of the process, let's move on to looking at the actual steps involved in deploying software using Group Policy.

Windows Installer

If you've installed newer application programs, such as Microsoft Office 2000, you probably noticed the updated setup and installation routines. Applications that comply with the updated standard use the *Windows Installer* specification and software packages for deployment. Each package contains information about various setup options and the files required for installation. Although the benefits may not seem dramatic on the surface, there's a lot of new functionality under the hood!

Windows Installer was created to solve many of the problems associated with traditional application development. It has several components, including the Installer service (which runs on Windows 2000 Server and Professional computers), the Installer program (msiexec.exe), which is

Part II

responsible for executing the instructions in a *Windows Installer package*, and the specifications for third-party developers to use to create their own packages. Within each installation package file is a relational structure (similar to the structure of tables in databases) that records information about the programs contained within the package.

In order to appreciate the true value of Windows Installer, let's start by looking at some of the problems with traditional software deployment mechanisms. Then we'll move on and look at how Windows Installer addresses many of these problems.

Application Installation Issues

Before Windows 2000 and Windows Installer, applications were installed using a setup program that managed the various operations required for a program to operate. These operations included copying files, changing Registry settings, and managing any other operating system changes that might be required (such as starting or stopping services). However, this method included several problems:

▶ The setup process was not robust, and aborting the operation often left many unnecessary files in the file system.

▶ The process of uninstalling an application often left many unnecessary files in the file system and remnants in the Windows Registry and operating system folders. Over time, this would result in reduced overall system performance and wasted disk space.

▶ There was no standard method for applying upgrades to applications, and installing a new version often required users to uninstall the old application, reboot, and then install the new program.

▶ Conflicts between different versions of dynamic link libraries (DLLs)—shared program code used across different applications—could cause the installation or removal of one application to break the functionality of another.

Benefits of Windows Installer

Because of the many problems associated with traditional software installation, Microsoft has created a new standard known as Windows Installer. This new system provides for better manageability of the software installation process and, as we'll see later in this chapter, allows systems administrators more control over the deployment process. Specifically, benefits of Windows Installer include the following:

Improved Software Removal   The process of removing software is an important one since remnants left behind during the uninstall process can eventually clutter up the Registry and file system. During the installation process, Windows Installer keeps track of all of the changes made by a setup package. When it comes time to remove an application, all of these changes can then be rolled back.

More Robust Installation Routines   If a typical setup program is aborted during the software installation process, the results are unpredictable. If the actual installation hasn't yet begun, then the Installer generally removes any temporary files that may have been created. If, however, the file copy routine starts before the system encounters an error, it is likely that the files will not be automatically removed from the operating system. In contrast, Windows Installer allows you to roll back any changes when the application setup process is aborted.

Ability to Use Elevated Privileges   Installing applications usually requires the user to have Administrator permissions on the local computer since file system and Registry changes are required. When installing software for network users, systems administrators thus have two options. The first is to log off the computer before installing the software and then log back on as a user who has Administrator permissions on the local computer. This method is tedious and time-consuming. The second is to temporarily give users Administrator permissions on their own machines. This method could cause security problems and requires the attention of a systems administrator.

Through the use of the Installer service, Windows Installer is able to use temporarily elevated privileges to install applications. This allows users, regardless of their security settings, to execute the installation of authorized applications. The end result is the saving of time *and* the preservation of security.

Support for Repairing Corrupted Applications   Regardless of how well a network environment is managed, critical files are sometimes lost or corrupted. Such problems can prevent applications from running properly and cause crashes. Windows Installer packages support the ability to verify the installation

Part II

of an application and, if necessary, replace any missing or corrupted files. This saves time and the end-user headaches associated with removing and reinstalling an entire application to replace just a few files.

Prevention of File Conflicts   Generally, different versions of the same files should be compatible with each other. In the real world, however, this isn't always the case. A classic problem in the Windows world is the case of one program replacing DLLs that are used by several other programs. Windows Installer accurately tracks which files are used by certain programs and ensures that any shared files are not improperly deleted or overwritten.

Automated Installations   A typical application setup process requires end users or systems administrators to respond to several prompts. For example, a user may be able to choose the program group in which icons will be created and the file system location to which the program will be installed. They may also be required to choose which options are installed. Although this type of flexibility is useful, it can be tedious when rolling out multiple applications. By using features of Windows Installer, however, users are able to specify setup options before the process begins. This allows systems administrators to ensure consistency in installations and saves time for users.

Advertising and On-Demand Installations   One of the most powerful features of Windows Installer is its ability to perform on-demand installations of software. Prior to Windows Installer, application installation options were quite basic—either a program was installed or it was not. When setting up a computer, systems administrators would be required to guess which applications the user *might* need and install them all.

Windows Installer supports a function known as *advertising*. Advertising makes applications appear to be available via the Start menu. However, the programs themselves may not actually be installed on the system. When a user attempts to access an advertised application, Windows Installer automatically downloads the necessary files from a server and installs the program. The end result is that applications are installed only when needed, and the process requires no intervention from the end user. We'll cover the details of this process later in this chapter.

To anyone who has had the pleasure of managing many software applications in a network environment, all of these features of Windows Installer are likely to be welcome ones. They also make life easier for end users and application developers who can focus on the "real work" their jobs demand.

Windows Installer File Types

When performing software deployment with Windows Installer in Windows 2000, there are several different file types you may encounter. These are as follows:

Windows Installer Packages (MSI)   In order to take full advantage of Windows Installer functionality, applications must include Windows Installer packages. These packages are normally created by third-party application vendors and software developers and include the information required to install and configure the application and any supporting files.

Transformation Files (MST)   *Transformation files* are useful when customizing the details of how applications are installed. When a systems administrator chooses to assign or publish an application, he may want to specify additional options for the package. If, for instance, a systems administrator wants to allow users to install only the Microsoft Word and Microsoft PowerPoint components of Office 2000, he could specify these options within a transformation file. Then, when users install the application, they will be provided with only the options related to these components.

Patches (MSP)   In order to maintain software, *patches* are often required. Patches may make Registry and/or file system changes. Patch files are used for minor system changes and are subject to certain limitations. Specifically, a patch file cannot remove any installed program components and cannot delete or modify any shortcuts created by the user.

Initialization Files (ZAP)   In order to provide support for publishing non–Windows Installer applications, *initialization files* can be used. These files provide links to a standard executable file that is used to install an application. An example might be `\\server1\software\program1\setup.exe`. These files can then be published and advertised, and users can access the *Add/Remove Programs* icon to install them over the network.

NOTE
Please note that ZAP files do not support many of the features of MSI files, so you should use MSI files whenever possible. See technical article Q231747 on Microsoft's TechNet for more information.

Application Assignment Scripts (AAS)   *Application assignment scripts* store information regarding the assignment of programs and any settings that are made by the systems administrator. These files are created when Group Policy is used to create software package assignments for users and computers.

Each of these types of files provides functionality that allows for the customization of software deployment. Windows Installer packages have special properties that can be viewed by right-clicking the file and choosing Properties (see Figure 10.1).

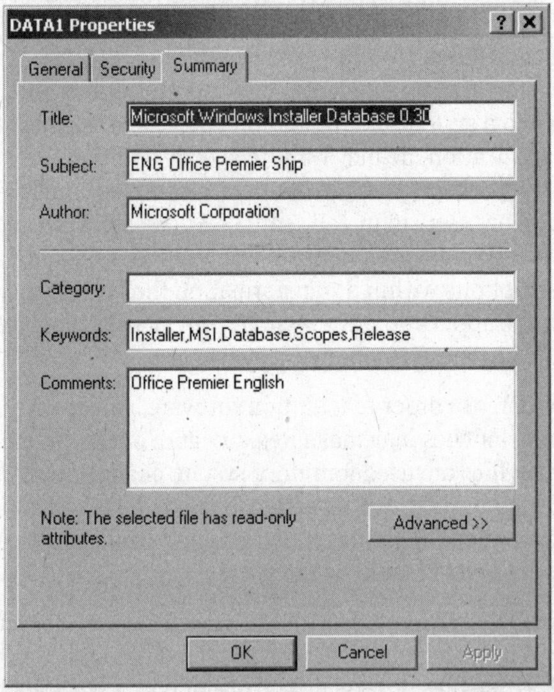

DATA1 Properties   ? X

General | Security | Summary

Title: Microsoft Windows Installer Database 0.30

Subject: ENG Office Premier Ship

Author: Microsoft Corporation

Category:

Keywords: Installer,MSI,Database,Scopes,Release

Comments: Office Premier English

Note: The selected file has read-only attributes.   Advanced >>

OK   Cancel   Apply

FIGURE 10.1:   Viewing the properties of a Windows Installer (MSI) package file

Deploying Applications

The functionality provided by Windows Installer offers many advantages to end users who install their own software. That, however, is just the tip of the iceberg in a networked environment. As we'll see later in this chapter, the various features of Windows Installer and compatible packages allow systems administrators to centrally determine applications that users will be able to install.

There are two main methods of making programs available to end users using Active Directory. They are *assigning* and *publishing*. In this section, we'll look at how the processes of assigning and publishing applications can make life easier for the IT staff and users alike. The various settings for assigned and published applications are managed through the use of Group Policy objects (GPOs).

Assigning Applications

Software applications can be assigned to users and computers. Assigning a software package makes the program available for automatic installation. The applications advertise their availability to the affected users or computers by placing icons within the Programs folder of the Start menu.

When applications are assigned to a user, programs will be advertised to the user, regardless of which computer they are using. That is, icons for the advertised program will appear within the Start menu, regardless of whether the program is installed on the computer or not. If the user clicks an icon for a program that has not yet been installed on the local computer, the application will automatically be accessed from a server and will be installed on the computer.

When an application is assigned to a computer, the program is made available to any users of the computer. For example, all users who log on to a computer that has been assigned Microsoft Office 2002/XP will have access to the components of the application. If the user did not previously install Microsoft Office, they will be prompted for any required setup information when the program is first run.

Generally, applications such as virus-protection software that are required by the vast majority of users should be assigned to computers. This reduces the amount of network bandwidth required to install applications on demand and improves the end-user experience by preventing the delay involved when installing an application the first time it is accessed. Any applications that may be used by only a few users (or those with specific job tasks) should be assigned to users.

Part II

Publishing Applications

When applications are published, the programs are advertised, but no icons are automatically created. Instead, the applications are made available for installation using the Add/Remove Programs icon in Control Panel. Software can be published only to users (not computers). The list of available applications is stored within Active Directory, and client computers can query this list when they need to install programs. For ease of organization, applications can be grouped into *categories*.

Both publishing and assigning applications greatly ease the process of deploying and managing applications in a network environment.

IMPLEMENTING SOFTWARE DEPLOYMENT

So far, we have discussed the issues related to software deployment and management from a high level. Now it's time to drill down into the actual steps required to deploy software using the features of Active Directory. In this section, we will walk through the steps required to create an application distribution share point, to publish and assign applications, and to verify the installation of applications.

Preparing for Software Deployment

Before you can install applications on client computers, you must make sure that the necessary files are available to end users. In many network environments, systems administrators create shares on file servers that include the installation files for many applications. Based on security permissions, either end users or systems administrators can then connect to these shares from a client computer and install the needed software. The efficient organization of these shares can save the help desk from having to carry around a library of CD-ROMs and can allow for installing applications easily on many computers at once.

TIP
One of the problems in network environments is that users frequently install applications whether or not they really require them. They may stumble upon applications that are stored on common file servers and install them out of curiosity. These actions can often decrease productivity and may violate software-licensing agreements. You can help avoid this by placing all of your application installation files in hidden shares (for example, software$).

Once you have created an application distribution share, it's time to actually publish and assign the applications. We'll look at that topic next.

Publishing and Assigning Applications

As we mentioned earlier in this chapter, software packages can be made available to users through the use of publishing and assigning. Both of these operations allow systems administrators to leverage the power of Active Directory and, specifically, Group Policy objects (GPOs) to determine which applications are available to users. In addition, the organization provided by organizational units (OUs) can help group users based on their job functions and software requirements.

The general process involves creating a GPO that includes software deployment settings for users and computers and then linking this GPO to Active Directory objects.

The overall process involved with deploying software using Active Directory is quite simple. However, you shouldn't let the intuitive graphical interface fool you—there's a lot of power under the hood of these software-deployment features! Once you've properly assigned and published applications, it's time to see the effects of your work.

Applying Software Updates

The steps described in the previous section work only when you are installing a brand-new application. However, software companies often release updates that need to be installed on top of existing applications. These updates could consist of bug fixes or other changes that are required to keep the software up-to-date. You can apply software updates in Active Directory by using the Upgrades tab of the software package Properties sheet in Group Policy.

You should also understand that not all upgrades make sense in all situations. There may also be some measure of choice among the users regarding which version they use when it doesn't affect the support of the network. Regardless of the underlying reason for allowing this flexibility, you should be aware that two basic types of upgrades are available for administrators to provide to the users.

Mandatory Upgrade   Forces everyone who currently has an existing version of the program to be upgraded according to

Part II

the GPO. Users who have never installed the program for whatever reason will be able to install only the new upgraded version.

Nonmandatory Upgrade   Allows users to choose whether they would like to upgrade. This upgrade type also allows users who do not have their application installed to choose which version they would like to use.

Verifying Software Installation

In order to ensure that the settings you made in the GPO for the Software OU have taken place, you can log in to the domain from a Windows 2000 Professional computer that is within the OU to which the software settings apply. When you log in, you will notice two changes. First, Microsoft Office 2000 will be installed on the computer (if it was not installed already). In order to access the Office 2000 applications, all a user would need to do is click one of the icons within the Program group of the Start menu (for example, the Microsoft Word icon). Note also that these applications will be available to any of the users who log on to this machine. Also, the settings apply to any computers that are contained within the Software OU and to any users who log on to these computers.

The second change may not be as evident, but it is equally useful. We assigned the Windows 2000 Administrative Tools program to the Software OU. We also created an account named juser within that OU. When you log on to a Windows 2000 Professional computer that is a member of the domain and use the juser account, you will be able to automatically install any of the published applications. You can do this by accessing the Add/Remove Programs icon in Control Panel. By clicking Add New Programs, you will see a display similar to that shown in Figure 10.2.

By clicking the Add button, you will automatically begin the installation of the Windows 2000 Administration Tools (see Figure 10.3). This is a useful way of allowing systems administrators to use the Windows 2000 Administration Tools to remotely manage Windows 2000 Server computers.

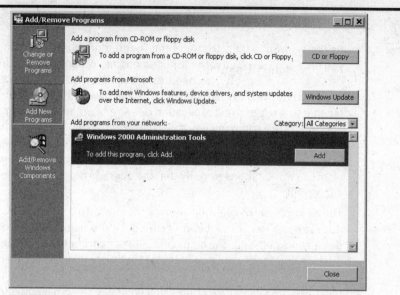

FIGURE 10.2: Installing published applications in Add/Remove Programs

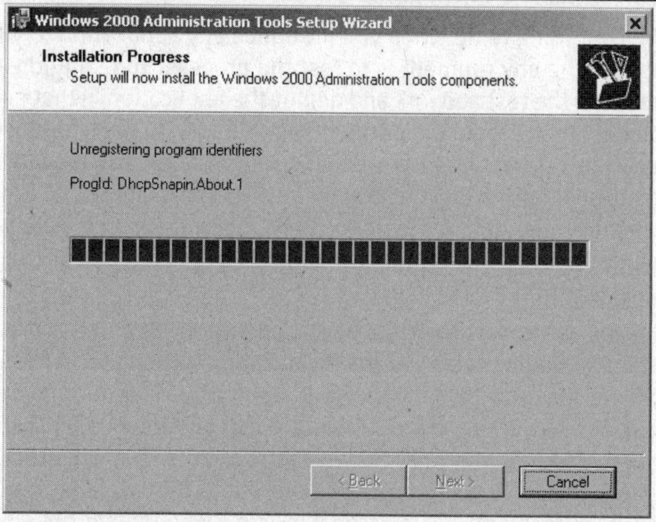

FIGURE 10.3: The automatic installation of Windows 2000 Administration Tools

SYSTEMATIC SOFTWARE DEPLOYMENT

As the network administrator of the Foundation Works Company, you have been involved with the migration from Windows NT to Windows 2000. Your role has been to set up the directory tree as designed by the network engineers. The plan was developed in a lab that was used to test replication issues and other architectural concerns. Your company has three sites that are built around the three locations of your company in New York, Chicago, and San Francisco. In the last phase of the migration, you have been testing all of the workstations to verify that the upgrade process has been successful.

The next phase of the migration is the move to a new suite of applications that have been certified by the vendors as Windows 2000–certified. The managers of the departments have been pushing you to get going and arguing that since they are certified, there should be no problem with the upgrades. You are resisting this pressure since the last time you went ahead with a software application install, there were issues surrounding the process that had to be dealt with before it functioned properly. And guess who gets the blame if anything goes wrong?

The best thing to do when you introduce any application to your networking environment is to test the process. You should gain access to the test network and deploy the application in that environment first. Create the packages and GPOs in that environment, and if you come across any problems, they can be resolved with the vendors without impacting any of the users on the network. While this may delay the deployment of applications, it will save you countless hours of unnecessary support calls if you send out packages with problems to your users.

This test environment should be thoroughly documented and published as a best practice in the organization so that you can resist the pressure from the managers who want to get it done as soon as possible. As the administrator, you are not only responsible for the actual manipulation of accounts and resources, but you are also responsible for how smooth the modifications to the system appear to the users. While you may seem invisible when things are working properly, rest assured that you are the most visible target to the user when things go awry.

CONFIGURING SOFTWARE DEPLOYMENT SETTINGS

In addition to the basic operations of assigning and publishing applications, there are several other options for specifying the details of how software is deployed. You can access these options from within a GPO by right-clicking the Software Installation item (located within Software Settings in User Configuration or Computer Configuration). In this section, we will examine the various options that are available and their effects on the software installation process.

Managing Package Defaults

On the General tab of the Software Installation Properties dialog box, you'll be able to specify some defaults for any packages that you create within this GPO. Figure 10.4 shows the General options for managing software installation settings.

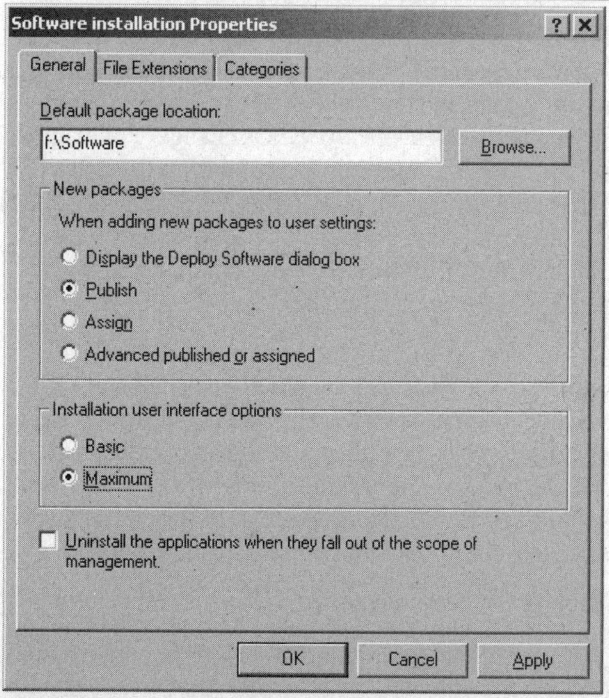

FIGURE 10.4: General options for software settings

The various options available include the following:

Default Package Location   This setting specifies the default file system or network location for software installation packages. This is useful if you are already using a specific share on a file server for hosting the necessary installation files.

New Packages Options   This setting specifies the default type of package assignment that will be used when adding a new package to either the user or computer settings. If you'll be assigning or publishing multiple packages, it may be useful to set a default here.

Installation User Interface Options   When an application is being installed, systems administrators may or may not want end users to see all of the advanced installation options. If Basic is chosen, the user will be able to configure only the minimal settings (such as the installation location). If Maximum is chosen, all of the available installation options will be displayed. The specific installation options available will depend on the package itself.

Uninstall The Applications When They Fall Out Of The Scope Of Management   So far, we have discussed how applications can be assigned and published to users or computers. But what happens when effective GPOs change? For example, suppose that User A is currently located within the Sales OU. A GPO that assigns the Microsoft Office 2000 suite of applications is linked to the Sales OU. Now I decide to move User A to the Engineering OU, which has no software deployment settings. Should the application be uninstalled, or should it remain?

If the Uninstall The Applications When They Fall Out Of The Scope Of Management option is checked, applications will be removed if they are not specifically assigned or published within GPOs. In our earlier example, this means that Office 2000 would be uninstalled for User A. If, however, the box is left unchecked, the application would remain installed.

Now let's look at some more options that are available for managing software settings.

Managing File Extension Mappings

One of the potential problems associated with the use of many different file types is that it's difficult to keep track of which applications work with which files. For example, if I received a file with the extension .abc, I would have no idea which application I would need to view it. And Windows would not be of much help, either!

Fortunately, through software deployment settings, systems administrators can specify mappings for specific *file extensions*. For example, I could specify that whenever users attempt to access a file with the extension .vsd, the operating system should attempt to open the file using the Visio diagramming software. If Visio is not installed on the user's machine, the computer could automatically download and install it (assuming that the application has been properly advertised).

This method allows users to have applications automatically installed when they are needed. The following is an example of the sequence of events that might occur:

▶ A user receives an e-mail message that contains an Adobe Acrobat file attachment.

▶ The Windows 2000 computer realizes that Adobe Acrobat Reader, the appropriate viewing application for this type of file, is not installed. However, it also realizes that a file extension mapping is available within the Active Directory software deployment settings.

▶ The client computer automatically requests the Adobe Acrobat software package from the server and uses Windows Installer to automatically install the application.

▶ The Windows 2000 computer opens the attachment for the user.

Notice that all of these steps were carried out without any further interaction with the user! You can manage file extension mappings by viewing the properties for any package that you have defined within the Group Policy settings. Figure 10.5 shows how file extension settings can be managed. By default, the list of file extensions that you'll see is based on the specific software packages you have added to the current GPO.

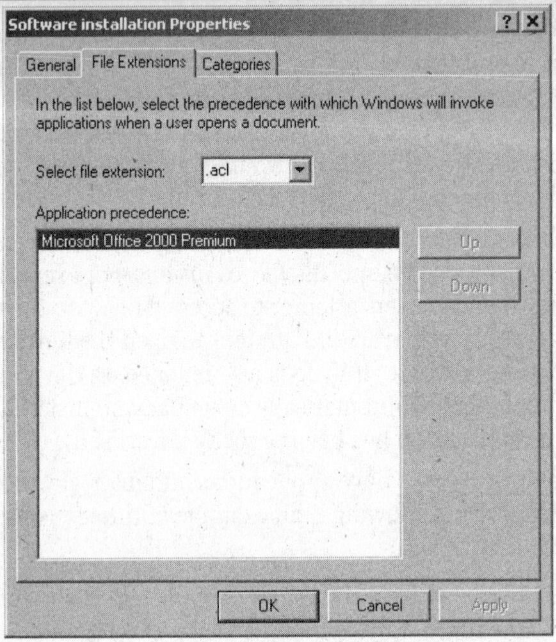

FIGURE 10.5:   Managing file extensions

Creating Application Categories

In many network environments, the list of supported applications can include hundreds of items. For users who are looking for only one specific program, searching through a list of all of these programs can be difficult and time-consuming.

Fortunately, there are methods for categorizing the applications that are available on your network. You can easily manage the application categories for users and computers by right-clicking the Software Installation item, selecting Properties, and then clicking the Categories tab. Figure 10.6 shows you how application categories can be created. It is a good idea to use category names that are meaningful to users because it will make it easier for them to find the programs they're looking for.

Once the software installation categories have been created, you can view them by choosing the Add/Remove Programs item in Control Panel. When you click Add New Programs, you'll see several options in the Category drop-down list (see Figure 10.7). Now when you select the properties for a package, you will be able to assign the application to one or more of the categories (as shown in Figure 10.8).

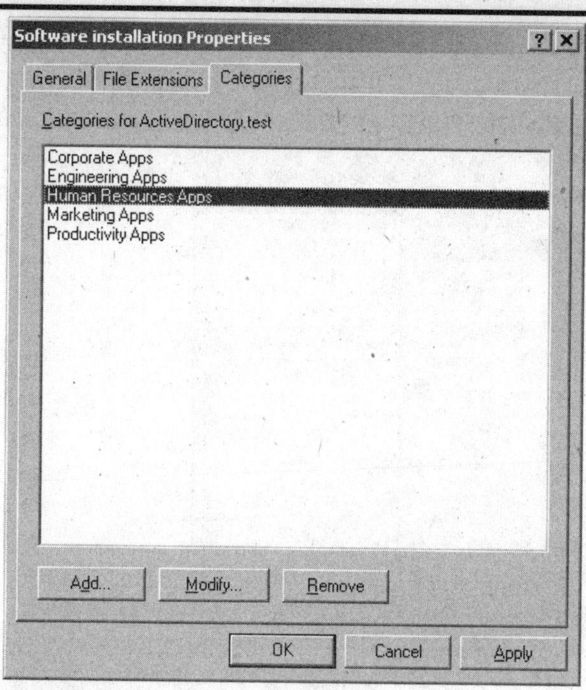

FIGURE 10.6: Creating application categories

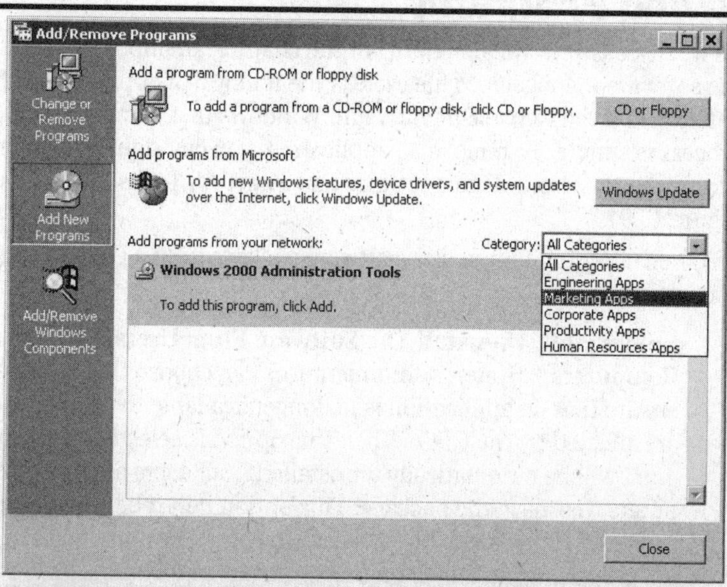

FIGURE 10.7: Viewing application categories in Add/Remove Programs

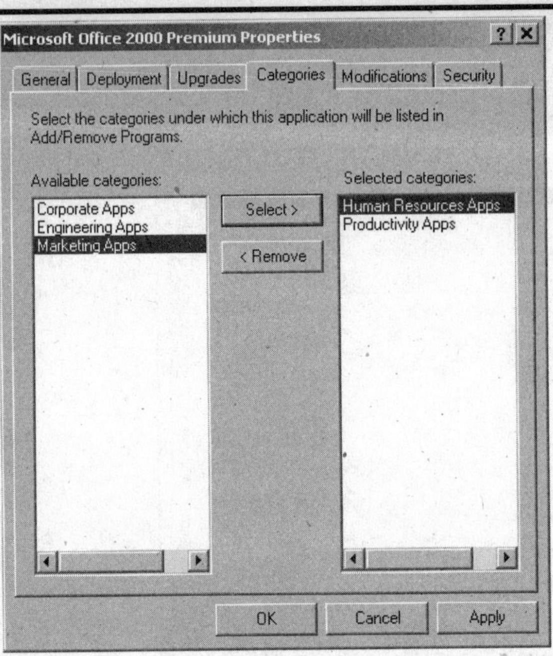

FIGURE 10.8:   Specifying categories for application packages

Removing Programs

As we discussed in the beginning of the chapter, an important phase in the software-management life cycle is the removal of applications. Fortunately, using the Active Directory and Windows Installer packages, the process is simple. To remove an application, you can right-click the package within the Group Policy settings and select All Tasks ➢ Remove (see Figure 10.9).

When choosing to remove a software package from a GPO, you have two options:

Immediately Uninstall The Software From Users And Computers   Systems administrators can choose this option to ensure that an application is no longer available to users who are affected by the GPO. When this option is selected, the program will be automatically uninstalled from users and/or computers that have the package. This option might be useful, for example, if the licensing for a certain application has expired or if a program is no longer on the approved applications list.

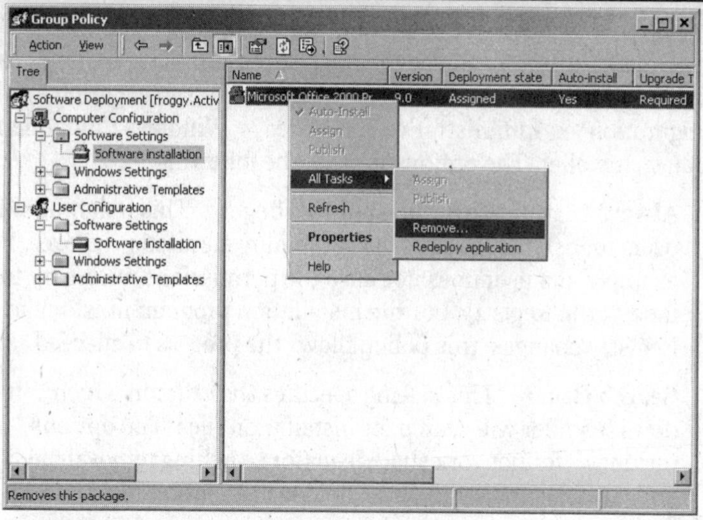

FIGURE 10.9: Removing a software package

Allow Users To Continue To Use The Software, But Prevent New Installations This option prevents users from making new installations of a package, but it does not remove the software if it has already been installed for users. This is a good option if the company has run out of additional licenses for the software, but the existing licenses are still valid.

Figure 10.10 shows the two removal options that are available.

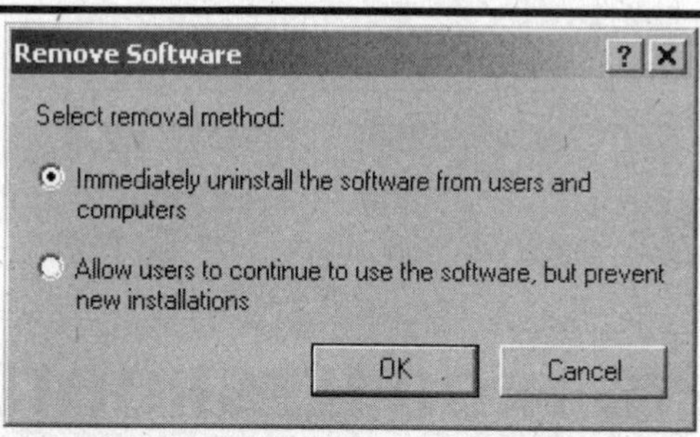

FIGURE 10.10: Software removal options

If you no longer require the ability to install or repair an application, you can delete it from your software distribution share point by deleting the appropriate Windows Installer package files. This will free up additional disk space for newer applications.

Windows Installer Settings

Several options that influence the behavior of Windows Installer can be set within a GPO. These options are accessed by navigating to User Configuration ➤ Administrative Templates ➤ Windows Components ➤ Windows Installer. The options include the following:

Always Install With Elevated Privileges   This policy allows users to install applications that require elevated privileges. For example, if a user does not have the permissions necessary to modify the Registry, but the installation program must make Registry changes, this policy allows the process to succeed.

Search Order   This setting specifies the order in which Windows Installer will search for installation files. The options include n (for network shares), m (for searching removal media), and u (for searching the Internet for installation files).

Disable Rollback   When this option is enabled, Windows Installer does not store the system state information that's required to roll back the installation of an application. Systems administrators may choose this option to reduce the amount of temporary disk space required during installation and to increase the performance of the installation operation. However, the drawback is that the system cannot roll back to its original state if the installation fails and the application needs to be removed.

Disable Media Source For Any Install   This option disallows the installation of software using removable media (such as CD-ROM, DVD, or floppy disks). It is useful for ensuring that users install only approved applications.

With these options, systems administrators can control how Windows Installer operates for specific users who are affected by the GPO.

OPTIMIZING AND TROUBLESHOOTING SOFTWARE DEPLOYMENT

Although the features in Windows 2000 and Active Directory make software deployment a relatively simple task, there are still many factors that systems administrators should consider when making applications available on the network. In this section, we will discuss some common methods for troubleshooting problems with software deployment in Windows 2000 and optimizing the performance of software deployment.

Specific optimization and troubleshooting methods include those that follow:

Test packages before deployment.   The use of Active Directory and GPOs makes publishing and assigning applications so easy that systems administrators may be tempted to make many applications available to users immediately. However, the success of using Windows Installer is at least partially based on the quality of the programming of developers and third-party software vendors.

Before unleashing an application on the unsuspecting user population, you should always test the programs within a test environment using a few volunteer users and computers. The information gathered during these tests can be invaluable in helping the help desk, systems administrators, and end users during a large-scale deployment.

Manage Group Policy scope and links.   One of the most flexible aspects of deploying software with Active Directory is the ability to assign Group Policy settings to users and computers. Since it is so easy to set up GPOs and link them to Active Directory objects, it might be tempting to modify all of your existing GPOs to meet the current software needs of your users. Note, however, that this can become difficult to manage.

An easier way to manage multiple sets of applications may be to create separate GPOs for specific groups of applications. For example, one GPO could provide all end-user productivity applications (such as Microsoft Office 2000 and Adobe Acrobat Reader) while another GPO could provide tools for users in the Engineering department. Now whenever the software requirements for a group change, systems administrators can just enable or disable specific GPOs for the OU that contains these users.

Roll out software in stages.   Installing software packages over the network can involve high bandwidth requirements and reduce the performance of production servers. If you're planning to roll out a new application to several users or computers, it's a good idea to deploy the software in stages. This process involves publishing or assigning applications to a few users at a time, through the use of GPOs and OUs.

Verify connectivity with the software distribution share.   If clients are unable to communicate with the server that contains the software installation files, Windows Installer will be unable to automatically copy the required information to the client computer, and the installation will fail. You should always ensure that clients are able to communicate with the server and verify the permissions on the software installation share.

Organize categories.   The list of applications that are available in a typical network environment can quickly grow very large. From standard commercial desktop applications and utilities to custom client-server applications, it's important to organize programs based on functionality. Be sure to group software packages into categories that end users will clearly recognize and understand when searching for applications.

Create an installation log file.   By using the msiexec.exe command, you can create an installation log file that records the actions attempted during the installation process and any errors that may have been generated.

Reduce redundancy.   In general, it is better to ensure that applications are not assigned or published to users through multiple GPOs. For example, if a user almost always logs on to the same workstation and requires specific applications to be available, you may consider assigning the applications to both the user and the computer. Although this scenario will work properly, it can increase the amount of time spent during logon and the processing of the GPOs. A better solution would be to assign the applications to only the computer (or, alternatively, to only the user).

Manage software distribution points.   When users require applications, they depend on the availability of installation shares. To ensure greater performance and availability of these shares, you can use the Windows 2000 Distributed File System (DFS). The features of DFS allow for fault tolerance and the ability to use multiple servers to share commonly used files from a single logical share point. The end result is increased uptime, better performance, and easier access for end users. In addition, the underlying complexity of where certain applications are stored is isolated from the end user.

Encourage developers and vendors to create Microsoft Installer packages.   Many of the benefits of the software deployment features in Windows 2000 rely on the use of MSI packages. To ease the deployment and management of applications, ensure that in-house application developers and third-party independent software vendors use Microsoft Installer packages that were created properly. The use of MSI packages will greatly assist systems administrators and end users in assigning and managing applications throughout the life cycle of the product.

Enforce consistency using MSI options.   One of the problems with applications and application suites (such as Microsoft Office 2000) is that end users can choose to specify which options are available during installation. While this might be useful for some users, it can cause compatibility and management problems. For example, suppose a manager sends a spreadsheet containing Excel pivot tables to several employees. Some employees are able to access the pivot tables (since they chose the default installation options), but others cannot (since they chose not to install this feature). The users who cannot properly read the spreadsheet will likely generate help desk calls and require assistance to add in the appropriate components.

One way to avoid problems such as these is to enforce standard configurations for applications. For example, we may choose to create a basic and an advanced package for Microsoft Office 2000. The basic package would include the most-used applications, such as Microsoft Word, Microsoft Outlook, and Microsoft Excel. The advanced package would include these applications plus Microsoft PowerPoint and Microsoft Access.

Create Windows Installer files for older applications.
Although there is no tool included with Windows 2000 to automatically perform this task, it will generally be worth the time to create Windows Installer files for older applications. This is done through the use of third-party applications that are designed to monitor the Registry, file system, and other changes that an application makes during the setup process. These changes can then be combined into a single MSI package for use in software deployment.

By carefully planning for software deployment and using some of the advanced features of Windows 2000, you can make software deployment a smooth and simple process for systems administrators and end users alike.

UNDERSTANDING APPLICATION ARCHITECTURE AND MANAGING SOFTWARE ROLLOUTS

The world of computing has moved through various stages and methodologies throughout the past several decades. Real-world business computing began with large, centralized machines called mainframes. In this model, all processing occurred on a central machine and "clients" were little more than keyboards and monitors connected with long extension cords. A potential disadvantage was that clients relied solely on these central machines for their functionality, and the mainframe tended to be less flexible.

Then, with the dramatic drop in the cost of personal computers, the computing industry moved more to a client-based model. In this model, the majority of processing occurred on individual computers. The drawback, however, was that it was difficult to share information (even with networking capabilities), and such critical tasks as data management, backup, and security were challenges.

Since then, various technologies have appeared to try to give us good features from both worlds. A new and promising method of delivering applications has been through the Application Service Provider (ASP) model. In this method, clients are relatively "thin" (that is, they do not perform much processing, nor do they store data); however, users still have access to the tools they need to do their jobs. The software provider is responsible for maintaining the software (including upgrades, backups, security, performance monitoring, etc.), and your company might engage an ASP through a monthly-fee arrangement.

In some respects during the past several years, we've moved back toward housing business-critical functionality on relatively large, central servers. However, we've retained powerful client machines that are capable of performing processing for certain types of applications. In a lot of cases, that makes sense. For example, users of Microsoft Office applications have several advantages if they run their applications on their own machines. Other applications, such as a centralized sales-tracking-and-management tool, might make

CONTINUED ➡

more sense to reside on a server. However, the fact remains that modern computers are marginally useful without software applications that make practical use of their power and features.

As an IT professional, it's important to understand the business reasons when evaluating an application architecture. Traditionally, the deployment of standard Windows applications was a tedious, error-prone, and inexact process. For example, if a user deleted a critical file, the entire application may have had to be removed and reinstalled. Or, if an application replaced a shared file with one that was incompatible with other applications, you could end up in a situation affectionately referred to as "DLL Hell." Microsoft has attempted to address the sore spot of application deployment and management with the use of the Active Directory and Windows Installer technology. However, it's up to developers and system administrators to take full advantage of these new methods.

As an IT professional, you should urge developers to create installation packages using the Windows Installer architecture. In many ways, it's much simpler to create an Installer package than it is to create the old-style setup programs. On the IT side, be sure that you take advantage of Active Directory's ability to assign and publish applications. And, when it comes time to update a client-side application, be sure to make use of Windows Installer's ability to generate patch files that can quickly and easily update an installation with minimal effort. This method can roll out application updates to thousands of computers in just a few days!

All of these features can cut down on a large amount of support effort that's required when, for example, a user needs to install a file viewer for a file that she received via e-mail. And, for applications that just don't make sense on the desktop, consider the use of Application Service Providers. Outsourced applications can allow you to avoid a lot of these headaches altogether. There's a huge array of options, and it's up to you to make the best choice for your applications!

SUMMARY

The real reason for deploying and managing networks in the first place is to make the applications that they support available. End users are often much more interested in being able to do their jobs using the tools they require than in worrying about network infrastructure and directory services. In the past, software deployment and management have been troublesome and time-consuming tasks.

In this chapter, we covered the following:

▶ Ways in which new Windows 2000 features can be used to manage the tasks related to software deployment and the benefits of the Windows Installer technology

▶ How Active Directory, Group Policy objects, and Windows Installer interact to simplify software deployment

▶ How to publish and assign applications to Active Directory objects

▶ The tasks associated with deploying, managing, and removing applications using Group Policy

▶ How to create a network share from which applications can be installed

▶ How to remotely control software deployment options and configuration through the use of Active Directory administration tools

▶ How to troubleshoot problems with software deployment

When implemented correctly, the use of the Active Directory software-deployment features can save much time, reduce headaches, and improve the end-user experience.

WHAT'S NEXT

In the following chapter, we will discuss moving from the PC model of running software to the thin client computing model of centralized processing.

Chapter 11
THIN CLIENT NETWORKING

*T*hin client networking refers to any network in which the lion's share of all application processing takes place on a server, instead of a client. The term refers to a network by definition, so it leaves out stand-alone small computing devices, such as personal data assistants (PDAs) and other specialized computers that use an operating system that is more streamlined than Windows. What makes thin client networking and computing "thin" is neither the size of the operating system nor the apps run on the client, but where in the network the processing takes place.

To a degree, thin client networking represents a return to the mainframe paradigm—applications are located on a central server and accessed by client machines with little in the way of local processing power. The analogy isn't completely accurate, as modern applications can do things that mainframes didn't support, such as word processing. However, the degree of control that thin client networking offers is mainframe-like.

· ·

Adapted from *Mastering Local Area Networks* by Christa Anderson with Mark Minasi

ISBN 0-7821-2258-2   784 pages $39.99

Why the move from centralized computing to personal computers and back again? Business applications drove the development of PCs; they simply couldn't work in a mainframe environment. Not all mainframes were scrapped, by any means, but the newer application designs were too hardware intensive to work well in a shared computing environment.

The return (to some extent, anyway) to thin client networking represents a recognition of two facts about PCs. First, they're a pain to administer. It's time-consuming to install and update locally stored applications. Also, PCs give network users a scary amount of control over their client environments to an extent that can mean a lot of reconfiguring when this control is abused. Second, many of the resources of client computers are wasted. As resource-hungry as modern applications are, they can't keep up with the high-powered CPUs and RAM available for client hardware. Particularly in environments wherein the network user is only actively doing something with the application from time to time, loading applications locally means that you're wasting resources supporting them.

Is thin client networking for everyone? Will it replace the PC-centric world or supplant the zero administration initiatives that are intended to reduce network administration costs? Almost certainly not. When using Microsoft's Terminal Services alone, thin client networking doesn't scale well enough to support many users, and it's definitely not suited to all applications or all environments. But for task-oriented applications or light user load, it can be very useful.

NOTE

Multiuser NT is not the only multiuser server operating system available; Unix, for one, supports terminal server functions. However, to keep things simple, this chapter will focus on NT-based thin client networking. Although the details for some other multiuser server products may be different, the essentials in terms of process and applicability will be the same.

DIAGRAMMING THE PROCESS

There are three parts to a thin client networking session:

▶ The *terminal server*, running a multiuser operating system

- ▶ The *client*, which can be running any kind of operating system
- ▶ The *display protocol*, which is a data link layer protocol that establishes a virtual channel between client and server when the client logs into the terminal server and establishes a session with the server

A session starts when a client computer logs into the terminal server (see Figure 11.1).

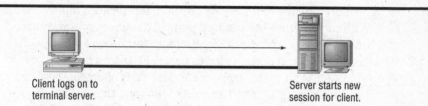

Client logs on to
terminal server.

Server starts new
session for client.

FIGURE 11.1:   A client initiating a session on a terminal server

During this session, client input in the form of mouse clicks and keystrokes is uploaded to the server via the virtual channel. The commands to render bitmaps showing the interface are downloaded to the client via the same virtual channel (see Figure 11.2).

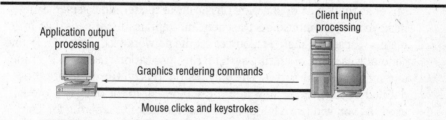

Client input
processing

Application output
processing

Graphics rendering commands

Mouse clicks and keystrokes

FIGURE 11.2:   Graphics instructions are executed on the client; all other processing is rendered on the server.

NOTE

In Windows Terminal Server, the multiuser version of NT 4, the image on the screen is updated about 20 times per second when the session is active. If the network client stops working, then the terminal server notes the inactivity and reduces the refresh rate to 10 times per second until client activity picks up again.

Image Processing

Once those commands are downloaded to the client, they're rendered using the client resources. The CPU and RAM installed in the client are almost wholly devoted to rendering these images. The processing demands placed on the client are reduced by two factors. First, the display is typically limited to 256 colors so the demands on the video card to produce complex color combinations won't be all that great. Second, at least some display protocols have a feature called *client side caching* that allows them to "remember" images that have already been downloaded during the session. With caching, only the changed parts of the screen are downloaded to the client during each refresh. For example, if the icon for Microsoft Word has already been downloaded to the client, there's no need for it to be downloaded again as the image of the desktop is updated. Data are stored in the cache for a limited amount of time and then eventually discarded using the Least Recently Used (LRU) algorithm. When the cache gets full, the data that have been there and unused the longest are discarded in favor of new data.

Session Handling

During the course of the session, the user can work on the terminal server as though he or she were physically at the terminal server, using its keyboard and mouse. As the client runs applications, loads data into memory, accesses shared resources on the network (see Figure 11.3), and generally uses the operating system, the applications use the CPU time and memory of the server. The only restrictions on the client are those defined by security settings and those inherent to the display protocol used. As you will learn later in this chapter under "Preparing for Thin Client Networking," not all display protocols have identical capabilities.

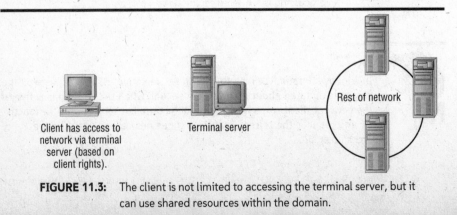

Client has access to
network via terminal
server (based on
client rights).

Terminal server

Rest of network

FIGURE 11.3: The client is not limited to accessing the terminal server, but it can use shared resources within the domain.

To the terminal server, each session is treated both separately and as part of the whole of demands placed on server resources. That is, each session is separate from any other sessions already running or that begin while that session is in progress (see Figure 11.4). However, all sessions use the same resources—CPU time, memory, operating system functions—so the operating system must divide the use of these resources among all of them. The number of sessions supported depends on how many sessions the hardware can support and how many licenses are available. When a session ends, the virtual channel to the client machine is closed, and the resources allocated to that session are released.

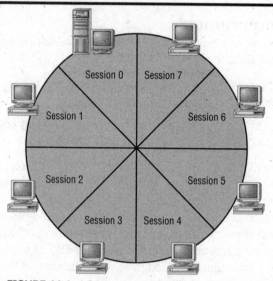

FIGURE 11.4: Sessions are separate, but they tap in to the same resource pool.

Note that in addition to each client session, there's also a session for the server's use. All locally run services and executables run within the context of this server session.

PREPARING FOR THIN CLIENT NETWORKING

Getting ready for thin client networking takes a little more preparation than an ordinary client/server network. Your client needs are lower, but the server needs, not surprisingly, are much greater and more complicated to arrange. The good news is that your network needs won't increase. In fact, if necessary, you can actually use a much slower connection than you'd ordinarily find comfortable with a traditional client/server network.

Server Requirements

On the server side, you'll need a multiuser operating system that supports the interface you want to present to network clients, enough hardware to support those clients, and a display protocol that will pass display data to the clients. These requirements are discussed in the following sections.

Hardware Requirements

First, there's the matter of supporting all the clients' hardware needs. To do that, you need to take into account the following:

▶ How much CPU power does the server need to support the compute cycles needed?

▶ How much RAM does the server need to support all client data and applications?

On average, you can figure on supporting about 12 to 15 clients per CPU in the machine, but the actual number will depend on how many compute cycles each client requires. This, in turn, is a function of both how often each client is using the computer and how compute-heavy are the applications each client is using. Thus, a server supporting clients for a bit of light word processing and periodic e-mail check-ins will be able to support many more clients than one used intensively throughout the work day for preparing Excel spreadsheets.

So far as memory is concerned, you'd better plan for using lots of it. Terminal servers typically have 256MB to 1GB of RAM installed; the exact amount you'll need depends on the applications the terminal servers are running, how much data each client loads into memory at a time, and how many sessions are active at any given time.

TIP

User training is one part of preparing for thin client networking. To get the most out of terminal server resources, encourage network clients to close applications and files that they're not currently using.

There is some good news: although each session in a multiuser operating system such as Windows Terminal Server is separate from all the other current sessions, objects used in more than one session can be shared. Therefore, the memory requirements for each application aren't quite as high as the memory requirements you'd see if you added up the virtual memory used among a like number of individual PCs. However, as is almost always true in a server, the more memory you have, the better the server will perform.

Software and Protocols

Once the hardware question is taken care of, there's still the matter of the software end of the support question:

▶ Will the server hardware be available to the clients connecting to the multiuser operating system?

▶ Will there be sufficient virtual memory addresses to support the client needs?

▶ Will the operating system support your clients' needs?

NOTE

Not all multiuser operating systems (or protocols used to support the client connection to them) are created equal. For example, some terminal services protocols do not support the use of audio or serial ports on the thin client machine. Different products may use one or several protocols, giving you the choices to fit your needs.

WINDOWS 2000 TERMINAL SERVICES

With the introduction of Windows 2000, terminal services was included for the first time in the core product. The differences between terminal services for NT and for 2000 are not significant in the context of this discussion; however, the inclusion of these services is. The fact that Microsoft decided to add this as a core OS offering says a lot about how far terminal servers have come. Throughout this section, comparisons will be made to terminal services in both NT and 2000. Most organizations will eventually move to Windows 2000, but until they do, a discussion of both is appropriate.

It's difficult to provide hard-and-fast rules that apply to all situations for these questions, but here's some background data you'll need to answer them for yourself. The questions depend on the multiuser operating system installed on the server and the display protocol you've got connecting server and client.

What Hardware Is Available?   Will server hardware be available to client machines? This depends on the hardware, the operating system, and how the server is set up to handle requests. The issue is that not all operating systems can handle requests from multiple users for all hardware. It's not the same thing as routing requests from multiple network clients. With multiple network clients, all the requests are in the "network" queue. Recall that all client work is being done on the multiuser server, so users are technically working locally even though the data is being displayed and manipulated by a separate client machine. Thus, with multiple local clients, the information goes to a "local" queue. Some hardware such as CD-ROMs, floppy drives, and serial and parallel ports were not originally designed to be shared among several people at once. This doesn't mean that they'll never work; however, it does mean that you may need to discuss your specific hardware needs with the suppliers of multiuser server operating systems to find out what you can reasonably demand from the operating system.

Virtual Memory Limitations   What about virtual memory addresses? For those of us used to thinking in terms of single-user clients or servers, the problem of running out of virtual memory addresses isn't one we spend a lot of time on. Physical memory, certainly, but server operating systems support 4GB of virtual memory addresses, and it's hard to imagine running short on that much virtual memory on a single-user system. Even when you cut that down to 2GB for user-related data after 2GB is reserved for core functions of the operating system, it's still a lot of virtual memory addresses.

NOTE

In NT 4 (with or without Windows Terminal Server installed), 2GB of virtual memory addresses may be used for user processes while 2GB are reserved for core functions of the operating system. With NT Enterprise Edition (or NT with Service Pack 3 loaded), this split can be made as 1GB for the operating system and 3GB for user-related needs.

Make it a multiuser system, however, and the story changes. Say that you've got 100 users logged in to a quad-processor system with a boatload of memory installed so that the physical resources aren't too strained. Each of those users requires 30MB of virtual memory for all the applications he or she is running—not an unreasonable amount, by any means. Factoring in the resources required by the operating system itself, you're getting perilously close to using up all 4GB of the virtual memory addresses that server operating systems can address. Run out of virtual memory addresses and, at best, the terminal server will generate Stop errors. At worst, it will crash.

The issue is this: Recall that, to the server, each session is kept separate from each other, but all sessions compete for the same pool of CPU time and memory space. To the terminal server, there is only one stack of virtual memory, not one for each session. Thus, the hardware might be able to support all the sessions, but the logic of the operating system can't. For the moment, there's not much to be done about this except to distribute users among terminal servers and train users to close open files and applications that they're not using. With Windows 2000, the virtual memory address area is larger than 4GB, so that will help the virtual memory crunch for Windows Terminal Server users.

Multiuser Server Operating System   Multiuser NT is a likely contender to answer the question, "What operating system will my terminal server run?" Two forms of multiuser NT are available:

- ▶ Citrix WinFrame

- ▶ Microsoft's Windows Terminal Server (WTS)

WinFrame, developed first, is a set of extensions to NT 3.51 that allow it to function in a multiuser environment. Microsoft licensed the technology back from Citrix to develop WTS, which is essentially the same thing but with the NT 4 interface. WTS is an add-on product from Microsoft for Windows NT 4 but has been included as an optional service that can be toggled for Win2K Server. Under the hood, WTS and Win2K running in single-user mode will be essentially the same operating system.

APPLICATION SCHEDULING IN MULTIUSER OPERATING SYSTEMS

One difference that exists between Windows 2000 Server and Windows 2000 Server in multiuser mode is related to thread

CONTINUED ▶

Part II

scheduling. One characteristic distinguishes a server operating system from a client operating system: the server operating system is optimized to give more priority to network-related functions than to personal applications. This is why you'll get better local performance out of a client operating system but better network performance out of a server operating system.

A terminal server presents a problem, though: it's a server running personal productivity applications like word processors and spreadsheets; it's not just sharing the .EXEs with network clients but running the applications locally. This is a problem for NT 4, as it's not really one thing or the other once the multiuser extensions are added. Thus, Windows 2000 Server's task scheduler is designed slightly differently from that of NT Server. Windows 2000 Server will allow you to adjust the scheduler; either personal productivity applications will run more quickly, or network services will. Which you choose will depend on whether you're using the operating system's terminal server capabilities.

There are some behind-the-scenes design changes to NT that allow it to function as a multiuser operating system (namely, to allow it to organize memory usage and object access among several users, not just one). But the crucial points about how it operates are not directly related to the operating system. The operating system the client sees will be the one that the terminal server is running, interface and all. The key differences in operation are largely a function of the features of the display protocol that allows the client and server to communicate.

Display Protocols   Recall that display protocols are the data link layer protocols that establish a virtual channel between the server and client, passing display information to the client for rendering and client input to the server for processing. NT-based multiuser operating systems support one of two display protocols: the Remote Display Protocol (RDP) and the Independent Computing Architecture (ICA).

NOTE
Familiar with the X protocol used with Unix terminal services? RDP and ICA have much the same function as the X protocol.

RDP, which comes with Microsoft's Windows Terminal Server product, is based on the Microsoft T.120 protocol originally developed for Net-Meeting, a video conferencing application. It supports only Windows clients (both 16-bit and 32-bit, including Windows CE), publishes the entire desktop to the client, and has limited communication between processes running on the client computer (if any) and processes running on the terminal server and displayed on the client.

ICA, the protocol at the base of Citrix's MetaFrame add-on to Windows Terminal Server, supports the following features, which RDP does not:

- ▶ Sound

- ▶ Access to multiple sessions

- ▶ Support for publishing individual applications instead of the entire desktop

- ▶ Support for non-Windows clients (DOS, Macintosh, Unix) to run Windows applications

- ▶ Shared Clipboard between local applications and those running on the terminal server

- ▶ Support for both IPX/SPX and TCP/IP

- ▶ Support for *session shadowing* (allowing an administrator to take over a terminal server session for troubleshooting purposes)

- ▶ Support for local printing from applications on terminal servers

- ▶ Persistent client-side caching to reduce network traffic related to screen updates

NOTE

RDP's design makes it technically capable of supporting multiple sessions, but the commercial product currently does not.

Why use RDP at all, if it's more limited than ICA? It comes with WTS, so you don't have to pay licensing fees for another display protocol. If your needs are simple (for example, Windows clients, no sound, no locally running applications, running a TCP/IP network), then RDP is perfectly acceptable.

Many of these limitations have been addressed with Windows 2000, and new enhancements to the RDP protocol are being made regularly. One such enhancement is the ability to run a terminal session through a

Part II

web browser. While this feature is not new to Citrix, it has been added with Support Pack 1 for Windows 2000.

- ▶ Session shadowing

- ▶ Local printing from remote applications

- ▶ Shared Clipboard between local and remote applications

- ▶ Sound

With Windows 2000, RDP has taken over some of the extra functionality presently restricted to ICA.

So far as speed goes, the conventional wisdom for a while has been that ICA is inherently faster than RDP. When the *Windows NT Magazine* labs performed a controlled test of the two protocols, however, this turned out to be not quite the case. Under some circumstances, RDP actually performs *better* than ICA. The difference lies in the number of windows that are displayed on the thin client. RDP is designed to send full-screen updates, so applications running in maximized mode and containing no child windows were painted more quickly with RDP than with ICA. Windowed applications, and applications with child windows, were redrawn more quickly with ICA than with RDP. These results were consistent regardless of the speed of the link between client and server. In short, if you're looking for speed, then choose RDP for running full-screen applications that don't spawn child windows, and ICA if redrawing windows will be necessary.

Client Requirements

The hardware requirements for a terminal server client vary depending on the client itself and what you're asking it to do. Memory and CPU requirements will depend on answers to the following questions:

- ▶ Will the client be running any applications locally?

- ▶ How complex will the display be? Will it include video or just still images?

The first question matters because the answer affects how resources will be used on the computer. As little stress as rendering images puts on a CPU or RAM, they put some on it—rendering images takes CPU time. If the CPU and RAM have to support local data processing as well, then they're going to need to be more powerful than the CPU and RAM in a terminal device that's not running any applications locally.

Windows terminals, which do not usually run applications locally, have lower client-side requirements than microcomputers running their own applications. They don't store data locally, so they don't have hard disks. Generally, they don't have external devices such as CD-ROMs or printers attached, either. Most often, a Windows terminal will be a CPU and some memory, with ports allowing a monitor, keyboard, and network to be attached. Ethernet over UTP is the most likely network connection to be available out of the box, but coaxial Ethernet connections or Token Ring are often available either as an existing option or by request.

Network Requirements

The good news about thin client networking is that it won't place heavy demands on your network. Information passes from client to server pretty steadily, but there isn't much information to pass. Thus, you can actually run a thin client network over a relatively slow connection, such as a VPN running over the Internet or a dial-up connection.

Display protocols won't transfer all data—they need a transport protocol. As noted in "Display Protocols," earlier in this chapter, both ICA and RDP support TCP/IP; ICA supports IPX/SPX; and neither support NetBEUI. For WAN or dial-up connections, both display protocols cooperate with a connection managed by PPP.

Choosing Thin Client Applications

Not all applications work equally well in a terminal server environment. The best applications have the following qualities:

▶ They are not demanding of compute cycles.

▶ They keep extraneous visuals to a minimum.

▶ They organize local and global data effectively.

▶ They refer to user names rather than to computer names.

Let's take a closer look at the reasons these features are important.

Compute Cycles

As all sessions are sharing CPU time, CPU cycles are much more in demand than they are on a single-user system. Thus, the applications running on a terminal server should be fairly low in their use of compute cycles.

Functions such as extensive number crunching and other calculations should be relegated to client-side applications.

NOTE

As of this writing, all clients with active sessions must contend equally for compute cycles. However, Windows 2000 Server supports functionality that can limit a session's use of common resources so that one session's excessive use of system resources doesn't impact all other sessions.

Unnecessary Visuals

Some visual updates are unavoidable: the screen changes that take place when you move from page to page with a web browser, the updates needed when you open a new document or new application, and so forth. For unavoidable screen updates, just make sure your thin clients are capable of processing the data required to render the images.

Some visual updates, however, are not required and don't really serve any useful purpose. Animations are probably the worst of these, as they require both compute cycles and screen updates. Applications should either not use animations at all or, if possible, those animations (such as the Office Assistant in Microsoft Office 97) should be turned off. Screen savers on client sessions are also a no-no for the same reason.

Information Storage

A good application for a multiuser environment is well behaved about where it stores information. Some applications assume a proportion of one machine, one user, but this obviously doesn't work in a multiuser environment. This can wreak havoc in the wrong circumstances, as data that should only be available to a particular user becomes available to anyone using a particular machine. Custom user information should be stored in a user-specific location, such as a user's home directory, not in the system directory.

User Identification

Another aspect of the "one machine, one user" assumption is related to messaging between users. Applications such as Windows Chat have a machine-centric view of the world—a chat session is established between two machines, not two users. In other words, you can't use Chat between two people logged in to the same terminal server because the application is actually running only on a single computer. The NET SEND command, in contrast, is user-centric, looking for the names of logged-in users instead of machine names. If you must use a machine-centric messaging application, you'll need to run it on client machines, not on a terminal server.

WHY USE THIN CLIENT NETWORKING?

Now you know what thin client networking is and what you need to support it. Now for the difficult question: Why should you go to all that work?

A year or two ago, when the idea of Windows-based thin client networking was starting to take off, you'd hear a lot about how it was a better idea than a traditional LAN because it allowed network clients to be so lightweight and thus so inexpensive.

Nope.

First, the price of new PCs capable of running client applications has dropped dramatically. You can buy a fully loaded PC for about $1000 now, sometimes including a monitor. A lower-end system can cost as little as $500 without a monitor. As memory prices rebound slightly, expect prices to rise accordingly, but desktop PCs simply aren't that expensive.

Second, Windows terminals and other thin client devices aren't all that cheap. Typically, a Net PC runs somewhere in the $300 to $500 range, not including a monitor. For that, you're getting a computer incapable of running anything without the help of an expensive multiuser operating system that runs on a fully loaded computer, often an SMP machine to maintain all its users.

Third, it's not cheap to junk existing machines and buy new ones and a new server operating system. It may be cheaper to keep existing PCs and perform spot upgrades to breathe new life into the machines you already have.

Clearly, the reason to go with thin client networking isn't a matter of reducing hardware costs. Rather than reducing the total cost of *ownership* (TCO), thin client networking reduces the total cost of administration (TCA). Thinking of it this way keeps you focused on where the money in the care and feeding of computers really goes. It's not the boxes that are expensive; it's taking care of them.

Reducing the Total Cost of Administration

The costs of a PC are a lot more than just hardware. They also involve the following:

- ▶ Fixing problems caused by user error
- ▶ Installing or upgrading applications
- ▶ Repairing broken PCs
- ▶ Upgrading PC hardware
- ▶ Resolving problems due to applications conflicting with other applications

Thin client networking helps you maintain control over the client computers in your network by centralizing everything about them in a single place. Applications, user settings—everything the clients need to use the network is centrally located, down to the operating system. Combined with system policies that control what users can and can't do to their desktops, this can dramatically reduce the amount of support your help desk people have to do. If inexperienced users can't delete desktop shortcuts or turn their screens black, then they don't have to call Support to fix the problem after they've done it.

The increased control can be applied at the hardware level, too. Thin clients can be ordinary PCs (which is sometimes desirable), but they can also be stripped-down machines that offer little more than a keyboard, mouse, and monitor. These restrictions prevent users from installing unauthorized applications or games (or introducing boot viruses to the computer). Terminal devices have an additional advantage in that their smaller footprint means that they take up less space than a full-blown PC. This makes them good clients for crowded areas like kitchens or stockrooms.

Breaking the Upgrade Cycle

Another reason to use thin client networking is to give those old client PCs a new lease on life. Most commercial application software seems to do nothing but get fatter, which means that your computer must get fatter to accommodate it. It's not just the applications, either: the data itself gets fatter, as multimedia becomes more prevalent. The problem is cyclical. Parkinson's Law, which describes the nature of work to expand to fill available time, can be applied to data—that is, it expands to fill available resources. So, you get more resources (memory, disk space) to meet the requirements of your data and then the data expands again.

In short, the obsolescence cycle for a PC is about two years, so this can get to be an expensive hobby. Unfortunately, it's also a hard one to break, as opting out of the upgrade cycle is hard to do when everyone else is upgrading. The word processor that's two generations behind might work perfectly well for in-house documents, but it won't necessarily be able to display the documents that your partner company sends you.

Computers aren't magically upgraded when they can't keep up with the latest application suite. If your PC can't keep up, then you have two options:

- ▶ Upgrade the PC

- ▶ Replace the PC

Upgrading is generally the cheaper of the two options in terms of hardware costs, but it's not necessarily cheaper in the long run. First, it costs time—a precious commodity for most of us—as you have to take the PC apart to add the new RAM or hard disk. Upgrading also eventually becomes difficult or impossible unless you replace the motherboard—tried to find 30-pin SIMMs for a 486 lately?

Buying new PCs every two years is the other option, but this option has hidden costs, as well. Buying a new PC isn't just a matter of buying a new box and plugging it in to the network; it requires making the new machine exactly like the old one. That means reinstalling applications, backing up locally stored data and user configuration settings and restoring them, and so forth.

NOTE

The issues involved in replacing an old PC with a new one are a convincing argument for central storage of all data and user configuration information, even if you're not doing thin client networking.

Now that you are thoroughly depressed, there is a way to leave this cycle, or at least to simplify keeping up with it. As all applications are run on a single server in thin client networking, the client machines themselves don't actually have to be capable of running the applications—or even an operating system that supports them. The only machine that needs to be upgraded to keep up with application demands is the server. Thus, with thin client networking, you can dramatically extend the life of your client computers.

Part II

Sample Applications for Thin Client Networking

If you're still not sure what you could do with thin client networking, consider the following situations, derived from case studies of real-world thin client networks.

NOTE
The full text of these scenarios, complete with hardware specifications and more details, is available at www.winntmag.com in the October 1998 and January 1999 issues.

Keeping Doctors on the Go

One Midwest clinic found itself in the position of needing to change the way it was storing data. For the previous 10 years or so, the clinic had been managing patient records and accounting with a combination of a mainframe and a few stand-alone PCs. The mainframe was getting old and unreliable, and the need for current patient information grew more crucial to manage the 10,000 patients the clinic saw each year.

The new solution had a couple of requirements. First, it had to offer reliable access to patient records so that hospital staff could do billing and other tasks that required patient information. Second, it had to give the staff physicians access to patient data without breaking the doctor-patient relationship. The doctors were accustomed to reading from a patient's file while at the patient's bed, and they weren't keen on the idea of interrupting that relationship by going to a client computer in another room. The end result was a combination of NT Workstation PCs for hospital staff and wireless Wyse thin client devices. The staff could use the PCs for fast and reliable access to patient data, while the doctors could carry the Wyse devices while making their rounds, making notes on the touch screen like a clipboard.

Giving Students Computer Access

One of the biggest hassles about traveling is lugging along the laptop computer. Even the lightest laptops are heavy, bulky to store on an airplane, and (in most cases) less comfortable to use than the average desktop computer. However, if you don't take your laptop with you when you travel, you can't do anything computer related.

One executive training center decided to make things easier on its students by providing them with PC access for their two-day stay. Each hotel room in the center had its own computer that the guests could use to run any of a suite of applications: e-mail, word processors, web browsers, and so forth. The guests were happy, but the network administrators were not. To keep each guest's data private, the network administrators had to wipe any files off each PC's hard drive after a guest had checked out. This was a major hassle when you consider that the center sees hundreds of guests a week and each only stays for a couple of days. Additionally, fixing broken and misconfigured computers took up a lot of administration time that could have been spent more usefully on designing network innovations.

To resolve this problem, the network designer decided to trade the PCs in each room in for thin client devices—network computers, in fact. The system policies for these users permitted them access to only a specific suite of applications, not any Control Panel settings. Two servers supplied login capabilities for the network; one provided file storage with user-specific home directories (with a script the training center staff developed) that could be automatically created at check-in and deleted at check-out. Four application servers provided access to network applications. With this configuration, users had limited control over the desktop (and thus limited ability to misconfigure the desktop), but they did have access to the applications they needed.

Centralizing Control of the Desktop

Not all thin client networks are homogenous—many, like the one in this example, represent a mixture of thin clients and fat clients as appropriate for users' needs. In this case, the network designers were lucky enough to be in a position to scrap their existing network—a collection of OS/2 servers, Windows 3.1 PCs, a mainframe, and some dumb terminals.

In the name of presenting a more consistent face to the network, and getting access to some applications that wouldn't run with either Windows 3.1 or dumb terminals, the company decided to replace the existing network. The company used a combination of Net PCs (devices that, like network computers, can run applications locally or remotely) and a terminal server. A few NT Workstation PCs were included for the power users who needed access to all applications and could be trusted not to misconfigure their computers. The rest of the user base was given the Net PCs and access to only selected applications. Some users objected to not being able to personalize their desktops (a common complaint when you use system policies to lock down part or all of the system configuration). However, most ended up being happy with the system's responsiveness and stability.

SUMMARY

Thin clients for everyone? Not at all. I don't believe in "magic bullets" that will solve all problems. Thin clients are suitable in networks where it's desirable, possible, and cost effective to centralize the network's computing resources, and for use with applications that perform well in a distributed computing environment. The more task oriented and intermittent your network client use, the better suited your network is to thin client networking.

Thin client networking isn't desirable for network clients running compute-heavy applications. It requires a very stable server environment, one that may be more power hungry than every network can afford. It also requires a network staff capable of maintaining a centralized server. In short, thin client networking doesn't always fit the needs of the network, or fit the needs of every person on the network. This is one reason it's worth your while to check out the possibility of running a network that's a hybrid of thin and fat clients.

WHAT'S NEXT

In the next chapter, we'll expand on thin client solutions as we look at Citrix MetaFrame XP. This add-on to Microsoft's Terminal Services adds enterprise-level administration capabilities to the thin client networking model.

Chapter 12

EXTENDING TERMINAL SERVICES

Many times over the past few years, as MetaFrame—and its predecessor WinFrame—has been introduced into companies, administrators have asked about MetaFrame's usefulness. That question arises especially now that Microsoft has introduced Windows NT 4.0 Terminal Server Edition and the Windows 2000 Server family. Both provide the basic functionality that allows a user's session to run on a server instead of the local computer. The key here is the word *basic*. An understanding of Citrix Systems history and its relationship with Microsoft will help to put this in perspective.

Terminal Services, as delivered through Microsoft, allows a client to run its session on a server and not tax the local resources of the desktop computer. As the user moves the mouse and types on the keyboard, the data is redirected to the server instead of the local computer processing the information. The server then processes the information it receives from the client and delivers screen updates for the user to see.

Adapted from *CCA: Citrix MetaFrame XP 1.0 Administration Study Guide* by Brad Price and John Price

ISBN 0-7821-4057-2   768 pages $59.99

NOTE

Having the server process information sent from a client system is called *client/ server technology* and is sometimes referred to as *thin client technology*.

As clients start sessions on the server running Terminal Services, the server reserves an area of memory for the session to run. This session is a complete user environment that includes the user's profile information. Each user's session is contained in a memory area on the server separate from all other users' sessions. All processing of applications and access to data is performed from the server session. These multiple sessions that are created on a server are made possible by a technology known as MultiWin.

DEVELOPMENT OF MULTIWIN AND METAFRAME

Citrix is the company that is responsible for the MultiWin technology. Ed Iacobucci, the founder of Citrix Systems, developed the original concept behind MultiWin and the product that developed from it, MetaFrame. From 1978 until 1989, he was employed by IBM, working in their Personal Computer Division, designing operating systems. It was in this capacity that he envisioned an operating system that would act as a mainframe, although based on the personal computer platform. When appointed head of the joint Microsoft/IBM project that was designing OS/2, he proposed adding the terminal services functionality to the new operating system. When it was decided that the project would not include this idea, he left IBM to start Citrix Systems.

Citrix Systems created a product called MultiView that would allow an OS/2 server to run multiple user sessions. OS/2 had not gained wide acceptance in the computer industry, and its future was not seen as very stable. Iacobucci needed to keep his company viable, so he entered into negotiations with Microsoft, which was trying to get their server operating system, Windows NT Server, off the ground. Microsoft saw the inclusion of a multiple-user session operating system as a way to improve the market position of their product. Microsoft licensed the NT kernel to Citrix and was so impressed with its technology that they bought 6 percent of the company.

In 1995, Citrix launched their vision, Citrix WinFrame. The product shipped as a stand-alone operating system that consisted of a redesigned Windows NT Server 3.51 kernel. This kernel was known as MultiWin.

Citrix enjoyed a great deal of success with WinFrame—so much so that they started working on a beta version of WinFrame 2.0 based on the Windows NT 4.0 kernel.

In February 1997, Microsoft informed Citrix that they would no longer license the Windows NT 4.0 kernel for use in WinFrame 2.0. Microsoft understood the impact that WinFrame had made and wanted to design and ship their own version of a multiuser operating system. Citrix's stock plummeted. Ed Iacobucci went on the offensive, and Citrix immediately went into negotiations with Microsoft. The outcome of those negotiations included the licensing of the MultiWin technology for use in future Microsoft products. Shortly after the agreement was finalized, Microsoft shipped Windows NT Server 4.0, Terminal Server Edition. This time, the product was also a completely independent operating system that separated itself from Windows NT Server 4.0 because of the redesigned kernel, but Microsoft was responsible for the distribution and support. The licensing extended to the Windows 2000 Server family.

What Citrix did not license to Microsoft is what sets Citrix apart from the crowd. Since Citrix is not allowed to ship their own version of terminal services, they have specialized in providing enterprise-level functionality to the terminal services provided by Microsoft. Such technologies as multivendor support, load balancing, installation management, and many others are provided to ease an administrator's job. These services are packaged under the auspices of MetaFrame. The original version of MetaFrame shipped as an add-on to Windows NT Server 4.0, Terminal Server Edition. The latest version of MetaFrame, MetaFrame XP, adds its enterprise functionality to both Windows NT Server 4.0, Terminal Server Edition and the Windows 2000 Server family running the Terminal Services service. When used with Windows 2000 Server, MetaFrame can take advantage of the new technologies Microsoft has implemented, such as the new domain structure and network security.

MetaFrame XP is marketed in three flavors: XPs, XPa, and XPe. The main difference among the three levels is the inclusion of various components. The size of the MetaFrame environment is usually the deciding factor for which product will be used.

The XPs version is the standard version of MetaFrame XP and is used in small MetaFrame environments. It ships with only the MetaFrame XP product—no additional pieces. Small organizations wanting to take advantage of the Independent Computing Architecture (ICA) protocol, additional client platform support, additional network protocol support, and seamless desktop features, yet do not have an immediate need for load balancing, utilize this version.

The XPa version ships with the Load Manager add-on. With this additional component, the MetaFrame servers in an organization can be load-balanced within the server farm. It's perfect for the medium-sized installation where the administrator wants centralized administrative control and ease of server load balancing.

The final product, XPe, includes all of the components for large enterprise-wide implementations of MetaFrame XP. These components include Load Manager, Installation Manager, Resource Manager, and Network Manager. Each of these tools provides additional functionality to the base MetaFrame XP product. Let's take a look at why MetaFrame XP is such a great product.

MetaFrame Benefits

In the previous chapter we discussed the benefits of terminal services, so let's look at what additional benefits MetaFrame brings to the thin client model. MetaFrame's benefits extend terminal services functionality and allow it to become an enterprise-level service. Without MetaFrame, an organization is restricted to using Microsoft Windows operating systems as the clients when accessing Windows Terminal Services. Support for other operating systems is gained from adding MetaFrame. Once it is added, Unix and Macintosh users have access to the same line-of-business applications that Windows users employ. Once the applications are standardized for all of the clients, administrators do not have to support a large variety of applications on different platforms, thus lowering their support costs.

Citrix retained the rights to numerous add-on products that extend the functionality of Terminal Services. These add-ons included the Citrix ICA protocol, Load Manager, Installation Manager, Resource Manager, and several other features. Let's take a brief look at these and other benefits in more detail.

Independent Computing Architecture

The Citrix design goal for MetaFrame is *Digital Independence*. Simply stated, this means that applications should be available on all computing platforms. Administrators are not limited to the traditional "They don't have Windows so they can't run Office" mentality. Standardizing applications reduces the amount of administration an administrator needs to perform in a varied computing platform environment. Controlling those applications from a centralized location eases an administrator's workload.

There are four primary areas identified in Citrix's goal for digital independence: Any Client Device, Any Network Connection, Any Network Protocol, and Seamless Desktop Integration. Let's take a look at each of these.

Any Client Device

While Microsoft has developed client software for virtually any Microsoft-based client, Citrix extends that ability to nearly every client type available. Table 12.1 lists the clients available when using MetaFrame.

TABLE 12.1: Clients Available Using MetaFrame

PLATFORM	CLIENTS
Windows 32-bit	Windows 9x, Windows NT 3.51, Windows NT 4.0, Windows 2000, Windows Me
Windows 16-bit	Windows 3.1, Windows for Workgroups 3.11, OS/2 2.1, OS/2 Warp Connect 3.0, OS/2 Warp Connect 4.0
Windows CE	Client device running Windows CE 2.0 or later; see OEM specs for availability
EPOC/Symbian	EPOC release 5.0
Java	Web browsers that support Sun's Java Virtual Machine or JDK 1.1 or later
Macintosh	68040 or PowerPC microprocessor systems running System 7.1.2 or later with Apple's Thread Manager, System 7.5.3, MacOS 8 or later
Unix	Linux, SCO UnixWare 7, Hewlett-Packard HP-UX 10.x or greater, Sun Solaris 2.5.1 and above, Sun SunOS 4.1.4, Silicon Graphics IRIX 6.2 and above, Digital Unix 3.2 and above, IBM AIX 4.1.4 and above
DOS	DOS 4.0 running on a 386 or better platform

Part II

With the inclusion of the Java client, any client with a web browser is able to access applications running on a Citrix MetaFrame server. Now you can run any operating system you choose and have access to applications that would normally run only on a Windows platform. MS-DOS 5.0 running Microsoft Office 2000 SR1, anyone?

Any Network Connection

The ideal thin client solution allows a client to connect from anywhere across any connection type. This would include any connection from a T1 to a slow modem connection. The ICA protocol is optimized to utilize very little bandwidth when passing data from the server to the client. Users can dial in from their home computers across a slow modem connection and still view their full desktop and run applications as though they were running the applications locally on their computers.

Any Network Protocol

The ICA protocol can be encapsulated within any routable protocol. An administrator can utilize an existing IPX/SPX, TCP/IP, NetBIOS, SLIP/PPP, or asynchronous network connection. When utilizing an asynchronous connection, there's no need for an administrator to configure a Remote Access Service (RAS) server for dial-up purposes.

Seamless Desktop Integration

Ideally, you do not want your users to know that they are actually running their applications on a server. If you can make them think that the applications are executing on their local computer, users are less likely to send inquiries concerning the applications to their IT department. *Seamless desktop integration* is the terminology Citrix uses when defining the user's experience working within a session. The interaction between the user's session and their local desktop should appear seamless, as though everything is running locally. The following topics define the technologies that are encompassed in this design goal.

Application Launching and Embedding   Imagine firing up a browser and pointing it to a web page that contains an icon for Microsoft Word. Immediately, Microsoft Word launches in a separate window on your desktop. All of the functionality of Microsoft Word is available to you. *Application launching* allows the application to start in its own window on the user's desktop independently of the web page. Launching an application is the most versatile means of accessing a program through a web page. When launching an application, the user can access other web pages and even close the web browser window while running the application. The connection to the Citrix MetaFrame server is maintained until the application is ended.

Or perhaps you access your corporate website and connect to a web page that has an Excel link listed. You click the link and an Excel spreadsheet appears within the main frame of the web page. *Application embedding* ties the application to the web page. Embedding an application into a web page allows you to limit the use of the application. Once the user leaves the web page, the application connection is lost. If the web page is closed, the application is closed also. MetaFrame XP allows an administrator to control how applications behave when accessed through a web page.

Resource Mapping and Redirection   *Resource mapping and redirection* is a term used to describe how MetaFrame interacts with the client's local resources. Drive mapping allows users to access their local hard drives with the same drive designations they had while running applications locally. Since most users are familiar with their C drive as the local drive on their computer, it is easier for everyone involved to have that designation still apply to the local hard drive on the user's computer. Virtual drives in the client's session represent the client's local drives. When the client accesses the virtual C drive while in a terminal session, they are accessing folders and files from their local hard drive. The server drives are mapped to other drive letters so that the client can still access them.

Printer mapping works similarly to drive mapping. A user's local printers are re-created in the user's sessions. Any documents sent to the printer are redirected to the user's local printer.

COM port redirection creates virtual ports on the server. When COM port redirection is used, the data is redirected to the user's local port. This allows the terminal session to use devices that are connected to the serial ports on the client's system.

Other resources that can be accessed by the server to give the user the impression that the applications are running locally are 16-bit stereo sound cards and the clipboard. Sound files pass from the server back to the client and are played through the stereo speakers. The clipboard can be utilized for copying information from applications that are running on the server and pasting that data to applications that are running locally on the client's computer, and vice versa.

Server Farms   For administrators who have multiple servers, a *server farm* can be used to group the servers into a centralized administrative unit. The servers can then be used to deploy and manage applications. During setup, the MetaFrame server can be added to a server farm. All servers in a server farm then share a data store. This data store acts as a repository for information for the applications, administrators, and servers within the server farm. An administrator can create the data store using any ODBC-compliant database, including Microsoft SQL Server, Oracle, and Microsoft Access. There are many benefits to using server farms, including load balancing and installation services, that we will look at in later chapters.

Scalability

When using Terminal Services alone, each client is directed to a server according to the settings within the Terminal Services client software. The only way to redirect a user is to change those parameters in the client software. Some administrators create multiple shortcuts on the user's desktop and direct them to connect to one server unless the session seems slow. In that case, they are directed to log out of that session and try the other server's shortcut on the desktop.

While the previous example will work, it is not a true load-balancing technique. Consider an organization that has five terminal servers and 100 users wanting to gain access to sessions. An administrator can configure the clients to connect to one of the servers so that only 20 users are accessing any one server at a time. This guarantees that the load on any of the servers will not become too great.

You may wonder, though, "What happens when users from one server are all logged on, but there are very few sessions started on any of the other servers?" One server will be loaded to its maximum while the others are barely taxed. This is not load balancing. MetaFrame has a load-balancing mechanism that directs a user to a server that is seen as the least busy, thus evening out the load on each server. If 40 users are logged on in this five-server environment, each server would have eight user sessions running. Each server is optimized and not overloaded, as resources are evenly distributed across the servers.

Throughout the remainder of the chapter, we will be discussing the technologies that make MetaFrame a necessary addition to Terminal Services.

THE TECHNOLOGIES

In the remainder of this chapter, you will be exposed to the technologies that make MetaFrame XP the great product that it is. These technologies extend the functionality of terminal services and deliver enterprise-level centralized administrative capabilities. Some of these are the same tools that were present within MetaFrame 1.8, some have been given facelifts and now have additional functionality, while others are completely new to MetaFrame XP.

Citrix has integrated these technologies so that they work with legacy MetaFrame environments such as MetaFrame 1.8. To make everything run smoothly, MetaFrame server farms now have two modes, native and mixed. In *mixed mode*, MetaFrame 1.8 servers can exist in the same server farm as MetaFrame XP servers. Only when the server farm no longer hosts MetaFrame 1.8 servers should the server farm be switched to *native mode*.

In this next section, we will identify the technologies that perform differently when in native mode than in mixed mode. So let's start by taking a look at the ICA protocol and dissecting the packet.

Identifying the Components of the ICA Packet

When Citrix was designing WinFrame, they knew that they needed a protocol efficient enough to travel over any transport protocol. In order to design a protocol that complex, they developed a set of standards, or criteria. Since Windows NT was the platform that Citrix was developing the ICA protocol for and TCP/IP was the protocol most widely used on that operating system, they decided that the first requirement would be that the protocol would have to build its own framing header. In the case of streaming protocols such as TCP, the packet was required to build its own frame set. *Framed protocols* such as IPX already have this functionality, so the framing header is not utilized.

Reliability was the second requirement since IPX/SPX was the second-most-popular transport protocol. Connectionless protocols such as IPX are then able to guarantee error-free transport of the encapsulated information. TCP, on the other hand, is a reliable connection-based protocol, so the reliable header is not used.

The other criteria that Citrix required in a protocol include the following:

Ensuring the server's ability to execute all application logic When an application launches within a session, all of the execution is performed on that server. The client computer does not process any of the information; it acts as a thin client only.

Keeping network traffic to a minimum This is achieved by transferring only screen updates, keystrokes, and mouse clicks between the client and the server. The client's only function is to interact with the user. Therefore, only the screen updates performed by the server and data input by the user are transferred across the network.

Ensuring the ability to utilize any transport protocol   These include TCP/IP, IPX, SPX, NetBIOS, NetBEUI, PPP, Async, ISDN, Frame Relay, ATM, and any other existing or developing protocols. ICA Packets can be encapsulated into any transport protocol.

Enabling the application to perform at LAN-like speed
This should be possible even when it's utilized through a low-bandwidth connection. The protocol efficiency should allow the client to interact with its session as though the user was accessing the applications locally.

Permitting the latest 16-bit and 32-bit applications to run on legacy clients that would not normally have the resources to execute them   Because the server processes the entire application logic, the client system does not need the additional resources to host the Windows NT/2000 operating system or the latest applications.

Pieces of the Packet

The ICA protocol, based on the criteria we just reviewed, is made up of multiple headers that surround a command byte and any command data. The following graphic illustrates the components of the ICA Packet:

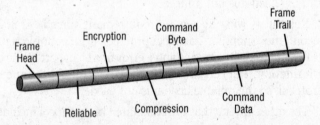

As shown, the packet contains the following headers:

Frame Head   The *Frame Head* header is used in stream-oriented communications such as TCP or Async to frame the data for reconstruction at the receiving computer.

Reliable   The *Reliable* header is used in connectionless protocols such as IPX to provide reliable, error-free delivery.

Encryption   The *Encryption* header is used as the preamble for managing any packets that contain encrypted data.

Compression   The *Compression* header is used as the preamble for managing any packets that contain compressed data.

Command Byte   The *Command Byte* header is the only required ICA command byte. This is the beginning of the base ICA protocol packet.

Command Data   The *Command Data* header contains optional data bytes associated with the specific command. The length of the data is dependent on the command.

Frame Trail   The *Frame Trail* header completes the packet for stream-oriented communications, such as Async and TCP.

The ICA Packet is built at the Presentation layer of the Open Systems Interconnection (OSI) model. This means that the protocol can be encapsulated within any of the transport protocols that exist in today's network environments. As the ICA Packet is built, it is passed through a series of drivers before it is encapsulated into the transport protocol. Depending upon the transport protocol and the additional technologies utilized, such as encryption, the command and command data have headers appended to them by these drivers. Just as with any protocol, the server adds these headers onto the packet. After the packet is encapsulated into the transport protocol, it is delivered to the client, which examines the headers and acts upon them to correctly access the command and command data.

The ICA Packet is the cornerstone for all of the technologies that Citrix has introduced over the years since WinFrame was developed. In the next few sections, we will take a closer look at some of these foundation technologies.

The Benefits of SpeedScreen

While a server is processing the data for a client, frequent screen updates can occur. Mouse movements and keyboard entries are reflected on the screen. The results of commands are displayed on the screen, and the windows and applications that are opened from double-clicking an icon are also shown. During these screen updates, if the server needed to refresh every pixel on the screen for every update, far too much network traffic would occur. Even though the ICA Packet can be compressed to reduce traffic, screen updates still occur very rapidly. Citrix took this factor into consideration and developed a technology for the MetaFrame 1.8 product known as *SpeedScreen*, which allows the server to update only the portions of the screen that have changed.

When screen repaint information is prepared for transmission to the client, each screen item is compared to previously transmitted data. If the data has not changed, the server will not retransmit the information and the client will not have to reprocess the information. Any data that has changed is reflected on the user's display. With these enhancements alone, users have four times the performance gains over non-SpeedScreen sessions.

Screen repaints are not the only performance-enhancing feature with SpeedScreen. MetaFrame XP introduced new functionality, *local text echo* and *mouse click feedback*. These new technologies extend and enhance an already robust idea and make MetaFrame an even more viable solution when used in a slow-link situation. Both are configurable at the server level and are known collectively as *SpeedScreen Latency Reduction*.

If SpeedScreen Latency Reduction is turned on, local text echo goes into action. As soon as a user logs on to a MetaFrame session, the server pushes a series of screen images, which represent the screen fonts, to the client system. As the user enters information, the client system examines the data that is captured by the keyboard and determines what should be displayed on the screen. When the server processes the information, the actual screen updates are sent to the client. For the most part, the client will not see any difference when the screen repaint occurs. Usually, the only differences occur when the font changes and the client has not been updated with the new screen information.

Mouse click feedback allows a user to see that the system is responding to a mouse-click action. This is especially useful on slow network links where the client system may not receive the screen update immediately. It may appear to the user that the mouse click was not received by the system. This becomes problematic when users are familiar with applications that run native on their computers. Since it appears as though the application did not respond to the mouse click, the user will again click the application. When it appears as though it is still not responding, the user will click again and again. This multiple clicking only causes further problems due to the additional data that is sent out for the server to process.

To alleviate this, mouse click feedback changes the pointer to an hourglass to indicate that the user has performed an action. After the server processes the client's action, the screen is updated to reflect that action, and the pointer returns to its normal shape. The major bonus to this feature comes from the server not having to process any additional mouse clicks. Hence, the users see what they think they should see, and the server processes only the data it should have to process.

These two SpeedScreen tools are configurable. From the client's Program Neighborhood, the options are applied for an entire application set or on the individual programs. You can set these options by opening Program Neighborhood and navigating to File ➤ Application Set Properties and selecting the Default Options tab. When applied at the application-set level, all applications within that set inherit the settings. If the properties for a published application are different than the application-set properties, the application overrides the set options. Program properties always override set properties. See the SpeedScreen Latency Reduction options in Figure 12.1.

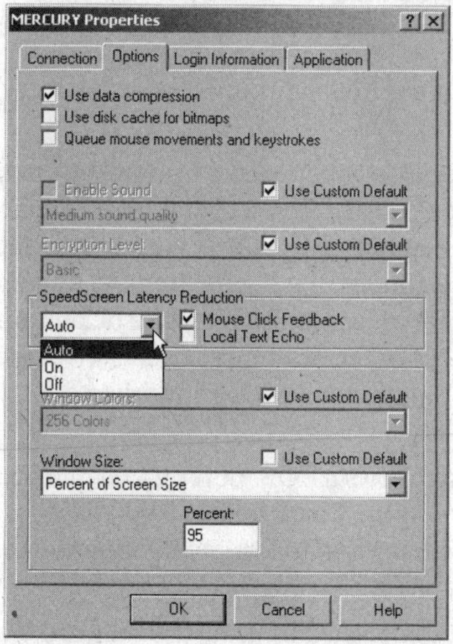

FIGURE 12.1: SpeedScreen Latency Reduction options

Client Resource Redirection and ICA Functionality

The server is responsible for performing the processing on behalf of the client, so all of the local resources for the server are made accessible to the user. There are instances when users need access to resources local to their workstations. MetaFrame provides file system redirection to some of the user's local resources by providing drive mapping, printer mapping, and COM port redirection.

Drive mapping gives an administrator the ability to control what the user sees when they access system drives during a session. Each drive the user has on their local computer is available to them in their Citrix session. If the drives on the server have been remapped, the user will access their local system drives using the same drive letter that they have on their local computer. Thus, the user's C drive will appear as C in the Citrix session. If the server's drive letters have not been remapped, the client's local system drives are mapped starting with the letter V and working backward through the alphabet. The only deviation from this would be if the client had a drive letter already in use at the time of the mapping. In this scenario, the client's C drive would appear as V, and their D drive would appear as U in the Citrix session. If U was already mapped before the connection to Citrix, then that letter would be skipped and the client's D drive would then connect to the next available letter, T. This mapping is handy when you want to transfer files or access files on your local computer while connected to a Citrix server.

Printer mapping applies the same theories to a printer. Just as you can connect to client drives, you can also connect and print to your local printer. Your print device is remapped to the Citrix server, so it appears in the client's printer list. You can set the connections to all of the printers defined on the computer or just to the Windows default printer. MetaFrame XP has alleviated a lot of the printing problems that this model created with MetaFrame 1.*x*. This is done with print driver deployment and management.

Finally, *COM port redirection* allows a COM port on a client computer to be redirected to a COM port on the Citrix server. A good use for this would be a mobile user downloading and uploading information in their PDA from their hotel room to the Citrix server back in the office.

Mapping of these items is accomplished by using the standard Windows device-redirection facilities. Client mappings appear as another network that represents the client devices. When you connect to a device, you will see (aside from the Microsoft network) a network with the name "client." The devices that can be connected appear as share points in the client network to which a drive letter or printer can be attached. You reach these options by opening Citrix Connection Configuration, right-clicking the connection you wish to configure, and choosing Edit. When the

Edit Connection screen appears, click the Client Settings button to open the Client Settings screen shown in Figure 12.2.

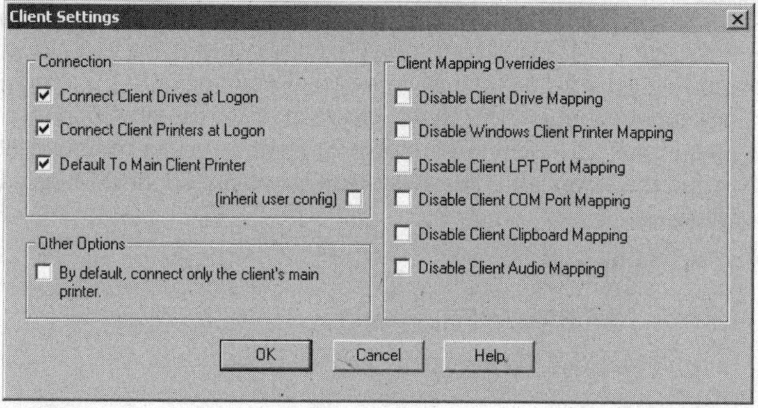

FIGURE 12.2:   Client mapping options in Citrix Connection Configuration

ICA utilizes client clipboard mapping, which allows cut-and-paste functionality between the ICA session and Windows clients. This permits a client to copy or cut and paste between a client application and an application that is running in an ICA session on the Citrix server.

Client audio mapping is also supported in ICA Clients. Audio support allows application sounds and WAV files to be played on the client devices. You can assign the following settings in the Citrix Connection Configuration utility.

Low   The low setting causes any waveform data passed to the client to be compressed to a maximum of 16Kbps before transmission. The CPU requirements and benefits are about the same as those for the medium setting, but the lower data rate allows for a low-bandwidth connection.

Medium   The medium setting causes any waveform data passed to the client to be compressed to a maximum of 64Kbps before transmission. This setting is recommended for most LAN-based connections, and it is the default setting.

High   The high setting allows the waveform data to be played on the client device in its native data rate. The high data rate requires about 1.3Mbps of bandwidth to play without disruption. This connection is recommended only when bandwidth is plentiful and sound quality is very important.

Features of Independent Management Architecture

Independent Management Architecture (IMA) is not just another fancy name that Citrix pulled out of their collective minds when trying to come up with a selling point for their latest version of MetaFrame. IMA is a completely new architectural model that replaces many of the key components of MetaFrame 1.8, and it is a protocol for server-to-server communications within the server farm. The subsystems that make up the IMA include the following:

- ICA Browser
- Server Management
- Application Management
- Runtime
- Persistent Storage
- Distribution
- Remote Procedure Call
- User Management
- Printer Management
- Citrix License
- Program Neighborhood
- Load Management

In Citrix's own words, IMA is "a unified, enterprise-wide platform for installation management, maintenance, support, and security for your organization's server-based computing and application hosting services." This reworking of some of the key components of MetaFrame has created a more robust enterprise-level product. Some of the functionality IMA has brought to MetaFrame includes:

- Centralized administration of MetaFrame XP IMA
- Centralized configuration storage for all Citrix servers through a data store
- Centralized license management and pooling
- Discovery of published applications from ICA Clients without User Datagram Protocol (UDP) broadcasts

▶ Logging of shadowed sessions

▶ Support for Simple Network Management Protocol (SNMP)

Let's take a look at each of these features in detail.

Centralized Administration

The new Citrix Management Console combines the functionality of several administrative tools: Citrix Licensing, Citrix Server Administration, Load Balancing, and Published Applications Manager. Since the console is Java-based, administrators are able to install it on Windows 2000, NT 4.0, and NT Server 4.0, TSE. With the tools located in a unified environment, the administrator is able to control the administration from one centralized tool instead of having multiple tools open at once. Figure 12.3 shows the Citrix Management Console with the nodes that are available to manage.

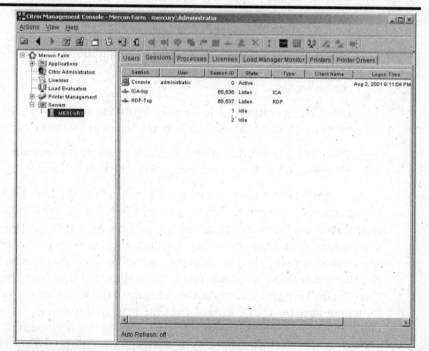

FIGURE 12.3: Citrix Management Console

You control all applications that are published in your MetaFrame XP server farm through the Citrix Management Console. This is also the utility that you use to define the administrators who are assigned to your server farm, as well as control license counts for client access to applications.

Centralized Configuration Storage

IMA acts as a central repository for configuration information for the server farm. All of the servers added to the farm report this information to the data store, which is a database that holds static and rarely changed information about the server farm. The data store can use either a Microsoft Access, Microsoft SQL Server, or Oracle database. In turn, this database is utilized in the farm in much the same manner as the Browser Service was used in MetaFrame 1.8. The data store holds the following information:

Published Application The Published Application section contains all of the configurable properties of the published application. These include the name of the application, user permissions, ICA connection properties, window size, color depth, encryption levels, and audio settings.

Pooled License The Pooled License section contains the license numbers and the total number of licenses available for pooling, which are reserved for individual servers.

Server Configuration The Server Configuration section holds information about the configuration of all servers in the server farm.

User Configuration The User Configuration section contains information about the configuration of all users in the server farm.

Printers The Printers section contains configuration and driver information for the printers available to the users.

Each MetaFrame XP server accesses the data store to send or retrieve configuration information. The servers are allowed to access the data store directly, or they can use another MetaFrame XP server as a proxy to access the data. These two access methods are known as direct access and indirect access. When configuring a server for direct access, known as putting it in direct mode, the server needs the Open Database Connectivity (ODBC) drivers installed for the database. If the administrator would rather not have the ODBC drivers installed on all of the servers, indirect mode will allow the server to indirectly access the data store through another server. One word of caution, however: the failure of the server configured with direct access will prevent the other servers from accessing the data store.

One of the key differences of MetaFrame XP over MetaFrame 1.8 is the way the servers in the farm handle information. In version 1.8, all of the servers in the farm held configuration information in their Registry. When the server came online, it would read the Registry and apply the configuration data to the server's Program Neighborhood. As changes were made, each server would notify the other servers in the farm of the changes. In addition, the master browser would keep a cached copy of the configuration information within an in-memory database. Although this allowed all of the servers to process information about all of the other servers in the farm and allowed clients to find published applications within the farm, there were issues with the amount of network traffic that was generated. All changes were sent to all servers as a complete change list, not an incremental one. The updates were also sent as UDP broadcasts, which limited the functionality of the update process.

With MetaFrame XP, servers no longer send all of the configuration information and configuration changes to every server. Instead, the configuration information is delivered to the data store. As servers are added to the server farm or started after a shutdown, they read the information contained in the data store and add it to their local host cache.

Each server within the server farm has a *local host cache*, which is actually a Microsoft Access database that holds a subset of the information contained in the data store. As information changes in the server farm, the server is notified of the changes, and it then downloads any changed information into the local host cache. This cached configuration is utilized for two purposes: to allow the server to still function when the data store is offline and to allow clients to resolve applications locally.

All MetaFrame XP servers replicate the information from the data store when they are first started. This information includes which servers are in the farm and the current published applications they host. The IMA service will continue to send updates to the server as changes are made to the server farm. When a client attempts to resolve access to an application, the server's local host cache can direct the client to the proper server since it contains information concerning the application configuration. This enhances the response time for the client when a published application is requested.

If the data store goes offline for any reason, MetaFrame XP servers can still perform the application resolution for up to 48 hours. After 48 hours, the licensing information expires and the server will not perform these functions until the data store is back online. The IMA service will continue to try to reestablish connection with the data store during this time. As soon as the data store comes back online, the server will refresh its licensing information and the local host cache. At that point, the client will function as normal.

Centralized License Management and Pooling

When the first MetaFrame XP server is added to the server farm, the MetaFrame XP server performs license pooling. All licenses available in the server farm are by default combined into a license group and available for all clients. This alleviates the problem of assigning a static number of licenses to each individual server. With licenses combined in one large database, any user can connect to the farm and gain access to resources on any server on the farm. Any user accessing resources will consume only one license, even if the resources they are accessing are physically located on different servers.

NOTE

For more information on client device licensing, see the section "Basics of Client Device Licensing" later in this chapter.

Discovering Published Applications

Whenever a client searched a MetaFrame 1.8 server farm for published applications, the client would send out a broadcast message that would be answered by a MetaFrame server that was configured as the master browser. This broadcast was sent out as a UDP broadcast. If the subnet that contained the client computer did not have a browser gateway installed, the client would not receive a full list of published applications. Published applications from other subnets would not be seen, only those published applications on the local subnet.

MetaFrame XP alleviates this problem by storing all of the server farm configuration information in the data store and then passing copies of it to all of the servers in the farm. When a client opens Program Neighborhood, the local MetaFrame server delivers a list of all of the published applications to the client.

The original version of the ICA browser is now replaced with IMA. Of course, Citrix includes support for the legacy browser, but by default the XP servers take over the master browser function in a mixed-mode server farm. Browser elections are still performed within the server farm, and MetaFrame XP is given the highest *election criteria*—a version number of 20. Since the MetaFrame XP server will win an election, MetaFrame 1.x servers should have their browser election setting configured so that they never become browsers in the farm. This will reduce the amount of network traffic generated when a MetaFrame 1.x server is rebooted.

IMA divides the farm into *zones* to ease administration and to reduce network traffic. Each zone defines a physical area in which servers are grouped. The zone's *data collector* gathers any changes made within the *server farm* and distributes the changes to other zones in the farm. Each zone has one data collector that is elected the same way a master browser was elected in previous versions of MetaFrame.

The election criteria for choosing a data collector are these:

1. Highest master number version: The number 1 is used for all MetaFrame XP servers.

2. Lowest master ranking: A server with the number 1 is the most preferred; a server with the number 4 is not preferred.

3. Highest host ID: The host ID is assigned at installation. It is a random number in the range of 0 through 65,536.

Elections are triggered in the following situations:

▶ A member server loses contact with the data collector.

▶ The data collector goes offline.

▶ A server is brought online within the server farm.

▶ The querydc -e command is invoked.

▶ The zone configuration changes, such as a change in the zone name, the election preference of member servers, or the server membership.

If a new data collector is elected, the servers will contact the data collector to verify that it is available. If the data collector is available, the servers will transmit their configuration information. If the data collector does not change, the servers that were online before the election will not send their configuration data. Servers that lost connection will send a complete update to the data collector.

Each of the data collectors has a connection to every data collector for each of the other zones in the farm. After an election is forced, if the existing data collector loses the election, it will contact the other data collectors and notify them of the change. Data collectors from other zones will then establish a connection with the new data collector.

As session information changes, the data collectors update one another. Communications among them are initiated immediately when any of the following changes occur:

▶ ICA Client logon or logoff

▶ ICA session reconnect or disconnect

Part II

- ▶ Server and application load changes
- ▶ License acquisition and release
- ▶ Server brought online or goes offline
- ▶ Published application changes
- ▶ IP and MAC address changes

Since each zone collector has a connection open to all other data collectors in the farm, all data collectors are aware of the server load, licensing, and session information for every server in the farm. If no communications have been received from a member server in a zone within a certain time interval, the zone's data collector pings (an internal function known as an IMA ping) that server to verify that it is online. The default time interval is once per minute. A single zone supports up to 256 member servers.

IMA reduces network traffic by taking advantage of the data collector model to distribute information quickly and efficiently. When a change is made on a member server, the member server sends the updated information to the data collector for the zone it is in. The data collector then sends update notifications to the data collectors for which it has connections. Each data collector that receives the update sends the update to the member servers in its own zone.

For example, when a Citrix administrator opens the Citrix Management Console and publishes a new print driver, the following steps occur:

1. The server writes information to the data store.

2. The server sends the change to its zone's data collector.

3. The zone's data collector distributes the change to all member servers in its zone.

4. The zone's data collector sends the change to all other zone data collectors.

5. The other zone's data collectors receive the change and distribute it to all member servers within their respective zones.

6. All member servers receive the change and update their local host cache as requested.

Normally, data collectors are synchronized through constant updates. Occasionally, an update sent from one data collector to another data collector can fail. Instead of flooding the network with constant requests to the failed server, the data collector waits a specified interval (five minutes by default) before attempting communication again.

Logging Shadowed Sessions

One of the most convenient features of MetaFrame is the ability to shadow a client. To *shadow* is to view the session of a client from within an administrator's session, more commonly know as a *shadowed session*. There are many benefits to shadowing. Companies have implemented shadowing for troubleshooting purposes, allowing remote control and providing users with application support. Many administrators take advantage of the ability to control a server from a remote computer. They can interact with the computer as though they were sitting locally and can control any resource on the computer with one tool.

ADMINISTRATORS ON THE GO

Most administrators like to sit and control everything on their network from one central location. Their workstation becomes their command center. For some smaller companies, however, the administrator may not have that luxury. The administrator may be the only tech support person at that location. Responsible for everything, they are too busy to have the luxury of a command center.

Steve is one such administrator. He is the lone wolf who fields every help desk question, fixes every problem with client machines and printers, and administers all of the systems on his network. He is one very busy person.

After installing Microsoft Windows 2000 Advanced Server on his network, Steve took advantage of Terminal Services so that if the occasion arose, he could load the client on a user's system and administer his servers and shadow other users having problems in their sessions. Though he did like the convenience, he did not like having to load the client software each time he used someone's computer that did not already have it installed. Loading the client also caused problems with those users who wanted to know what it did.

After purchasing MetaFrame XP and installing it to allow remote clients to use the web features, he came up with an idea to make his own life a little easier. He purchased a Compaq iPaq and loaded the Windows CE client on it. With the addition of a wireless network adapter, he is now able to administer his servers from anywhere in the building. Having the client software running on the Windows CE operating system allows him to view the entire remote desktop on the screen, or he can use the Panning and Scaling feature to have a full-size desktop.

CONTINUED ➡

Part II

> Now as he is walking through the building putting out fires, he can start a session on his handheld and manipulate any of his servers. If he needs to answer a call from a user who is having problems with an application, and that user is running a session, he can shadow that session and assist the user with their problem. Now he has the best of both worlds.

Shadowed sessions are not logged by default. To allow sessions to be logged to Event Viewer, the server must have the option enabled within the Citrix Management Console. You can reach this option by opening Citrix Management Console, right-clicking your server within the Servers node, selecting Properties, and choosing the MetaFrame Settings tab. Then click the Enable Shadow Logging On This Server check box, as shown in Figure 12.4. With this feature enabled, the application log records information concerning the session that is shadowed as well as the session that performed the shadowing. The event appears as an Event ID 1001. While shadowing can be a vital tool, logging can curtail any abuse.

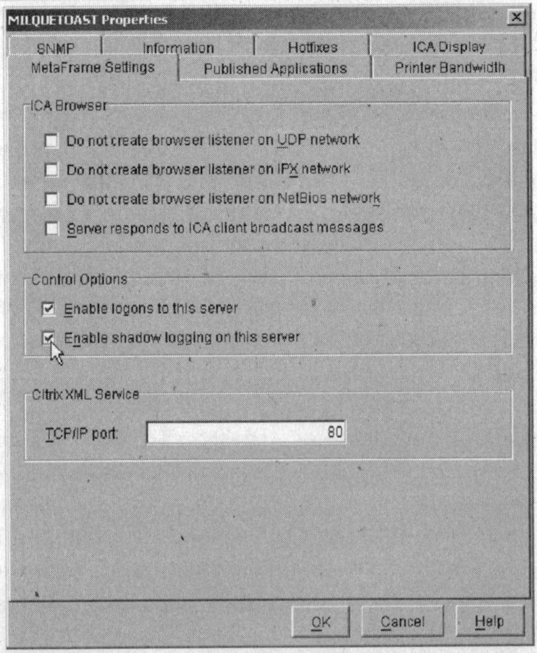

FIGURE 12.4:   Enabling shadowed session logging

Simple Network Management Protocol Support

Simple Network Management Protocol (SNMP) is a network tool that is used by many companies to monitor their networked devices. It has been in use for many years and is a well-proven protocol. Citrix provides support for SNMP monitoring of MetaFrame XP servers. Each of the servers in the server farm can provide administrative event notification to a third-party management console such as Hewlett Packard's HP OpenView product. The SNMP service loaded on a MetaFrame XP server also allows a basic level of administration of the server. If MetaFrame XPe is installed, Citrix Network Manager is available for use as an SNMP agent for the server farm. With this product, the entire server farm can be monitored and managed using SNMP.

Working with Listener Ports

When MetaFrame is installed, a special service is created, known as the *listener port*. By default, each protocol installed has one listener port created for it. This service monitors the packets received by the server's interfaces for client connection attempts.

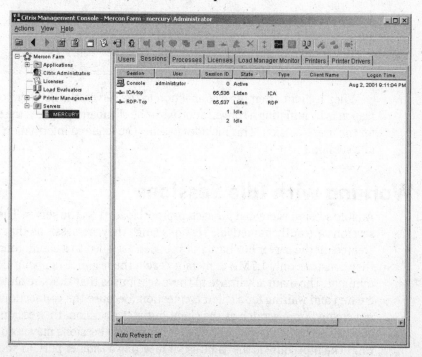

Part II

If users are reporting difficulties accessing the Citrix server, an administrator may need to reset a listener port. You can do this from within Citrix Management Console also.

When a client attempts a connection to the server, the listener port responds by initiating a conversation with the client and prepares the server for the user's session. This includes passing the required information to an idle session.

Working with Idle Sessions

An idle session is created for each protocol loaded on the server. These sessions are aptly named *idle sessions* since they are sessions that are created on the server but have not yet been assigned to a client. Since they consume only 1.7MB of memory each, the resource consumption is minimal. The main advantage to these sessions is that they are already created and waiting for a client connection. Because the connections are not created from scratch as the client initiates a session, the session can be activated much faster. Although it is rare, idle sessions may need resetting. The procedure is the same as for resetting a listener port, as shown in

Figure 12.5. Now let's look at what happens as a client attempts to create a session.

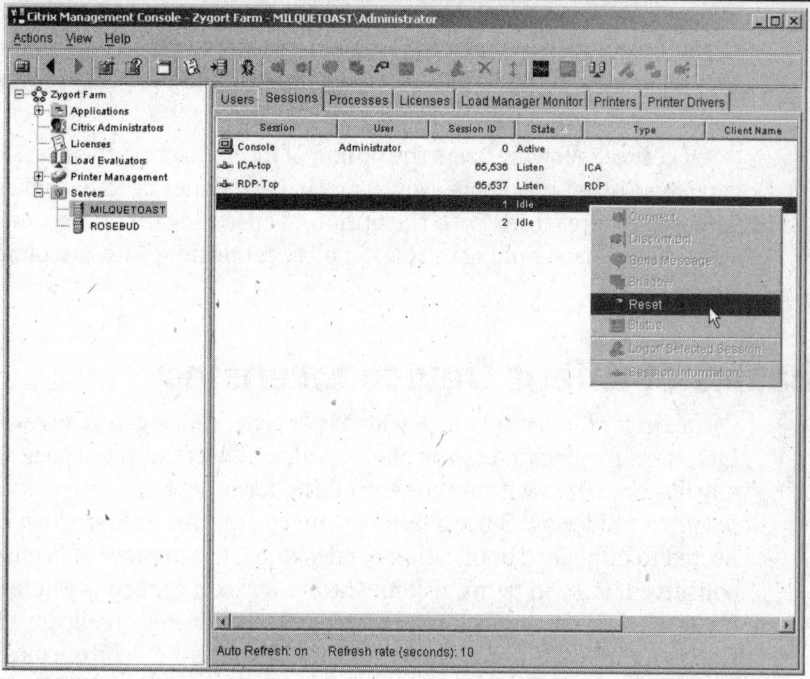

FIGURE 12.5: Resetting idle sessions from within the Citrix Management Console

Maintaining and Configuring ICA Sessions

As the listener port directs a client request to the idle session, the session state changes from Idle to ConnQ as the connection is in the process of connecting. Once connected, the session state changes to Conn. The session remains in this state while the user logs on. The session state will change one more time, this time to Active, when the user has successfully logged on to the server.

As long as the user is accessing applications within the session, the state of the connection will remain Active. Once the user logs off from the session, that session is discarded, and the resources reserved for it are released back to the operating system.

One other state that you may see when looking at the session information in Citrix Management Console is Disc, which stands for Disconnected.

Users can disconnect from their sessions, which keeps the session alive on the server, but the window in which they were viewing their session is closed on the client. As soon as the user logs back on to the server, the idle session that is presented with the session request redirects the user to their existing disconnected session. The user sees the same session they were running previously, with all applications that were processing still active.

Of course, allowing users the option of disconnecting their sessions can cause other problems. New users have a tendency to become confused when presented with the option to either log off or disconnect. Administrators should have rules in place for dealing with disconnected sessions.

Basics of Client Device Licensing

Client Device Licensing is analogous to per-seat licensing in Windows 2000. Licenses are allocated to the client, which allows the client to access any resource from within the server farm, regardless of which server the resource resides on. Since a user consumes only one license when connected to published applications or desktops, the number of licenses is conserved. Case in point, if Jami starts a session that runs Microsoft Excel, the server that is hosting the session allocates one license from the pool to Jami's account. After starting that session, she opens another session that runs WinZip. Even if the session controlling WinZip is on another server than the session running Microsoft Excel, Jami's account consumes only one license.

There is one exception to this rule. If the client connecting to the server farm is using client software from MetaFrame 1.0, the connections made to the servers in the farm must all be with the same protocol. If a user connects to Server A and Server B with TCP/IP, only one license will be consumed. As soon as the client connects to Server C using IPX/SPX, another license will be consumed, effectively wasting a license.

SUMMARY

As you have perused the pages of this chapter, you have been exposed to the technologies that, for the most part, work behind the scenes. Citrix's Independent Computing Architecture and Independent Management Architecture work together to give the end user a sense of working at their local workstation, while at the same time making administration of the entire enterprise easier for the administrator. These technologies and everything they have to offer, from client device licensing to shadowed sessions, are the building blocks for the chapters to come. As in any profession, the better you know how things work, the better your administrative acumen will be.

WHAT'S NEXT

In Chapter 13, we'll delve into greater detail about the networking environment. We'll take a look at enterprise applications that exist on a network, and we'll discuss how to evaluate a current network environment. We'll show you how to assess network services, the current TCP/IP infrastructure, and current network hardware. Finally, we'll discuss the layout of technical support and management systems.

Part II

Part III
Network Design, Maintenance, and Troubleshooting

Chapter 13

THE PRINCIPLES OF NETWORK DESIGN

T his chapter is a discussion about the nitty-gritty details of an enterprise. We start out by talking about the applications that are on a network (an important and often under-noticed subject). We then look at the network services and the existing TCP/IP infrastructure. We also examine *current* hardware situations, with an eye toward what you need to do to fix weaknesses. You need to identify any planned rollouts or upgrades, analyze the support structure, and describe the layout of network and systems management facilities.

Part III

Adapted from *MCSE: Windows 2000 Network Infrastructure Design Study Guide*, Second Edition by William Heldman
ISBN 0-7821-2953-6   784 pages $59.99

Defining Your Enterprise Network Applications

Let's begin with a discussion of what applications are on your network and how you can sort them into distinct cubbyholes that match functional profiles.

There are two separate distinctions that need to be made here:

▶ The application's scope, whether it is enterprise or workgroup

▶ Regardless of scope, whether the application is client/server or web-based

Enterprise vs. Workgroup Scope

Network applications can be split into two different varieties: enterprise and workgroup. This is a loose definition, but one that you can safely use in your network examinations.

An *enterprise application* is one that is used daily by a lot of people. Exchange is an enterprise application, but that's an obvious one. Another example is a front-end client that talks to an Oracle database. Often, organizations have customized an application that lives on the client's desktop and maintains connectivity either with the enterprise databases or with middleware that, in turn, talks to the databases. The scope of these kinds of applications is usually large, and they're generally enterprise-class applications, based on the application's volume of use. Think of enterprise applications as applications that have a mission-critical status, that are being used by large numbers of people, and that are in use almost all of the time during working hours.

How about Internet Explorer (IE)? Is that an enterprise application? I'd say no; it only brings web pages back to the local user and doesn't further the corporate good globally. An intranet application that lives on a web server and is used *with* IE is a different story. The number of users and daily volume of use could be vast.

A *workgroup application* lives on a server and serves a purpose specifically for one group of people. Financial applications are probably the most common of several good examples. Not everybody in the company needs to use server-based financial software—typically, only the accountants and payroll people. Nevertheless, the software is large and expensive, requires tons of training for the admins and end users, and needs a lot of care and feeding. Often a client-based GUI has to be installed and periodically upgraded. I've seen financial software that bundles extra features into Excel; the accountants and finance people then work with spreadsheets, coupled with the added financial package features.

Another good example is Visual SourceSafe (VSS) for developers. Few people in the company need VSS, but the software lives on a server and requires a lot of admin maintenance. How about engineering or statistical applications that supply important information to an entire group of engineers? Or legal software on CD that provides case information to lawyers? The list goes on, but the scope of these applications is *not* enterprise; they're local in nature and shouldn't be considered enterprise software.

> **NOTE**
>
> "Enterprise" can be defined many different ways, not just by number or scope of users. Besides the "volume of use" or "corporate good" definitions here, you could decide that the difference between enterprise and workgroup applications is determined by whether the application serves the whole company (enterprise) or a specific subgroup of the company (workgroup). Mission-criticality could be your criterion for "enterpriseness." Even Microsoft uses the term loosely!

Client/Server vs. Web-Based

A second distinction, independent of the scope of the application, is the way that the application is distributed across the environment. Do you have a *client/server* application or a web-based application? Let's start by differentiating the various client/server iterations, so you can get a feel for how complicated an applications disbursement can be:

> **2-tier client/server** A *2-tier client/server* typically means that a client software piece is installed on several computers and then this client component talks to the server. A database is usually involved. Exchange Server is a good example of 2-tier client/server. It includes a set of centralized databases (that are replicated to other servers, but that's a different story) and clients such as an Exchange client, the Outlook client, or Outlook Web Access (OWA). Clients can be homegrown with tools such as PowerBuilder or Visual Basic, or they can come with the application (as in the case of Exchange Server). Figure 13.1 illustrates a typical 2-tier client/server model.

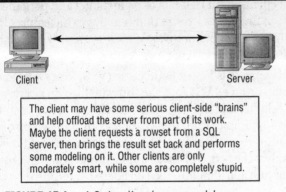

Client   Server

The client may have some serious client-side "brains"
and help offload the server from part of its work.
Maybe the client requests a rowset from a SQL
server, then brings the result set back and performs
some modeling on it. Other clients are only
moderately smart, while some are completely stupid.

FIGURE 13.1:   A 2-tier client/server model

3-tier client/server   Suppose that you have a database living
on a Unix server, and you want to get at it with your Windows NT
Workstation client. How can you do that? A third piece called
middleware is introduced into this client/server picture; middleware in a predominantly Windows environment usually resides
on a Windows NT computer. The user makes a request to the
middleware box, which in turn passes the request on to the Unix
host and then sends the result set back to the user. These three
components make up a *3-tier client/server* model, as illustrated
in Figure 13.2.

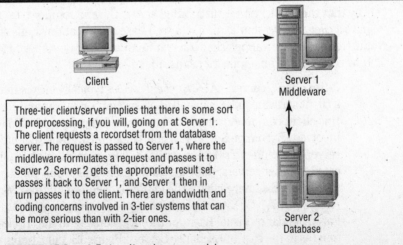

Client   Server 1
                                              Middleware

Three-tier client/server implies that there is some sort
of preprocessing, if you will, going on at Server 1.
The client requests a recordset from the database
server. The request is passed to Server 1, where the
middleware formulates a request and passes it to
Server 2. Server 2 gets the appropriate result set,
passes it back to Server 1, and Server 1 then in
turn passes it to the client. There are bandwidth and
coding concerns involved in 3-tier systems that can
be more serious than with 2-tier ones.

                                              Server 2
                                              Database

FIGURE 13.2:   A 3-tier client/server model

NOTE

In the Windows NT and Windows 2000 worlds, Gateway Services for NetWare is a great example of middleware. Conversely, Client Services for NetWare is simply a client, thus fitting into the 2-tier model.

You don't always have a client talking to NT middleware that then talks to Unix. You might find hundreds of different variations on a theme, but the point is that there are three players in the application system. The client component that the user uses can be homegrown (with Visual Basic, PowerBuilder, Oracle tools, Delphi, and others) or a client that actually comes with the application.

An *n*-tier client/server The phrase *n-tier client/server* is given to systems, like the one shown in Figure 13.3, with much more complicated levels than standard 2-tier or 3-tier systems. Suppose an interactive voice response (IVR) system comprises a 24-port T1 telephony card, a database repository on an NT server, a Unix flat file that is periodically downloaded to the database, and a client component that communicates with the system. Here you have deeper "granularity" than a simple 2-tier or 3-tier system; in fact, you could theoretically have a system that goes many levels deep. This is why it's called *n*-tier, because the design dictates how many tiers deep you go. Databases that replicate and consolidate with other databases might also qualify as *n*-tier systems. *N*-tier systems are highly complicated and require careful attention by server and application admins and DBAs.

Thin-client/server *Thin-client* computing is truly client/server computing, called "thin" because very little processing goes on at the client level and much processing takes place at the server. Thin clients access server applications via a web browser, the best example being access to an Exchange Server for e-mail. When you access an Exchange Server via OWA, you're accessing a database and using a browser to read it. You're not truly out on the Internet or even the intranet; you're using the browser software's limited skill for a different purpose. Terminal Services also employs thin-client technology. Relying

Part III

on the power of the server is what a thin client is all about. A thin-client/server system looks just like Figure 13.2, but instead of a GUI-based client, you hit the application with a browser.

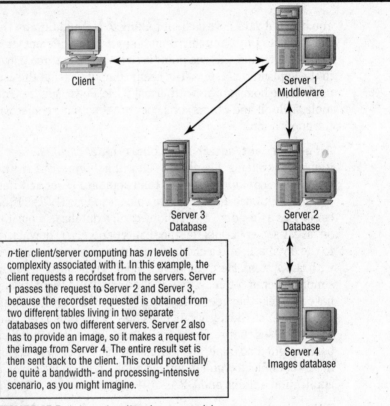

Client

Server 1
Middleware

Server 3
Database

Server 2
Database

Server 4
Images database

n-tier client/server computing has *n* levels of complexity associated with it. In this example, the client requests a recordset from the servers. Server 1 passes the request to Server 2 and Server 3, because the recordset requested is obtained from two different tables living in two separate databases on two different servers. Server 2 also has to provide an image, so it makes a request for the image from Server 4. The entire result set is then sent back to the client. This could potentially be quite a bandwidth- and processing-intensive scenario, as you might imagine.

FIGURE 13.3:   An *n*-tier client/server model

NOTE

You can purchase *thin-client computers*, pizza-box-sized computers that don't have a hard drive but do have RAM, a CPU, and the ability to boot the network via BootP (or, alternately, via PXE in the Windows 2000 world). These computers are touted as low cost, and users can't corrupt them by installing files that shouldn't be there.

Web-based Web-based applications also rely on a browser, but their functionality rises entirely from coding paradigms that center on the Web, things like ASP, HTML, XML, Java, and VBScript. When you use a browser to access an intranet application that talks to a database, you're using 3-tier client/ server (because your browser requests a row from a database and the web application on the server carries out the request and brings back the result set), but you're working in a strictly web-based environment.

APPLICATION CLIENTS

When dealing with client/server applications, there are two questions that the Windows 2000 network designers need to keep in mind. The first question is: What client are the users using? Is it a homegrown application that was developed using software like Delphi, Visual Basic, or PowerBuilder, or was it developed with something else? Homegrown client components can be scary from a design perspective because you don't know whether the client will continue to cooperate in the upgraded environment. If the programming staff in your client/server shop has developed some custom front ends, it's a really good idea to test the client accessing the databases on a Windows 2000 server to make sure things will continue normally. I'd also test the client on a Windows 2000 Professional workstation, just to make sure that it can play in that sandbox when the time arrives to upgrade the user machines.

With off-the-shelf client software, you have a little bit better opportunity to find out what sorts of compatibility issues you'll run into. The company that wrote the software should be able to give you a good idea of the client component's capability of working with Windows 2000, and I'd definitely check this out before the project went too far.

The second question is: Will the server software itself behave in the Windows 2000 environment? Some cases may be a slam dunk; others may be complicated. Suppose, for example, that you have some middleware that you need to use to talk to a Unix database. It works just fine on NT, but when you port it to Windows 2000 for testing, it breaks. What's the deal? This could be a long, arduous, tricky road. What about Microsoft SQL Server 7? If you're using it for your current databases, will you run into difficulties if you migrate the databases to a Windows 2000 box? Presumably you won't, but it's worth testing anyway.

BackOffice and Off-the-Shelf Server Applications

Some applications are designed to run in a heavy enterprise environment. All of the Microsoft BackOffice suite is, of course, built that way. But there are many other server software programs that reside on NT boxes and provide large user support for a specific function. It's important to identify these applications and then check with the vendor to make sure they're going to be able to keep up with the Windows 2000 environment. Test these applications before things get too far down the road just to make sure everything will work.

When working out your Windows 2000 design on paper, a big part of the activity that you'll perform is describing all of the different applications that are installed on servers throughout your enterprise. You need to determine the type and scope of each application, its use in the company, and whether it's going to cooperate with Windows 2000. You'll probably need to do some testing on the application in a Windows 2000 environment (something that might be much harder to set up than you first imagine) to make sure it's going to be okay with the change.

One last component of this kind of thinking has to do with parallel processing. It's practically—if not completely—impossible for you to have a small body of users hitting one production database that's in the Windows 2000 environment *and* have another body hitting a copy of the same database in NT. You're asking for trouble if you consider allowing parallel user processing and somehow consolidating the databases after they've gone home or even after you've finished a piecemeal upgrade. It's a lot safer to extensively test the deployment first and then plan a cutover date when the old application or database is locked out from users and the new one goes live.

Evaluating the Current Network Environment

Now it's time to do a finer analysis of your network. If you're not the internetworking and/or infrastructure keeper of the knowledge, that person's going to have to be available when you begin this undertaking. There are three separate issues you need to concern yourselves with: infrastructure, protocols, and hosts.

Evaluating Your Infrastructure

The infrastructure is the way that the various buildings your company occupies are wired, the health of the various switch closets, the backbone that connects the switch closets, and the switches, hubs, and routers that build the switching matrix of each building. When designing Windows 2000 for your company, select a building for examination. Take a walk through the building, getting a feel for where the wiring closets are and how they're wired. Are the patch panels old? What about the terminations into those patch panels? How about the connectivity between the switch closets? Is it fiber-optic or copper? Cat 3 or Cat 5? Are you running a totally switched environment—one where you have no hubs whatsoever in any part of the building—or do you still have some hubs you have to replace? Worse, are you still completely on hubs? How about your switch layout? Do you have one or two core switches that the closet switches hook into, or is everything running off of closet switches? Figure 13.4 shows three wiring closets, two of which are "user closets," where users connect from their office to the switches in the closet. Data travels the backbone to the core switch and then to the servers.

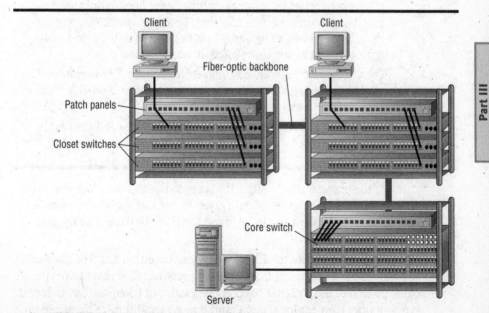

FIGURE 13.4:   A typical network infrastructure model

Older networks that started out as Cat 3 and have steadily gone through wiring upgrades to Cat 5 are the ones you need to worry the most about, in terms of assuring yourself that the network is healthy and happy. For a client computer to obtain satisfactory 100Base-T service to the desktop, the following is required:

- ▶ The connecting cable from the NIC to the computer has to be Cat 5.

- ▶ The wiring from the jack in the user's office to the patch panel has to be Cat 5.

- ▶ The patch cable from the patch panel to the switch has to be Cat 5.

CLOSET SWITCHES

Closet switches usually have a high number of ports. Users connect to the ports on the closet switches via a jumper cable that runs from the patch panel node corresponding to the user's wall plate to a port on the closet switch. The closet switches have one (or more) cables that connect to special ports on the patch panel. The patch panels connect to one another via Ethernet or fiber-optic cable. You can have redundant runs of either. The core switch has one (or more) connections going into the patch panel as well. Servers often hook to a port on the core switch for higher speed.

Cat 5 wiring throughout is required for 100Base-T or 1000Base-T (gigabit) speeds. Fiber-optic cable is a much better choice for backbone connections.

In gigabit backbone environments, servers can feasibly connect to the core switches via gigabit network cards.

All of the planets have to align. It's scary to think about older buildings that have a bizarre mixture of dark coax, in-use Cat 3, and some Cat 5. The whole wiring plant has to be up on Cat 5 for 100Base-T or Gigabit Ethernet.

You can get switches to talk to each other via either Cat 5 or fiber-optic cabling, but fiber-optic cabling is greatly preferred. You must have special cards in each of the switches to accept a fiber input (there are two different types of fiber connectors: type SC and type ST) and they're more expensive, but when the company you hire runs the fiber, they add extra pairs within the cable so that you have a fallback in the event that the pair you're on fails. That's good fault tolerance, and it's better than having a dark, spare Ethernet cable running through the ceiling. It's very plug and play because your fiber-optic installer will terminate the other fiber pairs in the fiber patch panel, and picking up the entire network is as easy as swinging the connectors from the dead patch panel terminator to the spare on both sides of the house. Very cool from a fault-tolerance perspective. If you have switches that support multiple fiber connections, you could even run a redundant link across the backbone and protect yourself from any downtime whatsoever (provided both cables don't fail at once).

Infrastructures can be complicated. You have to watch the connections at the patch panel terminators to make sure they're professionally installed. You want to run plenum Cat 5 through ceilings. Don't run the wire *parallel* to any lights or up chases with phone lines (crosstalk occurs in both cases), only across lights. You should *always* outsource your fiber-optic cable installations, and I recommend that you outsource *all* cable installations. Your cable plant is your lifeblood, so have an expert build it.

The switches you pick need to come from reputable vendors and should be periodically replaced with newer technology. Just like computers, your switch gear needs to be on a three-year replacement plan.

Why switches instead of hubs? Because hubs are dumb, passive devices that simply relay packets. They have no intelligence whatsoever. Switches have a CPU in them that manages the bandwidth, and they're a godsend for networks. They're an order of magnitude more expensive than hubs, but they're worth every penny. Generally, you price switches by the port cost. You add up your users, servers, printers, and other peripherals, and that's how many ports you need (called *port density*). You should buy enough switches to service your current needs as well as expansion. Just like servers, you don't want to go with clone switches; go with tier 1 vendors (3Com, Intel, Cisco, etc.).

Routers are an entire science unto themselves. Would you like chassis-based or stand-alone? Do you need to do wire-speed routing (on a layer 3 card in a switch chassis), or are you happy with standard 10Base-T throughput? What vendor should you use? What WAN protocols does the thing need to know? What LAN protocols should it pass? The list goes on and on. Are you a CCNA or CCIE? No? You might want to consider outsourcing your router purchase, configuration, and maintenance. Keep in mind that contractors offering router configuration services might not be much further ahead of the curve technically than you are, so shop around for somebody who has solid credentials.

While we're on the subject of infrastructure hardware, I recommend that you consider hardware-based firewalls. The Cisco PIX firewall is a great example and is in use all over the world. Wire-speed firewalls give you the comfort of firmware-based protection, knowing that you won't have a Dr. Watson or some other problem. Certainly, hardware breaks, but hardware firewalls are eminently more uncrackable and faster than software.

WARNING

Pay attention to your infrastructure (the cable plant, switches, routers, and patch panels), and it'll take care of you. Go bottom dollar, and you'll rue the day you put the cheap gear in production.

Evaluating Protocols

You will commonly deal with the following four major categories of protocols:

- ▶ LAN protocols (used on the network itself)
- ▶ WAN protocols (used by the routers and frame relay gear to get your packets to outlying destinations)
- ▶ Communication protocols (used by modems)
- ▶ Specialized protocols

By and large, you probably won't mess around too much with the WAN protocols. Routers convert most LAN protocols into packets that the WAN can understand, so you don't have many concerns there.

One thing you'll have to consider are networks with older protocols still hanging around. For example, suppose you had a Banyan VINES deployment at one time, and you've still got a couple of legacy VINES boxes being used by outlying employees. But you want to upgrade the router. Guess what? Either you will not be able to host the VINES protocol over the new router, or you'll have to pay some hefty cash to have support for VINES included. And that includes VINES TCP/IP, a proprietary TCP/IP implementation that works only with VINES and that routers still don't understand without add-on software. So you either stick with the old stodgy 10Base-T router, or you figure out a way to bag the VINES servers once and for all. It's a tough call that network designers have to make and develop a project plan for.

But what about LAN protocols? Now that you're in the thick of planning a Windows 2000 rollout, the best thing you can do is migrate toward a straight TCP/IP environment. Windows 2000 can deal with many legacy protocols, but they require drivers provided by the company requiring the protocol. VINES is one famous legacy example: Windows 2000 does *not* provide native support for VINES, but if VINES were to provide Windows 2000 support then you wouldn't have a problem. The implication isn't that Windows 2000 will only support a handful of protocols; it's rather that a handful of protocols are the ones that occupy the vast majority of the computing world. Exotic protocols require third-party support. You might be able to hook up with your vendor for protocols that are specific to legacy applications or peripherals. But if the application can also use TCP/IP (and most can), then why complicate things? Of course, some legacy applications have to stay around—some forever. That's life, but all in all, *now* is the time to jettison all unsupported protocols and go with a flat TCP/IP stack on your network.

It's up to you to ascertain which protocols are on the LAN side of the house and make plans to get rid of unsupported protocols. This may involve a server-to-server visit, just to find out what's on each computer and thus what's running on the LAN.

LAN Protocols

NetBEUI is still supported, but it is outdated. Sure, it was fast and required no configuration, but it wasn't routable.

IPX/SPX is also supported, for backward compatibility to legacy NetWare boxes. NetWare went straight TCP/IP a few years back, and they've never gone back to IPX. But there are *scads* of old NetWare 3.11 boxes still hanging around, running only IPX and with users needing to access them. You'll use IPX/SPX in a legacy NetWare environment, but only long enough to convert the NetWare boxes to TCP/IP (or to Windows 2000). Windows 2000 supports the IPX/SPX protocol with the Microsoft implementation of IPX/SPX, a protocol called NWLink.

An AppleTalk network integration is included for continued support of Macintosh clients. Both Intel-based and Apple clients can share files and printers using this feature.

Communication Protocols

The *Point-to-Point Tunneling Protocol (PPTP)* is supported in Windows 2000. Its single purpose is to assist with the nailing up of virtual

Part III

private networks (VPNs). PPTP has been around the Microsoft camp for several years now and works well.

A second VPN protocol, newer than PPTP, is the *Layer 2 Tunneling Protocol (L2TP)*. It too is used for VPNs, but L2TP does not rely on vendor-specific encryption technologies. Microsoft expects the L2TP protocol to wind up being the industry VPN standard.

The *RADIUS* protocol is predominantly used for dial-up users accessing a third-party RAS server device, but ISPs also use it for tunneled network users. All three protocols—PPTP, L2TP, and RADIUS—use the tunneling method. What this means is that the user's packets are buried deep in TCP/IP packets as they fly along the Internet. At the place where they knock on the door of the network, they are authenticated and unbundled and the data is read.

Specialized Protocols

Simple Network Management Protocol (SNMP) is still supported in Windows 2000. With this protocol, your network-monitoring software such as HP OpenView can obtain information from network gear and other equipment that has the ability to send SNMP traps.

The Hewlett-Packard DLC protocol is also included for backward compatibility with DLC connections to shared printers.

There are other specialized protocols such as the exotic infrared-device protocols IrDA-FIR and IrDA-SIR, but for the most part, the protocols in this section are the ones you'll be using most often.

Evaluating Hosts

The word "hosts" is a TCP/IP word. Whenever anyone says the word "host," you generally think of "computer." Technically, anything with an IP address is a host. However, *host* most often refers to a node (server, workstation, printer, etc.) on the network. That's why the old Unix file that resolves fully qualified domain names (FQDNs) to IP addresses is called hosts; it lists the hosts on your network. Although the hosts file was great, it's antiquated.

You need to assess the kinds of hosts you have on the network. This is categorically done by assessing what kinds of *operating systems* are loaded on your computers.

Linux is growing steadily in popularity. Do you have Linux hosts operating in your environment? If you do, then they're probably going to make

LPR print calls to your shared NT printers. They'll also probably mount NFS volumes (Unix's way of sharing out files for access by others), and you'll find that you can map to these NFS volumes and grab data—provided they're set up accordingly. Linux hosts that use StarOffice and whose users don't have a regular Windows 9*x* or NT box with which to run Office will probably run into file-sharing issues with others on the network that need to see their documents.

Do you have Macintosh hosts? These users have very unique requirements, but Windows 2000 has provided accessibility (just as Windows NT did) so that your Mac users can access files and printers just like your Windows users do.

Old-time mainframers call the mainframe itself "the host." A mainframe is considered a host, just like any other computer on the network. How do your users currently connect to the mainframe? If they're using some kind of 3270 or 5250 emulation software, be sure you check to make sure it's going to live on in the Windows 2000 world. Since everything's done through TCP/IP these days, the issue isn't nearly as complicated as it sounds. It's just a matter of making sure the GUI works in the Windows 2000 world like it did in the NT or 9*x* world.

What about other hosts that have proprietary protocols associated with them, such as the VINES hosts talked about earlier? Unless they can speak native, nonproprietary TCP/IP, the chances are the company that developed them will have to write software that makes them compatible with Windows 2000. And that's always dicey, because you really don't want other exotic protocols loaded on your systems—you want native TCP/IP and only TCP/IP. The astute Windows 2000 designer would take this opportunity to find replacements for those old software components that aren't dancing at the same disco as Windows 2000.

THE NEW ADMINISTRATOR'S POSITION

You've been hired by a small startup company to administer their network. The company is a small software-development company that's very high-tech. You're expecting to see really great infrastructure when you arrive at your first day on the job, but you're disappointed to find cables sticking out of the RJ-45 connectors, poorly terminated patch panels, old-fashioned hubs, and a variety of other problems throughout the office. The majority of the wiring is Cat 3, with Cat 5 between the two switch closets.

CONTINUED →

You're told on your first day's orientation that the company would like to migrate as quickly as possible to Windows 2000. You wonder how they're getting any computing done at all on their seven Windows NT 4 servers, based upon the incredibly poor infrastructure!

You meet with your boss, the CFO, and explain that the wiring plant is in incredibly decrepit shape. You want to replace all of the Cat 3 wiring with Cat 5. Next you want to add a fiber-optic run on the backbone but keep the existing Cat 5 for backup purposes. You want to get rid of the hubs and purchase enough switches for all 100 users on the net, about five switches. (No core switches are needed.) This will bring the network up to 100Base-T or 1000Base-T capability. Then, and only then, do you want to go forward with the Windows 2000 rollout, and that will only happen after you've assessed the servers, the network's protocols, and all of the other pertinent discovery items. You tell the CFO the cost of the cable plant rewire is about $18,000, and the switches will cost around $10,000. Project total costs will be around $28,000–30,000 and will take about two weeks to complete. You can install the switches, but you'll outsource the wiring updates.

Assessing Network Services

The purpose of this section is to talk about services consisting of either software or hardware that comes to the aid of the network in order to formulate a stronger, better-functioning system. Let's discuss some of the various network services categories.

Network Monitoring

Network-monitoring services typically consist of network-monitoring software coupled with a computer that's designated to handle only the influx of SNMP and remote network monitoring (RMON) traffic from the LAN. The combination of the network-monitoring software and hardware is called a *network management system (NMS)*. Some companies have many NMS computers housed in one area, strictly for the purpose of monitoring their huge networks. Sound pretty dull? Oh yeah, like watching paint dry. Is it necessary? You bet it is. Many NMS computers in one location is called a *network operations center (NOC)*.

Network devices report their status to the NMS via the SNMP protocol. Management information bases (MIBs) loaded on the NMS know how to prepare and present the freshly reported data. The most common NMS software around the world is HP OpenView or CA Unicenter TNG, though there are others.

Metrics Monitoring

The concept of metrics focuses on determining how much uptime the servers have had the luxury of experiencing. There are two methods of determining uptime, each at opposite ends of the scale. You could opt to manually keep track of every time a server went down, how long it was down for, and what the cause of the outage was. It would be easy to keep track of this kind of thing in a spreadsheet. Then, at the end of the month, you could go through and tally up the amount of time a server was down in, say, minutes and then calculate the percentage of that downtime over the whole month. For example, suppose you had a server that went down for 15 minutes in the month of April. Since there are 30 days in April and 1,440 minutes per day, there were 43,200 minutes in that month. Divide 43200 by 15, and you come up with 0.00035. Now multiply by 100, and you get the downtime as a percent: 0.035. Subtract this number from 100 and you get 99.965 percent uptime, quite remarkable for a server!

NOTE
Industry standards vary, but there are two basic delimiters that you'll hear when people talk about uptime statistics: *4-nines* means 99.99% uptime, and *5-nines* means 99.999% uptime. You probably won't be able to achieve 5-nines uptime (though phone companies do) and probably not even 4-nines. More than likely, you'll be in the 99.8% to 99.9% range. At 99.99% uptime, you have 53 minutes of downtime *per year*. Think about that number for a minute, and then decide whether you can realistically keep servers up for that kind of time. Purchasing high-quality equipment that's on the Microsoft hardware compatibility list (HCL) and keeping only one application on a server are good ways to increase uptime, but it's still difficult to hit even 3-nines or better.

The number of outages that occur on a specific server can be quite revealing information as well. If you know, for example, that a server was down four times in one month, you might find out that an application had been recently loaded on the server and that this was the cause for all the outages. What you'd do to correct that problem is another story, but at least you think you have a handle on what's causing all the outages.

A more elegant solution is that of software that handles metrics monitoring. NetIQ, BMC Patrol, and ManageX are all designed to give you excellent granularity in terms of watching critical servers and services, handling problems with them, and alerting you of the issues.

TCP/IP Services

TCP/IP services include DHCP, WINS, LDAP, and DNS. The most interesting of these are DHCP and DNS. In legacy environments where DNS servers are already running and handling things nicely, you might have a really hard time convincing people that you think DNS should move to Windows 2000. However, Windows 2000 DNS does have some nice features, which are discussed later in this book.

Lucent Technologies offers a replacement DNS/DHCP/WINS application called QIP, which lives on servers and takes the place of regular NT services. It shows the kind of thought that people have put into TCP/IP services.

Some switch and router gear can host TCP/IP services. Again, it's not feasible for switches to do your DNS work because you need Windows 2000 to do it for you.

Security Monitoring

Security monitoring, in my mind, has to do with the alerting that goes on with proxy and firewall servers. Recently, for example, there was a rash of attacks on web servers. These attacks are called *SYN attacks* (short for synchronization) and essentially amount to a request that a host makes for connection to another host (typically a server). If the hacker can duplicate enough bogus SYN requests and barrage the server with them, the server is so busy acknowledging SYNs that it can't do any other work. A firewall product would be expected to alert the administrator that some sort of attack was transpiring. Moreover, good firewall software should have some method of ascertaining when it's being hit by a SYN attack and dismantle the attack before it craters the network.

Another famous type of attack, one that had basically the same effect on servers a few years ago, was the ICMP (or ping) attack. Here you simply ping the host over and over again, hundreds of thousands of times. The poor computer is so busy answering pings that it cannot do anything else. Very clever, very easy, and terribly disruptive. The same kinds of security-checking features apply with the ICMP attacks as with SYN attacks. The firewall should be able to monitor for ICMP attacks and then proactively shut them down. Some companies don't respond to a ping because of the potential for this kind of attack. Their ICMP-defense software simply keeps anyone from being able to ping the box in the first place.

Fault-Tolerance Monitoring

When you install tools like HP's TopTools or Compaq's equivalent, Insight Manager, one of the things you do is monitor the fault-tolerant gear that's installed in the server. This is fault-tolerance monitoring. For example, HP's brand of RAID array adapters, NetRAID, responds to faults by alerting the TopTools agents if there is a problem.

SNMP could be said to be acting in a fault-tolerance monitoring capacity when it sends out a trap alerting the administrators that a redundant link (a special port on switches that allows you to set up a second, fallback link into them) has gone down. When this happens, of course, the switch represents a single point of failure (SPOF) and needs to be addressed quickly.

Web Monitoring

A new kind of monitoring activity that administrators have to be cognizant of is monitoring the company's websites, both internal and external. With websites, you're interested in a variety of things. You'd like to know how many people hit the site on a daily basis and where they "clicked through" to. You want a feel for the performance of your pages—how fast they load and how accurate they are, in terms of whether they generate script errors and so forth. You also would like to capture any visitor information that you can get. Most importantly, you need to keep the sites from being hacked and changed in some ways.

Some of the things that hackers do may sound like they're pretty funny. As a not-so-good website developer, I can tell you that there's a heck of a lot of work that goes into developing even a cheesy little site, and it's devastating to see somebody else tank all of your hard work.

ASSESSING THE TCP/IP INFRASTRUCTURE

Assessing the TCP/IP infrastructure is probably one of the simpler tasks that you'll be involved with in your Windows 2000 network design. You need to know where critical servers are and what their names and

IP addresses are. You need to know the network IDs and subnet masks in use on the network. You need to know what the router, firewall, and proxy server IP addresses are.

Here are the kinds of things you'll be watching out for:

▶ Critical servers are the DNS, DHCP, and WINS servers in the environment. Find out these servers' names (both NetBIOS and FQDN) and IP addresses and where they're located. While you're locating this information, also identify the server scopes: where they are, what they're composed of, and the various global or scope settings that are applied.

▶ Identify all of the network IDs. Also find out what subnet masks are in use throughout the various parts of your network.

▶ Obtain all of the critical connector server information such as router addresses (typically the network ID with a .1 address—e.g., 10.1.1.1). You'll also want to know the NetBIOS and FQDN names and the IP addresses of the various proxy servers and firewalls on the network.

▶ Obtain the IP addresses of the printers and the locations of their LPR, DLC, or HP ports.

▶ List the IP addresses and NetBIOS and FQDN names of the servers.

▶ If a BootP server is in use for thin-client workstations that have no hard drive and use BootP to boot off of the network, you need to identify the server names and IP addresses.

▶ Identify any RAS servers, their names, and IP addresses. While identifying these boxes, it'd be a good idea to jot down the phone numbers that are associated with the servers.

ASSESSING CURRENT HARDWARE

Depending on the size of your network (and whether or not you have Systems Management Server installed), you might have to spend several weeks getting information about the hardware on your network. You need to diagram several different categories of hardware in order to have a more complete understanding. In larger installations, a complete view might be impossible, but it's at least possible to ascertain what servers are in the domain. Once you know that, the very least that you should do is find out what hardware the servers have.

The point of this exercise is to find weak spots on the network that need to be addressed before you go forward with the design and deployment. In terms of budgets, if you're going to ask for the money for the upgrade, also ask for the hardware upgrade dollars you're going to need to support this new NOS.

When assessing your current hardware and future hardware needs, here are some areas to concentrate on:

Servers are the most critical part. Figure out which servers are on the network. Identify the brand; write down how much RAM is in each, how many CPUs and their speed, the hard disks and their size and remaining space, and whether they have FAT or NTFS partitions. Note any special peripheral equipment on the box, such as hardware RAID controllers, DAT or DLT tape drives, fax cards, and so forth. Determine whether your servers fit the Windows 2000 hardware guidelines. It might be a good idea to arrange the servers by function, i.e., file, print, application, database, and web.

Identify networked printers by type, manufacturer, and model. If you can obtain the printer's duty cycle (the number of pages it is rated for monthly) that's a great piece of information to have on hand. If you know roughly how many pages are printed in a day and you know the printer's duty cycle, you can very quickly tell whether a printer is overworked and ready for replacement. You should also jot down the amount of RAM the printer has, the driver it's using, the amount and type (laser or ink) of any cartridges, whether it's connected by an internal card or an external network box, and the card type (JetDirect, for instance). From the print server, you should also get the IP address and port that the printer is using. Don't forget specialized printers such as plotters.

Ascertain the type of switches and hubs you have on the network. You're interested in the port density of each switch, the types of ports (fiber, Ethernet, etc.), the types of uplink cards, the brand name, model number, firmware revision level, and how you get into the switch or hub's user interface to maintain it (telnet, web, etc.). Hubs connected to hubs connected to hubs should make you sit down and do a complete infrastructure redesign, *then* go into the Windows 2000 design.

Document your routers.　It is good to know the router's WAN connectivity, overall throughput speed, model number, and manufacturer. The type of routing protocol it's using would be good information to jot down as well. For years, Cisco used a proprietary routing protocol that didn't work well with the other router vendors like 3Com. This kind of routing protocol information may come in handy at router update time or in the event you decide to do some Windows 2000 routing.

Revisit your tape backup systems.　Windows 2000 is a much bigger NOS than NT and requires much bigger tape-backup horsepower. Make sure your current backup strategy can handle it. DLT is practically the only way to go for enterprise backups these days, and the Windows 2000 deployment presents an excellent opportunity for you to make sure backups are adequate for the new network paradigm.

Evaluate your RAS servers.　Stand-alone devices that provide telecommuting interfaces into your network—such as those made by Shiva, US Robotics, and 3Com—are also going to come into play on the new Windows 2000 network. Write down the model and manufacturer of the RAS server. If the server is using a database to validate telecommuting users, state so; if it's using NT authentication software, then note that. You need to know how many ports are on the server, what kinds of modems it is using, the relevant firmware revisions to the box, and the telephone numbers (and if they're hooked to a hunt group), including toll-free numbers.

List miscellaneous devices.　There are all kinds of devices that come to mind. For instance, manufacturing lines, sometimes called *packout lines*, often have specialized computers on them that handle the flow of the line. Test gear, imaging equipment, network scanners, and other exotic peripherals should be listed, along with their manufacturer, model, and a description of what they do.

IDENTIFYING EXISTING AND PLANNED UPGRADES AND ROLLOUTS

It's possible that you work for such a large operation you can't possibly know all the things that are going on from an IT perspective. And yet, Windows 2000 is going to mandate that you somehow get a handle on at least the major undertakings. For example, suppose that you have a development group that's planning to go forward with a huge computer telephony integration (CTI) application sometime in the next few months. They've spent several weeks looking for the ideal product/vendor mix that will provide the application zest and business fit that they're looking for. Now all of a sudden, you're going to saunter in and apply a NOS that their system may not work with. In the best case, you'll be guilty of bad timing. In the worst case, if you try this with a business unit that has a high profile, you could see your upgrade project killed!

It is crucial that you identify any existing or planned upgrades or rollouts that might be affected by your Windows 2000 plans. Let's identify the difference between an upgrade and a rollout:

Upgrade   An *upgrade* is something that happens to an already extant system or device—an improvement over a *like* existing system. If you have 3Com switches in your closets and the network folks are going to go through and apply the latest rev of firmware, that's an upgrade. If your database people are on Oracle 8 and they're changing to Oracle 11, that's an upgrade. An HP 5SI network printer that's being replaced by an HP 8000 is an upgrade.

Rollout   Implementing a new hardware device, a new way of doing a business task, or a new software application is a *rollout*. Suppose that for years your parts department simply wrote down the parts they worked with on a form. The forms were entered into a spreadsheet that somebody kept track of on a PC. But when too many people needed to see the results of that spreadsheet and there came to be too many parts people, a client/server system was needed. So developers were brought in and the system was developed (VB over SQL Server, of course). When the developers were ready to go live with the new system, they were said to be in *rollout stage*.

Whenever your company moves ahead with its network, you can categorize the progress as either an upgrade or a rollout. The biggest difference is, if the structure existed before, it's an upgrade. If this is a new product, it's a rollout.

Perhaps a bigger issue than identifying upgrade vs. rollout is dealing with the network change. If your company has already told you that it plans on making a specific change to the network, like upgrading your DNS servers to Windows 2000, then it's something you should be aware of and you can plan for. The harder part is planning for future upgrades and rollouts. It's not likely that you can predict the future; otherwise you would be working as a psychic instead of in the computer field. However, when designing your network, keep in mind how aggressive the company has been historically in upgrading and expanding the network. This will give you a good indication of what to expect in the future. Past results do not guarantee future performance, but past results do give you valuable clues.

ANALYZING THE TECHNICAL SUPPORT STRUCTURE

After you've analyzed the equipment and code, it's time to find out what people and procedures your company uses to maintain all that. Who is going to support all of this equipment and provide a place for developers to display their wares?

You must ask yourself, as you prepare your Windows 2000 upgrade plans, what kind of technical support is in place for the administrators who are going to have to own the system, and for the users who are going to use it? These are two separate technical support domains and require two different assessments and answers.

Network Manager Support

What technical support do you and your deployment managers require for the Windows 2000 rollout? Is today's technical support environment adequate? In other words, how much support do you think you'll need as you go forward with the rollout and begin to get people used to the new system? You're undoubtedly going to encounter problems—how ready for those problems are you? How much technical support from Microsoft can you afford? Will you have contractors helping you and will they agree to provide support for a limited time after deployment? If you're bringing Windows 2000 into an environment that includes third-party applications, will the vendor support the application on Windows 2000? How much support can you expect? This may be the time to examine the possibility of replacing applications that you're not happy with and that you know won't work in the Window 2000 arena.

The answers to the questions in the preceding paragraph may or may not be easy to find. This is where it's important for you to do some research. Again, it's hard to predict the future, but past clues can play a large role in planning ahead. As an example, if your company traditionally requires a great deal of outside support, either from Microsoft or from other consultants, the chances are you will continue to do so. One solution would be to implement a new training regimen to go along with your upgrade.

End-User Support

The second kind of technical support is the structure that your users expect. Do you have help-desk personnel in place, and if so, are they aware of the changes that are coming their way? Chances are good that if you deploy Windows 2000 correctly, the users won't notice the change on the servers, but they'll obviously notice Windows 2000 Professional. That's what communicating the changes and training are all about—putting your users on a knowledge level where they can use the network the way they used it before the rollout.

Considering that end users (as opposed to network personnel) constitute the majority of your employees, this could be a problem area. Many users will feel uncomfortable knowing that you are upgrading the network, whether it affects them much or not. There are a couple of keys to making the end users feel more relaxed when it comes to upgrading their network. First of all, conduct meetings to explain (in general terms) what is happening and provide a forum to answer all of their questions. If they need training to make their new network experience easier, then provide sessions for that as well. Most importantly, make sure your help-desk people are trained about potential new issues and are sensitive to the end users' concerns.

ANALYZING THE CURRENT NETWORK MANAGEMENT

Finally, you need to figure out how the network is being managed today and how the Windows 2000 change is anticipated to affect the network managers.

Depending on the size of your network, you'll find that network managers fall into several different categories. It's important to identify the various layers of network management that are involved at your location, who manages what, and the depth of each person's knowledge when it comes to Windows networks and TCP/IP. A training chart is called for, one that has "Current" and "Windows 2000" as column headers. Write the network manager's name, the type of management he or she is responsible for, and the level of knowledge currently possessed. Then you can write in the Windows 2000 column how much training is required for this person and how much involvement will probably happen on the new network. Let's pinpoint some of the kinds of network management tasks that various people might be performing:

Backup Managers   These people are responsible only for the backup of the network. It's possible that these are Unix people who happen to also back up the NT network, a very feasible paradigm.

Internetwork (Data-Comm) Managers   These people are responsible for the routers and WAN connections, though they may not be responsible for the infrastructure. There may be a logical separation of the two camps (internetwork and infrastructure).

Infrastructure Managers   These people manage the overall infrastructure of the network. They handle the cable plant, the wiring closets, the patch panels, and the hubs and switches.

Applications Managers   Someone is responsible for the enterprise applications on the network. Often they have one or, at most, two separate applications that they manage. There might be several different applications managers. A really great example of an application that requires specialized management is an IVR system. These people might not know much at all about how Windows NT functions, let alone Windows 2000, and you can rest assured that they probably don't know much about servers. But the interconnection between the IVR software and telephony—now that's something they're keenly aware of.

Print Managers In larger companies, believe it or not, there are people who do nothing but handle print queues all day long. If you've ever hassled with JetAdmin software over a new printer on the network, you'll know how challenging this job can be.

Database Administrators (DBAs) DBAs set up tables, create namespaces, write stored procedures, perform business analysis on new database systems, and so forth. They're usually very skilled in terms of the database software and they can be wonderful resources for you. Generally they have a good understanding of enterprise concepts.

NOS Managers Some companies have people who strictly handle the setting up of servers and the installing of the NOS. These people would not be terribly application-aware, but chances are they would be highly aware of the changes coming their way in Windows 2000.

E-mail Managers E-mail systems can grow to be so large and ponderous that dedicated administrators are required. This part of network management would then be relegated to the e-mail managers.

Web Managers For both Internet and intranet sites, dedicated web administrators are sometimes required.

Telephony Systems Managers Telephony systems managers are the rare breed of individual who are responsible for the telephony systems and associated interfaces into the corporate network. Generally, telephony people either have an incredibly up-to-date knowledge of Windows NT, or they don't know a thing about it. Windows NT 4 was highly CTI-aware, and Windows 2000 is even more so.

Security Managers These folks create and manage user accounts, groups, NTFS permissions, mainframe logons, Internet usage accounts, and so forth.

Software Management In addition to the activities that some of the previously listed human managers perform, you may have software management involved in your network as well. HP OpenView, CA Unicenter, and other management software products can help perform some of the tasks that human managers might be involved in. Systems that help manage the enterprise in this way are called *enterprise management systems (EMS)*. EMS installations are complicated, typically requiring a dedicated person or two in order to manage them.

It's perfectly reasonable, especially on smaller networks, for one person to occupy many roles. But on larger networks, you might have a "cast of thousands" who all work together for the good of the corporate network. It's possible that one entity might not even know that another exists. Nevertheless, all of these various management components need to know and be aware of the ramifications of a Windows 2000 network that's barreling their way.

SUMMARY

This chapter's goal was to discuss all the ramifications of the infrastructure design on the existing and planned technical *environment*—with emphasis on *technical* environment. What you're really being asked to do here is to take a huge overall look at the network and make determinations about its present and its future. How will the Windows 2000 rollout be affected by the various components, and how will the components be affected by the rollout? A Windows 2000 designer must look at many things when making these kinds of determinations.

This chapter started out by looking at the enterprise applications on the network. You need to discern the difference between an enterprise application and a workgroup application. While both applications are important, the enterprise application obviously has more weight in decisions relative to a Windows 2000 rollout. There are different types of applications as well: client/server, web, and back-office applications are three of the major delineations that can be made.

Next, we discussed the evaluation of the current network environment. This topic includes describing the infrastructure, the protocols in use (Windows 2000–supported protocols are largely unchanged from Windows NT 4, with the exception of the addition of VPN protocols), and hosts. Hosts are nothing more than computers. In computerese, the word "hosts" is a TCP/IP term for any node on the network with an IP address.

We talked about assessing network services, identifying several that need to be looked at when considering a Windows 2000 rollout. Among them were network monitoring, metrics monitoring, various TCP/IP services such as DHCP and DNS, security monitoring, fault-tolerance monitoring, and web monitoring. All are important to the health and well-being of the network.

We then discussed the assessment of the current TCP/IP infrastructure. There are many details to examine here, chief of which is the placement of DNS. Unix-based DNS is no longer the best option in a Windows 2000 world. Some shops have brought in third-party DHCP managers that live on Windows NT servers—this too needs to be examined. The overall network ID, subnet mask, and VLAN characteristics are highly important to the design of the new network.

We also talked about assessing current network hardware: servers, printers, internetworking gear, infrastructure gear, specialized hardware, and RAS servers. You need to identify existing and planned rollouts and upgrades.

We talked about the technical support structure and its two facets: the user component and the network manager component. By far, the network managers will need the most technical support as you go forward with your rollout, but users need to also be aware of the many issues surrounding the rollout.

Finally, we discussed the very relevant topic of how your network is being managed today. Depending on the size of the network, it's possible that you have a wide variety of manager types, and each network administration function may be performed by separate people, by one person, or by a group.

WHAT'S NEXT

Now that you have the basic concepts of network design, the next chapter begins to explain the options available to you for networking your home or a small office.

Part III

Chapter 14
HOME NETWORKING TECHNOLOGIES

O ver the years, there have been many types of networks. Some have come into wide popularity and then gone away more or less completely, replaced by newer and better approaches. Today, there are four common approaches to home networking: traditional Ethernet cables, phoneline networking, powerline networking, and wireless networking. In this chapter, you will learn about phoneline, powerline, and wireless networks (Ethernet networks are discussed in Chapter 3) and how to select the best home networking technology for your situation. Before you decide which type of home network technology is best for you, you should understand how each type of network works.

Part III

Adapted from *Mastering Home Networking*
by Mark Henricks
ISBN 0-7821-2630-8   544 pages $29.99

YOUR HOME NETWORKING OPTIONS

Home networking is still at a relatively early stage in its evolution compared to technologies such as, say, floppy disks. Over many years, floppies have evolved from 8-inch flexible envelopes created by IBM and capable of holding only 100KB of data to today's standard 3.5-inch 1.44MB diskettes.

The old days of floppies are similar to where we find ourselves in home networking. There are a number of competing approaches to networking, including standard Ethernet cable networking, home phoneline networking, powerline networking, and wireless networking. Each offers its own special benefits and limitations. Some, for instance, allow you to set up your network without installing any new wires. Others offer better performance, more mobility, lower cost, or other advantages. Unfortunately, each of them suffers incompatibility problems with the others—you can't freely mix and match different types of networks without encountering problems, some of them unmanageable.

Unlike, say, the choice between PC or Macintosh, the choice of a network type is not based primarily on personal preference. Each variant has significant differences in performance, convenience, and special features compared to the rest. Once you understand how you'll use the network and your requirements for installation, cost, and other concerns, you should be able to make a definitive choice among these technologies.

None of this is impossible to sort out. You simply have to understand the pluses and minuses of the various types of home networks. Then you have to decide what you want your network to do. After that, it's simply a matter of matching needs to capabilities.

UNDERSTANDING PHONELINE NETWORKS

Phoneline networking uses the existing wiring of your home phone system to connect your computers into a network. For that reason, it's known as one of the "no new wires" network technologies along with powerline and wireless.

Most phoneline networks are based on technology developed by Tut Systems. Tut, which is based in Pleasant Hill, California, doesn't sell its products directly to consumers. Instead, it sells components to other companies that use them to create products for sale down at your local computer store. Tut came out with its first phoneline network offering in 1992. The HomeRun technology Tut introduced in 1997 has proven very popular with many phoneline networking consumer product vendors.

NOTE

It's hard to overstate the value of the fact that phoneline networking uses already available wiring. It's estimated that in the United States alone, some $200 billion has been invested in the last 25 years in installing copper phone wiring to cover the so-called "last mile"—the distance between homes and the telephone company switching stations known as central offices.

Although networking using home phone lines is a relatively new idea, the technology has come a long way in a short time. The Home Phoneline Networking Alliance (HomePNA) is a group of large computer companies, like Intel and Compaq, that has pushed to establish standards in an effort to make home networking easy and available to almost everyone. This has helped push phoneline networking into the public's eye and has made a fairly broad array of equipment readily available through retail channels.

The distinguishing feature of phoneline networks is that they don't require any new wiring other than a cord running from the computer's NIC to the telephone jack. Nor do they need hubs or other external hardware. This makes them exceptionally easy and convenient, as well as inexpensive, to install. Yet they let you do all the essential network tasks, including sharing Internet connections, files, and peripherals; they also let you play online games with other networked computers.

THE HOME PHONELINE NETWORKING ALLIANCE

The Home Phoneline Networking Alliance is a nonprofit association of companies working together to help ensure adoption of a single, unified phoneline networking industry standard and rapidly bring to market a range of interoperable home networking solutions. It was founded in June 1998 by 3Com, AMD, AT&T Wireless, Compaq, Conexant, Epigram, Hewlett-Packard Co., IBM, Intel, Lucent Technologies, and Tut Systems. More than 70 companies of various

CONTINUED ➡

Part III

types (networking, telecommunications, hardware, software, and consumer electronics) have since joined the alliance. Rapid strides have been made to refine, improve, and standardize the technology. A move to introduce home networking products based on HomePNA has also been made. For more information, visit www.homepna.org.

Phoneline network performance lags behind Ethernet somewhat, however. Early products on the market ran at approximately 1Mbps, about 10 percent of the performance of a regular Ethernet network. Phoneline networks aren't all that slow, however, when you consider that 1Mbps is almost 20 times as fast as a 56K modem. And the technology is constantly improving.

How Phoneline Networks Work

Phoneline networks work by piggybacking a network signal over the same wiring used for your home's telephone system. You can still use your phone system for telephone calls, fax transmissions, and modem connections, even while your computers are communicating over the same wires. That's because the phoneline network cards use a high-frequency signal that telephones can't detect (as shown in Figure 14.1), so the signal doesn't interfere with your phone's or fax's normal operation.

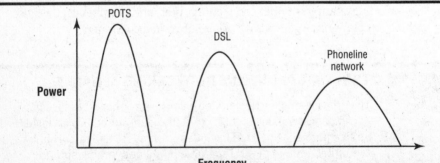

FIGURE 14.1:   Phoneline networks, Digital Subscriber Lines (DSL), and Plain Old Telephone Service (POTS) can share the same lines because each uses a different set of frequencies.

Specifically, the Plain Old Telephone Service (POTS) uses the frequencies from 20Hz to 3.4KHz. Digital Subscriber Line (DSL) high-speed data service occupies from 2.5KHz to 1.1MHz (million hertz). Phoneline network takes the highest road of all, working above 2.4MHz.

Unlike Ethernet networks, which use a variety of connectors, phoneline networks use regular telephone cabling. The technology developed by Tut is what makes high-speed data transfer work over what are otherwise non-data-grade copper wires.

Some new PCs are sold with built-in phoneline networking capability. If you have an older PC, or a new one without built-in phoneline networking, you need to install a phoneline network interface card in each PC you want to connect. Some phoneline network devices plug into a parallel port or USB port, so you don't have to open up the PC case. Otherwise, you install the phoneline card just like an Ethernet card, modem, or other expansion card. After creating your network interface connection on each PC, you plug each one into a nearby telephone jack and install the software.

NOTE

Phoneline networks access the media using CSMA/CD, just like the Ethernet method. In fact, phoneline networks can be considered basically Ethernet networks running over telephone wires, with the main difference being slower data transfer rates. This is significant, in that it allows phoneline networks to use much of the vast quantity of Ethernet-compatible software and hardware on the market.

Phoneline networks use the existing wiring of your home phone system to connect your computers into a network. Phoneline networks are exceptionally quick and easy to install and offer reasonably good performance. They are compatible with much Ethernet technology as well. By the time you read this, phoneline networks that provide speeds up to 100Mbps, matching regular Ethernet, will be available.

UNDERSTANDING POWERLINE NETWORKS

Like phoneline networks, powerline networks work by piggybacking a network signal over your home's existing wiring. In this case, however, the signal travels over the electrical power lines.

How Powerline Networks Work

People have known how to transfer data over electrical power lines for more than 20 years. The technology has been used for a number of things, including setting up home automation systems. But powerline networking hasn't been widely adopted for computer networking because, until recently, it has been too expensive, slow, and unreliable.

A number of vendors offer various types of powerline networking for the home. They include the following:

X-10   A 20-year-old technology initially developed for simple purposes, such as turning on lights and controlling home appliances. It's very slow compared to newer approaches.

Intellon CEBus   A much faster powerline network than X-10, reaching up to 10Mbps transfer rates in tests.

Echelon LonWorks   A control network designed to work with a computer network such as Ethernet or phoneline. It is used for networking lights, security systems, sprinkler systems, and other home appliances.

Powerlines use a scheme similar to phoneline networks to transmit data over electrical lines without disrupting—or being disrupted by—the ongoing use of the lines for transmitting power. Basically, the powerline network transmits over higher frequencies than those that are used for power transmission (see Figure 14.2).

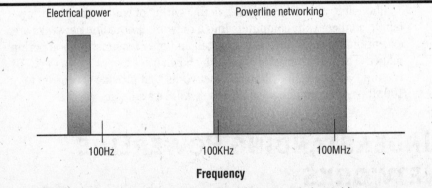

FIGURE 14.2:   Powerline networks share data transmissions with power transmissions by using a different set of frequencies.

Except for the fact that they run on power lines rather than phone or data transmission cables, powerline networks work much like other networks. Users can share files and printers, send e-mail, play games, and share high-speed Internet connections. Unlike most Ethernet networks, they don't require hubs. And some powerline networks don't even require the installation of network interface cards. They simply attach to the computer through a parallel port, then plug into a wall power outlet to hook to the network. And, they're designed to work with Windows 95/98 networking. So powerline networks are much the same as other networks, on the surface at least.

When it comes to performance, however, it's a different story. Although some powerline networking equipment vendors have reached Ethernet-like speeds in tests, in the real world, data transfer rates of 350Kbps or so are more typical. These speeds may be adequate for many home networkers, but they're certainly far less than what is offered by some of the other technologies.

Powerline networks have been around for years, but they are undergoing a renaissance of interest due to higher speeds and lower costs offered by new refinements.

UNDERSTANDING WIRELESS NETWORKS

Wireless networks are the ultimate no-new-wires approach—they don't require any wires at all. Using radio frequencies to connect computers rather than wires, they allow computers on the network to be almost anywhere.

How Wireless Networks Work

Modern wireless networks started at the same time and place as Ethernet—at the University of Hawaii as ALOHA Net. This wireless radio network was designed to tie together computers at seven campuses on four islands. Ethernet migrated to a wired environment, but ham radio operators, often using homemade black boxes called terminal node controllers, experimented with ways to turn their home personal computers into nodes on wireless wide area networks.

Wireless networking got a big boost in 1985, when the Federal Communications Commission (FCC) began allowing public use of the Industrial, Scientific, and Medical band of the radio spectrum. This bit of spectrum sits just above the area used by cellular phones, from 902MHz to 5.85GHz. One of the good things about this move was that it allowed networkers to send radio transmissions in this band without getting a license from the FCC.

One of the first results of the frequency allocation was the creation of wireless wide area networks. Companies such as Ardis and RAM Mobile Data set up wireless networks that in some cases spanned the entire country. Then they began selling the ability to wirelessly communicate between PCs, printers, and other devices. Customers were mostly businesses because of the high cost of the services. But it did get people aware of the advantages of wireless networking, which allowed them to be anywhere, any time, unconnected by wires, and still communicate with other resources on the network (see Figure 14.3).

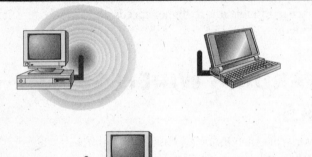

FIGURE 14.3: Computers connected in a simple wireless home network use radio waves instead of wires to communicate with stationary desktops and roaming laptop computers. Additional nodes may be needed to interface with the telephone network or other wired network.

Another push came in 1997, when the IEEE published its 802.11 standard for wireless local area networks (LANs). This was what the market had been waiting for, and within a year a large number of companies had come out with wireless networking products. These were cheaper than renting access to the private networks run by Ardis, RAM, and others like them. But they were still too expensive for home networkers. It took until late 1998 and early 1999 for the first truly affordable wireless radio home networking products to hit the market.

HOME RF WORKING GROUP

Like phoneline networking, wireless networking has a group of large, powerful companies who have banded together to promote the technology. The Home RF Working Group, whose members include Microsoft, Intel, and Motorola, wasn't quite as speedy as the HomePNA organization in getting its specification finalized, however. So Home RF decided to pare back the speed requirements for its initial specification, dubbed shared wireless access protocol (SWAP). Home RF originally planned to specify a speed of between 1Mbps and 2Mbps. The new specification allows speeds from 800Kbps to 1.6Mbps. The change will allow wireless networking vendors to come up with specification-meeting products several months earlier, providing the phoneline networking crowd with some competition. For more information, visit www.homerf.org.

Wireless networks require that a radio transceiver is installed in each computer or other device attached to the network. Once these adapters are installed and the necessary software is configured, you're ready to run a simple peer-to-peer network—no wires to run, new or old. (Exceptions include cables that might be run to an external antenna or to a wireless interface to the wired network, such as a wireless modem.)

Most wireless networks today use the 2.4GHz band. At first, wireless networks used the 902MHz band, but the need for more bandwidth drove them to a higher, wider band. The 2.4GHz band means higher cost and shorter range for wireless networks, but this band is available around the world, while the 902MHz range is generally only allowed to be used for wireless networking in North America. The 2.4GHz band also offers wider bandwidth. It is the band endorsed by the IEEE 802.11 specification for wireless networks. A visual representation of the wireless network radio spectrum is shown in Figure 14.4.

Part III

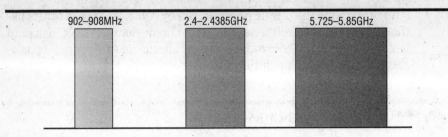

Wireless network radio spectrum

FIGURE 14.4:   Wireless networks use the 902MHz, the 2.4GHz, and eventually, the 5.725GHz bands.

Wireless networks adhering to the SWAP specification promulgated by the Home RF Working Group use the carrier sense multiple access with collision avoidance (CSMA/CA) method to allow data nodes to access the network. The CSMA/CA works similarly to the carrier sense multiple access with collision detection (CSMA/CD) method that Ethernet networks use. With collision avoidance, nodes on the network check for traffic before sending data. The nodes wait to receive a clear to send (CTS) packet before sending the data across the network. Collision detection, on the other hand, first senses to see if there is a signal currently being sent, attempts to transmit the data, and then listens to see if another node transmits information at the same time. If the node detects network traffic, it backs off for a random amount of time before sending its own data again. Because most collisions occur immediately after the network is freed up, this very short delay reduces collisions at the expense of some performance.

Using a laser-powered, straight-line narrowcasting link—a particular kind of high-bandwidth wireless transmission technology—it's possible to achieve performance with a wireless network that rivals Fast Ethernet. However, that kind of performance comes at far too high a price (in dollars and practicality) to be of much interest to home networkers. A more realistic expectation would be a data transfer rate of 1Mbps to 2Mbps, under good circumstances. And, while wireless can go around many obstacles that would stop a wired network, such as a historical building facade, its performance can degrade seriously in the face of such seemingly ephemeral obstacles as a poorly placed file cabinet, or a newly constructed room divider.

Range is a more significant issue with wireless than with wired networks. The maximum range of most home wireless networks, at about 150 feet, is much less than the maximum distance wired networks can cover. Also, because you are untethered, you are likely to roam around the house and yard while using the network.

WARNING

The U.S. military doesn't necessarily adhere to the FCC decisions opening bands of the spectrum up for public use. If you're going to operate a wireless network on a military base, you'll need to ask for a special permit. Otherwise, you might interfere with military radio transmissions.

Security is not as big a problem as you might think, considering that your data is being sprayed out broadcast-style by radio transmitters. That's doubly true when you reflect that the same frequency bands that some cordless phones use are the ones used by wireless networks. In fact, the technology that makes home wireless networks possible is basically an extension of cordless phone technology and the technology behind commercial-grade wireless LANs. However, by using digital encryption and changing frequencies 50 times a second, wireless networks can achieve levels of security comparable to some wired networks in spite of sharing the air with cordless phones.

Wireless networks have a unique set of features compared to all other network technologies. They've been around almost as long as any net-working technology but are only now becoming feasible for home use. Performance is going up and prices are coming down rapidly; the next few years should see many wireless home networks up and running.

UNDERSTANDING HYBRID WIRELESS-WIRED NETWORKS

Hybrid wireless-wired networks are the go-anywhere, do-anything net-work. They offer the performance of a wired network where you need it, plus the freedom of a wireless connection where that is required.

How Hybrid Networks Work

In reality, most wireless networks are, and have always been, hybrid wireless-wired systems. In most cases, a transceiver-equipped PC or other device, called an access point, connects to a wired network, such as the telephone network or a wired LAN, using standard cabling. This access point can receive and transmit data between the wireless and wired worlds.

In home use, you're most likely to mix and match wired and wireless equipment when it comes to connecting to a modem wired to the phone network or a cable television high-speed Internet service. You may also want to connect the network computers directly to a printer without going through a wireless-equipped PC. For either use, you can install a bridge that connects to both the wireless network and, through regular cabling, the printer, modem, or other device connected to a wired network.

You may also prefer to have most of your PCs on a wired network, but also connect a laptop computer, as shown in Figure 14.5, or perhaps a computer that is located an inconvenient distance away, through a second, wireless network. This is not quite so simple. If you want to set up a hybrid network, your PCs will need to work with two network cards, one for the wireless network and one for a wired network. *Multihoming*, as the practice of having more than one NIC per PC is called, is tricky with Windows 95/98 PCs.

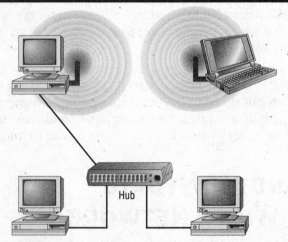

FIGURE 14.5: A hybrid wireless-wired network allows you to have most of your PCs on a wired network but also to connect a laptop computer to the network.

Hybrid networks have many uses. If you have a wireless network, odds are good that you'll go beyond a simple peer-to-peer pure wireless setup and find some way to add a wired interface to the system. If you want to run two networks, one wired and one wireless, it may be more complicated, but the advantages of having roaming where you need it and performance where you need it may outweigh the trouble.

WEIGHING THE PROS AND CONS

Each of the four common types of networks used in the home—Ethernet, phoneline, powerline, and wireless (along with the hybrid wireless-wired networks)—has enough history, standardization, performance, and convenience to make it viable for home networking scenarios. Though four distinct and, for the most part, incompatible approaches may seem to present an unnecessarily confusing number of choices, each of these network varieties has its own legitimate reason for being.

Choosing the type of home network you'll install is more than a matter of picking the fastest or the cheapest or the easiest. At this point, there simply is no hands-down, best-for-everybody, home networking choice. For many people, speedy Ethernet using 10BaseT or perhaps 100BaseT will be the best bet. For others, inexpensive and convenient phoneline networking is a wise choice. Users who want to roam untethered by any kind of cable will want wireless—or, more likely, a hybrid wireless-wired network. This section specifically looks at the pluses and minuses of each approach and sums them up to help you make the final choice.

Sizing Up Ethernet

Ethernet is the most widely used local area network in the world, and for good reason.

Ethernet Pluses

Ethernet is time-tested, reliable, and inexpensive, and it offers the best performance of any available home network. You can buy the equipment to wire a home for Ethernet at any sizable computer store, consumer electronics outlet, or hobbyist shop.

Ethernet Is Reliable   The technology behind Ethernet goes back more than 30 years, during which time it has been used and has developed a reliable reputation in all sorts of circumstances. There are many trained technicians, a wealth of diagnostic gear and techniques, and lots of informal experts you can turn to for help if and when you need it.

Ethernet Is Relatively Inexpensive   Ethernet isn't the cheapest networking alternative; however, it isn't expensive when compared to the cost of a new PC, another printer or scanner, or a high-speed Internet connection. And its costs are actually less per computer than wireless networks.

Ethernet Offers Good Performance　Ethernet stands above all the competition when it comes to performance. Only the latest phoneline networks can match the 10Mbps speed of regular Ethernet. None of the alternatives can come close to the 100Mbps speed of Fast Ethernet. (Not to mention Gigabit Ethernet, which, although not a practical option for most home networks, is 1000 times as fast as the first-generation phoneline networking standard.)

The 10Mbps speed of Ethernet should be more than adequate for the vast majority of home networks. If you need more speed to transfer big files, run an in-home video network, or perhaps play bandwidth-hogging head-to-head games, you may opt for Fast Ethernet. The cost differential between the two is not all that significant, compared to the speed advantages you gain. To begin with, you will probably use the same cable. The cards cost basically the same—only a few dollars difference in price. Fast Ethernet hubs, on the other hand, are somewhat more expensive. Still, a Fast Ethernet hub with ports to hook up four devices is going to run you only around $75. Those kinds of costs aren't all that important. In fact, by the time you read this, or not long after, Fast Ethernet may cost the same as regular Ethernet.

Ethernet Minuses

If Ethernet were the best choice for all home networks, there wouldn't be any need for this analysis. And it turns out that Ethernet does have some drawbacks and limitations that need to be considered before making the choice of a home networking approach.

Ethernet Requires Cables　Ethernet is the only one of the popular home networking schemes that requires new wiring between all the computers on the network. This is a significant obstacle in many residences, especially those with computers that are widely separated. The problem isn't the distance—computers on a 10BaseT Ethernet network can be separated by 300 feet or more. It's the problem of getting the cable through the barriers between.

It's no problem, of course, just to string a cable between two or more computers in the same room. But unless you like crawling through the attic, teetering on a ladder in the basement, or stapling possibly unsightly cable all along the exterior of your home—not to mention the hassle of drilling and pulling cable through walls and floors or ceilings—then installing a network of Ethernet cables is likely to be a significant obstacle.

RENTING AND BUILDING

Two special cases concerning wiring for a network deserve mention. If you are renting your home or apartment, you may need to get permission from your landlord before drilling holes or performing other work to install cabling for a network. Also, if you are building a new home, consider having the wiring installed before the dry-wall goes on. Installing a network cable system during construction is much cheaper, easier, neater, and more convenient than even the simplest retrofit installation. Prior to wiring or rewiring, you should also check the local fire codes for building. Some locations are forbidden from containing certain types of wiring.

To sum up, Ethernet offers these significant features:

▶ Proven technology

▶ Broad compatibility with the most popular networking standard

▶ Excellent performance

▶ Higher installation costs and trouble

Ethernet is an excellent choice if you don't mind running wires throughout the house, or if all the PCs to be networked are located very close to one another. If you live in a place that can't be wired easily, and high performance is not a critical concern, then one of the "no-new-wires" networks described below may be a better choice.

Sizing Up Phoneline

Phoneline networks have received considerable attention from computer manufacturers and others who want to push home networking. Phoneline networks can be easy to install, offer adequate performance, and are relatively inexpensive.

Phoneline Pluses

Phoneline has the best performance of the no-new-wires technologies (which also include powerline and wireless), and it is also low-cost and widely available. Its data transfer rate will soon match regular Ethernet's 10Mbps, and because it requires no new wires, it will always be cheaper than cabled Ethernet.

Phoneline Uses Existing Wiring

The big advantage to phoneline networking is that it uses existing wiring. Many homes are wired adequately for phones, so it is possible that every PC that needs to be on the network can reach a suitable phone jack. For those that can't, it's easier and cheaper to wire a room for a new phone jack than it is to install a wired network.

Phoneline Is Relatively Inexpensive

Already, you can buy a PC with built-in phoneline networking, including software, for an extra fee of less than $50. In a year or two, phoneline networking could cost half that per station. Because it needs no new wiring, it's always likely to be less costly than cabled Ethernet. And, because phoneline NICs are cheaper than wireless network transceivers, it will probably also underprice wireless networks.

Phoneline Standards Are Relatively Stable

With big players like Compaq and Intel lining up behind phoneline, it's a safe bet that standards are going to be set and maintained. The creation and maintenance of standards protects you against having an outmoded network that can't be upgraded or work with newer, better network equipment. This has proven important in the Ethernet world, where many manufacturers have come out with dual-speed hubs and NICs to allow networkers to upgrade when and how they choose, instead of having to replace the entire network at once. Standards also encourage competition, as equipment manufacturers feel confident that whatever they make will work with the competition.

NOTE

If you recall the flap over 56K modem standards, you know how important standards can be. Two competing standards for transmitting data over phone lines at a nominal 56Kbps were offered by rival firms. Neither took off, especially when it was announced that a joint standard would be agreed to. The result was that, for almost a year, modem sales almost completely dried up and consumers were reluctant to purchase a costly, cutting-edge modem that might prove incompatible with the new standard. In any case, most 56K modems could be upgraded to the new V.90 standard when it was released. When that happened, modem sales took off, prices dropped very low, and nearly anybody could afford a faster modem.

Phoneline Minuses

Phoneline limitations include the fact that all the PCs on the network have to be connected to a phoneline that has the same number. If you have several lines in your house, not all of which are run to each phone jack, this could be a problem. Another issue is how you will use the phoneline network with high-speed Internet connections, especially cable modem. In order to connect a PC to both the phoneline network and the cable modem interface card, you will probably need two NICs in the PC—a trick called multihoming.

Phoneline Performance Lags behind Ethernet   Recently, phoneline network vendors have introduced products that claim to offer speeds competitive with regular Ethernet, which runs at 10Mbps. It remains to be seen how well these will work in practice, however. Meanwhile, 100Mbps Fast Ethernet is becoming more widespread, inexpensive, and standardized than ever. Given the limitations of most home phone wiring, it's probably safe to say that phoneline networks are always going to have lower performance than networks set up with cabling designed for high-speed data communications.

Phoneline Requires Handy Phone Jacks   The average home has only two to four phone jacks. So, although odds are that at least one of your PCs is close to a phoneline so you can reach the Internet through a modem, it's not likely that a phone jack will be handy to all your PCs. That's especially true if your PC is located in a bedroom, garage, work room, or any place besides the kitchen, living room, master bedroom, or home office. You can always run a wire to a phone jack in another room, but if you're going to do that, you might as well run Ethernet cables.

Summing Up Phoneline

Phoneline has powerful forces pushing it as the home network of choice. Its main advantages include:

- ▶ It requires no new wires, assuming your home is well supplied with telephone jacks.

- ▶ Standardization is progressing rapidly, with some computer makers already offering it built in.

- ▶ Performance is second only to Ethernet.

- ▶ It's inexpensive and relatively easy to set up.

Part III

If having the utmost in performance isn't essential, or if you simply can't bring yourself to drill holes in walls and ceilings to wire a network, phoneline networking is a convenient, cost-effective approach for many home networkers.

Sizing Up Powerline

Powerline networking is nearly as old as Ethernet, but it has been changing as rapidly of late as the much newer phoneline networking technology. It has important advantages when it comes to ease of setup and convenience, especially regarding the number of points where you can access the network.

Powerline Pluses

Powerline is one of the no-new-wires technologies, which makes it attractive to many home networkers right off the bat. It's also unusually easy to get powerline up and running. And the power grid, which provides the wires used to connect computers on powerline networks, is simply the biggest, most ubiquitous network of them all. That's a powerful combination that makes this technology worth a look.

Powerline Uses Existing Wiring   When it comes to the sheer number of outlets or ways to reach existing wires, nothing comes close to powerline. Almost all homes have far more A/C outlets than they do phone jacks. Newer homes commonly have one or more power outlets on almost every interior wall, including bathrooms, kitchens, and garages. Many have exterior power outlets as well, providing the opportunity to access your network from the back porch or patio.

Powerline Networks Are Easy to Install   Powerline networks can be very simple to set up—as easy as plugging a connector into your PC's parallel port, plugging the adapter on the end of the cable into a power outlet, and running the setup program. It's hard for any other networking technology to claim to be that easy. Many phoneline networks, for instance, require you to open the back of your PC to install an adapter card. And this process is far easier than installing an Ethernet cabled network. If ease of installation is a paramount consideration, take a look at powerline.

Powerline Minuses

Although it sounds ideal to be able to simply plug your PC into a nearby A/C outlet and start networking, in practice powerline networking is often not that perfect. Before you settle on a powerline network, consider the issues of standardization, performance, reliability, and security.

Powerline Networking Lacks Standardization   So far, no single standard has emerged as dominant in the powerline networking arena. Most of the companies offering powerline networks use their own approach for signaling, each of which is incompatible with the others. They include Adaptive Network's hybrid token-passing scheme and the Ethernet-like peer-to-peer CSMA/CD approaches of Intellon and Echelon. Intelogis uses a client-server approach that places the bulk of the processing load on a PC server, reducing the costs of the rest of the network gear.

This lack of interoperability means, among other things, that if you purchase a powerline networking system, you'll probably have to buy any expansion or add-on equipment from the same vendor. In addition, the lack of a dominant standard means that should you later wish to switch to a new, faster powerline networking technology, you may have to scrap your whole network to do so. Other technologies, such as Ethernet, have preserved backward compatibility with older approaches by using such tools as dual-speed hubs and NICs.

Powerline Performance Lags   Powerline networking is catching up fast to the other networking technologies when it comes to speed. But, so far, the 10Mbps standard of regular Ethernet and the newer phoneline networks has only been demonstrated for powerline networks in lab tests. While you may not need 10Mbps now, it's a safe bet that before long, you'll find some use for any extra bandwidth you can get.

Meanwhile, of course, the other networking approaches—Ethernet in particular—aren't standing still. Fast Ethernet's 100Mbps transfer rate is something powerline networkers can't really think of at the moment.

Noise Plagues Powerline Networks   Powerlines were designed for transmitting power, of course, not data. This creates a number of problems when it comes to using those wires for computer networks. Among them are high levels of noise, distortion, and attenuation, or the tendency of the signal to fade out quickly.

Noise enters power lines from a variety of sources, including dimmer switches, intercoms (some of which also use the powerline to communicate), baby monitors, and electrical motors attached to the power grid. Networking vendors use various techniques to clean up their signals and protect them from noise, but none so far is as clean as a wired Ethernet system.

Powerline Has Security Issues   When you're using a powerline network, you may be exposing yourself to higher security risks than with other networks. Powerline networks can't connect devices that have a power-company transformer located between them. This usually is no problem for home installations, although it can be for businesses. But it does raise security issues because in many neighborhoods more than one home shares a transformer. If one of your neighbors is on the same transformer, they may also share your network wiring and be able to easily snoop on your network. Powerline networks usually use data-encryption and other security techniques to control this risk.

Summing Up Powerline

Powerline may be for you if the following circumstances apply:

- ▶ You aren't overly concerned about high performance.
- ▶ You don't want to go to the trouble of pulling wires or opening PCs.
- ▶ You have lots of A/C outlets and few phone jacks.

Powerline is a promising technology with lots of useful advantages that may make it a viable way to network for many home users.

Sizing Up Wireless

Wireless is unique among networking technologies in that it allows true mobility. It's not the cheapest, the fastest, or the easiest, but it does match up fairly well across the board, and it has that one major plus.

Wireless Pluses

Free roaming is the big advantage of wireless, but these untethered networks can also be very easy to install. With the advent of new low-cost home RF networks, installing wireless networks is inexpensive as well.

Wireless Needs No Cables Cables are both good and bad. They can carry data at faster rates than wireless networks, but they are also points of trouble. Cables can get worn, their connectors can disconnect or become loose, a short or flaw in one of them can bring the entire network down. People trip on them, roll their chairs on them, or place electrical transformers so near them that data flowing through the cable gets corrupted by the electromagnetic interference. The fact that wireless isn't exposed to these particular risks is a good reason for many home networkers to look at it.

Furthermore, wireless may be the only logical choice in many situations. If you can't drill holes and don't have adequate phone or power wiring, which may be the case in some old buildings, it's either go wireless or go without. Similarly, if you only plan to be in your residence for a short while but want to set up a network anyway, then wireless makes an excellent ad-hoc, temporary, and exceptionally easy-to-relocate network.

Wireless Is Easy to Install A simple peer-to-peer wireless PC network may be the easiest of all home networks to install. You simply install the transceiver cards in the PCs, or, in the case of a laptop, insert a PC card into the PCMCIA slot on the side, power up the machines, and run the software—and you're done.

Wireless Allows Untethered Roaming When cellular phones first came out, the idea that you could easily and (relatively) cheaply make a phone call from just about anywhere was astonishing and powerful. In the same way, being able to check your e-mail or transfer a file you need to a wirelessly networked computer is highly empowering and engaging. Given the short range of most wireless networks, perhaps a cordless phone is a better analogy. But, still, if you ever want to be able to develop a spreadsheet or shoot-em-up at Quake while relaxing in a backyard hammock, a wireless network may be your only way to achieve what you want out of your home network.

Wireless Minuses

If wireless is going to become the *de facto* standard in home networking—and some believe it will—it's going to have to overcome some significant limitations and risks. Chief among the problems is performance, followed by cost, interference, and range limitations.

Wireless Performance Is Lacking   You're not going to get the performance, in terms of data transfer rate, from a wireless network that you would get from regular Ethernet or one of the new, higher-speed phone-line networks. Wireless is also more subject to interference. Placing a transceiver too close to a wall, near a transformer used by another electrical device, on a different floor, or just behind too many sheetrock walls can cause signals to drop out and the workstation to fall off the network.

You can fix some of these problems by using external antennas, but that defeats some of the purpose of using easy-to-install wireless, and it won't necessarily help roaming workstations. And, unfortunately, there's almost no way to tell in advance whether wireless will work in your home without just trying.

Wireless Is Costly   Wireless until recently has been prohibitively expensive for home networking. Now, however, the prices have been more than halved, and you can set up a simple two-PC network for around twice what a wired network would be. Given the disadvantages of wired, this isn't much of a premium. However, if you're on a budget, or if you take into consideration the performance limits of wireless as well as the premium price, wireless may be too costly for many home networks.

Wireless Has Range Limitations   The typical home wireless network has a rated distance of approximately 150 feet within which network transmissions can be reliably sent and received. This is going to be adequate for many non-billionaire homes, certainly, but conditions such as obstructions or sources of electromagnetic interference can reduce that range significantly.

Wireless Standards Are Still Evolving   The IEEE 802.11 standard provides a good base for wireless networking, especially for business LANs. As the price of 802.11 equipment comes down, more home networks may start adopting it as the standard. Efforts to come up with a standard more suitable for home networks, by the Home RF Working Group, have had trouble meeting expectations so far. The Home RF Working Group's initial SWAP specification for home wireless networks ran only between 800Kbps and 1.6Mbps, about half of what was expected. The current HomeRF specifications allow speeds comparable to the 802.11 standard at 10Mbps.

Summing Up Wireless

To sum up, wireless offers these significant features:

- ▶ No new wires needed
- ▶ Excellent portability
- ▶ Higher equipment costs
- ▶ Higher potential for interference

Sizing Up Hybrid Wireless-Wired

Hybrid wireless-wired networks offer unique advantages to people in certain situations. Matching two different technologies can be challenging, however, so you'll want to carefully consider whether a single type of network may be able to solve your particular problems. For instance, if simply adding a few more ports to your network would do the trick, you could choose to go with an all-powerline or all-phoneline network instead of trying to mix and match a wired network with wireless.

Hybrid Wireless-Wired Pluses

The fact is, the advantages of having a wireless-wired hybrid network are such that you're unlikely to have a pure wireless network for long. Eventually, you're going to want to hook up to a cable or DSL modem, or you will want to attach a printer without using a PC as a print server. When that happens, you'll need some kind of bridge between the two systems, and then you'll have gone hybrid. A more advanced two-network hybrid setup offers additional advantages (chiefly the fact that you retain the option of roaming or reaching out to otherwise inaccessible areas with the wireless portion of the network), but you can save money or improve performance by going wired on the rest.

Hybrid Wireless-Wired Minuses

There's no free lunch, and the all-things-to-all-people promise of hybrid wireless-wired networks does come with a price tag. To begin with, when you connect wireless and wired networks, the traffic between them will occur at the speed of the slower network (most likely the wired). So you'll be unable to capture any performance advantage from the wired network on your wireless workstations. Also, any wireless network suffers from interference and a higher cost than a wired-only network.

Summing Up Hybrid Wireless-Wired

A hybrid network is not for everyone, but its unique mix of access to a wired network and untethered freedom make it a solid choice for certain users. Its major features are as follows:

- Roaming with laptops, but using desktops in wired network

- Interconnecting with modems, printers, and other non-PC devices

- Facing the sometimes challenging technical difficulties of interfacing two networks

HOW TO MAKE A SMART DECISION

There's nothing irreversible about making the decision of which network you will install in your home. You can always remove the NICs, yank the wires out of your walls if necessary, and try something else if you decide you've made a mistake. Then again, it would be better to do it right the first time. Making the decision well involves a simple six-step process:

1. First, decide what your needs are. For instance, is performance paramount for that bandwidth-gobbling game you love to play online?

2. Next, match your needs against the features of the various home network approaches. For instance, if you want to network to a PC that's in the workshop across a cement driveway, wireless is a good match.

3. Consider carefully the most appropriate locations for network nodes. You wouldn't want to choose a phoneline network only to find out that a key location, such as a child's bedroom, doesn't have a phone outlet.

4. Think about what type of devices you will want to attach to your network. You may be pretty disappointed if you plan to hook your video camera up to a powerline network, because this technology's low-end performance is poorly suited to the bandwidth needs of transmitting video over a network.

5. Before you make your decision, look into the future. Will your network be adequate in a few years' time? What is the likely upgrade path?

6. Finally, shop around to make sure you're getting the best service, support, and price available.

WHAT'S NEXT

In Chapter 15, we will look at how to troubleshoot your network. We'll explore some basic troubleshooting techniques, review a common troubleshooting model, and describe common resources to make trouble-shooting networks easier and more effective.

Part III

Chapter 15

NETWORK TROUBLESHOOTING

There is no doubt about it. The only way to get good at troubleshooting computers and networks is the same way to get good at any other art: practice, practice, practice. And as with any art, you must learn some basic skills before you can start practicing.

This chapter introduces you to some items to keep in mind when troubleshooting networks. In this chapter, we'll examine some basic troubleshooting techniques. First, we'll look at how to check quickly for simple problems. Then, we'll discuss a common troubleshooting model that you can use to identify many network problems. Finally, we'll look at some common troubleshooting resources and tips and tricks that you can use to make troubleshooting easier. Let's start with how you go about narrowing down the problem.

Part III

Adapted from the *Network+ Study Guide*,
Third Edition by David Groth
ISBN 0-7821-4014-9   624 pages $49.99

NARROWING DOWN THE PROBLEM

Troubleshooting a network problem can be daunting. That's why it's best to start by trying to narrow down the source of the problem. You do this by checking a few key areas, beginning with the simple stuff.

Checking for the Simple Stuff

The first thing to check, as most people will tell you, is the simple stuff. There's a saying that goes, "All things being equal, the simplest explanation is probably the correct one." For computers, it's rather hard to categorize simple stuff because what's simple to one person might be complex to another. I like to define simple stuff (as it relates to troubleshooting) as those items that you don't think to check, but when it turns out that one of those items is the problem, you say, "Oh, DUH!" Almost everyone can agree on a few items that fall into this category:

- ▶ Correct login procedure and rights
- ▶ Link lights/collision lights
- ▶ Power switch
- ▶ Operator error

CAN THE PROBLEM BE REPRODUCED?

The first question to ask anyone who reports a network or computer problem is, "Can you show me what 'not working' looks like?" If you can reproduce the problem, you can identify the conditions under which it occurs. And if you can identify the conditions, you can start to determine the source.

Unfortunately, not every problem can be reproduced. The hardest problems to solve are those that can't be reproduced, but instead appear randomly.

The Correct Login Procedure and Rights

To gain access to the network, users must follow the correct login procedure exactly. If they don't, they will be denied access. Considering everything that must be done correctly and in the correct order, it's a miracle that anyone logs in to a network correctly at all. There are so many opportunities for making a mistake.

First, a user must enter the username and password correctly. As easy as this sounds, users frequently enter this information incorrectly, don't realize it, and report to the network administrator that the network is broken or that they can't log in. The most common problem is accidentally typing the wrong username or password incorrectly. In some operating systems, this can happen when you accidentally leave the Caps Lock key pressed. An example of this is Unix, in which passwords are case-sensitive; the user will not be able to log in, unless his or her password is in all capital letters.

Additionally, in NetWare and Windows NT the network administrator can restrict the times and conditions under which users can log in. If a user doesn't log in at the right time or from the right workstation, the network operating system will reject the login request, even though it might be a valid request in terms of the username and password being spelled correctly. Additionally, a network administrator might restrict how many times a user can log in to the network simultaneously. If that user tries to establish more connections than are allowed, access will be denied. Any time a user is denied access to the network, they are likely to interpret that as a problem, even though the network operating system might be doing what it should.

To test for these types of problems, first check to see if the username and password are being typed correctly and whether or not the Caps Lock key is pressed. Try the login yourself from another workstation (assuming that doesn't violate the security policy). If it works, you might try asking the user to check to see if the Caps Lock light on the keyboard is on (indicating that the Caps Lock key has been pressed). If that doesn't solve the problem, check the network documentation to see if the aforementioned kinds of restrictions are in place.

TIP

If intruder detection is enabled on the network, the user's account will be locked after a specified number of incorrect login attempts. In this case, the user cannot log in until the administrator has unlocked the account, or until a certain amount of time specified by the administrator has elapsed, after which the account is unlocked.

Part III

The Link and Collision Lights

The *link light* is a small light-emitting diode (LED) found on both the NIC and the hub. It is typically green and is labeled *link* (or some abbreviation). A link light indicates that the NIC and hub (in the case of 10BaseT) are making a logical (Data Link layer) connection. You can usually assume that the workstation and hub are communicating if the link lights are lit on both the workstation's NIC and the hub port to which the workstation is connected.

NOTE
The link lights on some NICs aren't activated until the operating system driver is loaded for that NIC. So, if the link light isn't on when the system is first turned on, you may have to wait until the operating system loads the NIC driver.

The *collision light* is also a small LED, typically amber in color. It can usually be found on both Ethernet NICs and hubs. When lit, it indicates that an Ethernet collision has occurred. It is important to know that this light will blink occasionally, because collisions are somewhat common on busy Ethernet networks. However, if this light stays on continuously, there are too many collisions happening for legitimate network traffic to get through. This can be caused by a malfunctioning network card or another malfunctioning network device.

WARNING
Be careful not to confuse the collision light with the network activity or network traffic light (usually green). The network activity light indicates that a device is transmitting. This particular light should be blinking on and off continually as the device transmits and receives data on the network.

The Power Switch

To function properly, all computer and network components must be turned on and powered up. As obvious as this is, network administrators often hear a user complain, "My computer is on, but my monitor is dark." In this case, our response is to ask, "Is the monitor turned on?" After a pause, the voice on the other end usually says sheepishly, "Oh. Thanks."

Most systems include a power indicator such as a Power or PWR light, and the power switch typically has a 1 or an On indicator. However, the unit could be powerless even if the power switch is in the On position.

Thus, you need to check that all power cables are plugged in, including the power strip.

TIP

Remember that every cable has two ends, and both must be plugged in to something.

When troubleshooting power problems, start with the most obvious device and work your way back to the power service panel. There could be any number of power problems between the device and the service panel, including a bad power cable, bad outlet, bad electrical wire, tripped circuit breaker, or blown fuse. Any of these items can cause power problems at the device.

Operator Error

The problem may be that the user simply doesn't know how to perform the operation correctly; in other words, the problem may be due to *OE (operator error)*. Those in the computer and networking industry have devised several colorful expressions to describe operator error:

- ▶ EEOC (Equipment Exceeds Operator Capability)
- ▶ PEBCAK (Problem Exists Between Chair And Keyboard)
- ▶ ID Ten T Error (written as ID10T)

Assuming that all problems are related to operator error, however, is a mistake. Before you attribute any problem to operator error, ask the user to reproduce the problem in your presence, and pay close attention. You may find out that the user is having a problem because he or she is using an incorrect procedure—for example, flipping the power switch without following proper shutdown procedures. You may also find out that the user was trained incorrectly, in which case you might want to see if others are having the same difficulty. If the problem and solution are not obvious, try the procedure yourself, or ask someone else at another workstation to do so.

Part III

NOTE

This is only a partial list of simple stuff. You'll come up with your own expanded list over time, as you troubleshoot more and more systems.

Is Hardware or Software Causing the Problem?

A hardware problem typically manifests itself as a device in your computer that fails to operate correctly. You can usually tell that a hardware failure has occurred because you will try to use that piece of hardware, and the computer will issue an error indicating that this has happened. Some failures, such as hard-disk failures, may give warning signs—for example, a Disk I/O error or something similar. Other components may just suddenly fail. The device will be operating fine and then simply fail.

The solution to hardware problems usually involves either changing hardware settings, updating device drivers, or replacing hardware. As we have discussed in previous chapters, I/O address, IRQ (interrupt requests), and DMA (direct memory access) conflicts can cause computers (including workstations and servers) to malfunction. Change the hardware settings to solve these types of problems.

If the hardware has actually failed, however, you must get out your tools and start replacing components. If this is not one of your skills, you can send the device out for repair. In either case, because the system can be down for anywhere from an hour to several days, it's always prudent to have backup hardware on hand.

Software problems are a little more evasive. Some problems might result in General Protection Fault messages, which indicate a Windows or Windows program error of some type. Also, a program might suddenly stop responding (hang), or the entire machine might lock up randomly. The solution to these problems generally involves a trip to the manufacturer's support website to get software updates and patches or to search for the answer in a knowledge base.

Sometimes software will give you a precise message regarding the source of the problem, such as the software is missing a file or a file has become corrupt. In this case, you can either provide the file or, if necessary, reinstall the software. Neither solution takes long, and your computer will be up and running in a short time.

TIP

Sometimes fragmented memory, which occurs after you open and close too many programs, is the source of the problem. The solution may be to reboot the computer, thus clearing memory. Be sure to add this to your network-troubleshooting bag of tricks.

Is It a Workstation or a Server Problem?

Troubleshooting this problem involves first determining whether one person or a group of people are affected. If only one person is affected, think workstation. If several people are affected, the server or, more generally speaking, a portion of the network is probably experiencing problems.

If a single user is affected, your first line of defense is to try to log in from another workstation within the same group of users. If you can do so, the problem is related to the user's workstation. Look for a cabling fault, a bad NIC, or some other problem.

On the other hand, if several people in a group (such as a whole department) can't access a server, the problem may be related to that server. Go to the server in question and check for user connections. If everyone is logged in, the problem could be related to something else, such as individual rights or permissions. If no one can log in to that server, including the administrator, the server may have a communication problem with the rest of the network. If it has crashed, you might see messages to that effect on the server's monitor, or the screen might be blank, indicating that the server is no longer running. These symptoms vary among network operating systems.

Which Segments of the Network Are Affected?

Making this determination can be tough. If multiple segments are affected, the problem could be a network address conflict since network addresses must be unique across an entire network. If two segments have the same IPX network address, for example, all the routers and NetWare servers will complain bitterly and send out error messages, hoping that it's just a simple problem that a router can correct. This is rarely the case, however, and, thus, the administrator must find and resolve the issue. Also keep in mind that the continuous broadcasting of error messages will negatively impact network performance.

If all users of the network are experiencing the problem, it could be related to a different device, such as a server that everyone accesses. Or, a main router or hub could be down, making network transmissions impossible.

Additionally, if the network has WAN connections, you can determine if a network problem is related to the WAN connection by checking to see if stations on both sides can communicate. If they can, the problem isn't related to the WAN. If they can't communicate, you must check everything between the sending station and the receiving one, including the WAN hardware. Usually, the WAN devices have built-in diagnostics that can indicate whether the WAN link is functioning correctly to help you determine if the fault is related to the WAN link or to the hardware involved.

Cabling Issues

After you determine whether the problem is related to the whole network, to a single segment, or to a single workstation, you must determine whether the problem is related to network cabling. First, check to see if the cables are properly connected to the correct port. More than once, I've seen a wall phone cable plugged into a modem in the In jack.

Additionally, patch cables from workstation to wall jack can and do go bad, especially if they get moved or tripped over often. This problem is often characterized by connection problems. If you test the NIC and there is no link light (discussed earlier in this chapter), the problem could be related to a bad patch cable.

It is also possible to have a cabling problem in the walls where the cabling wasn't installed correctly. If a network cable was run over a fluorescent light, for example, the workstation attached to that cable might have problems only when the lights are on. The problem is that the fluorescent lights produce a large amount of EMI and can disrupt communications in that cable. This kind of problem may manifest itself only at times when most lights need to be on.

Next, check the MDI/MDX port setting on small, workgroup hubs, a potential source of trouble that is often overlooked. This port is used to uplink, for example, to a hub on the network's backbone. The port setting has to be set to either MDI or MDX, depending on the type of cable used for the hub-to-hub connection. A crossover cable (discussed later in this chapter) requires that the port be set to MDI; a standard network patch cable requires that the port be set to MDX (sometimes labeled MDI-X). You can usually adjust the setting via a regular switch or a DIP (Dual Inline Package) switch. Check the hub's documentation.

NOTE

Some hubs just have a port labeled MDX, since the MDI setting is really just another standard port for all intents and purposes. If you connect hubs using a standard patch cable, you must connect the MDX port to a standard port on the backbone hub.

TROUBLESHOOTING STEPS

In the Network+ troubleshooting model, there are eight steps:

1. Establish symptoms.
2. Identify the affected area.
3. Establish what has changed.
4. Select the most probable cause.
5. Implement a solution.
6. Test the result.
7. Recognize the potential effects of the solution.
8. Document the solution.

To facilitate our discussion of the troubleshooting steps, let's assume that a user has called you, the network administrator, to complain about not being able to connect to the Internet.

Step 1: Establish Symptoms

Obviously, if you can't identify a problem, you can't begin to solve it. Typically, you need to ask some questions to begin to clarify exactly what is happening. In our example, we should ask the user the following:

- ▶ Which part of the Internet can't you access?
- ▶ A particular website? A particular address? Any website?
- ▶ Can you use your web browser?

We find out that the user cannot access the corporate intranet or get to any sites on the Internet. He can, however, use his web browser to access the corporate FTP site, which he has bookmarked (by IP address 10.0.0.2). We can, therefore, rule out the web browser as the source of the problem.

Step 2: Identify the Affected Area

Computers and networks are fickle; they can work fine for months, suddenly malfunction horribly, and then continue to work fine for several more months, never again exhibiting that particular problem. And that's why it's important to be able to reproduce the problem and identify the affected area. Identifying the affected area narrows down what you have to troubleshoot.

Part III

One of your goals is to make problems easier to troubleshoot and, thus, get users working again as soon as possible. Therefore, the best advice you can give when training users is that when something isn't working, try it again and then write down exactly what is and is not happening. Most users' knee-jerk reaction is to call you immediately when they experience a problem. This isn't necessarily the best thing to do, because your response is most likely, "What were you doing when the problem occurred?" And most users don't know precisely what they were doing at the computer because they were primarily trying to get their job done. Therefore, if you train users to reproduce the problem first, they'll be able to give you the information you need to start troubleshooting it.

In our example, we find out that when the user tries to access the corporate intranet, he gets the following error message:

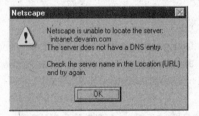

We're in luck—we can re-create this problem.

TIP

It is a definite advantage to be able to watch the user try to reproduce the problem, because you can determine whether the user is performing the operation correctly.

Step 3: Establish What Has Changed

If you can reproduce the problem, your next step is to attempt to determine the cause by determining what has changed. Drawing on your knowledge of networking, you might ask yourself and your user questions such as the following:

Were you ever able to do this?   If not, then maybe this is not an operation the hardware or software is designed to do. You can inform the user that the system won't do the operation (or that she may need additional hardware or software to do it).

If so, when did you become unable to do it?   If the computer was able to do the operation and then suddenly could not, the conditions that surround this change become extremely important. You may be able to discover the cause of the problem if you know what happened immediately before the change. It is likely that the cause of the problem is related to the conditions surrounding the change.

Has anything changed since you were last able to do this? This question can give you insight into a possible source for the problem. Most often, the thing that changed before the problem started is the source of the problem. When you ask this question of a user, the answer is typically that nothing has changed, so you might need to rephrase it. For example, you can try asking, "Did anyone add anything to your computer?" or "Are you doing anything differently from the way you normally proceed?"

Were any error messages displayed? This is one of the best indicators of the cause of a problem. Error messages are designed by programmers to help them determine what aspect of a computer system is not functioning correctly. These error messages are sometimes clear, such as "Disk full" (indicating that the disk cannot store any more files on it because it is full). Or they can be cryptic, such as "A random bit has been flipped in the I/O subsystem of memory junction 44FA380h" (this is a fictitious error, but you may encounter those just as complex). If you get a cryptic error message, you can go to the software or hardware vendor's support website and usually get a translation of the "programmerese" of the error message into English.

Are other people experiencing this problem? This is one question you must ask yourself. That way you might be able to narrow down the problem to a specific item that may be causing the problem. Try to duplicate the problem yourself from your own workstation. If you can't duplicate the problem on another workstation, it may be related to only one user or group of users (or possibly their workstations). If more than one user is experiencing this problem, you may know this already because several people will be calling in with the same problem.

Is the problem always the same? Generally speaking, when problems crop up, they are almost always the same problem each time they occur. But their symptoms may change ever so slightly as conditions surrounding them change. A related question is, "If you do x, does the problem get better or worse?" For example, you might ask a user, "If you use a different file, does the problem get better or worse?" If the symptoms become less severe, it might indicate that the problem is related to the original file being used.

These are just a few of the questions you can use to isolate the cause of the problem.

In our example, we find out that the problem is unique to one user, indicating that the problem is specific to his workstation. When we watch him as he attempts to reproduce the problem, we notice that he is typing the address correctly. The error message leads us to believe that the problem has something to with DNS (Domain Name Service) lookups on his workstation.

Step 4: Select the Most Probable Cause

After you observe the problem and isolate the cause, your next step is to select the most probable cause for the problem. Trust me, this gets easier with time and experience.

You must come up with at least one possible cause, even though it may not be correct. And you don't always have to come up with it yourself. Someone else in the group may have the answer. Also, don't forget to check online sources and vendor documentation.

In our example, we determined earlier that the cause was improperly configured DNS lookup on the workstation. The correction, then, is to reconfigure DNS on the workstation.

Step 5: Implement a Solution

In this step, you implement the solution. In our example, we need to reconfigure DNS on the workstation by following these steps:

1. Choose Start ➤ Settings ➤ Control Panel ➤ Network to open the Network dialog box.

2. Click the TCP/IP binding for your network card (indicated by TCP/IP ➤ *name of network card*).

3. Click Properties to open the TCP/IP Properties dialog box for that binding.

4. Click the DNS Configuration tab.

As you can see in Figure 15.1, DNS has been disabled on this workstation. At this point, it doesn't matter how it was disabled. We could probably assume that the user did something by accident to cause this to happen or that it was the result of a software installation, but anything is possible. To re-enable DNS, click the Enable DNS button. You may have to reboot the workstation to get the changes to take effect.

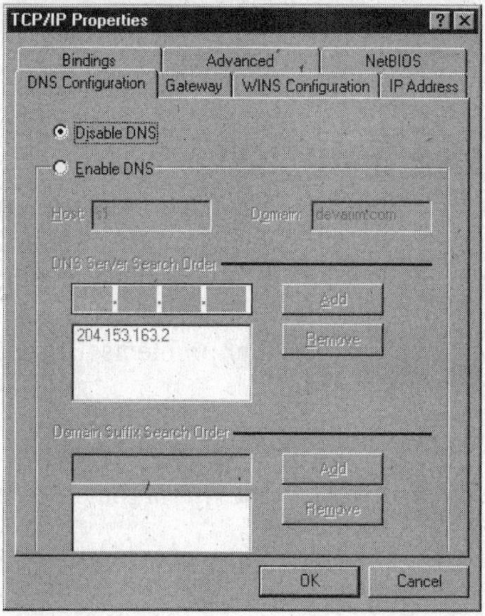

FIGURE 15.1: TCP/IP DNS properties for the misconfigured workstation

Step 6: Test the Result

Now that you have made the changes, you must test your solution to see if it solves the problem. In our example, we'd ask the user to try to access the intranet (since that was the problem reported). In general terms, ask the user to repeat the operation that previously did not work. If it works, great! The problem is solved. If it doesn't, try the operation yourself.

If the problem isn't solved, you may have to go back to step 4, select a new possible cause, and redo steps 5 and 6. But it is important to make note of what worked and what didn't so that you don't make the same mistakes twice.

Step 7: Recognize the Potential Effects of the Solution

The fundamental flaw of any network technician is the ability of the technician to solve only the one problem and not realize what other

Part III

problems that solution may cause. It is possible that the solution may be worse than the problem. As the saying goes, "Sometimes the cure is worse than the disease."

Before fully implementing the solution to a problem, make sure you are completely aware of the potential effects of the solution and the other problems it may cause. If it causes more problems than it fixes, the solution probably isn't the best solution for the problem.

Step 8: Document the Solution

Network documentation is very important. You'll definitely want to document problems and solutions so that you have the information at hand when a similar problem arises in the future. With documented solutions to documented problems, you can assemble your own database of information that you can use to troubleshoot other problems. Be sure to include information such as the following:

▶ A description of the conditions surrounding the problem

▶ The NOS version, the software version, the type of computer, and the type of NIC

▶ Whether you were able to reproduce the problem

▶ The solutions you tried

▶ The ultimate solution

THE TROUBLESHOOTER'S RESOURCES

In the process of troubleshooting a workstation, a server, or other network component, you have many resources at your disposal. In this section, we'll take a brief look at some of them. Those you use depend on the situation and your personal preferences. You will eventually have your own favorites.

Log Files

Log files can indicate the general health of a server. Each log file format is different, but, generally speaking, the log files contain a running list of all errors and notices, the time and date they occurred, and any other pertinent information. Let's look at a couple of the log files from the most commonly used network operating systems, NetWare 5 and Windows NT 4.

NetWare Log Files

NetWare uses three log files that can help you diagnose problems on a NetWare server:

- ▶ The Console Log file (CONSOLE.LOG)
- ▶ The Abend Log file (ABEND.LOG)
- ▶ The Server Log file (SYS$LOG.ERR)

We'll look at these log files in greater detail in the following chapter.

Windows NT/2000 Log Files

Windows NT and 2000, like other network operating systems, employ comprehensive error and informational logging routines. Every program and process theoretically could have its own logging utility, but Microsoft has come up with a rather slick utility, Event Viewer, which, through log files, tracks all events on a particular Windows NT or 2000 computer. Normally, though, you must be an administrator or a member of the Administrators group to have access to Event Viewer.

To use Event Viewer, follow these steps:

1. Choose Start ➢ Programs ➢ Administrative Tools (Common) to open the Select Computer dialog box:

Part III

Select Computer	⊠
	OK
Computer:	Cancel
	Help
Select Computer:	
🖳 ACME 📁 S1 🖳 WORKGROUP 📁 HAL9000 This is your computer identification	
☐ Low Speed Connection	

2. In the Computer field, enter the UNC (Universal Naming Convention) name of the computer whose events you want to view.

NOTE

You can also simply double-click the computer's name in the list in the Select Computer section.

3. If you are connected to a Windows NT/2000 network over a slower link, such as a slow WAN link or a dial-up connection, click the Low Speed Connection check box to optimize Event Viewer for running over the lower-speed connection.

4. Click OK.

5. To view a log file, select it from the list.

6. To view a different log file, choose Log ➤ Select Computer.

The first time you open Event Viewer, you will automatically be brought to the System Log. Subsequently, when you open Event Viewer, the first log you see is the one you were last viewing.

WARNING

Even though this list displays Windows 95/98 computers, you cannot view log files on those computers because their logging system isn't designed to interface with Event Viewer.

Using Event Viewer, you can take a look at three types of files:

▶ The System Log

▶ The Security Log

▶ The Application Log

TIP

To view the log files of any Windows NT machine from your Windows 95/98 client, copy the Server Tools from the Windows NT Server CD to your hard disk and create a shortcut for them. The Server Tools directory is located in the \CLIENTS\SRVTOOLS\ directory on the Windows NT Server Installation CD.

The System Log This log file tracks just about every event that occurs on that computer. System Log tracks three main types of events:

▶ Information (an event occurred, especially when a service fails)

▶ Warning (an event occurred that could cause problems)

▶ Error (a component has failed and needs immediate attention)

In a log file, the icon that precedes the date indicates the event's type. Figure 15.2 shows the three types of events found in the System Log.

```
ⓘ  Information

⊙  Warning

◉  Error
```

FIGURE 15.2: Sample Log event types and their associated icons

NOTE
Two other types of events (Audit Success and Audit Failure) normally appear only in the Security Log (discussed later in this chapter).

Figure 15.3 shows a sample System Log. This list contains several categories of information, including the date and time the event occurred, the source of the event (which process the event came from), which user (if applicable) initiated the process, the name of the computer the event happened on, and the Event ID number (in the Event column). The Event ID number is the unique error type of a particular event. For an explanation of each Event ID number, check the Help file, or go to www.microsoft.com/technet/ and search for Event ID.

If you want more detail on a specific event, double-click it. Figure 15.4 shows the event detail for the following event in Figure 15.3:

    1/7/9911:33:15 AMDiskNone7N/AS1

The note in the Description box indicates that Windows NT found a bad disk block. Even though this is an error event, it is not serious. One bad block is not a problem, unless several disk blocks start going bad at once. The Data box lists the exact data the Event Viewer received about the error condition. This may be useful in determining the source of the problem. More than likely, if you have a serious problem that you can't fix, this is the information that you will send to the vendor (or to Microsoft) to help troubleshoot the problem.

Part III

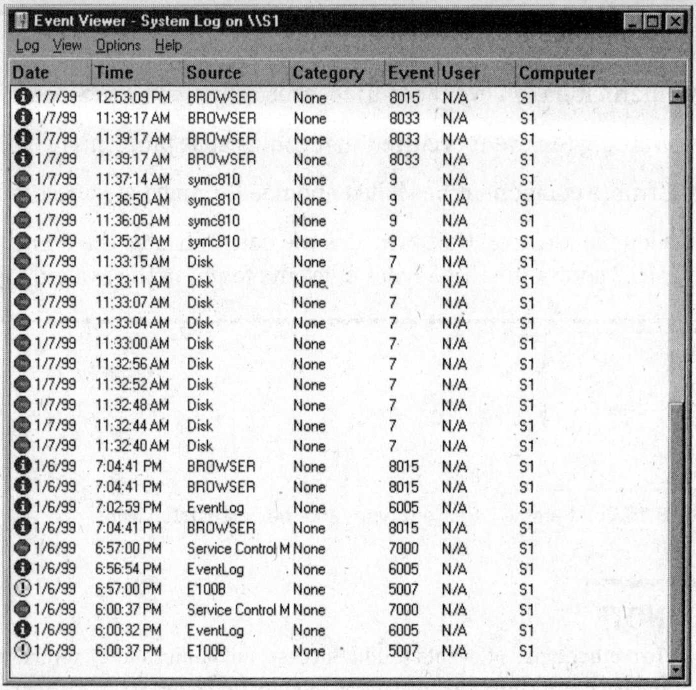

FIGURE 15.3:   A sample System Log (note the different error types and event IDs)

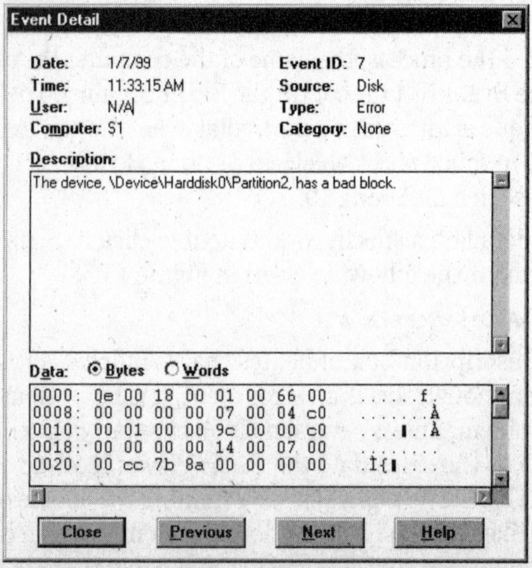

FIGURE 15.4:   The Event Detail dialog box for an event listed in Figure 15.3

The Security Log This log tracks security events specified by the domain's Audit policy. The Audit policy is set in User Manager For Domains and specifies which security items will be tracked in Event Viewer. To set the Audit policy, follow these steps:

1. Choose Start ➤ Programs ➤ User Manager For Domains to open User Manager For Domains.

2. Choose Policy ➤ Audit to open the Audit Policy dialog box:

3. Indicate the events that you want logged and check the Success or Failure check boxes to track the success and failure of those events. Since these are security settings, most often you'll want to log failures.

4. Click OK, and these events will be logged for all users and systems in the domain.

After you set the Audit policy for a domain, you can view the Security Log for any computer in that domain. Follow these steps:

1. Choose Start ➤ Programs ➤ Administrative Tools (Common) to open the Select Computer dialog box.

2. In the Computer field, enter the UNC (Universal Naming Convention) name of the computer whose events you want to view.

3. If you are connected to a Windows NT network over a slower link, such as a slow WAN link or a dial-up connection, click the Low Speed Connection check box to optimize Event Viewer for running over the lower-speed connection.

Part III

4. Click OK.
5. Choose Log ➢ Security to open the Security Log (see Figure 15.5) for that computer.

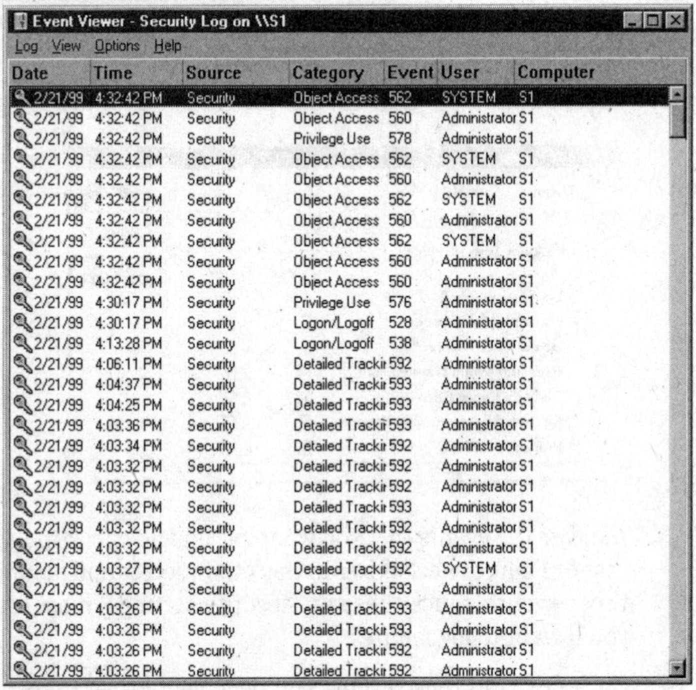
Event Viewer - Security Log on \\S1

Log View Options Help

Date	Time	Source	Category	Event	User	Computer
2/21/99	4:32:42 PM	Security	Object Access	562	SYSTEM	S1
2/21/99	4:32:42 PM	Security	Object Access	560	Administrator	S1
2/21/99	4:32:42 PM	Security	Privilege Use	578	Administrator	S1
2/21/99	4:32:42 PM	Security	Object Access	562	SYSTEM	S1
2/21/99	4:32:42 PM	Security	Object Access	560	Administrator	S1
2/21/99	4:32:42 PM	Security	Object Access	562	SYSTEM	S1
2/21/99	4:32:42 PM	Security	Object Access	560	Administrator	S1
2/21/99	4:32:42 PM	Security	Object Access	562	SYSTEM	S1
2/21/99	4:32:42 PM	Security	Object Access	560	Administrator	S1
2/21/99	4:32:42 PM	Security	Object Access	560	Administrator	S1
2/21/99	4:30:17 PM	Security	Privilege Use	576	Administrator	S1
2/21/99	4:30:17 PM	Security	Logon/Logoff	528	Administrator	S1
2/21/99	4:13:28 PM	Security	Logon/Logoff	538	Administrator	S1
2/21/99	4:06:11 PM	Security	Detailed Trackir	592	Administrator	S1
2/21/99	4:04:37 PM	Security	Detailed Trackir	593	Administrator	S1
2/21/99	4:04:25 PM	Security	Detailed Trackir	593	Administrator	S1
2/21/99	4:03:36 PM	Security	Detailed Trackir	593	Administrator	S1
2/21/99	4:03:34 PM	Security	Detailed Trackir	592	Administrator	S1
2/21/99	4:03:32 PM	Security	Detailed Trackir	592	Administrator	S1
2/21/99	4:03:32 PM	Security	Detailed Trackir	592	Administrator	S1
2/21/99	4:03:32 PM	Security	Detailed Trackir	593	Administrator	S1
2/21/99	4:03:32 PM	Security	Detailed Trackir	592	Administrator	S1
2/21/99	4:03:32 PM	Security	Detailed Trackir	592	Administrator	S1
2/21/99	4:03:27 PM	Security	Detailed Trackir	592	SYSTEM	S1
2/21/99	4:03:26 PM	Security	Detailed Trackir	593	Administrator	S1
2/21/99	4:03:26 PM	Security	Detailed Trackir	593	Administrator	S1
2/21/99	4:03:26 PM	Security	Detailed Trackir	593	Administrator	S1
2/21/99	4:03:26 PM	Security	Detailed Trackir	592	Administrator	S1
2/21/99	4:03:26 PM	Security	Detailed Trackir	592	Administrator	S1

FIGURE 15.5: The Security Log in Event Viewer

As you can see, this log looks similar to the System Log in most respects. The main differences are the icons and the types of events recorded here. To view the detail for an event, double-click it.

The Security Log displays two types of events:

- Success Audit (the event passed the security audit)
- Failure Audit (the event failed the security audit)

Figure 15.6 shows the icons associated with each of these types of events. When an item fails a security audit, something security-related failed. For example, a common entry (assuming the Logon Failure check box is checked in the Audit Policy dialog box) is a Failure Audit with a value of Logon/Logoff in the category. This means that the user failed to log on. If you look at the log shown previously in Figure 15.5, you can see that a user successfully logged on as administrator and that no failures have occurred.

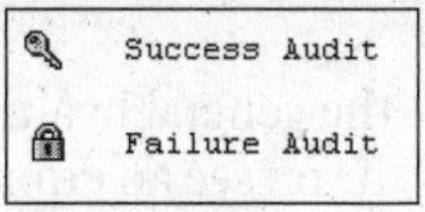

Success Audit

Failure Audit

FIGURE 15.6: The Security Log event types and their associated icons

This log is especially useful in troubleshooting when someone can't access a resource. If your domain security policy has been set to log Failures of Use Of User Rights, you can see every instance of a user not having enough rights to access a resource. The username appears in the User column of the Failure Audit event for the resource the user is trying to access.

The Application Log This log is similar to the other two logs, except that it tracks events for network services and applications (for example, SQL Server and other Back-Office products). It uses the same event types (and their associated icons) as the System Log. Figure 15.7 shows an example of an Application Log.

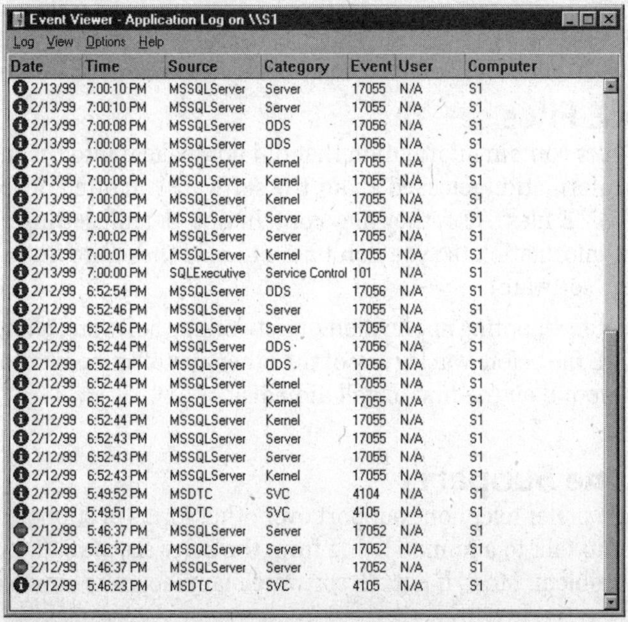

FIGURE 15.7: A sample Application event log

Part III

To access the Application Log, in Event Viewer, choose Log ➤ Application. The Sources column indicates which service logged which event. For example, in Figure 15.7, you can see three error events that came from Microsoft SQL Server (the MSSQL entry).

All together, the log files present a picture of the general health of a Windows NT or 2000 server. Generally speaking, if you see an error message, open Event Viewer and check the System Log. If you don't see the event here, check the other two logs.

Manufacturers' Troubleshooting Resources

In addition to viewing log files, you can use several types of troubleshooting tools that manufacturers make available for their network operating systems. You can use these resources to augment your own knowledge, as well as to solve those pesky problems that have no pattern or few recognizable symptoms. Each type of resource provides different information or different levels of support. Let's examine the most popular, including:

▶ README files

▶ Telephone support

▶ Technical support CD-ROM

▶ Technical support website

README Files

README files contain information that did not make it into the manual. The latest information released about the software can often be found in the README files. Also, they may contain tips, default settings, and installation information (so you don't have to read the entire first chapter to install the software).

When troubleshooting application or networking software, check out the README file before you try any of the other manufacturers' resources. It is usually found on the first installation disk or CD.

Telephone Support

Many people prefer telephone support over other forms of support. You actually get to talk to a human being from the software manufacturer about the problem. Most, if not all, software manufacturers have toll-free support numbers. The people on their end of the line can provide anything from basic how-to answers to complex, technical answers.

Unfortunately, because of their popularity, technical support phone lines are often busy. When the line is finally free, you might, however, find yourself in "voicemail hell." We've all been through it: Press 1 for support for products A, B, and C. Press 2 for Products D, E, and F, and so on and so on. Most people don't want this and hang up. They prefer to speak with a human being as soon as the call is answered. Today, phone support is often not free (the number to reach support might be, but the support itself is not), but must be purchased via either a time-limited contract or on an incident-by-incident basis. This is particularly true for network operating system software support. To solve this problem, companies have devised other methods, such as the technical support CD-ROM and website, which we will discuss next.

The Technical Support CD-ROM

With the development of CD-ROM technology, it became possible to put volumes of textual information on a readily accessible medium. The CD-ROM was, thus, a logical distribution vehicle for technical support information. In addition, the CD was portable and searchable. Introduced in the early 1990s, Novell's Network Support Encyclopedia (NSE) CD-ROM was one of the first products of this kind. Microsoft's TechNet came soon after. Both companies charge a nominal fee for a yearly subscription to these CDs (anywhere from $100 to $500).

To be sure, the first editions of these products (as with the first editions of most software products) left much to be desired. Search engines were often clumsy and slow, and the CDs were released only about twice a year. As these products evolved, however, their search engines became more advanced, they included more documents, and they were released more often. And, probably most important, manufacturers began to include software updates, drivers, and patches on the CD.

The Technical Support Website

The technical support CDs were great, but people started to complain (as people are wont to do) that because this information was vital to the health of their network, they should get it for free. Well, that is, in fact, what happened. The Internet proved to be the perfect medium for allowing network support personnel access to the same information that was on the technical support CD-ROMs. Additionally, websites can be instantly updated and accessed, so they provide the most up-to-date network support information. Since websites are hosted on servers that can store much more information than CD-ROMs, websites are more powerful than their CD-ROM counterparts. Because they are easy to access and use and because they are detailed and current, websites are now the most popular method for disseminating technical support information. As examples, you can view Novell's technical support website at `http://support.novell.com/` and Microsoft's technical support website (TechNet, a monthly subscription) at `http://support.microsoft.com/technet/`.

Hardware Troubleshooting Tools

In addition to manufacturer-provided troubleshooting tools, there are a few hardware devices we can use to troubleshoot the network. These are actual devices that you can use during the troubleshooting process. Some devices have easily recognizable functions; others are more obscure. Four of the most popular hardware tools are:

▶ A crossover cable

▶ A hardware loopback

▶ A tone generator

▶ A tone locator

The Crossover Cable

Sometimes also called a cross cable, a *crossover cable* is typically used to connect two hubs, but it can also be used to test communications between two stations directly, bypassing the hub. A crossover cable is used only in Ethernet UTP installations. You can connect two workstation NICs (or a workstation and a server NIC) directly using a crossover cable.

A normal Ethernet (10BaseT) UTP cable uses four wires—two to transmit and two to receive. Figure 15.8 shows this wiring, with all wires going from pins on one side directly to the same pins on the other side.

The standard Ethernet UTP crossover cable used in both situations has its transmit and receive wire pairs crossed so that the transmit set on one side (hooked to pins 1 and 2) is connected to the receive set (pins 3 and 6) on the other. Figure 15.9 illustrates this arrangement. Note that four of the wires are crossed as compared with the straight-through wiring of the standard 10BaseT UTP cable shown in Figure 15.8.

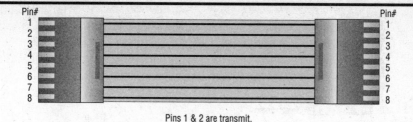

Pins 1 & 2 are transmit,
Pins 3 & 6 are receive

FIGURE 15.8:   A standard Ethernet 10BaseT cable

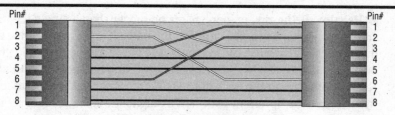

Pins 1 & 2 connect to pins 3 & 6
Pins 3 & 6 connect to pins 1 & 2

FIGURE 15.9:   A standard Ethernet 10BaseT crossover cable

TIP

Be sure to label a crossover cable as such to ensure that no one tries to use it as a workstation patch cable. If it is used as a patch cable, the workstation won't be able to communicate with the hub and the rest of the network.

You can carry a crossover cable in the tool bag along with your laptop. If you want to ensure that a server's NIC is functioning correctly, you can connect your laptop directly to the server's NIC using the crossover cable. You should be able to log in to the server (assuming both NICs are configured correctly).

The Hardware Loopback

A *hardware loopback* is a special connector for Ethernet 10BaseT NICs. It functions similarly to a crossover cable, except that it connects the transmit pins directly to the receive pins (as shown in Figure 15.10). It is used by the NIC's software diagnostics to test transmission and reception capabilities. You cannot completely test a NIC without one of these devices.

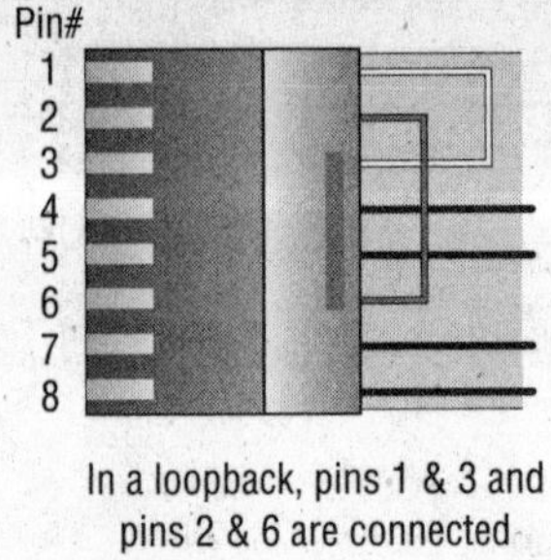

Pin#
1
2
3
4
5
6
7
8

In a loopback, pins 1 & 3 and
pins 2 & 6 are connected

FIGURE 15.10:   A hardware loopback and its connections

Usually, the hardware loopback is no bigger than a single RJ-45 connector with a few small wires on the back. If a NIC has hardware diagnostics that can use the loopback, the hardware loopback plug will be included with the NIC. To use it, simply plug the loopback into the RJ-45 connector on the back of the NIC and start the diagnostic software. Select the option in your NIC's diagnostic software that requires the loopback, and start the diagnostic routine. You will be able to tell if the NIC can send and receive data through the use of these diagnostics.

Tone Generator and Tone Locator

This combination of devices is used most often on telephone systems to locate cables. Since telephone systems use multiple pairs of UTP, it is nearly impossible to determine which set of wires goes where. Network documentation would be extremely helpful in making this determination, but if no documentation is available, you can use a tone generator and locator.

NOTE
Don't confuse these tools with a cable tester that tests cable quality. You use the tone generator and locator only to determine which UTP cable is which.

The *tone generator* is a small electronic device that sends an electrical signal down one set of UTP wires. The *tone locator* is another device that is designed to emit a tone when it detects the signal in a particular set of wires. When you need to trace a cable, hook the generator (often called the *fox*) to the copper ends of the wire pair you want to find. Then move the locator (often called the *hound* because it chases the fox) over multiple sets of cables (you don't have to touch the copper part of the wire pairs;

this tool works by induction) until you hear the tone. A soft tone indicates that you are close to the right set of wires. Keep moving the tool until the tone gets the loudest. Bingo! You have found the wire set. Figure 15.11 shows a tone generator and locator and how they are used.

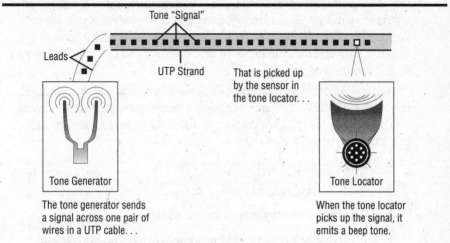

The tone generator sends a signal across one pair of wires in a UTP cable. . .

When the tone locator picks up the signal, it emits a beep tone.

FIGURE 15.11:   Use of a common tone generator and locator

WARNING

Never hook a tone generator to a cable that is hooked up to either a NIC or a hub! Because the tone generator sends electrical signals down the wire, it can blow a NIC or a hub. That is why tone generators are not usually used on networks. Cable testers are used more often. We'll discuss cable testers later in this chapter.

Software Troubleshooting Tools

In addition to these hardware troubleshooting tools, you can use software programs to gain information about the current health and state of the network. These tools fall into two main categories:

▶ Protocol analyzers

▶ Performance-monitoring tools

We use the term *network software diagnostics* to refer to these tools.

Protocol Analyzer

Any software that can analyze and display the packets it receives can be considered a *protocol analyzer*. Protocol analyzers examine packets from protocols that operate at the lower four layers of the OSI model (including Transport, Network, Data Link, and Physical) and can display any errors they detect. Additionally, most protocol analyzers can capture packets and decode their contents. Capturing packets involves copying a series of packets from the network into memory and holding the copy so that it can be analyzed.

You could, for example, capture a series of packets and decode their contents to figure out where each packet came from, where it was going, which protocol sent it, which protocol should receive it, and so on. For example, you can find out:

- ► The nature of the traffic on your network
- ► Which protocol is used most often
- ► If users are accessing unauthorized sites
- ► If a particular network card is jabbering (sending out packets when there is no data to send)

Two common examples of protocol analyzers are Sniffer, a Network General product, and Novell's LANalyzer.

Performance-Monitoring Tools

In addition to protocol analyzers, many network operating systems include tools for monitoring network performance and can display statistics such as the number of packets sent and received, server processor utilization, the amount of data going in and out of the server, and so on. NetWare comes with the MONITOR.NLM utility, and Windows NT comes with Performance Monitor. Both monitor performance statistics. You can use these utilities to determine the source of the bottleneck when users complain that the network is slow.

NOTE

To start the MONITOR.NLM utility in NetWare, simply type **LOAD MONITOR** at the console prompt. To start the Performance Monitor program in Windows NT, you must first be logged in as Administrator (or a member of the Server Operators group). Once you are logged in, choose Start ➤ Programs ➤ Administrative Tools ➤ Performance Monitor.

TROUBLESHOOTING TIPS

Now that we have covered the basics of network troubleshooting, we should go over a few troubleshooting tips. These tips will give you more "ammo" while you're hunting for network problems and using the various steps of the troubleshooting model discussed earlier.

Don't Overlook the Small Stuff

If you'll remember, the first thing we discussed in this chapter was small stuff. Often a problem is caused by something simple, such as a power switch in the wrong position, a card or port not functioning (as indicated by a link light that's not lit), or simply operator error. Even the most experienced administrator has forgotten to turn on the power, left a cable unplugged, or mistyped a username and password.

Finally, make sure that users get training for the systems they use. That may seem like an extra bother, but an hour or two of training goes a long way toward preventing problems. The number of incidents of EEOC will decline with a little user training.

Prioritize Your Problems

It is unlikely that as a network administrator or technician, you will receive problem calls one at a time. Typically, when you receive one call, you already have three people waiting for service. For this reason, you must learn to prioritize.

You start this process by asking some basic questions of the person reporting the problem so that you can determine its severity. If the current problem is minor and you have two more serious problems already facing you, your priorities are obvious.

You establish priorities to ensure that you spend your time wisely. The order in which you attempt to solve your networking problems, from highest priority to lowest, might look something like this:

- ▶ Total network failure (affects everyone)

- ▶ Partial network failure (affects small groups of users)

- ▶ Small network failure (affects a small, single group of users)

- ▶ Total workstation failure (single user can't work at all)

Part III

▶ Partial workstation failure (single user can't do most tasks)

▶ Minor issue (single user has problems that crop up now and again)

Mitigating circumstances can, of course, change the order of this list. For example, if the president of the company can't retrieve her e-mail, you'd take the express elevator to her office as soon as you hang up from the call. Also, a minor, persistent problem might move up the ladder.

Remember also that some simple problems may take more effort than larger problems. You may be able to bring up a crashed server in a matter of minutes, but a user who doesn't know how to make columns line up in Microsoft Word may take up to an hour or longer to train. The latter of these problems might get relegated toward the bottom of the list because of the time involved. It is more efficient to solve problems for a larger group of people than to fix this one user's problem immediately.

Some network administrators list all network service requests on a chalkboard or a whiteboard. They then prioritize them based on the previously discussed criteria. Some larger companies have written support-call tracking software whose only function is to track and prioritize all network and computer problems. Use whatever method makes you comfortable, but prioritize your calls.

Check the Software Configuration

Often, network problems can be traced to software configuration (as with our DNS configuration example earlier in this chapter). When you are checking for software problems, don't forget to check configuration, including the following:

▶ DNS configuration

▶ WINS configuration

▶ HOSTS file

▶ AUTOEXEC.BAT (DOS and Windows)

▶ CONFIG.SYS (DOS and Windows)

▶ STARTUP.NCF, AUTOEXEC.NCF, and server parameter settings (NetWare)

▶ The Registry (Windows 95/98 and NT/2000)

Software configuration settings love to hide in places like these and can be notoriously hard to find (especially in the Registry).

Additionally, in text configuration files, look for lines that have been commented out (either intentionally or accidentally). A command such as REM or REMARK or the asterisk or semicolon characters indicate comment lines in a file.

TIP

The HOSTS file uses a # (pound sign) to indicate a comment line, as does NetWare's NCF files.

Don't Overlook Physical Conditions

You want to make sure that from a network design standpoint, the physical environment for a server is optimized for placement, temperature, and humidity. When troubleshooting an obscure network problem, don't forget to check the physical conditions under which the network device is operating. Check for problems such as the following:

- ▶ Excessive heat
- ▶ Excessive humidity (condensation)
- ▶ Low humidity (leads to ESD problems)
- ▶ EMI/RFI problems
- ▶ ESD problems
- ▶ Power problems
- ▶ Unplugged cables

Don't Overlook Cable Problems

Cables, generally speaking, work fine once they are installed properly. Rarely is the cabling system the problem, unless someone has made some change to it. If you suspect that the cabling system is the problem, try replacing the patch cables at the workstation and hub first. These are easiest to get to (and replace). If that solves the problem, you know the problem was related to the patch cable. It was either faulty or the wrong type.

Part III

If the patch cable isn't the problem, use a cable tester (not a tone generator and locator) to find the source of the problem. Wires that are moved can be prone to breaking or shorting. A short can happen when the wire conductor comes in contact with another conductive surface, changing the path of the electrical signal. The signal will go someplace else instead of to the intended recipient. You can use cable testers to test for many types of problems, including:

- Broken cables
- Incorrect connections
- Interference levels
- Total cable length (for length restrictions)
- Cable shorts
- Connector problems

NOTE
As a matter of fact, cable testers are so sophisticated that they can even indicate the exact location of a cable break, accurate to within 6 inches or better.

Check for Viruses

Many troubleshooters overlook virus scanning because they assume that the network virus-checking software should have picked up any viruses. We're reminded by the network virus-scanning software of the bio-filters in the transporter on *Star Trek: The Next Generation*. They work great as long as the computer has the latest information on what the virus is and how to eliminate it. On many occasions, though, the ship's doctor or engineer had to reprogram the bio-filters to recognize some new virus that the crew of the *Enterprise* had come across.

The same thing happens with network virus-scanning software; to be effective, it must be kept up-to-date. Updates are made available almost daily. You must run the virus definition update utility to keep the virus definition file current.

If you are having strange, unusual, irreproducible problems with a workstation, try scanning it with an up-to-date virus scan utility. You'd be surprised how many times people have spent hours and hours troubleshooting a strange problem, only to run a virus scan utility, find and clean one or more viruses, and have the problem disappear.

SUMMARY

In this chapter, you learned about the proper methods of troubleshooting network problems. In the first section, you learned the proper method to start to fix any network problem by eliminating what the problem is *not*. You learned how to narrow the problem down to its essentials and therefore further define it.

Next, you learned a systematic approach to troubleshooting, using an eight-step troubleshooting model to troubleshoot almost any problems you may encounter on your network. After that, you learned about several resources that you can use to help you during the troubleshooting process. You learned about the websites and other support tools available for most vendors' products.

Finally, you learned a few troubleshooting tips that will help make the troubleshooting process go more smoothly. As you venture out into the "real world," keep these tips in mind, as they will help make you an expert troubleshooter.

WHAT'S NEXT

In the next chapter, we'll continue honing our troubleshooting skills as we look in greater detail at finding and fixing problems in a NetWare networking environment.

Part III

Chapter 16
DIAGNOSING REAL-WORLD PROBLEMS

No matter how carefully you plan, how carefully you build your network, and how carefully you train your users, things will go wrong. In fact, having things go wrong is a normal part of your network operations. When things don't go wrong, you should worry.

When something on the network is not working properly, you must change hats from strategic thinker to ambulance driver. Even if the problem is not much of a problem to the network as a whole, the affected user needs to be reassured. Psychology is important. When users have a problem, they don't want to hear that it isn't a big problem, because it is big to them. They want to hear that you understand their problem and are working to fix that problem. They will be reasonable (probably) if you acknowledge their distress ("I feel your pain") and inform them of your actions to resolve the problem.

Adapted from *Mastering NetWare 6* by James E. Gaskin
ISBN 0-7821-4023-8   864 pages $69.99

In the last chapter, we looked at network troubleshooting. Here we take it one step forward and look at troubleshooting in a NetWare environment.

GENERAL TROUBLESHOOTING TIPS

What changed? This question must spring immediately into your mind when a problem appears. Something almost always changes. Computer hardware has gotten so reliable that it's rare to find outright physical failures. Disk drives still wear out and power supplies still die, but hardware failure will not be a problem at the top of your list of aggravations.

I contend that you don't manage a network; you manage network changes. If nothing is changing, there's no troubleshooting to do. When nothing changes, you can focus on the future and try to keep up with your computer trade magazines. When you're adding users, software, and hardware, there will always be something to fix.

There are, however, occasions when a hardware component does cause your problem, even if it isn't a component failure. How about someone moving a wiring concentrator plug from a UPS to a wall plug? When the power blips and takes your concentrator offline, is that a component failure? Yes, and no. Something changed, and you can't blame that on component failure.

Many network managers have developed a "top-10" list of troubleshooting or prevention tips. Rather than stopping at 10, here's everything I could find, think of, or steal. Let's start with preventive measures.

A TROUBLESHOOTING SCENE

Let's look at a troubleshooting situation as a scene from a movie, or, more appropriately, a sitcom.

(SCENE: Irate user who can't boot his computer to the network.)

YOU: "What's the problem?"

USER: "Your stupid network is broken." (User registers disgust and waves an arm toward the defunct computer.)

YOU (sitting at the computer): "Your hard disk seems to be dead."

CONTINUED ➡

This is the time many network managers try to defend their network, pointing out that the user's problem is caused by and limited to the user. Your "stupid" network had nothing to do with this problem. However, resist this urge. The user is angry, and he will now be embarrassed. Anything you say in defense of the network will be seen by the user as "rubbing my nose in it."

YOU: "Let me configure a spare computer, so you can get logged in to the network. We'll order a new hard disk for you, and I'll bring your system back as soon as possible."

USER: "Thanks for your prompt attention to this matter. I apologize for disparaging the network, but I was upset by this disk failure. Please forgive me. Allow me to buy you lunch today in apology."

(ACTION: Glowing sunshine warmly colors the scene. Birds sing. Flowers bloom. Theme music swells.)

Perhaps this scenario is a bit far out, even for Hollywood. But the idea of not defending your network against an angry user is a good one. Angry people often need to blow off steam, and you're a good target. You aren't the boss, so you can't fire them. You aren't an immediate co-worker, so the user won't be embarrassed every morning afterward. You are a fairly safe target for the user's anger. Anything you say in defense of your network, or that insinuates that the problem is self-caused, will only make the user angrier. This is a "no-win" situation for you, at least in the short term.

Letting the user win doesn't make you a doormat. The network administrator's favorite fable is "The User Who Cried Wolf" for good reason. You will soon learn which users howl the loudest with the smallest problems. When several problems arrive at once, as they often do, you may safely put these users at the bottom of the help list. After all, you have already documented your multiple quick responses, right? How can they complain if they were served quickly many times and only served slowly when a larger network crisis appeared? Well, they will complain, but no one will listen to them, because you have documentation. That's the beauty of CYAWP (Cover Your A** With Paper).

Part III

Prevention Tips

The following are some prevention strategies you can try.

Ask your management to decide on a downtime "comfort level."   The faster you want to resurrect the network, the more money you must spend in preparation. A maximum of a few minutes of downtime can be guaranteed by using the two-node Cluster Services license included with NetWare 6 and by having backup hardware for every system wiring component. Downtime will stretch to several hours if you have some, but not all, of your replacement equipment available. Downtime will stretch to a day or more if you rely completely on outside resources.

Have your management decide which users must get back to work first.   In case of a serious network problem, you may be able to support only a few users. Which users will those be?

Know what you have.   Inventory all your network hardware and software. How else will you buy spare parts and get updated replacement drivers?

Expect everything and everyone to let you down.   If you expect the worst, you're prepared for anything. You're also pleasantly surprised almost all the time, since the worst rarely happens.

Anything that *can* fail *will* fail.   Be prepared for any LAN component to fail, be stolen, or be tampered with.

Know your component failure profiles.   On a server, failures are likely to be (in order): disks, RAM, the power supply, or network adapters. The same applies to a workstation, but only one user is inconvenienced.

Balance your network to eliminate as many single points of failure as possible.   Many network administrators spread every workgroup across two wiring concentrators, so one failure won't disable an entire department. You can also spread a group's applications across multiple servers, which is easy to do with NetWare 6.

Spend the money necessary to back up your system every night.   The quickest way to recover from corrupt or lost data files is by using a complete backup made the night before. Most restores will be user files deleted by accident. The previous night's tape will solve that problem if the NetWare SALVAGE command doesn't do the job.

Test your backup and restore software and hardware.   How long does it take to completely restore a volume with your backup hardware and software? You can't bring a replacement hard disk online until the restored files are in place.

Duplicate system knowledge among the administrative staff.   If a person, even you, is the single point of failure, take precautions. I know you feel you're always there, but do you want to come back from your honeymoon to replace a disk drive? Start some cross-training.

Your suppliers will let you down sometime, somehow. Support organizations have problems, too. Don't bet the ranch on your dealer stocking a replacement drive that they "always" have. If you must have one without fail, have it on your shelf.

Find sources of information before you need them.   Check out Novell's website, and participate in NetWare-oriented bulletin board services and Internet newsgroups. The more you know, and the more places you can go for quick information, the better off you are.

Document everything far more than you think necessary. Write down everything about your network, then fill in the blanks. Assume that your manager must recover the network while you're on your honeymoon (definitely without your beeper or cell phone). Will your documentation provide the manager with enough information? If some or all of your documentation is stored electronically, reprint the information after every substantial change and store the paper in a safe location. It's hard to read electronic documentation from a dead server disk.

Keep valuable network information in a safe.   Your password, some backup tapes, boot disks, software licenses, proof of purchase forms, and a copy of your network documentation should be in a safe—literally. Only network administrators and your manager should have access to this safe.

Make your network as standardized as possible.   Hardware and software consistency is not the hobgoblin of small minds; it's the savior of the harried administrator. Standardized configuration and policy files make life easier. It may be impossible to keep them consistent, but try. Find a good network adapter card and stick with it. Make as few different Windows Desktop arrangements as you can.

Make a detailed recovery plan in case of a partial or complete network disaster and test your recovery plan. Companies with workable recovery plans stay in business after a disaster. Those with no recovery plans are rarely in business two years after the disaster. But you'll never be sure that the plan works until the plan is tried. Do you want to try the plan after office hours in a test or while the CEO is looking over your shoulder? Test the plan as well as the people involved.

Put step-by-step instructions on the wall above every piece of configurable equipment. Every server, gateway, or communications box should have a complete operational outline on the wall above the equipment. It should cover all steps necessary for a computer novice to take the system down and/or bring the system back up. Large companies with a night support staff will find this particularly useful.

Tips for Solving Problems

Network problems can be both physical (cable) and virtual (protocols). This makes troubleshooting more fun than normal.

No matter how prepared you are, something will go wrong. It's nothing personal—it's just life. When faced with a problem, the following hints may be of some help.

What changed? I said this at the beginning, but it's worth repeating. When there's a problem, 99 percent of the time, somebody changed something somewhere. Scientists have disproved the idea of "bit rot," where software that did work goes sour and mutates into software that doesn't. However, it's common for workstation software to be pushed beyond its capabilities or to be modified by new applications. But that is a change, isn't it?

When you hear hoofbeats, look for horses before you look for zebras. Check the simple things first; hoofbeats are more likely to come from horses than from zebras (at least in Texas, where I'm writing this). Is the plug in the wall? Is the power on? Is the monitor brightness turned up? (I once drove across town in a snowstorm to turn up the brightness on a Unix system monitor.) Is this the right cable? Is the cable plugged in on both ends? Is a connection loose? You get the idea—nothing is too simple to verify before going on to the next step.

Isolate the problem.   Does this problem happen with other machines? Does it happen with this same username? Will this system work on another network segment? Will the server talk to another workstation? Can you ping the system having trouble?

Don't change something that works.   If you change a configuration parameter and that doesn't fix the problem, change the parameter back to what it was. The same goes for hardware. No use introducing new variables from new hardware or software while you're still trying to find the problem. Let me say this again: if you change something and it doesn't fix your original problem, change it back. It may look okay now, but you will more often than not mess up more than you fix if you change things all over the place.

Check your typing.   Typos in the configuration files will cause as much of a problem as the wrong command. Your software won't work well if your path includes \WINCOWS rather than \WINDOWS.

Read the documentation.   Equipment documentation may not be good enough, but it's better than nothing. Print out the readme files from the installation disks and keep the printout with the manuals. It's much easier for manufacturers to put crucial manual modifications in the readme file than in the manual.

Look for patches.   Check Novell's website for files to update your troublesome hardware. Call the vendor of third-party products for new drivers for network adapters and drive controllers.

Refer to previous trouble logs.   Keep a log of problems and solutions for your network. Even a new problem may be related to an old problem you've solved before.

Trust, but verify, everything a user tells you.   People interpret the same events different ways. What is unnoticed by a user may be a crucial bit of information for you. If a user tells you a screen looks a certain way, take a look for yourself.

Call your NetWare dealer early in the process. Buying your NetWare hardware and software from a local dealer gives you the right to call and ask for help. This is especially true during and just after installation. If you have a good relationship with your dealer, the support people should answer specific questions (such as, "Does this network adapter have a different driver when used in the server?") without charge. Be prepared to pay for support if your questions are open-ended ("Why doesn't this server talk to the workstation?") or you request a technician to come and look at your system.

Check out a Novell Support Connection subscription. Tons of information are on every update. Patches, white papers, compatibility reports, and tips of all kinds are there if you look.

Call Novell technical support. It's better to spend the money on 1-800-858-4000 than to leave your network down for a second day. But don't call until you've gone through the documentation, the Novell website, and all local support resources. It's embarrassing to find out during a paid support call that the solution is in the manual.

Do things methodically, one by one. Don't make a "brilliant" leap of deductive reasoning; that's a high-risk/high-reward procedure. Las Vegas casinos are rich because suckers play long odds. Keep following the plan, and don't try to be a hero.

LEARNING YOUR NETWORK'S NORMAL OPERATION

Do you know what your car sounds like when it's working properly? Do you know the beeps and buzzes your computer makes as it boots? Do you know how your body feels as you struggle out of bed?

Of course you do. You know these things from regular repetition. More important, you know that when one of those sounds or feelings is not right, something needs to be checked out.

Your network is the same way. You must learn how it is when it's normal so you can quickly tell when it isn't normal.

Tracking Aids

Several obvious things help you track the details of your network's normal operation.

Paper, in this case network documentation, is more necessary than you may imagine. You have about 2000 items to remember for every user. If you have a lot of users, learn to write down everything, or every day will be a rough day.

An activity log is vital to managing large networks. This log doesn't need to be fancy, just consistent. If you keep the log on paper, you should regularly put it in a database to organize and comment on the results of each action. Having it available on the system makes it easier for other administrators to share, but having a backup copy on paper (current copy, of course) keeps it useful when the system dies.

Help desk software is becoming inexpensive enough for small- and medium-sized companies. By tracking every support call from users, you maintain a single database with all trouble calls listed, cataloged, and indexed. Most important, this type of software tracks and shares the little, but aggravating, configuration details for many software packages that cause your network problems. If you have more than two network managers, you can benefit from help desk software.

Tracking Downtime

Networks are often judged harshly by old mainframers, since one or more stations or printers may be unavailable at any one time. To some, especially those who wish to cast aspersions on your network, this will count as downtime and be held against you. Don't let them define downtime to fit their terms. In fact, let's define downtime and another type of network time:

- *Downtime* is the time when a network service or resource is unavailable to any user.

- *Crosstime* is the time when a service object, such as a printer, is down, but the user has easy options to use comparable services.

If a server is down, but all users can log in through eDirectory, they are not down. The few users who need access to volumes on the down server do suffer downtime; everyone else suffers crosstime. Routing to another printer in place of your normal printer is not downtime; it's crosstime.

You should track the times that resources are down, but you must put this information into context. If you have 10 servers, and one server is down for one day, your servers are 90 percent available that day. If that is the only down day in a 30-day month, the monthly total for server availability is 99.67 percent available (299 available server days divided by 300 possible server days). This is very acceptable, even to mainframe bigots.

TIP

If the mainframe people give you too much trouble, ask for their remote-access uptime. It's usually lousy. They'll blame it on the phone lines. Just laugh and walk away.

Of the 2,000 details you must track for users, about 1,950 of them are tied to their workstations, especially if they run a Windows operating system. Don't feel bad if you never feel in control of Windows workstations on your network. With the added complexity that comes with the Registry, it is often difficult to get a handle on exactly what is happening on a particular computer. Thank you, Microsoft, for foisting on us a system where every new application can (and regularly does) overwrite critical system files for other applications.

Regardless of the hassle factor, you must make some baseline of your workstations, servers, and network in general. You might want to check some of the third-party server management software available, but you can also monitor your network fairly well with the tools NetWare provides.

Tracking Normal Server Performance

It's easy to ignore the server when it's running as it should. You have so many other little problems, such as printers that act strangely and users who behave even more strangely, that you leave the server alone.

Although it's easy not to pay attention to the server, it isn't advisable. You must spend a few minutes now and then checking on the server when it's running well so you'll have some idea of what it should look like under normal circumstances. Believe me, when it's down and you can't figure out why, you'll wish you had a few screen shots and configuration files saved in a notebook on your desk (hint, hint).

Monitoring Programs

MONITOR was your best bet for tracking server performance during the day (now the NetWare Remote Manager's Health Monitor screens work better). Many network managers leave MONITOR on-screen all the time. Even the snake-like screen saver (SCRSAVER.NLM) indicates server activity. The longer and faster the snake gets, the more server activity going on.

When the MONITOR program is running, four important performance indicators are evident from the General Information screen:

▶ The Utilization field shows how much CPU time is being spent servicing the network. This is half of the network load, with disk activity being the other half. If this number regularly stays over 50 percent for more than a minute or two at a time, you need more horsepower. It's possible for this number to run over 100 percent, so don't overreact if you see 103 percent utilization sometime.

▶ The Total Cache Buffers field is an indicator of file performance. The lower this number, the slower file performance will be. If less than half of your cache buffers are in the Total category, you need to get more RAM.

▶ The Current Service Processes number indicates outstanding read requests. When a read request comes in but there is no way to handle it immediately, a service process is created to perform the read as quickly as possible. Having too few cache buffers will run up this number. If you have plenty of RAM but increasing service processes, you need disk channel help. Upgrade the controller or disk, or move high-load applications to another server.

▶ Packet Receive Buffers hold packets from workstations until they can be handled by the server. They will be allocated as needed, but a gradually increasing number indicates that the server isn't keeping up with the load. Two thousand buffers are allocated automatically to support the Enterprise Web Server.

Figure 16.1 shows the MONITOR main screen, with the General Information window open to show all statistics. You can press Tab to shrink or expand this window. Shrink it to use the Available Options menu.

The other screen you may leave open in MONITOR is the Disk Cache Utilization Statistics view. You can see the Disk Cache Utilization menu choice at the bottom of Figure 16.1. If the Long Term Cache Hits figure stays above 90 percent, you have a server that's well configured for file service.

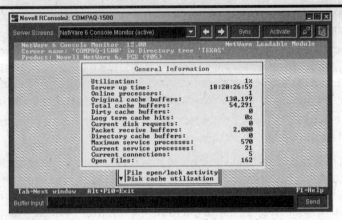

FIGURE 16.1: The standard server performance check

You should take a few screen shots of your server's MONITOR screen now and then. Using RConsoleJ makes this easy (old-timers used to scratch the numbers in stone tablets, since there was no way to capture a server console screen to a printer before RCONSOLE, the IPX-based predecessor to RConsoleJ). Make a few of these screen shots for each server now and then, with a notation of the date and time. Connections and open files are shown at the bottom of the window. Both of these are good load indicators for referencing the server activity.

If you prefer, you can use NetWare Remote Manager's Health Monitor and Multiple Server Monitor screens to monitor your servers. In this utility, you can see all of the important parameters at a glance, with links to click for more information. A traffic light indicates the status of each parameter, glowing green for good, yellow for suspect, or red for bad.

Server Log Files

NetWare automatically creates three server log files: SYS$LOG.ERR, VOL$LOG.ERR, and TTS$LOG.ERR. One more server log file, CONSOLE.LOG, is optional.

NOTE

The BOOT$LOG.ERR file in the SYS:\SYSTEM directory holds comparatively little information. The ABEND.LOG is one error file I hope you never see. ABEND.LOG is moved to the SYS:\SYSTEM directory when the server is restarted after an ABEND (ABnormal ENDing). This term is an old mainframe term, believe it or not. How it got loaded into NetWare in the early versions is anyone's guess.

SYS$LOG.ERR   SYS$LOG.ERR contains file server errors and general status information. This log file is stored in the \SYSTEM directory and can be viewed with ConsoleOne or any file viewer.

The SYS$LOG.ERR file is normally checked using the ConsoleOne program, but this viewer can't show a long log file. The beginning of the log file will not be shown, on the assumption that you are more interested in immediate history. If you wish to see the entire log file, you must use a text viewer.

Figure 16.2 shows the error log file for GW2K displayed in ConsoleOne. Vertical scroll bars are available to allow you to see more of the file. The text viewer always complains the log length makes it impossible to show, so some must be truncated.

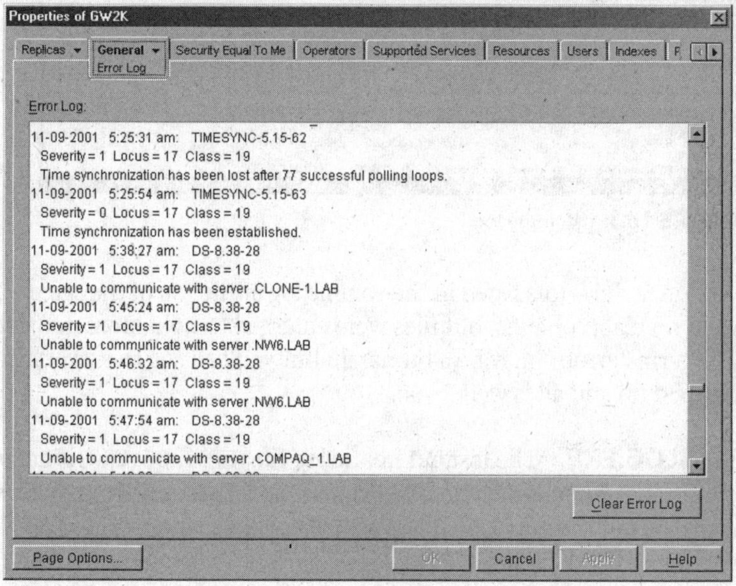

FIGURE 16.2:   Errors and server information

Notice that items that are not normally considered errors are tracked in this file. The first two messages complain that Time Synchronization dropped, then time became synchronized again. The other complaints concern servers revised or moved out of the LAB network but not yet out of eDirectory.

VOL$LOG.ERR   The volume log, VOL$LOG.ERR, shows volume errors and status information. It is created automatically and stored in the root of each traditional NetWare volume. There are no special viewers or ways to reach this log except to read it as a text file, but you won't need to read it often.

Figure 16.3 shows an example of a volume log in the life of a lab server. It's up, it's down, it's up, it's down, it's up—but mostly it's up. Most of your volume log will indicate this yo-yo type of activity. It may stretch over several years, since many volumes stay mounted for months at a time.

```
MS Command Prompt - list vol$log.err                        _ □ ☒
LIST      31      101     04-27-:0 11:51  ♦ VOL$LOG.ERR
Volume SYS mounted on Tuesday, March 21, 2000   9:29:12 pm.
Volume mount had the following errors that were fixed:
Problem with file Q_80B9.SRU, (TTS file...was not changed)
  length kept = 0, had allocated = 65536
Problem with file Q_80B9.SYS, (TTS file...was not changed)
  length kept = 0, had allocated = 65536
Problem with file _T-00004.TMP, length extended.
Problem with file _T-00004.TMP,  old length = 0, new length = 65536
Problem with file CONSOLE.LOG, length extended.
Problem with file CONSOLE.LOG,  old length = 0, new length = 327680

Volume SYS dismounted on Wednesday, March 22, 2000   5:04:59 am.

Volume SYS mounted on Wednesday, March 22, 2000   9:40:12 am.

Volume SYS dismounted on Thursday, March 23, 2000   2:08:02 am.

Volume SYS mounted on Thursday, March 23, 2000   7:14:54 am.

Volume SYS dismounted on Saturday, March 25, 2000   9:04:51 pm.

Volume SYS mounted on Monday, March 27, 2000   7:39:52 am.
Command▶                        Keys: ↑↓←→ PgUp PgDn F10=exit F1=Help
```

FIGURE 16.3: Volume log

Notice the errors listed in the volume log at the top of the screen. There were no real problems, but files were enlarged to hold more information. The term "errors" may be a bit harsh, but you can see that everything got cleaned up and all is well.

TTS$LOG.ERR   The last automatic log file, TTS$LOG.ERR, is activated only on those servers where TTS (Transaction Tracking System) is enabled, meaning only on traditional NetWare filesystem volumes (not on NSS volumes). If TTS is started, the log is started. Those servers without TTS enabled will not have the log file.

This file is stored in the root of each traditional NetWare volume with TTS active and can be viewed with a file viewer.

TTS guarantees that transactions are completely finished or completely undone back to the pretransaction state, the precursor to the journaling filesystem used in NSS. The log file lists times and data file names rolled back because of an incomplete transaction. This file won't have much inside it, except a time and date stamp of when TTS was started or shut down. These times will match those in the volume log.

CONSOLE.LOG   CONSOLE.LOG is a bit different. It keeps a copy of all console messages that normally scroll by quickly as the server boots. This is an optional log file, which is started by the line LOAD CONLOG in the AUTOEXEC.NCF file. This log file is stored in the \SYS:ETC directory and can be viewed using INETCFG or with a file viewer. Figure 16.4 shows a part of the CONSOLE.LOG file.

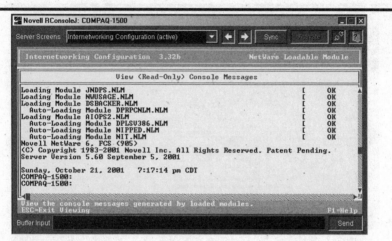

FIGURE 16.4:   Console comments in a file

This viewer is in the INETCFG utility, loaded at the server console. To see the file, type **LOAD INETCFG** at the console or go through RConsoleJ (choose View Configuration ➢ Console Messages). All the messages sent to the console are tracked here.

As the screen in Figure 16.4 says, the log is shown as read-only. You can open the log in the \SYS:ETC directory with a file viewer if you wish. You can also use a text editor to make notes about the log process before you print the log for safekeeping.

Server Configuration File Copies

Printing logs for safekeeping is a good idea. Having a clean server boot record may come in handy someday when you're trying to re-create a load sequence for a long list of NLMs.

The log files just mentioned are easy to find and print. There are a couple of other quick options, as well. Figure 16.5 shows the option to copy all SET parameters to a file.

The MONITOR utility offers a chance to copy all parameters to a file every time you leave the Select A Parameter Category menu of the Server Parameters option. When you choose to copy all parameters to a file, the SETCMDS.CP file is copied to the SYS:\SYSTEM directory. That location is the default, but you can change that path. Once the file location is chosen, every SET command is listed with the current setting.

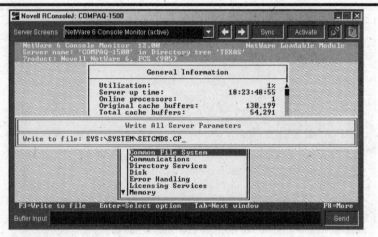

FIGURE 16.5:   Take advantage of this option

There isn't any help information in this file, and the file is nearly 9KB of ASCII text (on my server), but it's good to have. Some of the SET parameters can be a real problem if they are incorrect. Having a clean copy of the parameters for each of your servers is handy if a problem should arise.

You can also do this from NetWare Remote Manager. Select Set Parameters from the menu on the left, and the 14 configuration screens will appear under the heading of Category Name. At the end of the 14 screens, the Save Settings To A File On Volume SYS: option awaits, just below a bar labeled Set Parameter Control.

The AUTOEXEC.NCF file is kept in the \SYS:SYSTEM directory. It's easy to find, so make a quick printout of it every time it changes. Put it in the server notebook. Keep the old ones, so you can return to a former configuration if necessary.

The easiest way to get a copy of STARTUP.NCF is while the server is down. This file is kept in the \NWSERVER directory of the DOS partition by default. You may have placed it in a different directory during installation, but look in \NWSERVER first. If it is there, copy it to floppy disk and print it later. Your alternative is to look at it in the Install program (choose NCF File Options ➤ Edit STARTUP.NCF File). From there, you can print the screen.

If you have used the INETCFG utility to manage your protocols, the AUTOEXEC.NCF file will have all the protocol statements commented out with the number sign (#). There is a message telling you to check the INITSYS.NCF and NETINFO.CFG files in the \SYS:ETC directory. There is also a warning in the message not to edit those files directly, but to use the INETCFG utility. However, you can certainly print these files and put the printouts in your server notebook.

Tracking Normal Workstation Details

An easy place to check the performance of a workstation is through the MONITOR screen on a server. When you choose Connections and press Enter on the user connection name, you'll see the connection details.

Alternatively, you can use NetWare Remote Manager to view server connections. Start the NetWare Remote Manager program either directly or through Web Manager, and click the Connections menu item in the left frame under Manage Server. You'll see an information screen similar to the one shown in Figure 16.6.

What does this tell us? Well, first, if you see the user's name on the connection list, the network connection must be in fairly good shape. The connection time is listed, as is the connection type from workstation to server. The resulting kilobytes read and written aren't shown in Remote Manager, but they do appear in MONITOR, where these numbers update in real time.

The bottom of the window shows open files, and again, this display is updated in real time in MONITOR but a bit more slowly in Remote Manager. If you click a filename, the Record Lock Information window will pop up. If the user stops an application or otherwise closes files, those changes will appear in the window after a Remote Manager update.

NOTE

Notice the identifying address for the workstation: 10.00.01.57. It's odd for an old NetWare dog like me to see an IP address there, but I can still learn a new trick now and then.

Part III

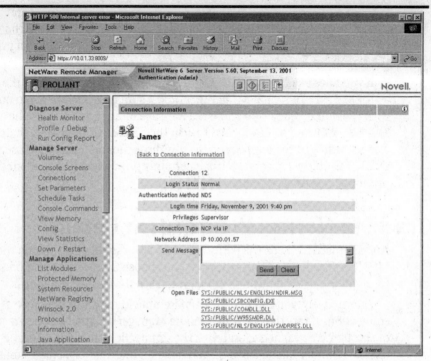

FIGURE 16.6: A healthy, active workstation connection

Workstation Configuration File Copies

During installation of each workstation or shortly thereafter, it's a good idea to make a backup copy of the important configuration files. For Windows 95/98 computers, this means creating an Emergency Boot/System Disk, either during the installation of the operating system or through the Add/Remove Programs applet in the Control Panel. This principle is continued for Windows NT Workstation computers, except that the disk is called the Emergency Repair Disk (ERD). That's also the name for the Windows 2000/XP version of this disk, but you make it through the Backup utility. Each of these is a disk that contains the configuration information for the computer and can be used during the repair processes in the event that you experience the dreaded catastrophic failure.

Yes, these workstation disks are just one more thing to keep track of, but they will come in handy. As these disks start piling up, your urge to develop and enforce a standard workstation configuration will grow.

Windows NT/2000 Utilities

If you have Windows NT Workstation computers in your network, you have some extra tools for determining how those workstations are operating: Performance Monitor and Windows NT Diagnostics. Windows 2000 offers corresponding System Monitor and Performance Logs and Alerts utilities.

NOTE

Since this is a book about NetWare, not Windows NT or 2000, this is not the place to find full coverage of the Windows NT/2000 utilities. For details, refer to the NT/2000 online documentation or perhaps some books cleverly titled *Mastering Windows NT* and *Mastering Windows 2000*, both from Sybex.

Performance Monitor is used to track NT counters that monitor all aspects of the computer, from the percentage of CPU time being used by applications to the number of packets being sent through a network interface. It displays the information retrieved from these counters in a real-time chart, as shown in Figure 16.7.

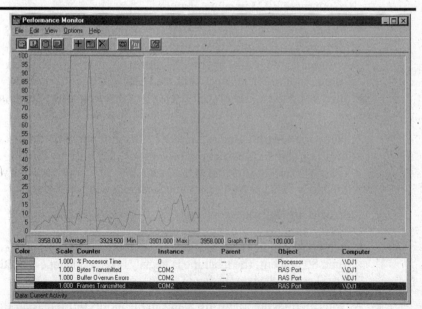

FIGURE 16.7:   The Windows NT Performance Monitor

To start Performance Monitor, select Start ➢ Programs ➢ Administrative Tools (Common) ➢ Performance Monitor. In Windows 2000, choose Control Panel ➢ Administrative Tools ➢ Performance utility.

You can add counters to the chart by clicking the plus sign on the menu bar and selecting the appropriate object and counter. An *object* is a system component, such as the network interface or processor. A *counter* is a particular function of that object that is tracked, such as the number of bytes transmitted per second.

NOTE   Some objects in Performance Monitor allow you to track more than one instance of the object. These occur when there is more than one of a particular object installed in a system, such as multiple hard disks, network interfaces, or processors.

Here are some of the more useful counter and object pairs to track with Performance Monitor:

Memory–Page Faults/sec   The average number of page faults per second for the current processor instance. If this number is more than double what you see during normal operation, it's time to put more RAM in your computer.

Network–Bytes Total/sec   The total amount of traffic through the computer's network adapter, both inbound and outbound. When this counter begins to approach the theoretical maximum for your network medium, it's time to consider increasing the speed of your network or dividing it into separate segments.

Network–Output Queue Length   The number of packets awaiting transmission across the network. If there are more than two packets queued at any particular time, network delays are likely and a network bottleneck should be investigated.

Processor–%Processor Time   The percentage of time since Performance Monitor started that the CPU has been busy handling nonidle threads. If this counter is continuously greater than 80 percent, the machine is heavily taxed and steps should be taken to alleviate the load.

As you can imagine, there are many, many more counters than the ones listed here. The best way to make the most of Performance Monitor is to take the time to familiarize yourself with all the available objects and counters.

TIP

There are two objects that relate to the operation of the hard disks in your system: Physical Disk and Logical Disk. Because of their tax on system performance, these counters must be enabled manually and should be disabled immediately after the measurements are taken. To enable the disk counters, run DISKPERF –Y from a command prompt and reboot the computer. To disable the counters, run DISKPERF –N.

Tracking Normal Network Performance

When Network General released their Sniffer products in the late 1980s, I worked for a company that sold them. Every customer I visited had the same question: "How busy is my network?" At the time (1988), Sniffers cost between $15,000 and $32,000 and came in a Compaq 286 luggable that weighed more than 20 pounds (and did a major number on your shins if you didn't carry it carefully).

People still want to know how busy their network is, but they don't need to spend thousands of dollars unless they want special protocol decoders and intelligent network analyses. If you just want to see how many packets are whizzing through your network and which stations are generating those packets, software-only traffic monitors are readily available.

Many companies make competitive software-only analyzers. Some other products I'm familiar with are Intel's LANDesk, Triticom's LANdecoder32, and even Microsoft's Network Monitor, which is included with Windows NT. EtherPeek, TokenPeek, and LocalPeek from the AG Group do the same job from both Macintosh and Windows platforms. The Sniffer, now part of Network Associates, still carries the high-end lead banner (a personal feeling, not based on exhaustive testing), but there is plenty of competition in all price ranges.

COMPONENT FAILURE PROFILES

That's an ugly phrase, "component failure," but it does happen. Your job as network administrator includes figuring out what will fail when and how to fix it quickly.

Guide to Managing PC Networks by Steve Steinke, with Marianne Goldsmith, Michael Hurwicz, and Charles Koontz (published by Prentice-Hall PTR), is a book about managing PC networks of all kinds. This book includes one section that has details of expected faults in a mythical network, based on research in the late 1990s. The graphs don't list exact percentages, but I can guess fairly well. What are the causes of network downtime? In order, these are the reasons for downtime and the percentage each item is responsible for:

47 percent	Cabling or physical infrastructure
20 percent	Servers
13 percent	Drivers, network operating system
13 percent	Improper configuration
3 percent	Routers
2 percent	Hubs
2 percent	Wide area links

Do you believe these numbers? I would like to see the data behind these statistics because I would bet that cable problems cause more than half of the network downtime. Some studies rate cabling as the cause of 90 percent of network downtime, but those studies are paid for by people who are selling either high-grade cable or physical plant management products. See the section about cabling problems later in this chapter for some tips.

One area this list doesn't address is users, since they aren't a component that will fail. However, they will cause plenty of downtime, one way or the other.

Part of the relatively low failure rate for cabling may be explained by another chart in the book, named "Causes of Cabling Fault Events on a Mythical Network." Once again, here are my estimates of the percentages:

88 percent	Coax Ethernet
8 percent	Token Ring
4 percent	10BaseT Ethernet

These numbers I do believe without question. Anyone who has ever crawled under desk after desk looking for the loose BNC Thin Ethernet connector that is causing the network problems is a strong advocate for 10BaseT Ethernet. Fortunately, none of the popular cabling schemes being promoted today are a shared-bus system like coax Ethernet. Is it any wonder twisted-pair Ethernet swamped coax and Token Ring in the marketplace?

On the server itself, the breakdown of breakdowns goes this way:

69 percent	Disk drives
18 percent	RAM
11 percent	Network interface boards
2 percent	Power supply

This list makes sense. The two highest failure rates belong to the only moving part (disk drive) and the part most sensitive to overheating (RAM). However, it isn't only heat that will cause RAM to stop a server. The cause can be voltage fluctuations, components running beyond their specifications, or just plain component failure.

COMMON WORKSTATION PROBLEMS AND SOLUTIONS

You will have more problems from users running Windows than from Macintosh, Unix, or Linux users. But you knew that already, didn't you? Primarily, Windows presents the most problems because it's the most popular platform and because it must track the most variable hardware and software resources.

NOTE
Novell actually had a disproportionate amount of tech support people dedicated to OS/2 during the rollout of NetWare 4.10. But IBM's fading desktop fortunes changed that statistic for NetWare 5 and forevermore.

Some problems and solutions are common to all PC workstations. Again, we're assuming a workstation was working, then developed a problem.

The following sections cover the most common workstation problems and provide some suggestions for solving them.

Workstation Can't Connect to the Server

The following are typical workstation connection problems and some solutions to try.

Check the workstation cable to the wall. Many patch cables that run between the workstation and the wall plug have been kicked out of their sockets. Others have been rolled over by a desk chair one too many times. Check that the plug for the patch cable is plugged into the wall. My friend Greg Hubbard says all 10BaseT Ethernet cards should have a speaker. That way, when you plug the Ethernet card into a phone plug, you'll hear the dial tone and realize your mistake. (Of course, if your phone still uses RJ-11 jacks—the ones that are smaller than 10BaseT RJ-45 connectors—this won't be a problem.)

Check the link between the wall plug and the wiring closet. Has anyone added cabling anywhere in that part of the building? It's common for new cabling installation to bump and loosen old cabling.

Verify that the port on your wiring concentrator is working. Switch the problem connection with a known good connection into a known good port.

Check the frame type.   Have the protocol details under the Networking program in Windows been changed? Is this workstation now trying to reach a new server? The default frame type for early versions of NetWare 4 was not Ethernet 802.3. Since NetWare has used that frame type since the beginning of time, many managers forget to check frame types when upgrading from NetWare 3. The same may be happening with the move to TCP/IP in many companies.

Verify the login name and password.   Wrong login names or passwords will obviously prevent a user from connecting to the server. If the user can't remember his or her password, change it immediately.

Check for a locked account.   With intruder detection, stations may be locked out of the network after a configurable number of unsuccessful login attempts. When a user comes to you with a password problem, check to see if the account is locked.

Verify that all the workstation files were loaded properly. Error messages go by fast, and sometimes they are missed by users. Changes in the workstation may use some network memory.

Make sure the network adapter is seated properly. Adding a card to one slot often loosens cards in other slots. Remember that a card can look well seated from outside the case but actually be disconnected. Patch cables, when tugged on, can loosen network adapters.

Check timeout values for WAN links. WAN links are much less reliable than LAN links. If you're trying to reach a remote network service, always assume the WAN link is at fault before changing anything at the workstation. WAN links take longer, and some workstations may time out before reaching the remote server and getting authenticated properly. Increase the SPX timeout value.

Check routers. Routers, both local and remote versions, sometimes get flaky on one port or another. Test other connections running through the same router in the same manner. You may need to check the router and reset a port.

Check hubs. Wiring hubs rarely fail, but they sometimes become unplugged. Check to see if other computers connected to the same hub are able to communicate. Hubs are also liable to run out of space, and the wiring plan gets reworked on the fly to add another station or two. When this happens, your station may be left out of a concentrator altogether.

Verify that the server sees the workstation's request. Use the TRACK ON command on the server to monitor requests from clients. If you know the client's MAC address, you can watch the server monitor to ensure that connection requests are received and the server responds.

Reboot the workstation. This can't hurt, and you'll be amazed at what a reboot can fix.

Workstation Can't Use an Application

The following are workstation application problems and some solutions to try.

Find out what changed at the workstation. Some new utility may have changed a few critical DLLs. A new Windows application may have modified the Registry. All applications have the potential for wreaking disaster.

Check the user's rights.   Does the user have the trustee rights to run the application? If you assign trustee rights to the directory and not the file, this shouldn't be much of a problem. This problem usually occurs with new applications, because few applications properly handle setting the rights for the users. Make sure to check all the application directories created by the installation. It is becoming common to place some directories for the same application on the same level of the eDirectory tree, rather than placing all the directories under one main directory. You may need to grant rights to another directory or two so that the user has rights to use some of the application files in the oddly placed directory.

Be careful after upgrading an application.   The rights will probably be the same in the existing directories, but a new directory or two is often added during an upgrade. You'll need to grant trustee rights to those directories as well.

Check the flags.   Most applications should have flags set to Read-Only and Shareable. Data files will be marked Shareable and Write, but the application must support multiple-user file access. In particular, check upgraded applications, since new files in the new version will probably not have the proper flags set. Verify your tape-restore procedure, since some vendors don't copy the extended file attributes NetWare uses to set the flags. An application that was Read-Only when backed up may become Normal (Read, Write, Erase, and so on) after being restored by tape. If someone then accidentally erases some files, the application won't work.

Check the user's current directory.   Many users never understand the drive redirection used by NetWare. When you ask where a problem is for them, they'll say, "drive K." Make sure drive K still points to the same subdirectory. New users are especially vulnerable to changing directories within a drive mapping without realizing what they've done.

Check the application's need for installing at the volume root.   Some applications demand to be placed in the root directory. Others don't but have a limit to how deep they can be installed in a directory structure. Some say they can be installed anywhere, but references to other directories are based on indexing from the root of the directory. You will need to use fake root mapping if any of these problems occur.

Does the application need NetBIOS? Some applications, even on NetWare, still require NetBIOS (thank goodness these are almost completely gone). Check that out, and load NetBIOS on a test workstation. If NetBIOS is used and has worked before, verify that the workstation is loading NetBIOS properly. Workstation changes may have ruined some necessary client files. If NetBIOS is needed, set up batch files so NetBIOS can be loaded and then unloaded after the application is exited. There is no use wasting more RAM than you need to for NetBIOS.

Verify that the application files are not mangled and that the application isn't missing some files. If an application is corrupted, you must reinstall it. In a Windows application, the DLL files may be missing or some users may be picking up old versions of them through poor search mapping.

Check for file handles and SPX connections. Database programs in particular often eat a lot of file handles. Check the application's documentation in the off chance that the writers have done their job and listed this information.

See if the application directory looks empty. This means that the user doesn't have rights to the directory. Check the rights of the container or group for the user before making a change for one user alone.

Workstation Shows "Not Enough Memory" Errors

The following are typical memory problems and some solutions to try.

Check to see what has changed. If a working network client suddenly has too little memory, something has changed. Check drivers and other TSR (terminate-and-stay-resident) programs in the workstation. Many of these hide on the Taskbar today.

Unload sneaky resident programs. Some applications, such as fax and e-mail programs, sometimes leave little notification programs or utilities to fax from within your application on workstations. These can take up memory without explaining their presence to the user.

Beware of the network client software upgrade. New driver and client files often require more room than the previous

versions. You may wish to postpone an upgrade for some workstations that are critically short of memory. Make a note of
those workstations in your network logs.

Beware of new video boards.   Video boards and network interface cards often fight over particular memory locations in PCs.

Beware of new monitors.   High-resolution monitors can force
a video board to a higher resolution requiring more memory.
Then the upper memory for a network driver won't be available, forcing the driver to load low. The result is "RAM cram."
It doesn't matter whether you have a gigabyte of RAM in the
workstation if the monitor and network adapter both want the
same few bytes.

Windows Doesn't Work Right

Everything in Windows affects everything else. Users are constantly
adding utilities, screen savers, and wallpaper, all of which can mess up
something else.

Sometimes, the user is not at fault. Demo software programs under
Windows now often add DLL files, modify the Registry, and load more
fonts into the local Windows system. Did anyone ask for this? No. Do you
need to fix it? Yes.

Believe me, something is always changing in Windows. As much as
you're tempted, you can't always blame Microsoft for this. Every application vendor has its problems, and some problems aggravate Windows
more than others.

The following are some common problems and solutions to try.

Restart Windows daily.   Microsoft has not yet stopped the
memory leaks within Windows. Applications regularly leave fewer
resources available after they unload. Windows doesn't need to
leak, but careless programming is everywhere. Windows 95/98 systems require a daily reboot, but Windows 2000/XP systems don't.
Windows NT sits in the middle, and needs a reboot every few days.

**Check System Resources or Task Manager before and after
loading an application.**   This will give you an idea of the
application's resource needs. Then check again after the application is unloaded. It's likely that you'll have fewer resources
than when you started.

Check to see if the user has logged in from the wrong workstation. Shared Windows files on the server make great sense and save time for administration, but they are dependent on the correct workstation configuration. If a user logs in from a different workstation, details such as the permanent swap file will be different on that machine.

Check for new fonts. Many applications add special fonts to Windows. Each font loaded takes memory and slows performance. If your workstations have little RAM, pare down the fonts. One font family can take enough resources for an application to have trouble where it didn't have trouble before.

Don't use wallpaper if memory is critical. Wallpaper may take just enough memory to cause trouble in RAM-deficient systems. Until you can add more memory or upgrade the workstation, strip out all nonfunctional pieces of Windows.

Get a good uninstall program for Windows. Many applications, even when they uninstall themselves, don't clean up behind themselves very well. Cleanup has improved with later versions of Windows, as application guidelines now require an uninstall program. Programmers don't always follow that advice, of course, being programmers.

Printing Problems

The following are typical printing problems and some solutions to try.

Verify that the proper printer or print queue is captured properly. With Windows printing choices, it's easy for users to pick the wrong printer by accident. Verify that the chosen printer is the correct printer. It's best to use a login script to assign the default printers for your network and discourage too much printer experimentation among users.

Verify that the job is in the print queue and that a print server is connected. Use ConsoleOne to check the status of the print queue. See if the job has actually arrived and whether the correct print server is attached to the queue. In most cases, the job will arrive in the queue, but the print server is not processing the job. Upgrade to iPrint and NDPS to help the users struggle less.

Check the print job configuration.   If you have multiple print job configurations, verify that the proper one is still used by the user. This is something else that is easy to change by accident. Under Windows, verify these settings through the Printers Control Panel (Properties).

Check the printer hardware.   Is the printer plugged into the print server? Can other users print to this printer? Are the proper paper and font cartridge (if used) in place?

Check which page description language was used in the print job.   Sending PostScript output to a non-PostScript printer guarantees problems and the need to reset the printer. Do the users understand the different types of printers they have available and how to send print jobs to those printers?

COMMON SERVER PROBLEMS AND SOLUTIONS

Let me summarize the NetWare manuals' advice on server problems: Add more RAM. The manuals provide quite a bit more help than that, of course, but more RAM is a constant mantra for NetWare servers. Save yourself the headache—*get more RAM*.

As servers support more users, more RAM is necessary. As more NLMs are loaded, more RAM is necessary. More disk space means more RAM for traditional NetWare volumes even if not for NSS volumes.

Some applications, such as the NetWare NFS Services, demand a ton of RAM on their own (20 to 24MB of RAM just for NFS Services). Want to tune your NetWare Enterprise Web Server? RAM demands jump from 128MB to 256MB just for the web server. More insidious is the RAM-creep of little programs and utilities that gradually eat your available cache buffers until you reach rock bottom.

Your servers are the core of the network. Server hardware is not a place to save a few pennies. When your boss complains about the cost of quality components in the server, amortize the cost across all potential server users. The more users you expect to support, the less investment per user a quality server will require. And this isn't just sales talk. Your server is an investment in the knowledge-sharing infrastructure necessary to propel your company into the future.

NetWare is a resilient operating system, and server hardware is more reliable today than ever before. Even before you start considering mirrored or duplexed disk drives or a clustered system, off-the-shelf computer components work faster and longer today than ever before. However, this is of little comfort as you stand before a dead server, with the howling mob at your back. Problems do happen. You must learn to manage these problems before and after they occur.

ADD MORE RAM

I hate to sound like a broken record (or a CD with a tracking error, for you kids), but more RAM cures many server ills. More applications running on the server take more RAM, since the program must have a segment of RAM in which to run.

The move that replaced two or three NetWare 3 servers with one NetWare 4 server meant that one server must have the RAM of the earlier three, plus some to support NDS. Now, some companies are consolidating three NetWare 5 servers onto two NetWare 6 servers (mostly because NetWare 6's NDS now has a cache and responds much more quickly). This is why I advise you to put RAM on every budget request for everything else.

RAM needs go up over time, but not because the software changes. Every server adds disk space and NLMs now and then. Each time you add something, you check the RAM and it doesn't look too bad. Then you add another NLM and another few users, and it doesn't look much worse than it did last time. Unfortunately, your available RAM for file cache is now about half what you had when you started the server the first time. Your server gets gradually slower and flakier until you fix things. And how do you fix things? Add more RAM.

Server Availability: A Management Decision

Your management decides how available your servers will be. Your job is to maintain service to the agreed-upon level. How available is that?

The quick answer is 24-7, meaning every hour of the day, seven days a week. Do you need this? Think about the answer. When will you do maintenance? Must you keep the system available during tape backup? How will you add a new disk drive to a server?

Guarantee that your network will be available during normal business hours. If you have no one in the office at 3:00 a.m., why does the network need to be available? Would it be reasonable for your network to be generally available, but with no guarantees, after 7:00 p.m. and before 7:00 a.m. (excluding certain web servers and services, of course)? They must remain up forever (hello, NetWare 6 Cluster Services).

Every system needs maintenance. If your entire network must be up overnight, pick one window of time on the weekends or during an evening for maintenance. Network management demands accessibility to the servers, including taking them down now and then.

WARNING

If you work in a large company, network-hostile mainframe bigots will track every minute a server is down. They will point to the fact that your network is unavailable more than the mainframe. Remember, mainframes don't need to shut down to add new disks. I hope your situation isn't this bad, but such hostility happens in some companies. Mainframers are feeling a bit unloved lately (with good reason, perhaps) and will spend a lot of energy to discredit the networks that are replacing mainframes. Be prepared.

The Hardware Scale and the Costs

Even if your network consists of one server and 15 users, management personnel must decide how much availability they are willing to pay for. Nothing is certain with computers, but more guaranteed uptime translates into more cost.

Any chart showing dollars in the computer business is suspect, since prices generally fall. Those prices that don't fall reliably, such as the cost of memory chips, tend to gradually fall with occasional spikes to weaken the hearts of purchasing managers everywhere. Hard drives today are amazingly inexpensive, and the prices continue to drop. Today, you are able to get large (80GB or 120GB) IDE drives for about the same price as a 500MB drive only a few years ago.

The ascending hardware listing is explained this way:

Peer-to-peer networks   Low cost, low numbers of users supported comfortably and inexpensively.

Desktop PCs as dedicated servers   Common choice for low-end servers. Desktop PCs don't have as much space for hard disks or RAM. Power supplies are sometimes inadequate for multiple disk drives.

Mirrored or duplexed drives Disk mirroring (two drives, one controller) and disk duplexing (two drives, two controllers) improve performance and provide protection against a single disk failure stopping your server. With the dropping cost of hard drives, it's hard to justify trusting your network to a disk drive as a single point of failure.

PC server models Extra space for drives, more RAM, and beefier power supplies help these systems look and act more like servers. Always in a tower case, these systems look more expensive and rugged, making management happier with the investment.

RAID storage systems RAID (Redundant Array of Inexpensive Disks) systems go further to eliminate the disk as a point of failure and add performance. These systems are often able to swap hard drives while the server is running, eliminating downtime due to a bad disk.

Servers on steroids Companies such as Compaq, HP, Acer, Dell, and AST (among others) are placing their servers at the top of the food chain. Diagnostic software and hardware offer a level of control and management unattainable with regular PC servers. Many of these systems now offer multiple processors, boosting horsepower even higher if your software is able to use the extra CPUs.

Clustered servers The new replacement for SFT III (System Fault Tolerance, level III), clusters primarily aim at keeping critical applications, such as web servers, available. I've had the fun of playing with a killer Compaq ProLiant cluster, and I must say proper use of such equipment will eliminate downtime completely. The first two-node cluster license comes free with NetWare 6, but after that, Novell charges $5,000 per clustered-server license, so only the critical applications will pass budget muster.

The further up the scale you go, the more money you must invest in your network. This extra investment buys peace of mind and better performance. Management must make the decision on the proper amount of investment for your network. See if you can find a subtle way to remind the people making the decisions that you can't get a Rolls Royce for a go-cart price.

Operating System and RAM Problems

The following are typical operating system and RAM problems and some solutions to try.

ABEND messages occur.   An ABEND (ABnormal ENDing) is a system shutdown due to an internal error of some sort. The best course of action after an ABEND is to write down the ABEND error message number and look it up in the "System Messages" section of the online documentation. Reboot the server, then check for sufficient RAM. Verify current versions of NLMs and drivers. If new hardware or software has been added, restart the server without the new component as a test. If all else fails, you may need to reload the operating system, but that doesn't happen often.

Users can't see server.   Check the frame type in use. Multiple frame types are easily supported, but both clients and servers must use a common frame type in order to communicate. Check the LOAD and BIND statements to make sure nothing has changed. Some third-party utilities may un-BIND or un-LOAD drivers during installation or by accident. Driver errors may also cause a network interface card to disconnect.

Server can't see users or other servers.   Again, check the frame type in use. Also check the LOAD and BIND statements. Check that SAP (Service Advertising Protocol) is active and not disabled. Verify network numbering of internal and external network numbers for the server. Driver errors may also cause a network interface card to disconnect.

Server goes up and down for no reason.   Check the power supply. This fails more often in a server than you might think. If your server UPS isn't doing the job, low voltage may cause the power supply to reset the computer motherboard. You should have a dedicated circuit for all your server equipment. Also, keep the cleaning crew from using AC plugs in the server area. I once saw a cleaning crew unplug servers to power their vacuum cleaners.

Server Memory

As I've said many times before, the main thing to do when you're low on RAM is to buy more RAM quickly. Here are some suggestions for freeing some server memory temporarily (until you can add more memory to the server):

- ▶ Type **REMOVE DOS** or **SECURE CONSOLE** to release the DOS memory in the server for the file cache.

- ▶ Forcibly purge files on traditional NetWare volumes to free the directory entry table space. (This is not necessary on NSS volumes.)

- ▶ Unload NLM programs that are not needed, such as MONITOR (often left up). The X Server Graphical Console eats a ton of memory and may be the only reason you need the Java Virtual Machine loaded, which requires another ton of memory.

- ▶ Dismount volumes that are not being used (this suggestion is straight from the manual, as if you have extra disks hanging off your server that no one needs).

- ▶ Turn off block suballocation and specify a 64KB block size on traditional NetWare volumes. This requires the volume to be reinitialized, meaning all data on the volume must be backed up and restored. This measure saves RAM but is a lot of trouble, takes the server offline for quite a while, and runs a slight risk of losing data. However, you might try it if you need to add a new volume with the smallest RAM impact possible. This method does use quite a bit more disk space, especially if you turn off file compression to save that RAM as well.

- ▶ Move volumes from this server to a different server with more RAM.

- ▶ Migrate all your traditional NetWare filesystem volumes to NSS storage pools.

Disk Errors

For volume dismounts and other disk problems, try the following:

- ▶ If you have an external disk subsystem, verify that the power is on and the cables are still connected.

- ▶ Check for error messages on the console. Ordinary disk errors will force a volume to dismount.

▶ Verify settings for the controller and driver combination.

▶ Check for increased numbers of Hot Fix redirection areas used. Increasing Hot Fix numbers generally indicate your disk is dying and should be replaced. The manual offers instructions on increasing the Hot Fix redirection area; I say dump the drive or at least reformat it and start all over.

▶ Run VREPAIR on the traditional volume (not on an NSS volume). This loads from the console, and if your SYS: volume is having a problem, you will need to reference the file on the DOS partition or the floppy. Run VREPAIR at least twice each time you use it.

Running out of disk space is a problem you don't want to have. Don't let this sneak up on you. If it happens to your SYS: volume, the server usually shuts down. Even if it isn't your SYS: volume, it still causes extra work and other hassles.

Check your volume space regularly. To produce a quick report on your current volume, use this command:

    NDIR /VOL

This replaces the VOLINFO command from NetWare 3.x. Figure 16.8 shows the command and result for the ProLiant SYS: volume.

```
Command Prompt                                              _ □ ×
M:\>ndir /vol

Statistics for fixed volume PROLIANT/SYS:
Space statistics are in KB (1024 bytes).

Total volume space:                        8,757,888   100.00%
Space used by 57,625 entries:              1,183,936    13.52%
Deleted space not yet purgeable:                  64     0.00%
                                          ──────────
Space remaining on volume:                 7,573,952    86.48%
Space available to NT1:                    7,573,952    86.48%

Maximum directory entries:                    98,816
Available directory entries:                  41,191    41.68%

Space used if files were not compressed:   2,992,640
Space used by compressed files:              967,680
                                          ──────────
Space saved by compressing files:          2,024,960    67.66%

Uncompressed space used:                   1,047,168

Name spaces loaded: OS/2

M:\>
```

FIGURE 16.8: Good space left, and good compression

When space becomes a serious concern, type **PURGE /ALL** for each volume. If the command-line PURGE doesn't clear enough space, delete unnecessary files still taking up directory entry table space. Change the Minimum File Delete Wait Time SET parameter to 0 so that files can be purged immediately. This stops them from being kept whole and salvageable on the volume.

CABLING PROBLEMS

As mentioned in this chapter, cabling causes lots of network problems. Vendors of new cable will tell real horror stories of old cable and the problems it caused. Introduce those vendors to your boss. Make it your goal to eliminate any coax or low-grade twisted pair left in the network.

As was also mentioned earlier in this chapter, coax Ethernet causes more than 20 times the number of network outages than are caused by 10BaseT Ethernet. Log your time spent chasing cable problems for two weeks, and then figure out the cost of those problems in your time alone. This is especially effective if your company is faced with a need to hire more network technicians. Replacing the cable will probably keep down your head count.

The first step when your network is having problems is to check all cables to make sure that they are plugged in. Don't laugh. Cables that aren't plugged in never work. Here are some other suggestions for avoiding cable problems:

▶ Find a cable contractor you like and stick with that contractor. Cabling consistency counts for a lot. If you find a cabling contractor who does good work, tests the cables with digital equipment, and offers a good warranty, you're lucky. Don't switch contractors for a few cents per foot.

▶ Buy quality cable. Cheap cable is good for telephones but not for data networks. High-speed systems in development now will push quality cable and will quickly overload cable not up to par. Buy the best cable (Level 5 and above) now, and you're covered for the foreseeable future.

▶ Declare a truce with any hostile telecom folks in your company. Some companies have telecom and datacom departments that are openly hostile. If your company is that way, I'm sorry. Go to management and request a meeting with all parties involved. If you can get over your differences, you will find that the telecom folks can be a great help.

▶ Verify cable distances, especially on new runs. All UTP (unshielded twisted-pair) cable networks have a length limit, usually 100 meters (300 feet plus a little). Going slightly beyond that limit will cause random problems. Going far beyond that limit will stop the connection entirely. There are third-party products that extend the cabling distance over UTP. Buy one of those, or just add a powered wiring concentrator to help cover the extra distance.

▶ Take care to avoid interference for your cable runs. Strong interference will blitz your cable and disrupt your network. Did you ever hear stories about networks that always went down at dusk? The cable was routed by a light switch. When that light was turned on, the cable interference overloaded the network and blocked all the packets.

▶ Provide UPS systems for all powered wiring components. In a blackout, your server and your desktop machine will likely continue on battery power. But if the wiring concentrator is powerless, how will you connect to the server from your workstation?

FOR COAX ETHERNET OR ARCNET USERS

If you have coax Ethernet, or worse, ARCnet, you no doubt turned to this troubleshooting chapter quickly. Let me tell you what you may or may not want to hear: *upgrade*.

You have been told this several times before. You know this is necessary every time you crawl under a desk to check a BNC connector. You know coax ages, gets brittle, and breaks time after time. You just need to convince your management.

Put the boss's secretary on the worst coax leg of your network. This isn't dishonest, but it is in your self-interest. Every time you go up to the executive area to fix the network (again and again), be sure you know how much it will cost to replace the coax Ethernet with 10BaseT or 100BaseT Ethernet. Basically pennies, nowadays. Remember that number when you're crawling under the secretary's desk, and repeat it to the boss when you emerge.

Monitoring Network Cable Performance

The best way to stop network downtime remains preparation, and knowing what your network does regularly may be the most critical part of your preparation. Let's look at another method of cable-related preparation you may not have considered.

Wiring hubs have gotten far smarter while getting far cheaper. One of the hubs used in my lab is from LinkSys (www.linksys.com), and they included an SNMP module to manage the 24-port hub. Check out the details in Figure 16.9, and we'll discuss some of them.

The top frame of the browser reflects the front of the hub. Yes, the active lights on the left and the colored port plugs on the right mean something and change in real time. Plugs with 10BaseT connections are green; the 100BaseT links are blue.

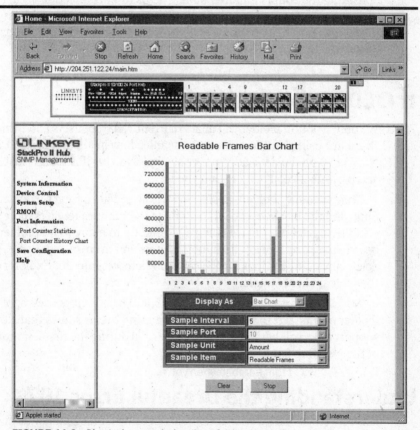

FIGURE 16.9: Physical network details unfolding every five seconds

Most of the informative details opened by the menu choices in the left frame are text oriented, with tables of packet details and the like. These are interesting on a fine-grained level but are not too graphically pleasing.

The screen shot in Figure 16.9, however, colors port summary information with five-second updates (configurable). The tallest (those with the most packets) ports are the servers in this picture, and they should be in your network as well. If one of those server bar lines drops down to nothing, your phone will magically start ringing. It happens every time.

SNMP modules add a couple hundred dollars to the cost of the 24-port hub, but they are worth it for at least your servers. LinkSys engineers allow you to control up to six 24-port hubs with one SNMP module, spreading the couple hundred dollars across 144 connections. That's getting too cheap to pass up. Show this page to your tightwad boss—I mean, aggressive fiscal management member—and see if that helps loosen the budget strings at least a little.

iFolder Fun and Games

Without a doubt, iFolder will amaze current NetWare users and intrigue those not using NetWare. Many companies may justify upgrading to NetWare 6 on iFolder's advantages alone, forgetting iPrint and clustering and performance. iFolder is that good.

Unfortunately, iFolder—as shipped with NetWare 6 First Customer Ship, and the late beta copies I examined—sometimes requires more effort than necessary to get going. One odd fix to many weird problems, based on reports on Novell Support forums and my own experience, is to delete any proxy settings for the copy of Microsoft Internet Explorer on the iFolder client system.

Novell support folks guess there is a 5,000-user limit per server of iFolder clients, but they aren't sure. One thing that is sure is that Novell support folks will have plenty of iFolder calls during the first few months of the NetWare 6 rollout.

Understanding the Dreadful Error 107

Error message "Check user error - 107" became far too familiar during my iFolder testing and configuration. What does "user error 107" mean in English? It means that something is messed up between eDirectory and your LDAP server, even when the LDAP server runs on the same NetWare server as the iFolder server.

> **TIP**
>
> Newsreader to the rescue: iFolder managers, set your newsreader to keep up with novell.support.internet.ifolder inside the support-forums.novell.com newsgroup hosted by Novell. You will need the help you find there.

The "something" that's messed up bounces around, depending on which Novell person gets involved, between eDirectory versions, LDAP implementation, and even whether the presented username is case sensitive or not. You may even need to edit one of the Apache configuration files, using a text editor such as Notepad, to ensure you get connected. If you wanted to feel like a Unix manager, start looking for the context settings for your NetWare login context inside the httpd_additions_nw.conf file.

Those of you hesitant to upgrade your current version of NDS to eDirectory 8.6 will lose this battle. Only the most recent eDirectory version will correctly (at least most of the time) start iFolder on the server when requested.

Sometimes, the advice from Novell for iFolder server problems is to unload and reload the LDAP.NLM utility. Sometimes things work better for me after rebooting the entire server, rather than just trying STOPIFOLDER and STARTIFOLDER to reload new changes (and some good luck helps, too).

More realistically, check for updates for all the LDAP services, and verify that the Allow Clear Text Passwords check box is checked in the LDAP Group for your server name. Find this setting in ConsoleOne, on the LDAP Group General page. Try turning off your proxy server settings for the client as well (some people say this helps). Obviously, keep an eye out for updates.

Waiting for Better iFolder Management Tools

When you see advice from Novell support to start editing the client Registry files, some product shipped too soon. I believe iFolder shipped a month or three too soon, if only for the lack of management tools available.

Sure, there are tools, but NetWare always had a management tool interface, no matter how clunky, from the days of the S/Net server (late

1980s for you youngsters). Asking users now to modify client Registry files and check the Context settings for server configuration files doesn't push Novell closer to the "ease of management" award at next year's Golden Globe ceremonies, does it?

Keep playing with iFolder, but keep watching Novell's help, download, and support sites for more help. The help will arrive, and iFolder will be an outstanding product by the time the second patch to all the systems has been downloaded and applied. But Novell usually cooks products all the way until they're ready to ship. This time, they seemed to pull iFolder out of the oven just before the oven timer rang.

NDS PROBLEMS AND SOLUTIONS

NetWare 6 provides two utilities that are handy for catching and repairing NDS problems. The DSTRACE (Directory Services Trace) utility traces server communications concerning NDS. DSREPAIR repairs database-related problems. You'll also find graphical versions of these utilities in iMonitor.

DSTRACE Tracks NDS Synchronization Processes

NetWare's TRACK ON console command has always been helpful. Watching server communications as clients connect to servers and servers exchange network routing information gives a nice, warm feeling that things are working as they should be.

That same warm feeling is now extended to the NDS communications between servers. The DSTRACE utility, run from the server console, will display server chat concerning NDS. Figure 16.10 is a screen full of (luckily) boring (and almost incomprehensible) NDS communications.

Look for a nice ending to all the processes: succeeded. This will be the hoped-for tail end of a DSREPAIR automatic repair session. All the directory services details, including all the schema operations, were listed by the DSREPAIR utility, discussed in the next section.

You can't see it here, but the word *succeeded* is in bright purple. Computer and partition names are all in blue. Purger operations are in hot pink. This isn't exactly graphical, but it certainly is colorful.

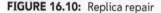

```
Novell RConsoleJ: PROLIANT                                    _ □ ×
Server Screens  DSTrace Console (active)        ▼  ←  →   Sync   Activate  🔍  📄
DCDuplicateContext for cac223e0, oldContext 17, newContext 21, flags 00000000
request DSAGetServerAddress by context 5 succeeded
ncp request, verb: 37 by context 21 succeeded
ncp request, verb: 37 by context 21 succeeded
ncp request, verb: 36 by context 17 succeeded
DCDuplicateContext for cac223e0, oldContext 17, newContext 20, flags 00000000
request DSAGetServerAddress by context 5 succeeded
ncp request, verb: 37 by context 20 succeeded
ncp request, verb: 37 by context 20 succeeded
ncp request, verb: 37 by context 20 succeeded
ncp request, verb: 37 by context 20 succeeded
DCFreeContext context 00000014 for cac223e0, idHandle 00000005, connHandle 00000
900
ncp request, verb: 36 by context 17 succeeded
DCDuplicateContext for cac223e0, oldContext 17, newContext 20, flags 00000000
request DSAGetServerAddress by context 5 succeeded
ncp request, verb: 37 by context 20 succeeded
ncp request, verb: 37 by context 20 succeeded
ncp request, verb: 37 by context 20 succeeded
ncp request, verb: 37 by context 20 succeeded
DCFreeContext context 00000014 for cac223e0, idHandle 00000005, connHandle 00000
900
DCFreeContext context 00000015 for cac223e0, idHandle 00000005, connHandle 00000
300
Calling DSAReadEntryInfo conn:13 for client
Buffer Input                                                        Send
```

FIGURE 16.10: Replica repair

Here are some reasons you may wish to watch such a boring but colorful display:

- ▶ To check whether the NDS replicas are finished with a process
- ▶ To watch for NDS errors, especially during and/or soon after adjusting or moving NDS objects

NDS-related system messages are numbered −601 through −699 and F966 through F9FE. Not all NDS system messages are bad news, just like regular NetWare system messages. However, you know the old story: No news is good news. If you see system messages that don't clear up as NDS settles down after changes, they are usually error messages. The System Messages section of the documentation describes all the system messages in mind-numbing detail.

Turning on DSTRACE

To see the NDS synchronization information using DSTRACE, go to the server console or start an RConsoleJ session. At the console prompt, type:

```
SET DSTRACE TO SCREEN = ON
```

To stop the trace, replace the ON with OFF. (Use the up arrow on the console to repeat the command, then just backspace over the ON to type **OFF**.)

If you wish to save this information for your server archives, or send the file to a support person, use this command at the server console:

```
SET DSTRACE TO FILE = ON
```

Part III

The file will be sent to DSTRACE.LOG in the SYS:SYSTEM directory. To write the file elsewhere, use this command:

```
SET DSTRACE FILENAME = path\filename
```

When you feel there is enough information in your file, repeat the DSTRACE TO FILE command, adding OFF. If you don't stop it, the file will wrap at about 500KB. Old information will be overwritten with new information as long as the log file is open.

NOTE

As with most log files, not everything is written faithfully to the log. If your log and screen information look good but things are still strange, trust your feelings rather than the log file.

Using a Graphical DSTRACE

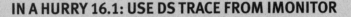

IN A HURRY 16.1: USE DS TRACE FROM IMONITOR

1. Log in as Admin or equivalent and open iMonitor.
2. Click the Trace Configuration button (the icon with arrows and a check mark) on the toolbar.
3. Provide the administrator name and password (if asked again).
4. Choose the DS Trace options switches with the check boxes.
5. Click the Submit command button to set the configuration.
6. Click the Trace On command button to start the trace.
7. Click the Trace Off command button to stop the trace.

The new iMonitor utility also includes a graphically configured DS Trace. Clicking the squiggly arrows with the check mark icon, next to the wrench on the toolbar, opens the Trace Configuration screen.

I'm still not sure what to call this. Novell calls it DS Trace most of the time, but it's just Track On and Track Off from the server console, albeit easier to customize. Look at Figure 16.11 and see if a better name springs to your mind.

Just above the DS Trace Options bar sit two command buttons (I rolled them out of sight to show more options). Submit tells the Trace

Configuration program to accept any changes in the check boxes for the next trace session. The second button says Trace On until you start the trace. Then it changes to Trace Off.

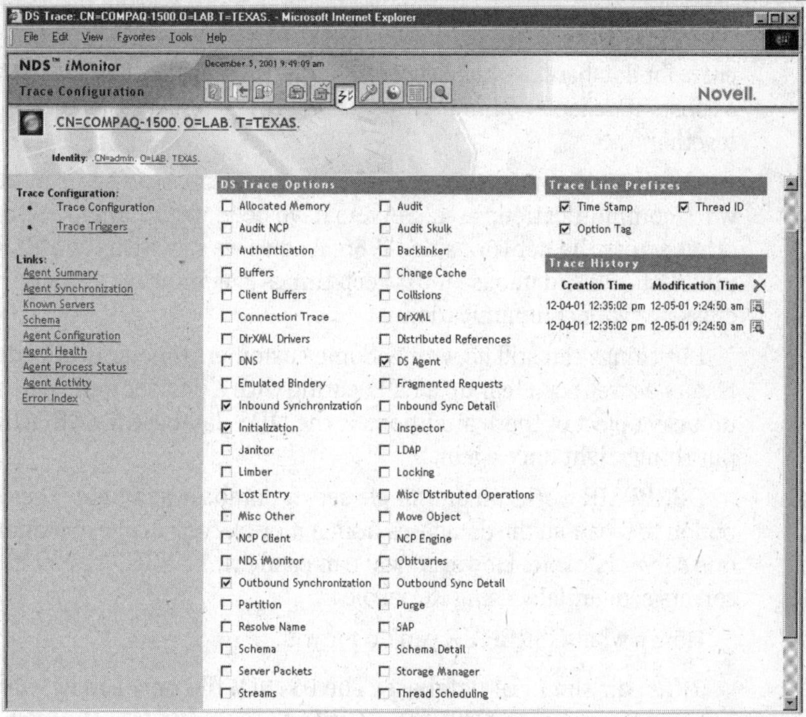

FIGURE 16.11: Configuring DS Trace via check boxes

Resulting log files wind up under the Trace History heading and stack up until you hit the red X for Delete All. One real advantage of the graphical DS Trace is that servers, other NDS objects, and error codes all have hyperlinks. Do you want to see details of a server? Click the hyperlinked name. Do you want an explanation for an NDS error message? Click the hyperlink.

Although the graphical utility is a welcome innovation, I do hesitate to rely solely on iMonitor for NDS repair functions. Clobbered servers may not have their web services up, making these graphical NDS control pages unavailable. Also, quick repairs on NDS should load and run faster under DSTRACE (or DSREPAIR) NLMs than under a browser window.

However, the new features, especially in DS Trace, make me happy. Many eDirectory hiccups can easily be handled without rebooting the server (most can, actually), so staying at my desk with iMonitor saves time, trouble, and shoe leather.

DSREPAIR Means Directory Services Repair

If you read the computer magazines, you know that distributed database technology is fraught with peril for database vendors. Trying to manage database pieces spread across multiple computers is beyond the ability of most commercial database vendors today. Part of the problem is the learning curve for database designers just starting to investigate using the network as a constant, reliable communications platform to tie all the database pieces together.

Novell has a considerable head start over database vendors in the network communications area. Servers have been negotiating with each other across the network since 1986. And as we saw with the DSTRACE utility, the NDS database must keep things synchronized through regular cross-network communication.

But things can still go wrong. Some customers (and network administrators as well) can tear up a ball bearing with a powder puff. When the unlucky object of these attentions is the NDS database, DSREPAIR will put things right once again.

DSREPAIR works on one single-server database at a time. There is no option to repair all the databases from remote servers in one operation from one server console. However, you can easily run DSREPAIR on multiple servers sequentially using RConsoleJ.

Here's what DSREPAIR can do for you:

- ▶ Repair the local database. The DS.NLM file on a server will be addressed by the DSREPAIR utility.

- ▶ Repair the local replicas. Examine and repair replicas, replica rings, and server objects. You can also verify that each replica has the same data as the others.

- ▶ Repair a single object to fix inconsistencies in the object's references.

- ▶ Search for local database objects. A browser function helps you locate and synchronize objects in the local database.

- ▶ Analyze the servers in each local partition for synchronization problems. View errors and list the partition name, server name, synchronization time, and errors with error codes.

- ▶ Write replica details to a log file. Detailed information about local partitions and servers is made available to check for database damage. If the local server has a wrong address for a remote server, you can check that here.

▶ Create a dump file of a damaged database. A compressed file is dumped, so you must use DSREPAIR to work with the file.

▶ Check the remote server ID list. Verify identification numbers for all remote servers and change those numbers as necessary.

Some NDS problems are less serious than others, and your eDirectory may continue to function. However, if you see a message saying that the server can't open the local database, go directly to DSREPAIR and start to work. Reinstalling the NDS database from a tape backup is more trouble, and that backup is probably slightly out of date. Try DSREPAIR before trying anything else.

Now that you know what DSREPAIR can do, here's what it can't do:

▶ Repair a remote NDS database

▶ Recover Unknown objects that do not have the mandatory object properties

DSREPAIR looks a lot like all the other NetWare C-Worthy utilities. Its opening screen shows the current version in the upper-left corner above the name of the tree and server being examined. The bottom of the screen shows helpful keystroke information and a brief description of the highlighted menu choice. Figure 16.12 shows the opening menu of DSREPAIR.

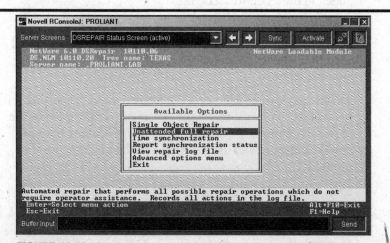

FIGURE 16.12: Preparing to repair the NDS database with DSREPAIR

Following are the DSREPAIR Available Options menu items:

Single Object Repair   Every eDirectory object has an Object ID. If details about a single Object ID get mangled for some reason, use this setting to straighten out and rework that Object ID.

Unattended Full Repair   Most of your work in DSREPAIR will be quick and simple, accomplished with this menu choice. In fact, if you start DSREPAIR and press Enter, your eDirectory will probably be back in shape in just a few seconds. Then you can press Enter again after reading the results of the operation and press Escape to exit DSREPAIR altogether.

Time Synchronization   Contacts every server in the local database and checks NDS and time synchronization details. If this server holds a replica of the [Root] partition, every server in the tree will be polled. Each server will be listed with its DS.NLM version, type of replica code, time source, whether time is synchronized, and the difference in time to the remote server. This process starts immediately when this option is selected, and the results are written to the DSREPAIR.LOG file.

Report Synchronization Status   Determines whether the NDS eDirectory tree is healthy by checking the synchronization status of each replica on each server. You must provide the Admin name and password to start this function. A log entry is added to the DSREPAIR.LOG file.

View Repair Log File   Shows the entire DSREPAIR.LOG file, allowing you to view all entries. The log file is controlled with the Log File Configuration option in the Advanced Options menu.

Advanced Options Menu   Opens another menu allowing you to manually perform each of the automatic repairs done by the first menu option. The advanced options give you more power and flexibility, as well as more potential for disaster. Use them carefully.

Exit   Exits DSREPAIR; you can cancel by entering No or pressing the Escape key.

Running the Unattended Full Repair

IN A HURRY 16.2: REPAIR THE NDS DATABASE AUTOMATICALLY WITH DSREPAIR

1. Type DSREPAIR from the console prompt.

2. Choose Unattended Full Repair (the default) and press Enter to start the repair operation.

3. Press Enter after reading the automatic repair results to view the log.

4. Press Escape to return to the main DSREPAIR menu.

When you press Enter on this first option, you won't be asked to verify your choice or to provide any information. The option is labeled Unattended and means just that. Press Enter, and the repair starts immediately.

During the repair process, the NDS database must be closed for obvious reasons. Just like any database record, if the file can be written to while it's being overhauled, dangerous things can happen.

Because the locking of the directory database will inconvenience users, it stays locked the shortest time possible. Repair of the GATEWAY2000 server took seven (yes, 7) seconds. Obviously, a small network with no real problems will take less time than a large network with a reason to use DSREPAIR.

Figure 16.13 shows the DSREPAIR process under way. The lines whiz by so quickly you can't read any of them during the process. The whizzing stops a time or two, but not long enough to consider the pause as a breakdown in the process. Although the display in the upper-right corner shows no errors, seven minor errors of no consequence to anything except the database were found and listed in the log file.

The bottom of the screen, depending on the operation running at that second, shows several interesting options:

F2=Options menu	Shows the DSREPAIR Options menu.
F3=Pause the screen	Stops the screen and the repair so you can examine the process.
Alt+F10	Exits DSREPAIR.
Esc=Stop repair	Abandons the repair and returns to the menu.

Part III

FIGURE 16.13:   Repair work in progress

NOTE

Little of what zooms by is helpful to a network administrator. But what great technical names: external synchronizer and attribute definitions are some of the functions that scroll by. I can almost hear Scotty now, yelling over the warp engines, "Cap'n, I canna keep the External Synchronizer up much longer! Our Attribute Definitions are blown!"

Using the Advanced Options Menu and Submenus

If the automatic full repair procedure doesn't fix your eDirectory problem, the Advanced Options menu is the next choice. You have little to lose at this point. Alternatively, your next step after the unattended repair is to restore from tape (not generally a good idea for directory services) or to delete the local database and copy it from another server. You might as well try a few advanced options before searching through the tape library.

Figure 16.14 shows the Advanced Options menu that appears as a submenu to the opening DSREPAIR program. The look is consistent with what you've seen before, including the identification information on the top and the help information at the bottom of the screen.

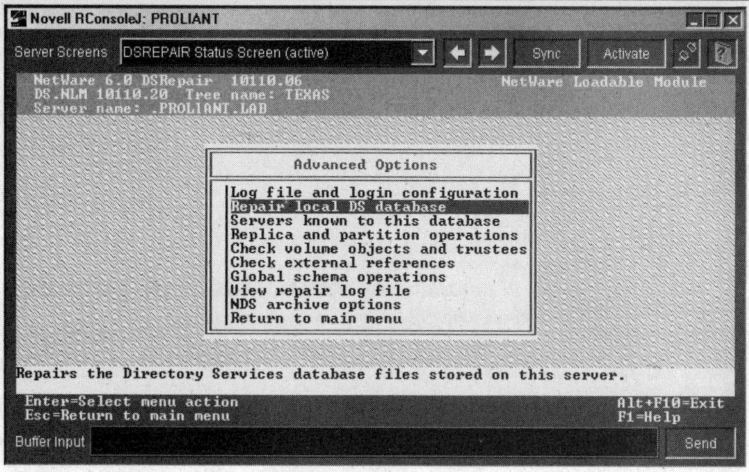

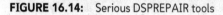

FIGURE 16.14: Serious DSPREPAIR tools

WARNING

Remember that each of the DSREPAIR options locks the eDirectory database. No one can be authenticated by NDS on this server during that time, since the database will be unavailable.

Before you choose any of the advanced options, you should definitely know what it does. The following sections describe the effects of each Advanced Options menu item.

Log File and Login Configuration   The default DSREPAIR log file, which will be created automatically for you, is SYS:SYSTEM\ DSREPAIR.LOG. If you wish to delete the log file, the first menu choice is one place to do so. Figure 16.15 shows the screen that appears when you choose Log File And Login Configuration from the Advanced Options menu.

The first field, Current File Size, cannot be changed here. The Reset The Log File? option, to delete the current log file, is the first choice you have. Pressing Enter by accident as you go into this submenu may teach you the value of the Salvage option in FILER.

Part III

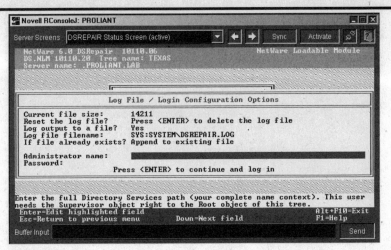

FIGURE 16.15:   Combo screen: log file configuration and directory login

The option to log output to a file (coincidentally named Log Output To A File?) of your own choosing is the same as is available in DSTRACE, but it provides a more complete capture of information. This file will be helpful if your eDirectory gets so messed up that you need help from Novell support technicians. You can send a copy of this file for their perusal. In the Log File Filename option, you may rename the log anything you wish or leave the default name. In the next option, if the named log file already exists, you can append or overwrite the file. If you don't want to specify the log file, a temporary one will be created during repair operations. This will be shown to you after the repairs are finished.

To continue, you must provide the Admin user's name and password. The name and password will be authenticated by the NDS database before you can save your log file changes.

Repair Local DS Database   This option does much of the same work as the Unattended Full Repair option on the main menu, with a few extra choices. One important distinction is that this option performs the repairs on a temporary file set, and you have the opportunity to back out before the temporary files become permanent. Figure 16.16 shows the choices you'll be able to make.

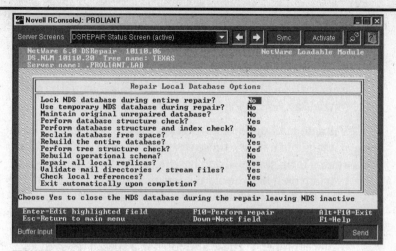

Novell RConsoleJ: PROLIANT

Server Screens | DSREPAIR Status Screen (active) | ← | → | Sync | Activate

```
NetWare 6.0 DSRepair  10110.06                    NetWare Loadable Module
DS.NLM 10110.20  Tree name: TEXAS
Server name: .PROLIANT.LAB
```

```
                    Repair Local Database Options
   Lock NDS database during entire repair?        No
   Use temporary NDS database during repair?      No
   Maintain original unrepaired database?         No
   Perform database structure check?              Yes
   Perform database structure and index check?    No
   Reclaim database free space?                   No
   Rebuild the entire database?                   Yes
   Perform tree structure check?                  Yes
   Rebuild operational schema?                     No
   Repair all local replicas?                     Yes
   Validate mail directories / stream files?      Yes
   Check local references?                        Yes
   Exit automatically upon completion?             No
```

Choose Yes to close the NDS database during the repair leaving NDS inactive

```
Enter=Edit highlighted field       F10=Perform repair      Alt+F10=Exit
Esc=Return to main menu            Down=Next field          F1=Help
```

Buffer Input | Send

FIGURE 16.16: NDS database repair options

Here are the questions and what your answers mean:

Lock NDS database during entire repair?   You used to have no choice, but now you have some. Keep it locked (choose Yes) if you're doing this when traffic should be light; keep it unlocked otherwise (choose No).

Use temporary NDS database during repair?   Saying Yes locks the database so a copy can be worked on and then can replace the original.

Maintain original unrepaired database?   If the old database has problems, why keep it? It eats a lot of disk space. Your answer here should be No.

Perform database structure and index check?   Yes, these are two areas that must be checked.

Reclaim database free space?   This should really say, "Delete unused database records?" because that's what it does.

Rebuild the entire database?   Repairs, cleans, and rebuilds the database, but this can take a while on a large network.

Perform tree structure check?   Verifies connectivity for all tree points to the appropriate database entries.

Part III

Rebuild operational schema?   The operational schema is the schema required for basic operation of NDS, making things very messy if rebuilt unnecessarily. Do this only under orders by Novell technical support; it's rarely needed.

Repair all local replicas?   Fixes all replicas stored on this physical server. Saying Yes is a good idea.

Validate mail directories/stream files?   Mail directories are not required by NDS; those were necessary in NetWare 3 for storing login scripts. If you have mail directories for an e-mail program built like the old bindery mail system, make sure this is set to Yes. If you have users who access the server through Bindery Services, they will need their login directories for login scripts as well. Stream syntax files, like login scripts, are a type of object property. These are stored in a special reserved area of the SYS: volume, along with the NDS database. If you choose Yes, orphaned stream syntax files are tagged and deleted.

Check local references?   This option takes more time, because it verifies the information within the local database. In large networks, it will extend the repair time, but this option should be set to Yes whenever time permits.

Exit automatically upon completion?   If you know enough or are so incurious as to not care what happens with the rebuild, change this to Yes. Otherwise, leave it alone. Even if you don't know a lot about how NDS works, you will be able to understand some of the log files and explanations given at the end.

After you've answered these questions, press F10 to perform the repair.

Servers Known to This Database   Here, you can fine-tune the local NDS database per server and see what the local server knows about the remote servers. Each of the known servers is listed, with its status and its local ID. See Figure 16.17 for a look at the server display as seen from PROLIANT.

The information imparted in this screen is easy to understand. The servers listed are those in the NDS database of PROLIANT. Three of the servers, according to the local database, are up. The local ID for each server is listed. Two other servers, in the process of being deleted, appear as Unknown. Those would bear investigating if I didn't know why they showed up as Unknown.

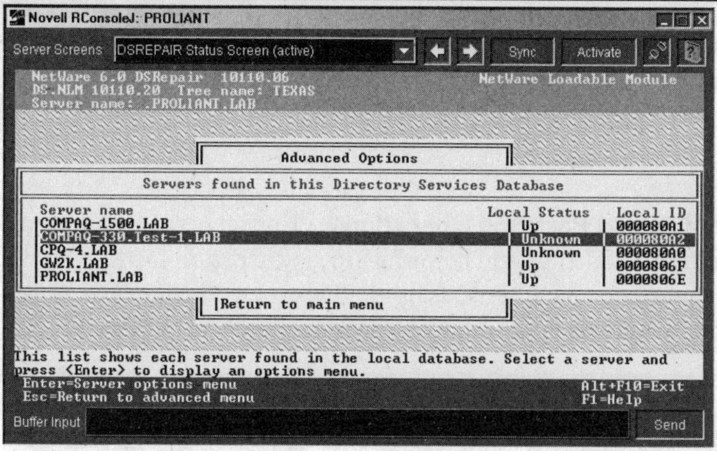

FIGURE 16.17: Know thyself and thy fellow servers in the NDS database.

It's possible for a server to be listed as up on this screen but really be down. It's possible to go the other way, with a server really active though shown as down here. Once the servers exchange some information, the display will match reality.

Pressing Enter while highlighting any of the listed servers opens up a new menu, named Server Options. The action occurs immediately after you press Enter, so if you're unsure, check the Help screens first by pressing F1.

The Server Options menu has these choices:

Time Synchronization and Server Status   Contacts every server in the local database and requests time and NDS information. If this server contains a replica of [Root], it will poll every server in the tree. The information presented here is the same as that shown from the main DSREPAIR menu choice of Time Synchronization.

Repair All Network Addresses   There needs to be an entry for each remote server in the local SAP tables. These tables match the remote server object's IPX network address and the address in the replica (when IPX protocols are used). If the addresses don't match, the RNA (Repair Network Address) function updates the local tables. If there is no name for an SAP address entry for a remote server, there is little else to be done.

Repair Selected Server's Network Address   Same as above, but for the highlighted server only.

View Entire Server's Name   Shows the full distinguished server name for the highlighted server; for example, PROLIANT.GCS.

Return to Server List   Backs out of this menu, or you can use the Escape key.

Replica and Partition Operations   This innocent-looking entry hides multiple submenus and powerful processes. Figure 16.18 shows the first of the submenus. After you choose this option, the Replicas Stored On This Server box opens, showing all the replicas on our local server.

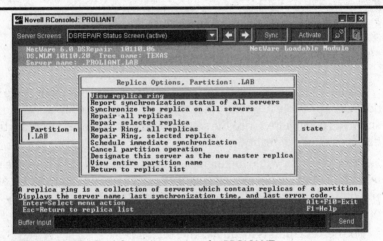

FIGURE 16.18: Specific replica options for PROLIANT

The first menu option, View Replica Ring, brings up a new term: *replica ring*. As you can read on the lower part of the screen, a replica ring is basically a group of replicas within a partition. Remember all the copies of replicas you can spread everywhere? These functions help keep them coordinated and functional.

You're not missing anything interesting in the background box, which explains that the LAB partition on this server holds a Read/Write replica and that it is On.

The main Replica Options menu has these choices:

View Replica Ring   Brings up a box labeled Servers That Have Replicas Of This Partition. Choose a server to see another submenu of choices, described in the following section.

Report Synchronization Status of All Servers   Runs a quick report and details time synchronization status of partitions.

Synchronize the Replica on All Servers   Reads the table of remote servers and replicas on the local server and forces all servers to synchronize with all other servers.

Repair All Replicas   Checks the replica information on each remote server defined in the local eDirectory database tables and makes any modifications necessary. If the local database hasn't been repaired in the last 30 minutes, repair it before trying this option.

Repair Selected Replica   Same as above, but for one high-lighted replica rather than all replicas.

Repair Ring, All Replicas   Repairs all the replicas on the ring, validating remote ID information. Run the Repair Local Database option before doing this.

Repair Ring, Selected Replica   Repairs the selected replica on the ring. Again, make sure you run Repair Local Database first.

Schedule Immediate Synchronization   Provides a good way to force synchronization, especially if you're watching the DSTRACE screen and are tired of waiting.

Cancel Partition Operation   Stops the partition operation on the selected replica, if the process hasn't gone too far.

Designate This Server As the New Master Replica   If the original Master replica is damaged or lost, this option makes this replica the Master replica. If the old Master replica comes back from a hardware failure, there will be two Master replicas, causing some confusion until the synchronization checks and forces the issue by deleting the original Master replica.

View Entire Partition Name   Shows the entire partition name, regardless of its length.

Return to Replica List   Backs up one menu (same as pressing Escape).

These operations force repairs and synchronizations while writing full details to the log file. They provide a rifle approach, as opposed to the shotgun approach of the Unattended Full Repair option.

Part III

As with VREPAIR in past NetWare versions, you may need to perform some operations several times. While the replica and partition information is updated throughout the network, small errors here and there may be magnified, or they may not appear until later in the process. So don't expect any of these options to be able to work magic and quickly fix your problem. Things take longer when working across a distributed network, and this is no exception.

Viewing a Replica Ring   Choosing the View Replica Ring choice, the first option on the Replica Options menu, brings up a list of servers. In our case, two servers have replicas of this partition.

Highlight the server and replica type of your choice, and still another new menu appears: Replica Options, Server (and the name of the current chosen server). Here we have nothing but actions, with no pause for reflection. If you've come down this many levels in your server operating system, you might as well go for it. These are your choices:

Report Synchronization Status on the Selected Server Gathers partition details on a specific server and replica.

Synchronize the Replica on the Selected Server   Same as above for a single, highlighted replica.

Send All Objects to Every Replica in the Ring   This may create high network traffic. All other replicas are relabeled as new replicas, and the old replicas are destroyed. The host server sends a new copy of the replica to the remote servers that had their old replicas deleted. Modifications made to the now-deleted replicas that didn't have time to get back to the host replica are gone.

Receive All Objects for This Replica   Again, this may create high network traffic. This option is the reverse of the above. The old replica is marked as deleted, and any objects are deleted. The Master remote replica replaces the host server replica.

View Entire Server Name   Another look at the server name, for those servers with names that can't fit in the small box of text in the earlier menu.

Return to Servers with Replicas List   Backs up one menu (same as pressing Escape).

Check Volume Objects and Trustees This Advanced Options menu choice tests and verifies that everything on the server's volumes is correctly listed in NDS, as illustrated in Figure 16.19. If a volume object can't be found, an attempt will be made to create one. All mounted volumes are checked for compliance. You must log into NDS to perform these checks.

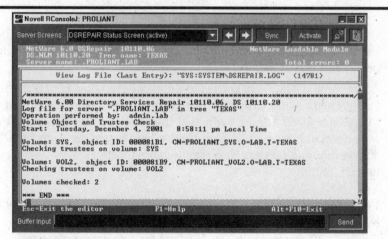

FIGURE 16.19: Volumes verified

The problem with new and faster servers and faster hard disks is that these volume checks whiz by too quickly to catch. Take a look at the log file to see the types of information checked for and verified. If there were any errors, they will appear in the log file.

Check External References When you choose Check External References from the Advanced Options menu, each external item referenced is checked to see if a replica containing the object can be located. If there is no joy, a warning will be given, but nothing dire happens immediately. Just keep working on your NDS repair until everything matches.

Global Schema Operations The *schema* consists of the rules governing objects and their relationships to NDS. It's important to have all servers on the same schema. Think of the schema as somewhat like the NDS program that tracks and controls all the objects. Having all servers on the same version of the program is smart, and it's also necessary. The submenu shown here appears when you choose Global Schema Options from the Advanced Options menu.

Part III

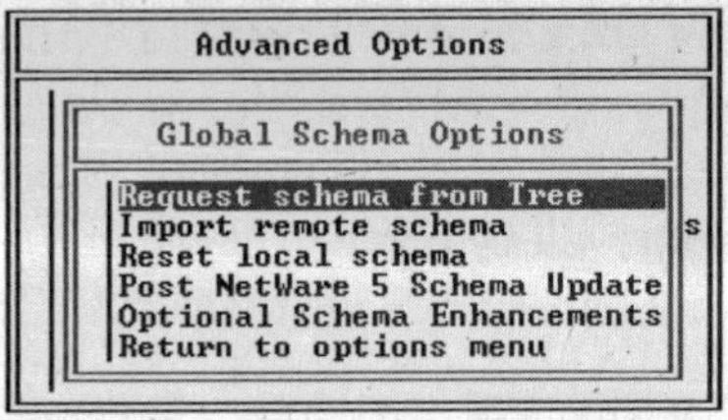

```
┌─────────────────────────────────────────┐
│            Advanced Options               │
│ ┌───────────────────────────────────────┐ │
│ │         Global Schema Options          │ │
│ │ Request schema from Tree              │ │
│ │ Import remote schema                 s│ │
│ │ Reset local schema                    │ │
│ │ Post NetWare 5 Schema Update          │ │
│ │ Optional Schema Enhancements          │ │
│ │ Return to options menu                │ │
│ └───────────────────────────────────────┘ │
└─────────────────────────────────────────┘
```

The first step in the upgrade looks at known servers in the tree and checks their schema version. If it's current, nothing happens, and the next server is checked.

Why would Novell engineers put a choice here, when the Help screen for the choice admits there will be network errors if all servers aren't up to the same level? The answer is that this is placed here for servers that were down or having an NDS problem when the updates were done. If at all possible, don't do any NDS maintenance unless all of your servers are up and running.

View Repair Log File   The DSREPAIR.LOG file keeps track of every result from every procedure run against the NDS on this server. Figure 16.20 shows results from looking for now-departed servers.

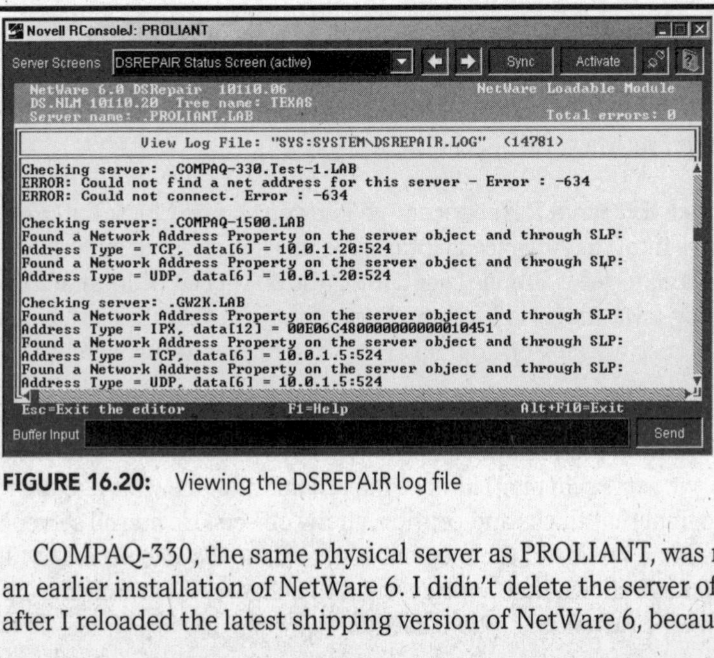

FIGURE 16.20:   Viewing the DSREPAIR log file

COMPAQ-330, the same physical server as PROLIANT, was merely an earlier installation of NetWare 6. I didn't delete the server officially after I reloaded the latest shipping version of NetWare 6, because I wanted to show some errors in DSREPAIR. That's my story, and I'm sticking with it.

The first three lines of the repair log show that COMPAQ-330 couldn't be found. No surprise there—it's hard to find something that no longer exists.

COMPAQ-1500 does exist, and the second block of repair log information shows the server seems fine and up-to-date.

The last and longest block of repair log information shows GW2K, an old Gateway 2000 Pentium 120 with 128MB of RAM. If you remember, NetWare 6 requires a minimum of 256MB of RAM. That's why GW2K remains a NetWare 5.1 server. Notice GW2K still runs both IPX and TCP/IP.

When you've finished viewing this file, press Escape and select to save the log file under the same name, or just exit.

Return to Main Menu Believe it or not, we are finished wandering in the world of partitions, replicas, schemas, and eDirectory databases. Once you choose the Return To Main Menu option or press Escape, you're out of the Advanced Options section. Back at the main menu, you'll see that we're out of DSREPAIR altogether.

Using a Graphical DSREPAIR

IN A HURRY 16.3: USE DSREPAIR FROM IMONITOR

1. Log in as Admin or equivalent and open iMonitor.

2. Click the DSREPAIR icon (wrench) on the toolbar.

3. Provide the administrator name and password (if asked again).

4. Choose the NDS Repair Switches with the check boxes.

5. Click the Start Repair command button.

Hidden within iMonitor is a fully graphical, almost complete copy of DSREPAIR. Novell marketing managers haven't made much noise about this utility, but they should, because it's pretty cool. (I guess there probably is not much publicity yet because iMonitor itself needs more awareness among administrators.)

Figure 16.21 shows the DSREPAIR window you can get to from iMonitor. See the little wrench on the toolbar in iMonitor? That's DSREPAIR, although iMonitor just calls it Repair.

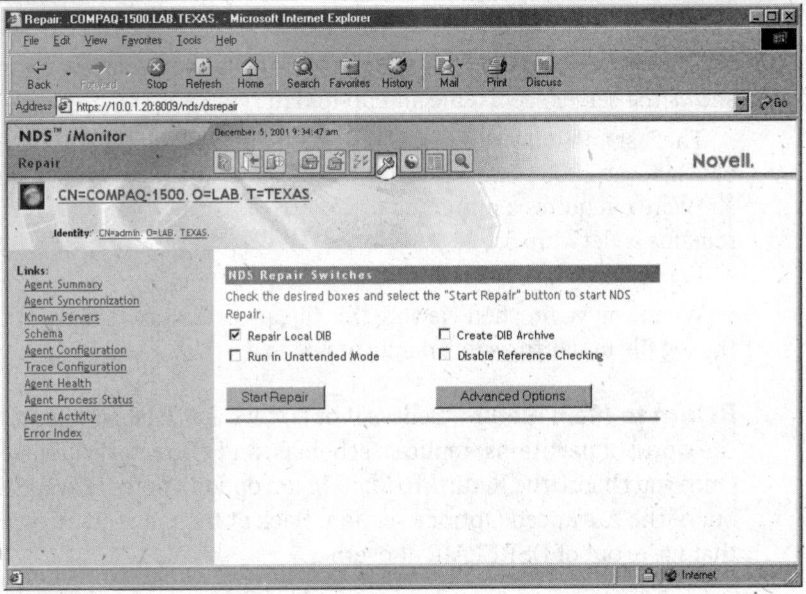

FIGURE 16.21: DSREPAIR goes Hollywood

Why would you use the console DSREPAIR if this version is here? Because the console version is more complete (all those advanced options, remember?) and may work on systems too crippled to support users. Besides, the more you use the console version, the more you appreciate the graphical option.

Running DSREPAIR functions from iMonitor provides the same log file as the console version. Unfortunately, you must go to the server console to view the log file, drilling through DSREPAIR.

One new and handy option for DSREPAIR in iMonitor is the Periodic Information capability, which is essentially a scheduling system for DSREPAIR. Click the Advanced Options command button to see the expanded screen display, as shown in Figure 16.22.

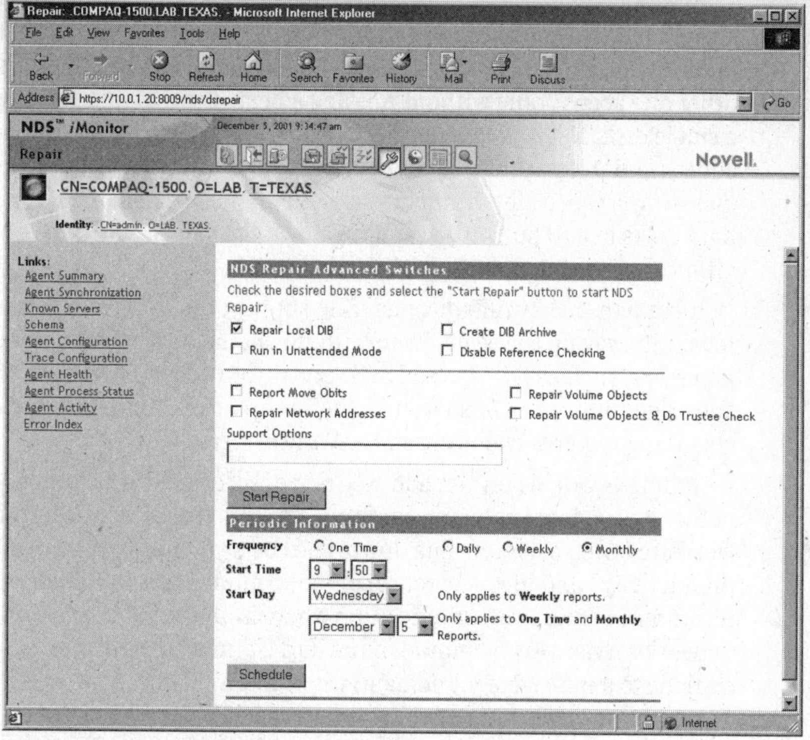

FIGURE 16.22: DSREPAIR Advanced Options within iMonitor

TELL YOUR BOSS: PRIOR PLANNING PREVENTS POOR PERFORMANCE

Every decision made during the design and implementation of your network impacts the performance and reliability of that network. Some of these choices are easy to evaluate: a fast multiprocessor server will perform better than a lower-end single-processor system. Other design choice ramifications don't appear until something has blown up, taking your network and peace of mind with it.

Keep in mind crosstime (as opposed to downtime) and explain the idea to your management. The option to support network clients through alternative servers and other resources is a sign of network flexibility, not fallibility.

Building fault-tolerance for your network means more work and more money. It's also the only way to guard against downtime. Mirrored or duplexed disk drives are a quick, easy example. If one drive dies, the other one keeps going without missing a beat. Try that in a server with a single disk. NetWare 6 and NSS 3.0 extend mirroring to partitions, adding fault tolerance to larger volumes across multiple disks. External disk arrays, especially with removable disks, mean you can now swap hard disks in and out without taking down the server. A volume may go offline for a moment, but not the server itself.

Including free, two-node clustering support into NetWare 6 jumps reliability way up the scale. Even without shared disk storage, some processes, such as DHCP and DNS servers, provide fail-over fault tolerance right out of the box. Well, actually two boxes, since two-node clustering requires two licensed NetWare servers.

Your network, when you add web server software, turns from a local network to a global network. Running e-commerce software on your NetWare 6 web server means downtime costs you hard dollars, not "lost productivity" and inconvenience. Remote options such as iFolder and iPrint mean employees or offices anywhere in the world depend on your network services every minute of the day. Uptime changed from a nice statistic to a management demand when the Web kicked into gear.

What can your boss do to help the troubleshooting process? Provide money for training (you and your users). Provide network analysis and management tools. Provide spare parts.

The best your boss can provide is a reasonable atmosphere. High expectations are met with high resources. Low resources lead to low results. Your management must make the decision on how important the network is and then provide resources accordingly.

In a typical company, management will try to force high expectations from low resources. That's possible for a time, especially if you're smart and work hard. However, one day the lack of spare parts and support tools will catch up to you. Your network will be down for at least one day. Your boss will try to blame you. Don't let that happen; point to the empty shelf labeled spare parts. Keeping a copy of your rejected proposals for network upgrades won't hurt, either.

WHAT'S NEXT

Now that we've covered the basics in network design, maintenance, and troubleshooting, let's stretch our knowledge to intranets, extranets, and interconnecting networks. The next section of this book will focus on bringing your networks right to your clients' desktops—even clients and potential clients halfway around the globe.

Chapter 17

DISASTER RECOVERY

This book started many years ago as a class on building, supporting, maintaining, and troubleshooting LANs. The people taking this class were all support people and network administrators, some coming up from the PC stand-alone world, some migrating to LANs from a mainframe environment, and some more experienced but looking to brush up on their skills. When we got to the part on disaster planning, whoever was teaching started a little exchange that went something like this:

"How many of you have disaster recovery plans in place?"

Most hands went up.

"How many of you have *written* disaster recovery plans in place?"

Many of the hands went down.

"How many of you have actually tested those plans and revised them where they didn't work?"

Most of the hands went down, most people looked sheepish, and it's a good bet that at least one of the people who still had their hands up was either lying or didn't hear the question.

Adapted from *Mastering Local Area Networks*
by Christa Anderson with Mark Minasi
ISBN 0-7821-2258-2   784 pages $39.99

Part III

There comes a time in everyone's life when a situation completely goes to pot. The server won't boot. The office burns down. The backups are destroyed. It's not fun to think about the file server going down in flames, but it's a heck of a lot better thinking about it ahead of time than explaining to your boss why you can't replace the network to its previous state. In this chapter, we'll talk about disaster recovery planning, including who's involved, what such a plan needs to encompass, and some possible solutions you can implement to avert or recover from disaster.

Exploring the Nature of Disaster

"Disaster" sounds terrifically melodramatic. If you think of disaster as limited to natural catastrophes or events on the order of the Oklahoma City or World Trade Center attacks, you might not think of disaster as being very close at hand.

A more realistic definition of disaster, with regard to computer networks, is any event or circumstance that could keep your company or organization from functioning for an undetermined length of time. That doesn't just encompass data loss, but anything that would interrupt operations; with that definition, disaster starts looking a lot closer.

You could divide the potential causes of disasters into three categories:

▶ Events

▶ Breakdowns

▶ Behavior

These categories aren't mutually exclusive, of course; an event could lead to a breakdown, or one breakdown could expose a behavior that exacerbates the disaster. For the purposes of recovering from a disaster, it doesn't always matter what caused it. For preparing for it, though, it does.

Event-Related Disasters

You probably already have a healthy appreciation of the power of nature to shut down a business. If you want an event-related disaster, a hurricane makes a good one. You have to shut down operations to evacuate; there's an excellent chance of water damage, or worse; you can't get needed supplies; and power shuts down. Then again, there are fires and earthquakes in California, tornadoes in the Midwest, freak spring snow-storms that shut down power and roads for much of New England for days, and flooding and electrical storms just about everywhere.

A disaster-causing event doesn't have to be as big as an earthquake or Hurricane George, either. A fire that starts in one building of an office park is certainly a threat, as is a broken water main that floods part of your building. Even if the disaster doesn't touch your office directly, you can still feel its effects. If you conduct your business remotely, one downed telephone line miles away is a minor disaster in terms of making it difficult or impossible to conduct business normally or at all. Events may not touch you directly, but they can cramp your style nonetheless.

Equipment Breakdowns

It is the nature of machinery—even solid-state machinery—to break down periodically. The more machinery you've got, the more likely it is that some of it will break at some point. The breakdown doesn't have to directly involve the machinery you need to function. For example, if the air conditioning goes out and it's hot outside, you may not be able to run the servers even if you can persuade the staff that they can function in 95-degree weather. Try to run a server for long in that environment, and you'll bake it.

The good news is that breakdown disasters are often the easiest to plan for. More so than human-related disasters, at any rate.

Behavior Problems

Most of us who've lived in one part of the country for even a year or two can anticipate weather-related problems. Broken equipment problems can be resolved with redundancy in equipment.

Human-related problems can be another matter entirely. There are the obvious ones like major flu outbreaks, or strikes, but thankfully those aren't often the worry of the network administrator or other technical staff unless they're the ones who are sick or on strike. However, deliberate sabotage (that DELETE *.* gambit), users ignoring safe computing advice and introducing viruses into the network, or someone bringing in unlicensed software, spreading it throughout the company, and bringing the wrath of the SPA down on your head are also human-related problems, and ones likely to directly concern you.

PREPPING FOR DISASTER— BACKUPS

Before you even think about a disaster recovery plan, you need to think about backups. Backups are so essential a part of a network administration plan that they should be an "of course" part of your network, not part of the disaster recovery plan.

In addition to the obvious role of permitting you to replace the network's data when someone puts a bullet through the file server's hard drive, backups are essential for a couple of less dramatic but still potentially bad situations:

▶ Replacing corrupted data, system, or template files

▶ Needing copies of files last used several years ago

These are small problems in comparison to the difficulty of replacing the entire company data files, but they are not always inconsequential, either.

Understanding Backup Types

There are four main types of backups (see Table 17.1). Each takes advantage of the file attribute archive bit to tune how the backup works.

TABLE 17.1:   Backup Types

BACKUP TYPE	COPY SET	RESETS ARCHIVE BIT?
Full	Copies all files selected for backup, regardless of whether their archive bit was set	Yes
Incremental	Copies only files with the archive bit set	Yes
Differential	Copies only files with the archive bit set	No
Daily	Copies only files with the archive bit and timestamped for the day of backup	No

NOTE

These are common backup types; some backup utilities may offer further options. For example, some backup programs make use of backup logs. In addition to using the archive bit, logging backups keep track of the last modification date and time of all backed-up files. By comparing this information to the current date of the file, the software can more accurately back up files. In addition, the log operation can prevent someone from tampering with, or otherwise defeating, the archive bit. The best software will use both in determining when a backup should occur.

It's not practical to copy every file every day, but you need a base set of all files on the system. Thus, an effective backup plan will incorporate more than one type of backup, most often a full backup at regular intervals (such as each week) and supplemented with a daily incremental or differential backup. Generally, daily backups are only useful if you're going on a trip and want to take copies of your most recently changed files with you, and not all backup software supports them anyway.

Backup types are important because part of outlining a backup plan lies in knowing what you want from your backups. What kind of flexibility do you want in your ability to restore data? For that matter, is flexibility or ease of use more important to you? How does the time it takes to back up figure in?

The easiest backup to restore is a full backup, because you're only restoring from a single source. Chuck in the same tape every day at 3 a.m. and you've always got a full backup. Of course, full backups typically take a long time and a lot of room—the more data you're backing up, the longer it will take. It's more of a problem to run one full backup every night with the same tape because you can't archive backups. If it turns out that the version of a file that you really need is the one saved Wednesday, not the one you backed up on Friday after you'd revised it, then you're out of luck. How many full backups are you prepared to store? More often, you'll make full backups at intervals and supplement them with incremental or differential backups, described below:

Incremental backups Create a record of the files that have changed since the last full or incremental backup was done. As such, they tend to be fairly small—certainly smaller than full backups and typically smaller than differential backups—and precise. They're useful when you want to find a single file to restore, but restoring an entire server's contents can be tedious, as you have to restore each incremental backup separately.

Differential backups   Back up all the files changed since the last full or incremental backup was done. Thus, they're the easiest type of backup to restore—all you need to do is restore the full backup, then the latest differential. The only catch arises if you're trying to restore a particular version of a file, as tracking down the version you want can be tricky.

NOTE
The backup combination with the greatest degree of flexibility and ease of use I've seen is the full/differential one described in the upcoming section, "Creating a Schedule."

Creating and Implementing a Backup Plan

What's important to a backup plan is functionality, whether that's functionality in terms of backup media, scheduling, or any other aspect. Study the systems other people have put in place. If a system works for someone else whose needs are like yours, then there's a good chance it will work for you.

One consultant was helping to install a network for a company in an industry that's historically been pretty paper-based. In the process, he was incorporating new client machines, helping the company get up to speed with networking, figuring out some thorny communications problems, and of course, developing a backup plan for the company.

The biggest problem he was running into (well, after the problem of convincing them that they needed a backup system in the first place, which was more of a problem than he anticipated) was that it seemed as though no one wanted to do things the simple way. The people in the soon-to-be technical support department had been reading about all the new alternative media solutions available, liking the idea of writable CD-ROMs or some such. Tapes, according to the tech support people, were boring; everyone was using tapes. They wanted to use something different.

The time that you're designing a backup plan is not the time to get creative. To be informed, yes. To look at the various options available and see what kinds of backup systems will suit you best, yes. But not to discount a system out of hand just because a lot of people are using it already.

Outlining the Plan

The first stage of creating the backup plan lies with figuring out frequency and timing of backups. How often do you need to back up data to keep the organization running? When can you back up this data with the least inconvenience to people?

The answer to the second question depends, to a degree, on your backup software. Some backup utilities will let you back up open files, somewhat simplifying the timing problem.

How Often Should I Back Up?

There's no set answer to the question of how often you need to back up—the answer depends on how much you can afford to lose. If you back up once a month, then you'd better hope you can re-create and/or live without a month's worth of data at a time. Most of us use some form of daily backups (perhaps supplemented with weekly full backups), but even that represents some data loss; you'd hate to lose what you create in a day. However, you'd hate even more to have to mess with running constant backups. As with security, the frequency of backups should represent the balance between the trouble it takes to do the backups, the value of the data you're protecting, and the likelihood that anything will happen to that data.

Timing Backups

Constant backups aren't usually a practical solution. Running backups interfere with people working because they consume CPU cycles and may add to network traffic (if the files being copied aren't on the same system as the backup system). They also require software that can back up open files.

For these reasons, few companies use real-time backups. Instead, they choose the time of day that is least likely to inconvenience the majority of users and at which files are most likely to be closed. If you have a centralized backup system for a WAN that spans several time zones, it may be impossible to choose a time at which no one is working, but you can at least minimize the overlap.

TIP

Some operating systems, such as Windows NT, run the file-sharing capability as a service that can be turned off and then turned on again. If users have left files open at the end of the day and your backup system doesn't support backing up open files, create a batch file that turns off the server service, runs the backup, then turns the server service back on.

Creating a Schedule   Table 17.2 shows a one-month sample backup schedule for a small office. An initial full backup (Full Backup Tape 1) must be done before you can adhere to this schedule.

TABLE 17.2:   A Sample Backup Schedule (Rotating Biweekly)

WEEK	DAY	BACKUP TYPE AND TAPE USED
Start of Cycle	Friday	Full Backup Tape 1
Week 1	Monday	Differential Tape 1
	Tuesday	Differential Tape 2
	Wednesday	Differential Tape 3
	Thursday	Differential Tape 4
	Friday	Full Backup Tape 2
Week 2	Monday	Differential Tape 5
	Tuesday	Differential Tape 6
	Wednesday	Differential Tape 7
	Thursday	Differential Tape 8
	Friday	Full BackupTape 3
Week 3	Monday	Differential Tape 1 (overwrite)
	Tuesday	Differential Tape 2 (overwrite)
	Wednesday	Differential Tape 3 (overwrite)
	Thursday	Differential Tape 4 (overwrite)
	Friday	Full Backup Tape 4
Week 4	Monday	Differential Tape 5 (overwrite)
	Tuesday	Differential Tape 6 (overwrite)
	Wednesday	Differential Tape 7 (overwrite)
	Thursday	Differential Tape 8 (overwrite)
	Friday	Full Backup Tape 5

On the Friday of Week 5, you'd overwrite Full Backup Tape 1 and restart the cycle. This backup schedule creates a two-week record of differential backups and a month record of full backups. An additional six-month archive might not be a bad idea either, for files that aren't often used or are discovered to be missing or corrupted only months—or even years—after their original use.

MORE RECOMMENDED BACKUP SCHEMES

Table 17.2 maps out a simplified version of one of Microsoft's two most recommended backup models: Grandfather/Father/Son (GFS). In GFS, "Grandfather" is a monthly full backup, "Father" is a weekly full backup, and "Son" is an incremental or differential daily backup. GFS uses a total of 12 tapes or other media to store all back-ups for a three-month period: four for daily backups, five for backups each weekend, and three for the monthly backups.

Another backup scheme Microsoft recommends is called the Tower of Hanoi (ToH), after the math puzzle by the same name. Although more complicated than GFS, ToH keeps a longer record of backups than the other backup scheme—32 weeks instead of 12 weeks. In ToH, five tapes (labeled A–E here) are used in the following order: A B A C A B A D A B A C A B A E. In this method, tape A is reused every two weeks, tape B every four weeks, tape C every 8 weeks, tape D every 16 weeks, and tape E every 32 weeks. ToH only plans for full backups, so you'll probably want to supplement each weekly full back-up with an incremental or differential daily backup.

To *really* keep things simple, get backup software that you can program to follow a certain backup scheme and prompt you for the correct tape. That way, you won't have to follow the plan quite so closely.

Choosing Backup Hardware

What are some good server-based backup devices? For practical purposes, a tape drive of some kind is probably your best bet: they're relatively inexpensive, have a high capacity, are reliable, and are widely supported.

Tapes aren't the only option, however. If there's a need for you to distribute the contents of your backups widely, then writable CD-ROMs might well be the perfect solution. Even though a CD-R holds less than 1GB and can be finicky for write options, you can be reasonably sure that just about all computers sold in the past three years will have a CD-ROM drive. The small capacity of Zip and Jaz cartridges makes the drives impractical for backing up servers. However, if your backup plan is client based instead of server based, the smaller removable drives may suit you well. The Jaz drive, especially, is large enough to back up user data, and if you use an external drive, it's easily swappable among SCSI-based client machines. If those backup options don't do anything for you, then you might consider backing up files to another disk, either on the server or on another networked computer entirely.

Ultimately, your choice of backup media will be influenced by its speed, capacity, and portability. These factors are discussed in the following sections.

Planning for Speed   If you're doing backups at night, fast backups might not be your first concern, but speed is likely to look a little more important when you're trying to *restore* data.

Speed is determined by two factors: the speed at which the media itself operates and the speed of the connection to the server. A switched fabric network connection will be fastest, but of the more likely options to be in use as of this writing, a SCSI connection will be fastest, with IDE second and a parallel port third. I recommend SCSI as the controller interface of choice for servers. Parallel ports aren't a practical solution for server backup interfaces, although they might work if you're backing up individual client machines that don't support SCSI.

The access time of the media also matters. How quickly can you get data on and off the media? The data transfer rate for various media will impact the rate at which data can be read from and written to the media.

NOTE
The write and read speed are adversely affected by the degree of compression.

Capacity Planning   How much data can one unit of the media hold? Will you be able to put all the backup data on a single unit, several units, or lots of units? The more data a backup storage unit can hold, the easier it will be to back up and restore data, as you'll have fewer media units to mess with. Backups will be simpler, as you won't have to swap units; it's faster to restore data if you can do it from one or two units, and it's much easier to store fewer units than more of them.

Planning for Portability   So far, tapes are ahead of most other media. Although their access times run somewhere in the Zip drive range, they're high capacity and widely supported. The only thing that tapes don't necessarily have is portability. There are so many different types of tapes and backup formats that tapes aren't an easy way to distribute data, except within the confines of a single company. For those purposes, writable CDs and removable drives are likely to be superior. Table 17.3 examines some possible alternatives to tapes.

TABLE 17.3: Characteristics of Common Non-Tape Backup Media

CRITERIA	HARD DISKS	CD-R/RW	ZIP	JAZ
Connection Types Available	IDE, SCSI, network	Parallel, IDE, SCSI	SCSI, parallel, USB, IDE	SCSI
Access Time	>9ms	250–350ms, depending on model	29ms (parallel)	15.5–17.5ms
Capacity	Up to 13GB for a single drive	650MB	250MB	2GB
Unit	Hard disk	CD	Disk-sized cartridge	Disk-sized cartridge

Not all backup packages support all media types. In Windows NT 4, NT Backup doesn't support any media but tapes, for example. You can't back up to a network or removable drive. This feature has been added to Windows 2000.

Choosing Backup Software

When choosing a backup utility, you need to keep in mind the product's flexibility and interoperability with the network components you've already got. Ask yourself the following about any backup applications you're considering:

▶ Compatibility:

   ▶ Does it work with my operating system?

   ▶ Is it compatible with any other backup systems that might already be in use?

- ▶ What backup types does it support?

- ▶ Does it work only on a per-server basis or can you use it to manage backups for multiple servers from a single console?

- ▶ What types of media will the application support?

- ▶ What tape format does it use?

▶ Flexibility:

- ▶ Can it schedule unattended backups?

- ▶ How much discretion does it give me in choosing files to be backed up (volume level, folder level, file level)?

- ▶ Will it retry busy (open) files?

- ▶ Will it back up open files?

- ▶ Does it copy data structures or make a binary image of the disk being backed up?

▶ Reliability:

- ▶ Does it have trustworthy error-correction available?

- ▶ Can you verify file integrity?

- ▶ Is it easy to use?

- ▶ Does it give you control over error correction?

- ▶ Does it keep dated revisions?

Most current network operating systems—even peer ones—have a native backup application you can use, so you don't necessarily have to shop for a separate one. NT's backup utility, for example, is a cut-down version of Seagate's BackupExec. For full functionality, including the ability to back up open files, you'd still need to purchase the Seagate version, but you can protect server data nicely with the NOS version of the utility.

Running the Plan

Once it's developed, running a backup plan is mostly a matter of administration, not technology. Plan for who's going to run the backup plan and where those backups will be stored, and practice restoring data.

Who's Minding the Store?   The backup administrator needs to be someone trustworthy, both because the fate of the company's data rests in her hands and because she'll need to have access to the server that's less restricted than that of the average user. Make sure that this person understands procedures, and that she knows whom to consult if she runs into problems. Procedures may include any of the following:

▸ Backing up data

▸ Verifying writes

▸ Storing and labeling archive tapes

▸ Rotating and reusing tapes

For that matter, make sure someone is available who can help. On one occasion, a backup administrator was having problems with the media, or the software—he wasn't sure which. The office expert on the backup utility traveled a lot and didn't have time to fix the problem when he was in the office, but the administrator figured that he'd catch the expert when the expert had time. You can probably write the ending; the file server crashed, the backups didn't work (the problem turned out to be poorly tensioned tapes, so the backups couldn't be restored), and it became a job for the data recovery people. Not pretty.

Finally, a responsible replacement backup administrator needs to be in place. If the main person is sick or on vacation, someone else needs to be ready immediately, not picked because he happened to be in the room when the usual person's absence is noticed. Otherwise, there's the danger that the job won't get done or won't be done properly.

TIP

Posting the backup schedule, with a place to initial after a backup is completed and verified, can help on two fronts. First, it's a reminder that the backups need to be done. Second, having the schedule on the wall lets you see at a glance when the files were last backed up, what type of backup it was, and who signed off on the job.

Practice Restoring Data   A key element to a successful backup plan lies in making sure that you can restore the data you're backing up. Problems could potentially arise due to operator error or hardware failure (remember those poorly tensioned tapes). It's nice to discover any such problems before the situation is critical. Thus, have the backup administrator verify the contents of all tapes and restore a file here and there (preferably one not changed since the backup was made).

Archiving and Storing the Backups   It won't do you much good if
you back up your disk but find that the backups are useless. If your office
is fire damaged, your backups won't help you if they sat on the shelf
above your computer. Nor will they help you if you keep the box with the
backups in it on a sunny windowsill—the disks will cook slowly in the sun
and become useless. On another track, if you don't label the disks well or
keep them organized, it will be difficult or impossible to find what you're
looking for when you need to restore.

What, then, can you do to make your backups as effective as possible?

Label your backups clearly. Include the name of the machine, the drive,
the date backed up, and the disk or tape number. A label or file card
might look like this:

FULL BACKUP of PALADIN D: 01/15/01 #4/6

Keep your backups in a safe, cool, dry place. It's best to keep important backups off site so that if your office burns down, your backups
don't burn with it. If you can't store them outside of your office building
for some reason, at least keep them on a separate floor so that they can
evade local disasters.

WARNING

If you buy a fireproof safe in which to keep backup tapes, make sure you get a
safe rated for data protection, not paper protection. Paper can stand fairly high
temperatures before combusting. Tapes can melt in sunlight, let alone the middle of a fire. A data safe will be much more expensive (around $300 instead of
$50), but the company data is worth at least that much.

Don't save backups you don't need; it will only confuse you later. If
your company formats a computer's hard disk and starts over, get rid of
the backups for that computer once you've established that nothing
important was on the drive.

Test your backups periodically to make sure that they work. Heat,
humidity, and electromagnetic fields can cause your data to deteriorate.
Disks and people are generally comfortable in similar climates. If you
wouldn't sit in your storage room for hours on end, your backups won't
enjoy it either.

Don't keep backups for years and expect them to remain intact without help. The magnetic images on your disks tend to neutralize each

other. A disk left on a shelf will slowly return to a *tabula rasa*. It would be as if you wrote in the sand on a beach; the writing would gradually fade unless you retraced it daily. You can give new life to your tapes by copying your backups to newly formatted media and then reformatting the old tape. Tapes are generally designed to last for two to three years.

Real-Time Data Protection Options

You may think of real-time backups as a practical impossibility—too expensive, too resource demanding, or the like. However, there are some methods you can use to maintain more-or-less constant updates of your data that will survive if a hard disk stops working. These methods have a couple of advantages. They not only provide data redundancy and improved up time, but also can improve network performance by introducing *load balancing*, distributing data access among multiple disks or servers. Ordinary backups, in contrast, only provide data redundancy.

Apply a Touch of RAID

RAID (Redundant Array of Inexpensive Disks) is a blanket term for the technology that allows you to combine the resources of multiple hard disks to improve overall disk reliability and/or performance. Hardware-based RAID is built on a RAID subsystem of SCSI disks, whereas software-based RAID uses software to build the array. RAID has the following characteristics:

- It can support the loss of one disk in the fault-tolerant array; the missing data can be supplied or re-created from the remaining disk(s).

- It is dependent on multiple physical disks working together. You can't combine logical volumes to create a RAID array, and if the physical disks aren't working together, they're Just a Bunch of Disks (JBOD).

- The physical disks in a RAID array do not have to be identical in size or type, but the logical divisions in the array must all be the same size. That is, each logical part of an array will be the same size as the other parts.

- You can use RAID to protect all or part of a physical disk.

TIP
You can create software-based RAID arrays with EIDE disks, but you'll get better performance if you use SCSI. SCSI supports multitasking for reads and writes on a single controller, whereas EIDE single-tasks.

RAID has become very common as disk prices have dropped and software-based RAID has made the technology more available to the average person. The two types of fault-tolerant RAID most often supported are disk mirroring and disk striping with parity. These are discussed in the following sections.

Disk Mirroring (RAID 1)   Disk mirroring protects all your data by writing it to two locations at once; every time you create or edit or delete a file, the changes are registered in both locations. It requires two physical drives explicitly associated in a mirror set. If anything happens to the data on one disk, you break the mirror set and a perfect and up-to-date replica of the data is available on the other disk. Mirror sets are inefficient in their use of disk space—the redundancy means that the data requires twice as much disk space as it would ordinarily—but they are an excellent means of data protection. In SCSI systems, they can also reduce read times because the read operation can be multitasked among two disks.

NOTE
If each disk in the mirror set has its own disk controller (so that a disk controller failure doesn't render both drives inaccessible), then it's called *disk duplexing*. Otherwise, the mirror set works as described above.

Stripe Sets with Parity (RAID 5)   Like disk mirroring, a stripe set with parity protects data by distributing the data among multiple disks. During write operations, data is written in stripes to each disk in the stripe set (stripe sets with parity must contain at least three physical disks). In addition to the original data, however, parity information for the data is also written to the disks and distributed among the physical disks like the original data, but stored separately from the particular data to which it applies. If one disk in the stripe set fails, then the parity information on the remaining disks can be used to reconstruct the missing data, so all data is still accessible. The proportion of parity information depends on the number of disks in the stripe set, as the parity is designed to make it possible to regenerate the data on a single disk. Therefore, a stripe set with three disks will use one-third of its capacity for parity information, while a set with 10 disks will use one-tenth for parity. The more disks in the stripe set, the greater the efficiency.

If more than one disk in the stripe set fails at a time, then the data is lost, but single disk failures are recoverable without any action required on your part. For example, say that you've created a four-disk array and used it as the foundation of a stripe set with parity. One of the disks dies. When you reboot the server and open the Disk Administrator, you'll see a message that a disk failed and that the missing data is being regenerated. People will be able to write to and read from the stripe set as though the missing disk were still there. Of course, you'll need to replace the dead disk as soon as possible. If a second disk fails, then the stripe set will be unrecoverable.

NOTE

The parity information is crucial to the fault tolerance. One type of RAID—disk striping without parity—is not fault tolerant. Instead, it's designed to improve disk throughput by spreading read and write operations over multiple disks. As the disks are codependent and contain no fault-tolerant information, these disk arrays must be backed up regularly—one disk failure will make the entire array inoperable.

The Pros and Cons of RAID Types   Should you use stripe sets with parity or disk mirroring? Disk mirroring has a lower initial cost, as the mirror set only requires a minimum of two disks instead of the minimum of three required for fault-tolerant stripe sets. Mirroring also has a speed advantage when it comes to write operations. In a SCSI-based mirror set, write options can be done more or less simultaneously because of SCSI's multitasking capabilities, so disk mirroring actually improves read and write speed. Stripe sets with parity, in contrast, take a performance hit for write options because they must keep recalculating the parity information as the data changes. Read operations aren't affected, but writes are slower than they would be if done to a single disk or in a mirror set. Finally, the calculations involved in supporting stripe sets place greater demands on server RAM and CPU time than does disk mirroring.

That said, stripe sets with parity are more common. Mirroring is very space inefficient, much more so than stripe sets, which become more efficient as more physical disks are added to the stripe set. The increased efficiency of space makes up for any performance hits, which aren't really large enough to be visible to the network client anyway. Cheap hardware means that the additional resources required to support stripe sets aren't really any deterrent to supporting the more efficient RAID method.

Data Replication

If you can't afford any downtime at all, then you have a couple of options. One is clustering (described in the next section) and another is data replication. *Replication*—copying data and data structures from one server to another—is a popular way to both maintain data integrity and also distribute the data load among several servers. The data is originally written to one server (called the *export server* in NT networks) and then copied to another (called the *import server*). You can set up server connections to manually divide client access between servers or use load balancing to automatically divide the client load among the servers.

Generally speaking, people tend to replicate two kinds of data: that which they can't afford to lose and that which benefits from load balancing. Because of network bandwidth constraints, ordinary data isn't often protected with replication—copying each change to a large file server can take up bandwidth needed for other purposes, and it's possible to protect file data with RAID. However, replication can be a useful way to protect database or mission-critical information such as WINS mappings or the directory of logon scripts. Rather than trying to serve all client requests from a central location, replication makes it possible to let multiple servers help with the job, while at the same time making sure that redundant copies of the database exist.

Create Redundant Servers with Clustering

Clustering is a bit like RAID carried a step further. Rather than creating arrays of multiple disks to provide fault tolerance and improved performance, clustering creates arrays of servers to provide fault tolerance and improved performance.

Not all clustering solutions are identical, either in function or in the way they're connected and interrelate. So far as function goes, there are three main types of clustering:

- ▶ Active/active
- ▶ Active/standby
- ▶ Fault-tolerant

All cluster types provide some support for fault tolerance, but the degree to which they do it—and the speed with which one server will take over for another if the first server fails—depends on the cluster type.

In an active/active cluster, all servers in the cluster are functional and supporting users all the time. If any server fails, the remaining server (or servers) continues handling its workload and takes on the workload from the failed server. It takes from 15 to 90 seconds for the remainder of the cluster to take over for the failed server. In an active/standby cluster, one server supports user requests or does whatever it's designed to do while another waits for the first server to fail. This doesn't improve failover time; if the first server dies, it still takes from 15 to 90 seconds for the second one to take over the workload of the first. (Any connections or services running on the standby server are terminated when the standby takes over.)

Fault-tolerant clusters are designed to have less than six minutes of downtime a year and they are different from active/active and active/standby clusters. In a fault-tolerant cluster, each server in the cluster is identical to all the rest of them and operates in tandem, performing precisely the same operation as all other servers in the cluster. Thus, if one server fails, the rest of the cluster can take over more or less instantaneously. Fault-tolerant clustering uses resources less efficiently than active/active or active/standby clustering, but in case of server failure causes no downtime. The other cluster types, in contrast, may be down for as long as a minute and a half—even 15 seconds of downtime is long enough to spoil a write operation. Table 17.4 compares the three types.

TABLE 17.4: Comparing Cluster Types

	ACTIVE/ACTIVE	ACTIVE/STANDBY	FAULT-TOLERANT
Primary/Secondary Server Operations	Are different	Are different	Are identical for full redundancy
Effect on Secondary Server If Primary Fails	Adds primary server's workload to its own	Discards its workload for that of the primary server	Are not affected, as both servers were doing the same thing before the failure
Requires Identical Systems?	No	No	Yes
Failover Time	15–90 seconds	15–90 seconds	<1 second

Part III

The type of cluster describes whether the cluster is designed to offer fault tolerance or improved performance and the way in which workload is balanced between members of the cluster. Cluster *products* differ in terms of their data-sharing techniques, the way in which the members of the cluster are connected, and how flexible they are as far as the hardware they support. Products also vary in the number of servers that may be in a single cluster—some clustering products only support two servers, a primary and a secondary—but the more expensive ones support more.

For data sharing, clusters may rely on replication, switching, or mirroring. In *replication*, the data written to the primary server's hard disk is replicated on that of the secondary server via the network connection between the servers. In *switching*, each member of the cluster has its own disk, but the disks are all connected to the same SCSI bus so that if the primary's disk fails, the secondary can take over. *Mirroring* works as described in the previous section, "Apply a Touch of RAID"—data is written simultaneously to the primary and secondary servers' disks.

The physical connection between the members of the cluster also varies with the product. Sometimes, the servers in the cluster will be connected with an ordinary network such as Ethernet. Sometimes, they'll be connected with proprietary connectors. Other solutions, such as a switched fabric connection, are also possible—whether they're supported depends on the product.

Similarly, the degree of flexibility in terms of hardware type supported will vary. Some clustering products only support a single kind of hardware—bad news, to be sure. Better are those that will support any two servers. Best are those that support servers with different platforms (say, one *x*86-based and one Alpha-based). Fault-tolerant clusters can't use this kind of flexibility, however, as the servers in the cluster must be identical.

Creating a Disaster Recovery Plan

Backups are an important aspect of preparing for disaster recovery, but not the only part; they have a place in the entire disaster recovery plan.

A *disaster recovery plan* is a detailed document spelling out how to restore the business to working order after a catastrophic event. It's important that it be written down so that the instructions are available even if the person who created the plan isn't available. It needs to be as detailed as possible so that the person executing the recovery doesn't necessarily have to be a computer expert.

NOTE
A complete disaster recovery plan involves nontechnical elements such as staffing, but I'll focus on the technical elements here.

A well-designed plan will have the following characteristics:

▶ The support of upper management

▶ A clear purpose

▶ A clearly defined chain of command and delegation of authority

▶ No single point of failure

▶ Flexibility in case conditions change

These elements aren't part of an ideal plan, but are essential to any disaster recovery plan that's going to work as needed.

Support from upper management is important, because you'll need their cooperation to develop and carry out the plan. A complete disaster recovery plan is too complicated and too involved with nontechnical concerns to be prepared fully in isolation from the rest of the company.

The clear purpose keeps the document on track. The plan shouldn't be a dissertation on network theory or nonessential tasks, but a tightly focused document explaining how to make the network operational again and detailing the steps required. Extraneous information may be saved for a "Meet Your Network" presentation for nontechnical staff members, or some such, but the plan itself should only include the essential instructions. Along the way to defining the plan's purpose, you'll need to answer the following questions:

▶ What is the purpose of the plan? Is it to restore the network to its complete state, or just to get it up and running for the moment, with more time to be taken later?

▶ What parts of the network need to be restored first? Some services are more essential than others, and some services are dependent on others.

Defining responsibilities, both for preparing for disaster and for recovering from it, expedites the recovery process. If everyone knows what jobs they have to do, then there's no time wasted in determining who's responsible for what. Defining responsibility also makes sure that everything gets done—there's less chance of important elements slipping through the cracks.

NOTE

One element of determining responsibility lies in defining response. When disaster strikes, everyone needs to know what's expected of them, whether it means staying home and out of the way, reporting elsewhere, or working around the people reassembling the network. Customers may also need to be notified if some product will be delayed or coming from another location due to the circumstances.

Well-defined roles in preparation and recovery are important, but every reliable system has some redundancy. The success or failure of the plan shouldn't rest on one person's shoulders, or on one piece of hardware; no single element should be allowed to prevent recovery. This means that:

▶ A chain of command exists, showing who takes over if one person isn't available.

▶ Recent backups are stored offsite to reduce the chance of a catastrophe that destroys the original data taking the backups with it.

▶ Damaged hardware must be quickly replaceable if need be.

Finally, a good plan is flexible. The best plan is modular, not too reliant on the skills of any one person, or reliant on any other specific set of circumstances. Companies grow, staff come and go, and hardware and software changes. The plan needs to be adaptable without requiring a complete rewrite every time the network evolves.

Who's Involved?

A disaster recovery plan is not the work of a single person. Instead, it represents the combined input from and efforts of a team:

▶ The people using the network

▶ The people who support the network

▶ The people who control the resources available

The number of people required to supply all these perspectives depends on your company's structure. Regardless of whether one person is in charge of each listed element, or one person is in charge of multiple duties, you really can't create a useful plan without input from all these sources.

> **NOTE**
>
> Don't forget to get input from one other source—the boss. Someone has to sign checks and approve equipment redundancies.

People Using the Network

The people in the best position to know what services are essential aren't always the people running the network. As the network administrator, you should know service dependencies, but what about knowing which data sources or other servers are most crucial? For that, you'll need input from the people using the network, or their representatives.

People Fixing the Network

The network support people are the technical voice of the disaster planning team. It's up to them (to you, that is) to know what recovery systems are required, what's available, how much the components will cost, and where to find more information. The network administrator should be able to supply feasibility information to the user contingent, letting them know what's physically possible (for example, no, we can't replicate the file server to an offsite server with a 33.6Kbps modem). Helping the people who control resources identify vendors and solutions is also part of the job of the support contingent.

The network administrator needs to know not only what's needed for disaster recovery, but also what's available now. For example, if the servers are SCSI based, then there's no point in buying backup IDE devices for them. An obvious point, but one sometimes missed. I recall one situation a few years ago in which a business manager bought some backup hard drives and controllers to have on hand in case the main ones failed. Unfortunately, the business manager didn't know what interface the existing controllers used. Thus, when the time came to replace one of the drive controllers with the backup, it turned out that the VL-Bus controller card that had been bought wouldn't work in the ISA/PCI server.

Part III

People Controlling Resources

The network administrator acts as one voice of reason, keeping tabs on what's technically feasible. The business manager acts as the voice of reason for cost and resource allocation. Sometimes the most effective disaster recovery plan isn't financially feasible. It's the job of the business manager to do the cost accounting required to make sure that the disaster recovery plan doesn't overprotect the network.

The business manager may also control the inventory of network hardware. Hardware inventory is important because it provides a reminder of how old hardware is, and also because it lets you know what parts need to be available (and perhaps, what can be cannibalized).

What's in a Plan?

The particulars of the plan will depend on the network design. Generally speaking, however, a disaster recovery plan will include the following:

▶ A statement of purpose describing the state to which the plan will restore the network

▶ Contact information for everyone involved in executing the recovery

▶ An organizational chart showing who's responsible for what elements of the recovery

▶ Instructions for recovery:

    ▶ Instructions for getting the various network servers (file, application, DHCP, WINS, web) back up and running again, including dependencies

NOTE
Dependencies are important! You need to make sure that in the process of recovery, the people restoring the network put the pieces back together in the proper order. Otherwise, the network may not function properly or at all.

    ▶ Instructions for restoring data from backups

    ▶ Instructions for regenerating data stored in a RAID array

Creating a disaster recovery plan takes a lot of time and effort—one plan can end up as a 145-page document—but when it comes time to get the network back up and running, perhaps without a full complement of the technical staff, it can be invaluable.

Some Final Thoughts on Designing Disaster Recovery Plans

Disaster recovery plans are essentially a really good piece of documentation. As such, they should be treated and tested as documentation. Make sure that the pieces work before forcing yourself to rely on them, and make sure you know what version of the product the documentation applies to.

First, test for accuracy. As each piece of the plan is written up, have someone else follow your instructions to make sure that you included everything and that your instructions are accurate. The ideal tester is someone who doesn't know how to do whatever the instructions describe—restoring backups, installing a DHCP server, or the like—because their inexperience will keep them from automatically filling in the blanks or correcting you where you're wrong, perhaps without even realizing that they're doing so. Second best is someone extremely picky, but you should never test the instructions yourself unless it's simply unavoidable. *Anyone* is better than you to fact-check your own instructions.

Second, test for feasibility. Can the plan work as you describe? Are all elements independent of special conditions? Do the pieces interoperate as envisioned? If the answer to any of these questions is "No," then redesign and test again.

Finally, keep a couple of dated hard copies of the plan in a safe place. If one copy is destroyed in the course of the disaster you're recovering from, you still have a copy of the plan. The dates are to let you know what version of the plan you've got, if more than one ever existed.

CALLING IN THE MARINES—DATA RECOVERY CENTERS

Disaster recovery isn't always fully successful. Perhaps your backups don't work or are destroyed themselves. One more option remains before you have to tell everyone that everything they were working on for the past month is irretrievably gone: data recovery centers. Data recovery centers are staffed by experts at getting data off media (most often hard disks, but not always) that can't be accessed by normal means.

Not all data recovery centers are the same. Some data recovery centers (in fact, the first data recovery centers) are staffed with people who are really, really good at getting dead hard disks back up and running. Using their skill, they can resuscitate the dead drive, copy its contents to other media, and then return the data—on the new media—to you.

TIP

If you're interested in learning how to do this kind of data recovery, Mark Minasi's *The Complete PC Upgrade and Maintenance Guide* (Sybex, 2002) includes an explanation of how you can bring drives back from the dead, at least long enough to get the data back.

Other data recovery services can retrieve data not recoverable with ordinary methods. These operate at a binary level, reading the data from the dead media (sometimes even opening the hard disk, if the problem is serious enough) and then copying the data to your preferred media. Turnaround time is typically no more than a day or two, plus the shipping time.

The cost of data recovery depends on the following:

► The method of recovery used (The places that just fix hard disks tend to be cheaper, but they can't always recover the data.)

► Turnaround time requested

► The amount of data recovered

TIP

Consider storing irreplaceable data on a different physical drive from data you can easily replace. A data recovery service can't selectively restore data. That is, if the data files and the system files are stored on a single physical disk, you can't save yourself a little money by asking the center only to recover the data files, even if those files are on two different logical partitions.

Until recently, you had to send the hard disk to the data recovery center to have its data retrieved, and this meant not having the data for at least a couple of days. Remote data recovery services can fix some software-related problems without requiring you to ship the drive anywhere or even take it out of the computer case. Using a direct dial-up connection, the data recovery center may be able to fix the problem across the telephone line. Currently, the only data recovery center that offers this capability is OnTrack (`www.ontrtack.com/rdr`).

SUMMARY

Disaster can take a variety of forms, some technical and some not. Whichever form it takes, your primary goal remains the same: getting the network back up and running. To do so, you'll need a combination of good backups and a good disaster recovery plan. Luck and skill are also helpful, but when neither is available, the backups and preplanning should help.

Most of the effort required for disaster recovery should take place *before* the disaster ever occurs. That's the time you should be making backups, testing those backups, and storing them carefully so that the data is easy to find and restore. Before the disaster is also the time that you may decide to implement a fault-tolerant system such as RAID, data replication, and/or server clustering.

In case these preparatory measures don't work, you'll need a well-planned disaster recovery plan. For best success, such a plan will be a detailed description of how to get the network back up and running as quickly and efficiently as possible, beginning with the most essential parts. If the plan isn't enough to let you fully restore your network's data, there are always the data recovery centers. It's a lot cheaper to preserve your data in the first place than to let a data recovery center get it back for you, but paying the money is better than the alternative of losing the data for good.

WHAT'S NEXT

If you've made it this far, then you have much of the ammunition you need to design a LAN, build it, and keep it up and running. Cabling is no longer a mystery to you, you know how to design the perfect server for your needs and pick the perfect clients, you have some ideas of applications to run on the network, and with a little luck and a lot of care and perseverance you'll keep the network organized and trouble free—or be able to fix it if it's not.

In Chapter 18, we will move into installing and configuring network adapters and network protocols.

Part III

Part IV

Intranets and Interconnecting Networks

Chapter 18

MANAGING NETWORK CONNECTIONS

For successful network connection management, you must understand how network protocols work. The OSI model helps you gain this understanding by conveying network protocols as modular in nature. Network adapters are hardware used to connect your computer to the network. You need a driver for the network adapter installed on your computer. Managing network connections also involves configuring your network protocols. The three protocols supported by Windows 2000 Professional are TCP/IP, NWLink IPX/SPX/NetBIOS, and NetBEUI.

This chapter begins with an overview of network protocols, including a discussion of network data flow and the OSI model. Then you will learn how to install and configure network adapters and network protocols.

Adapted From *MCSA/MCSE: Windows 2000 Professional Study Guide*, Second Edition by Lisa Donald with James Chellis

ISBN 0-7821-2946-3   912 pages $49.99

Part IV

REVIEWING NETWORKING PROTOCOLS

Communications over a network are accomplished using networking protocols. To understand the purpose of networking protocols, you should have a basic knowledge of the *OSI (Open Systems Interconnect) model*. The OSI model is not an actual product. It is a theoretical model that describes how networks work. There are several advantages to using the OSI model as a framework for understanding network protocols:

▶ Breaking down a large concept, such as a network, makes it easier to understand.

▶ Modularizing network functions allows you to apply specific technologies or protocols at specific layers in a mix-and-match manner.

▶ Understanding how one network system works and applying it to the OSI model allows you to easily apply that knowledge to other operating systems.

We'll start by looking at an example of how data flows through a network. Then we'll examine how the seven layers of the OSI model work to move data through a network.

Network Data Flow

Figure 18.1 illustrates an example of how data flows from Computer A on one network segment to Computer B on a separate network segment. In this example, the following steps are involved in moving the data from Computer A to Computer B:

1. Starting at Computer A, you create a message (file) using some type of program that offers file services. In this example, the message says, "Hello."

2. The computer doesn't understand the characters in "Hello," but it does understand ones and zeros. The message must be translated into ones and zeros through a protocol such as ASCII.

3. At the higher levels of communication, a connection (or session) is established. The connection determines when requests are made so that appropriate responses can be

made. Just like human conversations, computer communications are usually a series of requests and responses that must be answered sequentially.

4. Next you must determine if you want the connection to be reliable, called a *connection-oriented service*, or if you want the connection to use less overhead and assume that the connection is reliable, called a *connectionless service*.

5. Because Computer A and Computer B are on separate network segments, you must figure out how to route the message across an internetwork based on the best possible path available.

6. Once the message gets to the correct network segment, it must be delivered to the correct computer on the segment.

7. The message must travel over the physical connection that actually exists between Computer A and Computer B, which is at the lowest level of communication. The data moves through the cabling and network cards that connect the network. At this level, you are sending ones and zeros over the physical network.

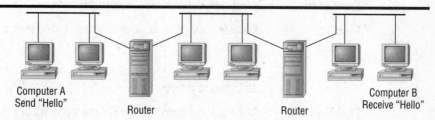

Computer A
Send "Hello"

Router

Router

Computer B
Receive "Hello"

FIGURE 18.1: Data flows from Computer A on one network segment to Computer B on another network segment.

The steps in this data-flow example correlate to the seven layers of the OSI model, discussed in the next section.

The OSI Model Layers

The seven layers of the OSI model are Application, Presentation, Session, Transport, Network, Data Link, and Physical. Each layer has a specific function in providing networking capabilities. Table 18.1 offers a couple of mnemonic phrases to help you remember the order of the layers.

Part IV

TABLE 18.1:   Mnemonics for the OSI Model Layers

LAYER	MEMORY TRICK (READ TOP TO BOTTOM)	MEMORY TRICK (READ BOTTOM TO TOP)
Application	All	Albert
Presentation	People	Prince
Session	Seem	See
Transport	To	To
Network	Need	Need
Data Link	Data	Don't
Physical	Processing	People

The Application Layer

The *Application layer* is used to support the following services:

File services	Store, move, control access to, and retrieve files
Print services	Send data to local or network printers
Message services	Transfer text, graphics, audio, and video over a network
Application services	Process applications locally or through distributed processing
Database services	Allow a local computer to access network services for database storage and retrieval

In addition, the Application layer advertises any services that are being offered and determines whether requests made by the client should be processed locally or remotely (through another network resource).

The Presentation Layer

The *Presentation layer* is used for four main processes:

Character-code translation	Converting symbolic characters such as the letter *h* into ones and zeros, as in 01101000, which is the ASCII code equivalent

Data encryption	Coding data so that it is protected from unauthorized access
Data compression	Reducing the number of packets required for transport
Data expansion	Restoring compressed data to its original format at the receiver's end

The Session Layer

The *Session layer* is responsible for managing communication between a sender and a receiver. Following are some of the communication tasks performed at this layer:

- ▸ Establishing connections
- ▸ Maintaining connections
- ▸ Synchronizing communications
- ▸ Controlling dialogues
- ▸ Terminating connections

When you create a connection, you authenticate the user account at the sending and receiving computers. Connection creation also involves determining the type of communication that will take place and the protocols that will be used by the lower layers.

Data transfer and dialogue control are used to determine which computer is making requests and which computer is making responses. This also determines whether acknowledgments are required for data transmission.

The Transport Layer

The *Transport layer* is associated with reliable data delivery. With reliable delivery, the sender and receiver establish a connection, and the receiver acknowledges the receipt of data by sending acknowledgment packets to the sender.

Depending on the protocol used, you can send data through the Transport layer using a *connection-oriented service* or a *connectionless service*. A connection-oriented service is like a telephone conversation, where the connection is established and acknowledgments are sent. This type of communication has a high overhead. A connectionless service does not establish a connection and is similar to communicating through the mail.

Part IV

You assume that your letter will arrive, but the communication is not as reliable as a telephone conversation (a connection-oriented service).

The Network Layer

The primary responsibility of the *Network layer* is to move data over an *internetwork*. An internetwork is made up of multiple network segments that are connected with a device, such as a router. Each network segment is assigned a network address. Network layer protocols build routing tables that are used to route packets through the network in the most efficient manner.

The Data Link Layer

The *Data Link layer* is responsible for establishing and maintaining the communication channel, identifying computers on network segments by their physical address, and organizing data into a logical group called a frame. *Frames* are logical groupings of the bits from the Physical layer. Frames contain information about the destination physical address and the source physical address, as well as all the data that has been used at the upper layers of the OSI model.

There are two main sublayers at the Data Link layer: the *Logical Link Control (LLC) sublayer*, which defines flow control, and the *Media Access Control (MAC) sublayer*, which is used for physical addressing.

The communication channel that is established at the Data Link layer is a low-level channel that manages whether or not a communication channel exists. All higher-level communication is handled at the Session layer. Computers are identified by their physical address, which is called the *MAC address*. Ethernet and Token Ring cards have their MAC addresses assigned through a chip on the network card.

The Physical Layer

The details of sending ones and zeros across a cable are handled at the *Physical layer*. The Physical layer is responsible for determining the following information:

- The physical network structure you are using
- The mechanical and electrical specifications of the transmission media that will be used
- How the data will be encoded and transmitted

INSTALLING AND CONFIGURING NETWORK ADAPTERS

Network adapters are hardware used to connect computers (or other devices) to the network. They function at the Physical and Data Link layers of the OSI model, as shown in Figure 18.2.

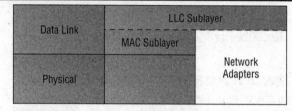

FIGURE 18.2:   Network adapters function at the Physical and Data Link layers of the OSI model.

Network adapters are responsible for providing the physical connection to the network and the physical address of the computer. These adapters (and all other hardware devices) need a *driver* in order to communicate with the Windows 2000 operating system.

In the following sections, you will learn about installing and configuring network adapters, as well as troubleshooting network adapters that are not working.

Installing a Network Adapter

Before you physically install your network adapter, it's important to read the instructions that came with the hardware. If your network adapter is new, it should be self-configuring, with Plug and Play capabilities. After you install a network adapter that supports Plug and Play, it should work the next time you start up the computer.

NOTE

New devices will autodetect settings and be self-configuring. Older devices rely on hardware setup programs to configure hardware. Really old devices require you to manually configure the adapter through switches or jumpers.

When you install a network adapter that is not Plug and Play, the operating system should detect that you have a new piece of hardware and start a Wizard that leads you through the process of loading the adapter's driver.

Part IV

Configuring a Network Adapter

Once the network adapter has been installed, you can configure it through its Properties dialog box. To access this dialog box, select Start ≻ Settings ≻ Control Panel ≻ Network And Dial-Up Connections ≻ Local Area Connection ≻ Properties and click the Configure button. Alternatively, right-click My Network Places and choose Properties, then right-click Local Area Connection, choose Properties, and click the Configure button.

In the network adapter Properties dialog box, the properties are grouped on four tabs: General, Advanced, Driver, and Resources. These properties are explained in the following sections.

General Network Adapter Properties

The General tab of the network adapter Properties dialog box, shown in Figure 18.3, shows the name of the adapter, the device type, the manufacturer, and the location. The Device Status box reports whether or not the device is working properly. If the device is not working properly, you can click the Troubleshooter button to have Windows 2000 display some general troubleshooting tips. You can also enable or disable the device through the Device Usage drop-down list options.

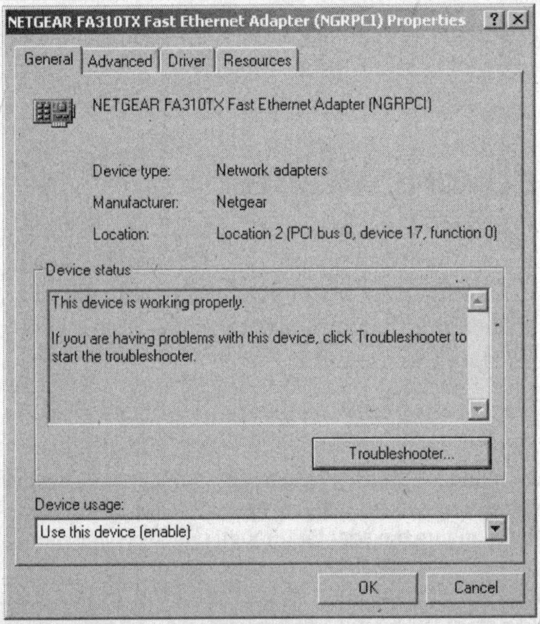

FIGURE 18.3:   The General tab of the network adapter Properties dialog box

Advanced Network Adapter Properties

The contents of the Advanced tab of the network adapter Properties dialog box vary depending on the network adapter and driver that you are using. Figure 18.4 shows an example of the Advanced tab for a Fast Ethernet adapter. To configure options in this dialog box, choose the property you want to modify in the Property list box on the left and specify the value for the property in the Value box on the right.

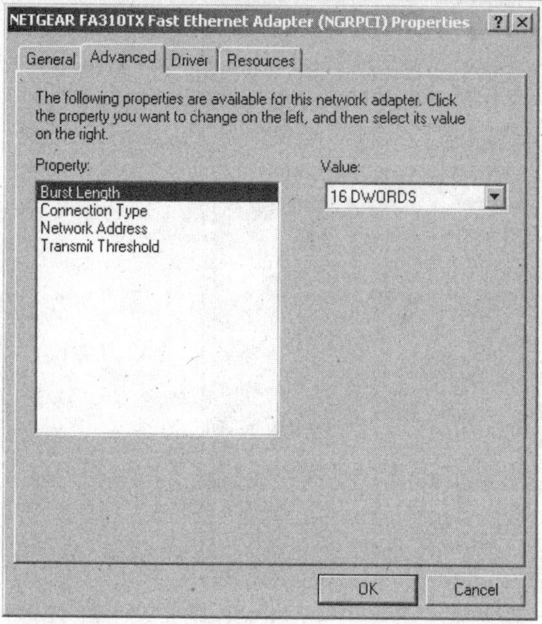

NETGEAR FA310TX Fast Ethernet Adapter (NGRPCI) Properties   **? ×**

| General | Advanced | Driver | Resources |

The following properties are available for this network adapter. Click the property you want to change on the left, and then select its value on the right.

Property:

Burst Length
Connection Type
Network Address
Transmit Threshold

Value:

16 DWORDS ▼

OK   Cancel

FIGURE 18.4:   The Advanced tab of the network adapter Properties dialog box

NOTE

You should not need to change the settings on the Advanced tab of the network adapter Properties dialog box unless you have been instructed to do so by the manufacturer.

Driver Properties

The Driver tab of the network adapter Properties dialog box, shown in Figure 18.5, provides the following information about your driver:

▶ The driver provider, which is usually Microsoft or the network adapter manufacturer

▶ The date that the driver was released

▶ The driver version, which is useful in determining if you have the latest driver installed

▶ The digital signer, which is the company that provides the digital signature for driver signing

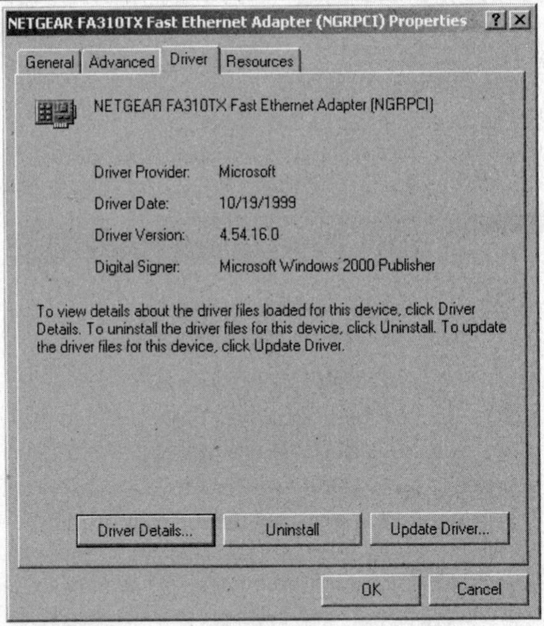

FIGURE 18.5:   The Driver tab of the network adapter Properties dialog box

Clicking the Driver Details button at the bottom of the Driver tab brings up the Driver File Details dialog box, as shown in Figure 18.6. This dialog box lists the following details about the driver:

▶ The location of the driver file, which is useful for troubleshooting

▶ The original provider of the driver, which is usually the manufacturer

▶ The file version, which is useful for troubleshooting

▶ Copyright information about the driver

The Uninstall button at the bottom of the Driver tab removes the driver from your computer. You would uninstall the driver if you were going to replace it with a completely new one. Normally, you update the driver rather than uninstall it.

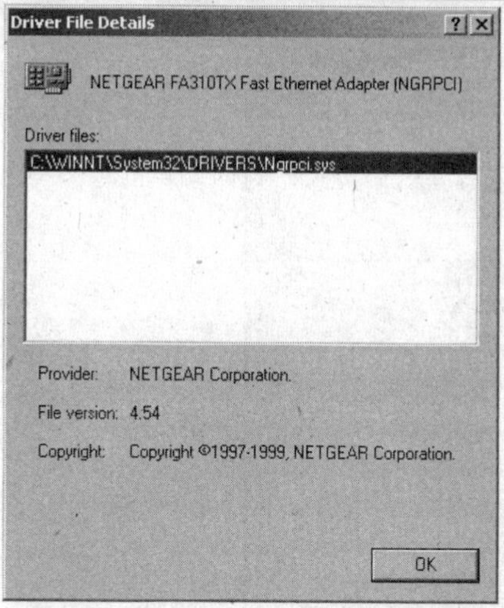

Driver File Details ? X

NETGEAR FA310TX Fast Ethernet Adapter (NGRPCI)

Driver files:

C:\WINNT\System32\DRIVERS\Ngrpci.sys

Provider: NETGEAR Corporation.

File version: 4.54

Copyright: Copyright ©1997-1999, NETGEAR Corporation.

OK

FIGURE 18.6:   The Driver File Details dialog box

To update a driver, click the Update Driver button at the bottom of the Driver tab. This starts the Upgrade Device Driver Wizard, which steps you through upgrading the driver for an existing device.

TIP

If you cannot find the driver for your network card or the configuration instructions, check the vendor's website. Usually, you will be able to find the latest drivers. You also should be able to locate a list of Frequently Asked Questions (FAQs) about your hardware.

Resource Properties

Each device installed on a computer uses computer resources. Resources include interrupt request (IRQ), memory, and I/O (input/output) settings. The Resources tab of the network adapter Properties dialog box lists the resource settings for your network adapter, as shown in Figure 18.7. This information is important for troubleshooting, because if other devices are trying to use the same resource settings, your devices will not work properly. The Conflicting Device List box at the bottom of the Resources tab shows whether any conflicts exist.

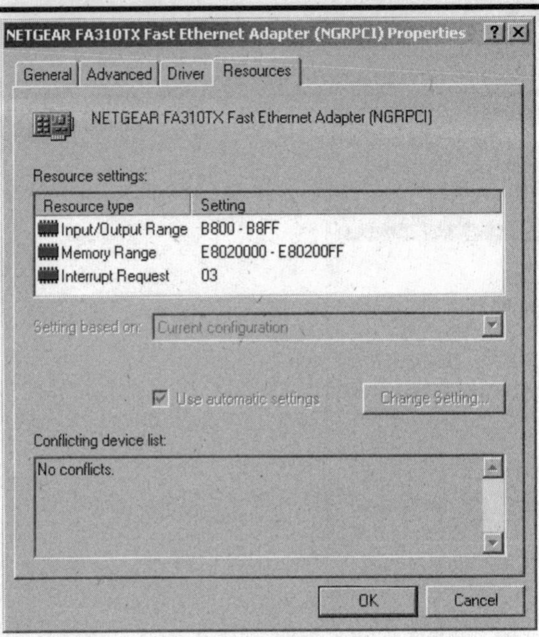

FIGURE 18.7:   The Resources tab of the network adapter Properties dialog box

Troubleshooting Network Adapters

If your network adapter is not working, the problem may be with the hardware, the driver software, or the network protocols. The following are some common causes for network adapter problems:

Network adapter not on the HCL   If the device is not on the hardware compatibility list (HCL), contact the adapter vendor for advice.

Outdated driver   Make sure that you have the most up-to-date driver for your adapter. You can check for the latest driver on your hardware vendor's website.

Network adapter not recognized by Windows 2000   Check Device Manager to see if Windows 2000 recognizes your device. If you do not see your adapter, you will have to manually install it (see "Installing a Network Adapter" earlier in the chapter). You should also verify that the adapter's resource settings do not conflict with the resource settings of other devices (check the Resources tab of the network adapter Properties dialog box).

Hardware that is not working properly   Verify that your hardware is working properly. Run any diagnostics that came with the adapter. If everything seems to work as it should, make sure that the cable is good and that all of the applicable network hardware is installed correctly and is working. This is where it pays off to have spare hardware (such as cables and extra network adapters) that you know works properly.

Improperly configured network protocols   Make sure that your network protocols have been configured properly. Network protocols are covered in detail in the next section of this chapter.

Improperly configured network card   Verify that all settings for the network card are correct.

Bad cable   Make sure that all network cables are good. This can be tricky if you connect to the network through a patch panel.

Bad network connection device   Verify that all network connectivity hardware is properly working. For example, on an Ethernet network, make sure the hub and port that you are using are functioning properly.

TIP

Check Event Viewer for any messages that give you a hint about what is causing a network adapter error.

ARE ETHERNET CARDS PROPERLY CONFIGURED?

You are the network administrator of an Ethernet network. When you purchase Ethernet cards, they are special combo cards that support 10Mbps Ethernet and 100Mbps Ethernet. In addition, the cards have an RJ-45 connector for using unshielded twisted pair (UTP) cables, and a BNC connector for using coaxial cable. Your network is configured to use 100Mbps Ethernet over UTP cabling. Sometimes when you install the new Ethernet cards, they are not able to connect to the network.

A common problem is experienced with the combo Ethernet cards. Even when the hardware configuration for IRQ and base memory

CONTINUED ➡

Part IV

are correctly configured and you have the right driver, the correct configuration for speed and cable type may not be detected. Within an Ethernet network, all of the Ethernet cards must transmit at the same speed and be connected to a hub that supports the speed of the cards that you are using. The cards must also be configured to support the cable type that is being used. You can verify these settings through the network adapter's Properties dialog box.

If the configuration is correct and you still can't connect to the network, you should check your network cables. It is estimated that between 70 and 80 percent of all network problems are related to cabling.

INSTALLING AND CONFIGURING NETWORK PROTOCOLS

Network protocols function at the Network and Transport layers of the OSI model. They are responsible for transporting data across an internetwork. You can mix and match the network protocols you use with Windows 2000 Professional, which supports three protocols: TCP/IP, NWLink IPX/SPX/NetBIOS, and NetBEUI. The following sections describe how to install and configure these protocols.

Using TCP/IP

TCP/IP (Transmission Control Protocol/Internet Protocol) is one of the most commonly used network protocols. TCP/IP evolved during the 1970s. It was originally developed for the Department of Defense (DoD) as a way of connecting dissimilar networks. Since then, TCP/IP has become an industry standard.

On a clean installation of Windows 2000 Professional, TCP/IP is installed by default. TCP/IP has the following benefits:

- ▶ It is the most common protocol and is supported by almost all network operating systems. It is the required protocol for Internet access.

- ▶ TCP/IP is scalable for use in small and large networks. In large networks, TCP/IP provides routing services.

▶ TCP/IP is designed to be fault tolerant. It is able to dynamically reroute packets if network links become unavailable (assuming alternate paths exist).

▶ Protocol companions such as Dynamic Host Configuration Protocol (DHCP) and Domain Name System (DNS) offer advanced functionality.

In the next sections, you will learn the basics of using TCP/IP and then how to configure and test TCP/IP.

Basic TCP/IP Configuration

TCP/IP requires an IP address and a subnet mask. You can also configure many other optional parameters, including the default gateway, DNS server settings, and WINS server settings.

IP Address   The *IP address* uniquely identifies your computer on the network. The IP address is a four-field, 32-bit address, separated by periods. Part of the address is used to identify your network address, and part is used to identify the host (or local) computer's address.

If you use the Internet, then you should register your IP addresses with one of the Internet registration sites. There are three main classes of IP addresses. Depending on the class you use, different parts of the address show the network portion of the address and the host address, as illustrated in Figure 18.8.

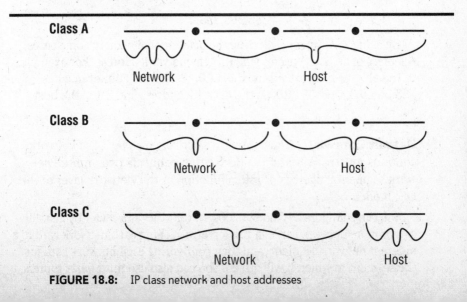

Class A

Network   Host

Class B

Network   Host

Class C

Network   Host

FIGURE 18.8:   IP class network and host addresses

Part IV

TIP
You can find more information about Internet registration at InterNIC's website, www.internic.net.

Table 18.2 shows the three classes of network addresses and the number of networks and hosts that are available for each network class.

TABLE 18.2:   IP Class Assignments

NETWORK CLASS	ADDRESS RANGE OF FIRST FIELD	NUMBER OF NETWORKS AVAILABLE	NUMBER OF HOST NODES SUPPORTED
A	1–126	126	16,777,214
B	128–191	16,384	65,534
C	192–223	2,097,152	254

Subnet Mask   The *subnet mask* is used to specify which part of the IP address is the network address and which part of the address is the host address. By default, the following subnet masks are applied:

Class A	255.0.0.0
Class B	255.255.0.0
Class C	255.255.255.0

By using 255, you are selecting the octet or octets (or, in some cases, the piece of an octet) used to identify the network address. For example, in the class B network address 191.200.2.1, if the subnet mask is 255.255.0.0, then 191.200 is the network address and 2.1 is the host address.

Default Gateway   You configure a *default gateway* if the network contains routers. A *router* is a device that connects two or more network segments together. Routers function at the Network layer of the OSI model.

You can configure a Windows 2000 server to act as a router by installing two or more network cards in the server, attaching each network card to a different network segment, and then configuring each network card for the segment to which it will attach. You can also use third-party routers, which typically offer more features than Windows 2000 servers configured as routers.

As an example, suppose that your network is configured as shown in Figure 18.9. Network A uses the IP network address 131.1.0.0. Network B uses the IP network address 131.2.0.0. In this case, each network card in the router should be configured with an IP address from the segment to which the network card is addressed.

You configure the computers on each segment to point to the IP address of the network card on the router that is attached to their network segment. For example, in Figure 18.9, the computer W2K1 is attached to Network A. The default gateway that would be configured for this computer is 131.1.0.10. The computer W2K2 is attached to Network B. The default gateway that would be configured for this computer is 131.2.0.10.

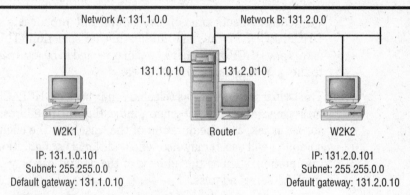

FIGURE 18.9:   Configuring default gateways

Advanced TCP/IP Configuration

Through TCP/IP, you can also configure advanced TCP/IP options, including these:

▶ Dynamic Host Configuration Protocol (DHCP)

▶ Domain Name System (DNS)

▶ Windows Internet Name Service (WINS)

Using DHCP   Each device that will use TCP/IP on your network must have a valid, unique IP address. This address can be manually configured or can be automated through DHCP. DHCP is implemented as a DHCP server and a DHCP client (Figure 18.10). The server is configured with a pool of IP addresses and their associated IP configurations. The client

Part IV

is configured to automatically access the DHCP server to obtain its IP configuration.

DHCP works in the following manner:

1. When the client computer starts up, it sends a broadcast DHCPDISCOVER message, requesting a DHCP server. The request includes the hardware address of the client computer.

2. Any DHCP server receiving the broadcast that has available IP addresses will send a DHCPOFFER message to the client. This message offers an IP address for a set period of time (called a *lease*), a subnet mask, and a server identifier (the IP address of the DHCP server). The address that is offered by the server is marked as unavailable and will not be offered to any other clients during the DHCP negotiation period.

3. The client selects one of the offers and broadcasts a DHCPREQUEST message, indicating its selection. This allows any DHCP offers that were not accepted to be returned to the pool of available IP addresses.

4. The DHCP server that was selected sends back a DHCPACK message as an acknowledgment, indicating the IP address, subnet mask, and the duration of the lease that the client computer will use. It may also send additional configuration information, such as the address of the default gateway or the DNS server address.

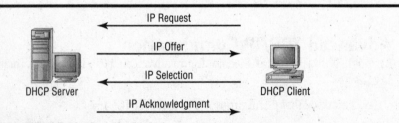

FIGURE 18.10:   The DHCP lease-generation process

NOTE

If you want to use DHCP and there is no DHCP server on your network segment, you can use a DHCP server on another network segment—provided that the DHCP server is configured to support your network segment and a DHCP Relay Agent has been installed on your network router.

TIP

If you are not able to access a DHCP server installed on a Windows 2000 Server within Active Directory, make sure that the DHCP server has been authorized. This is a new feature in Windows 2000.

DNS Servers *DNS servers* are used to resolve host names to IP addresses. This makes it easier for people to access domain hosts. For example, do you know what the IP address is for the White House? It's 198.137.240.91. Do you know the domain host name of the White House? It's www.whitehouse.gov. You can understand why many people might not know the IP address but would know the domain host name.

When you access the Internet and type in www.whitehouse.gov, there are DNS servers that resolve the host name to the proper IP address. If you did not have access to a properly configured DNS server, you could configure a HOSTS file for your computer that contains the mappings of IP addresses to the domain hosts that you need to access.

WINS Servers *WINS servers* are used to resolve NetBIOS names to IP addresses. Windows 2000 uses NetBIOS names in addition to host names to identify network computers. This is mainly for backward compatibility with Windows NT 4.0, which used this addressing scheme extensively. When you attempt to access a computer using the NetBIOS name, the computer must be able to resolve the NetBIOS name to an IP address. This address resolution can be accomplished by using one of the following methods:

▸ Through a broadcast (if the computer you are trying to reach is on the same network segment)

▸ Through a WINS server

▸ Through an LMHOSTS file, which is a static mapping of IP addresses to NetBIOS computer names

Configuring TCP/IP

Depending on your network setup, TCP/IP configuration is done either manually or dynamically. You can also use advanced TCP/IP options to configure DNS and WINS settings.

Part IV

Manual IP Configuration   You can manually configure IP if you know your IP address and subnet mask. If you are using optional components such as a default gateway or a DNS server, you need to know the IP addresses of the computers that host these services as well.

Advanced Configuration   Clicking the Advanced button in the Internet Protocol (TCP/IP) dialog box opens the Advanced TCP/IP Settings dialog box, shown in Figure 18.11. In this dialog box, you can configure advanced DNS and WINS settings.

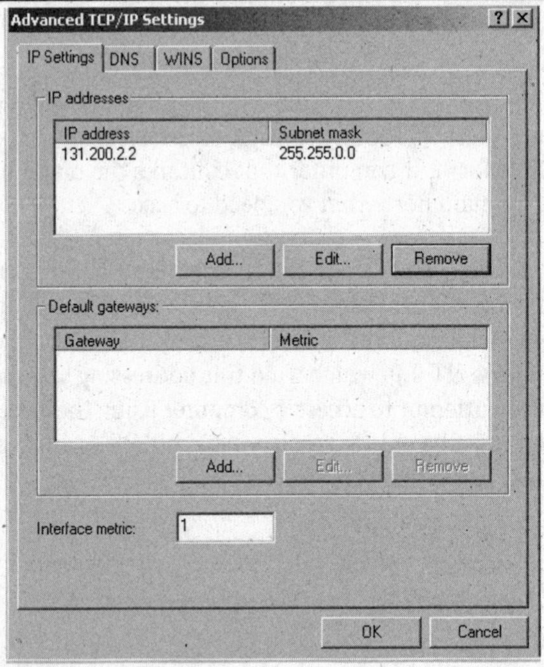

FIGURE 18.11:   The Advanced TCP/IP Settings dialog box

Advanced DNS Settings

You can configure additional DNS servers to be used for name resolution and other advanced DNS settings through the DNS tab of the Advanced TCP/IP Settings dialog box, shown in Figure 18.12. The options in this dialog box are described in Table 18.3.

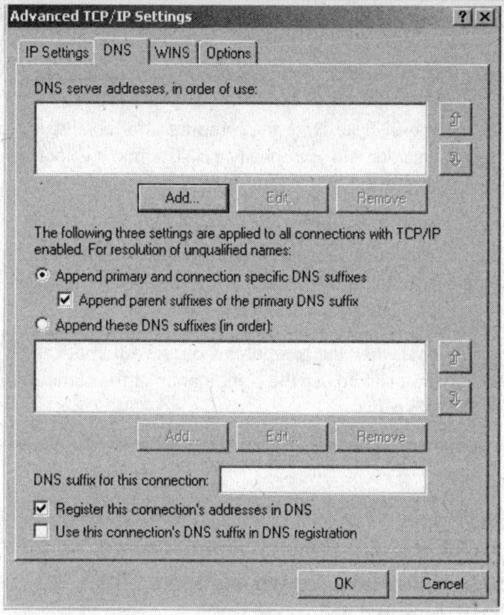

FIGURE 18.12: The DNS tab of the Advanced TCP/IP Settings dialog box

TABLE 18.3: Advanced DNS TCP/IP Settings Options

OPTION	DESCRIPTION
DNS server addresses, in order of use	Specifies the DNS servers that are used to resolve DNS queries. Use the arrow buttons on the right side of the list box to move a server up or down in the list.
Append primary and connection-specific DNS suffixes	Specifies how unqualified domain names are resolved by DNS. For example, if your primary DNS suffix is TestCorp.com and you type ping lala, DNS will try to resolve the address as lala.TestCorp.com.
Append parent suffixes of the primary DNS suffix	Specifies whether name resolution includes the parent suffix for the primary domain DNS suffix, up to the second level of the domain name. For example, if your primary DNS suffix is SanJose.TestCorp.com and you type ping lala, DNS will try to resolve the address as lala.SanJose.TestCorp.com. If this doesn't work, DNS will try to resolve the address as lala.TestCorp.com.
Append these DNS suffixes (in order)	Specifies the DNS suffixes that will be used to attempt to resolve unqualified name resolution. For example, if your primary DNS suffix is TestCorp.com and you type ping lala, DNS will try to resolve the address as lala.TestCorp.com. If you append the additional DNS suffix MyCorp.com and type ping lala, DNS will try to resolve the address as lala.TestCorp.com and lala.MyCorp.com.

TABLE 18.3 continued: Advanced DNS TCP/IP Settings Options

OPTION	DESCRIPTION
DNS suffix for this connection	Specifies the DNS suffix for the computer. If this value is configured by a DHCP server and you specify a DNS suffix, it will override the value set by DHCP.
Register this connection's address in DNS	Specifies that the connection will try to register its address dynamically using the computer name that was specified through the Network Identification tab of the System Properties dialog box (accessed through the System icon in Control Panel).
Use this connection's DNS suffix in DNS registration	Specifies that when the computer registers automatically with the DNS server, it should use the combination of the computer name and the DNS suffix.

Advanced WINS Settings

You can configure advanced WINS options through the WINS tab of the Advanced TCP/IP Settings dialog box, shown in Figure 18.13. The options in this dialog box are described in Table 18.4.

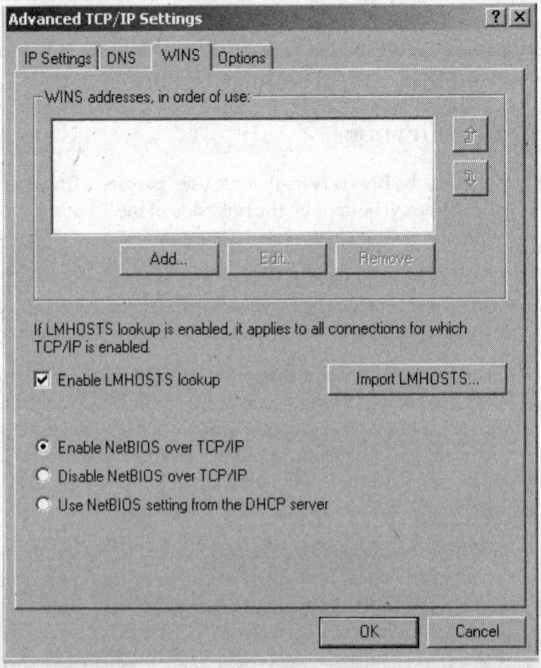

FIGURE 18.13: The WINS tab of the Advanced TCP/IP Settings dialog box

TABLE 18.4: Advanced WINS TCP/IP Settings Options

OPTION	DESCRIPTION
WINS addresses, in order of use	Specifies the WINS servers that are used to resolve WINS queries. You can use the arrow buttons on the right side of the list box to move a server up or down in the list.
Enable LMHOSTS lookup	Specifies whether an LMHOSTS file can be used for name resolution. If you configure this option, you can use the Import LMHOSTS button to import an LMHOSTS file to the computer.
Enable NetBIOS over TCP/IP	Allows you to use statically configured IP addresses so that the computer is able to communicate with pre–Windows 2000 computers.
Disable NetBIOS over TCP/IP	Allows you to disable NetBIOS over TCP/IP. Use this option only if your network includes only Windows 2000 clients or DNS-enabled clients.
Use NetBIOS setting from the DHCP server	Specifies that the computer should obtain its NetBIOS-over-TCP/IP and WINS settings from the DHCP server.

Dynamic IP Configuration   *Dynamic IP configuration* assumes that you have a DHCP server on your network. DHCP servers are configured to automatically provide DHCP clients with all their IP configuration information. By default, when TCP/IP is installed on a Windows 2000 Professional computer, the computer is configured for dynamic IP configuration.

If your computer is configured for manual IP configuration and you want to use dynamic IP configuration, take the following steps:

1. From the Desktop, right-click My Network Places and choose Properties.

2. Right-click Local Area Connection and choose Properties.

3. In the Local Area Connection Properties dialog box, highlight Internet Protocol (TCP/IP) and click the Properties button.

4. The Internet Protocol (TCP/IP) Properties dialog box appears. Select the Obtain An IP Address Automatically radio button. Then click the OK button.

Testing IP Configuration

After you have configured the IP settings, you can test the IP configuration using the IPCONFIG and PING commands.

The IPCONFIG Command   The IPCONFIG command displays your IP configuration. Table 18.5 lists the command switches that can be used with the IPCONFIG command.

Part IV

TABLE 18.5: IPCONFIG Switches

SWITCH	DESCRIPTION
/all	Shows verbose information about your IP configuration, including your computer's physical address, the DNS server you are using, and whether you are using DHCP
/release	Releases an address that has been assigned through DHCP
/renew	Renews an address through DHCP

The PING Command   The *PING* command is used to send an ICMP (Internet Control Message Protocol) echo request and echo reply to verify whether the remote computer is available. The PING command has the following syntax:

    PING IP address

For example, if your IP address is 131.200.2.30, you would type the following command:

    PING 131.200.2.30

PING is useful for verifying connectivity between two hosts. For example, if you were having trouble connecting to a host on another network, PING would help you verify that a valid communication path existed. You would ping the following addresses:

▶ The loopback address, 127.0.0.1

▶ The local computer's IP address (you can verify this with IPCONFIG)

▶ The local router's (default gateway's) IP address

▶ The remote computer's IP address

If PING failed to get a reply from any of these addresses, you would have a starting point for troubleshooting the connection error.

Using NWLink IPX/SPX/NetBIOS

NWLink IPX/SPX/NetBIOS Compatible Transport is Microsoft's implementation of the Novell IPX/SPX (Internetwork Packet Exchange/Sequenced Packet Exchange) protocol stack. The Windows 2000 implementation of the IPX/SPX protocol stack adds NetBIOS support.

The main function of NWLink is to act as a transport protocol to route packets through internetworks. By itself, the NWLink protocol does not allow you to access NetWare File and Print Services. However, it does provide a method of transporting the data across the network. If you want to access NetWare File and Print Services, you must install NWLink and Client Services for NetWare (software that works at the upper layers of the OSI model to allow access to File and Print Services). One advantage of using NWLink is that it is easy to install and configure.

Configuring NWLink IPX/SPX

The only options that you must configure for NWLink are the *internal network number* and the *frame type*. Normally, you leave both settings at their default values.

The internal network number is commonly used to identify NetWare file servers. It is also used when you are running File and Print Services for NetWare or are using IPX routing. Normally, you leave the internal network number at the default setting.

The frame type specifies how the data is packaged for transmission over the network. If the computers that are using NWLink use different frame types, they are not able to communicate with each other. The default setting for frame type is Auto Detect, which will attempt to automatically choose a compatible frame type for your network. If you need to connect to servers that use various frame types, you should configure Manual Frame Type Detection, which will allow you to use a different frame type for each network.

Using NetBEUI

NetBEUI stands for NetBIOS Extended User Interface. It was developed in the mid-1980s to connect workgroups that were running the OS/2 and LAN Manager operating systems. The NetBEUI protocol offers the following advantages:

- ▶ It is easy to install.

- ▶ There are no configuration requirements.

- ▶ It has self-tuning capabilities.

- ▶ NetBEUI incurs less overhead than TCP/IP and IPX/SPX and thus offers better performance.

- ▶ NetBEUI uses less memory than TCP/IP and IPX/SPX.

NetBEUI's main disadvantage is that it is not routable, so you cannot use it in networks that have more than one network segment. Also, NetBEUI is not as commonly accepted as the TCP/IP protocol.

Managing Network Bindings

Bindings are used to enable communication between your network adapter and the network protocols that are installed. If you have multiple network protocols installed on your computer, you can improve performance by binding the most commonly used protocols higher in the binding order.

To configure network bindings, access the Network And Dial-up Connections window and then select Advanced ➤ Advanced Settings from the main menu bar. The Adapters And Bindings tab of the Advanced Settings dialog box appears, as shown in Figure 18.14. For each local area connection, if there are multiple protocols listed, you can use the arrow buttons on the right side of the dialog box to move the protocols up or down in the binding order.

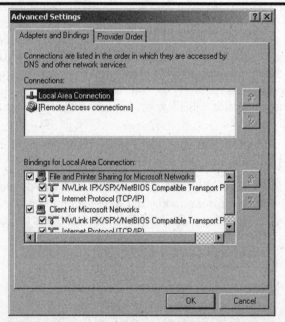

FIGURE 18.14:   The Adapters And Bindings tab of the Advanced Settings dialog box

SUMMARY

This chapter described how to manage network connections. We covered the following topics:

▸ How network protocols are used for network communications, including the movement of data through a network. We examined an overview of the OSI model.

▸ Installing, configuring, and troubleshooting network adapters. You install adapters that are not Plug and Play compatible through the Add/Remove Hardware Wizard. You configure a network adapter through its Properties dialog box.

▸ Installing, configuring, and testing network protocols. TCP/IP is the default protocol installed with Windows 2000 Professional. You can also install the NWLink IPX/SPX/NetBIOS and NetBEUI protocols.

WHAT'S NEXT

With Internet technologies making it easy for users to access all types of data, companies are adopting those technologies for internal use. Putting together an intranet can be very rewarding for users as well as administrators; however, the intranet needs to be designed and implemented correctly. The next chapter shows you how.

Chapter 19

INTRANET AND INTERNET SERVICES

Intranet sites are enterprise-wide websites accessible only by people within an organization. Intranets came about as a result of the need for improved corporate communications. As companies expand geographically, they face the challenges of providing company-wide information quickly and inexpensively—a feat not possible using traditional communication methods such as mailings, memorandums, faxes, or bulletin boards. Using an intranet, however, companies make information immediately accessible to all employees, regardless of their geographic location, and eliminate or significantly reduce the need for other forms of communication.

Although individuals or small groups generally develop and maintain public sites, employees often contribute content for intranets. For example, the information services department might actually run the intranet, but one or more employees in each department within an organization might assume responsibility for providing and updating pages pertaining to that department.

Adapted from *Mastering HTML 4 Premium Edition* by Deborah S. Ray and Eric J. Ray

ISBN 0-7821-2524-7   1,216 pages $49.99

Part IV

The result can be a hodgepodge of information that doesn't generally fit into a coherent information resource. Your goal as an information coordinator—whether you're the company owner, the head of information services, or the person who also develops and maintains the company's public site—is to ensure that the intranet is a valuable, uniform, usable information resource.

In the following sections, we'll look at how to coordinate content from contributors, suggest some ways that you can put out the word about what's new or updated on your intranet, and introduce intranet discussion groups. The "you" in these sections is the content coordinator for an intranet, and the "visitors" are employees or organization members who use an intranet.

Determining Intranet Content

Intranets provide substantial, company-specific information that helps employees do their jobs, automates processes, and provides updates or news. If your intranet is part of a corporate environment, a good starting point for content is the human resources department, where you're likely to find company policy manuals, training schedules, safety guidelines, evacuation plans, and much more.

You can also use an intranet to publish product or service descriptions. For example, when you place boilerplate (standardized) information about your products and services on your intranet, visitors can easily access it and use it in marketing materials, documentation, or whatever.

You might also publish information that's not pertinent to employees' jobs, but that employees would find useful:

▶ The cafeteria menu

▶ The company newsletter

▶ New contract announcements

▶ Annual budgets

▶ Company and retirement fund stock quotes

And if your intranet is connected to the Internet, you can also include links to industry news or to sister-company websites.

Your next step is to talk with employees about the information that they provide, distribute, and update to other groups within the company and about the information that they need and might (or might not) get from other departments. Ask about the following:

- ► Forms
- ► Reports
- ► Budgets
- ► Schedules
- ► Guidelines
- ► Procedures
- ► Policies
- ► Legacy documents

You can probably obtain some of this information using existing materials such as human resources handbooks, marketing brochures, company white papers, and so on.

ACCOMMODATING VISITOR NEEDS

Visitors to intranet sites generally have one thing in mind: they're looking for information necessary to do their jobs. They might, for example, use the information to write a report, develop marketing materials, plan their schedules, and so on. For this reason, make absolutely certain that the information you provide is accurate and timely.

Visitors also expect you to provide accessible information—information they can find consistently from day to day. As a starting point, develop the overall site organization, taking into account all categories of information you will provide. Be sure to leave room for growth—adding new categories and expanding existing categories. For example, in developing a navigation menu, include all the categories of information that you'll eventually need. If you end up including links that don't yet have content, provide a statement about the information coming soon, or better yet, specify a date when you'll provide the information. You can also include contact information for people who can answer questions in the interim.

Finally, visitors don't usually expect an intranet site to be flashy. After all, they're accessing the site because they need information, not because they expect to be dazzled. Plan a site design that is visually appealing, but don't go overboard with sounds, colors, and other special effects. Consider including your company's logo and using its color scheme, but beyond that, think functional, not fancy.

HELPING OTHERS CONTRIBUTE

As you saw in the previous sections, intranets are not usually the work of one person. Although you may be in charge of developing the site, others will actually provide and update the content. And not all contributors will have the same HTML proficiency; some will be novices, others will be experts. Striking a balance between consistency and creativity can be challenging. Here are some ideas that may help.

Provide Templates and Examples

If you maintain a consistent look and feel, your intranet will appear more established and polished than it actually is. Relying on information providers to care as much as you do about a consistent appearance is likely too much to hope for, so make it easy for them: provide templates.

Templates include all the structure tags and other tags that set up the general document format. You can provide templates for departmental home pages, for contact information, for current projects, or for any other pages that are common to several departments. You might also provide references to company-specific graphics and symbols. Using a template complete with these items, contributors can copy and paste the code into their documents and fill in the specific content. Figures 19.1 and 19.2 show a sample template and the resulting document format.

TIP

You can also provide templates for word-processing software such as Microsoft Word or WordPerfect. Contributors can then develop content in the word processor of their choice and easily save as HTML.

If your company has standardized on Netscape Navigator or Internet Explorer, consider providing Style Sheets to contributors. By supplying a Style Sheet, you help contributors concentrate on content and ensure a more consistent appearance throughout the site.

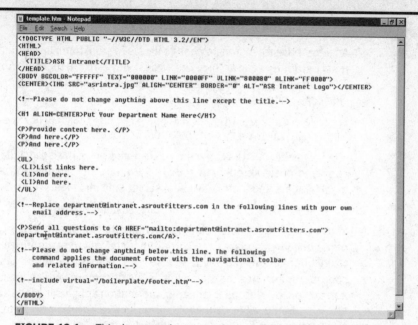

FIGURE 19.1:   This short template can save contributors time and effort.

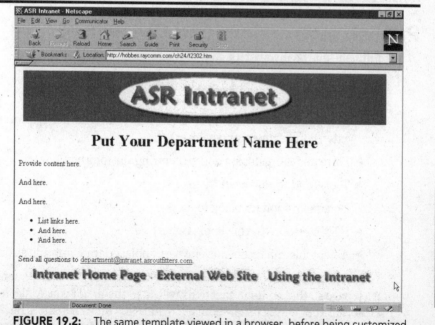

FIGURE 19.2:   The same template viewed in a browser, before being customized for specific departmental use.

Part IV

PROVIDING ACCESS TO IMAGES

An alternative to referencing image files is to store them in a folder that contributors can access. The easiest way is to put them all in a folder immediately off the server root, such as /graphics, and provide copy-and-paste text, like this:

```
<IMG SRC="/graphics/corplogo.gif" ALT="ASR Corporate
    Logo" ALIGN=LEFT HEIGHT=100 WIDTH=250>
```

Moving further into the copy-and-paste realm, you can also include copy-and-paste snippets of code to automatically include document headers and footers by using server-side includes.

```
<!--#include virtual="/includes/header.htm"-->
```

You provide the header, including anything that belongs at the top of the document such as the corporate logo, copyright, confidentiality information, and anything else your company requires. The contributor includes the single line in the document, and, when it appears on the Web, all the header information appears in place of the include tag. Check the web server documentation for more information about using server-side includes.

Publish Instructions and Guidelines

Publish—on the intranet, of course—instructions and guidelines for providing information on the intranet:

- ▶ Documentation for publishing information
- ▶ Acceptable versions of HTML (HTML 4, all Internet Explorer extensions, frames, or whatever)
- ▶ Formats for organizing and structuring the information
- ▶ Tools (and where to get them)
- ▶ Documentation for using tools
- ▶ HTML resources (this book, right?)
- ▶ Acceptable enhancements—images, applets, JavaScript, and so on

Also, specify that contributors include their contact information on each page so that content questions will go to them, not you. Make it clear that the "contact the webmaster" links are only for visitors having technical difficulties. Contributors need to give visitors a way to contact them—during and after hours.

Provide Conversion Services

Offer to convert existing documents to intranet pages. Most departments have pages of information that could easily be converted to HTML.

If you offer this service, you could be overwhelmed with documents to convert. We strongly recommend providing one-time conversion services to help departments get material out on the intranet, but rather than assuming the responsibility for ongoing document conversion, take the time to train the contributors thoroughly so that departments can support themselves.

Remind Contributors As Necessary

Most content providers contribute information to the intranet in addition to their regular duties. You can help them manage their sections of the intranet by sending them e-mail reminders. Include information about how frequently visitors access their information, which information is not accessed, and so on, which you (or the system administrator) can get from the access logs. If visitors aren't accessing certain pages, help find out why. Is the information outdated, hard to find, not needed? With this information, you can help weed out information that isn't being used and make room for more.

AUTOMATING PROCESSES

If you have programming resources available, consider automating some of the processes discussed in this chapter. For example, you can:

▶ Generate What's New lists

▶ Remind content providers of pages that haven't been updated in a specific amount of time

▶ Consolidate and summarize access logs, changes to pages, and new sections for reports to management

▶ Check incoming documents for compliance with corporate style, the correct version of HTML, and functional links

For more information, consult with your system administrator or internal programmers.

Part IV

ANNOUNCING NEW OR UPDATED INFORMATION

Visitors value new information, so be sure to notify them when the site is updated, and do so consistently. Even if visitors don't immediately need the information, making them aware that it's available might save them time later. Here are some ways to do so:

- ▶ Develop a What's New template that departments can use to feature new or updated information.

- ▶ Create New and Updated icons that contributors can include on their pages.

- ▶ E-mail employees regularly—say, weekly—and tell them what's new and updated.

- ▶ E-mail managers regularly about new and updated information, and request that they pass along the information to their employees.

SETTING UP A DISCUSSION FORUM

In a real-time discussion forum, visitors can interact, regardless of time zones or schedules, using the intranet as the communications medium. For example, visitors can hold informal meetings, chat about projects, or even get live feedback about a document draft—all from their offices at their convenience.

You can choose from several forum options, based on the software you implement. For example, you can use Matt's Script Archive or Selena's Public Domain Script Archive and adapt discussion forums from the scripts.

If you choose a more advanced software package, such as Ceilidh (pronounced kay-lee, available at www.lilikoi.com), visitors can post HTML documents and request that other people edit and comment—right there online. The result is that visitors can open forums to large groups and get immediate feedback. Other visitors can monitor discussions for developments or news pertaining to their projects. By conducting meetings online through an intranet, companies move toward a newer, more open approach to communication. A discussion in progress looks like Figure 19.3.

Figure 19.4 shows the form used to respond to a posting about the highly fictitious Baumgartner proposal.

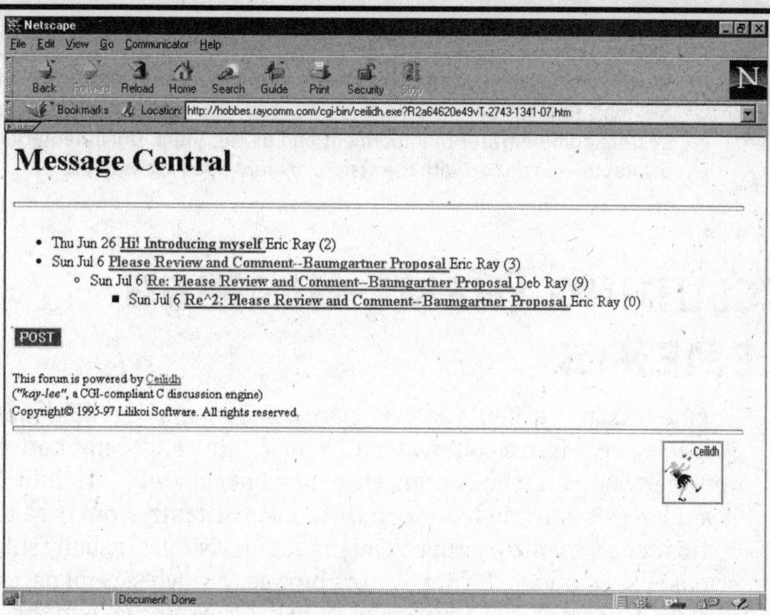

FIGURE 19.3: An ongoing discussion in Ceilidh

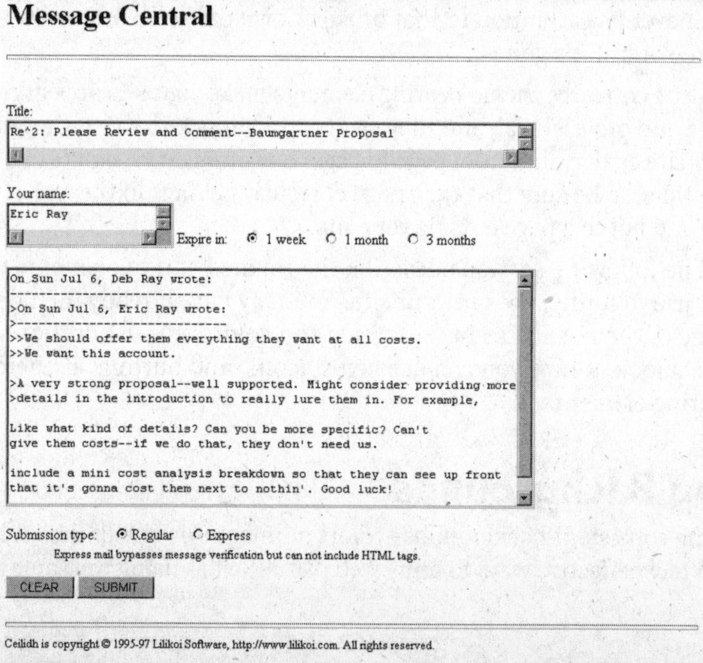

FIGURE 19.4: Responding to ongoing discussions is easy and fast.

TIP

When using scripts and server-side programs, such as Matt's Script Archive or Selena's Public Domain Script Archive, you may need assistance from your system administrator to implement and debug them. Documentation, when available, is included with the scripts or embedded in the code.

INCLUDING THEME-BEARING ELEMENTS

Theme-bearing elements are web page components that help unite multiple pages into a cohesive unit. Your visitors might not notice that you've included theme-bearing elements, but they will certainly notice if you haven't or if you have used them inconsistently from page to page. In this sense, theme-bearing elements set up visitors' (usually subconscious) expectations. If your visitors browse through several pages that contain a logo, they'll begin to expect to see the same logo in the same place on each page. They may not consciously notice that it's there, but they'll certainly notice if it's missing or in a different location, just as you never pay attention to that broken-down car at the house on the corner—until it's gone.

Used correctly, theme-bearing elements make your site appear complete and professional, and they also help visitors know that they are in *your* site as they link from page to page. A visitor can view only one page at a time, so be sure that each page obviously belongs to the rest of the site and not to a page outside your site.

The following sections describe the theme-bearing elements you can use to unify pages in your site. You may have already included some of them, such as backgrounds and colors, but in addition we'll take a look at how you can use logos, icons, and buttons as theme-bearing elements.

Adding Backgrounds

Using consistent backgrounds—colors or images—is one of the easiest and most effective ways to unify web pages, just as using the same color and style paper for multipage written correspondence identifies the material as a single package. Using a different background for each web page can lead to some unwanted results. Visitors might think they've somehow linked outside your site, or they might pay more attention to the differences in design than to your content.

NOTE

Have you ever received business correspondence in which the first page is on heavy, cream-colored, linen-textured letterhead, and the second page is on cheap 20-pound copier paper? Using different backgrounds for Web pages produces a similar effect—visitors will notice.

Whether you use a solid color or an image depends on the effect you want to achieve. Background colors are less obtrusive and can effectively mark pages as belonging to a specific site. Take a look at Figures 19.5 and 19.6, which show you how background colors and images create different effects.

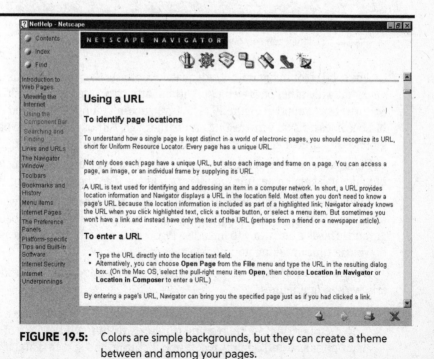

FIGURE 19.5: Colors are simple backgrounds, but they can create a theme between and among your pages.

Part IV

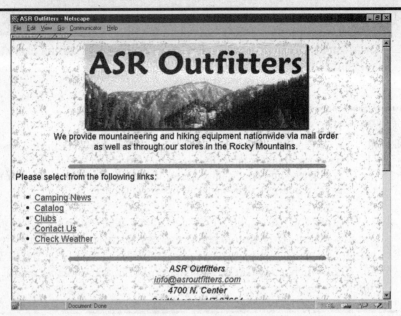

FIGURE 19.6:   Images create backgrounds that are more visually complex, yet they can complement—not overwhelm—page elements.

The solid color in Figure 19.5 adequately contrasts the page elements and helps unify the other page elements without attracting attention to itself. The textured background in Figure 19.6, however, doesn't unify the page elements but becomes a visually interesting part of the page. Although the image background isn't overwhelming in itself, it does make reading more difficult.

Some websites combine colors and images by using a mostly solid color but adding a small repeating graphic, such as the logo shown in Figure 19.7.

In using a small logo—which, in Figure 19.7, appears more like a watermark than an image—the image is less apparent and fades into the background. This is a great way to include a logo without significantly increasing download time or taking up valuable page space.

Regardless of whether you choose a color or an image background, follow these guidelines:

▶ Be sure that the background adequately contrasts with the text. Remember that online reading is inherently difficult because of monitor size and quality, resolution, lighting, and screen glare. If you use dark text, use a light background; if you use light text, use a dark background. If you have any doubt about whether the background contrasts adequately, it doesn't.

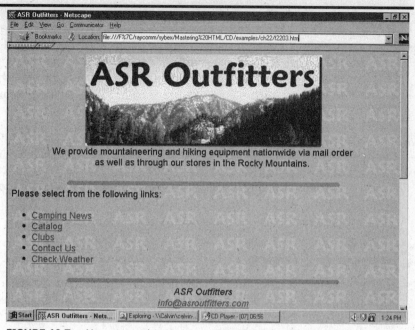

FIGURE 19.7: You can combine colors and images (or text) to create a subtle background.

▶ Be sure that the background complements—not competes with— other elements such as images. For example, if you include images, be sure that the background doesn't overwhelm them. Many times placing a busy or colorful background under equally busy or colorful images makes online reading more difficult.

▶ Be sure that the background matches the style and tone of the website content. A solid black background makes an impression, but doesn't necessarily soothe and calm the visitor. It's not a good choice, for example, for the ASR Outfitters pages because it's quite obtrusive.

▶ Be sure that the foreground text is large and bold enough to be easily read against the background. Use the <FONT> tag—or, better yet, Style Sheets—to increase the size and, optionally, set a font to help your visitors easily read text. A slightly increased font size can overcome the visual distractions of a textured or patterned background.

Part IV

▶ Be sure to choose a nondithering color (one that appears solid and nonsplotchy in web browsers). Because backgrounds span the entire browser window, the colors you choose make a big difference in how the background integrates with the page elements. If, for example, you use a dithering color as a background, the resulting splotches may be more apparent than the page's content. Your best bet is to choose one of the 216 safe colors.

▶ Be sure you view your web pages in multiple browsers and with varying color settings—particularly if you use an image background or don't choose from the 216 safe colors. A good background test includes changing your computer settings to 256 colors and then viewing all your pages again. Reducing the computer system's color depth may also degrade the quality of the background.

Choosing Colors

In most websites these days, colors abound—you see them in text, links, images, buttons, icons, and, of course, backgrounds. The key is to use color to enhance your web pages and identify a theme from page to page.

When developing a color scheme, consider which elements you want to color—text (regular text as well as links, active links, visited links), logos, buttons, bullets, background, and so on. For smaller color areas—text or links—you can choose any color you can imagine. For larger color areas, such as panes or backgrounds, stick to one of the 216 safe colors. The goal is to choose the colors you'll use for each element and use them consistently.

Most web-development software, from Netscape Composer to Microsoft FrontPage, comes with prepared color schemes. If you're not good with colors—if your significant other occasionally mocks your color choices when you get dressed—consider using these prematched colors. Because color is the primary visual element in your pages, problematic color choice will be woefully apparent to all visitors.

The colors you choose should match the site's content. For example, if you're developing a marketing site for a high-tech company, you'll likely choose small areas of bright, fast-paced colors (reds, bright greens, or yellows) that correspond to the site's purpose of catching and holding visitors' attention. If you're developing an intranet site, you'd likely choose mellow colors, such as beige and blue or dark green, because the site's purpose is to inform visitors, not to dazzle them.

If you choose particularly vivid colors, use them in small areas. As the old commercial goes, "a little dab will do ya!" A small expanse of red, for example, can attract attention and hold visitors to the page. A broad expanse of red—such as a background—will likely scare them off or at least discourage them from hanging around.

Including Logos

If you're developing a corporate website, consider using a logo on each page. In doing so, you not only help establish a theme, but you explicitly provide readers with the name of your company or organization throughout the site. Logos often include multiple theme-bearing elements: the logo itself, its colors, and the fonts or emphasis of the letters. Take a look at Figure 19.8, which shows a sample logo used on the ASR Outfitters page.

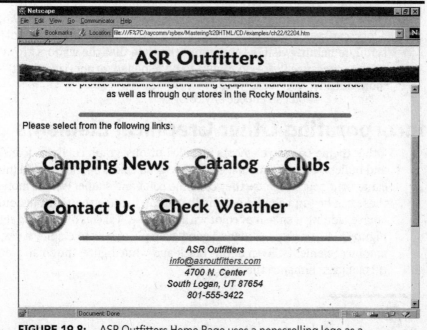

FIGURE 19.8: ASR Outfitters Home Page uses a nonscrolling logo as a theme-bearing element.

The logo helps set up other page elements. For example, the font appears in other places on the page, the colors are consistent throughout the page, and the image used as the foundation for the logo conveys the appropriate impression.

You may have no control over the logo you use—sometimes you're required to use your company's logo, for example. If you can develop a logo or enhance an existing logo, do so. Logos used online, particularly in websites, must carry more information about the company or organization and its style than a logo designed primarily for hard copy. A traditional logo includes paper choice, paper texture, and other elements establishing the organization's image—often, an online logo stands nearly alone without the help of other images or background images.

Where you place the logo depends on its emphasis. Many sites use a fairly large logo on the home page and a smaller version on subsequent pages. The logo thus appears on all pages, yet more space on subsequent pages is reserved for content.

An effective presentation is to combine small, classy logos with a clever arrangement of frames. For example, as shown in Figure 19.8, a logo can reside in a small frame at the top of a page that does not scroll, remaining visible throughout the time that the visitors are at the site. Because it does not have to be reloaded, other pages load more quickly.

Incorporating Other Graphical Elements

Other theme-bearing elements include buttons, graphical links, icons, and bullets. These elements, even more than colors and logos, add interest to your pages because they combine color and shape. What's more, these can be (and should be) small; you can include them throughout a page, adding a splash of color with each use. Take another look at Figure 19.8, a web page that's a good example of how to employ a few graphical elements. Even in this black-and-white figure, the small graphical elements enhance the page.

TIP

You can also enhance a page with animated GIF images, which add visual attraction without increasing load time.

Part of what makes a website usable is how easily visitors can access it, browse through it, and find the information they want. Most visitors access your site through a home page, which is typically a single HTML document that provides links to the other pages in the site. However, not all your visitors will drop in using the home page. For instance, they might go directly to a page they've viewed before, or they might access your site through a search engine and go straight to a specific page. In either case, you have little control over how visitors move through your site.

To ensure that your visitors can link to the information they're looking for and to encourage them to browse your site, you need to make your site easily navigable—that is, make accessing, browsing, and finding information intuitive and inviting. You can do this by using *navigation menus*, which are sets of links that appear from page to page.

Navigation menus come in two varieties:

▶ Textual, which is a set of text links

▶ Graphical, which is a set of images (or icons) used as links

Textual Navigation

Textual navigation is simply text that links visitors to other information in the website. As shown in Figure 19.9, a textual navigation menu doesn't offer glitz, but effectively conveys what information resides at the other end of the link.

Textual navigation, though somewhat unglamorous, offers several advantages over graphical navigation. Textual navigation is more descriptive than graphical navigation because, done right, the text clearly tells visitors about the information in the site. Textual navigation links can be as long as necessary to describe the information at the end of the link; the description is not limited by the size of a button. The smaller (thus faster to download) the button, the less text you can fit on it.

Textual navigation is also more reliable than graphical navigation because the link itself is part of the HTML document, not a referenced element, such as a navigation button.

Finally, text links download much faster than graphical navigation. The links download as part of the page, without the delays associated with images.

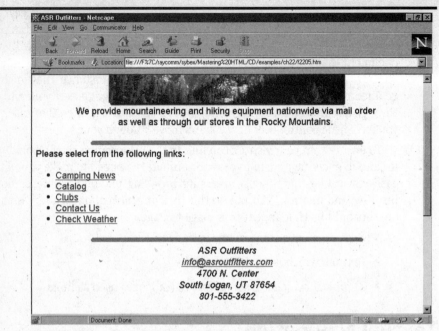

FIGURE 19.9: Textual navigation is often the most informative.

If you're considering using textual navigation, follow these guidelines:

▶ If your textual navigation menu appears as a vertical list, place the most important or most accessed links at the top.

▶ Make the text informative. Rather than calling links, "More Information," "Contact Information," and "Related Information," add specific summaries. For example, call these links "Product Specs," "Contact Us!," and "Other Sportswear Vendors." Whatever you do, don't use instructions such as "Click Here," which is uninformative and wastes valuable space. Additionally, words such as *Information* rarely do anything but take up space. After all, what would be at the other end of the link besides information?

▶ Provide the same menu—or at least a similar one—on each page. As your visitors link from page to page, they become familiar with the setup and location of the menu and actually (unconsciously) begin to expect that it contain certain information in a certain place.

▶ Customize the menu on each page so that the current page is listed, but not as a link. This helps visitors actually "see" where they are within the site; it also keeps menu locations consistent.

Graphical Navigation

Graphical navigation is a set of images that link to other information in the site. Most commonly, graphical navigation appears in the form of images with text on them, as shown in Figure 19.10. Graphical navigation can also be images that are pictures (called *icons*) representing what the buttons link to.

FIGURE 19.10: These navigation buttons include both text and images.

Graphical navigation has the distinct advantage of being visually more interesting than textual navigation. For example, because buttons and icons can include colors or patterns and can be almost any shape you can imagine, they are outstanding theme-bearing elements.

As colorful and interesting as graphical navigation might be, however, it has a few drawbacks. Primarily, it takes longer—sometimes much longer—to download than textual navigation. The download time depends on the file size and your visitor's connection speed, among other not-in-your-control variables.

Graphical navigation also tends be less informative than textual navigation. For example, if you're using buttons with text on them, you might be limited by the size of the button. The text can be difficult to read, depending on the size of the button and the resolution of the visitor's computer.

If you want to use graphical navigation, consider these guidelines:

▶ Be sure that button text is easily readable. Sometimes, when images used to create buttons are made smaller to fit within a navigation menu, the text becomes too small to read or the letters get pushed together. Your best bet is to try several button sizes to get a feel for which size is most effective.

▶ Be sure that the navigation menu integrates well with the other page elements. Images—including graphical navigation—are visually weighty page elements and often make other elements less apparent.

▶ Plan the navigation menu before you actually create it. Graphical navigation takes longer to develop than textual navigation, and it's much more difficult to change once it's in place. Even if all the pages aren't in place (or fully planned yet), at least create a placeholder for the navigation menu so that you don't have to revise the menu as you develop new content.

▶ Provide the same menu—or as close as possible—on every page. As with textual menus, visitors link from page to page and expect to see the same menu options in the same location on each page. Also, developing only one menu that you can use from page to page saves you time; you create it once and reuse it on each page.

TIP

Rather than creating several navigation buttons, you can create one image that includes several links. This single image with multiple links is called an *image map*.

Placing Navigation Menus

After you determine which kind of navigation menu to use, decide where to place the menu on your web pages. Regardless of whether you use textual or graphical navigation, be sure to place menus where visitors are most likely to use them.

Because navigation menus, particularly graphical ones, often take up a lot of valuable page space, be sure to choose menu location(s) that don't interfere with other page elements. Here are some considerations when choosing a location for navigation menus:

Top of the page   Locating a navigation menu at the top of pages is particularly useful because it is easy to find and access. Visitors who are casually surfing your pages can easily link in and out, and those who link to a page in error can easily get out of the page. The big advantage to using the top of the page (from the visitor's perspective) is that he or she isn't forced to wade through information to access the menu.

Middle of the page   This location is effective in long pages because visitors can read through some of the information, but are not forced to return to the top or scroll to the bottom just to leave the page. Usually, with mid-page navigation menus, you'll want to use targeted links.

Bottom of the page   This location works well in a couple of situations. For example, you can put the navigation menu at the bottom when you want visitors to read the material that precedes it. Keep in mind that visitors don't want to be forced to read information they're not interested in, but they don't mind browsing through a short page to get to a navigation menu at the bottom. Bottom navigation also works well on pages that already include many elements at the top, such as logos or descriptions; in this case, adding a navigation menu would crowd other important information.

Multiple locations   For most websites, you'll likely use a combination of these three locations, which is fine, as long as you use at least one consistently. You could, for example, place a menu at the top of all pages and place an additional menu at the bottom on longer pages. Or you might combine top and middle (or top, middle, and bottom) navigation locations for particularly long pages.

BALANCING FLASH WITH USABILITY

One of the most important principles of developing a website—particularly public and personal sites—is to balance flashy elements (ones that "dazzle" your visitors) with usability (which makes your site easy to use). If you've spent any time at all surfing the Web, you've probably noticed some really spectacular sites—ones that flash and make sounds and have moving pictures. However, you've probably also noticed that these flashing, beeping,

Part IV

moving sites have one significant drawback: they usually take forever to download. The result is that you end up waiting for the dazzling stuff, when all you were really looking for was the content.

AN ALTERNATIVE MENU LOCATION

If you use a framed website, place navigation menus separate from other web page elements. Visually separating the menu from other page elements enhances your website. Many websites display the navigation menu on the left side of the browser window, but the bottom can also be effective, as shown here:

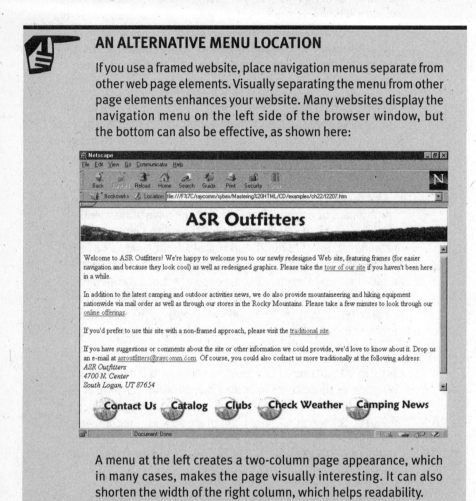

A menu at the left creates a two-column page appearance, which in many cases, makes the page visually interesting. It can also shorten the width of the right column, which helps readability.

Placing a navigation menu on the left or on the bottom can be less intrusive than placing it throughout the document. The menu, rather than being integrated with page elements, stands alone and can complement—not compete with—other page elements.

Finally, if the navigation menu appears in a separate frame, it can remain on screen at all times, regardless of which pages visitors link to or how far they scroll down a page.

Every other web surfer—including those who will surf your site—has had this experience. In a sense, glitz and flash have transformed web surfing into web waiting.

The key is to balance the number and kind of flashy elements you include with usability, which refers to how easily your visitors can get to the information throughout your website. Yes—absolutely—flashy elements attract visitors, similar to the way that color and creativity in printed marketing materials help lure in customers and keep them glued to every word. But if you include too many elements that slow loading time, visitors will get frustrated, leave your site, and probably won't return. Your goal is to make your site attractive and interesting but not to make visitors wait too long to access the information they want.

Sites that balance flash and usability include enhancements that download quickly and that are quickly available to most of your visitors. In balancing these, you'll find the following:

▶ Visitors spend more time in a balanced site than in one that lacks flash or usability.

▶ Visitors return to a balanced site more often than one that's difficult to use.

▶ Visitors spend more time in and return to a site that doesn't exclude some visitors from the effects. For instance, you're not likely to get many repeat visits from those using Internet Explorer if you've included only Netscape Navigator–supported effects or if you continually remind your visitors that the site was designed expressly for users of other browsers.

WARNING

Just because you *can* provide an effect doesn't mean you should. If the effect doesn't help convey information, improve your visitor's overall experience, or help project your public image, don't include it.

How to balance flash and usability? Consider which effects give you the flash, weigh the effects against download time, and consider the availability of the effects through different browsers. We can't tell you exactly how long each takes to download—too many variables exist such as file size, the type and the speed of the visitor's Internet connection, and the visitor's browser capability and computer resources. Table 19.1 summarizes the flashy effects you can add, the impact each can have on download time, and the availability in browsers.

TABLE 19.1:   A Summary of Web Page Enhancements

ENHANCEMENT	DESCRIPTION	AVAILABILITY
Images	These are the most common enhancements included in web pages because they add color and flash, yet they're fairly easy to obtain or create. For this reason, they're probably the biggest culprit of worldwide waiting because image files can grow to enormous sizes. You can, though, modify images and image files so that they take minimal time to download.	All graphical browsers.
Frames	These can slow things down slightly initially, but if used carefully can speed overall performance considerably because only new information must be downloaded with every new page, leaving logos and other elements in place in adjacent frames.	Available on most versions of Netscape Navigator and Internet Explorer.
Java applets	These slow down pages considerably, particularly for Netscape Navigator users. They can add power—both in terms of visual interest and through functional programs embedded in web pages—but at a high cost.	Available on most versions of Internet Explorer and Netscape Navigator and several other browsers.
JavaScript	This slows pages only slightly and can add attractive flash and glitz. However, many JavaScript effects are so overused as to be completely kitschy.	Available on most versions of Internet Explorer and Netscape Navigator. Some effects are less widely available.
ActiveX controls	These slow down pages, as do Java applets, but provide useful functionality.	Available on newer versions of Internet Explorer and on Netscape Navigator with the proper plug-in.

TABLE 19.1 continued: A Summary of Web Page Enhancements

ENHANCEMENT	DESCRIPTION	AVAILABILITY
Multimedia	Sounds, video, virtual reality worlds, and all the rest of the real flash slows pages nearly to a stand-still. If you're adding important information or if you segregate the flash so that only people who really want it will get it, it's okay, but use with extreme caution.	Available on newer browsers with the proper plug-ins or controls.
Cascading Style Sheets (CSS)	These offer great formatting capabilities and lots of flexibility, but aren't universally available. However, browsers that support them are becoming more common, making CSS formatting a possibility for many purposes.	Netscape Navigator 4 and newer and Internet Explorer 3 and newer. Specific capabilities vary greatly by browser.

Beware that some of these effects require visitors to have plug-ins installed on their computers. A *plug-in* is an extra program used to view effects within browsers that don't typically support the effect. If you decide to include a Shockwave animation, for example, visitors need the appropriate plug-in to view it. If they don't have the plug-in and want to view the animation, they're forced to download the plug-in off the Internet and install it one time for every browser they use.

Is this a hassle? Yes, without a doubt. Most of your visitors won't take the time to download and install plug-ins just to view your site, unless the information provided through the plug-in is essential. Of course, if your information is that important and can be conveyed without the plug-in, include it using a completely hassle-free method. Also, you can be fairly certain that your visitors won't open a page in Netscape Navigator and then reopen the same page in Internet Explorer just to view nifty effects.

What's Next

Now that we've discussed what you need to consider when designing intranet websites, let's move on to getting your website design online. In the next chapter, we'll cover the basics of creating and publishing Web content, including the different kinds of formatting options and the tools you'll need to publish you data.

Chapter 20

WEBSITE CONNECTIVITY

Near-universal access to the World Wide Web and other parts of the Internet has made the browser an essential office application. Why create an *intranet*-based web, though, if no one's going to see it but the people in the office?

In this chapter, we'll discuss what you can do with a corporate web and explain the basics of creating and publishing web content, including the kinds of formatting options that are open to you and the tools you'll need to publish the data. You won't come away from this chapter an expert on Java programming, but after reading this, you'll know what's involved in creating a page or site and have some ideas to explore.

NOTE

While this chapter focuses on creating an intranet or corporate website, the principles apply to extranet and Internet sites as well.

Adapted from *Mastering Local Area Networks*
by Christa Anderson with Mark Minasi
ISBN 0-7821-2258-2   784 pages $39.99

What Can You Do with a Corporate Web?

Although the first use for a web you may think of is publishing information about your company, that's only a small part of what you can do. Get creative and you can do any or all of the following:

- ▶ Post must-see information and get confirmation of who's read it and who hasn't.

- ▶ Host virtual meetings between people not able to meet in person.

- ▶ Automate initial queries to the help desk or other office information.

- ▶ Give people easy access to a corporate database.

- ▶ Run a corporate FTP site.

- ▶ Publish in-house research to allow people to share information.

NOTE

Several (not all) of the corporate web applications described in this chapter stem from case studies prepared for the "1999 NT Innovators" issue of *Windows NT Magazine*, which showcases ingenious uses of NT every January. If you'd like to read more about these inventive uses of corporate webs, visit www.winntmag.com and request InstantDoc #4690.

Can't think of anything else to do with a corporate web? Make it a testing ground for new ideas for the content of your Internet-accessible website. If you're not sure whether a concept is going to fly in the real world, why not publish it where only office people can see it, and ask for feedback? Better to find out in-house that an idea's a flop than on a network accessible to the entire world. You might even be able to save the idea from being a flop with the feedback you get.

Distribute Information Easily

Like e-mail, intranet web content can be a big paper saver. Rather than creating memos informing people of a change in company policy or inviting them to the company holiday party, you can create a web page with the information. This not only saves you the trouble of distributing the memos, but also allows you access to design elements not always possible in e-mail—without requiring people to have access to the application in which the original document was created. Posting the documents to the website also prevents people from getting cute and tampering with the original document.

Another advantage to publishing must-see documents on the company web is that you can confirm that people have read them—you're not limited to just posting the information and hoping it got to the people who needed to see it. Just create a section where people can click on a button saying, "Yes, I've read and understood this," to send a confirmation e-mail to the business manager or whomever else needs to know. You could do something similar to have people RSVP for the office party or get-together, creating a form in which people can indicate whether or not they'll be attending, how many guests they'll be bringing, and any other relevant information, such as preferred dates or dietary requirements. Anyone who's had to coordinate an office get-together will appreciate that kind of automation.

Bring People Together

Chat sessions can be a means of getting people together for meetings when physical meetings are difficult or impossible. A chat application is one way of doing this, but a web-based chat is another, and one that can be used by anyone with a browser, not just the people with the chat application installed. Video conferencing can also be supported via a web interface.

In fact, with web-based scheduling applications, the company web can also be used in group scheduling for those times when virtual meetings won't do the trick. Lotus Organizer, for example, has a web plug-in so that people can plan their schedules on their personal computers or PDAs and then upload the information to a web-based calendar.

TIP

Don't want just anyone able to see or read your calendar? Password-protect it for viewing and editing.

A corporate web provides still another means of getting people together—helping them find each other in the first place. Many big companies are a maze of cubicles or offices, and, in a large company, not everyone can know one another by sight. One solution to this problem is to prepare an online map of the corporate offices that shows the location of each person's office. Let users plug in a name, and the map highlights the location of that person's office *and* pulls up a picture of the person whose name you entered.

Reduce Support Costs

A web-based user help desk facilitates the support process. First, many user requests are predictable—they want access to a particular folder, can't reach their e-mail, or can't find a file. You can create a form listing common problems, inviting users to pick their problem from a list. If their problem isn't listed, they can explain it in a text box on the web page.

TIP

Using a web-based help desk allows people to complain about lack of e-mail access without using the telephone or relying on the e-mail they can't use.

Second, writing down the problem or choosing from a set of options encourages users to think about what's wrong and describe it more fully than they might over the telephone or in person. You often have to go through the initial process of isolating the problem, getting from "WordPerfect isn't working" to "WordPerfect is shutting down after a message comes up saying that the computer is low on resources." Isolating the problem can take several minutes, or even longer if the user and the support person both get frustrated. It's simpler, and less frustrating for everyone, to allow the user to write down the problem or choose his or her problem from a list. This won't completely eliminate the need to isolate some problems, but it should help. Telephone follow-up is always an option if more information is needed.

Third, submitting problems by web-based e-mail reduces both the time it takes to report the problem and the time required for the support person to listen to it. Additionally, e-mail is almost always available— the person reporting the problem doesn't have to wait for a free line to the support center to open up.

Simplify Database Access

An increasingly popular purpose for a corporate intranet web is to provide a front end to a database for salespeople or managers. It's a great improvement over printing out standard reports every month. A canned report may not answer a specific set of questions that a salesperson or manager has. Moreover, we're back to the distribution problem again—how do you get those reports to everyone in a widely distributed company? By fax? By e-mail? Who's going to take the time to create the reports?

TIP

At some corporations, users can send the database server queries via e-mail without having to know Structured Query Language (SQL) syntax. The users phrase the questions using standard language that will trigger a previously prepared query (but this language is very simple—much simpler than a complex query needs to be). More advanced users familiar with SQL syntax can e-mail queries using SQL and thus get custom reports.

Additionally, when people need to edit the database or create reports, with a properly designed web application they can do it without having to understand how to use a database front end, such as Access. The interface on the front end can be designed to translate the user-phrased queries into the SQL that databases use.

Distribute Files

It's entirely possible that you may want people to have access to certain files but not to the directories in which those files are stored. Perhaps the directories are across a slow WAN connection, or other files are stored in the directories that you don't necessarily want everyone to know exist. In such a case, you can set up an FTP site to function as a central repository for files coming in and going out. Users can upload and download files from a more-or-less public directory. The degree of security depends on how you configure it, whether access is dependent on a password, restricted to certain users, or open to anyone who logs in.

TIP

To keep data files consistent, replicate them from their original directories to the FTP site.

You needn't restrict your FTP site to text files. If you have fairly computer-savvy users on your network, you can store software upgrades in a central location. Users can run the Setup files from the FTP site, saving themselves the trouble of looking for their own disks or getting the support person to upgrade their applications.

Publish Research

One more use for the web is to share research between departments of a large organization. For example, several agencies in the U.S. Department of the Army share a corporate intranet. On this intranet is a web-based database called IntelLink that publishes the data collected by the analytical departments. Users of IntelLink, including policymakers, soldiers ("warfighters," to use the military jargon), management, and anyone else with access, can refer to a database of country reports, pictures, maps, and military hardware. Without this web-based application, these people would have to call the analysts to prepare reports for them. Obviously, the analysts still make custom reports and briefings, but often-requested information doesn't require any more work on the analysts' part.

WHY USE THE WEB?

You can share information and run virtual conferences with a corporate LAN that has file sharing, chat, and e-mail access enabled—no web required. Why bother building websites and applications? Mostly because a web creates a simple means of providing a consistent appearance for published data and an easy way of regulating access to that data.

Create a Consistent Look

Building a web interface for applications or information allows you to customize the interface to make it as simple or as complicated as you like. Ordinary LAN access requires people to have access to applications—either locally or on an application or terminal server—and to know how to use them. A web-based application interface means that people need only a browser, not one application for each type of resource access. Whether the network's users are accessing a database or sending e-mail, they can use their web browser to load the interface you've created. Not only does this limit the number of applications that must be accessible to network users, but it also means that the application front end can be as simple or as complex as your user base requires. For example, if users only need to prepare database reports for certain dates, you could create an interface with a place to plug in dates and a button that says, "Generate Report." It's not necessary to teach anyone how to use a database client.

Using web-based forms enhances consistency not only for the users but also for the people or applications receiving the information input by the users. For example, some e-mail applications support HTML and thus could display formatted party invitations or official memos. Even if your office uses such applications, however, e-mail is still an inferior form of communicating important information because it doesn't support forms. People can RSVP to your e-mailed invitation, but there's no way to force them to provide all the information you need. In contrast, a web-based invitation to a pot-luck dinner could include an RSVP section in which users could say that they were attending, indicate the number of people they were bringing, and choose a dish to bring from a list of options. The same invitation sent in e-mail demands a free-form response that might include all that information, some of it, or none of it. Similarly, canned reports that a user can choose from a list eliminate the possibility of user syntax errors. Get the syntax right on the back end and the user doesn't need to know it.

Securely Distribute Information

Web-based distribution of information provides not only consistency but also some additional layers of security. For example, recall that online documents are harder to tamper with than documents distributed in a user-editable form, and FTP sites allow documents to be made available without opening up the source directory. There's more:

► Pages can be protected to limit access to certain users or those who know a password.

► Canned queries can be the only interface to a database so that information not in the canned queries can't be part of a report.

► Chat rooms can be restricted to a set of users rather than being open to anyone.

In short, if you want to present a consistent yet customizable interface for data dissemination and retrieval, a corporate web is an excellent choice of medium. It's dynamic, almost endlessly forgettable, and can't be tampered with easily.

CREATING WEB CONTENT

Web content can be as simple as posting text and a few pictures or as complex as linking content from back-end applications or other pages. When creating content, think about who's going to be using the pages; from that, choose the tools you need to create the desired effect.

Planning Content and Design

As with preparing anything else complex, the first step in creating a website is not sitting down with Notepad or your favorite HTML editor and a copy of *HTML for Dummies*, but planning. Ask yourself the following questions:

- Who's going to be looking at this information?
- How should the content be organized?
- Will everyone have access to all content, or will some parts be shut off to all but a few people?
- Where will the content be coming from?

Thinking about all of this ahead of time will help you when it comes to figuring out how to organize material. Until you know who's going to be seeing the information, you can't plan an interface or plan for security. Until you know how the content will be organized and where it's coming from, you can't write the code that will make that content available.

Design Tips

A lot of good web design is related to simplicity and legibility. No matter how many websites there are that do nothing but play the theme from *Deliverance*, the grand majority of sites, including the ones on your intranet website, will be there for the purpose of imparting information. If your readers can't read that information easily, they'll give up. If they give up, then you might as well have saved yourself the trouble of creating the site in the first place.

Keeping Data Organized   Web pages are typically three-dimensional structures, built not only on their own contents but also with links to other pages. It's certainly possible to build an intranet website that's a collection of unrelated pages, but it'll be much easier to navigate the site if each page is part of a coherent whole.

TIP

Protected pages are one exception to this rule. If you don't want everyone to be able to view a particular page, one simple way of limiting access to it is to not link the page to other pages and to not publish its URL. (If the page's content is really private, password-protect it as well; this method will help keep out the idle curious if that's all you're worried about.)

Drawing a site map of your website's data sources, page links, and other pieces may help you keep organized when planning (see Figure 20.1). Once you've got the site's design mapped out, you're ready for some content and page design work.

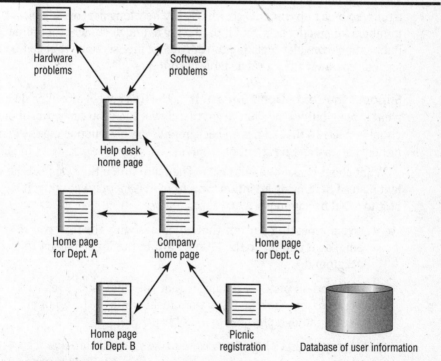

FIGURE 20.1:   Draw a site map of your website before worrying about content.

TIP

Some HTML editors, such as Microsoft's FrontPage, let you create and graphically arrange pages, simplifying the process of organizing the website.

Don't Overload Reader Buffers   Flicker and backlighting make reading on screen harder than reading hard copy; most people read from a monitor at about one-third the rate at which they can read print. Thus, one of the first rules of creating text is: Keep it simple. If at all possible, keep text on a single page so that people don't need to scroll down to read. If this isn't possible (for example, if you're coding a longish document for online dissemination), then use white space to break up the page a bit. Whatever you do, don't format the page so that people have to scroll horizontally to read it. Code the text to dynamically arrange itself in relation to the dimensions of the browser window.

Content organization is also important in getting the message across. The human brain can remember and absorb only about seven things at a time, so break up content accordingly. Eschew long lists of bullets and numbers for smaller sets, and if producing a long document for online publication, consider breaking the document into sections that can be loaded separately from a single table of contents.

Support the Text—Don't Squash It   The first goal of an online document is readability. Once you've got that down, then you can worry about visual impact. To that end, keep backgrounds simple, supporting the text rather than distracting attention from it.

What about background bitmaps? They can work if they support the text instead of drawing attention away from it. Generally speaking, it's best to avoid backgrounds that:

▶ Have a repeating pattern that competes with the font you're using, as it will make the letters hard to distinguish from the background.

▶ Are based on pictures or images that will distract the reader's attention from the text. If you want to illustrate the text, put pictures or photographs next to it, not beneath it.

▶ Are very bright or high contrast, hurting your reader's eyes.

▶ Are too close to the color of the text.

Speaking of color, you can't assume that subtle gradations of color will display the same way on every monitor. Keep the color scheme fairly bold or some elements may be lost in the translation.

Don't Overdo the Extras   Animations aren't as much of a bandwidth problem on intranet websites as they are on the Internet, but they're still potentially distracting. Flashing signs, spinning globes, or the like can be a nice touch in small quantities, especially if they're used to focus the reader's attention. If overused, they draw attention away from the text. If *really* overused, they cause headaches and grouchy users.

What about sound? I'm not a huge fan of sound on web pages in any case, and in the office environment, it's really undesirable (unless everyone has their own office). Any kind of sound effects are distracting to people around you, and not every computer has speakers that support sound well anyway.

Keep It Connected   Make it easy to navigate the site. Back buttons on pages are a good idea, but an even better idea is a site map that's accessible from anywhere in the site. If you're comfortable with frames, you can put a site map in a frame to one side of the currently displayed document. If frames are a bit beyond you, you can put links to important pages (such as the site's home page) on the top or bottom of each page in the site.

Intranet Content versus Internet Content

Now that you're thoroughly intimidated, the good news is that creating web content for an intranet potentially can be much easier than creating it for the World Wide Web. First, you've got greater control over your user base in that you know what browser they're likely to be using and what features it supports. Not all browsers present the same information exactly alike or support the same capabilities. For example, Netscape Navigator does not natively support ActiveX controls (although you can download an add-on that will support them). For another, Microsoft supports a nonstandard Java type, so Microsoft's Internet Explorer is chancy at best when it comes to supporting pages running Java—sometimes they work, and sometimes they don't.

NOTE

Java is a programming language that Sun Microsystems designed to run on any computing platform without recoding.

Second, although you don't want to create pages that will bring your office LAN to a screeching halt, a corporate intranet doesn't have nearly the bandwidth problems of a World Wide Web page accessible only from a telephone line. A connection that runs at 100Mbps will download a web page to a client's browser much more quickly than a 56Kbps modem.

Even if the intranet spans WANs, traffic on the WAN may be lighter than traffic on the Internet during peak hours. It's certainly more easily manageable.

Third, security on the office LAN may be less of a problem than it is on the World Wide Web. There are security holes related to web publishing that can lead to someone editing your web page's content. (*The New York Times* public website found this out in the fall of 1998 when they got hacked and had to take down their page to keep the rest of the world from seeing what had happened to it.) However, a LAN has fewer potential culprits than the entire Internet. Thus, your chances of being hacked are reduced by a potential prankster's knowledge that he or she is more likely to be caught as the result of hacking a page.

TIP

These differences are worth keeping in mind when planning to migrate sites from the LAN web to the World Wide Web. Pages that work really well on a LAN may not scale well to the Internet.

Text Markup Languages

People sometimes talk about "programming" a web page, but formatting text to be readable by a browser isn't really programming. As the names of the formatting languages suggest, they're *markup languages*. That is, they're composed of characters or other symbols inserted in the body of a document that indicate how the file should look when printed or displayed, or to define its logical structure (such as paragraphs and bullets). Without such a markup language, the data to be displayed would be raw text with no character or paragraph formatting.

A markup language defines document appearance with codes called *tags* that take a form like this: <tag> </tag>. The first tag indicates the point where the formatting should begin and the second one (with the slash) indicates where the coding should end. If you forget the second tag, the coding for the first tag is applied until the end of the document.

NOTE

The markup language can be applied to raw text either by hand using a text editor (such as Notepad) or with a graphical tool that adds the code when you visually arrange the text as you want it to appear. Graphical tools are easier to work with when you're learning, but they're not always as precise as text editors.

Hypertext Markup Language (HTML)

HTML is the granddaddy of web page coding and the backbone of most web pages. HTML allows you to publish text and figures, the contents of spreadsheets, or even create database reports to be read online. It's good for any kind of static information, both for organizing it and for formatting. HTML codes let you

- Set text size and font.
- Apply bold, italic, or underlined formatting to text.
- Define links to other pages.
- Insert images.
- Create a title for the page.
- Create tables.
- Insert metadata for use by search engines.

NOTE

Metadata is hidden data that does not appear on the web page, but may be picked up by a search engine to direct people to that site.

There are three types of HTML tags: those that format text or individual characters, those that format paragraphs or other chunks of text, and those that are invisible but provide other functionality, such as metadata for searches.

HTML has one significant advantage over all other markup languages: near-universal support. Just about any browser (certainly any modern and graphics-capable browser) supports the current version of HTML, something not true of Dynamic HTML (DHTML), XML, or Java and ActiveX. If you need your websites to be accessible to a variety of browser types, HTML is the way to go.

Dynamic HTML (DHTML)

Dynamic HTML makes HTML a bit more flexible. Rather than presenting a static web page to the world, you can use DHTML and make a page customizable by the person using it, without corrupting the original document source. For example, a page prepared with DHTML can include elements that a user can drag around on the page to rearrange its contents. When the page is refreshed, however, the changes are lost and the page is restored to its original appearance.

DHTML has support for the following features not included in HTML:

▶ Dynamic styles

▶ Precise positioning

▶ Data binding

▶ Dynamic content

Not sure what all this means? Fear not—it's explained next.

Applying Styles to Web Documents   *Dynamic styles* are based on the principles of cascading style sheets (CSS), applying style sheets to a page instead of formatting the various sections by hand. If you use a modern word processor, then you're probably familiar with style sheets that automatically format text blocks a certain way depending on the style you assign to them. This formatting can include text color, font, positioning, visibility, and just about anything else to do with how text can be presented. CSS, and by extension DHTML, is the same kind of thing, only applied to web pages instead of word processors.

DHTML's dynamic styles have capabilities not included in word processors. For example, you could mark up text to make links automatically change color when you position your mouse over them, or show text when you move your cursor over a certain blank space. The only catch to these styles is that they require you to put most documents in style sheets, a time-consuming task for those new to style sheets or who are having to convert documents.

Placing Text Where You Want It   Another feature of DHTML is its ability to define exactly where on a page an element will appear, using *x* (horizontal), *y* (vertical), and even *z* (3D) coordinates to define object placement. (Defining object placement in 3D allows you to make objects overlap.) Precise positioning makes wrapping text around images possible and repositions objects according to the size of the browse window.

NOTE

HTML without CSS does not support exact placement; the positioning of elements depends on the browser.

Embedding Data in a Page   To give users access to back-end information, such as that stored in a database, normal HTML pages must contact the server holding the original data and ask for permission to let users manipulate data. DHTML allows the data to be bound to a particular page, permitting users to work with the bound data without disturbing the source data or even touching the server storing the original data. Instead, the data source is part of the page and can be sorted and filtered like a database. Not only does this reduce load on the servers, but it also allows users to view and manipulate data without giving them access to the source.

Creating Dynamic Content   Style sheets allow the web publisher to easily change the appearance of a page or set of pages. Dynamic content allows the web user to change the appearance of a page by running a script in order to

- ▶ Insert or hide elements of a page.
- ▶ Modify text.
- ▶ Change the page layout.
- ▶ Draw data from back-end sources and display it based on a user request.

Unlike HTML, which can only change page contents before the page is downloaded to the user's browser, DHTML can accept changes at any time. When used with scripts that allow users to define the elements they want to see, dynamic content can provide a high degree of interactivity.

TIP

In the section, "Bring People Together," earlier in this chapter, we described a web-based map of a building that could display the location of a particular office and a picture of the person the user was trying to find. That map was created with DHTML, using the markup language's dynamic content feature.

EXtensible Markup Language (XML)

XML is a new web coding language that doesn't replace HTML (certainly not at this point—there's little evidence of it in live web pages) but supports it, making web pages a little more flexible.

Part IV

The idea is this: When you're formatting a page with HTML, you can change the appearance of text with the tags for boldface, italic, paragraph break here, and so forth. These tags don't really tell you anything about the text's content but only format its appearance. XML is not limited to tags that say what text is supposed to look like; instead, you can use it to tag the text with what it is (names, addresses, product names, etc.).

Why is this helpful? First of all, this metadata can make it easier for search engines to find predefined elements. If you searched your corporate website (created with HTML) for "name," looking for all the names mentioned, the search would return all the instances of the *word* "name," not names. If the site were coded with XML, however, the search would return any text tagged as a name. Second, tagging parts of speech is useful if you want to apply a rule (such as color or language) only to parts of a web document. Say that the online document is a short story in Spanish with translation in English. Rather than having to switch from Spanish to English support in the document, you could define all the parts of the story with a <story></story> tag and apply the Spanish rule to those parts only, with the translations remaining in English. Essentially, if your web page design would be made easier by making certain parts of its text isolated elements, then you could benefit from using XML.

Application and Scripting Languages

Want your web page to actually *do* something instead of just displaying text and images? You'll need to add support for some miniprograms. On the client side, this could take the form of ActiveX controls or Java applets. On the server side, the miniprograms might use a common gateway interface (CGI) front end to a program stored on the server, or a script embedded in the page itself with Microsoft's Active Server Pages (ASP).

Client-Side Web Applications

Client-side web applications and executables are downloaded from the web server to the client, to be executed on the client using the client machine's resources. Client-side applications may include such features as chat programs or other applications likely to be used more than once while a page is still open.

The Java Language   *Java* is a cross-platform language developed by Sun Microsystems. The concept behind Java is interoperability: Java *applets* (miniature applications) are able to run on any platform—DOS,

Windows, Unix, NT, or what have you. When a Java applet runs, it first creates an execution environment (called a *sandbox*) for itself, and then runs in the context of this sandbox. Theoretically, this sandbox has two effects. First, it lets an applet execute on any platform because the sandbox creates the operating environment the applet needs. Second, it keeps the applet from doing anything to the native operating environment, as it never actually touches it.

Java applets that you might already have encountered include Netscape Communicator's Netcaster as well as the trip planners used on some travel websites. Netcaster is the front end to Netscape *pull* technology (that is, pulling content from websites without requiring that you actually visit the sites). The trip planners take the preferences you enter and search a database of airline flights that correspond to your needs and then return the possible matches.

You might have heard various and sundry terms associated with Java. While this isn't intended to be a complete tutorial on Java, Table 20.1 explains some related terms.

TABLE 20.1:   Java-Related Terminology

TERM	DESCRIPTION	MORE INFORMATION
HotJava	The first browser to support Java. The browser itself is written in Java.	HotJava supports any combination of several different views (online applications), allowing you to customize the features available to those using the browser.
Java Beans	Components that can be used to assemble a larger Java application.	Simplifies Java programming by allowing developers to easily reuse code.
JavaScript	CA scripting language developed by Netscape. Not all browsers support JavaScript equally well; Netscape Navigator (unsurprisingly) is most reliable.	JavaScript can be used to support forms and timers, make calculations, and identify the browser being used, among other possibilities.

NOTE

Not all browsers support Java equally well. Internet Explorer's support for Java is spotty, and Microsoft's version of Java (J++) enables some features not found in Sun's Java but which depend on Windows functions. A browser running on a non-Windows operating system may not get full functionality from J++ applets.

Part IV

ActiveX Controls   ActiveX is similar to Java in that it's a way of attaching miniapplications to web pages, but it's not identical. Rather than being a platform-independent programming language, ActiveX is a set of controls that can make applications written in a variety of languages—C++, Delphi, J++, and Visual Basic, to name a few—accessible via the browser. ActiveX controls do *not* run in a sandbox; they run like any other application in the user operating environment.

Server-Side Web Applications

Server-side web applications execute on the server, using a server operating environment and resources. Server-side applications are more likely to be one-time applications, such as search engines. The advantage to server-side applications is their universality: the browser doesn't have to support the client-side application language. The approaches to storing and loading these programs may differ. CGI servers access an application stored on the server, whereas Active Server Pages store the script to be executed in the HTML page itself.

Common Gateway Interface (CGI)   *CGI* is a standardized way of passing information from a web user's input to a back-end application or script and then passing back information to the client's browser. For example, when you fill out an online registration form and click the Submit button, the information that you supplied may be passed via a CGI to a database. Once the information has been processed, you get a "Thank you!" message back, via the CGI.

CGI's biggest advantage is its consistent interface. It doesn't matter what platform the server is running on; the data can be passed from the user to the application, regardless. The functionality you can get using CGI to access a back-end application isn't necessarily different from what you might get from using a scripting language; it just works differently. A script is attached to a specific web page, but an application accessible through CGI is not linked to a specific page, rather to a specific gateway. Any web page can associate itself with that gateway.

Active Server Pages (ASP)   Some web pages have scripts embedded in them that can be run when conditions require it—when a user clicks a search engine's Find button, for example, or fills out a form and clicks OK. You can create an ASP file by including in an HTML document a script written in VBScript or another supported scripting language, and then renaming the document with the ".asp" suffix. When the user loads that page and fulfills the conditions, the script will run.

SUMMARY

By now, you should have a pretty good idea of how you could put a corporate web to work. Publish reports, sign up people for the company picnic, speed up support calls, create maps of the office—if you can think of an information-related need, you can probably think of a web application to support it.

To create those web applications, you'll use a combination of markup languages (HTML, DHTML, or XML) and programming languages. Programming languages can run either on the client or on the server, depending on whether you'd rather use client-side resources or server-side resources, and whether your client browsers will support the clientside applications. Server-side applications can either embed scripts directly in the home page or include a common interface to a program stored on the web server or on another machine. When creating these pages, don't forget to take your audience's needs into account—these pages are meant to make people's lives easier, not harder.

WHAT'S NEXT

In the next chapter, you will learn about using public key cryptography to protect the valuable data you have learned to create in this chapter.

Part IV

Part V
NETWORK SECURITY

Chapter 21

SECURITY WITH CERTIFICATES

Some security services require a way to authenticate users or protect data in transit. Just to name one instance, secure e-commerce depends on having some way to obscure credit card numbers and expiration dates in transit, so they can't be easily stolen. For example, the Secure Sockets Layer, used to protect and secure web traffic, is a way to authenticate each side of a transaction. Authentication and confidentiality can be implemented in several different ways, ranging from simple password exchanges to elaborate hardware-assisted security systems. One way is to use *digital certificates*, since they can provide both authentication and confidentiality. A *certificate authority*, or *CA*, is a service that lets you issue new certificates, revoke or cancel old ones, and monitor and control which certificates are doing what. Most major operating systems include functions for providing this service, including Novell, Microsoft, and Sun.

• •

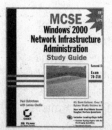

Adapted from *MCSE: Windows 2000 Network Infrastructure Administration Study Guide*, Second Edition by Paul Robichaux with James Chellis

ISBN: 0-7821-2949-8   816 pages $49.99

This chapter will explore the basic terms and concepts that underlie certificate servers. It will explain why encryption is important and how it's used to meet everyday business needs. It will also explain the terminology you need to understand to grasp what a certificate server can do.

SOME USEFUL BUZZWORDS

If the first step toward learning to use a certificate server is understanding the fundamentals of how digital certificates work, then the first step toward *that* is learning the right vocabulary to use when talking about certificates and CA operations. As anyone who's ever visited a doctor or attorney knows, being equipped with the right buzzwords makes a big difference in your understanding of key concepts.

Everything You Ever Wanted to Know about Encryption (and Then Some)

When most people hear the words "encryption" or "cryptography," they immediately think of secret-key cryptography. In a secret-key system, two people who want to communicate use a single shared key that must be kept secret. The same key is used to encrypt and decrypt data, so if a user loses the secret key or if it's stolen, the data it encrypts becomes vulnerable. Secret-key systems tend to be fast and flexible, but their dependence on a single key makes them better suited for applications where you can change the key frequently. In addition, secret-key systems can only be used for encryption, not authentication (more about that in a second).

Instead of the single secret key used in a secret-key system, public-key systems use *two* keys, combined into a single keypair:

► A *public key*, which is designed to be spread freely around

► A *private key* (also called a secret key), which must be held only by its owner and should never be publicly disclosed

These keys complement each other; for example, if you encrypt something with your public key, it can only be decrypted with the corresponding private key (which only you hold), and vice versa. The security of these keys depends on the mathematical relationship between the public and private keys. You can't derive one from the other, so passing out the public key doesn't introduce any risk of compromising the private key.

What You Can Do with a Public Key

There are two fundamental operations associated with public-key cryptography: encryption and signing.

▶ *Encryption* hides data so that only the intended party can read it. In public-key cryptography, for example, if Alice wants to send her boss Bob some private data, she uses Bob's public key to encrypt it, and then she sends it to him. Upon receiving the encrypted data, Bob uses his private key to decrypt it. The important concept here is that Bob can freely distribute his public key so that anyone in the world can send him encrypted data. If Alice and an attacker (let's call her Marlene) both have copies of Bob's public key, and Marlene intercepts an encrypted message from Alice to Bob, she won't be able to decrypt it. Only Bob's private key can do that, and he's the only person who holds it.

▶ *Signing* uses encryption to prove the origin and authenticity of some piece of data. If Alice wants the world to know that she is the author of a message, she signs it by encrypting it with her private key. She can then post the message publicly. This obviously doesn't provide any privacy, because anyone can decrypt the data using her public key. However, the fact that it can be decrypted using Alice's public key means that it must have been encrypted using Alice's *private* key, which only she holds—so it must have come from Alice.

In combination, signatures and encryption can be used to provide three features that customers demand, particularly for business-to-business e-commerce. These features include the following:

Privacy Properly encrypted data can't be read by anyone except the intended recipients. Because public keys can be posted freely, complete strangers can communicate privately just by retrieving each other's public keys and using them to exchange encrypted messages.

Authentication Transactions and communications involve two parties. Much of the time, it's desirable for one end or the other (or maybe both!) to verify the other's identity. For example, secure websites allow users to verify that the server's identity is as claimed. One way to implement authentication uses public keys: The client can encrypt a challenge message using the server's public key, then send it to the server. If the server can decrypt it and answer correctly, it demonstrates that the server has the proper private key, thus proving its identity.

Authentication also allows you to verify that a piece of data wasn't tampered with after it was sent. This kind of authentication is usually implemented as a digital signature, using the public-key signing operations mentioned earlier. Let's say that you want to digitally sign e-mail messages you send out announcing new revisions of your book. To do that, you use software built into your Eudora e-mail client that does the following:

1. It examines the message content you provide and passes it through a special type of algorithm called a *hash algorithm*. Hash algorithms generate a unique "fingerprint" (or hash) for any block of data; it's practically impossible to produce two different messages that have an identical hash.

2. It encrypts the message and the fingerprint using your private key.

Anyone who wants to verify that the message is from you can do the same steps in reverse: First your software decrypts the message using your public key, then it computes a hash for the message. If the new hash and the decrypted version match, it proves that (a) you sent the message, and (b) the message hasn't been modified.

Non-repudiation   Non-repudiation is one aspect of "conventional" business often overlooked by e-commerce users. For example, if we sign a paper contract and give you a copy, it's pretty hard for us to later say, "Hey, we didn't sign that." Digital signatures can provide the same legal binding for electronic transmissions, and they're being used to do so increasingly more often.

What about Certificates?

Think of a digital certificate as a carrying case for a public key. A certificate contains the public key and a set of attributes, like the key holder's name and e-mail address. These attributes specify something about the holder: their identity, what they're allowed to do with the certificate, and so on. The attributes and the public key are bound together because the certificate is digitally signed by the entity that issued it. Anyone who wants to verify the certificate's contents can verify the issuer's signature.

For a real-world analogy, look in your wallet. If you have a driver's license, you have the equivalent of a digital certificate. Your license contains a unique key (your license number) and some attributes (an expiration date, your name, address, hair color, and so on). It's issued by a trusted agency and laminated to prevent it from being tampered with. Anyone who trusts the agency that issued your license and verifies that the lamination is intact can rely on its authenticity. At that point, though, the analogy breaks down—in the real world, only the government can issue a driver's license, so everyone knows that a license issued by Paul's Really Good DMV isn't valid. How do you make the same determination with a digital certificate? Read on to find the answer!

Infrastructure? Sounds Complicated!

Certificates are one part of what security experts call a *public-key infrastructure* (*PKI*). This sounds more complicated than it actually is. We use infrastructure components every day, even if we don't think about them: For example, highways, the U.S. Postal Service, the sewer lines in your house, and the Internet backbone your ISP connects to are all infrastructure components of various kinds. A PKI just provides a fundamental set of services that application programmers can use to deliver privacy, authentication, and non-repudiation in their applications. Basically, the PKI has to be able to do the following three things:

Manage Keys A PKI makes it easy to issue new keys, review or revoke existing keys, and manage the trust level attached to keys from different issuers.

Publish Keys A PKI offers a way for clients to find and fetch public keys and information about whether a specific key is valid or not. Without the ability to retrieve keys and know that they are valid, your users can't make use of public-key services.

Use Keys A PKI provides an easy-to-use way for users to use keys—not just by moving keys around where they're needed, but also by providing easy-to-use applications that perform public-key cryptographic operations for securing e-mail, network traffic, and other types of communication.

As you might imagine, these services don't just appear out of thin air; they're provided by different components that together make up PKI. Scott Culp, one of Microsoft's security gurus, likes to point out that a PKI is a set of capabilities, not a single tangible thing or object. What components do you need to make a usable PKI?

What's in a PKI?

The plumbing infrastructure in your house or apartment has a large number of different components: sinks, toilets, supply pipes, municipal pumping stations, and so on. Likewise, a PKI has several different components that you can mix and match to achieve the desired results. A typical PKI implementation offers the following functions:

▶ *Certificate authorities* issue certificates, revoke certificates they've issued, and publish certificates for their clients. Big CAs like Thawte and Verisign may do this for millions of users; with your own PKI solution, you can set up your own CA for each department or workgroup in your organization if you want to. Each CA is responsible for choosing what attributes it will include in a certificate and what mechanism it will use to verify those attributes before issuing the certificate. CAs also build and maintain lists of revoked certificates (known as *certificate revocation lists*, or *CRLs*).

▶ *Certificate publishers* make certificates and CRLs publicly available, inside or outside an organization. This allows widespread availability of the critical material needed to support the entire PKI. In particular, a good certificate publisher will allow clients to automatically get the certificates they need. Microsoft's and Novell's CA and clients support certificate publishers that use the Lightweight Directory Access Protocol (LDAP).

▶ *Management tools* allow you, as an administrator, to keep track of which certificates were issued, when a given certificate expires, and so on.

PKI-savvy applications allow you and your users to do useful things with certificates, like encrypt e-mail or network connections. Ideally, the user shouldn't have to know (or even necessarily be aware of) what the application is doing—everything should work seamlessly and automatically.

The best-known examples of PKI-savvy applications are web browsers like Internet Explorer and Netscape Navigator and e-mail applications like Outlook and Outlook Express. These components all work together to provide a full set of PKI services.

Got a Question? Ask an Authority

How can you determine whether a certificate is valid or not? The answer lies in the concept of a *certificate hierarchy*. In a hierarchy, as shown in Figure 21.1, each certificate authority signs the certificates it issues using its own private key. Each CA actually has its own certificate, which contains the CA's public key. This CA certificate is itself signed by a higher-level CA. You can stack up any number of CAs in a hierarchy, with each CA certifying the authenticity of the certificates it has issued. Eventually, though, there must be a top-level CA, called a *root certificate authority*. Since there's nobody above the root CA in the hierarchy, there's nobody to vouch for its certificate. Instead, the root CA signs its own certificate, asserting that it is the root.

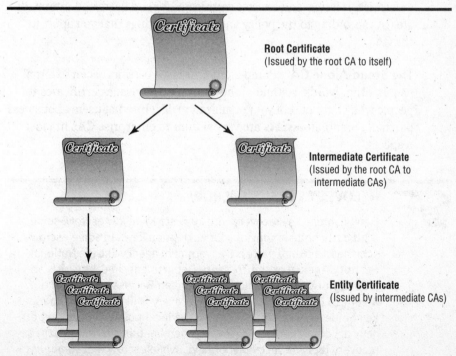

Root Certificate
(Issued by the root CA to itself)

Intermediate Certificate
(Issued by the root CA to intermediate CAs)

Entity Certificate
(Issued by intermediate CAs)

FIGURE 21.1: A simple certificate hierarchy.

The root CA is the CA at the top of the hierarchy; CAs lower in the hierarchy are variously called intermediate or subordinate CAs.

Alternative CA Types

Until now, you've been reading about only one type of CA. However, most PKI systems support two different *types* of CAs, and each type can operate in one of several different *roles*. The difference between types and roles is simple to understand. Cars and trucks are different types of vehicles. A single car or truck can be used in different roles: to carpool, to race, to put up on blocks as a lawn decoration, and so on.

Which type of CA you install determines whom you can issue certificates to and what they can be used for, so it's important to understand the distinctions between them. The only real configuration difference between the two is which set of policies it enforces, but the operational differences between them are important.

The Enterprise CA   The enterprise CA acts as part of the PKI for an enterprise. It issues and revokes certificates for end users and intermediate CAs according to the policy and security settings that you apply to the CA.

The Stand-Alone CA   Stand-alone CAs issue certificates for external use. In other words, a stand-alone CA is made to issue certificates to people who aren't part of your organization, like Internet users or business partners. Stand-alone CAs are very similar to enterprise CAs in most respects.

RECOVERY VERSUS ESCROW

Don't confuse key recovery with key escrow. In key escrow, some third party holds a copy of your encryption keys. In some escrow schemes, this third party is a government agency like the National Security Agency or the Treasury Department; in others, it's an industry organization like the American Bar Association or the American Banking Association. If recovery is like those magnetic key holders, escrow is like giving the local police department a copy of your key. A simple way to remember this difference is that recovery lets *you* recover *your* keys, while escrow lets *someone else* recover *your* keys.

WHAT'S NEXT

In this chapter, you learned the basic nature of a PKI solution. In most small networks, this system is created automatically by the operating system install, with very little intervention by the user. As your network grows, so does the complexity of a PKI system. When you understand the basic concepts, most PKI systems are very similar.

In the next chapter, you will continue to learn about security in a LAN environment using the tools of your NOS to protect your important data.

Chapter 22

FIREWALLS AND YOUR NETWORK

How secure is your network? What is available to secure your network from intrusions? These are some of the questions you face whenever you make that decision to connect your network to the public Internet. This chapter will help you understand the risks faced by different types of network administrators.

This chapter is broken down into two major sections. The first section, "Defining Your Security Requirements," will help you figure out what general type of security your business requires. The second section, "Configuring the Rules," will then explain exactly how to configure your border gateways to achieve that level of security. You may find that you'll read back and forth between the two sections to gain a full understanding of the problem.

Adapted from *Firewalls 24seven,* Second Edition
by Matthew Strebe and Charles Perkins
ISBN 0-7821-4054-8   576 pages $49.99

DEFINING YOUR SECURITY REQUIREMENTS

No two networks have exactly the same security requirements. A bank, for example, is going to be a bit more concerned than a retail clothing store about network intrusions. The type of security concern varies as well as the degree—in a University computing lab the administrator is just as concerned about *hosting* the source of hacking attacks as well as being the target of them.

To decide just how much effort to expend in securing your network, you need to know the value of the data in your network, the publicity or visibility of your organization, and the harm that could be caused by loss of service. You should also consider how much disruption or imposition you can live with on your network in the name of security.

Similar organizations have similar requirements, so you can compare the needs of your network to those organizational types listed below.

Home Offices

A home office is the simplest Internet connected network. Usually, a home office has two to three computers connected in a peer-to-peer fashion on a small LAN. These networks either have a modem attached to each computer so users can connect to the Internet or they have one computer or device that mediates access to the Internet whenever any of the users need an Internet connection. Sometimes the device that connects to the Internet is an inexpensive network hub and NAT router.

The typical home office budget can't afford to dedicate a computer to be a network firewall. Sometimes the Internet service provider is relied upon to keep the hackers out. However, this is not a particularly effective technique because ISPs vary in competence and workload, and they never customize security to fit your needs—they provide only a "one-size-fits-all" solution that is necessarily lax because they don't know how their customers will use the Internet.

Just because most firewalls are prohibitively expensive for home use doesn't mean you are helpless. There are several "mini-firewalls" that are intended to be installed on personal computers directly, as well as popular low-cost NAT routers which provide very strong default security. Small firewall-less networks can still (and should) install current operating system patches to protect the computers from TCP/IP attacks such as Ping of Death and the Out of Band attack. File sharing should be turned off for computers that are connected to the Internet (or, for more advanced operating systems such as Windows NT and Unix, those services should be disconnected from the network adapter or modem that is connected to the Internet). Any unnecessary services should also be turned off so network intruders can't exploit them.

A recent welcome development is the proliferation of devices that include simple stateful packet filters with Network Address Translation and Internet connectivity via dial-up modem or Ethernet connectivity to a cable or DSL modem. These inexpensive devices greatly increase the security of home office networks by hiding the identity of computers on the LAN and by foiling packet-based exploits, but they do not provide the full range of protection provided by full-spectrum firewalls.

The reason home office networks aren't exploited more often is because their network connections are usually intermittent, their connection speed is low so it takes a long time to hack into them, and they seldom provide services (such as websites) that hackers can exploit (with the notable exception of home offices that hook Windows computers directly to the Internet and do not turn off file and printer sharing, or Windows NT/2000 computers that leave IIS activated). Most hackers exploit random targets of opportunity, so a computer that spends most of its time detached from the Internet isn't going to make a very juicy target. The biggest threat to the home office network is from someone who knows about the network and has a specific reason to attack it. Disgruntled or former employees, business competitors, or an individual with a personal axe to grind are the most likely culprits.

Cable modem and DSL users have become a favored target of hackers, however, because their connection speeds are high, their connections are always on, they often have no security in place, and their computers are left in the default installation state without security patches applied.

The best way to permanently connect a home office telecommuter to a corporate network is to use a small firewall built to do exactly that, like the SonicWALL SOHO. These firewalls are complete, real firewalls that include IPSec and can be remotely managed through the VPN by the corporate IT staff. In this configuration, the home office is just like any other branch office—connected through a VPN to a firewall with a single public IP address and configured to perform Network Address Translation so the connection can be shared by a few computers. Unfortunately, these devices run about $500 each, so they're not particularly cost effective for many users.

The next best way is to use a small NAT device that can pass a single IPSec connection, like the Linksys Cable/DSL Router with IPSec pass-through. In this configuration, the device doesn't come with IPSec, but it will allow a single computer with an IPSec client to establish connections and route through it. It provides the inherent firewalling provided by all NAT devices and can be used to share a single Internet connection amongst multiple users. Neither your ISP nor the corporate IT group will see anything other than the single IP address of the NAT device, from which all connections including the IPSec connection will appear to come. This configuration is not really remotely manageable by the IT staff without potentially creating security problems, so it's most effective for users with some technical skill. This method will also work with proprietary VPN solutions like PPTP, L2TP, etc. as long as the NAT device can properly translate the protocol. This solution would cost about $150, including the price of the hardware NAT device and the license for the IPSec software client.

Small Service Businesses

Small service business networks, with a typical computer count of around a dozen or so, often have a dedicated computer for file and print services and, in many cases, a dedicated connection to the Internet. Although few small service businesses actually have firewalls, they all should. The potential loss of data and business productivity due to a network intrusion more than justifies the cost of one extra computer and some software.

You don't want to go overboard with security in a small service business, however, and very few small service businesses will go to great lengths to bulletproof their networks because a cost/benefit analysis will usually show that less stringent security is sufficient. Consider, for example, a heating and air-conditioning company that has a small network with an Internet connection. The company's computers have little that would interest either a random hacker or a rival company that might engage in industrial espionage. The network users want as few restrictions as possible on how they access the Internet, so it is difficult to justify draconian network policies.

TIP

The small service business network administrator should be concerned about security, but the appropriate policy for the firewall is to permit by default, and to specifically deny packets, protocols, and services on the firewall that the administrator judges to be dangerous.

Professional Firms

Like the small service business, a small confidential practice such as a law firm, accounting firm, psychiatry practice, or medical specialist may have a half dozen to a dozen or more computers connected in a LAN with an intermittent or permanent Internet connection. The small confidential practice should have a more stringent security requirement than the typical small business, however, because the practice's computers contain confidential information that invites specific and targeted attack from network intruders over the Internet.

TIP

Because of the sensitivity of the information and the attraction this type of network presents to hackers, the network administrator of a small confidential practice should be cautious (denying packets, protocols, and ports by default unless the rules established specifically allow them) or strict (not routing IP packets at all and allowing only proxied network traffic through the firewall) about security.

Manufacturers

A large network with 50 to 100 computers is a much more tempting target to the average hacker, especially if the network has expensive network equipment and VPN links to other large computer networks. This is the type of network used by medium-to-large corporations, and the very size and complexity of corporate networks make them easier for hackers to attack.

Large corporate networks also may be subject to specific targeted attacks for the purposes of industrial espionage or anticompetitive denial of service. Since corporations have more employees (and former employees) than smaller businesses do, the corporations are also much more likely to come under attack from insiders or former insiders.

A corporation with a lot of public visibility (such as Sony, Microsoft, Pepsi, or Disney) also has the problem of hackers trying to penetrate their networks for the greater bragging rights than would be achieved by hacking other, less well-known companies (such as McMaster-Carr or Solar Turbines).

TIP

Network administrators of large corporate networks need to take extra care that their networks are not compromised because the potential cost of lost productivity is proportionately greater in the larger networks than it is in small ones, and because the large corporate network makes a much more tempting target for hackers. A cautious (deny routing by default) or strict (no routing at all) policy is most appropriate for these kinds of networks.

Government Bureaus

The networks used by governmental bureaus have all of the characteristics of corporate networks (they are often large, have interesting hardware, and provide links to other networks), but governmental networks are also tempting targets because of their political nature. The Bureau of Reclamation has little to worry about, but the FBI, on the other hand, is under almost constant siege from the very hackers they chase. As a general rule, the more visible the organization, the more likely it is to attract the ire of a hacker with an agenda.

TIP

Network administrators of governmental bureaus should be either strict (allowing no routing) or paranoid (minimizing any sort of Internet risk, regardless of the constraints that places on their own network use), depending on the visibility and sensitivity of the organization. Special care should be taken to secure websites in order to deny hackers an easy way to embarrass the bureau and to advertise their own causes.

Universities or Colleges

University network administrators have the vexing problem of having to defend their systems from internal attacks as well as external ones. The periodic influx of new students ensures a fresh crop of hackers who will always be pushing at the security boundaries of the network. The students must have computers and access to the Internet, but the administrative staff of the school also needs a secure work environment.

Most schools cope with this problem by having two (or more) separate networks, each with a different security policy and with carefully controlled access between the networks. The public access student network typically has a severely restrictive policy and is frequently checked for viruses, Trojan horses, modified system settings, and so on.

TIP

The university or college network administrator usually takes a cautious (deny by default) or a strict (proxy only, no routing) approach to managing the school's administrative networks. The network administrator also takes a fairly open approach to managing the students' network, while taking special care to keep the networks separate and while keeping a close eye on the state of the student network.

Internet Service Providers

The ISP network administrator has a problem similar to that of the university network administrator. The ISP network administrator must keep hackers from the Internet at bay and internal hackers contained, for the customers of the ISP expect to be protected from each other as well as from the outside. In addition, customers expect to have full Internet access—they want to decide for themselves which protocols and services to use.

TIP

Most ISPs use a firewall to protect their network service computers (DNS server, mail server, and so on) in a cautious or strict configuration and use a packet filter in a more liberal configuration (permission by default) to stop the most obvious Internet attacks (Ping of Death, source-routed packets, malformed IP and ICMP packets, etc.) from reaching their clients. At the client's request, many ISPs will apply more strict security policies to the client connection on a per-client basis.

Online Commerce Companies

For most companies, the Internet connection is a convenience. For online commerce companies, the reliable operation of the connection and the services that flow over it are the lifeblood of the company. A used bookstore that accepts inquiries for titles over the Internet can afford for its website to be down every once in a while, but an online bookstore that transacts all of its business over the Internet cannot.

In addition to preventing denial-of-service attacks, the administrator of an online commerce network must be aware of a more dire threat—the theft of customer information, including financial transaction data (especially credit card numbers). Consumers expect that the data they provide to your online company will remain confidential, and there may be severe public relations problems if the data gets out, as well as legal repercussions if the company is found negligent in its security precautions.

An online commerce company often has two networks to protect—the internal network used by company employees and another network, perhaps located on the company premises or maybe located at an ISP, that provides the company's online interface to its Internet customers. Each network will have separate security policies; in fact, the online interface must be protected from unauthorized access from the interior network, and vice versa.

TIP

Because of the severe repercussions of both denial-of-service and data-theft attacks, the smart network administrator for an online commerce company will implement a strict (proxy only, no routing) firewall policy for the company's Internet servers. The administrator may establish a more permissive (cautious or concerned) policy for a separate administrative network if the staff needs freer Internet access for business activities that are not business critical.

Financial Institutions

As a general rule, if there is money or there are things worth money flowing over the network, the administrator is going to be particularly careful about who can access the network and how they go about it. The more money there is, the stricter the rules for access will be. Therefore, banks and credit unions never allow any direct Internet access to their financial networks (the ones that directly convey money from one account to another) or even to the administrative networks that bank officials use to perform more mundane tasks.

A growing trend in financial institutions is to allow customers to perform online banking through their web browsers over the Internet. This, of course, means that a web server of some sort must be linked both to the Internet and to the protected financial computers. If you work for a financial institution, you should be sure that every possible measure is taken to secure that web server and protect the customers' account information.

TIP

Those banking systems that allow any sort of Internet access implement strict (proxy access only) or paranoid (custom crafted with special purpose network software) policies to protect their computers.

Hospitals

In a hospital network, unlike all the previous types of networks, people can die if the computers stop working. For this reason, the patient care hospital networks that have medical equipment attached to them are seldom connected to the Internet in any form. Administrative networks may be connected, but those links are carefully secured because of the risk of divulging or destroying confidential patient data. The networks in research labs, however, are typically closely and permissively attached to the network because scientists work best in an open environment where information exchange is made easy.

TIP

Like those of banks and universities, the hospital network administrator breaks his networks into several mutually untrusting sections. Life-critical equipment simply is not connected to the Internet. A strict policy is adopted for administrative computers (they still need e-mail, after all), while research LANs have a cautious or concerned policy.

Military Organizations

Military networks, like hospital networks, can have terminal repercussions when security is penetrated. Like governmental bureaus, hackers or espionage agents often have a specific target or axe to grind with the military. But not all military networks are the same—the civilian contractors managing a contract to purchase, warehouse, and distribute machine tools will have a different set of security requirements than the Navy war college's academic network, and neither of those will be designed with anywhere near the level of paranoia that goes into constructing the real-time battle information systems that soldiers use to wage war.

TIP

The administrator of a military network must match the firewall policy of the LAN to the type of work performed on it. Classified and administrative networks will have at least a cautious (default deny) or strict (proxy only, no routing) policy, while Secret and above information systems will be divorced from the Internet entirely.

Intelligence Agencies

Some organizations have the dual goals of safeguarding their own networks while simultaneously finding ways to circumvent the walls keeping them out of other people's networks. You can be sure that the professional agents in these organizations have a dossier on and an action plan to exploit every operating system bug or protocol weakness there is. But knowing about a hole and plugging it are two different issues, and sometimes the hackers can steal a march on the spooks.

In an odd turn of fate, the NSA has in fact taken the Linux source code, tightened up security in areas they find important, and released the code back to the free software community. This has given hackers and open-source advocates a bit of indigestion—do you trust it because it is open and you can check the source code, or do you mistrust it because of its source?

TIP

It is a good bet that the administrators of these kinds of networks go one step beyond implementation of a strict firewall security—I would be very surprised if these secrecy professionals used any commercial software to firewall their networks. The truly paranoid will only trust software that they personally examine for back doors and weaknesses compiled with similarly inspected software tools.

CONFIGURING THE RULES

Once you've determined the degree of paranoia that is justified for your network (or networks if you manage more than one), you can set up the firewalling rules that keep the hackers out. Every firewall allows you to establish a set of rules that will specify what trans-firewall traffic will be allowed and what will not, as well as to establish and manipulate these rules.

In the remainder of this chapter, you'll learn about these rules generically and how you should establish them so that your firewall won't have any obvious and easily avoidable weaknesses. You'll also learn about the care and feeding of a running firewall and what you can do when you discover it has come under attack.

Rules about Rules

Every firewall worth its weight in foam packing peanuts will have a number of features or characteristics of rules in common. You need to understand these rules and features because they form the building blocks of the logic that will either keep the hackers out or let them in.

Apply in Order

When deciding whether or not to allow a packet to pass the firewall, well-constructed firewall software will start with the first rule in its rule set and proceed toward the last until the packet is either explicitly allowed, explicitly disallowed, or reaches the end of the rules (whereupon the packet is allowed or dropped by default). The rules must always be evaluated in the same order to avoid ambiguity about which rule takes precedence.

Some strong firewalls take a "best rule fitting the problem" approach rather than an ordered rule set approach. While this may in fact provide stronger security, it can be very difficult for an administrator to determine which rule will be applied in a specific circumstance.

Per Interface

Firewall software should be able to discriminate between packets by the interface they arrive on and interface they will leave from. This is essential because the firewall can't really trust the source and destination addresses in the packets themselves; those values are easily forged. A packet arriving on an external interface that says it is from inside your network is an obvious flag that something fishy is going on.

Per Type of Packet (TCP, UDP, ICMP)

Your firewall must be able to filter based on packet type because some are essential to network operation, while other types are just recipes for trouble. For example, you will want to allow ICMP echo reply packets to pass into your network from the outside (so your client computers can verify connectivity to outside hosts), but you may not want to pass ICMP echo request packets in to those same clients. After all, there's no sense letting hackers build a list of potential targets on your LAN. Some protocols use UDP on a particular port while others use TCP, and you don't want to let UDP traffic through on a port that has been opened for TCP or vice versa.

Per Source and Destination Addresses

Your firewall must classify traffic according to where it comes from and where it is going. You may want to allow external computers to establish connections to publicly accessible internal or DMZ web and FTP servers, but not to establish connections to internal client computers. You probably want to allow internal clients to establish connections going the other way, however. Your firewall should be able to permanently block troublesome hosts and networks from performing any access at all, and should be able to deny all access to sensitive computers inside your network that don't need Internet connectivity.

Per Source and Destination Ports

Similarly, you will want to control TCP and UDP packets according to which ports they're coming from and going to. You should allow external users to connect from any port on their own computers to just those internal ports that are used by externally visible services (such as HTTP and FTP). Don't allow external users to connect to just any port on internal computers, because Trojan horses such as Back Orifice work by opening up a port above 1023 (most operating systems restrict user programs from opening ports below this value) for hackers to connect to. However, users inside your network need to be able to initiate connections using source ports greater than 1023 with the destination port of any common TCP protocol ports (such as HTTP, FTP, Telnet, and POP). You might want to limit your users to just a few destination ports, or you may allow connections to arbitrary external ports.

Per Options

Originating hosts and routers can set a variety of options in the header of IP packets. Some options are notorious for being used to circumvent security, with source routing as the most abused of all the options. Most firewalls simply drop source-routed packets. Because none of the IP options are required for normal Internet traffic, strong firewalls simply drop any packets that have options set.

Per ICMP Message Type

As mentioned above, some ICMP packets are required for the Internet to cope with network problems. But many ICMP packets (sometimes the same essential packets) can also be used in unconventional ways to crash computers on your network. The firewall must be able to determine, based on the message type and how it is used, whether or not that ICMP packet is safe to pass.

Per ACK Bit for TCP

The firewall must be able to tell the difference between a packet that is requesting a connection and one that is merely sending or replying over an already established connection. The difference between these two types of packets is just one bit—the ACK bit. Packets requesting a connection have it cleared; all others have it set. You will use this rule characteristic most often with the source and destination characteristics to allow connections to only those ports you specify and in only the direction you allow.

Protocol Specific Proxying Rules

For strong security, packet-filtering rules aren't secure enough. The above packet rules only concern themselves with the header of IP or ICMP packets; the data payload is not inspected. Packet rules won't keep viruses out of e-mail nor will they hide the existence of internal computers. Proxies provide greater security but also limit any ICMP, IP, TCP, or UDP level attacks to the gateway machine. Proxies also ensure that the data flowing through the firewall actually conforms to the format specified by the protocols that the firewall is proxying for those ports.

Logging

A good firewall will not only block hazardous network traffic but will also tell you when it is doing so, both with alerts and with messages written to a log file. You should be able to log (at your discretion) every packet dropped or passed through the firewall. These logs should be able to grow large enough to track activity over days or weeks, but the logs should never be allowed to grow so large that they fill all of the firewall's hard drive space and crash the computer.

The alert mechanism should not only pop up windows on the firewall's console but also send e-mail to an arbitrary address (such as your pager e-mail gateway, if you are really serious about responding quickly to network attacks and you don't mind those occasional midnight false alarms).

Graphical User Interface

While not necessary for firewall security or performance, a graphical user interface for manipulating rule sets makes it much easier to set up and configure firewalls.

Rules for Security Levels

We've divided the spectrum of security into five levels that will be a good fit for most organizations. Using the first half of this chapter, you should be able to identify which of these levels applies most closely to your organization. Once you've matched your organization to one of the following security levels, you can use the rules we lay out as a starting point for your firewall policy. The general levels are as follows:

- ▶ Aware
- ▶ Concerned
- ▶ Cautious
- ▶ Strict
- ▶ Paranoid

For each security level we'll explore the rules, restrictions, and procedures that a network administrator will enact to provide that level of security in the network.

Aware

There are some things every security network administrator should do regardless of the degree of security warranted by the network contents or the type of organization the network serves. These actions and prescriptions plug obvious security holes and have no adverse effect on Internet accessibility. The security aware administrator should:

▶ Install the latest operating system patches on both the client and server computers in the network.

▶ Keep network user accounts off of Internet service computers such as web servers, FTP servers, and firewalls, and have separate administrative accounts with different passwords for these machines.

▶ Regularly scan the system logs for failed logon attempts to network services and failed connection attempts to web servers, FTP servers, etc.

▶ Regularly scan system user accounts for the unauthorized addition or modification of user accounts for network services.

▶ Disable all unnecessary services on network and Internet servers.

▶ Use virus scanners on your server (at least).

▶ Perform regular backups.

Concerned

A network administrator who is concerned about security will at least install a packet filter and take the above "security aware" steps. The packet filter will not stop a concentrated network attack from exploiting service protocol weaknesses, but it will stop the simplest denial-of-service attacks—those based on malformed or maliciously configured ICMP or IP packets.

A packet filter in its most lax configuration allows packets to pass by default unless a rule specifically tells the filter to drop them. Proxy servers may be used to enhance network services (by caching HTML pages, for example) but provide no extra security because network clients can easily bypass them. The packet filter can also lock out troublesome external IP addresses and subnets, as well as deny external access from the outside to specific internal computers such as file and database servers.

Packet Rules (Filtering)

The packet rules control the flow of several different kinds of packets through the filter or firewall. They are as follows:

- ▷ ICMP Rules
- ▶ IP Rules
- ▶ UDP Rules
- ▶ TCP Rules

ICMP   ICMP controls the flow of IP packets through the Internet. IP is therefore essential to the correct operation of the Internet, but ICMP packets can be forged to trick your computers into redirecting their communications, stopping all communication, or even crashing. The following rules (see Table 22.1) protect your LAN from many ICMP attacks.

Note that while we assume that the concerned (but not cautious) administrator allows packets to pass the firewall by default, the above rules work both for permit-by-default and deny-by-default configurations. Rules are (or should be) evaluated in order from first to last, and if an ICMP packet is not specifically allowed or denied in Rules 1–13, Rule 14 will cause it to be dropped. A short description of each rule follows.

1. Allow source quench: You want external hosts to be able to tell your client computers when the network is saturated.

2. Allow echo request outbound: You want your clients to be able to ping external computers to verify connectivity.

3. Allow echo reply inbound: You want your clients to be able to hear the reply of pinged hosts.

TABLE 22.1: ICMP Service Rules

Rule	In Interface	Out Interface	Src IP	Src Port	Dest IP	Dest Port	Opt	Ack	Type	ICMP Type	Act
1	*	*	*	*	*	*	*	*	ICMP	Source Quench	Pass
2	*	Ext	*	*	*	*	*	*	ICMP	Echo Request	Pass
3	Ext	*	*	*	*	*	*	*	ICMP	Echo Reply	Pass
4	*	Ext	*	*	*	*	*	*	ICMP	Destination Unreachable	Pass
5	Ext	*	*	*	*	*	*	*	ICMP	Service Unavailable	Pass
6	Ext	*	*	*	*	*	*	*	ICMP	TTL Exceeded	Pass
7	Ext	*	*	*	*	*	*	*	ICMP	Parameter Problem	Pass
8	*	Int	*	*	*	*	*	*	ICMP	Echo Request	Drop
9	Ext	*	*	*	*	*	*	*	ICMP	Redirect	Drop
10	Int	*	*	*	*	*	*	*	ICMP	Echo Reply	Drop
11	Ext	*	*	*	*	*	*	*	ICMP	Destination Unreachable	Drop
12	Ext	*	*	*	*	*	*	*	ICMP	Service Unavailable	Drop
13	Ext	*	*	*	*	*	*	*	ICMP	TTL Exceeded	Drop
14	*	*	*	*	*	*	*	*	ICMP	*	Drop

Part V

4. Allow destination unreachable inbound: These packets inform your clients that an exterior resource is not available.

5. Allow service unavailable inbound: These packets inform your clients that an exterior resource is not available.

6. Allow TTL exceeded inbound: These packets inform your clients that an exterior resource is too far away.

7. Allow parameter problem: These packets inform your clients that they are not sending correctly formatted packets.

8. Drop echo request inbound: Echo request ("ping") packets can be used to survey your internal network for computers to attack. Malformed ping packets are also often sent in an attempt to crash computers.

9. Drop redirect inbound (log it instead): You don't want external agents to be able to mess with your internal computers' routing tables without your supervision.

10. Drop echo reply outbound: Why make it easy for hackers to find computers to attack?

11. Drop destination unreachable outbound: You should protect the identity of interior networks just as you would the identity of individual interior hosts.

12. Drop service unavailable outbound: It is not a good idea to advertise to network attackers what services are available inside your network.

13. Drop TTL exceeded outbound: Hackers can determine the number of hops or LAN boundaries that exist inside your network by trying different TTL values.

14. Drop all other ICMP packets: Just to be safe. The ICMP packets you have specifically allowed should be sufficient.

IP   There are some rules that you will want to configure for all IP packets regardless of whether they contain TCP or UDP traffic inside them.

See Table 22.2 for an overview of the rules, then read further for an explanation of each.

These rules govern the general flow of IP traffic in and out of your network. If you want to forbid certain computers or networks from accessing your computers, you would place a rule there, as in rule 20.

15. Drop all source-routed packets: Nobody redirects packets around damaged connections anymore, they just fix the broken equipment. A source-routed packet is a red flag indicating a network intrusion attempt.

16. Drop all packets arriving on the external interface that have a source field indicating that the packet came from inside your network: If the packet claims it originated from inside your network, it should only come from the internal interface.

17. Drop all packets arriving on the internal interface that have a source field indicating that the packet came from outside your network: As in Rule 16, this behavior is an indicator that there's something fishy going on, and you're safest if you just drop the packet and log the event.

18. Drop incoming packets to interior computers that have no externally accessible services (file server, etc.): People outside your network have no business connecting to your LAN file server unless they do it through secure encrypted tunnels that you specifically set up for them.

19. Drop RIP, OSPF, and other router information exchange protocols: You don't need external agents reconfiguring your routers for you.

20. Drop packets from a specific host: This is where you put rules banning hosts and networks that have been bugging you.

21. Drop packets going both to and from internal addresses: These packets shouldn't be on the router in the first place. If they are, it's because some sort of hacking attempt is occurring.

UDP Once you have set rules for generic IP traffic, you will want to further specify some UDP rules to block egregious security holes, such as X-Windows, as shown in Table 22.3.

TABLE 22.2: IP Service Rules

Rule	In Interface	Out Interface	Src IP	Src Port	Dest IP	Dest Port	Opt	Ack	Type	ICMP Type	Act
15	*	*	*	*	*	*	Source Route	*	*	*	Drop
16	Ext	*	Internal	*	*	*	*	*	*	*	Drop
17	Int	*	*	*	Internal	*	*	*	*	*	Drop
18	Ext	*	*	*	Protected Servers	*	*	*	*	*	Drop
19	Ext	*	*	*	*	RIP, OSPF	*	*	*	*	Drop
20	*	*	192.168 .0.1	*	*	*	*	*	*	*	Drop
21	*	*	Internal	*	Internal	*	*	*	*	*	Drop

TABLE 22.3: UDP Service Rules

Rule	In Interface	Out Interface	Src IP	Src Port	Dest IP	Dest Port	Opt	Ack	Type	ICMP Type	Act
22	*	*	*	*	*	0–20	*	*	UDP	*	Drop
23	*	*	*	*	*	6000–6003	*	*	UDP	*	Drop
24	*	*	*	*	*	161–162	*	*	UDP	*	Drop

NOTE

By default, the concerned-but-not-cautious administrator allows packets to pass through the firewall, unless a rule specifically denies that kind of packet.

Each rule specifically denies a port or a range of ports (some firewalls require you to repeat the rule for each port specifically disallowed).

22. Drop packets using ports below 21: There are no services below port 21 that your average Internet user will find helpful.

23. Drop X-Windows (packets using ports 6000-6003): You don't want a hacker gaining control of your mouse and keyboard, do you?

24. Drop SNMP (packets using ports 161 and 162): You don't want network intruders to reconfigure your hubs and routers using this protocol either.

TCP The TCP rules you create are like the UDP rules with one difference—you can use the ACK bit of a packet to stop connections from being initiated from one direction or the other. Blocking inbound packets with the ACK bit cleared (C) for a particular port allows only outbound connections to be initiated, but allows subsequent data traffic for that connection—all of which will have the ACK bit set (S). See Table 22.4 for a typical set of TCP rules.

You'll note that some of the TCP ports here are the same as the UDP ports listed in the previous section—some protocols operate over UDP as well as TCP.

25. Drop packets using ports below 20: There are no services below port 20 that your average Internet user will find helpful.

26. Drop X-Windows (packets using ports 6000–6003): You don't want a hacker gaining control of your mouse and keyboard, do you?

27. Drop SNMP (packets using ports 161 and 162): You don't want network intruders to reconfigure your hubs and routers using this protocol either.

Part V

TABLE 22.4: TCP Service Rules

Rules	In Interface	Out Interface	Src IP	Src Port	Dest IP	Dest Port	Opt	ACK	Type	ICMP Type	Act
25	*	*	*	*	*	0–20	*	*	TCP	*	Drop
26	*	*	*	*	*	6000–6003	*	*	TCP	*	Drop
27	*	*	*	*	*	161–162	*	*	TCP	*	Drop
28	Ext	*	*	*	*	23	*	*	TCP	*	Drop
29	Ext	*	*	*	*	8080	*	*	TCP	*	Pass
30	Ext	*	*	*	*	>1023	*	C	TCP	*	Drop
31	Ext	*	*	*	*	20–21	*	C	TCP	*	Drop
32	Ext	*	*	*	Not SMTP Server	25	*	*	TCP	*	Drop
33	Ext	*	*	*	Not Web Server	80	*	*	TCP	*	Drop

28. Disallow incoming Telnet connections (incoming packets with destination port 23): Telnet is an insecure protocol because the account name and password exchange are not encrypted and neither is the data channel once a Telnet session is established. If you need secure exterior console access on Unix systems, use SSH (port 22) instead.

29. Specifically allow any internal services that use ports greater than 1023: This way you can use the next rule to stop back door software such as Back Orifice, which opens ports internally for remote unauthorized control of your computers. In the rule base above, we've shown an example of allowing external traffic to a web server running on port 8080. Your custom rules will vary depending upon your needs.

30. Drop SYN packets from outside to internal ports >1023: Most legitimate services are configured on ports <1024, so this rule stops connection requests to ports higher than 1023. Rule 28 and others like it (which must be placed before this rule) specifically allow any exceptions.

31. Disallow incoming FTP data connections thus allowing passive FTP only.

32. Disallow SMTP connections (port 25) from the outside to other than your mail server.

33. Establish service destination rules for other services such as HTTP.

Cautious

Most network administrators feel that the aforementioned rules are not enough; a dedicated hacker with time and resources can find a way around these rules. A cautious network administrator will take a more conservative track and block all traffic by default, only allowing the traffic that seems safe after careful consideration. This approach takes much more time and effort to set up correctly, but the result is a much more secure firewall.

Network Address Translation   One feature that cautious administrators really like is Network Address Translation, or NAT. This nifty feature allows you to expose just a handful (or even one) of IP addresses to the outside world, while it hides a whole LAN of tens, hundreds, or even thousands of computers behind it. To the computers on your LAN there is little difference between existing on a NAT hidden LAN and being directly connected to the Internet. The firewall keeps track of connections and rewrites packet source and destination and port values on the fly.

Fragmentation   A cautious network administrator won't allow fragmented packets into the network. Until recently, fragmented packets were considered safe because it was understood that only the first fragment of a fragmented packet needed to be examined and dropped if necessary. Any subsequent packet fragments would be dropped by the destination computers because they lacked an initial packet with the header information.

Because of a bug discovered in common TCP/IP protocol implementations (including that of Windows NT), that is no longer the case. The bug (since fixed) ignored improper fragment offset values, which allowed the second (or later) fragment to occupy the memory location of the first fragment and to provide the header information the network stack was looking for (header information that had not been checked by the firewall). Although the bug has been fixed, most cautious network administrators choose to reassemble fragmented packets at the firewall or just drop them since the fragmentation feature is largely obsolete.

ICMP, TCP, and UDP   Some of the packet rules listed in the previous sections become redundant when the cautious administrator denies all packets by default. You may want to leave them in your rule set so you can switch from deny-by-default to allow-by-default and back again when you are diagnosing network connectivity problems.

One rule that is not listed here (because it is denied by default) is that you shouldn't allow Telnet connections (connections to port 23) to travel through your firewall at all. Use the Secure Shell (SSH) instead because it provides much greater security for a remote terminal. In addition, we don't explicitly list the rule you should block access out to ports above 1023 because the commonly accessed services live below 1023. See Table 22.5 for a few additional rules that the cautious administrator will want to configure in the firewall.

34. Allow outgoing SMTP connections (port 25) from your mail server.

35. Allow NNTP from your news server to external news server (Port 119).

TABLE 22.5: The Additional Rules of a Cautious Administrator

Rules	In Interface	Out Interface	Src IP	Src Port	Dest IP	Dest Port	Opt	ACK	Type	ICMP Type	Act
34	*	*	SMTP Server	*	*	25	*	*	TCP	*	Pass
35	*	*	NNTP Server	*	Ext NNTP Server	119	*	*	TCP	*	Pass
36	*	*	Ext. NNTP Server	119	NNTP Server	*	*	*	TCP	*	Pass
37	Int	*	*	>1023	*	80	*	*	TCP	*	Pass
38	Ext	*	*	80	*	>1023	*	S	TCP	*	Pass

36. Allow NNTP from external news server to internal news server (Port 119).

37. Allow clients to establish HTTP connections (source port >1023 destination port 80).

38. Allow data traffic from an already established HTTP connection to travel back from port 80 on the Internet to the client port (>1023) on your LAN. It is usually not necessary to specify return channel rules on modern stateful firewalls.

You can repeat Rules 36 and 37 for any additional Internet services that you want internal clients to be able to connect to.

Service Rules (Proxying)

General rule: Disallow proxy requests from the Internet by filtering out packets with the ACK bit cleared that connect to your proxy from the external interface. This prevents hackers from connecting to your proxy server and using it to launder their connections.

Proxy DNS using a DNS server or a proxy server that supports DNS proxy transparently, but disallow zone transfers. You don't want anyone outside your network reconfiguring your network names.

Use SOCKS to proxy stream-oriented (circuit level) TCP and UDP going out of your network for protocols you intend to allow that do not have specific security proxy software.

Proxy SMTP by having your mail servers write e-mail messages to disk and having another mail process read and forward those messages inside the network. This prevents any single process from being compromised, which would allow a connection all the way through the machine. It also guarantees that any malformed e-mail will either crash the inbound process and be dropped or will be completely regenerated by the forwarding process without the deformity. This prevents buffer overrun conditions on mail servers inside your network.

Proxy NNTP by establishing an NNTP server in your demilitarized zone (DMZ). Inbound NNTP should be forwarded only to that machine, and internal newsreaders should only be able to read news at that machine. This prevents Trojan horses or other non-NNTP traffic from exploiting the open NNTP port on the packet filter.

Proxy FTP using a dedicated FTP proxy application in the firewall. FTP service filters on stateful firewalls may also be used as long as they are specific to the FTP protocol.

Proxy HTTP through a secure HTTP proxy. Your HTTP proxy should be capable of virus checking and stripping executable content.

Disable SOCKS proxies because of the wide protocol access SOCKS allow.

Do not provide POP access at your exterior border gateway. Your SMTP servers should be inside your DMZ. For remote users, force the establishment of an encrypted tunnel for mail access. This prevents e-mail from being exposed in an unencrypted form on the Internet. Internal users who wish to access their private POP accounts should use one of the many free gateway services available on the Internet so they can use their web browser to check their private e-mail.

Do not provide a Telnet proxy. Telnet is far too insecure to allow public access through your gateway.

Strict

The basic strategy for strict control is to completely disallow Network-layer routing between the public and private networks. Strict policies use only Application layer proxies (and not many of them) to provide only the most useful Internet services. Stateful packet filters should be used to protect the application proxies on the bastion host, which should perform no packet routing.

The bastion host may perform Network Address Translation to make itself "invisible" to internal hosts so that client applications don't have to be explicitly set to use a proxy. In this mode, the proxy host looks like a router to internal hosts; it receives all traffic as if it were going to forward it directly onto the public network. That traffic is redirected to proxy applications on the bastion host instead of being routed, so the connections are in fact regenerated to eliminate any undetected deformities. This mode also makes it easy to proxy difficult protocols like FTP and H.323.

Packet Rules (Filtering)

No routing should exist between the external public and internal private interfaces of the bastion host. The same ICMP and IP rules described for the previous section should be applied to protect the bastion host from denial-of-service attacks.

Service Rules (Proxying)

The basic strategy behind strict security is to proxy only the most useful protocols: HTTP and SMTP. These two protocols, which are easy to control and keep track of, allow most of the functionality of the Internet to be utilized. Your attack risk increases linearly with the number of special cases you define on your bastion host. So, the policy here is to limit to the utmost practical degree.

Proxy DNS using a DNS server, but disallow zone transfers. You don't want anyone outside your network reconfiguring your network names. Make sure your DNS proxy does not publish internal names.

Proxy HTTP through a secure HTTP proxy, like NAI Gauntlet. Strip all executable content including EXE, ActiveX, and Java applets. Consider putting a client in the DMZ where these restrictions don't apply if you need to download executable attachments or visit a site that requires Java or ActiveX.

Proxy SMTP by having your mail servers write e-mail messages to disk and another mail process read and forward those messages inside the network. Configure your mail server to strip all executable attachments and perform virus checking on ZIP compressed and office documents. The only allowable method to transfer executable content through the firewall should be in a non-executable form like BIN-HEX or a compressed format. This prevents users from clicking on Trojan horse attachments and executing them. The extra level of indirection ensures that they will at least manually inspect the files before running them.

Paranoid

The strategy for paranoid installations is to either not connect to the Internet or connect a separate "Internet only" network to the Internet. The U.S. government does both to protect its classified networks from the Internet: they are completely disconnected, and a separate pool of "disposable" machines are available for users to work on the Internet. You should simply use a pool of dedicated Internet machines behind a standard stateful inspection filter.

Packet Rules (Filtering)

Allow no direct routing between the public and private networks.

Service Rules (Proxying)

Allow no proxying between the public and private networks.

CASE STUDY: ALL THE KING'S FIREWALLS

As we wrote this chapter, we agonized over what case study to include: what could we talk about that would justify the "paranoid" strategy? Reality intruded on our behalf. While this chapter was being written, the Code Red (cross platform!) buffer-overrun worm appeared and passed unscathed through even the most rigorous firewalls in the world, wreaking havoc and causing uncountable millions of dollars in damages.

Worms are malicious programs that exhibit characteristics of both Trojan horses and viruses. In fact, the Nimda virus, another recent Internet plague, was both a worm and a Trojan horse that propagated using the methods of a virus that required user activation. An e-mail worm typically works like this:

An e-mail message appears in the victim's inbox containing the message text "I received your e-mail and shall send you a reply ASAP. Till then, take a look at the attached zip docs." The sender's address is the valid address of a close friend or co-worker. The attached executable file is called `zipped_files.exe`.

Upon clicking the attachment, the Trojan horse functionality is activated. The worm creates e-mail messages to everyone in the user's personal address book, thus propagating itself to all of them and appearing to come from the activating user. The worm also rifles through the shared directory structure on the computer and propagates itself to other machines on the local network.

The worm then goes on a rampage, destroying programming code, office documents, and other useful work-related materials, as well as modifying system files on the computers.

Because the virus is attached to e-mail and transmitted by the users who have privileged access through the firewall, it passes through even the strongest firewalls unmolested. Only those organizations whose administrators have insisted on stripping executable attachments from e-mail are safe.

The only way to truly protect an organization from Internet-based attacks is not to connect to the Internet. Using the paranoid model discussed above is protection against even the most devious schemes.

WHAT'S NEXT

In this chapter, we showed you how to identify the general type of security your business requires and to evaluate and determine the value of your network's data. We defined security requirements and discussed configuring your border gateways and firewalls to maintain the appropriate level of security.

In Chapter 23, we'll take a closer look at securing your network, specifically your NetWare 6 network.

Chapter 23

SECURING YOUR NETWARE 6 NETWORK

Security—what does it mean to you? Hackers sneaking in and deleting entire volumes? Illegal software on the system? What does security mean to your boss? Inventory asset tags on all the computers, so you know the location of every piece of hardware? Competitors tapping into your system and stealing the plans for the rollout of your new product line?

Security, like much of life, is a desirable abstract state sought through the use of material items. No two people think of the same thing when they hear the word *security*. Regardless of the situation, some people never feel secure. Other people may feel content and secure when actually their systems are vulnerable. The trick is to develop a sense of appropriate paranoia, without becoming obsessed.

In this chapter, we'll cover planning for security, filesystem and NDS security issues, managing security with ConsoleOne, virus protection, and security improvements in NetWare 6.

• •

Adapted from *Mastering NetWare 6* by James Gaskin
ISBN 0-7821-4023-8   864 pages $69.99

PLANNING SECURITY

Each company must make a decision about what security means and about the amount of effort that it will expend to reach a comfortable level of security. Securing your network, including all the physical and virtual items, will be expensive. This brings up another management decision point: how much security is enough?

Security: A Definition

How about a definition: "Security is an aspect of networking administration concerned with ensuring that the data, circuits, and equipment on a network are used only by authorized users and in authorized ways." This comes from the *Complete Encyclopedia of Networking* by Werner Feibel, published by Sybex (the folks who bring you this book).

Notice the order of items to be secured: data, circuits, equipment. Management often focuses security measures on physical items, such as computer hardware and telephone connections and modems. But if a computer is stolen, all that's necessary to replace that computer is money. Circuits must be protected from tampering and eavesdropping, and they must be available when needed.

If data is destroyed, years of work, effort, and thought are gone. Unfortunately, work, effort, and thought are not easily replaced.

Mr. Feibel suggests four threat areas to manage for your system security:

Threats to hardware   Theft, tampering, destruction, damage, unauthorized use, and ordinary equipment wear and tear.

Threats to software   Deletion, theft, corruption, and bugs.

Threats to information   Deletion, theft, loss, and corruption.

Threats to network operations   Interruption, interference, and overload.

Can you and your boss agree on these items? Do some of them seem outside the realm of security, such as ordinary equipment wear and tear? What about the threat of overload?

Some network managers think of security from a negative aspect only. Something is stolen or deleted. I don't believe that definition is wide enough to support the network needs of today.

Let's agree that system security means that the system is available to authorized users doing their job. Anything that interferes with this is a security problem. If a file server is stolen, people can't do their work. What if the file server is overloaded or erratic? Isn't the result the same? People can't do their work. What if the file server is safe and running well, but someone deletes (either accidentally or on purpose) some of the system files? The result is the same once again: people can't do their work.

Where Is Your Security Plan?

In 1988, the Internet Worm ran amok, clogging thousands of computers and data circuits for days. The Worm was not destructive but caused disruptions in computer services all across the Internet. Front-page stories were copied by paranoid managers and handed to network technicians with a question: "Where is our security plan?"

One of the responses of the Internet community to the Worm of 1988 was to establish CERT (Computer Emergency Response Team). This group responds to and helps resolve Internet security incidents. Part of the group's job is to help network administrators protect their systems against intruders before an attack is attempted.

The good news is that upgrading security takes surprisingly little work for most systems. Unfortunately, that's also the bad news. CERT estimates that 60 to 75 percent of network problems are caused by the following:

- Accounts with no passwords
- Poor passwords
- Unwatched guest accounts
- Poor user security management, especially giving users more rights than necessary

Are the listed problems familiar to you? Do you understand how easy these problems are to fix?

Before doing anything else, check the easy things. Many cars are stolen simply because the keys are left dangling from the ignition switch. Don't make things that easy in your network.

Should I Be Concerned Since My NetWare Network Is Connected to the Internet?

Yes, of course you should worry. Bad things sometimes happen to networks connected to the Internet. But you shouldn't be overly paranoid.

Your boss, however, will be overly paranoid. That's because the nontechnical press latches onto every hacker story like a starving pooch on a pork chop. You and I know these stories are poorly researched and written by journalists who either don't understand computers or don't trust them, so we ignore most of them. Bosses can't ignore them because their bosses read the same articles in the same papers, and misinformed hysteria feeds upon nontechnical misunderstanding, and everyone gets all worked up.

Prepare yourself every time the *Wall Street Journal* or *New York Times* runs a computer hacker or system crash story—your boss will come and ask how nervous you are about the horrible state of Internet security. If you're of a certain type of mind, that is the time to increase your budget considerably under the guise of improving security. Even if you're not of that type of mind regularly, chances like that don't come around often, so you should take a shot and ask for enough money to get a new server, firewall, and/or software upgrade.

The truth is that connecting any part of your network to the Internet requires plenty of extra work, caution, and responsibility. You must keep the bad people out and keep the irresponsible people in.

The Internet and Firewalls

No intelligent network manager will connect to the Internet without some type of firewall in place to provide security. If your company already has an Internet connection and you are adding your own NetWare network to the list of Internet-aware networks, a firewall is in place already. Talk to the network administrator in charge of your TCP/IP network, and get the details you need to feel good about network security.

Firewall is an unusually descriptive term, even for the term-spewing computer industry. In construction, a firewall stands against disasters by forming an impenetrable shield around the protected area (I got the impenetrable shield slogan from my deodorant). Most disasters in buildings revolve around fires; hence, the term firewall.

The goal of a firewall is simple: to control access to a protected network. Firewall managers use two philosophies during configuration:

- ▶ Allow everything except designated packets
- ▶ Block everything except designated packets

Today, the proper attitude is to block everything except designated packets. Novell's products come this way straight from the box. When you enable filtering, everything is blocked, and you must designate what is allowed to pass through the firewall and/or filtering software.

There are four types of firewalls. Table 23.1 shows each type of firewall matched up with where it functions in the OSI seven-layer model.

TABLE 23.1: Matching Security Filters and Network Layers

OSI MODEL LAYER	INTERNET PROTOCOLS	FIREWALLS
Application	HTTP, FTP, DNS, NFS, Ping, SMTP, Telnet	Application-level gateway, stateful inspection firewall
Presentation		
Session	TCP	Circuit-level gateway
Transport	TCP	
Network	IP	Packet-filtering firewall
Data Link		
Physical		

Let's see what each of these firewalls can do for you:

Packet filters (FILTCFG)   The lowest level, packet filters, was once enough to protect your network, but that is no longer true. IP addresses are used to allow or deny packets, and IP address spoofing (disguised packets) has ruined the idea of this level of protection being enough to protect your network.

Circuit-level gateways   Circuit-level gateways do more to control internal traffic leaving your protected network than to keep outsiders at bay. Rules for users, such as allowable hosts to visit and time limits, are handled at this level.

Application-level gateways   Application-level gateways are specific to network services, such as FTP or e-mail. These are most common today with web browsers, used by software meant to monitor or block web access to certain sites.

Stateful inspection firewalls   Finally, the most critical area is the stateful inspection firewall, used by Novell and few others. This software examines incoming packets to match them to appropriate outgoing packets and is able to examine packet contents to maintain control. The more options you have, the better your security, and NetWare gives you plenty of options. Of course, you'll need more time to configure more settings, but NetWare utilities will help with that chore.

Protect Your Corporate Network

If your network is the corporate network, check out Novell's Border-Manager software. You aren't familiar with this product? It adds a complete security- and performance-enhancing software server to any NetWare 4, 5, or 6 server.

You can run both the NetWare 6 server and BorderManager on the same hardware. Larger networks will want to separate the BorderManager software on its own server for performance reasons. One BorderManager server protects your entire network when configured correctly.

Keeping Up with Security Threats

Can one person, namely you, keep up with all the network miscreants out there? No, but there are more people on your side than you might imagine.

Enlist the resources of your firewall vendor, whether Novell for Border-Manager or another vendor. Keep up-to-date on all bug fixes, patches, and upgrades for your firewall software. Maintain proper security for the physical firewall system (lock it up in the server room or equivalent).

Also, watch the trade magazines and websites pertaining to security. Security information is all over the place if you keep your eyes open. Please don't be one of those who become paranoid *after* you get burned. Go ahead and start being paranoid, or at least well informed, before something serious happens to your network.

Here's a regularly repeated warning: *Watch your users carefully.* Some companies are using "internal" firewalls to keep employees out of sensitive areas. A serious security breach, where valuable information is stolen or compromised, almost always includes help from the inside. Every user is a potential thief. Always provide new services with tighter rather than looser security, and then loosen the leash as you and your management feel more comfortable with the security situation on your network. Most data thieves walk out rather than break in.

When the network is new, or a security problem has occurred, everyone is conscientious. After a time, however, human nature takes over and everyone gets sloppy.

Your network changes constantly, and each change is a potential security disaster. Add a new user? Did you take care to match the new user to an existing group with well-defined security and access controls? How about new files created by the users themselves? Do you have a plan for watching the access level of those files? Do users have the ability to allow other users access into a home directory? If so, no private file will be safe. Don't allow file sharing within each person's private directory. Send the file by e-mail or have a common directory in which users can place files to share. Do not allow them more file rights to the \PUBLIC directory, even though some will ask for it.

Watch new applications. Many vendors have modified NetWare rights for files and directories for years, especially during installation. Are these loopholes closed in the new application directories you created just last week? Take the time to check.

Passwords and Login Restrictions

All user accounts need to be protected so that only the authorized user can utilize the account. The most popular method of protecting the account is to assign a password to it, although other measures can be taken to restrict the use of the account. The following is a brief synopsis of how to protect accounts.

Passwords

Each user must have a password. Here are some tips for your passwords:

- ▶ The longer the password, the better. Novell's default minimum is five characters; try for six or lucky seven.

- ▶ Encourage the use of mixed alpha and numeric characters in the password.

- ▶ Set passwords to expire (the default is 40 days).

- ▶ Let the system keep track of passwords to force unique ones. The limit is 20.

- ▶ Limit the grace logins; two is enough.

Login Restrictions

Using login restrictions, you can limit users' network access and track the resources they use. Here are some tips for setting login restrictions:

- ▶ Limit concurrent connections for all users.

- ▶ Set an account expiration date for all temporary workers.

- ▶ Disable accounts for users away from the office who don't communicate remotely to your network.

THE ADMIN USER, ADMIN RIGHTS, AND THE SUPERVISOR RIGHT

The only user created with NetWare 6 is named Admin, short for Administrator. If you just climbed up the version tree from NetWare 3.1x, don't bother looking for SUPERVISOR, because Admin replaced SUPERVISOR.

Make the mental note that the Admin user is separate from the Admin rights over the network operating system and included objects. As you'll see later, the more advanced management techniques that arrived with object management and the Admin user are a way to block this SUPERVISOR equivalent from managing parts of the network. Oops.

The Admin user is a supervisor's supervisor, able to control the network completely as the old SUPERVISOR did in earlier NetWare versions. The Supervisor right, however, may be granted to any user for particular NDS eDirectory objects or containers. Being able to set up subadministrators for specific tasks can be a great help.

This flexibility of supervision is an important feature of NetWare 6 — one of the many features that place NetWare ahead of the competition. With global enterprise networking the norm for many companies today, the job of supervision is far beyond the abilities of any one person. NetWare 6 allows the supervision chores to be distributed in whatever method you prefer.

CONTINUED ➡

You can have different administrators for different parts of the tree, as well as different volumes, directories, or files. Admin may control the NDS design and overall setup but have no control over the files. Filesystem supervisors in each container will handle those chores. Admin in Chicago may share duties with Admin in Cleveland, with each responsible primarily for his or her own city but able to support the other network across the WAN if necessary.

UNDERSTANDING FILESYSTEM SECURITY

There are two main security areas for NetWare 6: filesystem and NDS security. If you are familiar with NetWare 3.x, you will be familiar with filesystem security. NetWare 4.1x added some attributes to support data compression and data migration features and changed a bit of the terminology, but most of the details and the security goals remain the same, even in NetWare 6. The main goal is to provide users access to and control of the proper files and directories.

NetWare files are protected in two ways:

▶ Users must be granted the right to use files and directories.

▶ File and directory attributes provide hidden protection.

What is hidden protection? Suppose that Doug has the right to create and delete files in the \LETTERS directory. If he writes a letter named SLS_GOAL.OCT and decides he doesn't like that file, he can delete it. Files can be deleted from within applications or from the DOS prompt. He can use Windows Explorer.

What if Doug's mouse slips a fraction within Explorer, and he tries to delete the SLS_GOAL.PLN file, the template for all the sales goal letters? Is the file doomed?

Not necessarily. If the network administrator (probably you) has set the attribute to SLS_GOAL.PLN as Read Only or Delete Inhibit, Doug can't delete the file. However, if Doug also has the right to modify the file attributes (a bad idea, knowing Doug), he could change the Read Only or Delete Inhibit designation and delete the file anyway. But he would need to work at deleting the file; he couldn't do it by accident.

When granting Doug rights to use the \LETTERS directory, we call him a *trustee* of the directory, given to him by way of a *trustee assignment*. He has been trusted to use the directory and files properly. The trustee concept works with objects and NDS items, as we'll soon see.

Someone in authority must grant Doug, or a group or container Doug is a member of, the rights to use the file, directory, or object in question. The administrator is the person who places trust in Doug, making him a trustee of the rights of the object. This is referred to as making trustee assignments to a directory, file, or object. The trustee assignments are stored in the object's ACL (Access Control List) property inside NDS eDirectory.

The rights granted to users flow downhill (kind of like *stuff* on a bad day). This means that the rights Doug has in one directory apply to all subdirectories. This idea works well, and the official name is *inheritance*. If your system is set up with \LETTERS as the main directory, and Doug has rights to use that directory, he will automatically have the same rights in the \LETTERS\SALES and \LETTERS\PROSPECT subdirectories. He will inherit the same rights in \LETTERS\SALES as he has in \LETTERS.

One way to stop Doug from having full access to a subdirectory is to use the IRF (Inherited Rights Filter). The IRF filters the rights a user may have in subdirectories and will be covered later in this chapter. The other way is to explicitly make a new trustee assignment to this subdirectory. A new assignment always overrides the inherited settings.

NOTE

NetWare 3.x had Inherited Rights Masks (IRMs). NetWare 4.1 and later have Inherited Rights Filters (IRFs). The name has changed, but the actions are the same.

[Public] is a special trustee, for use by all the users on the network, and can always be specified as a trustee of a file, directory, or object. Although it sounds similar to the group EVERYONE in earlier NetWare versions, containers act more like the EVERYONE group than [Public] does.

File and Directory Rights

The rights to use directories and files are similar, so we'll take a look at the directory situation first. Users' rights in dealing with files and directories are also similar, making explanations fairly simple.

Directory Rights for Users and Groups

There are reasons to grant rights to directories rather than files, not the least of which is the time savings. Even with wildcards available, I would rather set the rights of users to use a directory and all subdirectories than set their rights to the files in each directory.

What are these rights that users can have over a directory? And did that last sentence in the previous paragraph mean subdirectories? Yes it did. The directory rights available to users are summarized in Table 23.2.

TABLE 23.2: Directory Rights in NetWare 6

RIGHT	DESCRIPTION
Supervisor (S)	Grants all rights to the directory, its files, and all subdirectories, overriding any restrictions placed on subdirectories or files with an IRF. Users with this right in a directory can grant other users Supervisor rights to the same directory, its files, and its subdirectories.
Read (R)	Allows the user to open and read the directory. Earlier NetWare versions needed an Open right; Read now includes Open.
Write (W)	Allows the user to open and write files, but existing files are not displayed without Read authorization.
Create (C)	Allows the user to create directories and files. With Create authorization, a user can create a file and write data into the file (authority for Write is included with Create). Read and File Scan authority are not part of the Create right.
Modify (M)	Allows the user to change directory and file attributes, including the right to rename the directory, its files, and its subdirectories. Modify does not refer to the file contents.
File Scan (F)	Allows the user to see filenames in a directory listing. Without this right, the user will be told the directory is empty.
Access Control (A)	Allows the user to change directory trustee assignments and the IRFs for directories. This right should be granted to supervisory personnel only, because users with Access Control rights can grant all rights except Supervisor to another user, including rights the Access Control user doesn't have. The user can also modify file trustee assignments within the directory.

Let's see how these directory rights appear in ConsoleOne. Figure 23.1 shows the group Techies and the file and directory rights the members have. Why use ConsoleOne rather than NetWare Administrator? To get ready for the future, since ConsoleOne gets the Novell developer's attention today, while NetWare Administrator remains static. Like it or not, ConsoleOne is the future.

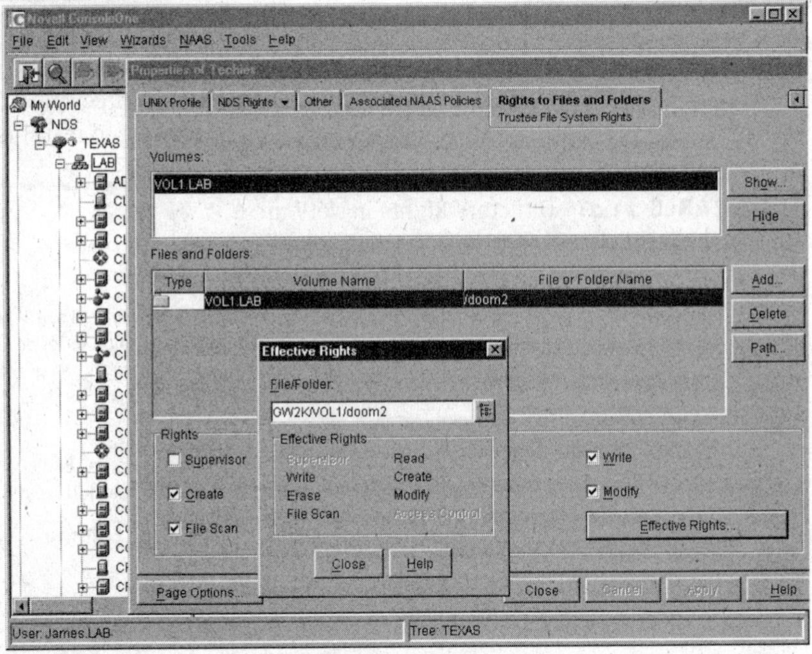

FIGURE 23.1:   An example of the rights a group can have.

The Effective Rights dialog box in Figure 23.1 appears when you click the Effective Rights command button in the Rights To Files And Folders tab of the Techies property page. The odd arrangement here helps show all the pieces without blocking the parent window. Unlike NetWare Administrator, ConsoleOne requires you to drill down through the volume to the directory in the Select Object dialog box (not shown here).

The Supervisor and Access Control check boxes are clear in the Rights area. This means that the group Techies does not have those two rights. Giving a group of users (especially a group of techs) the Supervisor right could be dangerous. Giving a person or group the Access Control right is equally dangerous. With the Access Control right, the user or group member can change his or her own rights and add more rights without your knowledge or consent.

NOTE

If you're just moving up from NetWare 3.x, you should be aware of a change to users' home directories rights: the home directories created during the initial user setup now have all rights, including Supervisor.

These rights apply to the directory where they are granted and to all subdirectories. Rights are inherited from the top directory levels through all the existing subdirectory levels.

The rights are displayed (in DOS with the RIGHTS command) as a string of the initials within brackets: [SRWCEMFA]. If some are missing, a space is put in their place. For instance, the most rights nonadministrative users generally have are [_RWCEMF_]. As you can see, underscores were put in place of the S (Supervisor) and A (Access Control) rights. If the generic user listed previously didn't have the rights to Erase in a particular directory, the listing would appear as [_RWC_MF_].

File Rights for Users and Groups

In contrast to directory rights, file rights address only specified files. Sometimes the files are identified individually, and sometimes they are specified by a wildcard group (*.EXE, for example). There are minor differences between how the rights are applied to a directory and to a file. Table 23.3 summarizes the file rights.

TABLE 23.3:   File Rights in NetWare 6

Right	Description
Supervisor (S)	Grants all rights to the file, and users with this right may grant any file right to another user. This right also allows modification of all the rights in the file's IRF.
Read (R)	Allows the user to open and read the file.
Write (W)	Allows the user to open and write to the file.
Create (C)	Allows the user to create new files and salvage a file after it has been deleted. Perhaps the latter should be called the Re-create right.
Erase (E)	Allows the user to delete the file.
Modify (M)	Allows the user to modify the file attributes, including renaming the file. This does not apply to the contents of the file.

TABLE 23.3 continued: File Rights in NetWare 6

RIGHT	DESCRIPTION
File Scan (F)	Allows the user to see the file when viewing the contents of the directory.
Access Control (A)	Allows the user to change the file's trustee assignments and IRF. Users with this right can grant any right (except Supervisor) for this file to any other user, including rights that they themselves have not been granted.

You might notice that the Create right is a bit different, and the Supervisor and Access Control rights apply to individual files. Why do we have the differences between directory and file rights?

The IRF and File and Directory Rights

Let's pretend that your filesystem is set up so that all the accounting data is parceled into subdirectories under the main \DATA directory in the volume ACCOUNTING. Many people on your network will need access to the information in these accounting files. Some will need to use the accounting programs, some will need to gather the information into reports, and others may need to write applications that use those data files.

Since directory rights flow downhill, this will be easy: give the group ACCOUNTING rights to use the \DATA directory, and the information in \DATA\AR, \DATA\AP, \DATA\GL, and \DATA\PAYROLL is available to everyone. But suddenly your boss realizes that giving everyone rights to see the information in \DATA\PAYROLL is not smart (your boss must be slow, because salary information paranoia runs pretty high in most bosses).

This is what the IRF was made for. The IRF controls the rights passed between a higher-level directory and a lower-level directory. In our example, that would be \DATA to \DATA\PAYROLL. The IRF does not grant rights; it strictly revokes them. The IRF default is to let all rights flow down unless otherwise instructed.

Figure 23.2 shows a simple look at our example. Everyone has access to all directories except for \DATA\PAYROLL. The IRF is blocking the rights for everyone in that directory.

Part V

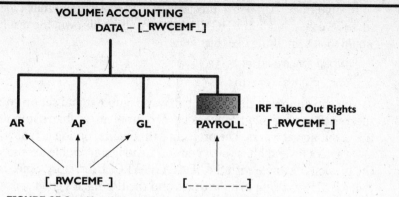

VOLUME: ACCOUNTING
DATA – [_RWCEMF_]

AR   AP   GL   PAYROLL

IRF Takes Out Rights
[_RWCEMF_]

[_RWCEMF_]   [_____]

FIGURE 23.2:   Keeping prying eyes out of PAYROLL.

There's a problem here: how does anyone see the \DATA\PAYROLL directory? The network administrator must specifically grant rights to the \DATA\PAYROLL directory for those users who belong there. The IRF filters between the parent directory and subdirectory. It does not dictate the rights assigned specifically to the subdirectory.

When you type RIGHTS from the DOS command line, you see your rights in the current directory listed with an explanation. If you have all rights in a directory, such as your home directory, the RIGHTS command will show something like the display for user Alex in Figure 23.3.

NOTE

Like Figure 23.3's old screenshot using Novell DOS? Yes, they had it for a while until they sold it to Caldera—the Linux people.

```
[Novell DOS] I:\HOME\ALEX>rights
GATEWAY2000\PROJECTS:\HOME\ALEX
Your rights for this directory:  [SRWCEMFA]
    Supervisor rights to directory.       (S)
    Read from a file in a directory.      (R)
    Write to a file in a directory.       (W)
    Create subdirectories and files.      (C)
    Erase directory and files.            (E)
    Modify directory and files.           (M)
    Scan for files and directories.       (F)
    Change access control.                (A)

[Novell DOS] I:\HOME\ALEX>
```

FIGURE 23.3:   Results of the RIGHTS command.

If you have no rights in a directory, such as if our friend Alex typed the RIGHTS command in the HOME directory above his own, the result would look something like this:

```
GATEWAY2000\PROJECTS:\HOME
Your rights for this directory: [  ]
```

You can approach the IRF in two ways: ignore it and set up your filesystem so that inheritance is never a problem, or take a minute to figure out how it works. The problem with the first option is that reality always rises up and bites you when you try to ignore problems, such as the previous example with the \DATA\PAYROLL directory. Since inheritance is always going to be with us, and the IRF makes good sense in certain situations, let's look at another view of the IRF.

First, let's add a complication: group rights. Users can be assigned rights directly, or they can get them through group memberships. The individual and group rights are additive. If you have one right granted individually and another granted through group membership, you effectively have both rights.

The IRF works against both the individual and group rights. The results of the individual plus group rights minus those taken away by the IRF are called the effective rights. Figure 23.4 stacks up the individual and group rights, subtracts the IRF, and shows the effective rights.

Individual Rights	[_RWCE_F_]	[_RWCEMFA]	[_RW_E_F_]
plus **Group Rights** +	[_____M_A]		[_R___MF_]
minus **IRF** −		[_____M_A]	[__W_EM__]
Effective Rights	[_RWCEMFA]	[_RWCE_F_]	[_R____F_]

FIGURE 23.4:   Stacking and subtracting rights.

Notice that the Supervisor (S) rights aren't mentioned anywhere. The IRF does not block the Supervisor rights, whether granted to the individual or a group. This is true only of the directory and file rights IRF. Later, you'll see that the object rights are a different story.

Directory and File Security Guidelines

No two networks are alike or use the same security profile. However, some general guidelines are applicable:

▶ Design your network top-down, from tighter security at the higher directories to looser security in the lower directories.

▶ Fight the urge to grant trustee rights to individuals. Always look for groups first, second, and third before you work with the individual user.

▶ Plan for inheritance. Grant Read and File Scan rights high and Create, Erase, and Modify rights lower in the NDS eDirectory tree.

▶ Avoid granting any destructive rights high in the directory structure.

▶ Remember that the Supervisor right for the filesystem cannot be blocked by the IRF. Grant that right carefully, if at all.

File Attributes As a Security Enhancement

File attributes in NetWare, as in DOS, detail the characteristics of a file or directory. NetWare administrators often call these attributes *flags*. The NetWare DOS command-line utility FLAG.EXE displays and modifies these attributes.

Since we've decided that security includes making sure all network resources are available, the safety of files on the file server is important. Someone besides you deleting or renaming files is a security problem.

File and directory attributes are not a defense for cases of willful destruction and sabotage. They are a defense against mistakes and typos by innocent users. Haven't you ever had a user type DEL *.* in a directory on drive G instead of drive C? Having some of the files set as Read Only or Delete Inhibit may lessen the damage from a confused user.

Attributes control what can and can't be done with files and directories. They are also a limited form of virus protection. Since most viruses work by modifying executable files, keeping those executables Ro (Read Only) will stop viruses from trying to rewrite files and save them back with the same name.

WARNING

Ro flags won't help with the new genre of Word macro viruses or with many of the other multitude of viruses out there. Flagging files Ro is never enough virus protection; it just helps a little.

Filesystem: Directory Attributes

As is the case with much of NetWare, there are attributes for directories as well as files. Again, this makes sense. Unlike the rights to use an object, most directory rights don't directly affect the files in the directory. The attributes dealing with compression and data migration obviously do impact individual files. Since compression may be set by volume, the Immediate Compress attribute may be used more often than the Don't Compress attribute. Table 23.4 lists the directory attributes with their abbreviations and descriptions.

TABLE 23.4:   Directory Attributes in NetWare 6

Attribute	Description
All (All)	Sets all available directory attributes.
Don't Compress (Dc)	Stops compression on any files in the directory. This over-rides the compression setting for the volume.
Delete Inhibit (Di)	Stops users from erasing the directory, even if the user has the Erase trustee right. This attribute can be reset by a user with the Modify right.
Don't Migrate (Dm)	Stops files within the directory from being migrated to secondary storage.
Hidden (H)	Hides directories from DOS DIR scans. NDIR will display these directories if the user has appropriate File Scan rights.
Immediate Compress (Ic)	Forces the filesystem to compress files as soon as the operating system can handle the action.
Normal (N)	Flags a directory as Read/Write and nonshareable. It removes most other flags. This is the standard setting for user directories on the server handling DOS programs.
Purge (P)	Forces NetWare to completely delete files as the user deletes them, rather than tracking the deletions for the SALVAGE command to use later.
Rename Inhibit (Ri)	Stops users from renaming directories, even those users who have been granted the Modify trustee right. However, if the user has the Modify trustee right, that user can remove this attribute from the directory and then rename the directory.
System (Sy)	Hides directories from DOS DIR scans and prevents them from being deleted or copied. The NDIR program will display these directories if the user has appropriate File Scan rights.

NOTE
The Don't Compress, Immediate Compress, and Don't Migrate attributes for files and directories were added when NetWare 4 introduced compression and advanced storage features.

Most of these directory attributes are seldom used to protect a directory from confused users. The options you will probably use the most are those that concern the operating system, such as Don't Compress and Immediate Compress. The Normal attribute will be used most often, if your network follows true to form.

Filesystem: File Attributes

Most flagging happens at the file level and doesn't get changed all that often. After all, once you set the files in a directory the way you want (all the .EXE and .COM files Read Only and Shareable, for instance), few occasions require you to change them.

The time to worry about file attributes is during and immediately after installation of a new software product. Many product vendors today advertise, "Yes, it runs with NetWare," and they normally set the flags for you during installation. However, it's good practice to check newly installed applications, just in case the developers forgot to set a flag or three. The available file attributes are listed in Table 23.5, with their abbreviations and meanings.

TABLE 23.5: File Attributes in NetWare 6

ATTRIBUTE	DESCRIPTION
All (All)	Sets all available file attributes.
Archive Needed (A)	DOS's Archive bit that identifies files modified after the last backup. NetWare assigns this bit automatically.
Copy Inhibit (Ci)	Prevents Macintosh clients from copying the file, even those clients with Read and File Scan trustee rights. This attribute can be changed by users with the Modify right.
Don't Compress (Dc)	Prevents the file from being compressed. This attribute overrides settings for automatic compression of files.
Delete Inhibit (Di)	Prevents clients from deleting the file, even those clients with the Erase trustee right. This attribute can be changed by users with the Modify right.

TABLE 23.5 continued: File Attributes in NetWare 6

ATTRIBUTE	DESCRIPTION
Don't Migrate (Dm)	Prevents files from being migrated from the server's hard disk to another storage medium.
Hidden (H)	Hides files from the DOS DIR command. The NDIR program will display these files if the user has appropriate File Scan rights.
Immediate Compress (Ic)	Forces files to be compressed as soon as the file is closed.
Normal (N)	Shorthand for Read/Write, since there is no N attribute bit for file attributes. This is the default setting for files.
Purge (P)	Forces NetWare to automatically purge the file after it has been deleted.
Rename Inhibit (Ri)	Prevents the filename from being modified. Users with the Modify trustee right may change this attribute and then rename the file.
Read Only (Ro)	Prevents a file from being modified. This attribute automatically sets Delete Inhibit and Rename Inhibit. It's extremely useful for keeping .COM and .EXE files from being deleted by users, and it helps stop a virus from mutating the file.
Read Write (Rw)	The default attribute for all files. Allows users to read and write to the file.
Shareable (Sh)	Allows more than one user to access a file simultaneously. Normally used with the Read Only attribute so that a file being used by multiple users cannot be modified. All the utility files in the \PUBLIC directory are flagged Sh (and Ro, Di, and Ri).
System File (Sy)	Prevents a file from being deleted or copied and hides it from the DOS DIR command. NetWare's NDIR program will display these directories as System if the user has appropriate File Scan rights.
Transactional (T)	Forces the file to be tracked and protected by the Transaction Tracking System (TTS).

File attributes are normally assigned to the files using a wildcard with the FLAG command, as in this example:

```
FLAG *.EXE RO Sh
```

This command says, "Change the file attributes of all files with the .EXE extension to be readable, but not writable, and to share the file by allowing multiple clients to use the program file concurrently."

TIP

When a user has a problem with a file, the first two things to check are the user's rights in that directory and the flags set on the problem file. One of these two settings, mismatched in some way, accounts for 80 percent or more of user file problems.

Let's look at how to type an exploratory FLAG command and examine the results. Figure 23.5 shows the command and result.

```
MS MS-DOS Prompt                                                    _ □ ×
  8 x 12 ▾   [] ▣ ▣ ⊠ ⬚⬚ A
J:\PUBLIC>flag m*.*

Files         = The name of the files found
Directories   = The name of the directories found
DOS Attr      = The DOS attributes for the specified file
NetWare Attr  = The NetWare attributes for the specified file or directory
Status        = The current status of migration and compression for a file
                or directory
Owner         = The current owner of the file or directory
Mode          = The search mode set for the current file

Files                    DOS Attr NetWare Attr        Status Owner         Mode
MAP.EXE                  [Ro----] [-----Di--Ri------]        .[Supervisor] 0
MFC42.DLL                [Ro----] [-----Di--Ri------]        .[Supervisor] N/A
MODIFY.BAT               [Rw---A] [-----------------]        .James.LAB    N/A
MSVCP50.DLL              [Ro----] [-----Di--Ri------]        .[Supervisor] N/A
MSVCRT.DLL               [Ro----] [-----Di--Ri------]        .[Supervisor] N/A
MSVCRT40.DLL             [Ro----] [-----Di--Ri------]        .[Supervisor] N/A

Directories              NetWare Attr      Owner

MGMT                     [-----------] .[Supervisor]

J:\PUBLIC>
```

FIGURE 23.5:   Checking the FLAG setting in the \PUBLIC directory.

In this example, we can see the file attributes for a few of the NetWare utility files. Most are Ro (Read Only), meaning they also have the NetWare attributes of Di (Delete Inhibit) and Ri (Rename Inhibit) set as well. Looking at the second set of attributes, you see this is true.

The MODIFY.BAT was created by me (James). You can tell because the flag is set to Rw (Read Write) and the Archive attribute is set, meaning the file changed since the last backup. The rest of the files in the example are owned by the Supervisor. The ownership for these files was set during installation.

To check for all the various FLAG command-line switches, from the DOS command line, type:

```
FLAG /? ALL
```

You'll see six screens' worth of information.

NOTE

Don't think that FLAG is the only way to change file attributes. The FILER, ConsoleOne, and NetWare Administrator utilities allow these same functions, just not as quickly and easily (in my opinion).

ConsoleOne's new beefy manifestation, like the weakling working out after being embarrassed, impresses me with its progress. Early versions of ConsoleOne couldn't get to the file level, but Novell engineers whipped that problem in NetWare 5.1. See Figure 23.6 for ConsoleOne's new file-control features.

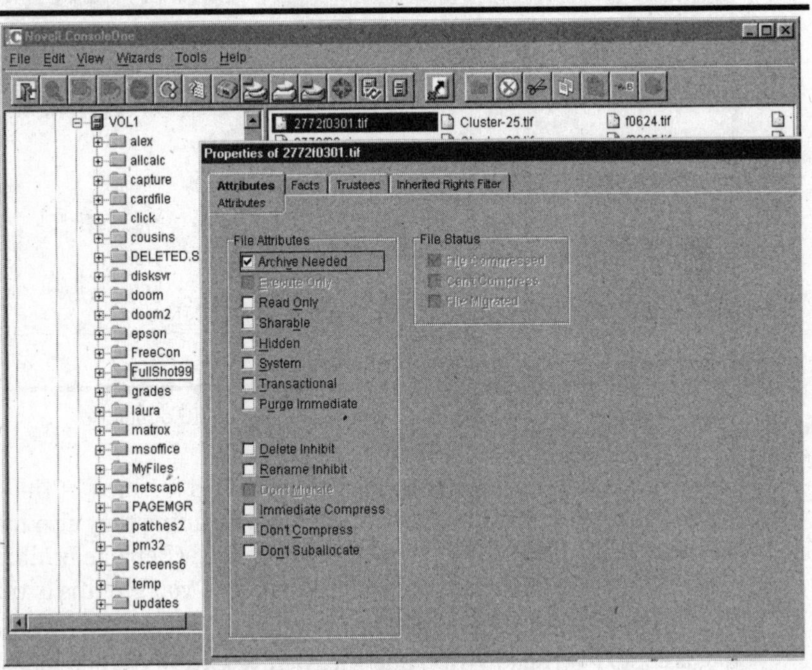

FIGURE 23.6:   ConsoleOne now displays file attributes.

Notice the strange icons on the ConsoleOne toolbar? The red X means delete, the scissors mean cut, the pages mean copy, and the A with a strikeout and the B means rename. Not the best iconography for rename, I grant you, but new and impressive overall.

UNDERSTANDING NDS SECURITY

Since NDS was new to NetWare 4, the idea of NDS security was new to old NetWare hands at the time, and it may still be new to those just jumping up from good old NetWare 3. NDS security is concerned with the management and protection of the NDS database and its objects.

The SUPERVISOR user in NetWare 3 was concerned about both file security (as we just discussed) and network resources security. The second part of the job included creating and managing users, setting network access privileges for all network users, and creating and managing network resources, such as printers and volumes.

The Admin user has, by default, all the rights and power of the SUPERVISOR user. In NetWare 6, however, the management can easily be split between NDS security and filesystem security. It's entirely possible to have one administrator with no control over file and user trustee rights and another administrator with no control over containers, Organizations, or Organizational Units. You can also set up subadministrators with complete control over their containers, having both file and property rights.

Let's be quite clear about this: filesystem and NDS security systems are (almost) completely separate from each other (the Supervisor right crosses the line). Just as filesystem security controls which users can control which files, NDS security controls the same functions for the NDS objects. Having the rights to control a container gives you no authority over a file kept on a volume in that container, unless rights are granted to that volume. The two security systems are not in any way related. Let me repeat: having control over the NDS attributes of an object (let's say a disk volume) does not grant the rights to the files contained in that volume.

The NDS database allows multiple management layers. You can create as many Organizations and Organizational Units as you want, nesting the Organizational Units as many levels as you want. As you'll see when I talk about how the IRF works on object and property rights, it's possible for the Admin of a network to have full control over the Organization and the first Organizational Unit, but no control over the final Organizational Unit. Make sure this is what you have in mind before setting up such a system, however. If you can't trust your Admin with access to everything, you have more problems than can be solved by NetWare.

Object Rights versus Property Rights

There are two types of rights in NDS: object rights and property rights. *Object rights* determine what a trustee (user with the proper rights) can do to an object, such as creating, deleting, or renaming the object. *Property rights* determine whether a trustee can examine, use, or change the values of the various properties of an object.

Only in one case does an object right intrude into the property rights arena: the Supervisor right. A trustee with the Supervisor right to an object also has full rights to all properties of that object. But unlike with file and directory rights, the Supervisor right can be blocked on object and property rights by the IRF.

The opposite of the Supervisor right is the Browse right. This is the default right for users in the network. It allows users to see, but not modify, objects in the NDS eDirectory tree.

Object rights concern the object as a whole in the Browser. Actions taken on an object in the Browser, such as moving a User object from one context to another, exemplify object rights.

Property rights concern the values of all the properties of an object. The User object that was moved in the last paragraph has hundreds of properties. The ability to change a property value, such as Minimum Account Balance or Telephone Number, requires property rights.

Objects have inheritance rights, meaning a trustee of one object has the same rights over a subsidiary object. If a trustee has rights over one container, that trustee has the same rights over any container objects inside the main container.

Let's play "Pick Your Analogy." Object rights are like moving boxes, and the box contents are properties. The movers have authority over the boxes (object rights) but not over the contents of the boxes (property rights). A mover supervisor, however, has the rights to the boxes and to the contents (property rights) of those boxes for management situations.

When you turn your car over to a parking lot attendant, you give that attendant object rights: your car can be placed anywhere in the parking lot. The attendant has full control over where your car is and if it needs to be moved while you're gone. You probably exclude the Delete right from the attendant, however. The property rights to your car, such as the items in your trunk, glove compartment, and backseat, do not belong to the parking lot attendant. You have granted the attendant some object rights to your car, but no property rights. Do you think armored car drivers have object rights or property rights to the money bags? Which would you prefer if you were a driver? What if you owned the bag contents?

To keep things consistent, object rights and property rights overlap only in the Supervisor right. The trick is to remember that sometimes a C means Create and sometimes it means Compare. Take a look at the official list of object rights in Table 23.6.

TABLE 23.6: Object Rights in NetWare 6

Right	Description
Supervisor (S)	Grants all access privileges, including unrestricted access to all properties. The Supervisor right can be blocked by an IRF, unlike with file and directory rights.
Browse (B)	Grants the right to see this object in the eDirectory tree. The name of the object is returned when a search is made, if the search criteria match the object.
Create (C)	Grants the right to create a new object below this object in the eDirectory tree. No rights are defined for the new object. This right applies only to container objects, because only container objects can have subordinates.
Delete (D)	Grants the right to delete the object from the eDirectory tree. Objects that have subordinates can't be deleted unless the subordinates are deleted first, just like a DOS directory can't be deleted if it still contains files or subdirectories.
Rename (R)	Grants the right to change the name of the object. This officially modifies the Name property of the object, changing the object's complete name.

The object rights tend to be used by managers, not by users. Create, Delete, and Rename rights are not the type of things normally given to users. The Browse object right is granted automatically to [Root], meaning everyone can browse the NDS eDirectory tree. Remember that the Supervisor object right automatically allows full access to all property rights. The property rights are listed in Table 23.7.

TABLE 23.7:   Property Rights in NetWare 6

RIGHT	DESCRIPTION
Supervisor (S)	Grants all rights to the property. The Supervisor right can be blocked by an IRF, unlike with file and directory rights.
Compare (C)	Grants the right to compare any value with a value of the property for search purposes. With the Compare right, a search operation can return True or False, but you can't see the value of the property. The Read right includes the Compare right.
Read (R)	Grants the right to read all the values of the property. Compare is a subset of Read. If the Read right is given, Compare operations are also allowed.
Write (W)	Grants the right to add, change, or remove any values of the property. Write also includes the Add or Delete Self right.
Add or Delete Self (A)	Grants a trustee the right to add or remove itself as a value of the property, but no other values of the property may be changed. This right is meaningful only for properties that contain object names as values, such as group membership lists or mailing lists. The Write right includes the Add or Delete Self right.

The Access Control List (ACL)

The ACL is the object property that stores the information about who may access the object. Just as Joe is a value of the Name property, the ACL contains trustee assignments for both object and property rights. The ACL also includes the IRF.

To change the ACL, you must have a property right that allows you to modify that ACL value for that object. Write will allow this, as will the Supervisor object right. Add or Delete Self is for users to add or remove themselves from a Members List property of a Group object.

Do you want to grant object or property rights to another object? You must have the Write, Add or Delete Self, or Supervisor right to the ACL property of the object in question.

Although it sounds as if the ACL is some list somewhere, it's really just one of many properties held by an object. Each object has an ACL. If a user is not listed in the ACL for an object, that user cannot change the properties of that object.

How Rights Inheritance Works

As I said before, rights flow downhill (ask a plumber what else flows downhill). Directory rights pass down to subdirectories, and container rights flow down to subcontainers. The only way to stop rights from flowing to a subcontainer is to use the IRF in the subcontainer. This forces users with rights to the parent container to also get the trustee rights to the subcontainer in a separate operation. That means the network supervisor (probably you) must go back and grant trustee rights to those users who need access to the subcontainer.

The system works well, with one exception: selected property rights are not inherited. If a user is granted trustee rights to an object for selected property rights only, those rights do not move down to the subcontainer or other objects. Figure 23.7 shows an example of the process of granting a user selected property rights.

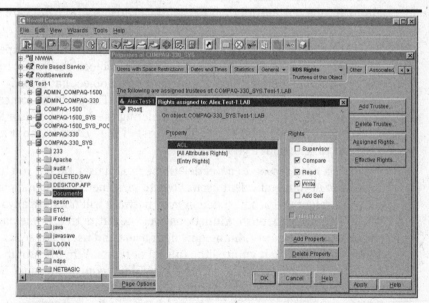

FIGURE 23.7: Granting limited rights that cannot be inherited.

Selected property rights always take precedence over inherited rights. Even without an IRF, setting particular trustee rights in one container puts those rights in effect, no matter which rights are assigned to the container above. ConsoleOne shows these rights assignments in a different way than we're used to, but you can see in Figure 23.7 that we just added property rights to the ACL property for the Documents volume for Alex. I clicked the Add Property button in the foreground dialog box to pop up the long list of rights to choose for Alex.

The IRF and Object and Property Rights

The IRF works the same with object and property rights as it does with file and directory rights. The IRF doesn't give rights to anyone; it only takes rights away.

You, as network manager, set the level of rights users should have to an object. If a particular user has more rights than that, the IRF will filter that particular user to the level of access you set.

The big difference in the IRF when dealing with the NDS object and property rights is the ability to block the Supervisor object right. This gives some departments a warm fuzzy feeling, since no one except their administrator can control their part of the eDirectory tree. But care must be taken in organizing your system.

NetWare helps safeguard against accidentally eliminating all supervision for part of your tree by not allowing you to block the Supervisor object right to an object unless at least one other object has already been granted the Supervisor right to that object. The problem comes if the other Supervisor object is deleted. Deleting the sole Supervisor for part of your NDS eDirectory tree leaves part of the system without management, which is not a good thing.

This is a good reason to never delete the Admin user, even if you have one or two Admin-equivalent users. Over time, something will happen to both equivalent users, and suddenly your network will not have anyone able to perform supervisory functions over the entire tree. Some paranoid people have both Admin-equivalent users and users not set as Admin-equivalent but granted the full set of rights. Why? If Admin is deleted or the properties are garbled, the Admin equivalency may be worthless as well.

So, when you grant someone the Supervisor trustee right to a section of the eDirectory tree, also grant them all other trustee rights. This precaution allows that person to maintain the ability to create, delete, rename, and modify objects, even if the Supervisor right is blocked by the IRF.

NDS Security Guidelines

Security management is not the most exciting stuff in the world, 99 percent of the time. The goal of this section is to help you ensure that the one percent of security management that is exciting—a security breach—happens only in the mildest way possible. Maybe only a bad joke breach.

Realize that few users need to create, delete, or modify objects (users, printers, and so on) during their normal workday. Those users who have occasion to need these trustee rights should be made an official or unofficial helper. The designation of "Power User for Marketing" will help that person feel better about spending extra time helping other users without getting paid for it. At least recognize those power users, since recognized helpers will help keep security strong, not tear it down. The big problems come when someone accidentally gets too many rights, not when the department's power user has defined a new printer.

A CNI (Certified NetWare Instructor) friend of mine offers these guidelines for granting rights:

▶ Start with the default assignments. Defaults are in place to give users access to the resources they need without giving them access to resources or information they do not need.

▶ Avoid assigning rights through the All Properties option. Avoiding All Properties will protect private information about users and other resources on the network.

▶ Use Selected Properties to assign property rights. This will allow you to assign more specific rights and avoid future security problems.

▶ Use caution when assigning the Write property right to the ACL property of any object. This right effectively gives the trustee the ability to grant anyone, including himself or herself, all rights, including the Supervisor right. This is another reason to use extreme care when making rights assignments with All Properties.

▶ Use caution when granting the Supervisor object right to a Server object. This gives Supervisor filesystem rights to all volumes linked to that server. This object rights assignment should be made only after considering the implication of a network administrator having access to all files on all volumes linked to a particular server. Furthermore, granting the Write property right to the ACL property of the Server object will also give Supervisor filesystem rights to all volumes linked to that particular server.

▶ Granting the Supervisor object right implies granting the Supervisor right to all properties. For some container administrators, you might want to grant all object rights except the Supervisor right and then grant property rights through the Selected Properties option.

▶ Use caution when filtering Supervisor rights with an IRF. For example, a container administrator uses an IRF to filter the network administrator's rights to a particular branch of the NDS eDirectory tree. If the network administrator (who has the Supervisor right to the container administrator's User object) deletes the User object of the container administrator, that particular branch of the NDS eDirectory tree can no longer be managed.

Here's my security slogan: Grant to containers or groups; ignore the individuals. The more individual users you administer, the more time and trouble it will take. I've known some NetWare managers to make groups holding only one person. That sounds stupid, but consider the alternative: when a second person comes, and then a third person, you'll find yourself handling each one by hand. If a group is in place, each new person who arrives takes only a few seconds to install and give all the necessary trustee rights and network resource mappings.

Whenever possible, handle security (access to network resources) through the container. If not a container, then a group. If not a group, look harder to make the need fit an existing group or develop a new group. The more adamant you are about securing your network by groups rather than by individual users, the lighter your network management burden. The more you use the container to grant rights, the neater things are.

MANAGING SECURITY WITH CONSOLEONE

When NDS first installs, there are two objects: Admin and [Public]. By default, the Admin object has Supervisor object rights to [Root], which allows Admin to create and administer all other network objects.

The [Public] object has the following object and property rights by default:

▶ Browse object rights to [Root], which allows all users to see the NDS eDirectory tree and all objects on the tree

▶ Read property right to the Default Server property, which determines the default server for the User object

When you create User objects, each has a certain set of default rights. These rights include what the User object can do to manage itself, such as Read and Write the user's login script and print job configuration. To get around in the eDirectory tree, users are also granted limited rights to [Root] and [Public]. Here's a summary of the default User object trustee, default rights, and what these rights allow a user to do:

▶ Read right to all property rights, which allows the reading of properties stored in the User object

▶ Read and Write property rights to the user's own Login Script property, which allows users to execute and modify their own login scripts

▶ Read and Write property rights to the user's own Print Configuration property, which allows users to create print jobs and send them to the printer

The [Root] object has one default property right: the Read property right to Network Address and Group Membership, which identifies the network address and any group memberships.

As you can see, the default NDS rights are fairly limited. A new user can see the network, change his or her own login script and printer configuration, and wait for help.

If that's too much—perhaps you don't want users to have the ability to change (and mess up) their own login scripts—change it. Merely revoke the User object's Login Script property right. Figure 23.8 shows the User object details, with the Write capability for the Login Script property revoked. The Read capability is necessary so that the user can log in.

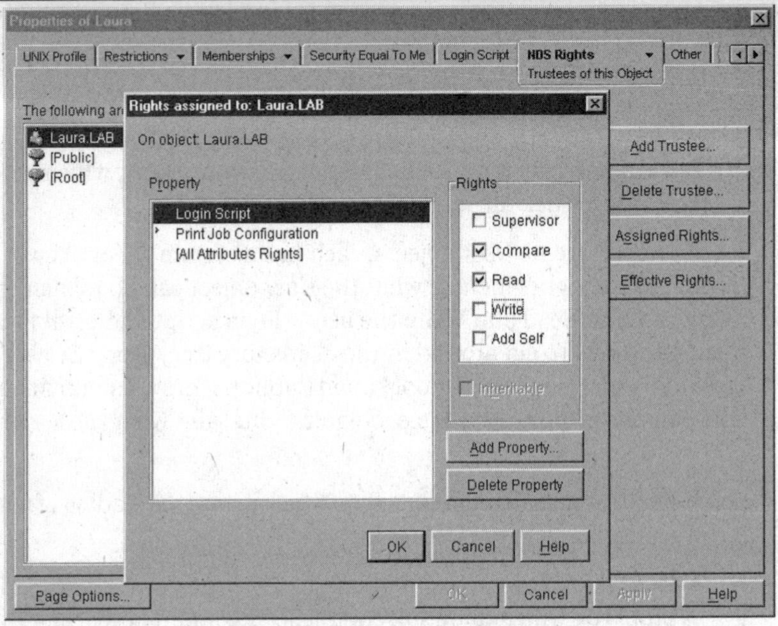

FIGURE 23.8:   Preventing Laura from changing her login script.

Revoking a Property Right

> **IN A HURRY 23.1: PREVENT USERS FROM MODIFYING THEIR OWN LOGIN SCRIPTS**
>
> 1. Open ConsoleOne from some Java Virtual Machine–enabled system.
>
> 2. Open the user's property page by right-clicking the User object name and selecting Properties.
>
> 3. Click the NDS Rights tab and choose Trustees Of This Object.
>
> 4. Highlight the User object and click the Assigned Rights button.
>
> 5. Click the property to modify (you may need to click the Add Property button).
>
> 6. Clear the Write check box while Login Script is highlighted.
>
> 7. Click OK to save the information.

Think of this process as a prelude to the other security-management tasks we're going to do in the following sections. First, you must start ConsoleOne from some Java Virtual Machine (JVM)–enabled system and highlight the User object that you want to modify. You must either right-click and choose Properties or use the File ➤ Properties menu choice.

When we get to the property page for the User object (as you can see in Figure 23.8 in the previous section), we want to change the Property Rights setting. It may sound odd, or at least different, but with Console-One, we need to check the Trustees Of This Object right under NDS Rights. Drill down to Laura.LAB.TEXAS. Then click the Assigned Rights command button, which opens the Rights Assigned To dialog box. Scroll through the list, find Login Script, highlight it, and review the rights.

The default is to have both Read and Write capabilities. By clicking the Write check box, that right is cleared from our user. The change will become active after the dialog box is saved with the new setting and the NDS database has a second to digest the change.

In Figure 23.8, I also opened the Rights Assigned To: Laura.LAB dialog box by clicking the Effective Rights button from the NDS Rights page. When I highlighted Login Script, the rights for user Laura to her own login script were shown: Compare and Read appeared in the Rights box. So now we know user Laura has the capability to read, and therefore execute, the login script, but not to change it.

TIP

The other way to prevent users from playing with their login scripts is to bypass them entirely. Remember the sequence of login script execution? The User object's login script comes last. Just use the EXIT command in the container login script, and the personal login script for everyone in the container will be bypassed. Users can then make all the changes they want in their login scripts, but it won't make a bit of difference.

Setting or Modifying Directory and File Rights

You can allow a user or group of users access to a directory in two ways:

- ► You can go through the user side and use the rights-to-files-and-directories approach.

- ► You can go to the directory to be accessed and use the trustees-of-this-directory angle.

Which method you use depends on whether you're making one directory available to many users or granting trustee rights to one set of users to a lot of other network objects. We'll take a look at both approaches.

From the Group or User's Point of View

IN A HURRY 23.2: GRANT TRUSTEE RIGHTS TO A VOLUME OR DIRECTORY

1. Open ConsoleOne.

2. Drill down in the left window to the Organizational Unit that contains the Group or User object.

3. Right-click the Group or User object and choose Properties.

4. Click the Rights To Files And Folders tab.

5. Click the Show command button and choose the correct volume in the Select Object dialog box.

6. Click the Add command button, and drill down to the correct directory or file.

7. Check the boxes near the rights you wish to grant.

8. Click the OK command button, or click the Apply button if you have more changes to make.

You can easily grant trustee rights for a single object to multiple volumes, directories, or files. The object gaining the rights should be a group of some kind, such as an Organization, an Organizational Unit, or a Group object, but it works for single User objects as well.

Start ConsoleOne as either the Admin user or another user with the Supervisor right to both the user side and the network resource side of this equation. Drill down until the group appears on the right side of ConsoleOne. We'll work with our Techies group in this example. Right-click that group, choose Properties, click the Rights To Files And Folders tab, and you'll see most of what appears in Figure 23.9.

First, click the Show command button to find and select the correct volume (COMPAQ-330_SYS: in this case). Then click the Add command button, select down to the directory level, and choose the Apache directory. Techs demand access to web pages and source code, so let them have it.

Notice that all rights are being granted to Techies. If you don't give them all rights, they'll just whine and complain until you change your mind and upgrade their rights. Give them all rights the first time, then let them worry about what happens if they screw up. They're programmers, so if they do screw up, they'll never admit a thing. That's what I'm doing in Figure 23.9—giving them all rights to the Apache directory.

Unlike in NetWare Administrator or other Windows utilities, ConsoleOne won't allow you to select multiple files or directories on the Rights To Files And Folders tab of the group's property page. You could use another utility, but I would rather you take the hint: don't change one file at a time, but focus on the directory.

The default rights to any new volume, directory, or file are Read and File Scan. Figure 23.10 shows that this is the case for the Techies group's effective rights to the Documents directory.

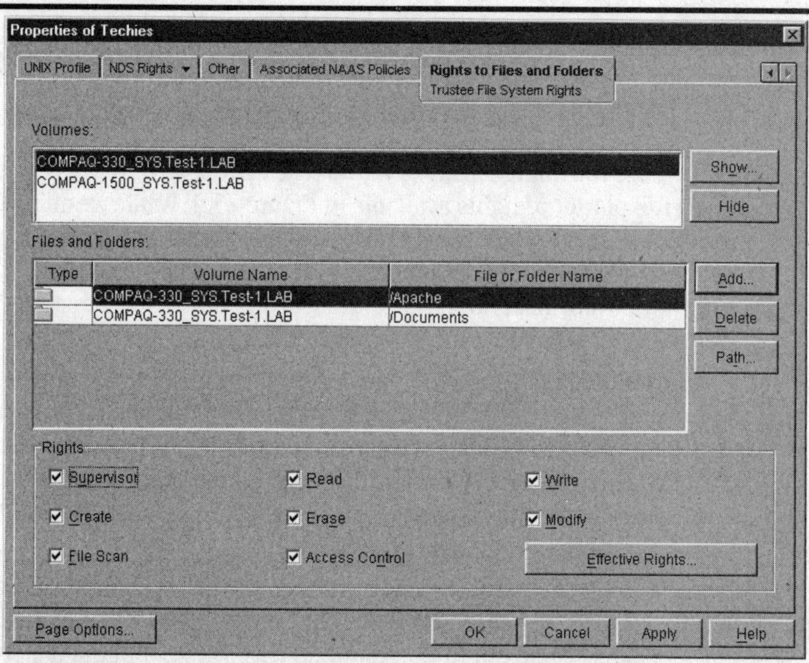

FIGURE 23.9: Granting Techies access to the Apache directory.

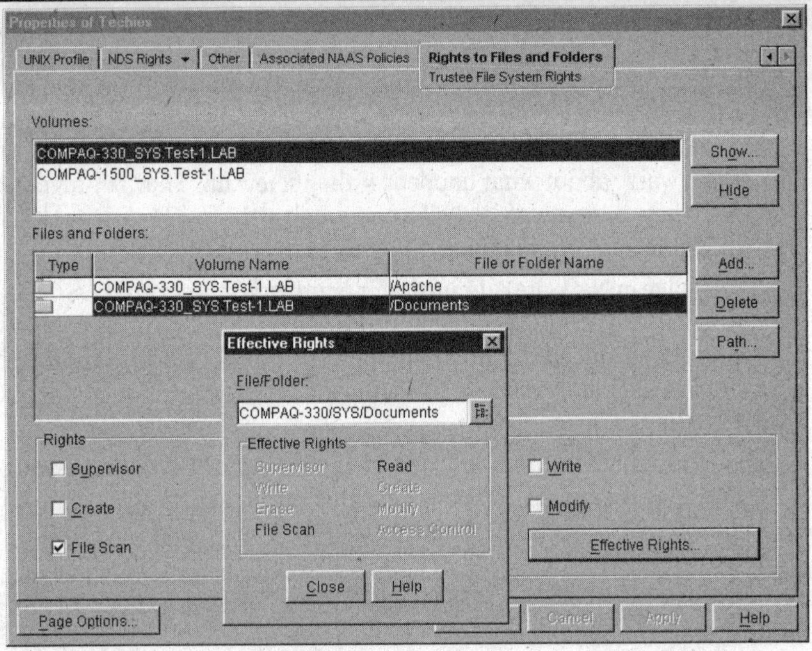

FIGURE 23.10:   Granted rights are bold; excluded rights are gray.

Contrast the limited array of rights (the default rights) in Figure 23.10 to the full platter of rights available in Figure 23.9. While we all agree Techies can make good use of their full access to the web server directory, giving them access to corporate documents may prove less useful. This is why they have almost no rights to the Documents folder. Trust me, writers hate to let techs attempt to write or edit their work.

Granting rights to a directory in another container is not a problem, but one more step may be needed. If the users want to map a drive to another container in their login script, they can't get there from here. You must create an Alias object for the remote volume and then map the groups and users to the Alias.

You can grant trustee rights to a Volume object rather than to a directory or file. If you do, the object with those rights has complete access to the root directory, meaning the entire volume. If you have enough volumes to parcel them out in that manner, that's great, but many networks grant rights to a directory. That allows plenty of accessibility for the users, since they can build a full directory structure, while still maintaining an easy method of control.

From the Directory or File's Point of View

IN A HURRY 23.3: GRANT TRUSTEE RIGHTS TO A GROUP OR USER

1. Open ConsoleOne.

2. Drill down to the volume or directory desired.

3. Right-click the directory or file and choose Properties.

4. Click the Trustees tab to check current trustees. Click the Add Trustee command button to add another trustee.

5. Drill down to the object to become a trustee of the directory.

6. Highlight the groups and/or users in the Select Objects dialog box and click OK.

7. To modify the rights, check or clear the check boxes in the Rights section. Repeat as necessary for each group or user.

8. Click OK to save the settings.

Approaching rights from the directory's (or file's) point of view is the best method to use when granting several users or groups trustee rights to the same volume, directory, or file. One screen allows you to choose multiple trustees at once and yet assign different rights to each of them. Although this technique can work with volumes and files, let's use a common scenario: making a group of users trustees to a directory.

Start the ConsoleOne program. Browse through the NDS eDirectory tree as necessary to locate and highlight the object that you want to make available to the new user or users. In our example, the Documents directory is the one to be shared with Sandi and now the Writers Organizational Unit (yes, an OU can have trustee rights, as we discussed earlier).

Once the volume is highlighted in the left pane, the directories will appear in the right pane. Pressing Enter will display the directories in the left pane, leaving the right pane still empty. Right-click the directory name (in either pane you prefer) and choose Properties.

We added Sandi and the Techies earlier, so she and that group appear as trustees of the directory. Click the Add Trustee command button to open the Select Objects dialog box, and then select the Writers OU, as shown in Figure 23.11. Once you've found it, click OK to add the Writers OU to the list of trustees for the Documents directory.

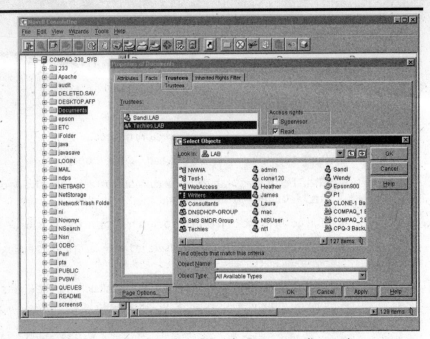

FIGURE 23.11:   Adding the Writers OU to the Documents directory's
Trustees list.

Once the new trustees are copied to the list, checking the Access Rights
boxes for each group will set the level of control the group has over the
directory. Since few groups should ever have Supervisor rights, leave that
box unchecked.

In ConsoleOne, the Access Rights check boxes do an excellent job
of showing the Effective Rights. In Figure 23.12, you can see that the
Writers OU has all rights, except Supervisor, to the directory.

Click OK to save and exit, or just click Close since the rights have
already been changed, and then reenter to check that all the rights you
planned to grant have in fact been granted. It's easy to skip a mouse-click
here and there, so make it a habit to check yourself.

Once again, granting rights to a directory in another container is not
a problem, but one more step may be needed. If the users want to map a
drive to another container in their login script, they can't get there from
here. You must create an Alias object for the remote volume and then
map the groups and users to the Alias.

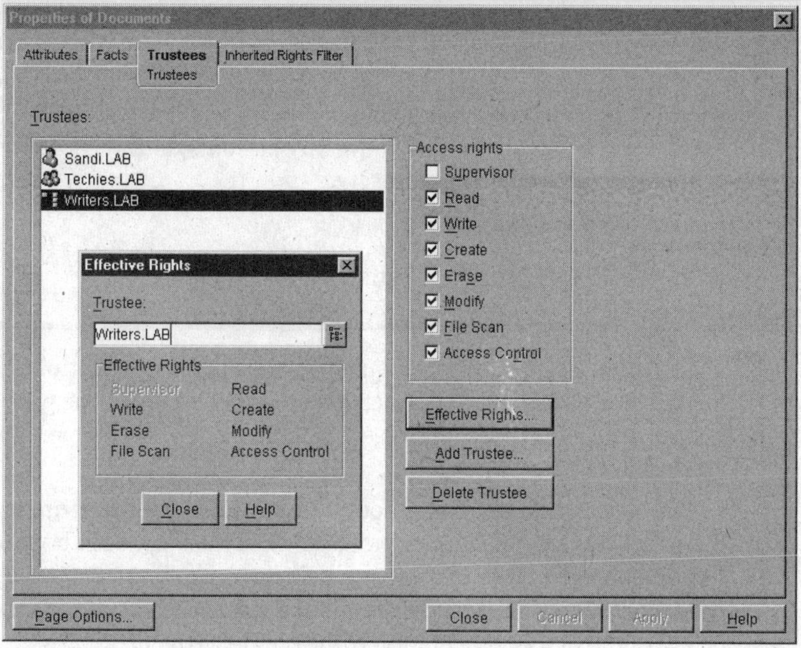

FIGURE 23.12:   The effective rights to the Documents directory for the Writers OU.

Setting or Modifying Object and Property Rights

IN A HURRY 23.4: GIVE AN OBJECT TRUSTEE RIGHTS TO OTHER OBJECTS

1. Open ConsoleOne.

2. Right-click the object to be given trustee rights to another object and choose Properties.

3. Click the NDS Rights tab and choose Trustees Of This Object.

4. Click the Add Trustee command button to open the Select Objects dialog box.

CONTINUED ➡

5. To find the object to become an assigned trustee, click the down arrow to open the eDirectory tree listing, or click the folder icon with the up arrow to move up one context level. Move up or down the tree as necessary.

6. Select the object and click OK.

7. Click OK to save the settings.

Sometimes, one network resource must be managed, controlled, or modified by multiple other objects. That's what we did in the previous section. And sometimes, one object must manage or control multiple other objects.

The network administrator does this, of course, for the entire network. But many users need some control over more than just their home directory. Even medium-power users can help by controlling a department printer or volume. Real power users can become de facto subadministrators with the proper cooperation with your department.

Do you want to give an object trustee rights to more than one other object at a time? Here's the place. This procedure allows you to grant trustee rights to multiple objects from one screen.

As the Admin user or equivalent, start ConsoleOne. Highlight the object, such as a user, a group, or a container, that you want to make a trustee of one or more other objects, right-click, and choose Properties. Then click the NDS Rights tab and select Trustees Of This Object from its menu.

The first step is to discover what the object already has rights to. This requires our first real search operation. Figure 23.13 shows the Select Objects dialog box open, with the user Laura's NDS Rights property page in the background. The Select Objects dialog box offers two ways to cruise the NDS eDirectory tree, and Figure 23.13 shows one of them.

When the dialog box opens, the current context displays. Use the down arrow at the end of the Look In box to display the full eDirectory tree down to your current context. If you need to go up only one context level, you can click the up-arrow icon to the right of the down arrow instead. Drill down, or slide up, the eDirectory tree until you find what you need. Since we're going to let Laura control some servers in a minute, we need to move up to the Test-1 Organization level.

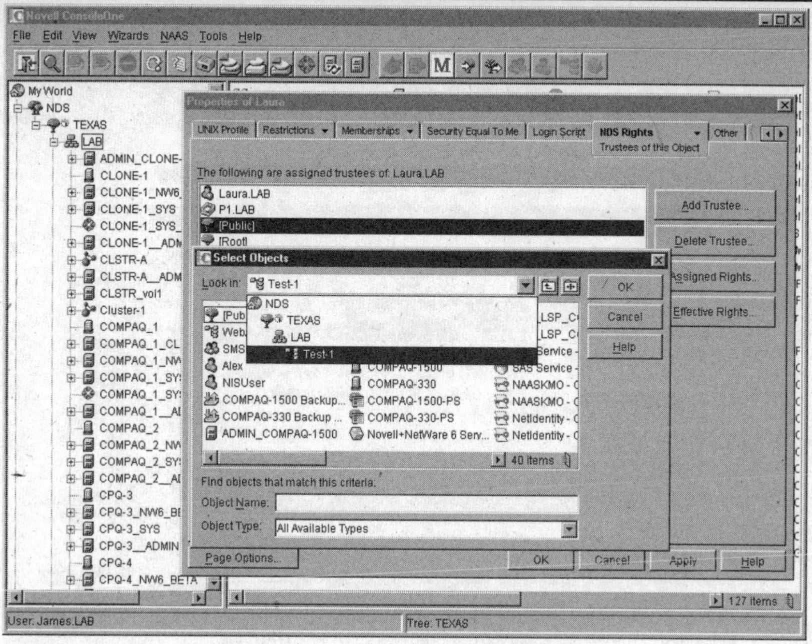

FIGURE 23.13:   Searching for other objects for Laura to control.

Our goal is to Add Trustee. Browse through the NDS eDirectory tree and highlight the object or objects to gain trustee rights over, as shown in Figure 23.14. In our example, Laura now gains some control over the COMPAQ-1500 and COMPAQ-330 servers.

Notice that we may once again tag several objects in one screen by using either the Ctrl-key-and-multiple-click or the Shift-key-and-inclusive-click technique. We can see the current context of the items we're choosing, not the context of the objects gaining the trustee rights. Click OK to save your choices and move them to the Trustees Of This Object property page for final configuration.

Figure 23.15 shows the final step in this process. We can configure both of our chosen objects concurrently. As long as one or more items in the Rights Assigned To list is highlighted, the check boxes will apply to all of the objects. Click the Assigned Rights button, then click the rights you want the object to have over the target object (in our example, the rights of Laura over COMPAQ-1500_SYS and COMPAQ-330_SYS). When you're finished, click OK to save and exit the object's property page.

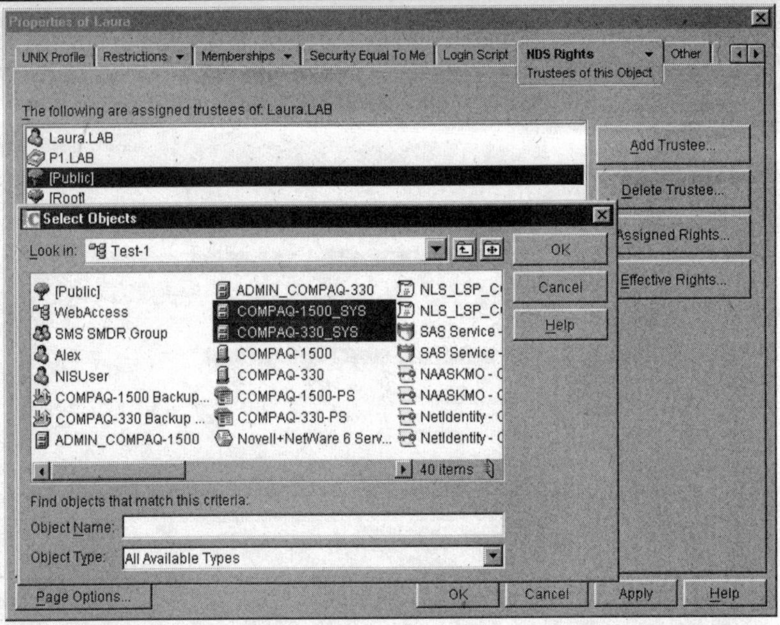

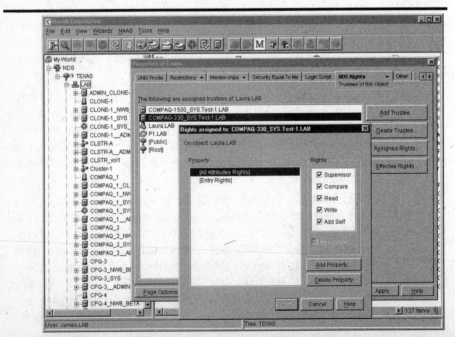

FIGURE 23.14: Laura selects volumes to control.

FIGURE 23.15: Granting trustee rights to more than one object at a time.

The same process works for modifying existing rights to objects. In that case, making sure you search the entire network for all objects is even more important. If you want to delete the assignment, highlight the previously Assigned Rights and click the Delete Property command button. The rights assignment, not the object itself, will be deleted.

PROTECTING YOUR NETWORK FROM VIRUSES

Viruses are always a concern, even if they are statistically insignificant. People worrying about viruses waste more time than viruses waste, although the proliferation of operating systems with Swiss cheese security (the initials are Microsoft) makes virus protection more critical than in years past. Knowing that a virus attack is rare doesn't make you feel any better or get your network back to normal any faster if it does happen. Time spent preventing viruses is much more fun than time spent cleaning up after one.

Some Precautions

You can take some precautions without adding optional software to your network or much time to your workday. Mark all .EXE and .COM files as Read Only. Viruses generally function by modifying executable files. If all your executable files are read-only, viruses have a much harder time getting started.

Keep a tight watch on users' access rights to system areas—there shouldn't be any. Only managers, with a proper understanding of virus prevention, should have access to system files.

Do not allow users to bring disks from outside and load them to the network before being tested. Some companies go so far as to lock floppy drives, not so that users can't steal from the company, but so that users can't load infected software. This method is difficult to enforce and not good enough to be your only prevention step. Better to offer a virus-free check station for users to test floppies than try to ban floppies altogether. If you ban them, people will just sneak them into the building. The same goes for CDs, the preferred method of program distribution today.

The days when users regularly downloaded unknown files from bulletin boards and booted their systems with those disks are long gone.

That's good. Commercially sponsored download sites now pride themselves on running a clean site. That's good also. But the number of files copied from unknown sources across the Internet is growing tremendously, and that's bad. Unix administrators often don't know which DOS and Windows files are on their systems, and they don't have the time or tools to test them for viruses. That's also bad.

Feel free to restrict or eliminate FTP (File Transfer Protocol) programs from your Internet suite of applications, except for those trustworthy users who understand the need for virus protection. Although you can't always stop users from downloading files with a web browser such as Netscape, keeping the FTP programs away from the general user population may help a little, even though few "regular" users ever attempt using FTP.

Virus-Protection Software

Special virus-protection software is available for networks, often in conjunction with software metering or network user management. If your company is overly concerned with a virus attack, the software may give some peace of mind. However, antivirus software used inconsistently is worse than none at all. When you have none, people are more careful. When you have antivirus software used poorly, people develop a false sense of protection.

Here are some of the virus-protection features the optional programs provide:

- ▶ Install and configure easily. NetWare versions are run as NLMs (new Java versions have yet to appear).

- ▶ Block unprotected clients from logging in to a protected server.

- ▶ Distribute protection to multiple servers and clients.

- ▶ Include an administration program for Windows as well as DOS.

- ▶ Send alerts to specified users when a questionable event occurs.

- ▶ Schedule when and how security sweeps are made.

- ▶ Report on status and other statistics.

There are two major camps regarding the primary means of protection against the virus-developer community. One idea is to track the signature of all viruses. The *signature* is a piece of code inside the virus that identifies that virus, usually included by the virus criminal as an ego enhancer. As more viruses are discovered, the signature database must grow. Those systems that scan for known virus signatures should receive regular database updates.

The other option is to register a *CRC* (cyclical redundancy check) of every executable file on the server when the file is installed. The CRC is checked each time the file is read from the server. If the CRC value changes, this means that the file has been tampered with. The alert sounds, and the software shuts down the use of that file.

I lean toward the CRC method, for several reasons. First, a new virus obviously can cause you problems, and this threat is eliminated with a CRC. Second, the overhead of checking a large virus database with every file-read request will only get heavier. As the demands on servers grow, this overhead will become burdensome. Finally, my friend John McCann was one of the first programmers to make quality add-on NetWare utilities, and he says the CRC method is better. Since he knows more about NetWare programming than anyone else I know, I'll take his word for it. (It's especially easy when I agree with his conclusion anyway.)

Do you have a favorite antivirus program? Do I? Not really. Be sure to check several major brands if you don't have virus protection already (and why don't you have protection already?). Those readers with multivendor networks (which usually means some Windows NT or 2000 servers) will find that many of the companies in this market make virus products for both NetWare and NT/2000.

Some people ask about the values of server-based versus client-based virus protection. We could even have separate sections extolling the virtues of both types of protection. But we won't, because I feel strongly that you can't trust users to do your job for you. Yes, the users will suffer if they have a virus attack on their personal system, but they will demand that you fix things for them. So, asking them to protect against virus attacks on the client is asking them to do your job for you. Even if they were willing, they don't have the mental discipline to do a good job. They'll trust a file from a friend, assuming their friend knows the file's history. That's usually a bad move, as recent virus writers have demonstrated by forwarding viruses through every contact in an infected system's Outlook address book (thanks again, Windows).

A critical part of virus protection is regular updates. Server-based products need a single update session to protect hundreds of clients.

This is much more efficient (and reliable) than upgrading hundreds of clients individually.

Verify that your virus protection works on the client when the user logs in. Kicking off a check of the client during the login process catches most of the viruses introduced by careless users. You won't catch them all, unfortunately, because if you make the process idiot-proof, your company will hire a better idiot. Just make sure the virus doesn't spread.

TIP

If your manager is particularly scared of a virus attack, use that fear to your advantage. Clip an article about a virus attack and the resulting damage to the company. Nearly every single report includes a line about how the company had an inadequate backup procedure in place, meaning extra loss. If you've been angling for a bigger tape backup system or an upgrade, play the cards you're dealt, and hit your manager with the tape backup request in one hand while waving the virus attack article in the other hand. Is this dishonest? Not at all. Some people need to be pushed into doing the right thing. You should take care to push your manager when he or she is already staggering. This way, you don't need to push noticeably hard, but you still get what your network needs. Our world will never be virus-free again, so you must keep upgrading your protection systems. Nudge and/or blackmail your management as necessary.

NetWare 6 Security Improvements

Ever-evolving features required Novell to add some bang to the security section of NetWare 4.1x and NetWare 5. Novell could have done this by adding a few extra security screens everyone ignores, marked the security matrix as "improved," and gone on with their business.

Security became much more prominent than that. Novell hired one of the original developers of the U.S. Government's "Red Book" security project. That developer, and other work done by Novell deep inside the operating system, helped certify NetWare 4.11 as a "C2 Red Book" network. This is a big deal. NetWare 6 must also be certified, but Novell officials declared this rating important and will submit NetWare 6 soon.

WHY IS C2 SECURITY CERTIFICATION A BIG DEAL?

First of all, it's a big deal because Microsoft made so much noise about Windows NT getting C2 security. The Novell folks can't stand for Microsoft to beat them in any purchase order check-off category, and that's what was happening. The fact that Windows NT was only C2 secure in stand-alone mode left the door open for Novell to top Microsoft, at least in the PR war. Not that the government followed their own regulations; departments regularly ignored the security guidelines and bought NT.

Second, it's a big deal for customers who support and use such security systems already, such as the government, the armed forces, and paranoid corporations. It's true that the government has a sizable NetWare installed base, and huge areas of some departments can't run computer equipment rated lower than C2.

Does C2 security do much for you? Probably not. Realistically, C2-level security is a giant hassle, and few companies go to that much trouble. If your company is one of the C2 adherents, you know of what I speak.

I will be amazed if your company increases your NetWare security profile up to the C2 level, unless you work for one of the aforementioned groups such as the military. For one thing, only C2-authorized software can run on a NetWare NTCB (Network Trusted Computing Base). All those NLMs you have? Gone, unless they've been certified.

Are you and the other administrators certified? Gone. Do you have NetWare 3.x networks still running on your corporate network? Gone. Only secure systems can run on a secure network. Do you have your server under lock and key? Gone until that's done. Have you limited access to remote console programs, such as RCONSOLE? Gone. See what I mean? It's more trouble than it's worth, at least for the majority of corporations.

Adding the JVM will make your NetWare 6 server more popular for all types of utilities for the server, including security. Distributed applications are all the rage today, and security is becoming a consideration in the design phase. This falls under the heading of "a good thing," as Martha Stewart would say.

NetWare 6 includes a certificate authority for added security, but don't confuse that with C2 security certification. Those certificates guarantee that traffic across the Internet came from whom you think it came from and have nothing to do with normal, intracompany network business. We won't go into much depth with the Internet security options, because that topic deserves a book or two or ten devoted to ways to secure Internet traffic.

WHEN SECURITY STINKS, MANAGEMENT SMELLS THE WORST

A "rock and a hard place" describes security. The tougher the security, the more people will hate the network. Looser security makes for happier users but more virus problems and file mishaps.

Remember, here we're speaking about NetWare security, not complete Internet security for all your web and e-mail servers. That subject has its own bookshelf.

Your company routinely allows access to every room of your building to the lowest paid, and least monitored, employees: cleaning crews. The biggest risk is crews employed by the building management, especially those who use temporary helpers. Do you have any idea what these people are doing? Does your management? Probably not.

This is one of the areas where hard choices must be made, and your management must make them. If your bosses won't do their jobs, push a little. If they still refuse, document the security measures in place, the reasons for those measures, and apply them absolutely. When users complain to their bosses, and their bosses complain to your boss, let your boss modify the procedure. Then get your boss to sign any changes. Accountability is shared; blame is yours alone.

Don't let management overcompensate for lousy security elsewhere by tightening the screws on the network. That's like a bank with a vault full of cash, while the bearer bonds, cashier checks, and negotiable securities are lying out in the open, ready to be picked up and carried away.

Force management to define a consistent security profile. It makes no sense to restrict network users to the bone while leaving the president's file cabinet unlocked. People looking to steal information, both from the inside and outside, will happily take paper or computer disks. While it isn't legal to steal a report off your computer system, it is legal to grab a printout of that same report out of the dumpster.

Inconsistent security control runs both ways. I once had a customer so worried about security that he refused to have a fax server on the network.

The owner was afraid of dial-in hackers going through the fax modem into the computer system. We finally convinced the owner that this was impossible.

The flip side was a major oil company in the mid-1980s that had the typical tight security on its mainframe. Terminal and user IDs were tracked, users were monitored, and passwords were everywhere—the whole bit. Then someone noticed it was possible to copy information from the mainframe to a PC connected with an IRMA board (an adapter in the PC that connected via coax to an SNA cluster controller, effectively making the PC a 3270 terminal). A management committee studied the matter and verified that yes, anyone could copy any information from the mainframe to disks and paper. The information could then be dropped in the trash, carried home, or sold to a competitor. All these options obviously violated the company's security guidelines.

What did the managers do? They decided to ignore the problem and placed no security on PCs with IRMA boards beyond what they had on the terminals the PCs replaced. It may be noble to trust the employees, but it was inconsistent security. Those users with PCs deserved security training and a warning about the severity of potential security leaks. They got nothing because corporate management was too lazy to do its job. If a problem developed, who would be blamed? You know—the computer managers who had no control over the decision.

WHAT'S NEXT

Remote access into a network has become a vital part of the corporate environment. Configuring remote access so that your clients can gain access to the resources they require can be challenging. A virtual private network session is an authenticated and encrypted communication channel across some form of public network, such as the Internet. Because the network is considered to be insecure, encryption and authentication are used to protect the data while it is in transit. The next chapter looks at remote access and ways of ensuring data security when using VPN technology.

Chapter 24
REMOTE CONNECTIVITY

It seems like it was only a few years ago that the concept of remote computing or dial-up connectivity was relatively unknown. As far as most of the world was concerned, there was no such thing as the Internet, the idea of telecommuting hadn't been born yet, and e-mail didn't exist. Remote connectivity and dial-up modems were vague, mysterious technologies as far as the average person was concerned. Once considered the tools of businesses and technically oriented individuals to simply get "data" from one location to another, these concepts have now become part of everyday life.

Technology has changed the world in some remarkable ways, but the most amazing way is how "connected" people are these days (or, at least, can be if they *want* to). Home computers are becoming more and more common, and the average home consumer can buy a dial-up modem just as easily as a toaster or CD player. Employees are being equipped with everything from laptops to palmtops and being sent out on the road, with

Adapted from *Mastering Windows 2000 Server*, Third Edition by Mark Minasi, Christa Anderson, Brian M. Smith, and Doug Toombs

ISBN 0-7821-2872-6   1,872 pages $59.99

the expectation that they should be just as connected on the road as they are when they're in the office. For better or for worse, this onslaught of technology has brought with it a demand for "easy connectivity—anytime, anywhere."

These demands have put a heavy burden on the backs of system administrators. Not only does the typical administrator have to handle day-to-day support issues *within* the office, but with so much work happening outside the office it seems to have made an already difficult job seem impossible at times. Unfortunately, there isn't a magical solution for everyone yet (I doubt there ever will be), but Microsoft's Remote Access Service (RAS) has been designed and improved over the years to help administrators deal with some of these demands.

Originally developed in the early days of Windows NT, RAS was initially bundled as part of the base operating system. I've always felt the reason for this (at least partially) was to give NT a competitive advantage against other network operating systems out on the market—namely Novell. When remote computing was first starting to take off, Novell was the primary player in the NOS market, and they had developed add-on products like NetWare Connect to support dial-up connections to NetWare networks. Products like NetWare Connect worked well and gave users the connectivity they needed, but these products had to be purchased separately, and the license costs often increased in direct proportion to the number of simultaneous dial-in connections that needed to be supported.

While I can't be absolutely certain this is the reason Microsoft chose to bundle RAS in with the operating system for free, it certainly seems like a reasonable assumption. As many recent court cases have highlighted, "bundling" is a popular Microsoft tactic to gain market share. Personally, I know of at least a few organizations that started deploying NT in its early days simply because of the number of things that were included for free with the operating system—things they would have had to pay extra for with any other network operating system. Whatever the reasons were, NT began to take off, and RAS capabilities grew with each new version of the operating system.

Microsoft has improved RAS with each new version of Windows NT to the point where it has grown into a full-featured remote access platform capable of handling even the most demanding environments. By the time Windows NT 4 was released, RAS was a solid, reliable part of the NT operating system. The Internet was a few years along in its transition from the government and education environment into the commercial world, and it was becoming more common for people to try to leverage their investments in Internet connectivity to meet their remote access needs. With the release of NT 4, Microsoft included support for Point-to-Point Tunneling Protocol as a means of encapsulating RAS packets and sending them over the Internet instead of a modem. The phrase "virtual private networking" started becoming a buzzword in the vocabulary of network administrators, and Microsoft improved on the virtual private networking capabilities of NT 4 by later releasing a routing update called Routing and Remote Access Service (RRAS).

With the advent of Windows 2000, Microsoft has put together the most comprehensive set of remote access capabilities to date, consolidating all the previous technologies and capabilities in an easy-to-use interface. But with *so* many options available, at times it can be hard to know which is your best choice. In the pages that follow, I'll discuss what some of your options are, some common scenarios you will probably run into, and the solutions for those problems.

COMMON APPLICATIONS FOR REMOTE ACCESS SERVICE

For the purposes of this text, we'll assume that Remote Access Service is divided into two distinct functions: accepting inbound calls and placing outbound calls. With the advent of Windows NT 4, Microsoft now commonly refers to the latter as Dial-Up Networking (DUN for short), and receiving inbound calls has pretty much always been referred to as Remote Access Service (or RAS). Even though RAS and DUN share some of the same setup and installation routines, when you see a reference to DUN, you can assume it is for an outbound call.

With that clarification taken care of, let's take a look at some of the tasks you can accomplish with the Remote Access Service in Windows 2000 Server.

Connecting to the Internet

One of the more commonly used capabilities of Dial-Up Networking is to allow your computer to dial in to an ISP—usually via Point-to-Point Protocol (PPP)—and communicate with distant servers and hosts across the Internet. Although this might commonly be used for simple browsing and file transfers on a server, it is becoming common for e-mail and proxy servers to function entirely over dial-up connections to the Internet.

Windows 2000 Server includes several functional improvements over previous versions of Windows NT when it comes to Dial-Up Networking. Features such as demand dialing, reestablishing failed links, and repetitively dialing nonresponsive numbers make Win2K Dial-Up Networking a robust platform for establishing Internet connections and keeping them online.

Accepting Incoming Calls from Remote Clients

Traveling workers, telecommuters, and late-night workaholics all share one thing in common: they all eventually need access to corporate resources from remote locations. Remote Access Service can serve as a platform to get these users connected into your internal networks and servers.

Whether you need to allow access to your NT network, Novell servers, Unix hosts, or any other internal devices, RAS can act as a universal gateway for all your inbound communication needs. By accepting inbound connections from several different devices (analog, ISDN, X.25, VPN) and routing the traffic to your internal network, RAS can provide seamless networking for your users. Workstations dialed into a network over RAS will work exactly the same as they would if they were connected directly to the network (albeit a bit slower—more on that later).

Connecting to a Private Network

In addition to connecting a Windows 2000 Server to the Internet, it's often necessary to connect one network to another—perhaps to transfer data to suppliers or clients. In any case, Windows 2000 Server can be connected to another private network just as easily as to the Internet and take advantage of the same link reliability features.

Acting As an Internet Gateway

In response to popular demand, Microsoft has added the capability for a Windows 2000 Server to share an Internet connection among clients connected to an internal network. By the addition of network address translation (NAT) capabilities in Win2K, Windows can now act as a sort of proxy for getting internal clients connected to the Internet.

NOTE

It is worthwhile to note that this "proxy" service for getting internal clients connected to the Internet over a shared connection is completely different from the Microsoft Proxy BackOffice application.

Although this service will primarily be of use to small and home offices, it is a dramatic (and welcome) addition to the suite of services contained in RAS.

Accepting VPN Connections from Remote Clients

Along with the advent of the Internet in the corporate world, the concept of virtual private networking has emerged and become one of the hottest areas in networking. Virtual private networking, loosely defined, is a means of running a secure, private network over an insecure public network. Or, in plain English, you can have clients get connected (securely) to your office network by simply having an Internet connection and a valid (public) IP address and then establishing a VPN session to your RAS server. The VPN session is secure and encrypted, so your private data is protected as it passes over the public network (i.e., the Internet).

Microsoft has leveraged their investments in RAS in the development of virtual private networking in Windows 2000. By incorporating PPTP and L2TP protocols within the operating system, you can effectively set up "virtual" modems that work over IP networks, instead of analog or digital circuits. The methodology and terms used to implement these virtual modems are the same that are used for regular modems, so learning how to implement virtual private networking is made easier.

Dialing Up a Remote Network and Routing Traffic

With the addition of the Routing and Remote Access Service update to Windows NT 4, Microsoft made it easier for a Windows NT Server to act as a router, connecting to remote networks as needed and routing traffic. This type of connection between locations is commonly referred to as wide area networking or WAN connectivity.

With no more hardware than a dial-up modem at each site, internal clients and workstations can access resources on remote networks through this capability. By simply programming your internal workstations and devices to use your Windows 2000 Server as a "gateway," RAS can accept client traffic destined for a remote network, establish a connection to that network, and then pass the traffic across the connection as necessary. Since most office-to-office connectivity has traditionally been handled via costly dedicated circuits, having this ability is a tremendous benefit.

Already, this capability is helping organizations act in a completely "virtual" capacity—appearing to have a centralized network of resources that are actually individual servers spread across several sites, joined by demand-dialed dial-up connections.

BANDWIDTH PLANNING AND CONSIDERATIONS

Before we begin discussing what types of hardware and software you need to start using RAS, it's important to make sure you have an understanding of when RAS would and wouldn't be a good solution. The two most important factors in determining this are speed and reliability.

No discussion of remote access would be complete without defining the two different types of communication that are often referred to when you hear the phrase "remote access." These are sometimes referred to as *remote-node* and *remote-control* technologies. They may sound similar, and as far as end users are concerned they're basically the same, but these two methods of remote access are in fact very different. Unfortunately, many administrators are often left with implementing vague management directives such as "make sure that our employees can work while they're on the road," which are amazing oversimplifications of remote access's complexities. It's important to understand the capabilities and limitations of each type of access so you can make the best decision for your needs.

Remote Node

RAS is a remote-node method of communication and a very flexible and versatile means of getting users or networks connected to one another. Overall, I prefer remote-node solutions over remote control for most

Part V

applications, but having an understanding of how remote node works will help you recognize the best time to use it.

One of the simplest ways to visualize remote-node communication is to view the phone line connecting a client to a network as a *very* long network cable. Like any normal network cable in your office, this one is plugged into two locations. It starts at the user's workstation or laptop, goes through the phone company, and then ends at a modem in your office. Visualize that entire connection as a network cable. That modem, in turn, is connected to a RAS server (or another similar device), and the RAS server is—presumably—connected to your network. The RAS server accepts the incoming data from that dial-in user and then simply "passes" their data onto a local network segment. The same is true for outgoing data. The RAS server will see any outgoing data destined for that user on the network and transmit it over the phone line. As far as end-user functionality goes, your network should work exactly the same way in the office as it does dialing in, albeit much slower.

Since typical office network connections these days are running at speeds of upwards of 10,000,000 to 100,000,000 bits per second, throughput can be amazingly fast. So fast, that it is easy to overlook the amount of data that is actually traveling across your network. Considering the fact that the best analog modems available today are only reaching speeds of 56,000 bits per second, throughput can be a problem with remote-node solutions. Basic math indicates that there's only about 1/20th of the bandwidth available over a 56K modem in comparison to a 10-megabit Ethernet connection. That simple fact has a direct impact on the speed and performance of applications being used on the network. For example, a 2.5-megabyte Word document might open up in just a few seconds on a 10-megabit Ethernet connection in an office, but on a 56K modem connection, that document could take upwards of a few minutes to open up.

 ### CALCULATING MODEM TRANSMISSION TIMES

Use the following formula to calculate modem transmission times:

$$\frac{\text{File size in "bytes"} \times 8}{\text{Speed of connection in "bits" (i.e., 56k = 56,000)}} = \text{Transmission time in seconds}$$

Case in Point: Choosing the Right Remote Access Solution

If you implement a RAS solution without having some of these facts in your arsenal, you could end up with a solution that is effectively useless. Consider, for example, the case of one of my clients—let's call them the XYZ Corporation. The XYZ Corporation was in the process of moving into a new building but had to leave their accounting software and data on the file server in their old building due to several licensing and political issues. The accounting software was an old FoxPro file-based program that had served them well for many years, but it was eventually being replaced when they moved.

Their initial desire was to just have users dial in to the network in the old building and work on the accounting application as they did before. However, since the accounting application was "file-based" as opposed to being "client-server" (more on that later), the amount of data going back and forth between their workstations and servers was simply too great to make a remote-node solution work for their application. Simple analysis of their traffic indicated that their primary users of the accounting software were easily transferring 20 to 40 megabytes worth of data across their network in *as little as an hour*. If you've ever downloaded a large application from the Internet over a modem, you know how long it takes to move that much data—you probably start your download overnight and check it again the next morning.

Remembering our calculations from earlier, only about 1/20th of the bandwidth was available to XYZ Corporation over a dial-up remote-node connection. Quite simply, they were not going to be able to move that much data over a modem and maintain usable response times—a remote-node solution was *not* going to work for this client with this specific application.

The key factor that worked against XYZ Corporation was the fact that their critical application was file-based instead of being client-server. I can't emphasize enough how important it is to understand the mechanisms that computers typically use to move data around, so let's walk through some example applications of each of these types, see how they work, and see why some don't work well with remote-node solutions while others do.

File-Based Apps versus Client-Server Apps

Consider, if you will, a simple Microsoft Access database of names and phone numbers that you have stored on your computer. For discussion purposes, we'll assume that you have not "indexed" this database (a process that makes searching databases faster) and are trying to look up the phone number for an individual with the last name of Toombs. To find this name and number, you'd launch your Microsoft Access application, open your phone number database, and then do a search on the last name. Once you submit your search, your CPU would talk to your hard drive controller, tell it to open the database on your hard drive, and retrieve the first record in the database. When the first record comes back, it turns out that it's for somebody named Anderson. The CPU realizes that Anderson doesn't equal Toombs, so it dumps the first record from its memory and then requests the second one. The second record is for Daily. Daily doesn't equal Toombs either, so once again the CPU would dump that record from memory and read the third one. And so on, and so on, until it finally got to the record for Toombs. Once it successfully finds Toombs, it displays the record on the screen.

The important factor to take note of is the repetitive process the CPU had to go through to get the data it needed. It had to keep communicating with the hard drive controller to get the next record, and then receive the response (the actual data) and check it. Given how speedy today's computers are, this all happens in the blink of an eye. But as you can see, there's a lot of communication that has to go on to make that simple operation work.

That communication, however, is all taking place between the internal components of your systems—from the CPU, across the data bus, through the hard drive controller, to the hard drive, and back again. Since these devices are directly connected to each other, they're very fast. However, suppose you move that phone number database off your hard drive and onto a file server so everyone in your office can access it. If you do the same search as before, each time Microsoft Access has to get a new record to check, the CPU will send a request to the network controller instead of the hard drive controller. The network controller will transmit the request to the server for the record and wait for the response from the file server. Once again, the CPU has to request this information over and over again from the network until it finally finds the record for Toombs. Since a hard drive on a network file-server probably isn't going to respond as fast as the hard drive in your computer, response time suffers.

To put some rough numbers to it, when the database was stored on the computer's internal hard drive you might have had a maximum of 20 megabits worth of bandwidth between the components inside your computer (hard drive, controller, bus, and CPU). Let's assume the last-name search took 1 second to complete. Once you move the database on your file server, your maximum bandwidth might have stepped down to only 10 megabits, assuming you're on a 10-megabit network. In theory, a search that took 1 second before could now take 2 seconds. That's still not too bad, and these are rough numbers (don't hold me to them), but they do illustrate the point we're about to make.

The 1-second query operation became a 2-second query operation when the phone number database was moved off the local hard drive and onto the network file server. Part of the reason for that is the fact that the bandwidth between our CPU and the actual data was cut in half, from 20 megabits to 10. Since the CPU had to keep requesting each record in the file, the bandwidth available between the CPU and the data source plays a key role. Now, what if someone was dialing in to the network and trying to perform the same query? If you recall the 1/20th figure discussed earlier in regards to 56K modems, you can probably see where this is heading. Cutting the bandwidth down from 10 megabits to 56 kilobytes could potentially increase our search time twentyfold. It's entirely possible that our simple query could take upwards of 40 seconds over the 56K dial-up connection.

Now, I'll be the first to admit that I'm oversimplifying things here considerably to make a point. In reality, our example query probably wouldn't take 40 seconds over a dial-up connection, but the response time would be noticeably sluggish. Even if it only took 10 to 15 seconds to retrieve the data, slowdowns like that eventually produce productivity problems. The key to all this is the fact that bandwidth is a huge factor in remote computing if you have any applications that are file-based. So what's the solution? Try to stick with applications that are client-server based.

In keeping with our name-lookup scenario above, let's assume that the data is stored in a SQL Server database instead of a standard Microsoft Access file. Using Microsoft Access (the *client* in client-server) as a "front end" on your workstation, you can submit the same query for the last name Toombs as before. However, instead of requesting each record individually this time and checking them one by one, Access will transmit a request to the SQL Server software (the *server* in client-server) for a specific record. Access will transmit a specific request such as "Get me the record(s) with a last name of Toombs." Small requests like those transmit very quickly, even over a slow connection (like a 56K modem). At that point, the responsibility of retrieving the correct data has shifted from the copy of Microsoft Access running on your CPU and is now in the hands of the SQL Server. Since the SQL Server presumably has high-speed access to the drives that store the data (most likely its own drives), it can find the answer in a few microseconds and then return an appropriate response back to Access.

The key thing to look for in determining whether an application is client-server or not is to see if there are two separate parts to the application. One part will run on your client workstations, and a second part will run on the server that stores your data (or at least on a server nearby with a high-speed connection on it). If there are two parts to your application, it is probably a client-server application and you shouldn't run into too many difficulties with remote-node users using it. However, if there aren't two parts to your application—if the only part is the client software that just uses directories and files on your file servers—you might run into performance problems using remote-node solutions.

Opening Word documents and Excel spreadsheets is—in effect—a file-based application, so it's worthwhile to look at your average document size to see how quickly it might transmit over a slow connection. Refer to the transmission times formula earlier in this section and figure out how long some sample documents would take to transmit over a modem. If most of your documents are simple and text-based, you probably won't run into too many performance issues. However, if your users typically work with large, multimegabyte documents on your server, you might need to consider other options.

Remote Control

If remote-node communications can be viewed as using a phone line as a long network cable, then remote-control communications should be viewed as using a phone line as a long keyboard, mouse, and video cable. Remote-control solutions, by definition, allow you to remotely take control of a workstation on your network over a dial-up connection. Software on a workstation would typically have some sort of remote-control software running on it (such as pcAnywhere) and a modem attached to it. This is sometimes referred to as the host PC, since it is typically waiting to host an incoming caller. Then, presumably from another location, another workstation with compatible remote-control software would call into the host PC.

Once the two PCs have negotiated a connection, the host would begin sending its screen data to the calling computer, in effect letting the person at that calling station see everything that is on the remote screen. The calling workstation would then pass any keystrokes or mouse movements to the host PC, which would perform those actions just as if the user were sitting at the host PC doing them him- or herself. In effect, the remote-control software is tapping into the keyboard, mouse, and video input/output of the host PC and making it available to a remote PC over a phone line.

Traditionally, remote-control solutions have been a bit more expensive to develop and scale due to the increased hardware requirements on each side. Whereas one RAS server with an adequate amount of modems would theoretically be able to handle 256 simultaneous inbound modem connections, having that many simultaneous connections using certain remote-control products could require 256 computers—one to receive each of the connections. That can be rather cost prohibitive in most cases, not to mention being difficult to manage. However, it is worth mentioning because in some cases it might be the only remote access solution that would work in your environment.

It is also worth mentioning that Microsoft is including some remote-control functionality in Win2K with the bundling of Terminal Server with the base operating system (hmmm...there's that "bundling" concept again). If you are in a position where a remote-node solution won't meet your needs, you might want to take a look at it and see if Terminal Server will work for you. Terminal Server can be a worthy option since it doesn't require a separate computer to handle each inbound connection; instead, it requires one huge computer, and everybody runs a Windows session on that device (note: there are some other third-party products that function in a similar manner).

Since you've gotten this far, I'm assuming that you feel RAS is the right solution for you and you're ready to start working with it and implementing it on your network. If that's the case, keep reading. Let's talk a bit about what type of hardware and circuits you're going to need to have in place to make this all work.

RAS HARDWARE REQUIREMENTS

One of the first things to determine in remote networking is where you plan on connecting to and how fast you want to connect. Often, one or both of those criteria will help you determine what your available

Part V

communications options are. In most instances, that will leave you with one of the following options:

Connection Type	Typical Maximum Speed	Typical Maximum Distance
Analog modem	Asymmetrical—53Kbps down, 33.6 up	Unlimited, usually domestic
ISDN	BRI—128Kbps, PRI—1.544Mbps	Unlimited, usually domestic
X.25	2400bps—64Kbps	Global
Serial cable	Serial port max—230Kbps in most cases	"Physically near (less than 50 feet)" according to Microsoft
Infrared	Varies	Very close, line-of-sight
Parallel cable	Up to 500Kbps	Very close
Frame relay	1.544Mbps	Global

Of course, it should go without saying that any devices you are considering purchasing for use with RAS should be checked against Microsoft's Hardware Compatibility List (HCL) to make sure they are compatible with Windows 2000. By checking for HCL compatibility, you can be sure your choice of hardware has been specifically tested for compatibility with Win2K and has met the standards Microsoft has deemed necessary to be considered "compatible."

Also, if you're purchasing modems from a manufacturer that has several different models to choose from, pick your product carefully. While some modems might cost more than others due to features like voice or fax capability, if you're looking at two different models from the same manufacturer with the same capabilities, I'd suggest buying the more expensive of the two. The reason for this is quite simple: lower-cost modems are often designed by manufacturers primarily for light-duty home use applications. These are usually the modems you will see on the shelves in retail computer outlets. They are marketed to consumers and designed with tolerances and specifications targeted at the average consumer's needs. This doesn't take into consideration the more demanding needs of using modems for routing links, mail servers, etc.

Case in Point: Choosing the Right Modems

Here's a real-life case in point from one of my clients. ABC Software Company was having several problems with users calling into their RAS server. They had purchased modems built by one of the top manufacturers (if I told you the name, 90 percent of you would recognize it), but they had purchased the consumer-grade modems off their local computer store's shelf for roughly $100 each. Well, ABC Software Company seemed to always be running into odd, unpredictable problems with their remote access users. These users were unhappy and constantly calling with support issues since their connections would randomly get dropped, they'd have trouble negotiating connections, sometimes the modems wouldn't answer at all, etc. Again, these modems on their RAS server were built by one of the top manufacturers, but they weren't the right tools for the job.

We decided to remove all the $100 modems and replace them with the $200 commercial-grade modems from the same manufacturer. The modems were the same speed and had roughly the same features, but as soon as we changed to the new modems all the odd problems with their dial-in users disappeared. Just like that. The moral of the story: Saving money is good, but not if it ends up costing you more in the long run.

With that out of the way, let's take a closer look at your hardware and circuit options, and then we'll jump into configuring RAS on your Windows 2000 Server.

Analog Modems

Analog modems are the most commonly used connection device on RAS servers these days, so a good portion of our examples and configurations throughout this chapter will be using them.

A primer on how modems operate is in order for those of you who are unfamiliar with the technology. Modems are devices that accept binary signals (ones and zeroes) from whatever device they are connected to, convert those binary signals into audible tones, and then transmit those tones over a phone line at a prescribed speed. (This process is described as "modulation" and is the derivative of the "mo" part of the word "modem.")

On the other side of the telephone line, another modem receives these audible tones and converts them back into the binary ones and zeroes they represent. Once they have been converted back ("demodulated"), they are passed through to the device the modem is connected to as binary data. As you probably guessed, this "demodulation" process represents the "dem" in the word "modem."

Therefore, to complete a remote access or dial-up networking connection via a modem, you will need the following:

▶ Modem on the transmitting computer

▶ Modem on the receiving computer (this may be out of your control, for example, if you are dialing in to an ISP)

▶ Telephone connection between the two modems

In today's world, analog modems can transmit *and* receive data over traditional phone lines at speeds anywhere from 300 to 33,600 bits per second (sometimes referred to as the baud of the modem). As we mentioned earlier, the modems on either end of the connection convert the stream of bits to analog signals and transmit them over the phone line at a prenegotiated speed.

ISDN

A few years ago, a 56K analog modem would be more than enough bandwidth for most remote data needs. However, as computers have grown in size and complexity, so have the files and data that computers typically need to move around. Downloading multimegabyte items from the Internet, such as Windows 2000 Service Packs, could literally take hours over a standard dial-up connection. Fortunately, Integrated Services Digital Network (ISDN) is an option to get more bandwidth without having to get a dedicated circuit in place.

Direct Options (Null Modem, Parallel, and Infrared)

Given the affordability and broad universal support for network cards these days, using a null modem or parallel cable to connect two computers has really become more of a niche than a mainstream use of RAS. However, there may be occasions when it is the only option—maybe you have a specialty device that can't support a network card and can only communicate with the outside world via a serial or parallel port. If that's the case, a null modem cable, parallel cable, or infrared connection between your systems can be used for a connection.

X.25

X.25 is a protocol that coordinates communication between multiple machines, routing information through a packet-switched public data network. Instead of establishing direct connections from one device to another, all devices in an X.25 network simply connect to a "cloud" and pass their data to the cloud. It is up to the company that maintains and manages the cloud to ensure that the data reaches the correct destination point. X.25 is a relatively outdated technology, which is why throughput speeds top out at 56K to 64K.

So, why use X.25? Well, even though it is an extremely slow transport medium, it is also an exceptionally reliable one. There is an extensive amount of error checking and correction that occurs as a part of the X.25 protocol, which makes it a worthwhile consideration in areas with poor telecommunication services. X.25 is available globally and in some cases may be the only reasonable option for connectivity in certain countries.

Frame Relay

Frame relay is quickly becoming a preferred option to X.25 connections, as it functions on roughly the same principle—each system passing data into a data cloud—but at much higher speeds. Frame relay can support connections ranging from 56Kbps all the way up to 1.544Mbps. Since frame relay only requires a single connection from each site into the cloud, it is an excellent choice for global connectivity, since dedicated wide area network links across continents could end up being prohibitively expensive to implement.

RAS INSTALLATION AND SETUP

Now that we've laid the groundwork for understanding how remote access works, it's time to start working through some of the sample applications discussed earlier.

Installing Devices for Remote Access

Since a modem is one of the most widely used tools for remote access services, we'll start by quickly walking through installing your modem on a Windows 2000 Server, making sure that the correct drivers are installed, ports are selected, etc.

To begin adding modems to your system, start by clicking the Start button on the Windows desktop. Choose the Settings ➤ Control Panel option, and then double-click the Phone And Modem options icon. If this is your first time using this option, you will be probably be prompted for information about your area code, what type of dialing the system should use (tone or pulse), etc. After you've entered some of that preliminary information, you will be taken to the Phone & Modem Options applet. Click the Modems tab. More than likely, you won't have any modems listed. Click the Add button to launch the modem installation wizard, as seen in Figure 24.1.

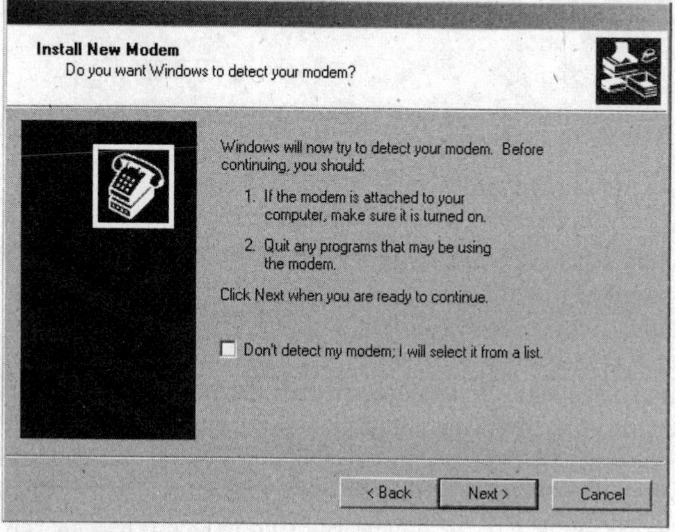

Install New Modem
Do you want Windows to detect your modem?

Windows will now try to detect your modem. Before continuing, you should:

1. If the modem is attached to your computer, make sure it is turned on.

2. Quit any programs that may be using the modem.

Click Next when you are ready to continue.

☐ Don't detect my modem; I will select it from a list.

< Back   Next >   Cancel

FIGURE 24.1: The Install New Modem Wizard

Depending on your preferences, you can either have Windows 2000 attempt to detect your modem automatically or you can select it manually from a list. If your modem is a bit older (as in, it was on the market before Win2K), you are probably safe letting Win2K attempt to find the correct driver for your modem. Leave the "Don't detect my modem; I will select it from a list" box unchecked and click Next to begin the detection process.

If your modem is newer than the release of Windows 2000, or if you prefer to configure these options yourself (*I* prefer setting all these things myself), check the "Don't detect my modem; I will select it from a list" box and click Next. You'll be taken to the screen shown in Figure 24.2.

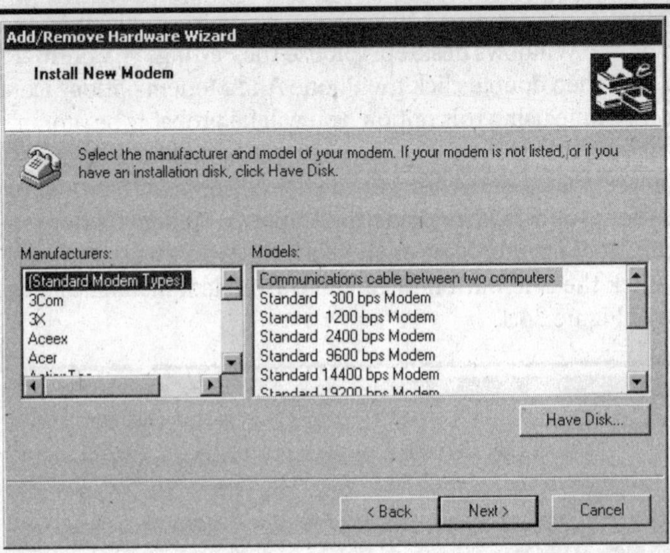

FIGURE 24.2: The Install New Modem selection screen

From here, you can choose from a myriad of different modem drivers. Find the driver that matches your modem, select it, and then click Next to install it. If for some reason an appropriate driver isn't listed for your modem, you can always use one of the standard modem drivers listed in the Standard Modem Types selection under Manufacturers. The standard modem drivers are reasonably good and are reliable in most circumstances. There are even standard modem drivers for 56K modems supporting the V.90, x2, and k56Flex standards. If your modem manufacturer included a driver disk along with the purchase of your modem, click the Have Disk button and insert your driver diskette in the appropriate drive. You will need to tell Windows to look in that location by giving it the appropriate path to check for the driver (usually A:\; consult your modem manufacturer's documentation for further information).

If you are installing your driver by hand, you will need to tell Windows what communications port this modem is connected to, as shown in Figure 24.3.

If you have identical modems on all your communications ports, you can select the All Ports radio button. Otherwise, you should select the port your modem is currently attached to. If you have multiple modems on many ports (but not "all ports"), hold down the Ctrl key while selecting each port. When you have selected the correct ports, click Next to complete the installation. You should receive a confirmation dialog box indicating that your modem has been successfully installed.

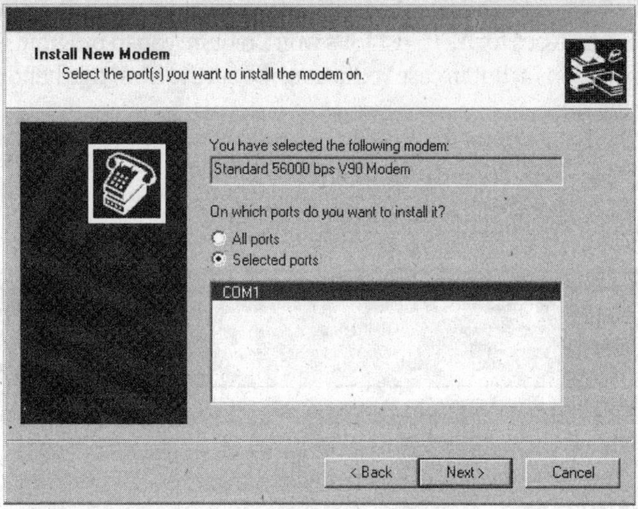

FIGURE 24.3:   Selecting communications ports

Now that you have a modem installed, it's time to take it for a test drive. One of the easiest things to do in Windows 2000 is define a dial-up connection to the Internet, so we'll start there first.

CONNECTING TO THE INTERNET

It's no secret that Win2K was designed with the Internet in mind. Given that fact, Microsoft has made it easy to get your computer connected to the Internet. If you are running a Windows 2000 Server as a proxy server so your internal clients can surf the Web or if you're running it as an e-mail server, dial-up connections to the Internet are an option worth looking into. Due to some readily available "fine tuning" parameters you can set for dial-up connections, you can create a rather reliable link to the Internet with just a modem. Let's get started.

The first thing you'll need to do before connecting to the Internet is set up an account with an Internet service provider (ISP). We won't go through the specifics of how to do that here, but once you have an account you will need a minimum of three things handy to create your dial-up connection to the Internet:

▶ A local access phone number to dial (whether analog or ISDN)

▶ A username and password combination

▶ Optionally, an IP address to assign to your dial-up connection, and DNS addresses to use (most ISPs won't require you to program this information in, but in case yours does, be sure to have this handy in advance)

When you're ready to build your connection to the Internet, choose Start ➤ Settings ➤ Network And Dial-Up Connections. You should get a window that looks like the screen in Figure 24.4.

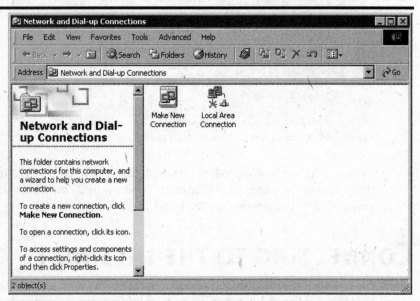

FIGURE 24.4:   The Network And Dial-Up Connections window

From here, double-click the Make New Connection icon to start the Network Connection Wizard, which will present you with a list of connection types you can establish. Select the Dial-Up To The Internet option and then click Next. This will launch the Internet Connection Wizard, which will walk you through the process of setting up an ISP account. The initial step of the wizard will ask you whether you want to define a new ISP account, transfer an existing ISP account, or configure your settings manually. For the purposes of being thorough, we'll walk through the manual setup option.

After selecting the "I want to set up my Internet connection manually" option, you will be asked whether you want to set up your Internet connection over a modem or a LAN. If you have in-house Internet connectivity that is already running, then a LAN would be the option you would want to choose. However, since we're discussing modems, let's walk through the modem configuration.

After you select the "Connect through a phone line and a modem" option and click Next, you will be taken through a three-step process to collect the information we discussed earlier, starting with the phone number as shown in Figure 24.5.

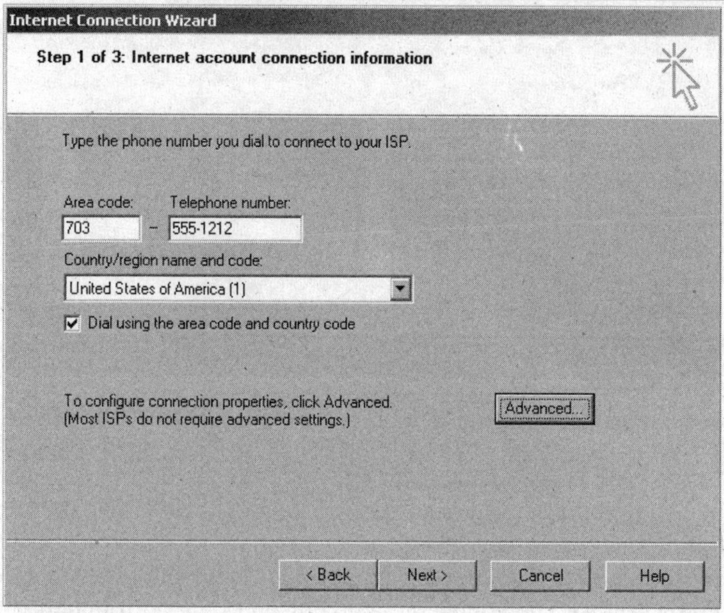

FIGURE 24.5: Entering account connection information

Enter the area code and phone number of your ISP's local access number in the fields provided. Select your appropriate country code, and leave the field "Dial using the area code and country code" checked unless you want to override Windows 2000's ability to check the area code of the number you're dialing against its current location and adjust the dialing string accordingly.

As we mentioned before, if you need to manually assign an IP address for your server or DNS server addresses to use, this is the screen from which to do it. Click the Advanced button, and you'll see a dialog box for setting the advanced connection properties of this dial-up connection. Click the Addresses tab, and you will see a screen like the one in Figure 24.6.

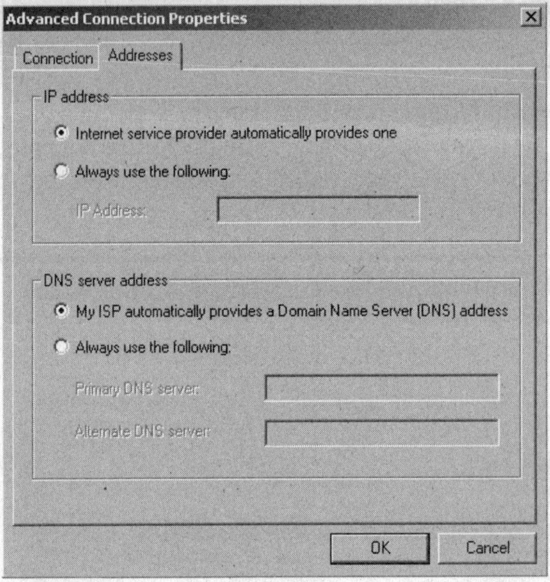

FIGURE 24.6: The Advanced Connection Properties screen

Even though most ISPs will assign you an address automatically, if your ISP requires you to manually assign yourself an IP address, click the Always Use The Following radio button in the top of the window and enter the appropriate address in the IP Address field. Some ISPs may still require you to enter DNS server information (DNS is how Windows 2000 translates names like www.microsoft.com into IP addresses). If so, click the Always Use The Following radio button in the bottom half of the window and enter your primary and secondary DNS server IP addresses exactly as your ISP provided them to you. Once you're finished with any advanced settings, click the Next button to proceed to step two of the Internet Connection Wizard, as shown in Figure 24.7.

Step two of the Internet Connection Wizard is rather straightforward. Here you will enter the user credentials (username and password) your ISP has provided you for use with your account. This information will be stored along with all the other information for this dial-up networking entry so Windows 2000 doesn't have to prompt you for it every time you want to make a connection. If you don't feel comfortable having this information stored on your machine, leave the password field blank. You will receive a warning dialog box asking whether you want to proceed with a blank password.

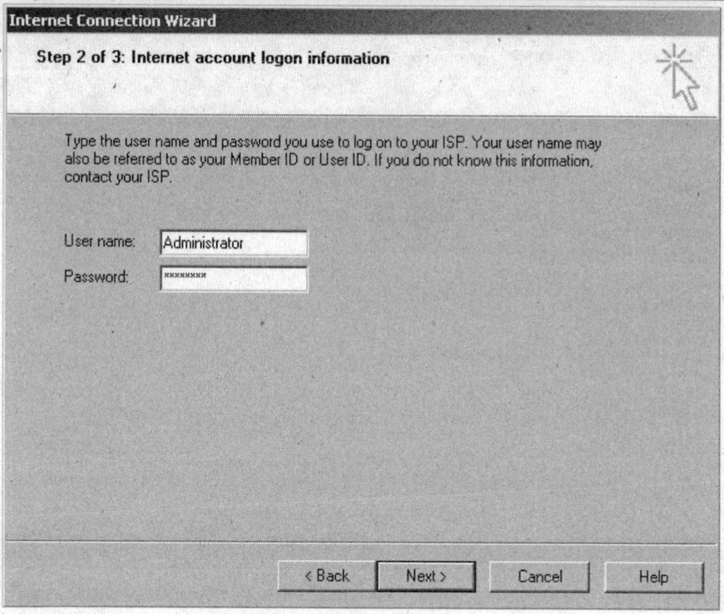

Internet Connection Wizard

Step 2 of 3: Internet account logon information

Type the user name and password you use to log on to your ISP. Your user name may also be referred to as your Member ID or User ID. If you do not know this information, contact your ISP.

User name: Administrator

Password: ×××××××

| < Back | Next > | Cancel | Help |

FIGURE 24.7:   Defining user credentials

When you've entered your user credentials, click Next to complete the last step of the Internet Connection Wizard: assigning a "friendly name" to this connection. You can choose whatever you want here. Later, you will reference this connection by the name you give it. Enter a descriptive connection name and then click Next.

If you have an Internet mail client installed on your system (namely Outlook Express), the Internet Connection Wizard will ask if you would like to configure your mail settings at this point. For the purposes of this chapter, we'll skip those settings for the time being—you can always set them later. The last thing you should see is a dialog box indicating that you have finished defining your connection.

Once you've completed defining your Internet connection, it should be shown as a grayed-out icon in the Network And Dial-Up Connections window, as shown in Figure 24.8.

At this point, you could double-click your new ISP connection and get connected to the Internet if you provided a password in step two of the Internet Connection Wizard. If that's the case, launch the icon and verify that it is working correctly. Once you're successfully connected, you should be able to connect to hosts on the Internet.

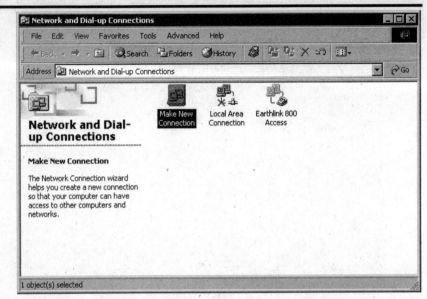

FIGURE 24.8: The Network And Dial-Up Connections window with a new
ISP entry

Optional Internet Connection Settings

After you've verified that your Internet connection is working properly,
there are some optional settings you might find useful for controlling the
behavior of this dial-up connection. Such items include:

- ▶ Programming a list of alternate numbers for Windows 2000 to
  attempt dialing

- ▶ Disconnecting idle connections (good for per-minute connections
  such as ISDN)

- ▶ Automatic redialing of busy or nonresponsive numbers

- ▶ Automatic reestablishing of connections that have dropped

All these features are useful enough by themselves. However, if
you're running a Windows 2000 Server that *depends* on having an
Internet connection available, you'll find these extra features useful.
It takes much less administration when a server can take care of establishing and reestablishing its own Internet connections without any
human intervention.

To get to these options, open the Network And Dial-Up Connections window again and right-click your ISP dial-up entry. Select the Properties option, and you should get to the dialog box shown in Figure 24.9.

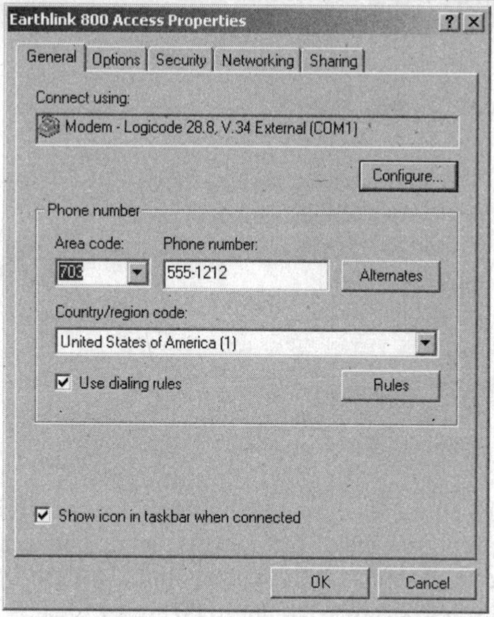

FIGURE 24.9:   Editing general properties of dial-up entries

If your ISP has several local phone numbers available for you to use, you can program Win2K to cycle through the entire list until it gets a connection. Click the Alternates button next to the phone number, and you should see a screen like the one in Figure 24.10.

From the Alternate Phone Numbers dialog box, you can enter as many numbers as you would like Windows 2000 to use to attempt to establish this connection. Click the Add button to add a new number to the list, and then use the arrow buttons on the right side of the dialog box to adjust the order of which number should be dialed first.

As an additional option, Windows 2000 can remember which number was successful last time you connected and try that one first if you check the Move Successful Number To Top Of List option. This will make sure that if for some reason one of your ISP's local access numbers goes offline for a while, it won't stay in the top of the list and Windows 2000 won't keep trying to dial that number first.

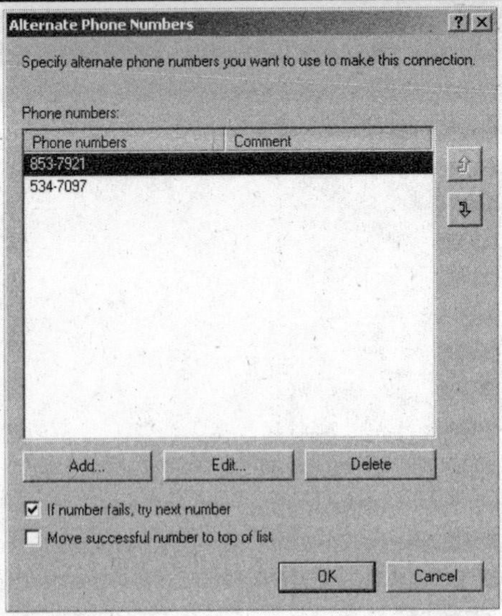

FIGURE 24.10: Entering alternate dial-up numbers

When you're finished entering alternate numbers, click the OK button to return to the main properties dialog box for this dial-up connection. To reach the rest of the editable items for this connection, click the Options tab. This should bring you to a screen similar to Figure 24.11.

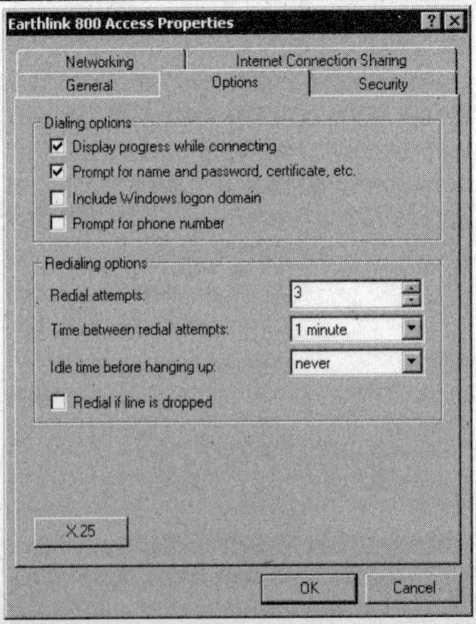

FIGURE 24.11: Editing options for dial-up entries

This dialog box has several options available, the most useful of which regard dialing, idle time-outs, and reestablishing broken connections. Let's go through these one by one and show how they can be used.

Prompt for Name and Password, Certificate, etc. When you first created this dial-up networking entry using the Internet Connection Wizard, one of the steps you should have gone through (step two) was for entering a username and password to use for this connection. If you decided not to enter your password directly into the settings for this dial-up networking entry, you will want to check this option. Otherwise, Windows 2000 will simply try to use a blank password when establishing this connection. Checking this option will cause Windows to prompt you for a username and password to use instead of the existing username and password stored with this dial-up networking entry.

Redial Attempts and Time between Redial Attempts If your local ISP has a problem with busy signals, you will appreciate these options. By choosing the number of times to attempt to redial and the time to wait between attempts, you can program Win2K to keep dialing your ISP until a number becomes available. Personally, I've found this setting to be extremely useful in times of inclement weather when everyone is stuck in their homes and clogging my ISP's lines.

Idle Time before Hanging Up If the same phone company that serves my area serves yours, then you are accustomed to paying for your ISDN access by the minute. These per-minute charges can add up to a rather substantial phone bill if your ISDN connection stays up all day. If your server only really needs to have a connection during business hours (for example, for proxy server clients browsing the Internet), set an appropriate idle time-out value here in minutes. Once the specified number of minutes has passed without any activity, Windows 2000 will drop the connection.

Redial If Line Is Dropped It's simply a fact of life—dial-up connections "drop" sometimes. It just happens, but it can cause considerable headaches if people are depending on this connection being up and you happen to be away when it goes down. Checking this option causes Win2K to automatically redial and reestablish your connection if it drops. Assuming something hasn't failed on the ISP side of your connection, your link should come back up automatically within about a minute.

For this feature to work, you must have the Remote Access Auto Connection Manager service running. This service doesn't automatically start on Windows 2000 Server by default, so you will need to enable it manually. To do this, enter the Computer Management administrative tool by selecting Start ≻ Programs ≻ Administrative Tools ≻ Computer Management or by right-clicking My Computer and selecting the Manage option. This will bring you into the Microsoft Management Console (MMC) for managing computers on your network. In the left pane of the MMC, you should see an option for Services under the Services And Applications group (you might need to expand Services And Applications to see it). Click the Services icon in the left pane, and you should see a listing of all the services running on your Windows 2000 Server in the result pane. The MMC screen should look like Figure 24.12.

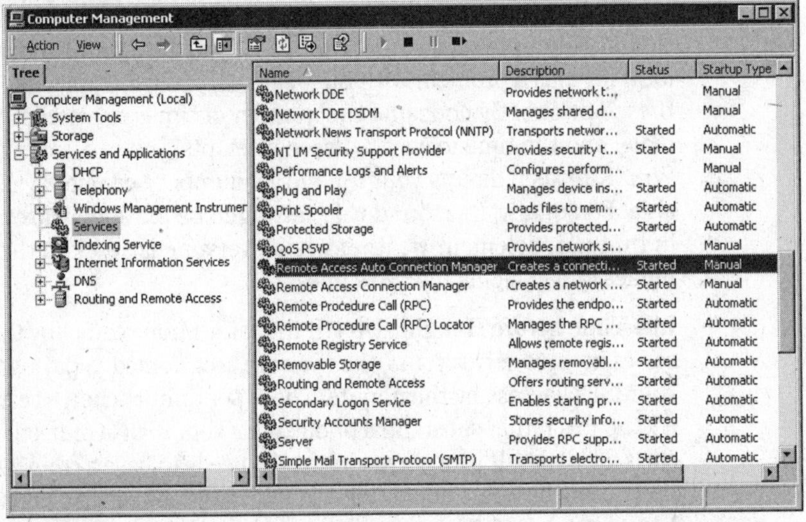

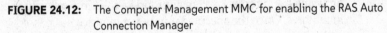

FIGURE 24.12:   The Computer Management MMC for enabling the RAS Auto Connection Manager

Find the Remote Access Auto Connection Manger service in the listing on the right, and double-click it to edit the properties. From here, you can start the service manually, and configure it to start up automatically every time your Windows 2000 Server boots up. The properties page for this service should look like Figure 24.13.

To start this service manually, click the Start button in the dialog box. If everything goes okay, the status of this service should change to Started. Now, to make sure that this service starts every time your Windows 2000

Server boots, select Automatic from the Startup Type pull-down box. Click OK to save your changes and then exit the Computer Management MMC.

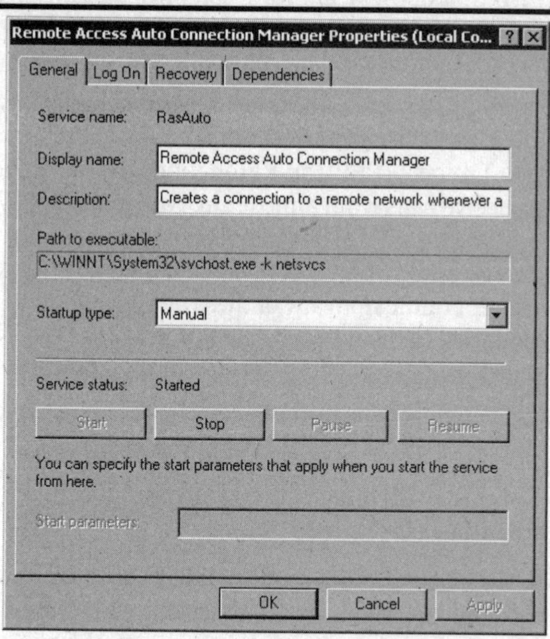

FIGURE 24.13: Service properties for the RAS Auto Connection Manager

To test the redial functionality, try establishing a connection with this ISP dial-up entry and then pulling the phone plug out of your modem. Wait a few seconds so that you're sure the carrier has dropped (if you have an icon in your Taskbar indicating you're connected, it should disappear) and then plug the phone line back in. Within a minute, Windows 2000 should attempt to reestablish this connection for you without any intervention whatsoever.

ACCEPTING INCOMING CALLS FROM REMOTE USERS

In today's business world there are several buzzwords that tend to make an administrator's job a bit more challenging. Phrases like telecommuting, mobile computing, and sales force automation are all centered around one common principle—getting corporate data into the hands of people who need it, exactly when they need it, wherever they are located. In terms of systems administration, this typically means accepting inbound connections from remote clients. If you have yet to face this administrative challenge, rest assured that in the near future you most likely will. The tendency toward remote computing simply shows no signs of slowing down anytime soon.

Whatever your dial-in needs are, Windows 2000 can act as a universal gateway to get remote clients into your network. Thanks to built-in support for Point-to-Point Protocol (PPP), an RFC-defined dial-up standard, Windows 2000 can receive calls from almost any type of device. Windows PCs, Macintosh systems, Unix hosts, and even personal digital assistants (PDAs) can all establish PPP connections to remote networks. Windows 2000 can accept traffic from any of these devices and route it to the devices on your internal network, whether they're NT servers, Novell servers, Unix hosts, etc.

To start accepting incoming calls from remote clients, you will need the following:

▶ Windows 2000 Server with remote access software configured to accept incoming calls

▶ Connection device of some sort (modem, ISDN, X.25, etc.) connected to the Windows 2000 Server to accept calls from the remote clients

▶ Client computer capable of establishing a PPP session (Windows 95, 98, and NT 4; Windows 2000 Professional; Macintosh; 3Com PalmPilot; etc.)

▶ Connection device of some sort (modem, ISDN, X.25, etc.) connected to the remote client and capable of establishing a connection to the corresponding device on the Windows 2000 Server

▶ Circuit (phone line, ISDN line, etc.) between the two devices

▶ User account on your Windows 2000 Server (or within your Active Directory) with dial-in rights granted to it

For the sake of brevity, we'll assume that you've gone through the detailed steps earlier in this chapter to add your modems (ISDN devices or whatever you might be using) to your Windows 2000 Server and they are functioning properly. With that out of the way, let's get started on accepting incoming calls from remote clients.

To be sure we're all working from the same baseline, we'll assume that you do not have the Routing and Remote Access Service installed on your computer. If you do have it installed, going through this procedure will stop your existing services and reinstall them with the answers provided to the configuration wizard.

Remote Access Server Installation and Setup

Start the installation for Routing and Remote Access Service by clicking Start ≻ Programs ≻ Administrative Tools ≻ Routing And Remote Access. You will see an MMC window appear, and you should see your server listed somewhere in the left pane. Right-click your server and select the Configure And Enable Routing And Remote Access option.

This will begin the RRAS installation process. This process is aided by a wizard that will help you configure the necessary services to allow remote clients to dial in. After a welcome dialog box (to which you will answer Yes), the first dialog box you will see should look similar to the screen shown in Figure 24.14.

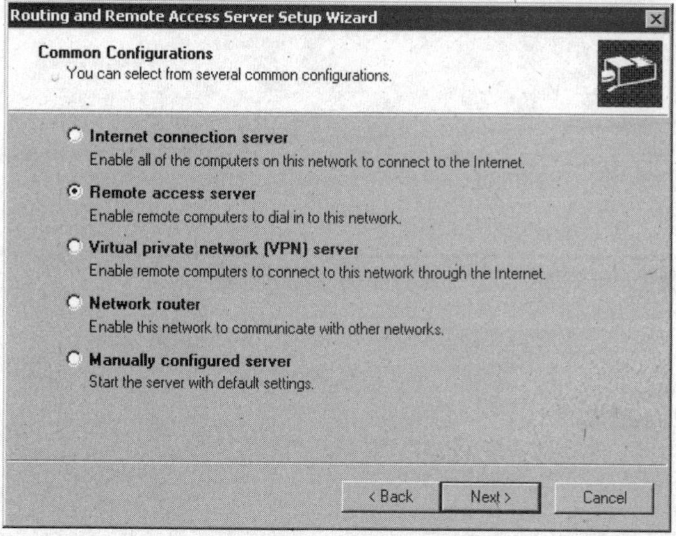

FIGURE 24.14: The RRAS configuration wizard: role of server

The first step of the configuration wizard is to determine what role your Windows 2000 Server will play. If you are simply looking to accept connections from dial-in clients, click the Remote Access Server radio button and then click Next to move on to the next step of the wizard.

Figure 24.15 shows the next step of the configuration wizard, which allows you to verify that the protocols installed on your server are correct for the type of remote access you are trying to provide to your dial-in clients. The only correct answer to this dialog box is to answer "Yes, all of the required protocols are on this list;" answering "No, I need to add protocols" will cause the wizard to stop at this step and abort the configuration process. Therefore, it is recommended that you select Yes and continue to the next step of the wizard, shown in Figure 24.16.

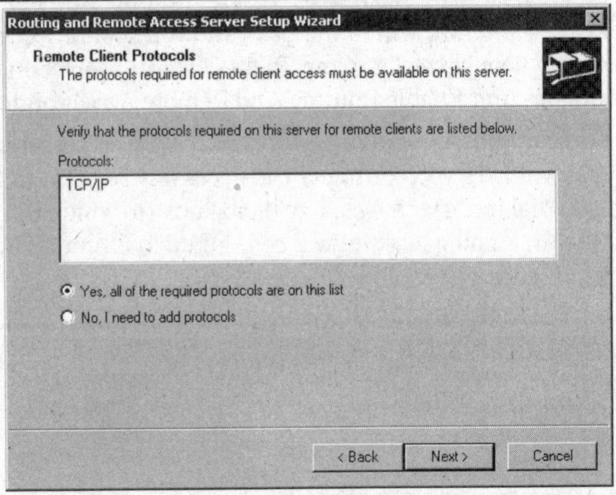

FIGURE 24.15:   The RRAS configuration wizard: configuring protocols

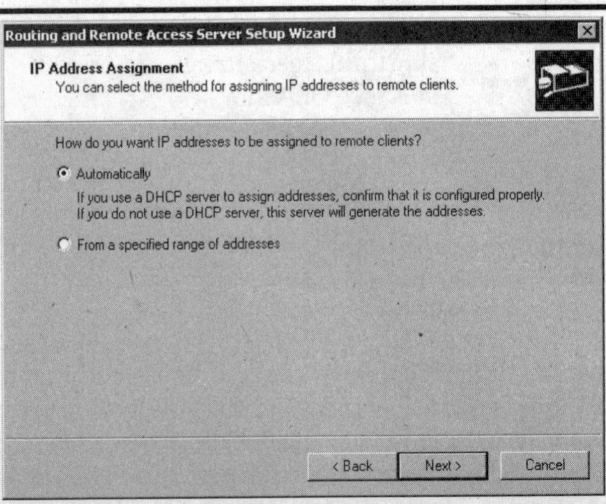

FIGURE 24.16:   The RRAS configuration wizard: IP address assignment

NOTE

You cannot, at this step of the wizard, specify only to use certain protocols. Although the dialog box might lead you to believe you can "select" which protocols to use, in reality the RRAS configuration wizard will automatically assume that you want to allow connections on all protocols. To remove protocols from your RRAS server, you will need to go back and manually reconfigure it after the wizard is through.

The next step of the wizard—assuming you have TCP/IP installed on your server—will ask you how to handle assignment of IP addresses to remote dial-in clients. Since every device on the network must have its own IP address, your dial-in workstations need a way to get addresses as well. By default, RRAS will want to assign addresses to your dial-in users automatically from a DHCP server. If you have a DHCP server running, you will probably want to accept the default Automatically option. Whether DHCP and RAS are running on the same server or on separate systems, the RAS service will attempt to obtain a DHCP-assigned address from the internal network and then pass it along to the remote client to use. The key with this option is to make sure you have a working DHCP server somewhere on your network and that it has enough IP addresses that can be used for dial-in connections.

Under some special circumstances, you might want to control which IP addresses RAS hands out to dial-in clients. For example, if you have developed login scripts or other automation routines that depend on IP addresses, having a preset range might be useful. Or you might have security policies in place on your networks that only allow certain IP addresses to connect to certain devices. Either way, if you need to make sure RAS clients always fall within a certain range of IP addresses, select the From A Specified Range Of Addresses option and then click Next to proceed to Address Range Assignment, shown in Figure 24.17.

Through address range assignment, you can enter a series of IP address ranges for RRAS to use when clients dial in to your network. You can make these ranges as small or as large as you would like—just so long as you know that they are usable addresses within your network. To add a range (or ranges) to your system, click the New button and enter a start and end range of IP addresses to use. The New Address Range dialog box will automatically calculate how many addresses are in the range you provided. In the example shown in Figure 24.17, I have already entered a range of 10.0.0.1 to 10.0.0.254 for this RRAS server to use. When you have finished entering your addresses, click Next to proceed with the next step in the wizard, shown in Figure 24.18.

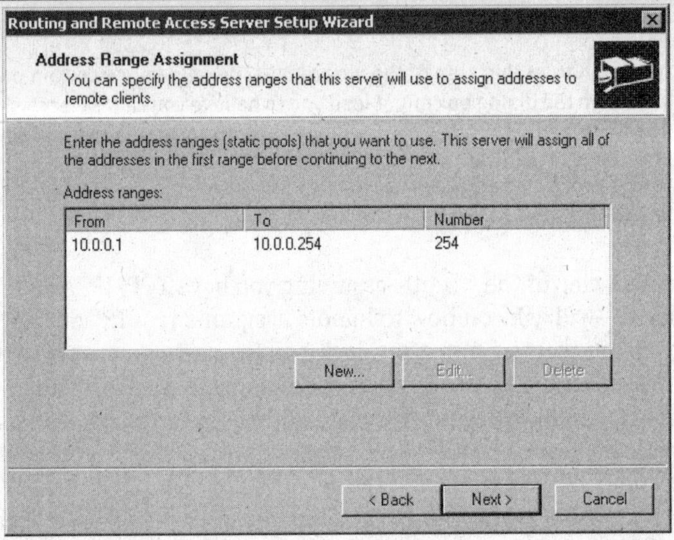

Routing and Remote Access Server Setup Wizard [X]

Address Range Assignment
You can specify the address ranges that this server will use to assign addresses to remote clients.

Enter the address ranges (static pools) that you want to use. This server will assign all of the addresses in the first range before continuing to the next.

Address ranges:

From	To	Number
10.0.0.1	10.0.0.254	254

New...   Edit...   Delete

< Back   Next >   Cancel

FIGURE 24.17: The RRAS configuration wizard: address range assignment

Routing and Remote Access Server Setup Wizard [X]

Managing Multiple Remote Access Servers
You can manage all of your remote access servers centrally.

A Remote Authentication Dial-In User Service (RADIUS) server provides a central authentication database for multiple remote access servers and collects accounting information about remote connections.

Do you want to set up this remote access server to use an existing RADIUS server?

⊙ No, I don't want to set up this server to use RADIUS now

○ Yes, I want to use a RADIUS server

ⓘ Windows provides a RADIUS solution called Internet Authentication Service (IAS) as an optional component that you can install through Add/Remove Programs.

< Back   Next >   Cancel

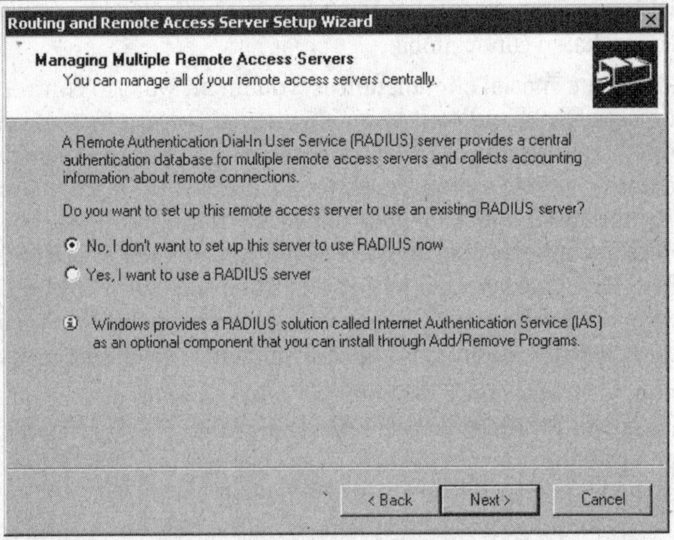

FIGURE 24.18: The RRAS configuration wizard: RADIUS services

Although the next step of the wizard might look like it's simply asking if you have a RADIUS server available on your network, it's actually asking far more than that. This step of the wizard is asking how you would like to handle dial-in authentications. Your choices are limited to two simple options.

If you are currently using RADIUS services on your network (Remote Authentication Dial-In User Service) for authentication and logging of other dial-in access, you can set up your RRAS server to use the existing RADIUS server instead of using its own authentication and logging mechanisms. To specify your own RADIUS information, select the "Yes, I want to use a RADIUS server" option and then click Next. Since RADIUS is outside the scope of this chapter, we'll assume that you will stick to using Windows 2000's own authentication and logging mechanisms. Therefore, you can leave the default "No, I don't want to set up this server to use RADIUS now" option and then click Next to continue.

Since the option for RADIUS selection is the final step of the wizard, your server should be configured after you click Finish on the final panel of the wizard.

NOTE

One of the more impressive things about Windows 2000 that was easy to overlook was the fact that the entire process for adding RAS services was completed without rebooting the server *at all*. I commend Microsoft on finally getting their operating system working so that it doesn't require a reboot after every minor change.

Granting Dial-in Permissions to User(s)

Once you've successfully installed the Routing and Remote Access Service, the next thing to do is grant dial-in permissions to a user account in your Active Directory tree. (We'll assume you already have an account created for this purpose.)

To grant dial-in permissions to selected users, choose the Active Directory Users and Computers MMC by clicking Start ➤ Programs ➤ Administrative Tools ➤ Active Directory Users And Computers. Navigate through the Active Directory tree to the user you want to grant dial-in permissions to and right-click the corresponding record. By selecting the option to edit the properties for this user, you'll be taken to a dialog box to edit options for this user. Click the Dial-In tab, and you should be left with a screen similar to the one in Figure 24.19.

By default, the user account you've selected will probably have the Deny Access option selected at the top of the dialog box. Click Allow Access to grant dial-in permissions to this user. You also have the option to edit some user-specific settings through this dialog box.

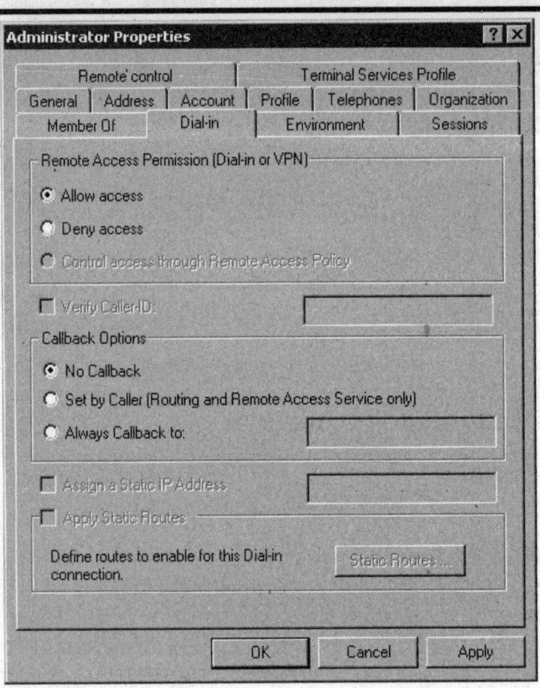

FIGURE 24.19:   Granting dial-in permissions via user properties

For example, if you'd like to implement an additional measure of security by making sure a certain user's remote access session always comes from a specific phone number, you have a few options available. First, if your modem and phone line supports caller ID service, you can simply select the Verify Caller-ID option box and enter the phone number this user must call in on. However, if you are using hardware that doesn't support caller ID or that service is unavailable in your area, you can achieve the same type of security by having your RAS server call the user back at a certain phone number. Selecting one of the Callback options available in the middle of the screen activates this feature.

If you have home users who dial in either via long distance or local long distance, callback options might also save you some money when it comes to your remote access costs. If the telephone service you have in your office has a better per-minute rate than the rates your users typically have in their homes, you can save money on your remote access connections by having your RAS server call users back at the cheaper rates.

In addition to callback options, you can also specify a fixed IP address for this specific user to receive. This is a new feature in Windows 2000 and can be exceptionally useful when setting up internal access policies based on IP address (firewall rules, etc.).

Now, take a moment and relax. Your server is set up to receive calls. You should be able to test this by calling the number associated with your RAS server from a standard phone and getting a carrier tone. If you don't hear a carrier tone, double-check your work and make sure everything is connected properly. If for some reason you still don't get a carrier tone when you call in, try rebooting the server (oddly enough, this happened to me once, and rebooting it corrected the problem).

Changing RAS Server Configurations after Installation

Wizards are both a blessing and a curse for the Windows operating system. Although they make complex tasks easier, they also tend to assume several answers for you with no chance to change those assumptions. The RRAS configuration wizard is guilty of this practice; it will make several assumptions for you as you configure your system. You may want to check these configurations to make sure they are exactly the way you want them to be.

If you need to change any of your configuration at a later time, you can easily do so by right-clicking your server in the Routing and Remote Access MMC and then selecting Properties. Through the RRAS properties dialog boxes, you can add or remove support for certain protocols for dial-up connections, increase authentication security, and fine-tune the PPP controls for establishing connections to client systems. We'll walk through each of these areas, starting with the controls for security shown in Figure 24.20.

Through this screen you can control several behaviors for the security and encryption used with your dial-up connections. Although there are pros and cons for using each (with the pros usually being increased security and the cons being limited client support), we'll discuss each option briefly so you can make your own judgements as to which is best to use.

By default, the authentication provider that should be automatically configured is Windows Authentication. If you have an external RADIUS server, you can change Windows to use the RADIUS server instead by selecting the RADIUS option from the pull-down box and then clicking the Configure button to define the RADIUS servers to use. Since RADIUS servers are out of the scope of this chapter, we'll simply stick to Windows Authentication methods.

Part V

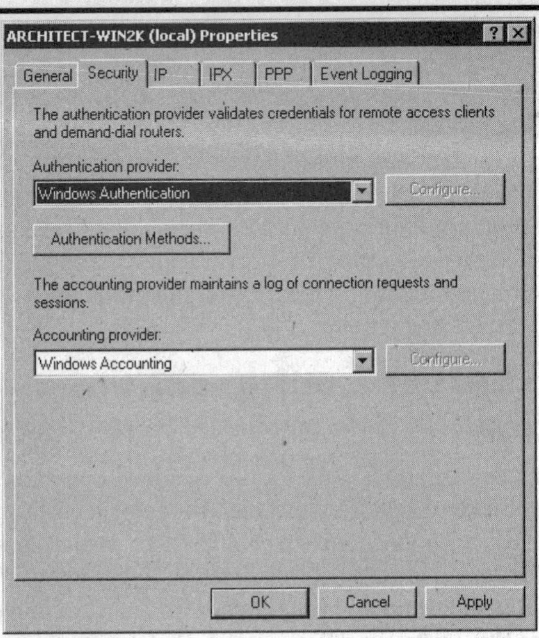

FIGURE 24.20:   Editing security properties for RAS service

By clicking the Authentication Methods button below the Authentication Provider pull-down box, you will be taken to a screen similar to the one shown in Figure 24.21.

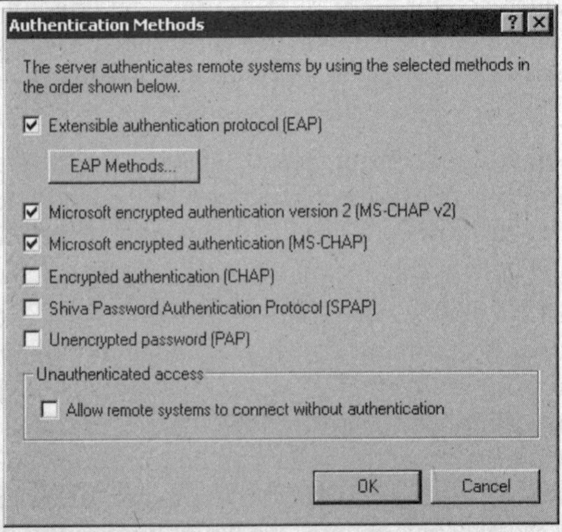

FIGURE 24.21:   Editing authentication types for RAS service

As you can see, there are several authentication options to choose from, as defined below:

Extensible Authentication Protocol (EAP)   Because security and authentication is a constantly changing field, embedding authentication schemes into an operating system is impractical at times. To solve this problem, Microsoft has included support for EAP, which is simply a means of "plugging in" new authentication schemes as needed. Currently, Windows 2000 Server only supports MD-5 Challenge and Transport Level Security (TLS, primarily used for smart-card support), but this option will allow for future authentication protocols to be plugged into the operating system easily.

Microsoft Encrypted Authentication (v1 and v2), MS-CHAP Microsoft's derivative of CHAP, or Challenge-Handshake Authentication Protocol (see below). Using MS-CHAP allows you to encrypt an entire dial-up session, not just the original authentication, which is especially important when it comes to setting up virtual private networking sessions. MS-CHAP v2 support is included in Windows 2000 for all types of connections and in Windows NT 4 and Windows 95/98 (with the Dial-Up Networking 1.3 upgrade) for VPN connections.

Encrypted Authentication (CHAP)   Defined in RFC 1334, and later revised in RFC 1994, the Challenge-Handshake Authentication Protocol is a means of encrypting authentication sessions between a client and server. Since this protocol is defined by an RFC, it enjoys a broad base of support among many operating systems and other devices.

Shiva Encrypted Authentication (SPAP)   SPAP, short for Shiva Password Authentication Protocol, is an encrypted password authentication method used by Shiva LAN Rover clients and servers. Windows 2000 Server can act as a server when Shiva LAN Rover clients are dialing in by providing the correct authentication sequence for them.

Unencrypted (clear text) Password (PAP)   Password Authentication Protocol (PAP) is one of the last two options listed, and it is also one of the least secure. It is no more secure than a simple conversation from your server saying, "What is your name and password?" to the client, the client responding with, "My name is Doug and my password is 'let-me-in'." There is no encryption of authentication credentials whatsoever.

Unauthenticated Access At first glance, this option wouldn't seem to make much sense—leaving a wide-open access point to your network with no authentication required whatsoever. However, when paired with caller ID verification, this option can make a simple and secure method for getting clients connected to your network.

If a dial-in user provides a username only, that username will be checked against the Active Directory. If there is a caller ID verification set for that user, the caller ID information will be checked and the connection will be accepted or rejected based on whether the information matches. If the user does not send a username at all, the Guest account will be used by default. Therefore, if you intend to use this option, you might want to disable the Guest account on your system (a good security practice to get in the habit of anyway).

Within the properties for the RAS service, you have the ability to fine-tune each protocol accepted by the RAS server and passed on to the internal network. By clicking the appropriate tabs (shown in Figure 24.22) for IP, IPX, NetBEUI, and AppleTalk, you can edit the following options for each protocol:

Allow *<Protocol>*-Based Remote Access and Demand Dial Connections (IP, IPX, NetBEUI, and AppleTalk) To enable or disable support for individual protocols, check the boxes for each protocol to allow and uncheck the boxes for each protocol to reject. If you used the automatic wizard to install Remote Access Service, you might find that Windows 2000 Server enabled support for all the protocols on your system by default. However, good security practices dictate only opening up support for the protocols you need, so it's probably a good idea to remove any protocols you aren't using.

Entire Network Access for Remote Clients (IP, IPX, NetBEUI, and AppleTalk) One way to increase the security of your dial-in system is to only allow dial-in users to access the dial-in server itself. For example, if traveling workers only need to access a set of word processing documents or spreadsheets, these could be kept on the remote access server. By unchecking the Entire Network Access For Remote Clients box, clients will only be able to access the RAS server itself.

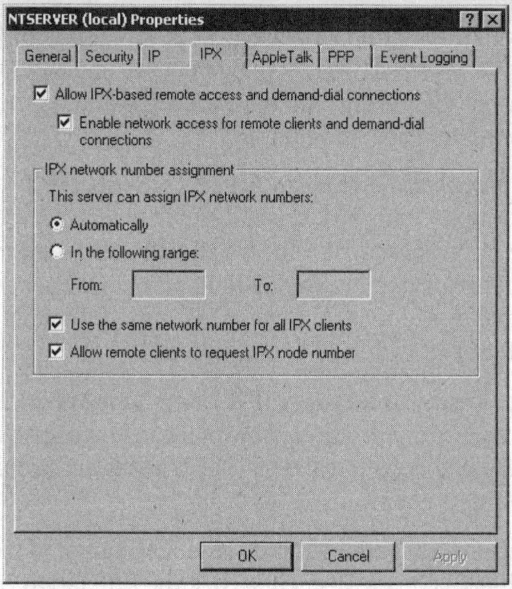

FIGURE 24.22: Editing security properties for RAS service

Additionally, this is a useful option for protecting certain types of servers. For example, perhaps you only want your dial-up users to access your Windows 2000 or NT network, which runs solely on TCP/IP. However, you might have Novell NetWare servers on your network running IPX that you don't want to allow access to. By removing access to the entire network for the IPX protocol, you can allow dial-in access to some systems and not others.

Dynamic Host Configuration Protocol—or—Use Static Address Pool (IP Only) As was previously discussed in the configuration of Remote Access Service, here you can select whether your RAS server will use a DHCP server to hand out IP addresses to dial-in clients or if it will manually assign addresses from a static pool. If you choose to assign addresses from a static pool, you will need to provide the correct TCP/IP network address range and subnet mask to use.

IPX Network Number Assignment—Automatic or in the Following Range (IPX only) Since IPX network numbers typically consist of two parts—a network address and a node number—you can configure what addresses RAS will assign to clients through this screen. If you have NetWare servers on your network, you may find it useful to assign a specific network number to your dial-in clients. For example, you might modify the login script on your NetWare servers to behave one way for internal clients and differently for dial-in clients, based on the IPX network number of the workstation.

Use the Same Network Number to All IPX Clients (IPX only)   If this option is checked, the RAS server will automatically assign the same network number to all IPX clients—either an automatic network number or one defined by allocating numbers. This will reduce the number of RIP announcement packets the RAS server will need to broadcast.

Allow Remote Clients to Request IPX Node Number (IPX only)   If your dial-in clients are capable of asking for a specific node number, check this option and your RAS server and dial-in client will negotiate a node address accordingly.

If you need to fine-tune the parameters for your RAS server to use when establishing PPP sessions with clients, click the PPP tab to edit the properties of these items, as shown in Figure 24.23. The default settings will be acceptable in most instances, but if needed you can enable or disable the following options.

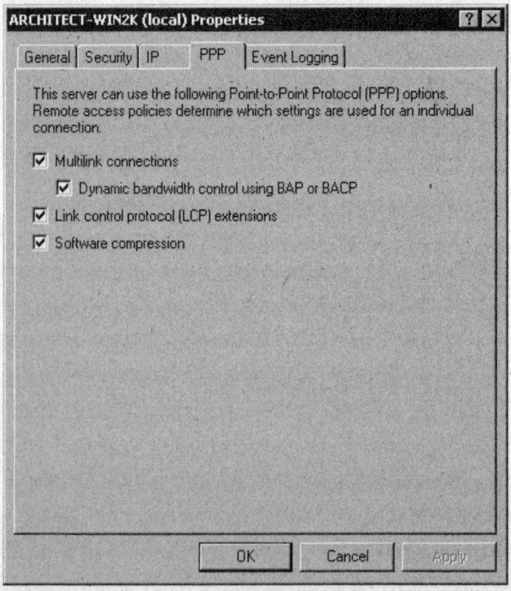

FIGURE 24.23:   Editing PPP properties for RAS service

Multilink Connections Multilink Point-to-Point Protocol (MPPP for short) was defined in RFC 1717 as a means of joining (often referred to as "bonding") two or more PPP sessions together to increase bandwidth. Effectively, you could double or triple your bandwidth between a client and a server if you had two or three modems at each location, two or three phone numbers, etc. This option must be selected if you want to be able to choose the next option.

Dynamic Bandwidth Control (BAP/BACP) Defined in RFC 2125, Bandwidth Allocation Protocol (BAP) and Bandwidth Allocation Control Protocol (BACP) are similar in nature to Multilink protocol in that they are both used to bond connections together for increased bandwidth. However, while Multilink protocol is a "fixed" solution that will automatically join all the channels it can together, BAP/BACP will only initiate additional connections as needed due to high bandwidth utilization. This is an excellent option if you have connections that are subject to per-minute charges and don't need to have them online all the time.

LCP Extensions Enabling Link Control Protocol (LCP) extensions is a necessary part of supporting callback security on a RAS server. If you are planning on having your system be able to call users back at a specified number, you must have this option enabled.

Software Compression Never missing an opportunity to define a protocol for something and create another standard, Microsoft has developed the Microsoft Point-to-Point Compression (MPPC) protocol to compress data as it travels across a remote access link. MPPC is defined in RFC 2118.

In addition to configuring protocol and authentication types to use, you may also want to configure what ports on your system are used to accept incoming RRAS calls. For example, you may have some modems that are to be used strictly for dial-in and others strictly for dial-out. Unfortunately, the RRAS configuration wizard will simply assume you want to use *all* your modems for dial-in purposes.

To alter the configuration of ports on your system, return to the Routing and Remote Access MMC and expand your server in the left pane of the window. Below your server, you should see an option for Ports. High-light that option and then select Properties from the Action pull-down menu (or by right-clicking the item). That should take you to a window similar to the one shown in Figure 24.24.

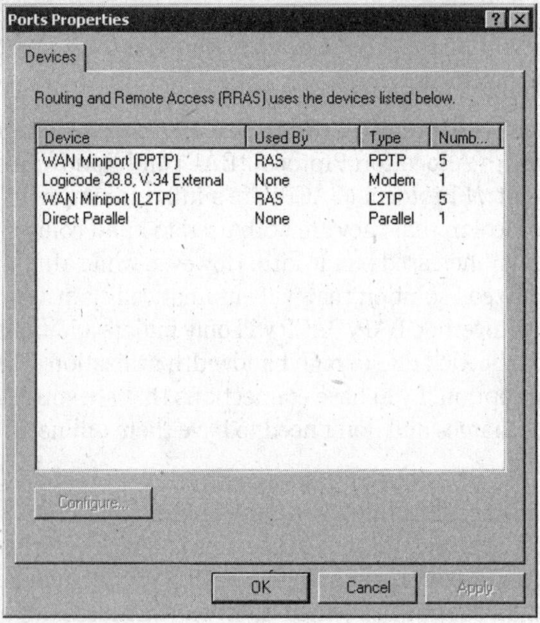

Ports Properties ? X

Devices

Routing and Remote Access (RRAS) uses the devices listed below.

Device	Used By	Type	Numb...
WAN Miniport (PPTP)	RAS	PPTP	5
Logicode 28.8, V.34 External	None	Modem	1
WAN Miniport (L2TP)	RAS	L2TP	5
Direct Parallel	None	Parallel	1

Configure...

OK   Cancel   Apply

FIGURE 24.24: Configuring RRAS ports via the Routing and Remote Access MMC

As you can see on this screen, all the interfaces that can support RRAS clients are listed for you to choose from. Highlight the interface(s) that you'd like to accept incoming calls from and then click the Configure button. This will open the individual properties page for this device. Check the box labeled Remote Access Connections (Inbound Only) and—if you can—enter the phone number for the line connected to that device in the Phone Number Of This Device field. The phone number will allow you to support BAP for devices to initiate additional connections to your server (although since this requires multiple modems and lines at each location, it might not be an option you need). Repeat this procedure for all the ports on your server.

Part V

NOTE

It is important to note that *all* types of ports are automatically configured for your RRAS server—including the VPN ports for PPTP and L2TP. If this server is accessible over the Internet, these ports will be "openings" that outsiders can use to try to authenticate to your network. I recommend that you change the Maximum ports value for L2TP to zero and for PPTP to one (the minimum value allowed in RC2), unless you specifically intend to implement virtual private networking (discussed later in this chapter).

Client Configurations

Now that you have a RAS server that's running smoothly, it's time to enable some clients and get connected into the network. While we can't cover every possible platform under the sun when it comes to remote access, we'll look at a few of the more common options, namely Windows NT 4 Workstation and Windows 9*x*. Windows 2000 Professional Dial-Up Networking will follow a routine very similar to the Windows 2000 Server Dial-Up Networking steps, outlined in detail in a later section, "Connecting to a Private Network."

All these client configurations assume that you have Dial-Up Networking already installed on your system and correctly configured. Assistance on installing Dial-Up Networking on other platforms is outside the scope of this book.

TIP

I frequently get calls from clients who have configured a user's home computer to dial in to the corporate network but are having trouble browsing the Network Neighborhood and seeing any resources. In most cases, this is due to the work-group and domain settings on the home system not matching the settings for workstations in the office. Make sure you use the same settings in both locations.

Windows NT 4 Workstation

From the Windows NT 4 desktop, double-click My Computer and then Dial-Up Networking to bring up the main Dial-Up Networking program. If this is the first time you are using Dial-Up Networking, you might get a message about your phonebook being empty—this is okay because it is simply Windows telling you it doesn't know how to dial anyone yet. If you get that message, click OK to continue, and that should leave you at the main Dial-Up Networking screen as shown in Figure 24.25.

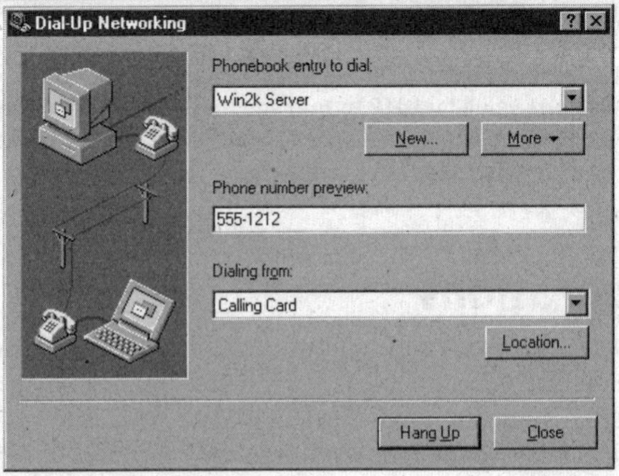

FIGURE 24.25: Dial-Up Networking in Windows NT 4 Workstation

To add a new entry for your Windows 2000 Server, click the New button to start defining a new phonebook entry. The initial screen will let you enter information such as a friendly name to use for this phonebook entry, the number to dial, which modem to use, etc. Enter the appropriate information as needed and then click the Server tab to enter information about the server you are calling into. Your phonebook entry screen should look similar to Figure 24.26.

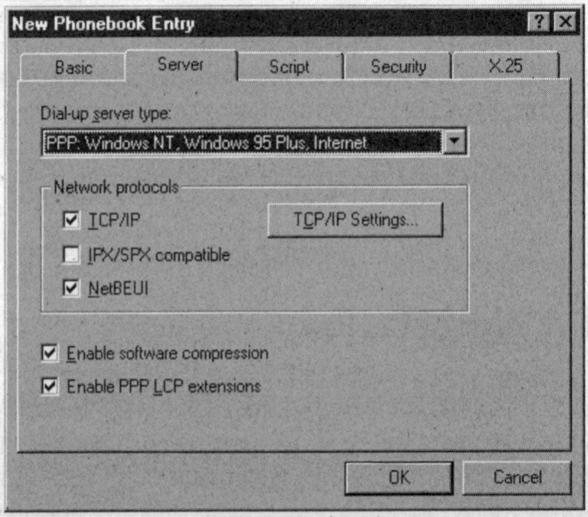

FIGURE 24.26: Selecting server options for a new phonebook entry, Windows NT 4 Workstation

By default, Windows NT 4 Workstation will assume you are going to be dialing into a PPP-compatible server, so it will use that selection as a default for the dial-up server type pull-down box. Also, NT Workstation will assume you want to use software compression and PPP LCP extensions (as seen by the check boxes in the bottom of the window). These are also acceptable defaults for most dial-up connections and can be left checked in most cases. These settings directly correspond to the PPP settings defined on the configured RAS server.

By far, the most important settings in this dialog are the network protocol settings. In general, these settings should correspond directly to the protocols configured when installing the RAS server service, as seen back in Figure 24.15. The client workstation obviously cannot connect on certain protocols if they are not installed on your server, so make sure you are using the same protocols in each location. If you plan on using TCP/IP (which I expect most readers will), click the TCP/IP Settings button to define protocol-specific parameters if necessary. The TCP/IP Settings screen should look like the one in Figure 24.27.

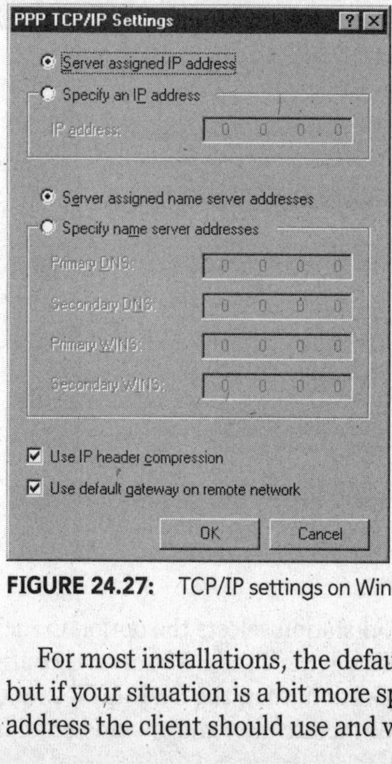

FIGURE 24.27:   TCP/IP settings on Windows NT 4 Workstation Dial-Up Networking

For most installations, the default TCP/IP settings should work fine, but if your situation is a bit more specific, you can enter values for the IP address the client should use and which DNS servers and WINS servers to use for name resolution. If you don't enter any settings for the DNS and WINS servers to use, the dial-up networking client will inherit the same values the RAS server uses itself. This is an important point, because if you are using DHCP to assign addresses, you might assume that any DHCP scope options you have added to your address space would be automatically passed along to your RAS clients. However, even if your RAS server is consulting your DHCP server for addresses to use, it will not pass DHCP scope options along to RAS clients. Settings for DNS servers and WINS servers to use will come directly from the same settings programmed into your RAS server. So, if you're using DHCP on your network, make sure you hard-code an IP address for your RAS server and program in the correct name server addresses.

Once you have set your server and protocol settings as necessary, click the Security tab to define the appropriate authentication options for your dial-in client. The security settings are shown in Figure 24.28. Just as the correct configuration for the server settings on the dial-up client depends on how your RAS server was configured, the security settings on the client will depend on how the security is configured on the RAS server as well.

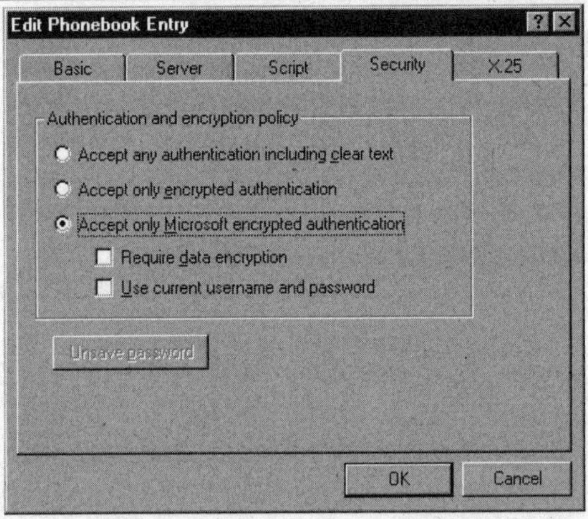

FIGURE 24.28:   Security settings on Windows NT 4 Workstation Dial-Up Networking

By default, Windows NT 4 Workstation selects the option to Accept Any Authentication Including Clear Text. If the RAS server is configured to only allow MS-CHAP authentication, then the Dial-Up Networking client will submit an MS-CHAP authentication and should be validated without any difficulty. If you run into problems logging in, make sure your authentication settings between your server and your client match on at least some level.

When you have completed making the necessary settings for this dial-up networking entry, click OK and then click Dial to dial in to your Windows 2000 Server. You will be prompted for a valid username, password, and domain name to log in with. Use the username(s) you granted dial-in permission to on your servers, click OK, and if everything goes according to plan, your Windows NT 4 Workstation should be connected!

Windows 9x

From the Windows 9x desktop, double-click My Computer and then Dial-Up Networking to bring up the Dial-Up Networking program. If this is the first time you are using Dial-Up Networking, you might be asked to enter information about your local area code, whether to use touch tone or pulse dialing, and any prefixes you need to dial. Simply fill in the information and click OK to continue. This should bring you to the Make New Connection window shown in Figure 24.29.

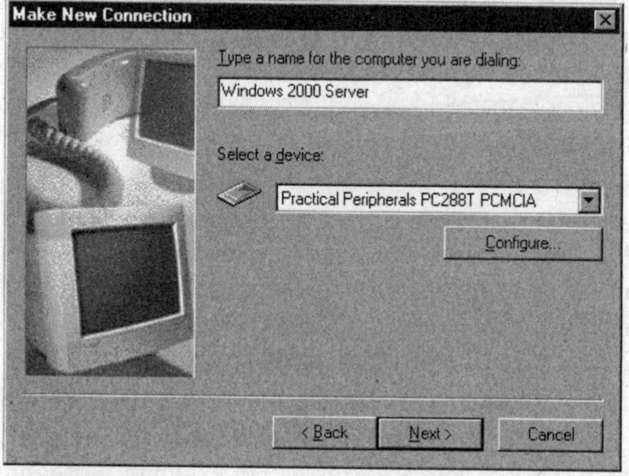

FIGURE 24.29: The Windows 9x Make New Connection window

At the first step of the Make New Connection dialog box, you can enter a friendly name for this Dial-Up Networking connection and select which modem you'd like to use. Enter this information and then click Next to continue to the next step, shown in Figure 24.30.

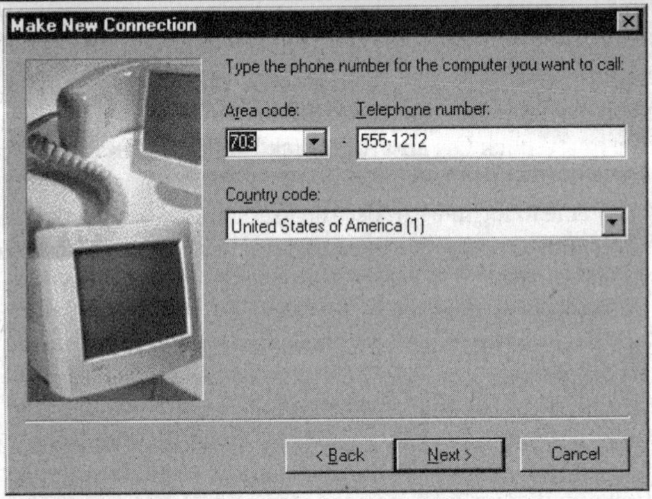

FIGURE 24.30:   Windows 9x Make New Connection, step two

In the second (and final) step, enter the area code and phone number of your RAS server and then click Next to complete the creation of this Dial-Up Networking entry. By default, Windows 9x will assume several things about this Dial-Up Networking entry, including which protocols and security settings you'd like to use. For example, Windows 9x will select all the protocols installed on your system and try to use them over this Dial-Up Networking connection.

If you'd prefer to configure these options yourself instead of having Windows 9x assume what you want, go back to the main Dial-Up Networking window (the one with the Make New Connection icon) and you should see an icon for your Dial-Up Networking session. Right-click the icon, and select Properties to edit the configuration. You will see the properties pages for this Dial-Up Networking connection, as shown in Figure 24.31.

From here, you can (and should) change the security and protocol settings to match those of your RAS server. For example, if you only run TCP/IP on your corporate network, you don't necessarily need to have NetBEUI and IPX selected in your Dial-Up Networking session. Configure the settings accordingly, and then launch your session to verify that it works.

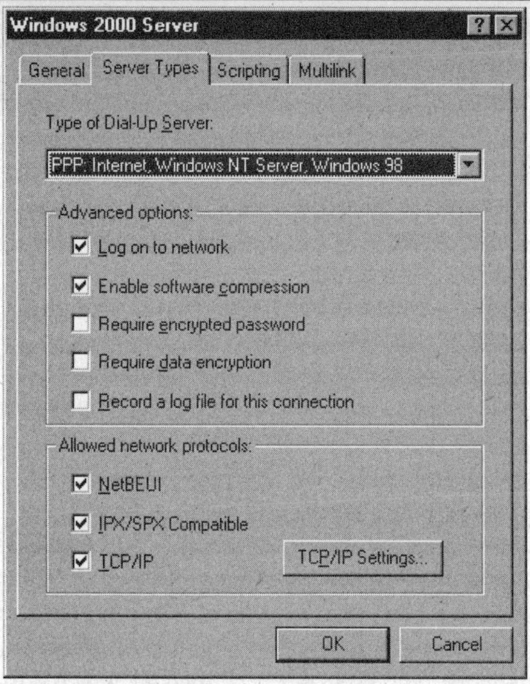

FIGURE 24.31: Editing Windows 9x Dial-Up Networking entry properties

Managing Connected Users

If you need to keep tabs on users connected to your network, the Routing and Remote Access MMC can give you an overview of all remote access connections currently connected to your server. Whether connections are coming into your systems from VPN connections, serial connections, analog modems, or ISDN lines, you can get an overview of all your remote connections from one convenient console.

To manage connected users, launch the Routing and Remote Access MMC, by selecting Start ➢ Programs ➢ Administrative Tools ➢ Routing And Remote Access. By expanding the details for your RAS server in the left pane, you should see a subitem for Remote Access Clients listed below your system, along with a number next to it in parentheses. This number indicates the number of dial-in users currently connected to your system. This screen should look similar to the one in Figure 24.32.

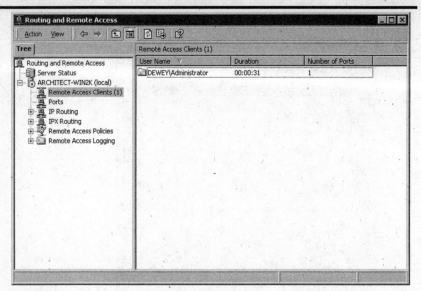

FIGURE 24.32: Managing remote access users through RRAS MMC

From this screen, you can get an overview of how long users have been connected to your network, who is currently connected, which ports are in use, etc. By double-clicking any of the listed connections on your system, you can get advanced details about that individual connection, such as what IP/IPX addresses were assigned to the system, how much data has been transferred, etc. You can disconnect an individual connection from the same properties page by clicking the Hang Up button, or you can disconnect a user by right-clicking that user's connection in the main list of connected users. In addition to being able to disconnect a user from the main listing of connected users, you can also send a message to an individual user or to all connected users by right-clicking a connection and selecting either Send Message or Send To All, respectively.

CONNECTING TO A PRIVATE NETWORK

Much like connecting to the Internet, at times you might need to connect your Windows 2000 Server to another private network. Maybe one of your servers needs to collect data from a client's systems or transmit product orders to a supplier. The private network might be another Win2K network, an NT network, a Novell network, or a network that contains a combination of servers and other systems. In any case, dial-up networking can get your Windows 2000 Server connected with a minimal amount of effort.

Before getting started, there are a few things you will need to have to complete making a connection to another network. Namely, you will need to have the following information available in advance:

▶ Access phone number to dial

▶ Username and password combination

▶ Protocols that will be used on the remote network

▶ Authentication the remote network will require

To get started, we'll once again be working through the Network Connection Wizard by clicking Start ➤ Settings ➤ Network And Dial-Up Connections and then choosing the Make New Connection icon. When the wizard starts, you should see the screen shown in Figure 24.33.

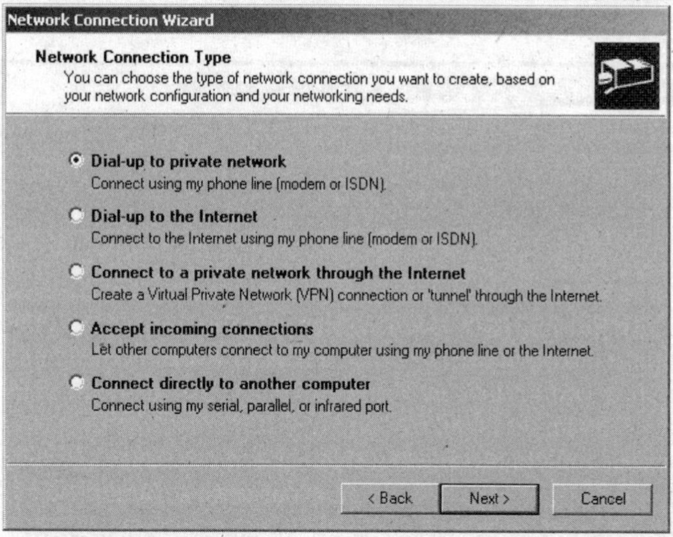

FIGURE 24.33: The Network Connection Wizard: connect to a private network

From this point, select the first option, Dial-Up To Private Network, and click Next to continue to the next step of the wizard, as seen in Figure 24.34.

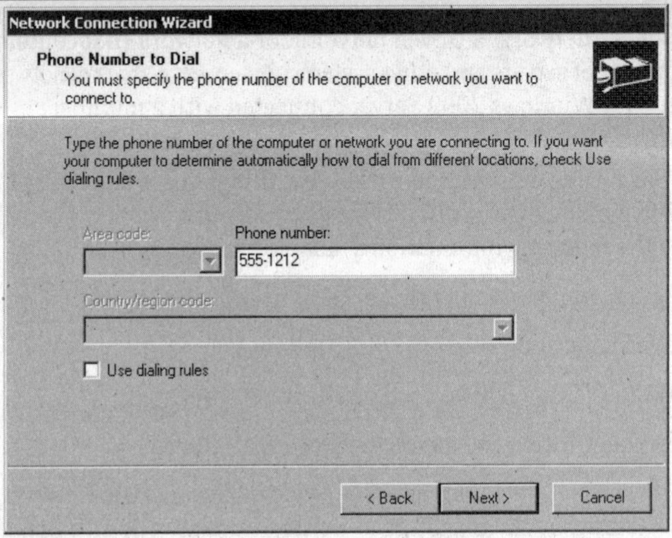

FIGURE 24.34:   The Network Connection Wizard: enter a phone number

Enter the phone number as prompted, and then click Next to get to the last step of the wizard, pictured in Figure 24.35.

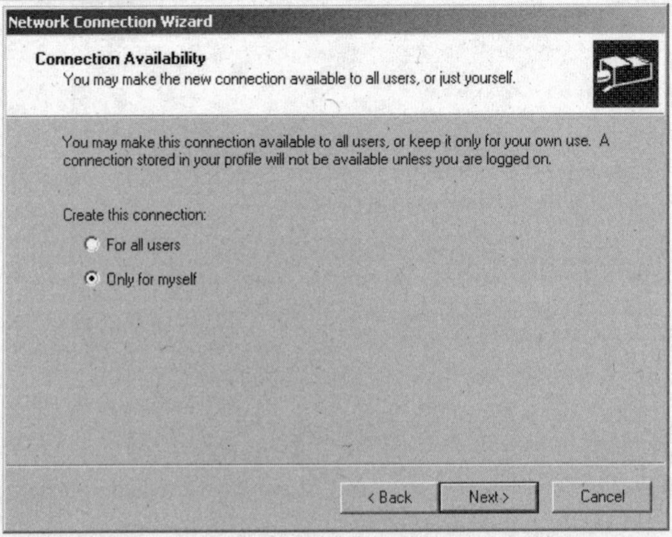

FIGURE 24.35:   The Network Connection Wizard: share the connection

The last step of the Network Connection Wizard will ask if you would like to make this dial-up connection available to all users or to keep it just for use by the machine itself. For the purposes of simply connecting a Windows 2000 Server to another network, select the Only For Myself option here. The other option, For All Users, would end up sharing this connection with other users on the network, a topic discussed in the next section ("Acting As an Internet Gateway"). Click Next when you are finished, and you will have successfully created a Dial-Up Networking entry.

However, Win2K will have assumed several things about your Dial-Up Networking entry that might not work for your specific situation. To double-check everything, edit the properties for this dial-up connection by right-clicking the icon for it in the Network And Dial-Up Connections window. Clicking the Networking tab on the properties page should bring you to a page similar to the one shown in Figure 24.36.

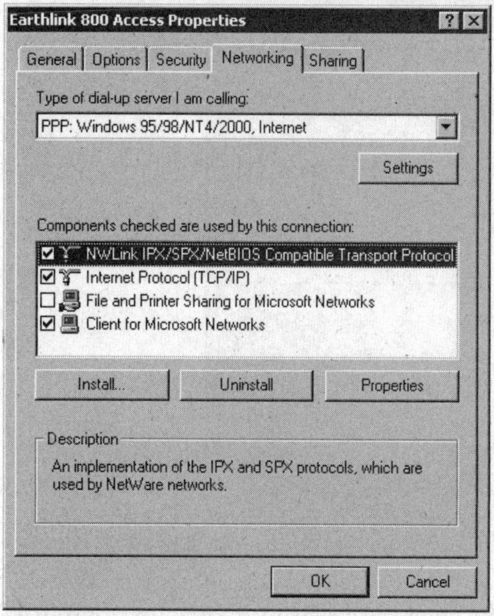

FIGURE 24.36:   Dial-Up Networking entry properties

Windows 2000 will assume you want to use several defaults when you try to connect to this remote network. For example, it will assume you want to use *all* the protocols loaded on your system for this connection, it will assume it can use unsecured passwords, etc. Some of these options might not make sense in specific situations. For example, if you are connecting to an IPX-only network, it doesn't make much sense to try and negotiate a TCP/IP connection. Even though Win2K will realize that it can't establish the TCP/IP connection, why even try?

To fine-tune this connection, remove or add specific protocols as needed by checking the boxes next to the protocols listed under the Networking tab of the Dial-Up Networking entry properties pages. If you are connecting to a remote TCP/IP network and the device you are dialing in to does not provide you with an IP address or DNS server addresses automatically, you can program these in by highlighting the TCP/IP protocol and then clicking the Properties button. This will bring you to the specific TCP/IP settings to use for this connection (Figure 24.37).

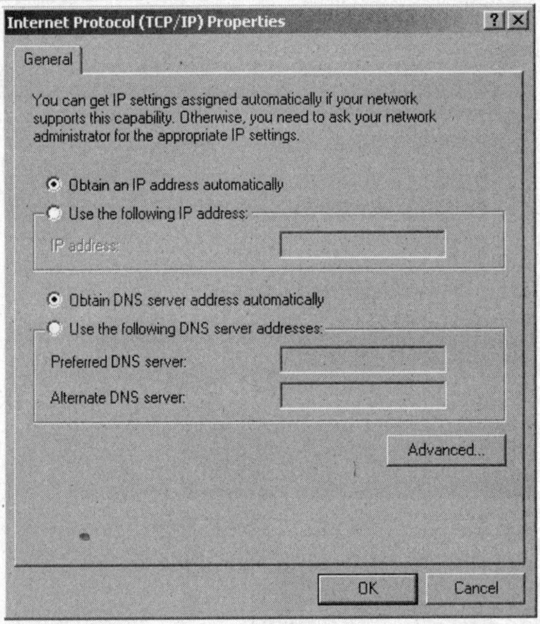

FIGURE 24.37:   Editing TCP/IP properties for Dial-Up Networking entries

On this screen you can enter the necessary information for your TCP/IP connection. If you are accessing a remote network that uses WINS servers but does not provide those addresses to you, enter them in the advanced TCP/IP settings area by clicking the Advanced button and then clicking the WINS tab.

Once you have your protocols configured correctly, click OK to get back to the main properties page for this dial-up connection. If you need to edit any other properties, such as the type of security or authentication to use, click the appropriate tabs and make those settings as necessary.

If you think this looks similar to the steps to connect to the Internet described earlier in this chapter, you are correct. Basically, all the mechanisms are the same in Dial-Up Networking, but different wizards will take a different approach to the settings that are applied by default. Therefore, some of the same advanced options discussed in the "Connecting to the Internet" section (reestablishing failed links, redialing nonresponsive numbers, etc.) are available for regular dial-up connections to private networks. As a matter of fact, you can even use the Dial-Up to a Private Network Wizard to define a connection to the Internet. Which brings us to our next topic.

ACTING AS AN INTERNET GATEWAY

One of the hottest little "niche" applications people always seemed to want to do with Windows NT 4 Server was to share an Internet connection with everyone else inside their organization. After all, NT servers were usually set up to share other resources (files, printers, etc.)—so it made sense that NT Server should have been able to share an Internet connection, right? Not exactly. With enough tweaking and some strict rules to follow, you *could* actually have NT Server dial an Internet connection and route traffic for internal hosts out to the Internet. However, the setup would be difficult and cumbersome, and it requires having valid (InterNIC-assigned) IP addresses available for everyone within the organization. Simply sharing a $20/month unlimited-access Internet account is not an option.

Now, Microsoft has included a variety of capabilities in Windows 2000 Server that make this task relatively easy. With the correct information about what type of connectivity you need to the outside world, Windows 2000 Server can act as an Internet gateway for your internal clients, leveraging an existing Internet connection among all the workstations in your organization.

NOTE

The Internet gateway capabilities of Windows 2000 Server worked so well that, in the course of writing the first edition of this chapter, I was actually using my Windows 2000 Server (Beta 3) as an Internet gateway for my laptop and other test machines.

Although Microsoft has included some great tools for sharing connections on your network, it is important to note several subtle hints Microsoft has included in their documentation for this feature of Windows 2000 Server. First and foremost, Microsoft often makes several references to small or home office networks, implying that this capability really isn't designed for use in medium-to-large environments. I would have to agree with them on this point; if you have a reasonable number of workstations on your network, you will probably be far better off going with a product such as Microsoft Proxy Server and a dedicated Internet connection.

The second point Microsoft makes repeatedly throughout their documentation is that "you should not use this feature in an existing network with other Windows 2000 Server domain controllers, DNS servers, gateways, DHCP servers, or systems configured for static IP." Since this configuration requires a very specific IP configuration to work correctly, implementing this on a network that doesn't conform to that configuration could cause lots of difficulty. I would agree with Microsoft on this point as well.

Although acting as an Internet router isn't one of the options normally available through the Make New Connection Wizard used throughout this chapter, fortunately one of the other options will configure most everything necessary. By using the steps detailed in the last section, "Connecting to a Private Network," and connecting to the Internet as the "private" network, you can make Windows 2000 act as an Internet gateway, routing traffic from your internal clients out to the Internet and back again.

Configuring Windows 2000 Server to Act As an Internet Gateway

Start with the same steps listed in the section "Connecting to a Private Network" and go all the way up to Figure 24.34, using a local access number for your ISP as the number of the private network to dial.

This time, when the Network Connection Wizard asks if you would like to make this connection available to all users (pictured in Figure 24.35), select For All Users instead of Only For Myself. This will enable the sharing properties for this connection. Click Next, and you should end up with a screen like the one in Figure 24.38.

On this screen, you will have two options for how this shared connection should be handled. The first option is simply to enable sharing for this connection; leave this option checked. The second option tells Windows 2000 Server when it should establish the connection. If this box is unchecked, the only way to establish the connection to the Internet will be manually. However, users typically expect connections to be available whenever they want them, so enabling the on-demand dialing option will allow Windows 2000 Server to automatically establish this connection as needed, with no outside intervention. If you are going to be implementing a shared Internet connection, you probably want to select this option. When you check the box for on-demand dialing and click Next, you will probably receive a warning dialog box similar to the one in Figure 24.39.

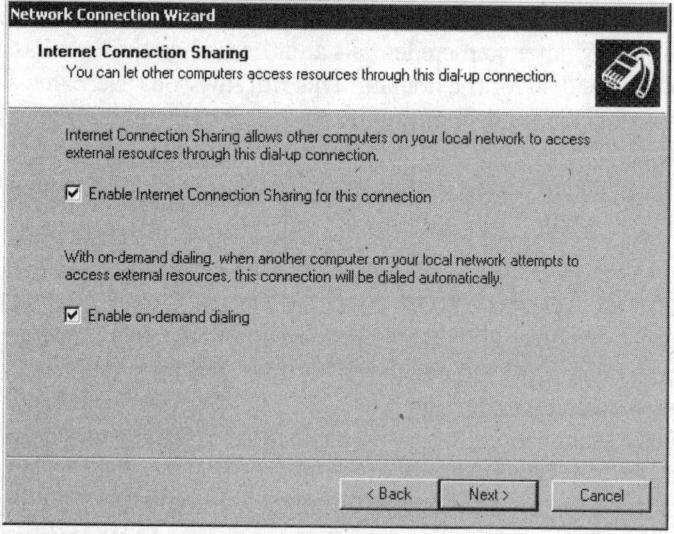

FIGURE 24.38: Defining sharing options

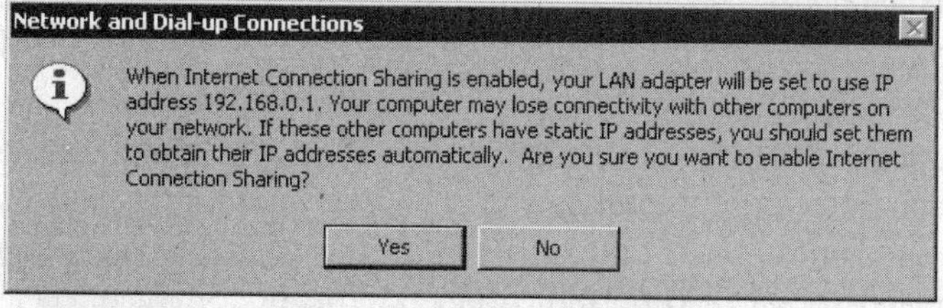

FIGURE 24.39: Static IP address change warning

This dialog box lets you know that Windows 2000 Server will need to make several changes to its IP configuration for this functionality to work, including specifying a fixed IP address to use for the server's internal network connection. If anyone is connected to your server at this point, make sure they are disconnected before continuing, otherwise they may lose their connections to the system. Click Yes to continue, and Windows 2000 Server will make the appropriate IP changes to support sharing an Internet connection.

The last step of the wizard should ask you to assign a friendly name to this connection. Go ahead and assign a meaningful name to this connection and then click Finish. Once you have completed the wizard, you should see an icon for your shared connection in the Network And Dial-up Connections dialog box. Launch the connection to verify that everything is working correctly. When you are prompted for your ISP username and password, enter your credentials and then check the Save Password box below the field for the domain. This will save your username and password for this connection so that when it is demand-dialed it will have what it needs. Once you have established that your ISP connection works correctly in and of itself, it's time to define a few rules as to what you want to allow across your Internet connection.

Defining Application and Service Configurations

By default, Windows 2000 Server will not automatically route any traffic from your client workstations to the Internet. You must define specific rules as to what type of traffic (i.e., what TCP/IP protocols) can go across your shared connection. To do this, begin by editing the properties for your shared Internet access connection by right-clicking the Dial-Up Networking icon in the Network And Dial-Up Connections window and then selecting Properties. Click the Sharing tab, and you should see settings for enabling shared access for this connection and on-demand dialing. At the bottom of the window is a button labeled Settings. By clicking the button, you can define settings for which applications and services can go across your shared Internet Connection. The Internet Connection Sharing Settings dialog box is pictured in Figure 24.40.

As a point of clarification, "applications" typically refer to connections that come from your internal network (for web browsing, e-mail, etc.) and are destined out to the Internet. However, sharing an Internet connection can also allow you to accept traffic from external hosts targeted at systems within your network. For example, maybe you have a small web server running in your organization that you would like people to be able to access. Using a shared Internet connection not only lets your users share access to the Internet, but it can be programmed to allow the Internet access to your internal shared resources as well.

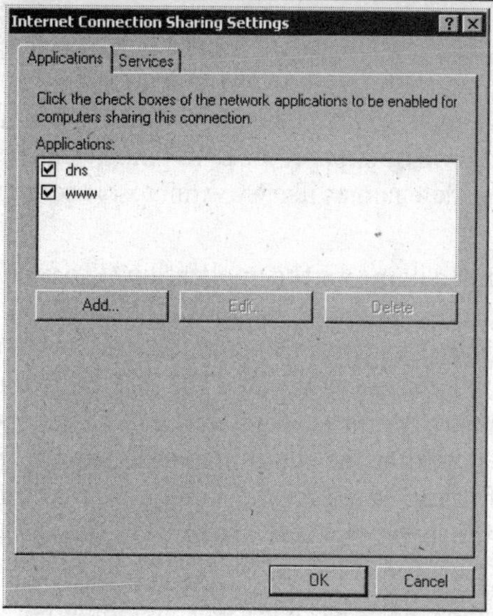

FIGURE 24.40: Configuring shared access settings

This is one of the reasons why it's important to define rules as to what is allowed in and out of your shared Internet connection. Let's start by adding a few rules to allow web browsing across the shared Internet connection. From the Settings screen, make sure you are looking at the Applications tab. More than likely you won't have any applications listed on your system (unlike the example in Figure 24.40). Press Add to add an application (in effect, a TCP/IP protocol) to your system. The dialog box to add a shared access application is shown in Figure 24.41.

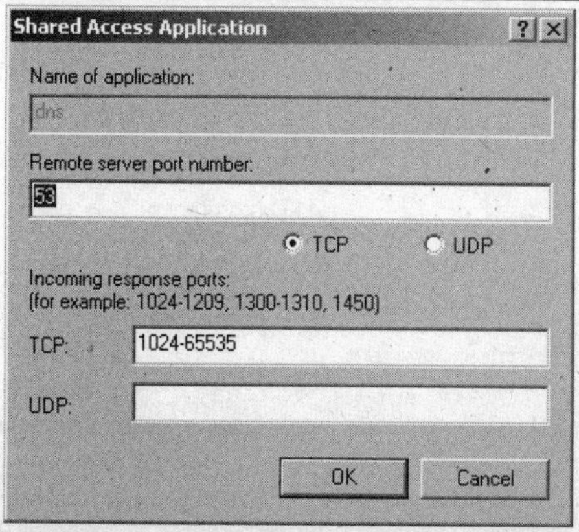

FIGURE 24.41: Adding a shared access application

To allow shared access for a TCP/IP application, Windows 2000 Server needs to know how that application functions. Specifically, Windows 2000 Server needs to know which ports the application uses and whether the application uses TCP or UDP connections. One of the first applications you will probably want to add will be support for DNS—the means by which clients and browsers can translate names like www.microsoft.com into IP addresses.

To add DNS support, enter a name for the application (I've used "dns" in Figure 24.40) and the port on the remote server that Win2K will be communicating with. For DNS, this port is 53, and the protocol to use for the request (with my ISP) is TCP, so I've selected the TCP radio button below the port. DNS responses from the target system will generally come back in on the same port that the client made the request from, which can be any number from 1024 to 65535. Therefore, I've put 1024-65535 in the TCP field for the incoming response to allow the DNS server to respond with the appropriate information.

As you can see, knowing how ports work is a key component of using shared Internet access. Some applications even get complicated by sending responses on UDP *and* TCP ports. For information on some commonly used Internet application ports and for the information necessary to configure your own applications as needed, see Table 24.1. Once you have configured an application for DNS, add applications as needed for the applications on your internal network.

TABLE 24.1: TCP/IP Well-Known Ports and Services

PROTOCOL TYPE	DESTINATION PORT/ PROTOCOL	RESPONSE PORT(S)/ PROTOCOL(S)
FTP	21/TCP	1024-65535/TCP
Telnet	23/TCP	1024-65535/TCP
SMTP	25/TCP	1024-65535/TCP
Gopher	70/TCP	1024-65535/TCP
HTTP	80/TCP	1024-65535/TCP
POP3	110/TCP	1024-65535/TCP
NNTP	119/TCP	1024-65535/TCP

If you need to have outside clients access services on a computer on your internal network, you will need to add definitions to the Services tab of the Internet Connection Sharing Settings dialog box. Unless you want people from the outside world connecting to your internal systems, I would recommend leaving this blank. But if you have a web server or FTP server that you need to have people connect to, this is the area to do it. Clicking the Services tab will take you to a screen almost identical to the one for Applications with several services listed on it. Clicking a service will allow you to define an internal host that Windows 2000 should direct that type of traffic to. Or you can click the Add button to add a service, and you will see a dialog box like the one shown in Figure 24.42.

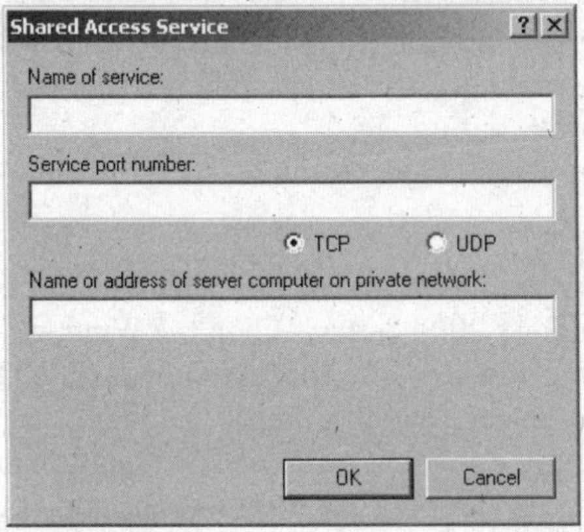

FIGURE 24.42: Adding a shared access service

Services work a bit differently from applications because external hosts won't connect *directly* to the IP address assigned to your internal workstation that has the destination service (especially since in most cases the internal IP addresses won't be routable addresses on the Internet). Instead, external systems will connect to your Windows 2000 Server on a specific port, and based on what port they connect to, Win2K will redirect the request to one of your internal systems. Therefore, the definitions for services vary a bit.

Start defining your service by giving it a name—for example, http, ftp, etc. In the field for service port number, put the port you will expect incoming connections to come to. Again, you can use Table 24.1 to determine which ports to use. If you wanted to allow incoming HTTP traffic, for example, you would put 80 in the field for service port. Finally, in the last field for adding a service, tell Windows 2000 which of your internal computers to redirect the request to by entering either the name or IP address of the correct internal network computer. If you are using DHCP to assign addresses to your internal computers, I would recommend referencing the system by name in this dialog box.

Once you have completed this definition, click OK and then make sure this service is checked in the Shared Access Services definition for settings. Now, if you have a connection that is demand-dialed, it's important to note that this won't typically work for incoming connections. That is, your ISP won't know that it should dial *your* server whenever someone on the Internet tries to access one of your systems. Therefore, if you are going to accept incoming service connections, I'd recommend having your Internet connection online at all times.

Once you have defined the appropriate application and service settings, it's time to configure your clients to direct their Internet traffic to your Windows 2000 Server for routing.

Configuring Clients

Once your server is ready, you will need to tell your clients to route their Internet traffic to your Windows 2000 Server. When the Windows 2000 Server receives these packets, it will realize that they are destined for the Internet and route them as necessary (initiating your demand-dialed connection if needed). You can either program each workstation manually or let DHCP do it for you by defining the correct scope and options to use.

The following information will work in your DHCP scope for getting your clients connected to the Internet (other slight variations would work as well; this is merely an example):

▶ Address range: 192.168.0.2 to 192.168.0.254

▶ Address mask: 255.255.255.0

▶ Default gateway: 192.168.0.1

▶ DNS servers to use: enter your ISP's DNS server addresses

To enter these settings manually on a Windows 2000 Professional, NT 4, or 9x client, edit the TCP/IP properties of your computer to change the IP address to something in the range listed above. The mask should be 255.255.255.0 as listed above, and the default gateway should be 192.168.0.1, the IP address your Windows 2000 Server will give itself once you enable shared access. In Windows NT 4 Workstation, this would look similar to the dialog box shown in Figure 24.43.

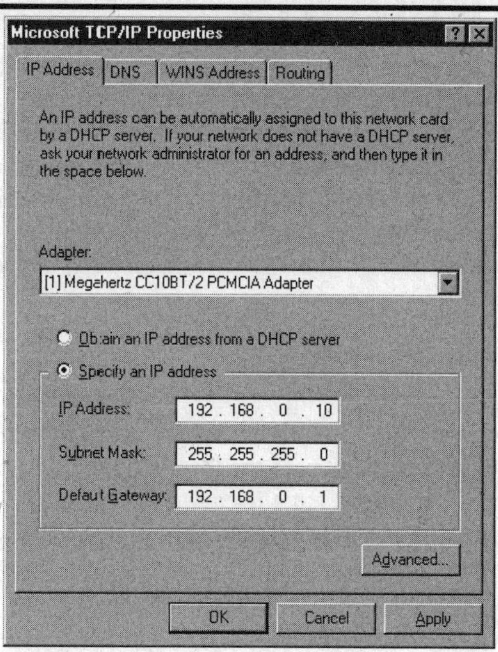

FIGURE 24.43:   TCP/IP settings for shared access on Windows NT 4 Workstation

The last setting to make is the DNS server setting. Since your workstation will need to look somewhere to translate host names into IP address, you will need to put the DNS server IP addresses for your ISP into your connection settings. In NT 4 Workstation, clicking the DNS tab and adding new DNS servers to your system does this. If you don't know the IP addresses of your ISP's DNS servers, I would recommend contacting them to ask them directly or see if they list the appropriate settings somewhere on their website.

Once you have the correct DNS and TCP/IP settings programmed in, reboot your workstation and log back in to the network. Once your computer is up and running, you should be able to allow access across your shared Internet connection for the protocols you defined on your server (DNS, web, etc.). You should see your Windows 2000 Server automatically initiate the connection as needed whenever one of your client systems tries to access the Internet.

ACCEPTING VPN CONNECTIONS FROM REMOTE CLIENTS

Virtual private networking is one of the hottest subjects in networking today. With the widespread presence of the Internet, it only makes sense that corporations and organizations would want to try to leverage existing investments in Internet connections for their corporate networks. But as exciting as VPN can be, it can also be a rather complex subject. Since it is basically a means of layering one logical network over another, the complexities of making a network connection are, in effect, doubled.

VPN Overview

Loosely defined, a VPN allows you to run a secure, private network over an unsecured public network. You can use virtual private networking to get clients connected to your network over the Internet and do it securely, even though the Internet is inherently an unsecured network.

One of the better analogies I've found for explaining the concepts of a virtual private network is to refer to them as "pipes." To conceptualize VPNs, think of two pipes, one large and one small. Now, imagine that the small pipe actually runs *inside* of the large one. It starts and ends at the same places the large pipe does, and it can carry materials on its own, completely independent of whatever is happening in the large pipe. As a matter of fact, the only thing the small pipe depends on the large pipe for is the determination of the start and end points. Beyond that, the small pipe can operate independently of the large pipe in terms of direction of travel, materials it carries, etc.

To add another layer to this analogy, let's assume that the large pipe is made out of a transparent material, and the small pipe is made out of metal. If anyone were to take a look at the pipe-within-a-pipe, they would easily be able to see whatever was moving through the outside (large) pipe. However, whatever was traveling through the inside pipe would remain a mystery.

If this is starting to make sense, you should be thinking to yourself that the large pipe represents the unsecured network (i.e., the Internet) and the small pipe represents the virtual private network. VPN is a way of tunneling data packets through a connection that already exists but that can't be used on its own for privacy reasons. Obviously, the Internet is a perfect example of a network that often can't be used on its own for privacy reasons.

So, what benefit does this have for the overworked network administrator? Well, for starters, it could reduce or eliminate your need to maintain a pool of modems at your site for remote dial-in users. Remote users don't need to call directly into your network to get connected; they can simply call in to a local ISP and get a valid Internet (unsecured) connection. Assuming you have a VPN/RAS server running on your network (and it's connected to the Internet), once the remote user has connected to their ISP, the client just has to establish the VPN (secured) session with the RAS server. The cost of maintaining modems and phone lines is shifted to the ISP. As long as your RAS server is connected to the Internet, you can support multiple incoming calls all over that one connection. Also, in keeping with this example, since the VPN session is being established over the Internet, there is no need for any long distance calls. If your remote user is hundreds of miles away, the cost to connect to your network is the same as if they were local, since the only call they would need to make would be to their ISP. This is a great way to support a geographically dispersed user base.

Microsoft has gone a long way toward making virtual private networking easy to implement in Windows 2000. However, if there is one piece of advice I could give everyone trying to implement virtual private networking, it is this: get a good, solid RAS server working and accepting incoming connections *first*. Use standard connections (analog modems, ISDN, etc.) on your RAS server first to make sure everything is functioning correctly. Once you are sure RAS is working correctly for standard connections, only then is it advisable to try implementing VPN connections. Since virtual private networking adds another layer of functionality "on top of" RAS, it is crucial to have a stable foundation to begin with. RAS can be peculiar in its behavior at times, so it is important to have all your configurations working correctly (DHCP address assignment, browsing, etc.). If only I had a nickel for every time I heard someone say "this VPN thing is messed up," only to find out that if they dial in to their network over a modem connection, they experience the exact same problems.

A Brief History of VPN: PPTP, L2F, and L2TP

When virtual private networking was first being developed back in the mid-1990s, two of the largest companies in the computer/networking industry tried to run with implementations of VPNs in the hopes that they would enjoy widespread implementation and therefore become an "industry standard." The two companies were Microsoft and Cisco, and each had their respective VPN technologies. Microsoft was approaching the VPN market from the operating systems point of view and had developed Point-to-Point Tunneling Protocol (PPTP) as a means to securely transmit data across unsecure networks. At the same time, Cisco was taking the lead in VPN from a strictly networking point of view with a protocol called Layer 2 Forwarding, or L2F.

Now, when either of these companies decides to develop an industry standard, they can usually get away with it if one doesn't already exist. No single standard had obtained a large enough share of the VPN market to be considered an industry standard, so the playing field was literally wide open. However, the sheer muscle and momentum that either one of these companies can put behind an initiative wasn't necessarily enough to displace the other. Each protocol had its strengths and weaknesses, and Microsoft and Cisco's offerings enjoyed moderate successes.

Now, I'm speculating a bit here, but I think that since neither industry giant was going to successfully displace the other in the VPN market, they decided it would be better to cooperate than compete. In any case, Microsoft and Cisco made the decision to collaborate on virtual private networking by merging their protocols, PPTP and L2F, into one hybrid protocol. The final product of that collaboration is Layer 2 Tunneling Protocol, or L2TP for short.

Windows 2000 Server includes L2TP support for establishing virtual private networking connections but also includes support for PPTP for backward compatibility with other operating systems. At the time this book was being written, L2TP was only supported in Windows 2000 (Server and Professional), and Microsoft had only made passing references to supporting it in Windows 98 or Me. Based on some of the white papers I've read recently, Microsoft isn't committing to L2TP support for Windows 98 or Me just yet. Therefore, the only option today for supporting legacy clients (NT 4, Windows 9x or Me) across a virtual private network is to include support for PPTP.

Okay, enough said. Let's assume you've got a good solid RAS server running and get on to the fun stuff.

Implementing VPN via PPTP and L2TP

If you went through the section "Accepting Incoming Calls from Remote Users," congratulations—you have 80 percent of what you need to support VPN connections in place already. When you install Remote Access Service, Windows 2000 Server should have added support for five PPTP connections and five L2TP connections by default. If you didn't go through the section to accept incoming calls from remote users, stop reading now and go back to complete the steps listed there. For the remainder of this section, we'll assume you have a functional RAS server in place.

We'll start by verifying that support for PPTP and L2TP is in place through the Routing and Remote Access MMC. Start the RRAS MMC by selecting Start ➤ Programs ➤ Administrative Tools ➤ Routing And Remote Access. In the left portion of the MMC window, you should see the name of your RAS server listed; expand the information for that server by double-clicking it. Right-click the listing for ports, and then select Properties to edit the ports (Figure 24.44).

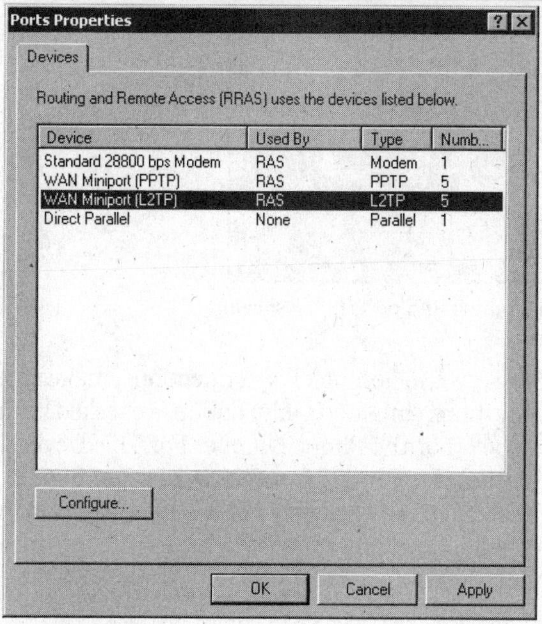

Ports Properties   ? ✕

Devices

Routing and Remote Access (RRAS) uses the devices listed below.

Device	Used By	Type	Numb...
Standard 28800 bps Modem	RAS	Modem	1
WAN Miniport (PPTP)	RAS	PPTP	5
WAN Miniport (L2TP)	RAS	L2TP	5
Direct Parallel	None	Parallel	1

Configure...

OK   Cancel   Apply

FIGURE 24.44:   Ports Properties

In the Ports Properties screen, you will see all the ports that Win2K has recognized and can use for Remote Access Service. Each device has a usage listed, a device name, a type, and several ports associated with it. By default, RAS should have PPTP and L2TP devices installed on your system and probably has five ports associated with each.

Depending on which type of connections you will be allowing and how many you want to allow, you can edit your protocols and circuits accordingly from here. For example, if you are only going to have Win2K clients connecting to your network over virtual circuits, you can stick with just supporting L2TP. However, if you need to support legacy clients accessing your network via virtual circuits, PPTP is your only choice. In any case, to edit the port properties for either type, double-click the item to edit or just highlight it and click the Configure button. This will take you into the port configuration screen shown in Figure 24.45 (the screen looks the same whether you are configuring PPTP, L2TP, or modem ports).

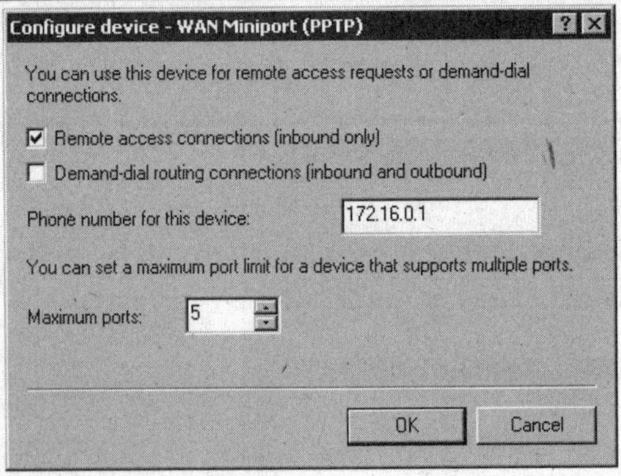

Configure device - WAN Miniport (PPTP)   ? X

You can use this device for remote access requests or demand-dial connections.

☑ Remote access connections (inbound only)
☐ Demand-dial routing connections (inbound and outbound)

Phone number for this device: 172.16.0.1

You can set a maximum port limit for a device that supports multiple ports.

Maximum ports: 5

[OK]   [Cancel]

FIGURE 24.45:   Configuring RAS ports (PPTP shown)

To configure your server to accept VPN connections, make sure the Remote Access Connections (Inbound Only) option is checked in the Configure Device dialog box. For the Phone Number For This Device field, enter the public Internet IP address of your server (assuming the Internet is the public, unsecured network you will be using). This is the IP address that clients will eventually connect to across the Internet for establishing VPN circuits.

TIP

I strongly recommend that you use a fixed IP address and Internet connection for your server. Yes, you *can* use a dial-up connection from your RAS server to the Internet, and you can even make dynamic IP addresses work for this. But with dynamic IP addresses, your server's IP address will change every time it has to reestablish its link, quickly becoming a management nightmare.

Depending on how many simultaneous virtual private networking connections you plan on supporting, adjust the Maximum Ports value accordingly and then click OK.

TIP

I would recommend disabling any and all VPN connections that you *don't* plan on using. For example, if you are only going to support L2TP connections from Windows 2000 clients, disable PPTP by unchecking the Remote Access Connections (Inbound Only) option on the properties page for PPTP. This will prevent anyone from trying to establish a connection to your server via PPTP without your knowing about it.

Client Configuration

To get a client workstation connected to a Windows 2000 Server running VPN protocols, you will need to have one of the following:

- ▶ Windows NT 4, Workstation, or Server (PPTP only)

- ▶ Windows 95 with the Dial-Up Networking 1.2 upgrade or better (PPTP only)

- ▶ Windows 98 (PPTP only now; L2TP *might* be included later)

- ▶ Windows 2000 Professional (PPTP or L2TP)

Since older operating systems such as Windows 95 and Windows NT 4 don't install PPTP by default, the first thing to do is add PPTP support to the client system. PPTP is a standard protocol, just like NetBEUI or NWLink, so the procedures for adding this new protocol are roughly the same.

Windows NT 4 Workstation   Assuming you already have Dial-Up Networking set up on your NT 4 Workstation, the first step to adding VPN support is to add the Point-to-Point Tunneling Protocol in the Control Panel ➢ Network applet. Start by clicking Start ➢ Settings ➢ Control Panel ➢ Network, and then click the Protocols tab. Clicking the Add button from the Protocols properties page will bring you to the Select Network Protocol dialog box, as shown in Figure 24.46.

Once you have selected the Point-to-Point Tunneling Protocol and clicked OK, NT 4 Workstation will ask you how many simultaneous virtual circuits you'd like to support in the dialog box in Figure 24.47.

However many circuits you choose here will determine how many virtual ports Windows NT 4 will add to its configuration. Each virtual port will be called VPNx, with x referring to the specific port number. In effect, they function similarly to modems running on COM ports (COMx), so think of these VPN devices as virtual modems. If you will only be connecting to one virtual private network at a time, choose 1 and click OK.

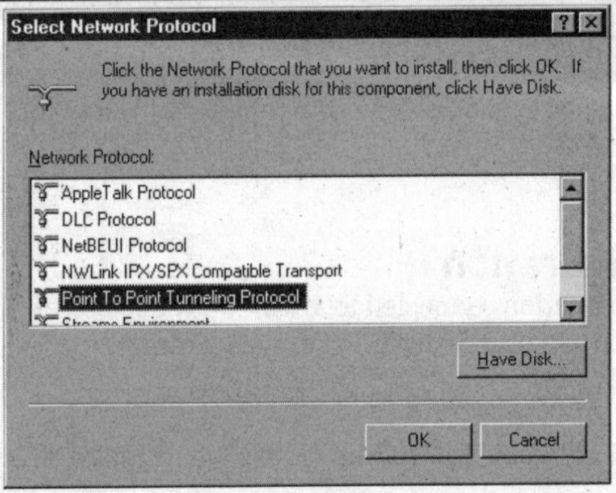

FIGURE 24.46:   The Select Network Protocol dialog box in NT 4 Workstation

FIGURE 24.47:   Configuring the number of virtual circuits to support

Once you have completed selecting the number of virtual circuits to support, NT 4 Workstation will invoke RAS setup to allow you to add your new virtual modem(s) to the RAS configuration, as shown in Figure 24.48.

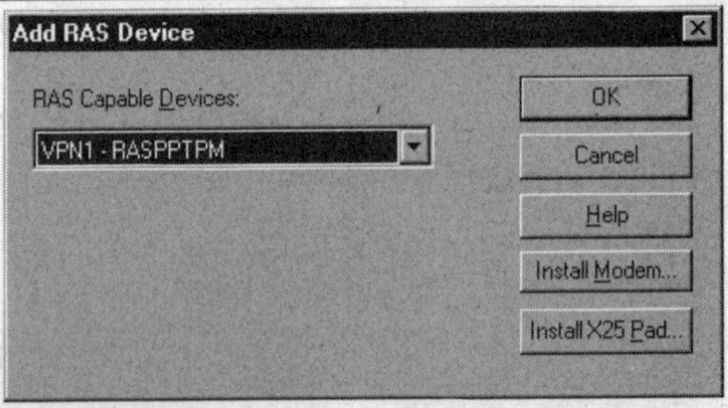

FIGURE 24.48:   Adding VPN devices to RAS in NT 4 Workstation

Click the Add button in Remote Access Setup and you should see your VPN device in the Add RAS Device window. If you see a modem or some other device there, try pulling down the list and then selecting your VPN device. Once you have your VPN device selected, click OK and it will be added to your RAS configuration.

Once you are back to the Remote Access Setup screen, highlight your VPN device and click the Configure button. This device should be configured for Dial-Out Only as shown in Figure 24.49.

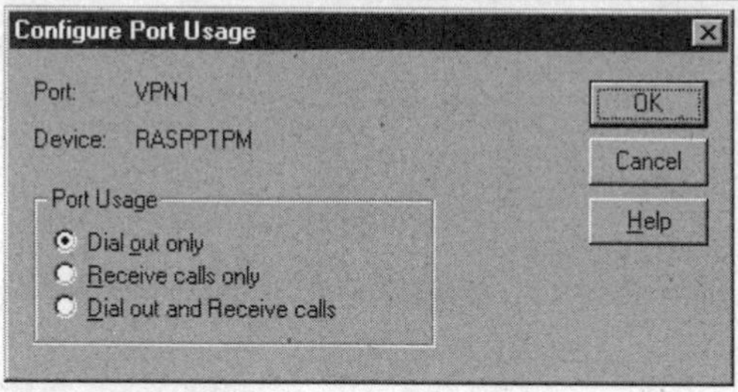

FIGURE 24.49: Configuring VPN devices for dial-out only in NT 4 Workstation

Once everything is set correctly, click OK and RAS will start the installation routine. This will most likely require a reboot of your computer, so go ahead and restart it and get back into Windows. To use your VPN device, the last step you need to perform is creating a Dial-Up Networking entry.

Double-click My Computer and then Dial-Up Networking to begin creating a new Dial-Up Networking entry. Creating a VPN Dial-Up Networking entry is almost identical to creating a regular Dial-Up Networking entry for a phone line, except that you will use an IP address instead of a phone number to dial and the VPN*x* device instead of a modem. This is shown in Figure 24.50.

As you can see, this Dial-Up Networking entry will call a VPN server at IP address 172.16.0.1, the same IP address used in the configuration of the RAS/VPN server earlier in this chapter. As long as the VPN device is selected in the Dial Using pull-down box, everything should be set for this connection.

The first step to actually making this connection is to make sure you have an actual, valid Internet IP address before doing so. If you need to use Dial-Up Networking to connect to an ISP for this, do that first. Once you have a valid IP address available, launch your VPN Dial-Up Networking Connection to get connected to your remote system. Once you provide a set of valid user credentials, you should end up getting connected at 10,000,000 baud (10 megabits, equivalent to the speed of a 10Base-T network).

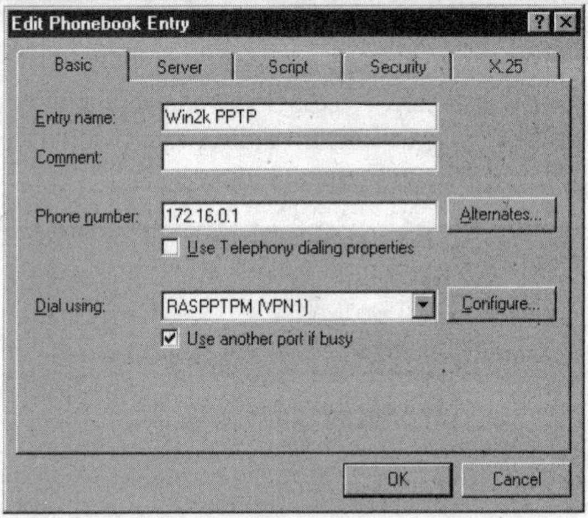

FIGURE 24.50: Creating a VPN Dial-Up Networking entry in Windows NT 4 Workstation

Windows 9x   Windows 9x takes a unique approach to implementing virtual private networking through the use of a Microsoft VPN adapter. Instead of adding support for PPTP or other protocols (like in other Microsoft operating systems), all you need to do is add the VPN adapter to your system to get connected.

NOTE

To add VPN support for Windows 95, you must have the Dial-Up Networking upgrade v1.2 or later installed on your system. VPN support is included in Windows 98 right out of the box.

Start by editing the network properties of Windows 9x by selecting Start ➤ Settings ➤ Control Panel ➤ Network. When the Network properties page comes up, click the Add button, and then select Adapter as the component type you'd like to install. Your screen should look like Figure 24.51.

In the list of adapters supplied, scroll down to Microsoft for the manufacturer, then select the Microsoft Virtual Private Networking Adapter listed on the right side of the screen. Click OK and Windows 9x will add the VPN adapter to its system. Of course, this will require a reboot for the changes to take effect.

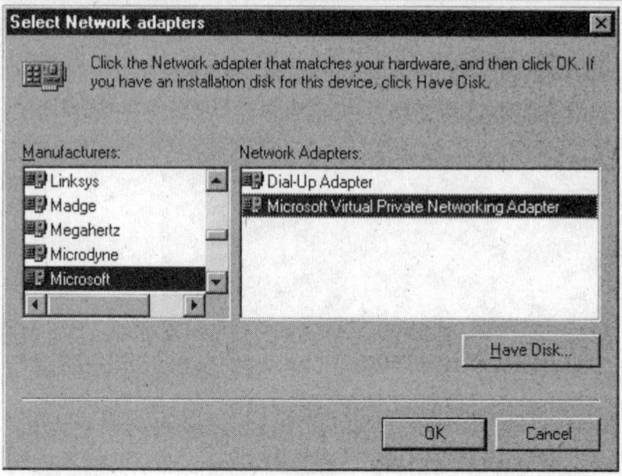

FIGURE 24.51: Adding the Microsoft VPN Adapter to Windows 9x

Once your system has rebooted, the next step to getting connected is creating a Dial-Up Networking entry to connect to your VPN server. From the Windows 9x desktop, double-click My Computer, then Dial-Up Networking, and then Make New Connection to launch the Make New Connection Wizard, shown in Figure 24.52.

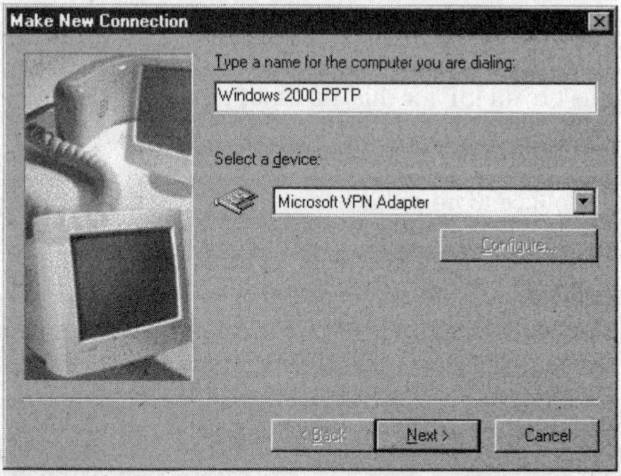

FIGURE 24.52: The Windows 9x Make New Connection Wizard

From the Select A Device pull-down box, choose the Microsoft VPN Adapter if it isn't already selected. Click Next to move to the next step of the wizard shown in Figure 24.53.

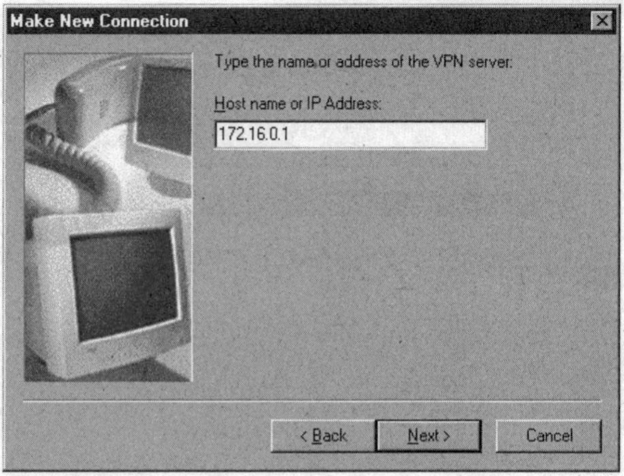

FIGURE 24.53:   Entering the IP address of a VPN server in Windows 9x

Enter the IP address or DNS name of your VPN server in the box as needed. In the example in Figure 24.53, we have used an IP address of 172.16.0.1, the same IP address used in the configuration of the RAS/VPN server earlier in this chapter. After entering the hostname or address, clicking Next will complete the wizard and place a VPN Dial-Up Networking entry on your system.

To make the VPN connection, you must make sure you have an actual, valid Internet IP address before doing so. If you need to use Dial-Up Networking to connect to an ISP for this, do that first. Once you have a valid IP address available, launch your VPN Dial-Up Networking connection to get connected to your remote system. Once you provide a set of valid user credentials, you should end up connected at 10,000,000 baud (10 megabits, equivalent to the speed of a 10Base-T network).

Windows 2000   Windows 2000 adds a few nice features to the client side of establishing VPN connections, namely the ability to automatically associate one DUN entry with another. For example, if you need to dial an ISP before you can connect with your virtual private network, Windows 2000 can join these two functions. The end result is that when you (or your users) need to connect to the virtual private network, doing so only requires launching one Dial-Up Networking session.

Like most of the remote access functionality in Win2K, to define a VPN connection, you will begin with Start ➣ Settings ➣ Network And Dial-Up Connections, and then the Make New Connection Wizard. From the first screen of the wizard, select the option to Connect To A Private Network Through The Internet as shown in Figure 24.54.

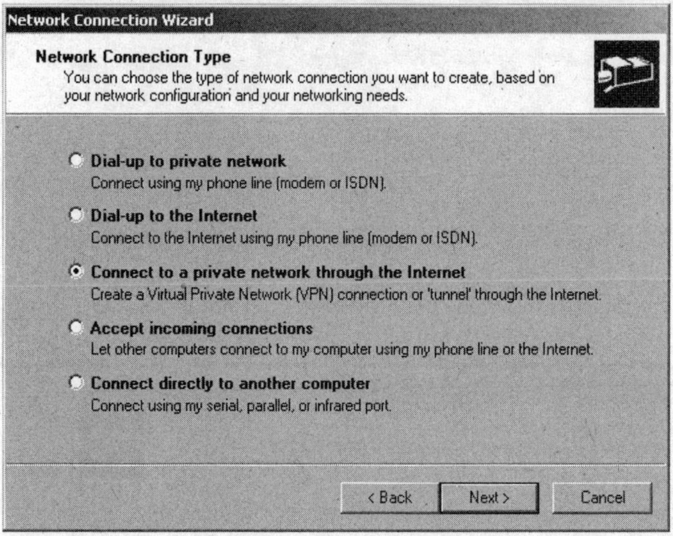

FIGURE 24.54: Creating a VPN connection on Windows 2000

Click Next to continue, and Win2K will then ask if you need to establish a public network (Internet) connection first before establishing the VPN connection, as shown in Figure 24.55.

If the Win2K device you will be connecting already has a valid, public Internet IP address, answer Do Not Dial The Initial Connection to this question. Otherwise, if you need to obtain an IP address first from an ISP, select Automatically Dial This Initial Connection and choose the connection that will get you connected to the Internet. Doing so will cause your VPN Dial-Up Networking connection to initiate an ISP connection first. Click Next to continue on to entering the IP address or host name of the target server, as shown in Figure 24.56.

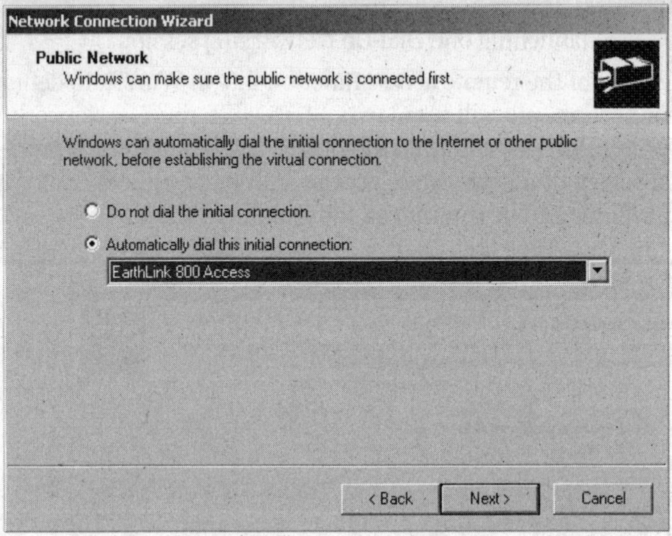

FIGURE 24.55: Creating a public connection before a VPN connection

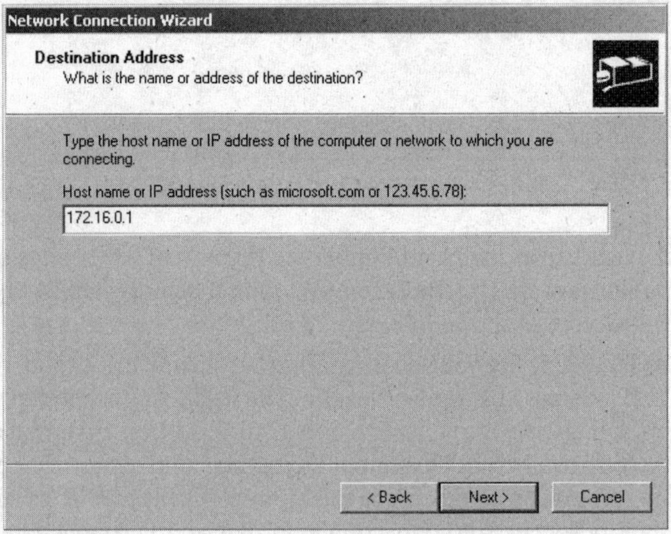

FIGURE 24.56: Entering the IP address of the VPN server

Much like many of the other client platforms we've already discussed, you will need to enter the IP address of your target system or a DNS-resolvable host name. As you can see, this Dial-Up Networking entry will call a VPN server at IP address 172.16.0.1, the same IP address used in the configuration of the RAS/VPN server earlier in this chapter. Click Next to continue, and the final step of the wizard will ask you whether you want to make this VPN connection available to all users or just yourself. For the purposes of this section, we'll assume that you just want to use the VPN connection for yourself, so click the Only For Myself radio button and click Next to finish creating the Dial-Up Networking entry.

When it comes time to actually establish this connection, if you selected the option to have Win2K dial an initial connection, you will see a dialog box like the one in Figure 24.57 asking you if the public network connection should be initiated first.

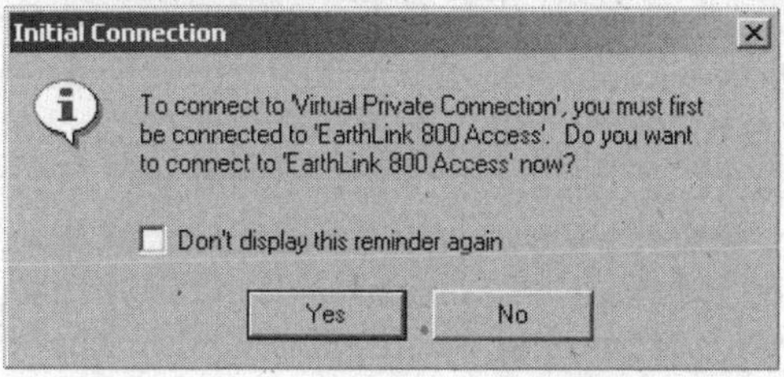

FIGURE 24.57:   Windows 2000 asking if an initial public network connection should be established first

VPN Performance Considerations

Our section on virtual private networking wouldn't be complete without taking a bit of time to discuss performance issues to consider. Although virtual private networking is a neat technology, unfortunately there are some times when it just might not make sense to use it. Careful planning and consideration should help you determine if it is a solution that can add value to your organization.

In the right set of circumstances, virtual private networking can provide fast, reliable, and secure connections to remote networks across the Internet (or another unsecured network). However, in the wrong set of circumstances, a VPN can make an already slow dial-up connection seem even slower.

So what are the right circumstances? In my professional opinion, the right circumstances are when you have high-speed connectivity on your RAS server at the very least and preferably when you have high-speed connectivity on both your RAS server and your DUN client. On occasions when I have been able to implement VPN circuits at locations with a T1 or better available at both the server and client ends, performance has been wonderful and the connections reliable. However, due to the protocol overhead involved with PPTP and L2TP and the inherent latency of the Internet, if you are planning on implementing a VPN with dial-up modems on each side of your connection, I would urge you to think twice.

"But wait," you might be thinking, "I want to implement a VPN to reduce costs, not increase them." Well, I wish I could say that Microsoft's VPN implementations were going to give you the performance you might expect over modem connections, but they just won't. Simply due to the additional complexities of encrypting the data, bundling the payload data inside a TCP/IP packet, and the latency of communications across the Internet, you can expect a decrease in your performance ranging anywhere from 10 to 50 percent. Now, without getting into all the technical details, it is worthwhile to note that this isn't entirely Microsoft's fault; after all, they can't be blamed for the fact that the Internet can be inherently slow at times (or can they?). However, even with the worst-case scenario of a 50 percent reduction in performance, if there is a T1 on each side of the virtual private network, the effective speeds of the network are still roughly in the 760Kbps range. However, if you're using a 56K modem on each side of the virtual private network, which probably won't connect much faster than 48Kbps, you can easily see how a 50 percent performance penalty can make a connection go from "slow" to "unusable."

Simply put, if you are using a modem on your RAS server and a modem on your DUN client, you will get your best possible speeds by having one dial directly into the other. By doing so, there is no protocol overhead getting in the way, nor is there the need for your data to travel across dozens of routers as it works its way to its destination. By creating a direct connection, data packets go directly from the DUN client to the target network.

However, everything in life is a trade-off, and it will be up to you to decide whether this will work adequately enough for your needs. After all, what is adequate to one person might be great to another and unacceptable to yet another. In either case, expect a performance penalty when implementing virtual private networking and plan your bandwidth accordingly.

Appendix A

BEYOND NETWORK
ADMINISTRATION

In the Middle Ages, feudal society revolved around the concept of villagers, called serfs, who were bound by law to work for their lord. They didn't necessarily lead bad lives (that depended mostly on how well the lord ran the demesne), but they weren't free to choose their daily activities, either. Free folks, who were usually skilled workers like carpenters, millers, or smiths, had far wider latitude—they could move if they wanted to, and they made a much better living than the serfs. Arguably, they had more freedom than the lords, who also were not free to move around.

Fast-forward to the 20th century. Modern corporations act much like feudal society, with employees who have no choice but to do as they're told or quit. Employees can't choose which

Adapted from *Serf to Surfer: Becoming a Network Consultant* by Matthew Strebe with Marc S. Bragg, Esquire and Steven T. Klovanish, CPA

ISBN 0-7821-2661-8   336 pages $19.99

projects they want to work on, how much they want to work, or how much they want to try to get for their services once they've accepted a job. Consultants are the free people of the corporate world. They move from job to job and company to company, taking on as much work as they want, charging what they can convince clients to pay, and taking time off whenever they want for activities like surfing the waves or the Web. In my book, *Serf to Surfer*, I detail what you can do to escape from feudal corporate work and how to establish yourself as a free agent. In essence, you will begin the progression from serf to surfer.

Anyone can become a consultant. There is no professional association you must join, no jury or council from whom to obtain a license, and, in most cases, there is no government regulation on most types of consulting. All you have to do is convince clients to pay you for your expertise. Unfortunately, that's more difficult than passing a licensing exam.

There's a popular notion that consultants do nothing and make a ton of money. Both points are true, but not at the same time. Consultants either do nothing or make a ton of money.

Successful consultants, those who know how to find new customers, retain old ones, and deliver solutions consistently, are always busy. They make a ton of money, and they have no time to spend it, so it just accumulates until they retire. Unsuccessful consultants complain about how they can't find work, how crappy their customers are, and how they'd be more successful if their car didn't keep breaking down.

Everything I am about to relate to you is designed to help make you successful as a consultant, because driving a crappy car sucks. I know this from experience. When I started consulting, I drove a used Hyundai Scoupe. Within a year, I bought a used Infiniti J30 (paid cash), and a year later, I traded that in for a new Mercedes Benz E-Class (financed, because the interest rate is lower than the return on my investments). I'm not mentioning this to brag about my success (yeah, right) but to show by example that no matter what your financial situation is now, you can use consulting to get to wherever you want to be.

This appendix will help you understand consulting and demystify the roles of people you may know who call themselves consultants. It will also explain what you need to know to become a network consultant, and help you decide whether you have both the talent and the personality to become successful at consulting.

How I Lost My Job and Found My Calling

The company I worked for was sinking faster than *Titanic* analogies. Since the company was a small defense contractor in San Diego, the military drawdown struck them swiftly and hard. Both of the military contracts the company had depended on were completed, and the management staff had no idea how to market for more business in the face of stiff competition from the large defense contractors who were now scrambling for a piece of a much smaller pie. Suddenly, the small contracts on which we subsisted (which the big contractors were overlooking because they were working larger contracts) were being snatched from us. It was like being the smallest orphan in the poorhouse.

The owner had refused a buyout offer from one of the largest defense contractors in the country over a difference in valuation, thus virtually assuring that we'd all lose our jobs. When the company had to hold my paycheck until the next payday rolled around, I decided to negotiate my own layoff since I could just as well do nothing if I wasn't going to get paid. The company was closed down for good less than four months later. I quit on the third anniversary of my hire date, and I had no idea what I was going to do next.

Just after I'd quit, a sales manager for a local network-cabling distributor called and said he'd heard that I was no longer encumbered with a job. He had a customer who needed help with a networking problem and asked if I could help. It seems that their network was extremely sluggish. I had no idea what the problem might be, so when they asked for a firm, fixed-price contract to solve it, I figured it would probably take me a week to figure out. I multiplied 40 hours per week by $62.50 to determine the contract price. (This number seemed unreasonably large at the time; it was what my former employer charged for my time when they billed my time to their customers. My employer paid me $25 an hour.) I then told them that if I didn't solve the problem, I wouldn't bill them. They were happy with that, so I started to work.

Less than four hours later, I'd identified a malfunctioning bridge that was transmitting broadcast storms. It connected an obsolete section of Thicknet cabling to the network and was hidden in a ceiling—none of the current IT staff even knew it was there. I had identified its Ethernet address using an Ethernet packet-sniffer diagnostic tool and wound up tracing cables until I stumbled across it in the ceiling. After shutting it off, the network became completely stable and fast again.

I went home, fired up my copy of Excel, and used the default Excel invoice template to write up a bill. After that, I realized I could make three weeks' pay in a day, and I would never have to sit in a cubicle again. I've never looked back.

When I first became unemployed—er, I mean, a consultant—I looked far and wide for a good book on consulting or the process one would go through to become one. I didn't find any good books on becoming a consultant. I did, however, find a few books with lots of meaningless facts (like what FoxPro programmers in New York charge per hour) and bad advice (like cold calling was apt to be my best strategy to find customers if I didn't happen to already know everyone in town). I threw those books out and decided to figure things out on my own since nearly none of the advice offered seemed to apply to me. (I now wish I'd kept the Tax chapter, but that's a story for a later chapter.)

I have vague memories of my former cubicle—staring fixedly at my monitor, filling out vacation request forms, and listening to irate customers complain about problems I was powerless to solve. I remember my boss telling me I didn't have enough vacation time on the books to get married and take a honeymoon. I remember taking a urinalysis for insurance purposes. I remember sitting through endless meetings trying desperately to keep my eyes open while people debated ceaselessly about matters that had nothing to do with my work or me. It's been three years for me though, so the memories are fading fast.

I love my lack of a job. I'm excited to get up in the morning, happy to execute my daily routine, and satisfied at the end of the day. I have a solid body of work to look back on proudly. The money I make is limited mostly by the amount of work I want to take on, and my customers feel like they're getting a great deal. Being a network consultant allows me to schedule my life the way I want to, and it allows me to work as much as I feel like working. Best yet, I make about four times what I made when I did the same thing for a company.

My work is different now. Although the phone is even more insistent now than it was then, the conversations are far more positive. The attitude of my customers is my responsibility—and because I can control the work I do, everything stays positive. I rush around quite a bit, but I like driving, and I don't mind the hurry. I don't waste much time at all—I spend time in traffic either on the phone updating customers or my schedule (on a hands-free cellular phone), or dictating books on consulting. While waiting at a customer's site, I respond to e-mail on a hand-held computer that I synchronize with my desktop computer at the end of the day. It's a hectic life, but I like hectic.

People ask me how I tolerate the uncertainty of working for myself (which they apparently equate to being unemployed). I have a hard time figuring out how they tolerate the uncertainty of a single paycheck. I've never liked putting all my eggs in one basket; when my former employer went out of business a few months after I was laid off, I realized that nothing is certain. At least as a consultant, I'm in charge of my destiny, as far as it can be made certain. Without sounding glib, having six customers pay me on a regular basis makes it nearly impossible to lose all my work at once. Even if I suddenly lost three of them for some inexplicable reason, I'd have plenty of income to get by and plenty of time to find more customers. To me, consulting is far less risky than working for a single company whose finances I don't control.

CONCERNING CONSULTING

Consulting is the business of providing specific expertise on a job-by-job basis. Unlike employees, consultants are hired to solve a very specific problem. That problem either has well-defined specifications, time periods, and budget constraints, or the consultant is hired to define the problem, time period, or budget needed.

Hiring a consultant makes sense for businesses when one or more of the following is true:

- ▶ The business needs to solve a problem in an area that none of the employees understands sufficiently.

- ▶ The business can't afford to hire an employee to solve the problem, or the problem isn't important enough to warrant a new hire.

- ▶ There are recurring short periods of time when the business requires outside expertise.

- ▶ The business needs help on a single, specific project with a defined time period and budget.

Businesses hire consultants because they are less expensive than hiring an employee to perform the same function—this is the case because the function is most likely short term, perhaps for a period of days, weeks, months, or even a year, but it's not permanent. For these short-term projects, hiring a permanent employee doesn't make sense because there won't be a long-term need for the specific expertise once the project is finished.

In other cases, there may be a continuous but infrequent need. For example, I consult for numerous small businesses that need me to stop in only once every two or three weeks to set up a new workstation, add new server software, or modify a firewall policy. Having someone sit around full time for these infrequent tasks doesn't make sense, so hiring a consultant part-time is less expensive.

Of course, as a network consultant, you'll work for yourself, so in addition to all of the technological knowledge you will need, you'll also need the following business skills, which I call "The Seven Business Skills I've Enumerated for No Very Good Reason":

Negotiation To make certain you provide what your clients need at a price that's fair for everyone.

Financial acumen To stay ahead of the myriad of expenses, receipts, tax issues, and accounting.

Ethics To keep your dealings above board and your attention to customer service in the right place.

Discernment To find the clients with whom you can work best.

Public speaking To address large audiences during training sessions and sales presentations.

Good humor To relieve stress and make people feel good about you.

Technical writing To document your results and provide information to your clients.

Chances are, you're more worried about the business skills than the technical skills. If you're already a network administrator, you're pretty familiar with what your job as a consultant will be. But negotiating a contract? Finding clients? Picking up on subtle clues that indicate a potential client has financial problems? Getting a client to pay? Doing taxes?

Don't worry. Everything in the above list is a learnable skill (yes, even the good humor part), and it's all easier than building a Linux-based file server with a RAID adapter and a wireless interface.

TYPES OF CONSULTANTS

The majority of consultants are freelance technical experts. Technical experts design, implement, and maintain hardware and software network systems for businesses; they are network consultants, systems integrators, and application developers.

In the course of my consulting, I've identified a few other types of people who call themselves consultants. If I were a conservative writer, I would, of course, euphemistically describe them according to their merits. But I prefer to throw gasoline on the raging debate about what actually constitutes consulting because it bothers me that the word consultant has recently (and unfortunately deservedly) become something of a joke in the business community.

In order to demystify the sort of consulting that *Serf to Surfer* covers, take a look at the list and descriptions that follow. See if you can classify yourself into one of the following five types of consultants. I've included recommended reading for those types of consultants who will not find *Serf to Surfer* useful:

- The Unemployee (Purchase *Job Interviews for Dummies* or *The Complete Idiot's Guide to Getting the Job You Want.*)

- The Glorified Temp (Purchase *Consulting for Dummies.*)

- Celebrity Experts and Soothsayers (Purchase *7 Habits of Highly Effective People* or *The Goal: A Process of Ongoing Improvement.*)

- The Application Developer (You'll find my book, *Serf to Surfer*, useful.)

- Network Consultants (*Serf to Surfer* is for you.)

Unemployees

Unemployees are unemployed middle managers or technical experts who don't actively consult, but they do hand out business cards with their own logo on them while they seek gainful employment. They might accept a contract job or two, but their primary goal is to get plugged back into permanent employment as soon as possible. Essentially, they describe themselves as consultants to avoid the embarrassment of being unemployed.

I personally don't find being unemployed embarrassing—some of my fondest memories are of being unemployed. If I could live without working, I'd do it in a heartbeat. If you're actually unemployed and don't really intend to become a consultant, don't muddy the waters by calling yourself a consultant. You'd be surprised how pleasant employers find forthright people looking for work without pretense.

Glory Temps

A new trend among temporary employment firms (also called "brokerages," as if humans were a commodity trade item; don't even get me started on "human resources") is to call their pool of temporary employees consultants and farm them out for a higher price than your usual Kelly temp.

People who work through brokerages or temporary agencies are not consultants, they are "glory temps." Temp doesn't sound as cool as consultant, but temporary employees who call themselves consultants muddy the term for real consultants. If you're paid via an IRS form W2, you aren't a consultant, you're a temp.

According to the IRS, if you work for a single employer for the period of a fiscal year, you are an employee, and if you work for just one client, you aren't a consultant; you're a contract employee. This may mean you pay your own taxes, but paying your own taxes doesn't make you a consultant, it just makes you self-employed. I know that thousands of contract programmers and application developers disagree with me, and because the word consultant is somewhat fuzzy, they have their case.

Celebrity Experts and Soothsayers

Management consultants who use the early success of their technical books or high-profile jobs to make themselves a permanent niche in the speaking and writing fields are called "celebrity" experts. You can't decide to become a celebrity expert—you must have already achieved success as a consultant or writer before you can begin your nationwide speaking tour.

These celebrity experts become soothsayers when they find themselves sucked into the vacuous realm of the mahogany-paneled, high-rise Fortune 500 boardroom explaining technology to those who believe they are the masters of the world because their expertise is money. In this way, management consultants are the soothsayers to the modern emperors of capitalism. As with any feudal society, this role actually trickles down to small business fiefs, so you may actually find cut-rate management consultants hovering around little presidents as well.

You can identify the management consultants by their characteristic use of the word "paradigm." If you ever hear this word come out of the same person's mouth twice, they're either a management consultant or they want to be one. You'll find these consultants making ill-defined or blatantly obvious statements like, "We need to rethink our process for maximum efficiency."

Application Developers

Application developers create custom business solutions for their clients. They do everything from designing databases, to writing custom workflow software, to creating e-commerce solutions and websites. Custom application development is often necessary for businesses that want to encode their unique business model in software.

The line between an application developer and a systems integrator/network consultant is very blurred. Technically, one group deals mostly with software and the other deals mostly with hardware. Most practicing consultants do both, however, depending upon their specific expertise.

Avoid becoming the dreaded Addiction Developer, however. Addiction Developers build themselves jobs by delivering systems nobody else can work on. The binding thread among this group is that they tend to build themselves permanent clients—once their system is implemented, it's nearly impossible to extricate the consultant without abandoning the system. Because the system is proprietary, and because the consultant is the only one who knows it inside and out, it's prohibitively expensive to have anyone else provide further development.

Developing a group of clients who are addicted to your work is a great way to keep getting paid forever. But a better and more ethical way to ensure a paycheck is to create systems that are lucid enough for any competent consultant to understand, to document those systems completely, and then to rely on good business relationships to keep you working.

Network Consulting

Network consulting, also called systems integration, is the practice of designing, installing, maintaining, upgrading, and repairing computer networks and their associated software, and peripherals like servers, printers, and client computers.

Network consulting is different than most other forms of consulting. Unlike contract programmers who are little more than temps forced to pay their own taxes, network consultants rarely work full time for a single employer for more than a few weeks at a time. Unlike celebrity experts (like me, for example), who act as soothsayers to upper management, network consultants solve concrete problems. And unlike application developers who often wind up addicting customers with software that nobody else can maintain, network consultants are generally easily replaced. These differences make the practice of network consulting somewhat unusual among the computer consulting trades.

A typical network consultant has from two to ten regular customers, averaging around five. Usually, these consultants are called in to either establish a new network or reengineer an existing deficient network. After the initial work is complete, the consultant usually remains on either a retainer or with an established hourly fee for administration and maintenance. The point of hiring a freelance expert is to avoid paying a full-time network administrator or chief technology officer (depending upon the size of the business and the scope of the work involved). By hiring 1/5 of an expert, the company saves money and avoids having geeks wander around the office all the time.

Freelance technical experts like network consultants don't get oodles of billable hours from a single employer the way contract employees do, so their rates are necessarily higher. If you're looking for cushy chair consulting, learn Visual Basic—network consultants are always on the go.

To do this work, you need to completely understand the following:

Network cabling   Especially Ethernet and Fast Ethernet.

Data link equipment   Including repeaters, hubs, bridges, and switches.

Network equipment   Like routers, firewalls, and network printers.

Computer components   Like processors, RAM, motherboards, hard disk drives, and network adapters.

High-end computer hardware   For servers like RAID adapters and tape backup controllers.

Network operating systems   Including Windows NT, Unix, and Novell NetWare.

Network server application and Internet software   Like e-mail services, web servers, and groupware applications like Exchange and Lotus Notes.

Client operating systems   Like Windows, Unix, and the MacOS.

Client application software   Like Microsoft Office, Internet client software, and financial software.

Wide area networking technology   Like leased lines, xDSL, and various alternative carrier options.

Don't worry about knowing everything on the above list at first. As long as you have a fast brain and you know at least half of the above, you're ready to start. Pick your clients well to make sure you're inside your range of experience, and learn as you go.

CAN YOU CONSULT?

So you don't waste your time reading further if in fact you should not be a consultant, take the following personality quiz. This quiz is not technology specific—rather, it weeds out those psychological profiles that might have an especially difficult time marketing themselves. Remember: if you fail this quiz, it's not your fault—it's society.

The quiz is even easier than the ones you'd find in *Cosmo*: read the question, formulate your response, and then quit if your answer isn't (a). If you don't make it to the end of the quiz, read this only for the funny parts and don't think about quitting your job.

1. If you went a month without making any money, would you:

   A. Learn to love mac & cheese

   B. Get divorced

   C. Starve to death

2. Have you ever brought a weapon to work?

   A. No.

   B. Yes.

   C. Does it count if I bought it at work?

3. Do you believe that you've been contacted by nonhuman intelligent beings of any sort?

   A. No.

   B. Yes. (Explain: _____)

   C. I have strange scars I can't account for.

4. How many pets do you own?

   A. 0-4

   B. 4-8

   C. 9+

5. How many times have you been convicted of a felony?

   A. 0-1

   B. 2-3

   C. 4+

6. With whom do you live?

   A. Self, domestic partner, roommate, kids

   B. Parents

   C. Other members of my commune/church

7. Complete this sentence: I believe the world is...

   A. Round/spherical

   B. Flat

   C. Hollow, with an interior sun and a subtechnological society living in peace on the inside

8. How often do you shower?

   A. Daily

   B. Weekly

   C. Other

9. Why do you want to be a consultant?

   A. For the independence

   B. Sounds cool to say you're a consultant

   C. Because I keep getting fired

10. Have you ever changed your name to match that of a beloved celebrity?

   A. No.

   B. No, but I've thought about it.

   C. Yes, because Cassidy is easier to spell.

11. Have you ever had a sex change?

   A. No.

   B. Yes.

   C. I'm back to my original sex.

Now remember: this quiz isn't designed to make you feel badly about your lifestyle choices, it's to prepare you for the fact that your lifestyle may be a marketing problem in today's business environment. Of course, your lifestyle choices may be normal in your neighborhood, so your marketing mileage may vary depending upon where you live. Feel free to try anyway, and if you find your niche, you have my greatest respect.

In an ideal world, factors like religious preference, sexual preference, and body-piercing preference wouldn't matter. But we don't live in an ideal world, and no law exists to protect consultants from discrimination. If a client doesn't like something about you, they don't have to hire you, and there's absolutely nothing you or anyone else can do about it. If very few people in a contracting position agree with your lifestyle choices and your eccentricity can't be hidden, you won't maintain enough work to keep consulting.

FROM THE TRENCHES

The following story is true.

As the network administrator for the College of Law at the University of Utah, my fellow consultant and friend (who shall remain nameless) was on the steering committee for the development of a work automation application for the college of administration. One of the developers, a consultant whom I will refer to as "Bob," was a competent and hardworking member of the team. The team met every Friday to discuss progress, feature changes, and so forth.

CONTINUED ➡

One Friday, Bob showed up to the meeting wearing a dress, makeup, and heels. At the beginning of the meeting, he announced that from that point on, he was to be referred to as "Roberta." He then calmly went about explaining the features of the new version of the software while the other members of the team sat in stunned silence, gripping their coffee mugs and trying to maintain their composure. After finishing the presentation, "Roberta" left the meeting. The group was unable to provide useful comment on the software at the end of the meeting, because they'd been totally distracted during it.

CONCLUSION

When you become a consultant, you're in charge of the trade-off between time and money—you can sell or keep as much time as you want. Want four-day weekends? Take them. Want to accumulate money faster than a car's grille collects gnats? Work seven days a week.

Because the demand for good network integrators is so strong, you won't have to worry about competition; in all of my consulting career, I've never had to compete against another consultant. The only competition I have had was the customers' preconceived notion of how much service should cost. By avoiding the metric they used to compute that cost (the hourly rate) by using firm, fixed-price agreements and retainers, I've managed to provide better, faster service, lower overall costs for my clients, and higher profits for me.

Appendix B
GLOSSARY OF NETWORKING TERMS

Adapted from the *Network+ Study Guide*, Third Edition by David Groth

ISBN 0-7821-4014-9   624 pages $49.99

10Base2 Ethernet   An implementation of Ethernet that specifies a 10Mbps signaling rate, baseband signaling, and coaxial cable with a maximum segment length of 185 meters.

10BaseFL   An implementation of Ethernet that specifies a 10Mbps signaling rate, baseband signaling, and fiber-optic cabling.

10BaseT   An implementation of Ethernet that specifies a 10Mbps signaling rate, baseband signaling, and twisted-pair cabling.

100BaseVG   Star topology using round-robin for allowing systems to transmit data on the network.

100VG (Voice Grade)   IEEE 802.12 standard for 100BaseVG networks.

100VGAnyLAN   A networking technology that runs 100Mb Ethernet over regular (Cat 3) phone lines. It hasn't gained the industry acceptance that 100BaseT has. *See also* AnyLAN.

A

access control list (ACL)   List of rights that an object has to resources in the network. Also a type of firewall. In this case, the lists reside on a router and determine which machines can use the router and in what direction.

ACK   *See* acknowledgment.

acknowledgment (ACK)   A message confirming that the data packet was received. This occurs at the Transport layer of the OSI model.

ACL   *See* access control list.

Active Directory   The replacement for NT Directory Service (NTDS) that is included with Windows 2000. It acts similarly to NDS (Novell Directory Services) because it is a true X.500-based directory service.

active hub   A hub that is powered and actively regenerates any signal that is received. *See also* hub.

active monitor   Used in Token Ring networks, a process that prevents data frames from roaming the ring unchecked. If the frame passes the active monitor too many times, it is removed from the ring. Also ensures that a token is always circulating the ring.

adapter Technically, the peripheral hardware that installs into your computer or the software that defines how the computer talks to that hardware.

address Designation to allow PCs to be known by a name or number to other PCs. Addressing allows a PC to transmit data directly to another PC by using its address (IP or MAC).

address record Part of a DNS table that maps an IP address to a domain name. Also known as an A (or host) record.

ad hoc RF network A network created when two RF-capable devices are brought within transmission range of each other. A common example is handheld PDAs beaming data to each other.

ADSL *See* asymmetrical digital subscriber line.

alias record *See* CNAME record.

antivirus A category of software that uses various methods to eliminate viruses in a computer. It typically also protects against future infection. *See also* virus.

AnyLAN Another name for 100VGAnyLAN created in 802.12. *See also* 100VGAnyLAN.

Application layer The seventh layer of the OSI model, which deals with how applications access the network and describes application functionality, such as file transfer, messaging, and so on.

ARCnet The Attached Resource Computer Network, which was developed by Datapoint Corporation in the late 1970s as one of the first baseband networks. It can use either a physical star or bus topology.

ARP table A table used by the ARP protocol. Contains a list of known TCP/IP addresses and their associated MAC addresses. The table is cached in memory so that ARP lookups do not have to be performed for frequently accessed TCP/IP and MAC addresses. *See also* media access control, Transmission Control Protocol/Internet Protocol.

asymmetrical digital subscriber line (ADSL) An implementation of DSL where the upload and download speeds are different. *See also* digital subscriber line.

Asynchronous Transfer Mode (ATM) A connection-oriented network architecture based on broadband ISDN technology that uses constant size

53-byte cells instead of packets. Because cells don't change size, they are switched much faster and more efficiently than packets across a network.

ATM   *See* Asynchronous Transfer Mode.

Attachment Unit Interface (AUI) port   Port on some NICs that allows connecting the NIC to different media types by using an external transceiver.

B

backbone   The part of most networks that connects multiple segments together to form a LAN. The backbone usually has higher speed than the segments. *See also* segment, local area network.

Backup Domain Controller (BDC)   Computer on a Windows NT network that has a copy of the SAM database for fault tolerance and performance enhancement purposes. *See also* Security Accounts Manager.

backup plan   Term used to describe a company's strategy to make copies of and restore its data in case of an emergency.

backup window   The amount of time that an administrator has available to perform a complete, successful backup.

bandwidth   In network communications, the amount of data that can be sent across a wire in a given time. Each communication that passes along the wire decreases the amount of available bandwidth.

baseband   A transmission technique in which the signal uses the entire bandwidth of a transmission medium.

baseline   A category of network documentation that indicates how the network normally runs. It includes such information as network statistics, server utilization trends, and processor performance statistics.

bearer channel (B channel)   The channels in an ISDN line that carry data. Each bearer channel typically has a bandwidth of 64Kbps.

blackout   *See* power blackout.

blank   These are often referred to as slot covers. If a PC card is removed, there will be an opening in the computer case. This will allow dirt and dust to enter the computer and prevent it from being cooled properly. Some computer cases have the blanks as part of the case, and they must be broken off from the case before a bus slot may be used to insert a PC card into it.

BNC connector   Tubular connectors most commonly used with coaxial cable.

bonding   A procedure where two ISDN B channels are joined together to provide greater bandwidth.

bounded media   A network medium that is used at the Physical layer where the signal travels over a cable of some kind.

bridge   A network device, operating at the Data Link layer, that logically separates a single network into segments, but lets the two segments appear to be one network to higher layer protocols.

broadband   A network transmission method in which a single transmission medium is divided so that multiple signals can travel across the same medium simultaneously.

broadcast address   A special network address that refers to all users on the network. For example, the TCP/IP address 255.255.255.255 is the broadcast address. Any packets sent to that address will be sent to everyone on that LAN.

brouter   A device that combines the functionality of a bridge and a router, but can't be distinctly classified as either.

brownout   *See* power brownout.

bus   Pathways in a PC that allow data and signals to be transmitted between the PC components. Types of buses include ISA and PCI.

bus topology   A topology where the cable and signals run in a straight line from one end of the network to the other.

C

cable   A physical transmission medium that has a central conductor of wire or fiber surrounded by a plastic jacket.

cable map   General network documentation indicating each cable's source and destination as well as where each network cable runs.

cable tester   A special instrument that is used to test the integrity of LAN cables. *See also* time-domain reflectometer.

carrier   Signal at a frequency that is chosen to carry data. Addition of data to the frequency is modulation and the removal of data from the frequency is demodulation. This is used on analog devices like modems.

Carrier Sense Multiple Access/Collision Avoidance (CSMA/CA)   A media access method that sends a request to send (RTS) packet and waits to receive a clear to send (CTS) packet before sending. Once the CTS is received, the sender sends the packet of information.

Carrier Sense Multiple Access/Collision Detection (CSMA/CD)   A media access method that first senses whether there is a signal on the wire, indicating that someone is transmitting currently. If no one else is transmitting, it attempts a transmission and listens for someone else trying to transmit at the same time. If this happens, both senders back off and don't transmit again until some specified period of time has passed. *See also* collision.

categories   Different grades of cables that determine how much protection is offered against interference from outside the cable. Category 1 allows voice data only. Category 2 allows data transmissions up to 4Mbps. Category 3 allows data transmissions up to 10Mbps. Category 4 allows data transmissions up to 16Mbps. Category 5 allows data transmissions up to 100Mbps.

cell   Similar to a packet or frame, except that the ATM cell does not always contain the destination or source addressing information. It also does not contain higher-level addressing or packet control information.

central office   The office in any metropolitan or rural area that contains the telephone switching equipment for that area. The central office connects all users in that area to each other as well as to the rest of the PSTN. *See also* Public Switched Telephone Network.

Channel Service Unit (CSU)   Generally used with a T1 Internet line, it is used to terminate the connection from the T1 provider. The CSU is usually part of a CSU/DSU unit. It also provides diagnostics and testing if necessary.

checkpoints   A certain part or time to allow for a restart at the last point that the data was saved.

checksum   A hexadecimal value computed from transmitted data that is used in error-checking routines.

circuit switching   A switching method where a dedicated connection between the sender and receiver is maintained throughout the conversation.

Classless Internetwork Domain Routing (CIDR)   The new routing method used by InterNIC to assign IP addresses. CIDR can be described as a "slash x" network. The x represents the number of bits in the network that InterNIC controls.

client   A client is a part of a client/server network. It is the part where the computing is usually done. In a typical setting, a client will use the server for remote storage, backups, or security such as a firewall.

client/server network   A server-centric network in which all resources are stored on a file server and processing power is distributed among workstations and the file server.

clipper chip   A hardware implementation of the skipjack encryption algorithm.

clustering   A computing technology where many servers work together so that they appear to be one high-powered server. If one server fails, the others in the cluster take over the services provided by the failed server.

CNAME record   A DNS record type that specifies other names for existing hosts. This allows a DNS administrator to assign multiple DNS host names to a single DNS host. Also known as an *alias record*.

coaxial cable   Often referred to as coax. A type of cable used in network wiring. Typical coaxial cable types include RG-58 and RG-62. 10Base2 Ethernet networks use coaxial cable. Coaxial cable is usually shielded.

collision   The error condition that occurs when two stations on a CSMA/CD network transmit data (at the Data Link layer) at the same time. *See also* Carrier Sense Multiple Access/Collision Detection.

collision light   A light on a NIC or hub that indicates when a collision has occurred.

concentrator   *See* hub.

connectionless   Communications between two hosts that have no previous session established for synchronizing sent data. The data is not acknowledged at the receiving end. This can allow for data loss.

connectionless services   *See* connectionless, connectionless transport protocol.

connectionless transport protocol   A transport protocol, such as UDP, that does not create a virtual connection between sending and receiving stations. *See also* User Datagram Protocol.

connection-oriented   Communications between two hosts that have a previous session established for synchronizing sent data. The data is acknowledged by the receiving PC. This allows for guaranteed delivery of data between PCs.

connection-oriented transport protocol   A transport protocol that uses acknowledgments and responses to establish a virtual connection between sending and receiving stations. TCP is a connection-oriented protocol. *See also* Transmission Control Protocol.

controller   Part of a PC that allows connectivity to peripheral devices. A disk controller allows the PC to be connected to a hard disk. A network controller allows a PC to be connected to a network. A keyboard controller is used to connect a keyboard to the PC.

Control Panel   A special window inside Microsoft Windows operating systems (Windows 95 and above) that has icons for all of the configurable options for the system.

core OS   The core component, or kernel, of NetWare.

cost   A value given to a route between PCs or subnets to determine which route may be best. The word *hop* is sometimes used to refer to the number of routers between two PCs or subnets. *See also* hop.

country codes   The two-letter abbreviations for countries, used in the DNS hierarchy. *See also* Domain Name Service.

CRC   *See* cyclical redundancy check.

crossover cable   The troubleshooting tool used in Ethernet UTP installations to test communications between two stations, bypassing the hub. *See also* unshielded twisted-pair cable.

crosstalk   A type of interference that occurs when two LAN cables run close to each other. If one cable is carrying a signal and the other isn't, the one carrying a signal will induce a "ghost" signal (crosstalk) in the other cable.

CSMA/CA   *See* Carrier Sense Multiple Access/Collision Avoidance.

CSMA/CD   *See* Carrier Sense Multiple Access/Collision Detection.

cyclical redundancy check (CRC)   An error-checking method in data communications that runs a formula against data before transmissions. The sending station then appends the resultant value (called a checksum) to the data and sends it. The receiving station uses the same formula on the data. If the receiving station doesn't get the same checksum result for the calculation, it considers the transmission invalid, rejects the frame, and asks for a retransmission.

D

datagram   A unit of data smaller than a packet.

Data Link layer   The second layer of the OSI model. It describes the logical topology of a network, which is the way that packets move throughout a network. It also describes the method of media access. *See also* Open Systems Interconnect.

data packet   A unit of data sent over a network. A packet includes a header, addressing information, and the data itself. A packet is treated as a single unit as it is sent from device to device. Also known as a *datagram*.

Data Service Unit (DSU)   It transmits data through a Channel Service Unit (CSU) and is almost always a part of a single device referred to as a CSU/DSU.

D channel   *See* delta channel.

default gateway   The router that all packets are sent to when the workstation doesn't know where the destination station is or when it can't find the destination station on the local segment.

delta channel (D channel)   A channel on an ISDN line used for link management. *See also* Integrated Services Digital Network.

demarcation point (demarc)   The point on any telephone installation where the telephone lines from the central office enter the customer's premises.

denial of service (DoS) attack   Type of hack that prevents any users—even legitimate ones—from using the system.

destination port number   The address of the PC to which data is being sent from a sending PC. The port portion allows for the demultiplexing of data to be sent to a specific application.

DHCP   *See* Dynamic Host Configuration Protocol.

dialogs   Communications between two PCs.

digital subscriber line (DSL)   A digital WAN technology that brings high-speed digital networking to homes and businesses over POTS. There are many types, including HDSL (high-speed DSL) and VDSL (very high bit-rate DSL). *See also* plain old telephone service, asymmetrical digital subscriber line.

directory   A network database that contains a listing of all network resources, such as users, printers, groups, and so on.

directory service   A network service that provides access to a central database of information, which contains detailed information about the resources available on a network.

disaster recovery   The procedure by which data is recovered after a disaster.

disk striping   Technology that enables writing data to multiple disks simultaneously in small portions called stripes. These stripes maximize use by having all of the read/write heads working constantly. Different data is stored on each disk and is not automatically duplicated (this means that disk striping in and of itself does not provide fault tolerance).

distance vector routing protocol   A route discovery method in which each router, using broadcasts, tells every other router what networks and routes it knows about and the distance to them.

DIX   Another name for a 15-pin AUI connector or a DB-15 connector.

DNS   *See* Domain Name Service.

DNS server   Any server that performs DNS host name–to–IP address resolution. *See also* Domain Name Service, Internet Protocol.

DNS zone   An area in the DNS hierarchy that is managed as a single unit. *See also* Domain Name Service.

DoD Networking Model   A four-layer conceptual model describing how communications should take place between computer systems. The four layers are Process/Application, Host-to-Host, Internet, and Network Access.

domain   A group of networked Windows computers that share a single SAM database. *See also* Security Accounts Manager.

Domain Name Service (DNS)   The network service used in TCP/IP networks that translates host names to IP addresses. *See also* Transmission Control Protocol/Internet Protocol.

dotted decimal   Notation used by TCP/IP to designate an IP address. The notation is made up of 32 bits (4 bytes), each byte separated by a decimal. The range of numbers for each octet is 0–255. The leftmost octet contains the high-order bits and the rightmost octet contains the low-order bits.

DSL   *See* digital subscriber line.

D-type connector   The first type of networking connector, the D-type connector, is used to connect many peripherals to a PC. A D-type connector is characterized by its shape. Turned on its side, it looks like the letter *D* and contains rows of pins (male) or sockets (female). AUI connectors are examples.

dual-attached stations (DAS)   Stations on an FDDI network that are attached to both cables for connection redundancy and fault tolerance.

dumb terminal   A keyboard and monitor that send keystrokes to a central processing computer (typically a mainframe or minicomputer) that returns screen displays to the monitor. The unit has no processing power of its own, hence the moniker "dumb."

duplexed hard drives   Two hard drives to which identical information is written simultaneously. A dedicated controller card controls each drive. Used for fault tolerance.

duplicate server   Two servers that are identical for use in clustering.

dynamically allocated port   TCP/IP port used by an application when needed. The port is not constantly used.

dynamic ARP table entries   *See* dynamic entry.

dynamic entry   An entry made in the ARP table whenever an ARP request is made by the Windows TCP/IP stack and the MAC address is not found in the ARP table. The ARP request is broadcast on the local segment. When the MAC address of the requested IP address is found, that information is added to the ARP table. *See also* Internet Protocol, media access control, Transmission Control Protocol/Internet Protocol.

Dynamic Host Configuration Protocol (DHCP)   A protocol used on a TCP/IP network to send client configuration data, including TCP/IP address, default gateway, subnet mask, and DNS configuration, to clients. *See also* default gateway, Domain Name Service, subnet mask, Transmission Control Protocol/Internet Protocol.

dynamic packet filtering   A type of firewall used to accept or reject packets based on the contents of the packets.

dynamic routing   The use of route discovery protocols to talk to other routers and find out what networks they are attached to. Routers that use dynamic routing send out special packets to request updates of the other routers on the network as well as to send their own updates.

dynamic state list   *See* dynamic routing.

E

EEPROM   *See* electrically erasable programmable read-only memory.

electrically erasable programmable read-only memory (EEPROM)   A special integrated circuit on expansion cards that allows data to be stored on the chip. If necessary, the data can be erased by a special configuration program. Typically used to store hardware configuration data for expansion cards.

electromagnetic interference (EMI)   The interference that can occur during transmissions over copper cable because of electromagnetic energy outside the cable. The result is degradation of the signal.

electronic mail (e-mail)   An application that allows people to send messages via their computers on the same network or over the Internet.

electrostatic discharge (ESD)   A problem that exists when two items with dissimilar static electrical charges are brought together. The static electrical charges jump to the item with fewer electrical charges, causing ESD, which can damage computer components.

e-mail   *See* electronic mail.

EMI   *See* electromagnetic interference.

encoding   The process of translating data into signals that can be transmitted on a transmission medium.

encryption key   The string of alphanumeric characters used to decrypt encrypted data.

endpoint   The two ends of a connection for transmitting data. One end is the receiver, and the other is the sender.

ESD *See* electrostatic discharge.

Ethernet A shared-media network architecture. It operates at the Physical and Data Link layers of the OSI model. As the media access method, it uses baseband signaling over either a bus or a star topology with CSMA/CD. The cabling used in Ethernet networks can be coax, twisted-pair, or fiber-optic. *See also* Carrier Sense Multiple Access/Collision Detection, Open Systems Interconnect.

Ethernet address *See* MAC address.

expansion slot A slot on the computer's bus into which expansion cards are plugged to expand the functionality of the computer (for example, using a NIC to add the computer to a network). *See also* network interface card.

extended AppleTalk network An AppleTalk network segment that is assigned a 16-bit range of numbers rather than a single 16-bit number.

F

failover device A device that comes online when another fails.

failover server A hot site backup system in which the failover server is connected to the primary server. A heartbeat is sent from the primary server to the backup server. If the heartbeat stops, the failover system starts and takes over. Thus, the system doesn't go down even if the primary server is not running.

Fast Ethernet The general category name given to 100Mbps Ethernet technologies.

fault-resistant network A network that will be up and running at least 99 percent of the time or that is down less than 8 hours a year.

fault-tolerant network A network that can recover from minor errors.

FDDI *See* Fiber Distributed Data Interface.

Fiber Channel A type of server-to-storage system connection that uses fiber-optic connectors.

Fiber Distributed Data Interface (FDDI) A network topology that uses fiber-optic cable as a transmission medium and dual, counterrotating rings to provide data delivery and fault tolerance.

fiber-optic   A type of network cable that uses a central glass or plastic core surrounded by a plastic coating.

file server   A server specialized in holding and distributing files.

File Transfer Protocol (FTP)   A TCP/IP protocol and software that permit the transferring of files between computer systems. Because FTP has been implemented on numerous types of computer systems, files can be transferred between disparate computer systems (for example, a personal computer and a minicomputer). *See also* Transmission Control Protocol/Internet Protocol.

firewall   A combination of hardware and software that protects a network from attack by hackers who could gain access through public networks, including the Internet.

FQDN   *See* Fully Qualified Domain Name.

frame relay   A WAN technology that transmits packets over a WAN using packet switching. *See also* packet switching.

frequency division multiplexing (FDM)   A multiplexing technique whereby the different signals are sent across multiple frequencies.

FTP   *See* File Transfer Protocol.

FTP proxy   A server that uploads and downloads files from a server on behalf of a workstation.

full backup   A backup that copies all data to the archive medium.

Fully Qualified Domain Name (FQDN)   An address that uses both the host name (workstation name) and the domain name.

G

gateway   The hardware and software needed to connect two disparate network environments so that communications can occur.

global group   A type of group in Windows NT that is used network-wide. Members can be from anywhere in the network, and rights can be assigned to any resource in the network.

ground loop   A condition that occurs when a signal cycles through a common ground connection between two devices, causing EMI interference. *See also* electromagnetic interference.

H

hardware address   A Data Link layer address assigned to every NIC at the MAC sublayer. The address is in the format xx:xx:xx:xx:xx:xx; each xx is a two-digit hexadecimal number. *See also* media access control, network interface card.

hardware loopback   Connects the transmission pins directly to the receiving pins, allowing diagnostic software to test if a NIC can successfully transmit and receive. *See also* network interface card.

heartbeat   The data transmissions between two servers in a cluster to detect when one fails. When the standby server detects no heartbeats from the main server, it comes online and takes control of the responsibilities of the main server. This allows for all services to remain online and accessible.

hop   One pass through a router. *See also* cost, router.

hop count   As a packet travels over a network through multiple routers, each router will increment this field in the packet by one as it crosses the router. It is used to limit the number of routers a packet can cross on the way to its destination.

host   Any network device with a TCP/IP network address. *See also* Transmission Control Protocol/Internet Protocol.

Host-to-Host layer   A layer in the DoD model that corresponds to the Transport layer of the OSI model. *See also* DoD Networking Model, Open Systems Interconnect.

HTML   *See* Hypertext Markup Language.

HTTP   *See* Hypertext Transfer Protocol.

hub   A Physical layer device that serves as a central connection point for several network devices. A hub repeats the signals it receives on one port to all other ports. *See also* active hub.

Hypertext Markup Language (HTML)   A set of codes used to format text and graphics that will be displayed in a browser. The codes define how data will be displayed.

Hypertext Transfer Protocol (HTTP)   The protocol used for communication between a web server and a web browser.

I

IBM data connector   A proprietary data connector created by IBM. This connector is unique because there isn't a male version and female version; any IBM connector can connect with another IBM connector and lock together.

ICMP   *See* Internet Control Message Protocol.

IEEE   *See* Institute of Electrical and Electronics Engineers, Inc.

IEEE 802.x standards   The IEEE standards for LAN and MAN networking.

IEEE 802.1 LAN/MAN Management   Standard that specifies LAN/MAN network management and internetworking.

IEEE 802.2 Logical Link Control   Standard that specifies the operation of the logical link control (LLC) sublayer of the Data Link layer of the OSI model. The LLC sublayer provides an interface between the MAC sublayer and the Network layer. *See also* media access control, Open Systems Interconnect.

IEEE 802.3 CSMA/CD Networking   Standard that specifies a network that uses Ethernet technology and a CSMA/CD network access method. *See also* Carrier Sense Multiple Access/Collision Detection.

IEEE 802.4 Token Bus   Standard that specifies a physical and logical bus topology that uses coaxial or fiber-optic cable and the token-passing media access method.

IEEE 802.5 Token Ring   Specifies a logical ring, physical star, and token-passing media access method based on IBM's Token Ring.

IEEE 802.6 Distributed Queue Dual Bus (DQDB) Metropolitan Area Network   Provides a definition and criteria for a DQDB metropolitan area network (MAN).

IEEE 802.7 Broadband Local Area Networks   Standard for broadband cabling technology.

IEEE 802.8 Fiber-Optic LANs and MANs   A standard containing guidelines for the use of fiber optics on networks, which includes FDDI and Ethernet over fiber-optic cable. *See also* Ethernet, Fiber Distributed Data Interface.

IEEE 802.9 Integrated Services (IS) LAN Interface   A standard containing guidelines for the integration of voice and data over the same cable.

IEEE 802.10 LAN/MAN Security   A series of guidelines dealing with various aspects of network security.

IEEE 802.11 Wireless LAN   Defines standards for implementing wireless technologies such as infrared and spread-spectrum radio.

IEEE 802.12 Demand Priority Access Method   Defines a standard that combines the concepts of Ethernet and ATM. *See also* Asynchronous Transfer Mode, Ethernet.

IETF   *See* Internet Engineering Task Force.

Institute of Electrical and Electronics Engineers, Inc. (IEEE)   An international organization that sets standards for various electrical and electronics issues.

Integrated Services Digital Network (ISDN)   A telecommunications standard that is used to digitally send voice, data, and video signals over the same lines. *See also* delta channel.

intelligent hub   A hub that can make some intelligent decisions about network traffic flow and can provide network traffic statistics to network administrators.

internal bridge   A bridge created by placing two NICs in a computer.

internal modem   A modem that is a regular PC card that is inserted into the bus slot. These modems are inside the PC.

International Organization for Standardization (ISO)   The standards organization that developed the OSI model. This model provides a guideline for how communications occur between computers.

Internet   A global network made up of a large number of individual networks interconnected through the use of public telephone lines and TCP/IP protocols. *See also* Transmission Control Protocol/Internet Protocol.

Internet Architecture Board (IAB)   The committee that oversees management of the Internet. It is made up of two subcommittees: the Internet Engineering Task Force (IETF) and the Internet Research Task Force (IRTF). *See also* Internet Engineering Task Force, Internet Research Task Force.

Internet Control Message Protocol (ICMP)   A message and management protocol for TCP/IP. The Ping utility uses ICMP. *See also* Ping, Transmission Control Protocol/Internet Protocol.

Internet Engineering Task Force (IETF)   An international organization that works under the Internet Architecture Board to establish standards and protocols relating to the Internet. *See also* Internet Architecture Board.

Internet Protocol (IP)   The protocol in the TCP/IP protocol suite responsible for network addressing and routing. *See also* Transmission Control Protocol/Internet Protocol.

Internet Research Task Force (IRTF)   An international organization that works under the Internet Architecture Board to research new Internet technologies. *See also* Internet Architecture Board.

Internet service provider (ISP)   A company that provides direct access to the Internet for home and business computer users.

internetwork   A network that is internal to a company and is private.

Internetwork Packet eXchange (IPX)   A connectionless, routable network protocol based on the Xerox XNS architecture. It is the default protocol for versions of NetWare before NetWare 5. It operates at the Network layer of the OSI model and is responsible for addressing and routing packets to workstations or servers on other networks. *See also* Open Systems Interconnect.

inverse multiplexing   The network technology that allows one signal to be split across multiple transmission lines at the transmission source and combined at the receiving end.

IP   *See* Internet Protocol.

IP address   An address used by the Internet Protocol that identifies the device's location on the network.

ipconfig   A Windows NT utility used to display that machine's current configuration.

IP proxy   All communications look as if they originated from a proxy server because the IP address of the user making a request is hidden. Also known as *Network Address Translation (NAT)*.

IP spoofing   A hacker trying to gain access to a network by pretending his or her machine has the same network address as the internal network.

IPX   *See* Internetwork Packet eXchange.

IPX network address   A number that represents an entire network. All servers on the network must use the same external network number.

ISDN   *See* Integrated Services Digital Network.

ISDN terminal adapter   The device used on ISDN networks to connect a local network (or single machine) to an ISDN network. It provides power to the line as well as translates data from the LAN or individual computer for transmission on the ISDN line. *See also* Integrated Services Digital Network.

ISP   *See* Internet service provider.

J

Java   A programming language, developed by Sun Microsystems, that is used to write programs that will run on any platform that has a Java Virtual Machine installed.

Java Virtual Machine (JVM)   Software, developed by Sun Microsystems, that creates a virtual Java computer on which Java programs can run. A programmer writes a program once without having to recompile or rewrite the program for all platforms.

jumper   A small connector (cap or plug) that connects pins. This creates a circuit that indicates a setting to a device.

JVM   *See* Java Virtual Machine.

K

kernel   The core component of any operating system that handles the functions of memory management, hardware interaction, and program execution.

key   A folder in the Windows Registry that contains subkeys and values, or a value with an algorithm to encrypt and decrypt data.

L

LAN   *See* local area network.

LAN driver   The interface between the NetWare kernel and the NIC installed in the server. Also a general category of drivers used to enable communications between an operating system and a NIC. *See also* network interface card.

Large Internet Packet (LIP)   A technology used by the IPX protocol so that IPX can use the largest possible packet size during a transmission. *See also* Internetwork Packet eXchange.

laser printer   A printer that uses a laser to form an image on a photo-sensitive drum. The image is then developed with toner and transferred to paper. Finally, a heated drum fuses toner particles onto the paper.

Layer 2 Switch   A switching hub that operates at the Data Link layer and builds a table of the MAC addresses of all the connected stations. *See also* media access control.

Layer 3 Switch   Functioning at the Network layer, a switch that performs the multiport, virtual LAN, data pipelining functions of a standard Layer 2 Switch, but it can perform basic routing functions between virtual LANs.

LCP   *See* Link Control Protocol.

line conditioner   A device used to protect against power surges and spikes. Line conditioners use several electronic methods to clean all power coming into the line conditioner.

line noise   Any extraneous signal on a power line that is not part of the power feed.

line voltage   The voltage, supplied from the power company, that comes out at the outlets.

Link Control Protocol (LCP)   The protocol used to establish, configure, and test the link between a client and PPP host. *See also* Point-to-Point Protocol.

link light   A small light-emitting diode (LED) that is found on both the NIC and the hub. It is usually green and labeled "Link" or something similar. A link light indicates that the NIC and the hub are making a Data Link layer connection. *See also* hub, network interface card.

link state route discovery   A route discovery method that transmits special packets (Link State Packets, or LSPs) that contain information about the networks to which the router is connected.

link state routing   A type of routing that broadcasts its entire routing tables only at startup and possibly at infrequently scheduled intervals. Aside from that, the router only sends messages to other routers when changes are made to the router's routing table.

link state routing protocol   A routing table protocol where the router sends out limited information, such as updates to its routing tables, to its neighbors only.

Link Support Layer (LSL)   Part of the Novell client software that acts as sort of a switchboard between the Open Datalink Interface (ODI) LAN drivers and the various transport protocols.

Linux   A version of Unix, developed by Linus Torvalds. Runs on Intel-based PCs and is generally free. *See also* Unix.

LIP   *See* Large Internet Packet.

local area network (LAN)   A network that is restricted to a single building, group of buildings, or even a single room. A LAN can have one or more servers.

local groups   Groups created on individual servers. Rights can be assigned only to local resources.

local loop   The part of the PSTN that goes from the central office to the demarcation point at the customer's premises. *See also* central office, demarcation point, Public Switched Telephone Network.

log file   A file that keeps a running list of all errors and notices, the time and date they occurred, and any other pertinent information.

logical bus topology   Type of topology in which the signal travels the distance of the cable and is received by all stations on the backbone. *See also* backbone.

logical link control (LLC)   A sublayer of the Data Link layer. Provides an interface between the MAC sublayer and the Network layer. *See also* media access control, topology.

logical network addressing   The addressing scheme used by protocols at the Network layer.

logical parallel port   Port used by the CAPTURE command to redirect a workstation printer port to a network print queue. The logical port has no relation to the port to which the printer is actually attached or to the physical port. *See also* physical parallel port.

logical port address   A value that is used at the Transport layer to differentiate between the upper-layer services.

logical ring topology   A network topology in which all network signals travel from one station to another, being read and forwarded by each station.

logical topology   Describes the way the information flows. The types of logical topologies are the same as the physical topologies, except that the flow of information, rather than the physical arrangement, specifies the type of topology.

LSL   *See* Link Support Layer.

M

MAC   *See* media access control.

MAC address   The address that is either assigned to a network card or burned into the NIC. This is how PCs keep track of one another and keep each other separate.

mail exchange (MX) record   A DNS record type that specifies the DNS host name of the mail server for a particular domain name.

MAU   *See* Multistation Access Unit.

media access   The process of vying for transmission time on the network media.

media access control (MAC)   A sublayer of the Data Link layer that controls the way multiple devices use the same media channel. It controls which devices can transmit and when they can transmit.

media converter   A networking device that converts from one network media type to another. For example, converting from an AUI port to an RJ-45 connector for 10BaseT.

member server   A computer that has Windows NT server installed but doesn't have a copy of the SAM database. *See also* Security Accounts Manager.

mesh topology   A network topology where there is a connection from each station to every other station in the network.

modem   A communication device that converts digital computer signals into analog tones for transmission over the PSTN and converts them back to digital upon reception. The word "modem" is an acronym for "modulator/demodulator."

multiple-server clustering   A system in which multiple servers run continuously, each providing backup and production services at the same time. (Expensive servers, therefore, are not sitting around as designated "backup" servers, used only when an emergency arises.) If a server fails, another just takes over, without any interruption of service.

multiplexing   A technology that combines multiple signals into one signal for transmission over a slow medium. *See also* frequency division multiplexing, inverse multiplexing.

multipoint RF network   An RF network consisting of multiple stations, each with transmitters and receivers. This type of network also requires an RF bridge as a central sending and receiving point.

Multistation Access Unit (MAU)   The central device in Token Ring networks that acts as the connection point for all stations and facilitates the formation of the ring.

N

name resolution   The process of translating (resolving) logical host names to network addresses.

NAT   Acronym that means Network Address Translation. *See* IP proxy.

National Computing Security Center (NCSC)   The agency that developed the Trusted Computer System Evaluation Criteria (TCSEC) and the Trusted Network Interpretation Environmental Guideline (TNIEG).

National Security Agency (NSA)   The U.S. government agency responsible for protecting U.S. communications and producing foreign intelligence information. It was established by presidential directive in 1952 as a separately organized agency within the Department of Defense (DoD).

nbtstat (NetBIOS over TCP/IP statistics)   The Windows TCP/IP utility that is used to display NetBIOS over TCP/IP statistics. *See also* network basic input/output system, Transmission Control Protocol/Internet Protocol.

NCP   *See* NetWare Core Protocol.

NCSC   *See* National Computing Security Center.

NDPS   *See* Novell Distributed Print Services.

NDS   *See* Novell Directory Services.

NDS tree   A logical representation of a network's resources. Resources are represented by objects in the tree. The tree is often designed after a company's functional structure. Objects can represent organizations, departments, users, servers, printers, and other resources. *See also* Novell Directory Services.

nearline site   When two buildings can almost be seen from one another. Obstructions in between are few.

NetBEUI   *See* NetBIOS Extended User Interface.

NetBIOS   *See* network basic input/output system.

NetBIOS Extended User Interface (NetBEUI)   Transport protocol based on the NetBIOS protocol that has datagram support and support for connectionless transmission. NetBEUI is a protocol that is native to Microsoft networks and is mainly for use by small businesses. It is a nonroutable protocol that cannot pass over a router, but does pass over a bridge since it operates at the Data Link layer. *See also* network basic input/output system.

NetBIOS name   The unique name used to identify and address a computer using NetBEUI.

netstat   A utility used to determine which TCP/IP connections—inbound or outbound—the computer has. It also allows the user to view packet statistics, such as how many packets have been sent and received. *See also* Transmission Control Protocol/Internet Protocol.

NetWare   The network operating system made by Novell.

NetWare 3.x   The version series of NetWare that supported multiple, cross-platform clients with fairly minimal hardware requirements. It used a database called the bindery to keep track of users and groups and was administered with several DOS, menu-based utilities (such as SYSCON, PCONSOLE, and FILER).

NetWare 4.x The version series of NetWare that includes NDS. *See also* Novell Directory Services.

NetWare 5.x The version series of NetWare that includes a multiprocessing kernel. It also includes a five-user version of Oracle 8, a relational database, and the ability to use TCP/IP in its pure form.

NetWare Administrator The utility used to administer NetWare versions 4.x and later by making changes to the NDS Directory. It is the only administrative utility needed to modify NDS objects and their properties. *See also* Novell Directory Services.

NetWare Core Protocol (NCP) The upper-layer NetWare protocol that functions on top of IPX and provides NetWare resource access to workstations. *See also* Internet Packet eXchange.

NetWare Link State Protocol (NLSP) Protocol that gathers routing information based on the link state routing method. Its precursor is the Routing Information Protocol (RIP). NLSP is a more efficient routing protocol than RIP. *See also* link state routing.

NetWare Loadable Module (NLM) A component used to provide a NetWare server with additional services and functionality. Unneeded services can be unloaded, thus conserving memory.

network A group of devices connected by some means for the purpose of sharing information or resources.

Network Address Translation (NAT) *See* IP proxy.

network attached storage Storage, such as hard drives, attached to a network for the purpose of storing data for clients on the network. Network attached storage is commonly used for backing up data.

network basic input/output system (NetBIOS) A Session layer protocol that opens communication sessions for applications that want to communicate on a network.

network-centric Refers to network operating systems that use directory services to maintain information about the entire network.

Network File System (NFS) A protocol that enables users to access files on remote computers as if the files were local.

network interface card (NIC)   Physical device that connects computers and other network equipment to the transmission medium.

Network layer   This third layer of the OSI model is responsible for logical addressing and translating logical names into physical addresses. This layer also controls the routing of data from source to destination as well as the building and dismantling of packets. *See also* Open Systems Interconnect.

network media   The physical cables that link computers in a network; also known as *physical media*.

network operating system (NOS)   The software that runs on a network server and offers file, print, application, and other services to clients.

network software diagnostics   Software tools, either Protocol Analyzers or Performance Monitoring Tools, used to troubleshoot network problems.

Network Support Encyclopedia (NSEPro)   *See* Novell Support Connection.

NFS   *See* Network File System.

NIC   *See* network interface card.

NIC diagnostics   Software utilities that verify the NIC is functioning correctly and test every aspect of NIC operation. *See also* network interface card.

NIC driver   *See* LAN driver.

NLM   *See* NetWare Loadable Module.

NLSP   *See* NetWare Link State Protocol.

non-unicast packet   A packet that is not sent directly from one workstation to another.

NOS   *See* network operating system.

Novell Directory Services (NDS)   A NetWare service that provides access to a global, hierarchical directory database of network entities that can be centrally managed.

Novell Distributed Print Services (NDPS)   A printing system designed by Novell that uses NDS to install and manage printers. NDPS supports automatic network printer installation, automatic distribution of client printer drivers, and centralized printer management without the use of print queues.

Novell Support Connection   Novell's database of technical information documents, files, patches, fixes, NetWare Application Notes, Novell lab bulletins, Novell professional developer bulletins, answers to frequently asked questions, and more. The database is available from Novell and is updated quarterly.

NSA   *See* National Security Agency.

N-series connector   Used with Thinnet and Thicknet cabling that is a male/female screw and barrel connector.

nslookup   Allows you to query a name server to see which IP address a name resolves to.

NT Directory Services (NTDS)   System of domains and trusts for a Windows NT Server network.

NTDS   *See* NT Directory Services.

O

object   The item that represents some network entity in NDS. *See also* Novell Directory Services.

octet   Refers to eight bits; one-fourth of an IP address.

ODI   *See* Open Datalink Interface.

OE (operator error)   When the error is not software or hardware related, it may be a problem with the user not knowing how to operate the software or hardware. OE can be a serious problem.

offline   The general name for the condition when some piece of electronic or computer equipment is unavailable or inoperable.

Open Datalink Interface (ODI)   A driver specification, developed by Novell, that enables a single workstation to communicate transparently with several different protocol stacks, using a single NIC and a single NIC driver.

OpenLinux   A version of the Linux network operating system developed by Caldera.

Open Systems Interconnect (OSI)   A model defined by the ISO to categorize the process of communication between computers in terms of seven layers. The seven layers are Application, Presentation, Session, Transport, Network, Data Link, and Physical. *See also* International Organization for Standardization.

OSI *See* Open Systems Interconnect.

oversampling Method of synchronous bit synchronization in which the receiver samples the signal at a much faster rate than the data rate. This permits the use of an encoding method that does not add clocking transitions.

overvoltage threshold The level of overvoltage that will trip the circuit breaker in a surge protector.

P

packet The basic division of data sent over a network.

packet filtering A firewall technology that accepts or rejects packets based on their content.

packet switching The process of breaking messages into packets at the sending router for easier transmission over a WAN. *See also* frame relay.

passive detection A type of intruder detection that logs all network events to a file for an administrator to view later.

passive hub A hub that simply makes physical and electrical connections between all connected stations. Generally speaking, these hubs are not powered.

password history List of passwords that have already been used.

patch Software that fixes a problem with an existing program or operating system.

patch cable A central wiring point for multiple devices on a UTP network. *See also* unshielded twisted-pair cable.

patch panel A central wiring point, containing no electronic circuits, for multiple devices on a UTP network. Generally, patch panels are in server rooms or located near switches or hubs to provide an easy means of patching over wall jacks or hardware.

PDC *See* Primary Domain Controller.

peer-to-peer network Computers hooked together that have no centralized authority. Each computer is equal and can act as both a server and a workstation.

peripheral Any device that can be attached to the computer to expand its capabilities.

permanent virtual circuit (PVC)   A technology used by frame relay that allows virtual data communications (circuits) to be set up between sender and receiver over a packet-switched network.

PGP   *See* Pretty Good Privacy.

physical address   *See* MAC address.

physical bus topology   A network that uses one network cable that runs from one end of the network to the other. Workstations connect at various points along this cable.

Physical layer   The first layer of the OSI model that controls the functional interface. *See also* Open Systems Interconnect.

physical media   *See* network media.

physical mesh topology   A network configuration in which each device has multiple connections. These multiple connections provide redundant connections.

physical parallel port   A port on the back of a computer that allows a printer to be connected with a parallel cable.

physical port   An opening on a network device that allows a cable of some kind to be connected. Ports allow devices to be connected to each other with cables.

physical ring topology   A network topology that is set up in a circular fashion. Data travels around the ring in one direction, and each device on the ring acts as a repeater to keep the signal strong as it travels. Each device incorporates a receiver for the incoming signal and a transmitter to send the data on to the next device in the ring. The network is dependent on the ability of the signal to travel around the ring.

physical star topology   Describes a network in which a cable runs from each network entity to a central device called a hub. The hub allows all devices to communicate as if they were directly connected. *See also* hub.

physical topology   The physical layout of a network, such as bus, star, ring, or mesh.

Ping   A TCP/IP utility used to test whether another host is reachable. An ICMP request is sent to the host, who responds with a reply if it is reachable. The request times out if the host is not reachable.

Ping of Death   A large ICMP packet sent to overflow the remote host's buffer. This usually causes the remote host to reboot or hang.

plain old telephone service (POTS)   Another name for the Public Switched Telephone Network (PSTN). *See* asymmetrical digital subscriber line, digital subscriber line, Public Switched Telephone Network.

plenum-rated coating   Coaxial cable coating that does not produce toxic gas when burned.

point-to-point   Network communication in which two devices have exclusive access to a network medium. For example, a printer connected to only one workstation would be using a point-to-point connection.

Point-to-Point Protocol (PPP)   The protocol used with dial-up connections to the Internet. Its functions include error control, security, dynamic IP addressing, and support for multiple protocols.

Point-to-Point Tunneling Protocol (PPTP)   A protocol that allows the creation of virtual private networks (VPNs), which allow users to access a server on a corporate network over a secure, direct connection via the Internet. *See also* virtual private network.

polling   A media access control method that uses a central device called a controller that polls each device in turn and asks if it has data to transmit.

POP3   *See* Post Office Protocol version 3.

port   Some kind of opening that allows network data to pass through. *See also* physical port.

Post Office Protocol version 3 (POP3)   The protocol used to download e-mail from an SMTP e-mail server to a network client. *See also* Simple Mail Transfer Protocol.

POTS   *See* plain old telephone service.

power blackout   A total loss of power that may last for only a few seconds or as long as several hours.

power brownout   Power drops below normal levels for several seconds or longer.

power overage   Too much power is coming into the computer. *See also* power spike, power surge.

power sag   A lower power condition where the power drops below normal levels for a few seconds, then returns to normal levels.

power spike   The power level rises above normal for less than a second and drops back to normal.

power surge   The power level rises above normal and stays there for longer than a second or two.

power underage   The power level drops below the standard level. *See also* power sag.

PPP   *See* Point-to-Point Protocol.

PPTP   *See* Point-to-Point Tunneling Protocol.

Presentation layer   The sixth layer of the OSI model; responsible for formatting data exchange such as graphic commands and conversion of character sets. Also responsible for data compression, data encryption, and data stream redirection. *See also* Open Systems Interconnect.

Pretty Good Privacy (PGP)   A shareware implementation of RSA encryption. *See also* RSA Data Security, Inc.

Primary Domain Controller (PDC)   An NT server that contains a master copy of the SAM database. This database contains all usernames, passwords, and access control lists for a Windows NT domain. *See also* Security Accounts Manager.

print server   A centralized device that controls and manages all network printers. The print server can be hardware, software, or a combination of both. Some print servers are actually built into the network printer NICs. *See also* network interface card.

print services   The network services that manage and control printing on a network, allowing multiple and simultaneous access to printers.

private key   A technology in which both the sender and the receiver have the same key. A single key is used to encrypt and decrypt all messages. *See also* public key.

private network   The part of a network that lies behind a firewall and is not "seen" on the Internet. *See also* firewall.

protocol   A predefined set of rules that dictates how computers or devices communicate and exchange data on the network.

protocol analyzer   A software and hardware troubleshooting tool that is used to decode protocol information to try to determine the source of a network problem and to establish baselines.

protocol suite   The set of rules a computer uses to communicate with other computers.

proxy   A type of firewall that prevents direct communication between a client and a host by acting as an intermediary. *See also* firewall.

proxy cache server   An implementation of a web proxy. The server receives an HTTP request from a web browser and makes the request on behalf of the sending workstation. When the response comes, the proxy cache server caches a copy of the response locally. The next time someone makes a request for the same web page or Internet information, the proxy cache server can fulfill the request out of the cache instead of having to retrieve the resource from the Web.

proxy server   A type of server that makes a single Internet connection and services requests on behalf of many users.

PSTN   *See* Public Switched Telephone Network.

public   For use by everyone.

public key   A technology that uses two keys to facilitate communication, a public key and a private key. The public key is used to encrypt a message to a receiver. *See also* private key.

public network   The part of a network on the outside of a firewall that is exposed to the public. *See also* firewall.

Public Switched Telephone Network (PSTN)   This is the U.S. public telephone network. It is also called the plain old telephone service (POTS). *See also* central office.

punchdown tool   A hand tool used to terminate twisted-pair wires on a wall jack or patch panel.

PVC   *See* permanent virtual circuit.

Q

QoS   *See* Quality of Service.

quad decimal   Four sets of octets separated by a decimal point; an IP address.

Quality of Service (QoS)   Data prioritization at the Network layer of the OSI model. Results in guaranteed throughput rates. *See also* Open Systems Interconnect.

R

radio frequency interference (RFI)   Interference on copper cabling systems caused by radio frequencies.

RAID   *See* Redundant Array of Independent (or Inexpensive) Disks.

RAID levels   The different types of RAID, such as RAID 0, RAID 1, etc.

README file   A file that the manufacturer includes with software to give the installer information that came too late to make it into the software manuals. It's usually a last-minute addition that includes tips on installing the software, possible incompatibilities, and any known installation problems that might have been found right before the product was shipped.

reduced instruction set computing (RISC)   Computer architecture in which the computer executes small, general-purpose instructions very rapidly.

Redundant Array of Independent (or Inexpensive) Disks (RAID)   A configuration of multiple hard disks used to provide fault tolerance should a disk fail. Different levels of RAID exist, depending on the amount and type of fault tolerance provided.

regeneration process   Process in which signals are read, amplified, and repeated on the network to reduce signal degradation, which results in longer overall possible length of the network.

remote access protocol   Any networking protocol that is used to gain access to a network over public communication links.

remote access server   A computer that has one or more modems installed to enable remote connections to the network.

repeater   A Physical layer device that amplifies the signals it receives on one port and resends or repeats them on another. A repeater is used to extend the maximum length of a network segment.

replication   The process of copying directory information to other servers to keep them all synchronized.

RFI   *See* radio frequency interference.

RG-58   The type designation for the coaxial cable used in thin Ethernet (10Base2). It has a 50ohm impedance rating and uses BNC connectors.

RG-62   The type designation for the coaxial cable used in ARCnet networks. It has a 93ohm impedance and uses BNC connectors.

ring topology   A network topology where each computer in the network is connected to exactly two other computers. With ring topology, a single break in the ring brings the entire network down.

RIP   *See* Router Information Protocol.

RISC   *See* reduced instruction set computing.

RJ (Registered Jack) connector   A modular connection mechanism that allows for as many as eight copper wires (four pairs). RJ connectors are most commonly used for telephone (such as the RJ-11) and network adaptors (such as RJ-45).

roaming profiles   Profiles downloaded from a server at each login. When a user logs out at the end of the session, changes are made and remembered for the next time the user logs in.

route   The path to get to the destination from a source.

route cost   How many router hops there are between source and destination in an internetwork. *See also* hop, router.

router   A device that connects two networks and allows packets to be transmitted and received between them. A router determines the best path for data packets from source to destination. *See also* hop.

Router Information Protocol (RIP)   A distance-vector route discovery protocol used by IPX. It uses hops and ticks to determine the cost for a particular route. *See also* Internet Packet eXchange.

routing   A function of the Network layer that involves moving data throughout a network. Data passes through several network segments using routers that can select the path the data takes. *See also* router.

routing table   A table that contains information about the locations of other routers on the network and their distance from the current router.

RSA Data Security, Inc.   A commercial company that produces encryption software. RSA stands for Rivest, Shamir, and Adleman, the founders of the company.

S

sag   *See* power sag.

SAM   *See* Security Accounts Manager.

Secure Hypertext Transfer Protocol (S-HTTP)   A protocol used for secure communications between a web server and a web browser.

Security Accounts Manager (SAM)   A database within Windows NT that contains information about all users and groups and their associated rights and settings within a Windows NT domain. *See also* Backup Domain Controller.

security log   Log file used in Windows NT to keep track of security events specified by the domain's Audit policy.

security policy   Rules set in place by a company to ensure the security of a network. This may include how often a password must be changed or how many characters a password should be.

segment   A unit of data smaller than a packet. Also refers to a portion of a larger network (a network can consist of multiple network segments). *See also* backbone.

self-powered   A device that has its own power.

Sequenced Packet eXchange (SPX)   A connection-oriented protocol that is part of the IPX protocol suite. It operates at the Transport layer of the OSI model. It initiates the connection between the sender and receiver, transmits the data, and then terminates the connection. *See also* Internet Packet eXchange, Open Systems Interconnect.

sequence number A number used to determine the order in which parts of a packet are to be reassembled after the packet has been split into sections.

Serial Line Internet Protocol (SLIP) A protocol that permits the sending of IP packets over a serial connection.

server A computer that provides resources to the clients on the network.

server and client configuration A network in which the resources are located on a server for use by the clients.

server-centric A network design model that uses a central server to contain all data as well as control security.

service Services add functionality to the network by providing resources or doing tasks for other computers. In Windows 9x, services include file and printer sharing for Microsoft or Novell networks.

service accounts Accounts created on a server for users to perform special services, such as backup operators, account operators, and server operators.

Session layer The fifth layer of the OSI model, it determines how two computers establish, use, and end a session. Security authentication and network naming functions required for applications occur here. The Session layer establishes, maintains, and breaks dialogs between two stations. *See also* Open Systems Interconnect.

share-level security In a network that uses share-level security, instead of assigning rights to network resources to users, passwords are assigned to individual files or other network resources (such as printers). These passwords are then given to all users that need access to these resources. All resources are visible from anywhere in the network, and any user who knows the password for a particular network resource can make changes to it.

shell Unix interfaces that are based solely upon command prompts. There is no graphical interface.

shielded When cabling has extra wrapping to protect it from stray electrical or radio signals. Shielded cabling is more expensive than unshielded.

shielded twisted-pair cable (STP) A type of cabling that includes pairs of copper conductors, twisted around each other, inside a metal or foil shield. This type of medium can support faster speeds than unshielded wiring.

S-HTTP   *See* Secure Hypertext Transfer Protocol.

signal   Transmission from one PC to another. This could be a notification to start a session or end a session.

signal encoding   The process whereby a protocol at the Physical layer receives information from the upper layers and translates all the data into signals that can be transmitted on a transmission medium.

signaling method   The process of transmitting data across the medium. Two types of signaling are digital and analog.

Simple Mail Transfer Protocol (SMTP)   A program that looks for mail on SMTP servers and sends it along the network to its destination at another SMTP server.

Simple Network Management Protocol (SNMP)   The management protocol created for sending information about the health of the network to network management consoles.

single-attached stations (SAS)   Stations on an FDDI network that are attached to only one of the cables. They are less fault tolerant than dual-attached stations.

skipjack   An encryption algorithm developed as a possible replacement for Data Encryption Standard (DES) that is classified by the National Security Agency (NSA). Not much is known about this encryption algorithm except that it uses an 80-bit key.

SLIP   *See* Serial Line Internet Protocol.

SMTP   *See* Simple Mail Transfer Protocol.

SNMP   *See* Simple Network Management Protocol.

socket   A combination of a port address and an IP address.

SONET (Synchronous Optical Network)   A standard in the U.S. that defines a base data rate of 51.84Mbps; multiples of this rate are known as optical carrier (OC) levels, such as OC-3, OC-12, etc.

source address   The address of the station that sent a packet, usually found in the source area of a packet header.

source port number   The address of the PC that is sending data to a receiving PC. The port portion allows for multiplexing of data to be sent from a specific application.

splitter   Any device that electrically duplicates one signal into two.

SPS   *See* Standby Power Supply.

SPX   *See* Sequenced Packet eXchange.

Standby Power Supply (SPS)   A power backup device that has power going directly to the protected equipment. A sensor monitors the power. When a loss is detected, the computer is switched over to the battery. Thus, a loss of power might occur (typically for less than a second).

star topology   A network topology where all devices on the network have a direct connection to every other device on the network. These networks are rare except in very small settings due to the huge amount of cabling required to add a new device.

state table   A firewall security method that monitors the states of all connections through the firewall.

static ARP table entries   Entry in the ARP table that is manually added by a user when a PC will be accessed often. This will speed up the process of communicating with the PC since the IP-to-MAC address will not have to be resolved.

static routing   A method of routing packets where the router's routing is updated manually by the network administrator instead of automatically by a route discovery protocol.

straight tip (ST)   A type of fiber-optic cable connector that uses a mechanism similar to the BNC connectors used by Thinnet. This is the most popular fiber-optic connector currently in use.

subnet mask   A group of selected bits that identify a subnetwork within a TCP/IP network. *See also* Transmission Control Protocol/Internet Protocol.

subnetting   The process of dividing a single IP address range into multiple address ranges.

subnetwork   A network that is part of another network. The connection is made through a gateway, bridge, or router.

subnetwork address   A part of the 32-bit IPv4 address that designates the address of the subnetwork.

subscriber connector (SC)   A type of fiber-optic connector. These connectors are square shaped and have release mechanisms to prevent the cable from accidentally being unplugged.

supernetting   The process of combining multiple IP address ranges into a single IP network.

surge protector   A device that contains a special electronic circuit that monitors the incoming voltage level and then trips a circuit breaker when an overvoltage reaches a certain level called the overvoltage threshold.

surge suppressors   *See* surge protector.

switched   A network that has multiple routes to get from a source to a destination. This allows for higher speeds.

symmetrical keys   When the same key is used to encrypt and decrypt data.

SYN flood   A denial of service attack in which the hacker sends a barrage of SYN packets. The receiving station tries to respond to each SYN request for a connection, thereby tying up all the resources. All incoming connections are rejected until all current connections can be established.

T

TCP   *See* Transmission Control Protocol.

TCP/IP   *See* Transmission Control Protocol/Internet Protocol.

TDMA   *See* Time Division Multiple Access.

TDR   *See* time-domain reflectometer.

telephony server   A computer that functions as a smart answering machine for the network. It can also perform call center and call routing functions.

Telnet   A protocol that functions at the Application layer of the OSI model, providing terminal emulation capabilities. *See also* Open Systems Interconnect.

template   A set of guidelines that you can apply to every new user account created.

terminal emulator   A program that enables a PC to act as a terminal for a mainframe or a Unix system.

terminator   A device that prevents a signal from bouncing off the end of the network cable, which would cause interference with other signals.

test accounts   An account set up by an administrator to confirm the basic functionality of a newly installed application, for example. The test account has equal rights to accounts that will use the new functionality. It is important to use test accounts instead of administrator accounts to test new functionality. If an administrator account is used, problems related to user rights may not manifest themselves because administrator accounts typically have full rights to all network resources.

TFTP   *See* Trivial File Transfer Protocol.

Thick Ethernet (Thicknet)   A type of Ethernet that uses thick coaxial cable and supports a maximum transmission distance of 500 meters. Also called 10Base5.

Thin Ethernet (Thinnet)   A type of Ethernet that uses RG-58 cable and 10Base2.

Time Division Multiple Access (TDMA)   A method to divide individual channels in broadband communications into separate time slots, allowing more data to be carried at the same time. It is also possible to use TDMA in baseband communications.

time-domain reflectometer (TDR)   A tool that sends out a signal and measures how much time it takes to return. It is used to find short or open circuits. Also called a *cable tester*.

Time to Live (TTL)   A field in IP packets that indicates how many routers the packet can still cross (hops it can still make) before it is discarded. TTL is also used in ARP tables to indicate how long an entry should remain in the table.

token   The special packet of data that is passed around the network in a Token Ring network. *See* Token Ring network.

token passing   A media access method in which a token (data packet) is passed around the ring in an orderly fashion from one device to the next. A station can transmit only when it has the token. If it doesn't have the token, it can't transmit.

The token continues around the network until the original sender receives the token again. If the token has more data to send, the process repeats. If not, the original sender modifies the token to indicate that the token is free for anyone else to use.

Token Ring network   A network based on a physical star, logical ring topology, in which data is passed along the ring until it finds its intended receiver. Only one data packet can be passed along the ring at a time. If the data packet goes around the ring without being claimed, it is returned to the sender.

tone generator   A small electronic device used to test network cables for breaks and other problems that sends an electronic signal down one set of UTP wires. Used with a tone locator. *See also* tone locator, unshielded twisted-pair cable.

tone locator   A device used to test network cables for breaks and other problems; designed to sense the signal sent by the tone generator and emit a tone when the signal is detected in a particular set of wires.

topology   The physical and/or logical layout of the transmission media specified in the physical and logical layers of the OSI model. *See also* Open Systems Interconnect.

Trace Route   *See* tracert.

tracert   The TCP/IP Trace Route command-line utility that shows the user every router interface a TCP/IP packet passes through on its way to a destination. *See also* Transmission Control Protocol/Internet Protocol.

trailer   A section of a data packet that contains error-checking information.

transceiver   The part of any network interface that transmits and receives network signals.

transient   A high-voltage burst of current.

transmission   Sending of packets from the PC to the network cable.

Transmission Control Protocol (TCP)   The protocol found at the Host-to-Host layer of the DoD model. This protocol breaks data packets into segments, numbers them, and sends them in random order. The receiving computer reassembles the data so that the information is readable for the user. In the process, the sender and the receiver confirm that all data has been received; if not, it is re-sent. This is a connection-oriented protocol. *See also* connection-oriented transport protocol.

Transmission Control Protocol/Internet Protocol (TCP/IP)   The protocol suite developed by the DoD in conjunction with the Internet. It was designed as an internetworking protocol suite that could route information around network failures. Today it is the de facto standard for communications on the Internet.

transmission media   Physical cables and/or wireless technology across which computers are able to communicate.

Transport layer   The fourth layer of the OSI model, it is responsible for checking that the data packet created in the Session layer was received error free. If necessary, it also changes the length of messages for transport up or down the remaining layers. *See also* Open Systems Interconnect.

Trivial File Transfer Protocol (TFTP)   A protocol similar to FTP that does not provide the security or error-checking features of FTP. *See also* File Transfer Protocol.

trunk lines   The telephone lines that form the backbone of a telephone network for a company. These lines connect the telephone(s) to the telephone company and to the PSTN. *See also* Public Switched Telephone Network.

T-series connections   A series of digital connections leased from the telephone company. Each T-series connection is rated with a number based on speed. T1 and T3 are the most popular.

TTL   *See* Time to Live.

twisted-pair cable   A type of network transmission medium that contains pairs of color-coded, insulated copper wires that are twisted around each other. A twisted-pair cable consists of one or more twisted pairs in a common jacket.

type   A DOS command that displays the contents of a file. Also, short for *data type*.

U

UDP   *See* User Datagram Protocol.

Uniform Resource Locator (URL)   A URL is one way of identifying a document on the Internet. It consists of the protocol that is used to access the document and the domain name or IP address of the host that holds the document, for example, `http://www.sybex.com`.

uninterruptible power supply (UPS)   A natural line conditioner that uses a battery and power inverter to run the computer equipment that plugs into it. The battery charger continuously charges the battery. The battery charger is the only thing that runs off line voltage. During a power problem, the battery charger stops operating, and the equipment continues to run off the battery.

Unix   A 32-bit, multitasking operating system developed in the 1960s for use on mainframes and minicomputers.

unshielded   When cabling has little protection of wrapping to protect it from stray electrical or radio signals. Unshielded cabling is less expensive than shielded.

unshielded twisted-pair cable (UTP)   Twisted-pair cable consisting of a number of twisted pairs of copper wire with a simple plastic casing. Because no shielding is used in this cable, it is very susceptible to EMI, RFI, and other types of interference. *See also* crossover cable, electromagnetic interference, radio frequency interference.

upgrade   To increase an aspect of a PC, for example, by upgrading the RAM (increasing the RAM), upgrading the CPU (changing the current CPU for a faster CPU), etc.

UPS   *See* uninterruptible power supply.

uptime   The amount of time a particular computer or network component has been functional.

URL   *See* Uniform Resource Locator.

user   The person who is using a computer or network.

User Datagram Protocol (UDP)   Protocol at the Host-to-Host layer of the DoD model, which corresponds to the Transport layer of the OSI model. Packets are divided into segments, given numbers, sent randomly, and put back together at the receiving end. This is a connectionless protocol. *See also* connectionless transport protocol, Open Systems Interconnect.

user-level security   A type of network in which user accounts can read, write, change, and take ownership of files. Rights are assigned to user accounts, and each user knows only his or her own username and password, which makes this the preferred method for securing files.

V

vampire tap   A connection used with Thicknet to attach a station to the main cable. It is called a vampire tap because it has a tooth that "bites" through the insulation to make the physical connection.

virtual COM   Serial port that is used as if it were a serial port, but the actual serial port interface does not exist.

Virtual LAN (VLAN)   Allows users on different switch ports to participate in their own network separate from, but still connected to, the other stations on the same or connected switch.

virtual private network (VPN)   Using the public Internet as a backbone for a private interconnection (network) between locations.

virus   A program intended to damage a computer system. Sophisticated viruses encrypt and hide in a computer and may not appear until the user performs a certain action or until a certain date. *See also* antivirus.

virus engine   The core program that runs the virus-scanning process.

volume   Loudness of a sound, or the portion of a hard disk that functions as if it were a separate hard disk.

VPN   *See* virtual private network.

W

WAN . *See* wide area network.

web proxy   A type of proxy that is used to act on behalf of a web client or web server.

web server   A server that holds and delivers web pages and other web content using the HTTP protocol. *See also* Hypertext Transfer Protocol.

wide area network (WAN)   A network that crosses local, regional, and international boundaries.

Windows Internet Name Service (WINS)   A Windows NT service that dynamically associates the NetBIOS name of a host with a domain name. *See also* network basic input/output system.

Windows NT   A network operating system developed by Microsoft that uses that same graphical interface as the Desktop environment, Windows 95/98.

Windows NT 3.51   The version of Windows NT based on the "look and feel" of Windows 3.*x. See also* Windows NT.

Windows NT 4   The version of Windows NT based on the "look and feel" of Windows 95/98. *See also* Windows NT.

Windows NT Service   A type of Windows program (a file with either an .EXE or a .DLL extension) that is loaded automatically by the server or manually by the administrator.

winipcfg   The IP configuration utility for Windows 95/98 that allows you to view the current TCP/IP configuration of a workstation.

WinNuke   A Windows-based attack that affects only computers running Windows NT 3.51 or 4. It is caused by the way that the Windows NT TCP/IP stack handles bad data in the TCP header. Instead of returning an error code or rejecting the bad data, it sends NT to the Blue Screen of Death (BSOD). Figuratively speaking, the attack nukes the computer.

WINS   *See* Windows Internet Name Service.

wire crimper   Used for attaching ends onto different types of network cables by a process known as crimping. Crimping involves using pressure to press some kind of metal teeth into the inner conductors of a cable.

wireless access point (WAP)   A wireless bridge used in a multipoint RF network.

wireless bridge   Performs all the functions of a regular bridge but uses RF instead of cables to transmit signals.

workgroup   A specific group of users or network devices, organized by job function or proximity to shared resources.

workstation   A computer that is not a server but is on a network. Generally a workstation is used to do work, while a server is used to store data or perform a network function. In the most simple terms, a workstation is a computer that is not a server.

World Wide Web (WWW)   A collection of HTTP servers running on the Internet. They support the use of documents formatted with HTML. *See also* Hypertext Markup Language, Hypertext Transfer Protocol.

worms   Similar to a virus. Worms, however, propagate themselves over a network. *See also* virus.

WWW   *See* World Wide Web.

X

X Window   A graphical user interface (GUI) developed for use with the various flavors of Unix.

Appendix C

INFORMATION ON THE INTERNET

This appendix contains a selection of the networking resources available on the World Wide Web, broken out by category to help you find the information you are looking for quickly and easily. To be consistent with the rest of this book, I have not specified the protocol used to access each Web site; unless a different protocol is specified, you can simply assume that HTTP will work in all cases. Just add `http://` to the beginning of each Web address in your browser when you access a site.

The Web is in a constant state of flux as URLs change and Web sites disappear. The better-organized sites will simply post a link to the new location if they make substantive changes, and you can use that new link to go right to the new or reorganized site. Other sites reorganize themselves periodically as a part of their housekeeping; the information you want is still available, but you have to look in another place to find it or use the site's built-in search engine to find it.

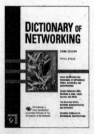

Adapted from *Dictionary of Networking* by Peter Dyson
ISBN 0-7821-2461-5   464 pages $29.99

When all else fails, use one of the Web sites listed in the "Portals and Search Engines" section of this appendix. In it you will find a list of the sites you can use to search the Web for documents using keywords, phrases, or even Boolean expressions. See each individual search engine site for details.

HARDWARE COMPANIES

This section lists the major manufacturers and suppliers of networking and computer hardware.

Acer Group	www.acer.com.tw
Adaptec, Inc.	www.adaptec.com
Advanced Micro Devices, Inc.	www.amd.com
Apple Computer, Inc.	www.apple.com
Ascend Communications, Inc.	www.ascend.com
AST Research	www.ast.com
Cabletron Systems	www.cabletron.com
Canon, Inc.	www.canon.com
Cirrus Logic, Inc.	www.cirrus.com
Cisco Systems, Inc.	www.cisco.com
Compaq Computer Corporation	www.compaq.com
Dell Computer Corporation	www.dell.com
Dialogic Corporation	www.dialogic.com
Gateway, Inc.	www.gateway.com
Hewlett-Packard Company	www.hp.com
Integrated Device Technology	www.idt.com
Intel Corporation	www.intel.com
IBM	www.ibm.com
Iomega Corporation	www.iomega.com
Lexmark International, Inc.	www.lexmark.com

Lucent Technologies, Inc.	www.lucent.com
Microcom, Inc.	www.microcom.com
Micron Technology	www.micronpc.com
Motorola, Inc.	www.motorola.com
National Semiconductor Corporation	www.national.com
NEC Corporation	www.nec.com
Packard-Bell	www.packardbell.com
Quantum Corporation	www.quantum.com
Rockwell Semiconductor Systems	www.nb.rockwell.com
Samsung Electronics	www.samsung.com
Seagate Technology, Inc.	www.seagate.com
Silicon Graphics, Inc.	www.sgi.com
Sun Microsystems, Inc.	www.sun.com
SyQuest Technology, Inc.	www.syquest.com
Toshiba Corporation	www.toshiba.com
U.S. Robotics Corporation	www.usr.com
ViewSonic Corp.	www.viewsonic.com
Western Digital Corp.	www.wdc.com

SOFTWARE AND SERVICE COMPANIES

This section lists the major providers of networking operating systems, applications software, and online and other services.

America Online	www.aol.com
Baan Company	www2.baan.com
Banyan Systems, Inc.	www.banyan.com
Caldera, Inc.	www.caldera.com
CompuServe, Inc.	www.compuserve.com

Computer Associates International	www.cai.com
Gartner Group, Inc.	www.gartner.com
Informix Software, Inc.	www.informix.com
Inprise Corporation	www.inprise.com
Learning Tree International	www.learningtree.com
Marimba, Inc.	www.marimba.com
Microsoft, Inc.	www.microsoft.com
Netscape Communications Corporation	www.netscape.com
Network Associates, Inc.	www.networkassociates.com
Novell, Inc.	www.novell.com
Oracle Corporation	www.oracle.com
PC Connection	www.pcconnection.com
PeopleSoft, Inc.	www.peoplesoft.com
PointCast, Inc.	www.pointcast.com
RealNetworks, Inc.	www.real.com
Red Hat Software	www.redhat.com
RSA Data Security	www.rsa.com
SCO	www.sco.com
SAP	www.sap.com
Sybase, Inc.	www.sybase.com
Symantec Corporation	www.symantec.com
White Pine Software	www.wpine.com

INTERNET ORGANIZATIONS

Here you will find URLs relating to the main Internet organizations.

| Internet Society | www.isoc.org |
| Internet Architecture Board | www.iab.org/iab |

Internet Engineering Steering Group	`www.ietf.org/iesg.htm`
Internet Engineering Task Force	`www.ietf.org`
Internet Research Task Force	`www.irtf.org`
International Ad Hoc Committee	`www.iahc.org`
Internet Assigned Numbers Authority	`www.iana.org`
World Wide Web Consotium	`www.w3.org`

STANDARDS GROUPS AND TRADE ORGANIZATIONS

This section provides URLs for the major network-related standards groups and trade associations.

ANSI	`www.ansi.org`
ATM Forum	`www.atmforum.com/home.html`
CERN	`www.cern.ch`
CERT	`www.cert.org`
EIA	`www.eia.org`
FCC	`www.fcc.gov`
IEEE	`www.ieee.org`
IrDA	`www.irda.org`
ISO	`www.iso.ch`
ITU	`www.itu.ch`
NCSC	`www.ncsc.com`
Object Management Group	`www.omg.org`
Open Group	`www.opengroup.org`
TIA	`www.tiaonline.org`

PORTALS AND SEARCH ENGINES

The distinction between a Web portal and a search engine continues to blur, so they are grouped together in this section.

Alta Vista	www.altavista.digital.com
America Online	www.aol.com
ESPN	www.espn.com
Excite	www.excite.com
GoTo.com	www.gogt.com
Hotbot	www.hotbot.com
Ivillage	www.ivillage.com
Lycos	www.lycos.com
Northern Light	www.nlsearch.com
Snap!	www.snap.com
Yahoo!	www.yahoo.com

OPEN SOURCE SOFTWARE

This section contains details on where to find open-source software, as well as URLs for some of the organizations supporting open source and free software.

Open Source Initiative	www.opensource.org
Slashdot	www.slashdot.org
O'Reilly Open Source Center	opensource.oreilly.com
The Apache Project	www.apache.org
GNU	www.gnu.org
Linux Online	www.linux.org
The Linux Kernel Archives	www.kernel.org
The Linux Documentation Project	www.linuxdoc.org

Linux Web pages	www.linux-center.org
The Perl Institute	www.perl.org
Netscape's Mozilla Project	www.mozilla.org
XFree86	www.xfree86.org
FreeBSD Project	ftp.freebsd.org
Open BSD	www.openbsd.org

LOCAL EXCHANGE CARRIERS

This section lists the companies providing local carrier services throughout the United States.

Ameritech, Inc.	www.ameritech.com
Bell Atlantic Corp	www.bell-atl.com
Bell South	www.bellsouth.com
NYNEX Corp	www.nynex.com
Pacific Bell	www.pacbell.com
SBC Communications, Inc.	www.sbc.com
U.S. West Communications Group	www.uswest.com

INTEREXCHANGE CARRIERS

This section lists the carriers that provide long-distance service in the United States.

AT&T Corp	www.att.com
LDDS WorldCom, Inc.	www.wcom.com
MCI Telecommunications Corp.	www.mci.com
Sprint Communications Company	www.sprintbiz.com
MFS Communications Company	www.mfsdatanet.com
Norlight Telecommunications, Inc.	www.norlight.com

Appendix D
CERTIFICATION PROGRAMS

This appendix presents information on the many and varied computer and networking certification programs available in the industry. Table D.1 lists the abbreviations and complete names for the most common certification programs, and Table D.2 lists all the network-related certification programs offered by each company or computer-industry organization.

Adapted from *Dictionary of Networking* by Peter Dyson
ISBN 0-7821-2461-5   464 pages $29.99

TABLE D.1:   Certification Program Abbreviations

ABBREVIATION	CERTIFICATION PROGRAM
A+	A+ Certification
AASE	Associated Accredited Systems Engineer
ABCP	Associate Business Continuity Professional
ACE	Advanced Certified Engineer
ACTE	Ascend Certified Technical Expert
ASE	Acredited Systems Engineer
BAC	Baan Advanced Certification
BBC	Baan Basic Certification
BNCE	Bay Networks Certified Expert
BNCS	Bay Networks Certified Specialist
CATE	Certified Advanced Technical Expert
CBCP	Certified Business Continuity Professional
CBE	Certified Banyan Engineer
CBS	Certified Banyan Specialist
CC	Certified Consultant
CCIE	Cisco Certified Internetworking Expert
CCP	Certified Computing Professional
CDA	Certified Database Administrator
CDIA	Certified Document Image Architect
CE	Certified Expert
CINA	Certified IRIX Network Administrator
CISA	Certified Information System Auditor
CISA	Certified IRIX System Administrator
CISSP	Information Systems Security Professional
CJD	Certified Java Developer
CJP	Certified Java Programmer
CLP	Certified Lotus Professional
CLS	Certified Lotus Specialist
CNA	Certified Novell Administrator

TABLE D.1 continued: Certification Program Abbreviations

ABBREVIATION	CERTIFICATION PROGRAM
CNE	Certified Novell Engineer
CNI	Certified Novell Instructor
CNP	Certified Network Professional
CNX	Certified Network Expert
CPDA	Certified Powerbuilder Developer Associate
CPDP	Certified Powerbuilder Developer Professional
CPTS	Certified Performance and Tuning Specialist
CS	Certified Specialist
CSA	Certified Solaris Administrator
CSE	Certified Solutions Expert
CSE	Certified Systems Expert
CSE	Certified Switching Expert
CSNA	Certified Solaris Network Administrator
CSS	Certified Switching Specialist
CU	Certified User
CUE	Certified Unicenter Engineer
MBCP	Master Busines Continuity Professional
MCNE	Master Certified Novell Engineer
MCP	Microsoft Certified Professional
MCSD	Microsoft Certified Solutions Developer
MCSE	Microsoft Certified Systems Engineer
MOE	Microsoft Office Expert
MOES	Microsoft Office Expert Specialist
MOPS	Microsoft Office Proficient Specialist
N+	Network+ Certification
NCIP	Novell Certified Internet Professional
PSE	Professional Server Expert
PSS	Professional Server Specialist
RCDD	Registered Communications Distribution Designer

TABLE D.2:   Computer and Networking Certification Programs

COMPANY	CERTIFICATION PROGRAM NAME
Baan	Baan Basic Certification
	Baan Advanced Certification in Enterprise Logistics
	Baan Advanced Certification in Enterprise Finance
	Baan Advanced Certification in Enterprise Tools
	Baan Advanced Certification in Enterprise Modeler
Banyan	Certified Banyan Specialist
	Certified Banyan Specialist: Windows NT
	Certified Banyan Engineer
BICSI	Registered Communications Distribution Designer
	Registered Communications Distribution Designer: LAN Specialty
Cisco	Cicso Certified Internetworking Expert: WAN Switching Expert
	Cicso Certified Internetworking Expert: ISP Dial Expert
	Cicso Certified Internetworking Expert: Routing and Switching Expert
Compaq	Associate Accredited Systems Engineer Specializing in Novell IntranetWare
	Associate Accredited Systems Engineer Specializing in Microsoft Windows NT
	Accredited Systems Engineer Specializing in Novell IntranetWare
	Accredited Systems Engineer Specializing in Microsoft Windows NT
Computer Associates	Certified Unicenter Engineer
CompTIA	A+ Certification
	Certified Document Image Architect
	Network+ Certification
CNX Consortium	Certified Network Expert
Disaster Recovery Institute International	Associate Business Continuity Professional
	Certified Business Continuity Professional
	Master Business Continuity Professional
Hewlett-Packard	HP OpenView Certified Consultant: Unix
	HP OpenView Certified Consultant: Windows NT
	HP OpenView Certified Consultant: Unix and Windows NT

TABLE D.2 continued: Computer and Networking Certification Programs

COMPANY	CERTIFICATION PROGRAM NAME
IBM	Certified Solutions Expert: Net Commerce
	Certified Solutions Expert: Firewall Resources
	IBM Certified AIX User
	IBM Certified Specialist: AIX System Administration
	IBM Certified Specialist: AIX Support
	IBM Certified Specialist: AS/400 Associate System Operator
	IBM Certified Specialist: AS/400 Professional System Operator
	IBM Certified Specialist: AS/400 Associate System Administrator
	IBM Certified Specialist: AS/400 Professional System Administrator
	IBM Certified Specialist: OS/2 Warp Server Administration
	IBM Certified Expert: OS/2 Warp Server
	IBM Certified Specialist: OS/2 LAN Server Administration
	IBM Certified Expert: OS/2 LAN Server
	IBM Certified Systems Expert: OS/2 Warp
	IBM Certified Advanced Technical Expert: RS/6000 AIX
	Professional Server Expert
	Professional Server Expert: Novell NetWare
	Professional Server Expert: OS/2 Warp Server
	Professional Server Expert: Windows NT Server
Informix	Database Specialist: Informix Dynamic Server
	System Administration: Informix Dynamic Server
	Informix-4GL Certified Professional
Institute for Certification of Computing Professionals	Certified Computing Professional
International Information Systems Security Certification Consortium	Certified Information Systems Security Professional

TABLE D.2 continued: Computer and Networking Certification Programs

COMPANY	CERTIFICATION PROGRAM NAME
Information Systems Audit and Control Association	Certified Information Systems Auditor
Learning Tree International	Internet/Intranet Certified Professional
	Internetwork Certified Professional
	Local Area Networks Certified Professional
	PC Service and Support Certified Professional
	Unix Systems Certified Professional
	Wide Area Networks Certified Professional
Lotus	Certified Lotus Specialist
	Certified Lotus Professional: Application Developer
	Certified Lotus Professional: Principal Application Developer
	Certified Lotus Professional: System Administrator
	Certified Lotus Professional: Principal System Administrator
	Certified Lotus Professional: cc Mail System Administrator
Microsoft	Microsoft Certified Professional +Internet
	Microsoft Certified Systems Engineer +Internet
	Microsoft Certified Systems Engineer
	Microsoft Certified Solutions Developer
	Microsoft Office Proficient Specialist
	Microsoft Office Expert Specialist
	Microsoft Office Expert
Network Professional Association	Certified Network Professional
Novell	Certified Novell Administrator
	Certified Novell Engineer
	Certified Novell Instructor
	Novell Certified Internet Professional
	Novell Internet Architect

TABLE D.2 continued: Computer and Networking Certification Programs

COMPANY	CERTIFICATION PROGRAM NAME
	Novell Internet Business Strategist
	Novell Intranet Manager
	Master Certified Novell Engineer
	Novell Web Designer
Oracle	Certified Database Administrator
	Certified Application Developer
SCO	Advanced Certified Engineer: Server Track
	Advanced Certified Engineer: OpenServer Track
	Advanced Certified Engineer: UnixWare Track
Silicon Graphics	Certified IRIX System Administrator
	Certified IRIX Network Administrator
Sun Microsystems	Certified Java Programmer
	Certified Java Developer
	Certified Solaris Administrator
	Certified Solaris Network Administrator
Sybase	Certified PowerBuilder Developer Associate
	Certified PowerBuilder Developer Professional
	Certified Database Administrator
	Certified Performing and Tuning Specialist
Xylan	Xylan Certified Switch Specialist
	Xylan Certified Switch Expert

Appendix E

ASCII Character Set

Table E.1 shows the first 32 characters (0–31) from the American Standard Code for Information Interchange (ASCII), also known as the control characters.

Table E.2 shows the 7-bit standard ASCII character set (comprising characters 32–127), which is implemented on all computers that use ASCII.

Table E.3 shows characters 128–255 of the 8-bit IBM extended ASCII character set.

Adapted from *Dictionary of Networking* by Peter Dyson
ISBN 0-7821-2461-5   464 pages $29.99

TABLE E.1: ASCII Control Characters

DECIMAL	CHARACTER	CONTROL COMBINATION
0	NUL (Null)	Ctrl+@
1	SOH (Start of heading)	Ctrl+A
2	STX (Start of text)	Ctrl+B
3	ETX (End of text)	Ctrl+C
4	EOT (End of transmission)	Ctrl+D
5	ENQ (Enquire)	Ctrl+E
6	ACK (Acknowledge)	Ctrl+F
7	BEL (Bell)	Ctrl+G
8	BS (Backspace)	Ctrl+H
9	HT (Horizontal tab)	Ctrl+I
10	LF (Line feed)	Ctrl+J
11	VT (Vertical tab)	Ctrl+K
12	FF (Form feed)	Ctrl+L
13	CR (Carriage return)	Ctrl+M
14	SO (Shift out)	Ctrl+N
15	SI (Shift in)	Ctrl+O
16	DLE (Data link escape)	Ctrl+P
17	DC1 (Device control 1)	Ctrl+Q
18	DC2 (Device control 2)	Ctrl+R
19	DC3 (Device control 3)	Ctrl+S
20	DC4 (Device control 4)	Ctrl+T
21	NAK (Negative acknowledgement)	Ctrl+U
22	SYN (Synchronous idle)	Ctrl+V
23	ETB (End transmission block)	Ctrl+W
24	CAN (Cancel)	Ctrl+X
25	EM (End of medium)	Ctrl+Y
26	SUB (Substitute)	Ctrl+Z
27	ESC (Escape)	Ctrl+[
28	FS (File separator)	Ctrl+/
29	GS (Group separator)	Ctrl+]
30	RS (Record separator)	Ctrl+^
31	US (Unit separator)	Ctrl+_

TABLE E.2:   Standard 7-Bit ASCII Character Set

DECIMAL	CHARACTER	DECIMAL	CHARACTER
32	space	62	>
33	!	63	?
34	"	64	@
35	#	65	A
36	$	66	B
37	%	67	C
38	&	68	D
39	`	69	E
40	(	70	F
41	)	71	G
42	*	72	H
43	+	73	I
44	,	74	J
45	~-	75	K
46	.	76	L
47	/	77	M
48	0	78	N
49	1	79	O
50	2	80	P
51	3	81	Q
52	4	82	R
53	5	83	S
54	6	84	T
55	7	85	U
56	8	86	V
57	9	87	W
58	:	88	X
59	;	89	Y
60	<	90	Z
61	=	91	[

TABLE E.2 continued: Standard 7-Bit ASCII Character Set

DECIMAL	CHARACTER	DECIMAL	CHARACTER
92	\	110	n
93	]	111	o
94	^	112	p
95	_	113	q
96	`	114	r
97	a	115	s
98	b	116	t
99	c	117	u
100	d	118	v
101	e	119	w
102	f	120	x
103	g	121	y
104	h	122	z
105	i	123	{
106	j	124	|
107	k	125	}
108	l	126	~
109	m	127	DEL

TABLE E.3:   IBM Extended ASCII Character Set

DECIMAL	CHARACTER
128	Insert Character ASC 128
129	Insert Character ASC 129
130	Insert Character ASC 130
131	Insert Character ASC 131
132	Insert Character ASC 132
133	Insert Character ASC 133
134	Insert Character ASC 134
135	Insert Character ASC 135

TABLE E.3 continued: IBM Extended ASCII Character Set

DECIMAL	CHARACTER
136	Insert Character ASC 136
137	Insert Character ASC 137
138	Insert Character ASC 138
139	Insert Character ASC 139
140	Insert Character ASC 140
141	Insert Character ASC 141
142	Insert Character ASC 142
143	Insert Character ASC 143
144	Insert Character ASC 144
145	Insert Character ASC 145
146	Insert Character ASC 146
147	Insert Character ASC 147
148	Insert Character ASC 148
149	Insert Character ASC 149
150	Insert Character ASC 150
151	Insert Character ASC 151
152	Insert Character ASC 152
153	Insert Character ASC 153
154	Insert Character ASC 154
155	Insert Character ASC 155
156	Insert Character ASC 156
157	Insert Character ASC 157
158	Insert Character ASC 158
159	Insert Character ASC 159
160	Insert Character ASC 160
161	Insert Character ASC 161
162	Insert Character ASC 162
163	Insert Character ASC 163
164	Insert Character ASC 164
165	Insert Character ASC 165

TABLE E.3 continued: IBM Extended ASCII Character Set

DECIMAL	CHARACTER
166	Insert Character ASC 166
167	Insert Character ASC 167
168	Insert Character ASC 168
169	Insert Character ASC 169
170	Insert Character ASC 170
171	Insert Character ASC 171
172	Insert Character ASC 172
173	Insert Character ASC 173
174	Insert Character ASC 174
175	Insert Character ASC 175
176	Insert Character ASC 176
177	Insert Character ASC 177
178	Insert Character ASC 178
179	Insert Character ASC 179
180	Insert Character ASC 180
181	Insert Character ASC 181
182	Insert Character ASC 182
183	Insert Character ASC 183
184	Insert Character ASC 184
185	Insert Character ASC 185
186	Insert Character ASC 186
187	Insert Character ASC 187
188	Insert Character ASC 188
189	Insert Character ASC 189
190	Insert Character ASC 190
191	Insert Character ASC 191
192	Insert Character ASC 192
193	Insert Character ASC 193
194	Insert Character ASC 194

TABLE E.3 continued: IBM Extended ASCII Character Set

DECIMAL	CHARACTER
195	Insert Character ASC 195
196	Insert Character ASC 196
197	Insert Character ASC 197
198	Insert Character ASC 198
199	Insert Character ASC 199
200	Insert Character ASC 200
201	Insert Character ASC 201
202	Insert Character ASC 202
203	Insert Character ASC 203
204	Insert Character ASC 204
205	Insert Character ASC 205
206	Insert Character ASC 206
207	Insert Character ASC 207
208	Insert Character ASC 208
209	Insert Character ASC 209
210	Insert Character ASC 210
211	Insert Character ASC 211
212	Insert Character ASC 212
213	Insert Character ASC 213
214	Insert Character ASC 214
215	Insert Character ASC 215
216	Insert Character ASC 216
217	Insert Character ASC 217
218	Insert Character ASC 218
219	Insert Character ASC 219
220	Insert Character ASC 220
221	Insert Character ASC 221
222	Insert Character ASC 222
223	Insert Character ASC 223
224	Insert Character ASC 224

TABLE E.3 continued: IBM Extended ASCII Character Set

DECIMAL	CHARACTER
225	Insert Character ASC 225
226	Insert Character ASC 226
227	Insert Character ASC 227
228	Insert Character ASC 228
229	Insert Character ASC 229
230	Insert Character ASC 230
231	Insert Character ASC 231
232	Insert Character ASC 232
233	Insert Character ASC 233
234	Insert Character ASC 234
235	Insert Character ASC 235
236	Insert Character ASC 236
237	Insert Character ASC 237
238	Insert Character ASC 238
239	Insert Character ASC 239
240	Insert Character ASC 240
241	Insert Character ASC 241
242	Insert Character ASC 242
243	Insert Character ASC 243
244	Insert Character ASC 244
245	Insert Character ASC 245
246	Insert Character ASC 246
247	Insert Character ASC 247
248	Insert Character ASC 248
249	Insert Character ASC 249
250	Insert Character ASC 250
251	Insert Character ASC 251
252	Insert Character ASC 252
253	Insert Character ASC 253
254	Insert Character ASC 254
255	Insert Character ASC 255

Appendix F

EBCDIC Character Set

Table F.1 shows all 256 characters that make up the Extended Binary Coded Decimal Interchange Code (EBCDIC) character set.

Adapted from *Dictionary of Networking* by Peter Dyson
ISBN 0-7821-2461-5   464 pages $29.99

TABLE F.1:   EBCDIC Character Set

Decimal	Character	Decimal	Character
0	NUL (null)	28	IFS (interchange file separator
1	SOH (start of heading)	29	IGS (interchange group separator)
2	STX (start of text)	30	IRS (interchange record separator)
3	ETX (end of text)	31	IUS/ITB (interchange unit separator/intermediate transmission block)
4	SEL (select)		
5	HT (horizontal tab)		
6	RNL (required new line)	32	DS (digit select)
7	DEL (delete)	33	SOS (start of significance)
8	GE (graphic escape)	34	FS (field separator)
9	SPS (superscript)	35	WUS (word underscore)
10	RPT (repeat)	36	BYP/INP (bypass/inhibit presentation)
11	VT (vertical tab)		
12	FF (form feed)	37	LF (line feed)
13	CR (carriage return)	38	ETB (end of transmission block)
14	SO (shift out)		
15	SI (shift in)	39	ESC (escape)
16	DLE (data length escape)	40	SA (set attribute)
17	DC1 (device control 1)	41	SFE (start field extended)
18	DC2 (device control 2)	44	MFA (modify field attribute)
19	DC3 (device control 3)	45	ENQ (enquiry)
20	RES/ENP (restore/enable presentation)	46	ACK (acknowledge)
21	NL (new line)	47	BEL (bell)
22	BS (backspace)	50	STN (synchronous idle)
23	POC (program-operator communication)	51	IR (index return)
24	CAN (cancel)	52	PP (presentation position)
25	EM (end of medium)	53	TRN (transport)
26	UBS (unit backspace)	54	NBS (numeric backspace)
27	CU1 (customer use 1)	55	EOT (end of transmission)
		56	SBS (subscript)

TABLE F.1 continued: EBCDIC Character Set

DECIMAL	CHARACTER	DECIMAL	CHARACTER
57	IT (indent tab)	109	-
58	RFF (required form feed)	110	>
59	CU3 (customer use 3)	111	?
60	DC4 (device control 4)	112–120	not assigned
61	NAK (negative acknowledge)	121	`
		122	:
62	not assigned	123	#
63	SUB (substitute)	124	@
64	SP (space)	125	
65	RSP (required space)	126	=
66–73	not assigned	127	
74		128	not assigned
75	.	129	a
76	<	130	b
77	(	131	c
78	+	132	d
79	| (Logical OR)	133	e
80–89	not assigned	134	f
90	!	135	g
91	$	136	h
92	*	137	I
93	)	138–144	not assigned
94	;	145	j
95	(Logical NOT)	146	k
96	-	147	l
97	/	148	m
98–105	not assigned	149	n
106	| (broken pipe)	150	o
107	,	151	p
108	%	152	q

TABLE F.1 continued: EBCDIC Character Set

DECIMAL	CHARACTER	DECIMAL	CHARACTER
153	r	213	N
154–160	not assigned	214	O
161	~	215	P
162	s	216	Q
163	t	217	R
164	u	218–223	not assigned
165	v	224	\
166	w	225	NSP (numeric space)
167	x	226	S
168	y	227	T
169	z	228	U
170–191	not assigned	229	V
192	{	230	W
193	A	231	X
194	B	232	Y
195	C	233	Z
196	D	234–239	not assigned
197	E	240	0
198	F	241	1
199	G	242	2
200	H	243	3
201	I	244	4
202	SHY (syllable hyphen)	245	5
203–207	not assigned	246	6
208	}	247	7
209	J	248	8
210	K	249	9
211	L	250–254	not assigned
212	M	255	EO (eight ones)

INDEX

Note to the Reader: Page numbers in **bold** indicate the principle discussion of a topic or the definition of a term. Page numbers in *italic* indicate illustrations.

About the Contributors

Some of the best—and best-selling—Sybex authors have contributed chapters from their books to *Networking Complete*, Third Edition.

Dave Barnett, RCDD, has been in the wire and cable industry for nearly 20 years. The Director of Product Engineering for the Electrical Group of Superior Essex, he also writes for books and magazines, runs a cabling Web site (www.CablingCentral.com), and is co-owner of PnP Networks, Inc., which specializes in home and small business networking.

Jim Blaney is an independent consultant specializing in network implementation and integration. He is the co-author of *The Complete Network Upgrade & Maintenance Guide* and *Windows 98 Developer's Handbook*, from Sybex.

Chris Brenton is a Certified Novell Engineer (CNE), Microsoft Certified Systems Engineer (MCSE), and Cisco Design Specialist (CDS). He has authored and coauthored a number of books for Sybex, including *Mastering Network Security*, *Multiprotocol Network Design and Troubleshooting*, and *The Complete Network Upgrade & Maintenance Guide*. As a Technology Specialist for Alpine Computers, he serves as a security consultant to clients and a mentor to the engineering staff.

Michael Chacon, MCT and MCSE, is senior solutions manager for Netigy Corporation. He is an internationally known advisor, lecturer, and columnist.

James Chellis is the co-author of numerous MCSE study guides from Sybex Network Press, including the best-selling *MCSE Core Requirements* box set and *CCNA: Cisco Certified Network Associate Study Guide*. He is also President of EdgeTek Inc., a national training company specializing in training and courseware development.

Anil Desai, MCSE, MCSD, MCDBA, is a consultant working in Austin, Texas. He is also a regular contributor to Microsoft Certified Professional magazine. He is the author of several other books, including *MCSE: Accelerated Windows 2000 Study Guide*, *Windows NT Network Management: Reducing Total Cost of Ownership* and *SQL Server 2000 Backup and Recovery*.

Lisa Donald, is a Microsoft Certified Trainer and Microsoft Certified Systems Engineer. She has worked extensively with numerous Fortune 500 companies and other prominent organizations, including Digital, Apple, the U.S. Postal Service, and the U.S. Naval Academy.

James E. Gaskin, a Dallas-area consultant and author specializing in networking technology, wrote *Mastering NetWare 5* and *IntranetWare BorderManager* for Sybex Network Press. For six years he served as the networking columnist for *Open Systems Today* (formerly *Unix Today!*). He is also a long-time instructor at NetWorld+Interop, specializing in NetWare and Internet integration and security. He has been installing, configuring, and explaining NetWare since 1986, beginning with Advanced NetWare 4.61a, which shipped on a handful of 5.25-inch low-density floppy disks for the hot new server, the IBM XT.

Gary Govanus is an independent Microsoft Certified Trainer (MCT), Microsoft Certified Systems Engineer (MCSE), Certified Novell Instructor (CNI), and Master Certified Novell Engineer (MCNE). He is co-author of *MCSE Exam Notes: NT Server 4*, *MCSE Exam Notes: NT Workstation 4*, and *MCSE Exam Notes: NT Server 4 in the Enterprise*. He is also the author of *MCSE Exam Notes: TCP/IP for NT Server 4* and *TCP/IP 24seven*.

David Groth is President and Chief Geek of Practical Training Solutions, a global franchise system of training centers, and the author of Network+ Study Guide, i-Net+ Study Guide, and other certification titles from Sybex. He holds many technical certifications, including Network+, A+, MCP, and CNI.

Bill Heldman, MCSE and MCT, is a senior NT administrator for a large telecommunications company in Denver, Colorado. He has authored numerous books for Sybex, including *MCSE: Exchange 2000 Server Design Study Guide*, *MCSE: ISA Server 2000 Administration Study Guide*, and *IT Project+ Study Guide*.

Mark Henricks, author of *Mastering Home Networking* from Sybex, is a full-time writer covering technology and business issues, including *Business Plans Made Easy*. He has written on business and technology for magazines including *Entrepreneur*, *American Way*, *Popular Science*, *The New York Times*, *Sports Illustrated for Kids*, *Southwest Airlines Spirit*, and *Men's Health*. He is also a former contributing editor of *PC World* and Technology columnist of *Kiplinger's*.

Robert King is a Microsoft Certified Trainer (MCT), Microsoft Certified Systems Engineer (MCSE), Certified Novell Instructor (CNI), and Master Certified Novell Engineer (MCNE). He co-authored *MCSE Exam Notes: NT Server 4*, *MCSE Exam Notes: NT Workstation 4*, *MCSE Exam Notes: NT Server 4 in the Enterprise*, and *MCSE Exam Notes: Exchange Server 5.5*. He has over ten years of experience teaching and working with Microsoft technologies. Robert and Gary Govanus also co-authored MCSE: Windows 2000: Network Security Design Exam Notes.

Mark Lierley, CNE, CNA, CNI, MCSE, MCP, MCT, A+, Net+, CIW has been teaching computer networking and related computer topics for the last 8 years.

In addition to his certifications, he has been working as a consultant specializing in Novell & Microsoft integration. Born in Colorado, he now lives in Phoenix, AZ.

Jim McBee, MCSE+Internet and MCT, is a consultant and trainer based in Honolulu, HI. He specializes in Windows NT/2000 and Exchange Server. Jim is the author of Exchange Server 5.5 24Seven and contributed to Mastering Netware 5, both from Sybex.

Mark Minasi, MCSE, is one of the world's leading Windows authorities. He teaches NT/2000 classes in 15 countries, keynotes at industry gatherings, and writes regular columns for Windows 2000 magazine and other prominent publications. His firm, MR&D, has taught tens of thousands of people to design and run Windows networks. Among his eight other Sybex books are Mastering Windows NT Server 4; Mastering Windows 2000 Server, Linux for Windows NT/2000 Administrators: The Secret Decoder Ring, and The Complete PC Upgrade and Maintenance Guide.

Dan Newland is an independent consultant and trainer. He holds MCSE, MCT, CNA, Server+, and A+ certifications and has worked on a number of titles for Sybex, most recently MCSE 2000 Jumpstart: Computer and Network Basics. Most recently he co-authored the *A+ Complete Study Guide*, Second and Deluxe Edition with David Groth.

Charles Perkins, an MCSE, is coauthor of *NT 4 Network Security* and numerous Sybex Network Press MCSE study guides. Formerly director of Computing Services for the University of Utah College of Law, he is now a consultant specializing in Windows NT and security.

Brad Price is a Citrix Certified Instructor Administrator and Microsoft Certified Trainer. He works as a Technical Education Consultant, specializing in Windows 2000, Exchange, and Citrix Administration.

John Price is also a Citrix Certified Administrator and Microsoft Certified Trainer. He works as a trainer and a Network Engineer Consultant, specializing in Citrix enterprise implementations.

Deborah S. Ray and Eric J. Ray are owners of RayComm, Inc., a technical communications consulting firm that specializes in cutting-edge Internet and computing technologies. Together they have co-authored more than 10 computer books, including the first and second editions of *Mastering HTML 4* from Sybex.

Paul Robichaux is a noted networking expert and the author of more than twenty books, including *Remote Access 24seven*, also from Sybex. In addition, he has written numerous white papers for Microsoft.

Matthew Sheltz, MCP, is a software engineer and systems administrator for EdgeTek Education.

Matthew Strebe is an MCSE who began his career in the U.S. Navy, installing the Navy's first fiber-optic LAN aboard a ship. He is the co-author of *NT 4 Network Security* and the author of *NT Server 4 24seven* and *Firewalls 24seven*. He is also the co-author of numerous Sybex Network Press MCSE study guides, as well as the owner of Netropolis, a network-integration firm specializing in high-speed networking and Windows NT. He and Mr. Perkins were members of the same hacking cabal in high school.

TELL US WHAT YOU THINK!

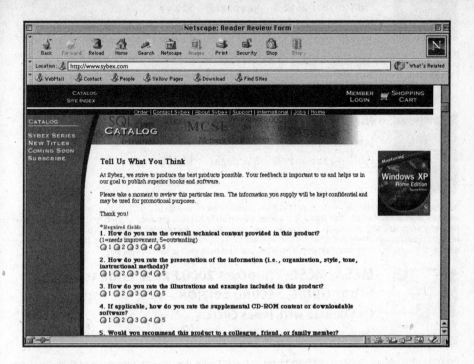

Your feedback is critical to our efforts to provide you with the best books and software on the market. Tell us what you think about the products you've purchased. It's simple:

1. Go to the Sybex website.
2. Find your book by typing the ISBN number or title into the Search field.
3. Click on the book title when it appears.
4. Click **Submit a Review.**
5. Fill out the questionnaire and comments.
6. Click **Submit.**

With your feedback, we can continue to publish the highest quality computer books and software products that today's busy IT professionals deserve.

www.sybex.com

SYBEX Inc. • 1151 Marina Village Parkway, Alameda, CA 94501 • 510-523-8233

SYBEX®

MASTERING™ HOME NETWORKING

MARK HENRICKS

ISBN: 0-7821-2630-8   544 pages $29.99

Now that many homes have two or more computers, home networks are spreading like wildfire. By networking your computers together, you can share files, high-speed Internet connections, and peripherals such as printers and scanners, saving your household time, effort, and money. And where home networking used to involve expertise with protocols, wires, and power tools, new networking products let you build an effective network in minutes—without drilling, without pulling cables, and in some cases even without using wires.

MASTERING™ NETWARE® 6

JAMES E. GASKIN

ISBN: 0-7821-4023-8   864 pages $69.99

NetWare 6 is a major release in the history of NetWare, providing improvements that will be appreciated by users and administrators alike. Mastering NetWare 6 is the latest edition of the NetWare resource long recognized for its comprehensiveness, practicality, and humor. You'll benefit from James Gaskin's instruction on standard NetWare techniques, in-depth examinations of new and advanced features, and the tips and tricks for which he's famous. If you're serious about getting all you can out of the latest version of NetWare, you'll set out with this book by your side.

MCSA/MCSE: WINDOWS 2000 PROFESSIONAL STUDY GUIDE, SECOND EDITION

LISA DONALD WITH JAMES CHELLIS

ISBN: 0-7821-2946-3 $49.99

Here's the book you need to prepare for Exam 70-210, Installing, Configuring, and Administering Microsoft Windows 2000 Professional. This study guide provides in-depth coverage of every exam objective—all the information you need! This book is packed with practical information, supplying you with all of the confidence you'll need to apply it in the real world. You will find hundreds of challenging review questions, both in the book and on the CD-ROM. Take advantage of our cutting edge exam preparation software, including a testing engine, electronic flashcards, and simulation software.

MASTERING™ HTML 4 PREMIUM EDITION

DEBORAH S. RAY, ERIC J. RAY

ISBN: 0-7821-2524-7   1,216 pages $49.99

This comprehensive edition is completely updated with coverage of all the essential HTML issues: formatting fundamentals, forms, frames, tables, image maps, integrating Java and Active X, using JavaScript 1.3, Internet Explorer 5 and Communicator 4.5 tags, and adding multimedia effects. You will find special topics only available in this Premium Edition, including XML and DOM, expanded DHTML coverage, and HTML development tools. On the CD you will find electronic versions of the Master's Reference to HTML tags, style sheets, JavaScript, HTML special characters, searchable HTML color codes, and a huge collection of powerful Web utilities (including WinZip, Paint Shop Pro, and a number of HTML editors).

FIREWALLS 24SEVEN™

MATTHEW STREBE, CHARLES PERKINS

ISBN: 0-7821-4054-8   576 pages $49.99